HUGMAN'S INTERNATIONAL BOXING ANNUAL 1990

The heavyweight champion of the world, "Iron" Mike Tyson Tom Casino

Edited by Barry J. Hugman

HUGMAN'S SPORTING PUBLICATIONS LIMITED

First published in Great Britain by
Hugman's Sporting Publications Ltd
24 Nottinghill Gate
London W11 3JQ

British Library Cataloguing in Publication Data
Hugman, Barry J. (Barry John)
Hugman's International Boxing Annual 1990
I. Boxing — Records
I. Title

ISBN 1 872290 00 0

Typeset by Area Graphics Ltd, Arden Press Way, Letchworth, Hertfordshire SG6 1LH
Printed in Great Britain by Cowells of Ipswich.

Contents

Acknowledgements

In this, the third edition of *Hugman's International Boxing Year*, I have made every effort not to forget anyone involved in making the book possible, and list accordingly.

Ron Olver — Assistant Editor of the *British Boxing Yearbook*; British correspondent of the *Ring*, America; former Assistant Editor of both *Boxing News* and *Boxing World*; author of *The Professionals*, *Boxing* (Foyles) and the boxing section of *Encyclopaedia Britannica*; a member of the British Boxing Writers' Club, the Commonwealth Championships Committee and the BBBC Benevolent Fund; Vice-President of several ex-boxers' associations — who, with his great experience of boxing, and of boxing people, was the ideal man to put together The Hall of Fame section within this book.

Fred Snelling, the author of *White Hope* and *A Bedside Book of Boxing*, among many others, has once again produced the month-by-month narrative in his own inimitable fashion. He began writing prior to the war and follows a long tradition of outstanding penmanship that has entertained the boxing public since the days of bare fist fighting. O.F. Snelling, or Fred, as he prefers to be called, spends most of his spare time these days, producing boxing magazines for several ex-boxers' associations, a task he delights in.

Eric Armit, who is undoubtedly one of the leaders in compiling international records, has yet again assembled nearly 450 for The World's Leading Fighters section. He is the man to whom boxing authorities and promoters turn to for an accurate record of any fighter that they are proposing to use. It was around 1958 that Eric began to compile boxing records and by 1962 he was involved with *Boxing News*, through his good friend, Ron Olver. Since then he has written countless articles for various worldwide boxing magazines as a recognised authority and is a member of the World Boxing Council Ratings Committee.

For the last two years I have relied heavily on Peter Goldfield for all of the USA based boxers' individual photographs. Peter has again supplied many great pictures for the latest book and can be reached at 3161 Alabama Road, Camden, New Jersey 08104.

Other magical action shots from the States were captured on film for the *International Boxing Annual* by Tom Casino. Tom lives at 9 Everett Street, Jersey City, New Jersey 07304.

Chris Farina, who looked after our action requirements, in Las Vegas with style, lives in Las Vegas at 4000 Vaquero Avenue.

Both Tom Casino and Chris Farina also supply magnificent colour action from America for *Boxing Monthly*. We feel that they are among the elite of photographers operating throughout the world of boxing.

Also supplying photos for both the *International Boxing Annual* and *Boxing Monthly* is David Jacobs and his top-team at Action Images Ltd., 12 Cambridge Terrace, Bury Street West, London N9. David specialises in the best of British boxing and is always to be found ringside, at not only big-fights, but at small hall shows, also.

Sporting Pictures (UK) Ltd., 7a Lambs Conduit Passage, London WC1R 4RG, through Steve Brown, looked after our other needs.

Other special mentions, regarding photographs, should be made of Peter Shaw of the World Boxing Fan Association; Derek Rowe (Photos) Ltd, and Harry Goodwin.

As in previous editions, a special mention must be made of Edwin Cook and Ray Hedley for their expert handling in the area of picture layouts and design.

Preface

Once again it gives me much pleasure to welcome you, the fans, to the third edition of *Hugman's International Boxing Annual*, formerly known as the International Boxing Year.

The past year has been a most exciting one for me, as I finally decided to bring this title and the *British Boxing Yearbook*, along with all my other works, under one banner. Edward Crawshaw was the entrepreneur behind this move and almost as soon as the ink was dried, he and I set about producing Britain's first ever monthly colour boxing magazine.

First published in May, 1989, *Boxing Monthly* has flourished due to the obvious need for a quality magazine, with plenty of colourful action from around the world, plus regular ratings, every British Fight report, world-wide results, great boxing stories, features on boxers and many other goodies.

It is our intention, ultimately, to provide a full service, not only in Britain, but throughout the world of boxing, that overshadows all else done previously, of which, *Boxing Monthly*, the *British Boxing Yearbook* and the *International Boxing Annual* form the cornerstone.

As in previous years, *Hugman's International Boxing Annual* summarizes the major world title action between January and April, 1988, within the introduction, while The World Boxing Season covers all world title fights between May, 1988 and April, 1989. And if the reader merely wishes to glance through these sections, there are 48 great colour shots, taken from the given period, to delight in.

The greatest problem we have, when compiling The World's Leading Fighters section, is who to leave out. In this day and age of three major boxing commissions, a fighter can come virtually from nowhere to win a title. For this edition, Eric Armit has selected nearly 450 boxers, covering 17 weight divisions, who, even if not champions already, could aspire to a title shot within the next twelve months.

It is intended to eventually portray potted biographies of all the world champions, since gloves, within the Hall of Fame section. And since the book was first published, Ron Olver has produced 36 stories, including the twelve within this edition.

An essential item is the inclusion of all world title bouts since 1890. The results are in weight order and alongside each entry is recorded the name of the body, or bodies, who gave the contest world title status.

It will be noticed that although the World Boxing Organisation (WBO) title contests are shown within boxer's records, where applicable, they are not recorded with the World Championship Boxing section. The explanation for this is that the WBO has only recently been formed, and until it proves itself alongside the other three world bodies, we will not accord it the same status.

I wrote in the first issue of *Boxing Monthly* that although the WBA, WBC and the IBF were doing a good job promoting boxing in general, and helping fighters to remain active, they were purely organising, in the main, world title eliminators, not world title bouts. At present there is only one universally recognised world champion, in Mike Tyson, and it should be the united aim of any body worth its salt to allow their champions to box off against the opposition's best in an effort to decide who is the top man at any given weight, at any given time.

It stands to reason that the more bodies there are operating merely serve to dilute world championship boxing, but if politics prevailed, the international scene would be very healthy.

The outstanding fighters of the current period, in no particular order, are Mike Tyson, Evander Holyfield, Michael Nunn, Julio Cesar Chavez, and among the little men, Sot Chitalada and Myung-Woo Yuh. The last named has successfully defended the WBA light-flyweight title on eleven occasions.

Famous names like "Sugar" Ray Leonard, Roberto Duran and Thomas Hearns are still plying their trade at the highest level, many moons after first arriving on the fistic scene. Close on 17 years since he first won the WBA lightweight title, the Panamanian, Duran, won the WBC version of the middleweight title last February when he defeated the champion, Iran Barkley, following a thrilling twelve-rounder.

There also appear to be several lively prospects who will certainly liven up their weight divisions. At light-heavy, Michael Moorer, from the Kronk stable, looks as though he could go all the way, while there are exciting young fighters like Jeff Harding, a light-heavy from Australia, and middleweights Nigel Benn and Michael Watson from England, who could all go close.

Coming back to Mike Tyson, it has often been said that the state of boxing is reflected by its heavyweight division. Well, there is no doubt that the heavyweight champ is an exciting fighter, who has created great interest in the sport worldwide, but he could just be running out of opposition. After destroying both Michael Spinks and Britain's Frank Bruno during the period covered within these pages, he needs much stiffer tests. Carl Williams is next in line to challenge, but the boxing world are really awaiting the prospect of a Tyson-Holyfield confrontation to discover how good the champion really is.

As in the previous editions, I close by wishing the fans, the boxers and everybody involved in the sport of boxing, much prosperity for 1989–90.

Is Boxing Brutal?

"Boxing brutalises" — or so the legend goes — by Brian Donald

That this is a fevered figment of the anti-boxing lobby's imagination, can be proven by a modern parable.

At the beginning of this century, two male children were born. One in North Africa, the other in Germany.

Raised in the slums of Tunisia, from an early age, the North African learned to fight on the hot dusty streets in order to survive.

In stark contrast, the young German lived in a comfortable middle-class home where deprivation was being permitted only one piece of "Kugelhuf" cake by the servants.

From an early age the young Teuton was exposed to his parents' holiness, and was probably on his knees praying, while his Tunisian counterpart was doing a more violent form of genuflection under street-fighting blows to the head.

The carnage of the First World War did nothing to cool the religious fervour of the young German. Indeed, he became even more pious, steeping himself in uplifting theological tracts.

Five hundred miles away, the youthful Tunisian, having now emigrated to France, was steeped in activities of a vastly different hue.

At approximately the same time that the North African was hooking heads and bodies in French rings, our holy young Teuton was dreaming of "hooking" souls, as he contemplated joining a German Missionary Society in Africa.

Circumstances ultimately prevented this and our holy young man joined an organisation of a different kind — "The Schutz-Staffel" — better known as the "SS".

In the meantime, the transplanted Tunisian won and lost both a fortune and the world flyweight title as he fought against the likes of Frankie Genaro, Johnny King, and Manchester's Jackie Brown.

By a strange quirk of fate, Tunisian and Teuton finally met: one from the tough, violent mileu of the professional ring — the other from the morally uplifting theology library.

They met not at an evangelical prayer meeting, but on a cold, windswept railway ramp. A ramp in the infamous death camp of Auschwitz — the ante-room to a living hell for untold millions of innocent men, women and children.

The date was 4 February, 1943 and the Tunisian ex-world champion had arrived from Paris via the dubious courtesy of a Gestapo-sponsored cattle truck. There in Auschwitz he would die at the hands of the depraved disciples of the erstwhile budding theologian, for Rudolf Hess had become commandant of this establishment which practised violence of an intensity and variety that made Graziano versus Zale or Foreman versus Frazier, seem like conventions for pansies!

It is the moral conundrum which causes me to reject the "boxing brutalises" theory.

If boxing really brutalised, then how come Victor "Young" Perez, who had spent a lifetime in gyms and rings around the world, was the victim of organised violence sponsored by a man whose youth was accompanied by hymns rather than punches?

Yet there is another more important reason why boxing does not brutalise those who participate in it: the "Uncle Toby Factor".

What is the "Uncle Toby Factor"?

In the 18th century, Laurence Sterne, in his novel *Tristram Shandy,* donated the character of "Uncle Toby" to posterity.

Uncle Toby spends all his waking hours reading about and the playing at war in his back garden, which is landscaped as a facsimile of an 18th century battlefield.

Toby mines and counter-mines; attacks and counter-attacks his imaginary enemies, but in one of literature's most celebrated moments, when Uncle Toby spots a common housefly in his bedroom, which is fruitlessly trying to assault its way through the window glass in order to escape, this man who had fought countless bloody battles in his head, opens the window to permit the escape of the demented insect.

In truth, the vast majority of boxing fans, and television viewers, are latter-day Uncle Tobys. They may watch in horrified fascination as Robert de Niro, alias Jake la Motta, beats his wives and brother in *Raging Bull,* but they would never dream of emulating this violence in their own homes.

Anyone who runs an amateur boxing club encounters the "Uncle Toby Factor" daily. Witness the boy who has the build and potential, and even initially the desire, but who proves too soft-hearted ever to be permitted inside a competitive ring.

Any club trainer will also confess that for every ring tiger he presents in the novice class, at least a dozen hopefuls have faded from the scene, having concluded that watching *Fight Night* is much less harrowing than actually taking shots on the chin, even with 16 ounce sparring "pillows". Indeed, boxing owes an enormous debt to the greatest "Uncle Toby" of them all: Nat Fleischer of *Ring* magazine fame.

Despite having witnessed, judged, refereed, and written about more professional boxing matches than almost any other man in history, Mr Fleischer — according to his son-in-law, Nat Loubet — blanched at even the mildest curse word. Hardly symptomatic of a brutalised individual!

So the next time someone in your company wails about "boxing brutalising young men", just remind them that Caligula was never a contender — Terry Downes was! I know under whose roof I would rather have spent an evening!

Introduction

Once again there is no denying that professional boxing is in a healthy and prosperous condition. Attractive contests continue to be waged worldwide, and some of the reigning champions — indeed, one or two non-champions at the moment — may be considered to be among the best of all time.

Admittedly, the game is still plagued by too many "ruling bodies". Instead of the number lessening, as we might have hoped for, yet another has added to the number! In addition, we now have so-called "international" champions, as distinct from the accepted world champions. The way things are going, there is no limit to the extravagances to which influential figures will aspire to stage a contest which will put rear-ends on to seats and TV customers putting coins into the slot.

To Joe Public, the whole thing, while ridiculous, is still acceptable. To the dedicated boxing man, and the true fighter aspiring to undisputed dominance, the situation borders on the tragic.

The designated champions of one or another of the so-called "Alphabet Boys": the WBA, the WBC, and the IBF, are mostly quite content to bask in the limelight of what really amounts to a mere third of the available and *potential* wattage-power. Time was, sad to say, when a champion of the world gloried in his position, and ducked nobody at all. It is sad to say, because today far too often a claimant in one division will studiously avoid meeting another at the same poundage.

The whole business sometimes tends to grow a trifle laughable to the cynical insider. But very, very occasionally, and quite apart from the phenomenal and all-conquering Mike Tyson, we get a man like the former cruiserweight, Evander Holyfield, who not only believes that he is the finest man at his poundage, but sets out and absolutely proves it.

Further, the heavyweight championship being what it is, the richest prize in sport, any reigning title-holder becomes fair game for every sensational journalist who gets the slightest whiff of a meaty story. This is not to suggest that "Iron" Mike Tyson is a blameless and blushing rose, who wants nothing more than to be left alone in peace. But in my opinion he is far more sinned against than sinning.

From his mighty achievements, and through his powerful physique, he would at first appear to be mature, but people seem to forget that the man up there pounding an opponent into oblivion is still

Larry Holmes (left) tries to stave off the onrushing Mike Tyson, who eventually got to the former heavyweight champion, destroying him in the fourth

Sporting Pictures (UK) Ltd

Marlon Starling won the WBA welterweight title from the much fancied Mark Breland, who was kaoyed in eleven rounds

Peter Goldfield/USA

little more than a kid in years and experience of the world. It was no small undertaking to have smashed his way to pre-eminence and a multi-million dollar fortune by the time he was barely out of his 'teens, and to win the hand, and the rest of her, of a young lady who must assuredly rank as one of the most erotically-beautiful of all women at present on the public scene.

Heady stuff, indeed, for a callow youngster who opens the newspapers each morning and reads such absurd inventions about his exploits, that while some part of him is flattered by the attention, another part insists: "They gotta be outa their minds!"

Add to all this the sudden death of his one true living friend, the only man he ever really listened to: his co-manager, Jim Jacobs, and I am not at all surprised at the onset of trauma.

More than half a century ago, a cynical but very observant newspaperman, one Don Skene, said: "Elephants never forget, fight fans never remember." This is perfectly true. Today, Mike Tyson is struggling through many, many personal problems. He has been painted as a brutal villain; he married a beautiful woman, who then took on the appearance of a *femme fatale,* and slipped in the wedge of disruption between her man and his career-advisers.

Readers of the newspapers, today lap it all up as a novelty: by definition, a new thing! They have either forgotten, or never even knew, that in the early 1920s, rather than in the late 1980s, the current heavyweight champion, a certain Jack Dempsey, was subjected to almost precisely the same journalistic rigmarole.

There was little radio then, and no TV. Still, the papers did their damnedest! *That* was "the media" getting on for 70 years back.

Then, we had the crop-headed, blue-jowled, beetle-browed and scowling "Manassa Mauler", an alleged wartime-slacker and double-dyed villain. Thousands came and paid a million to see him pound a luckless adversary, but most of the cash customers were hoping to see *him* get the chop! When, in his exuberant glory, he travelled to Hollywood, and met and married the glamorous star, Estelle Taylor, the papers were only too glad to publicise the nuptials. Eventually Estelle decided to take over her hubby's career, and queried why Dempsey should pay over so much of his earnings to the wily but somewhat crude Jack Kearns, the man, incidentally, who had picked him up as a penniless small-time fighter and ex-hobo and had been responsible for making him a millionaire.

To a few observers, the present-day Tyson saga is all too familiar. This is not to suggest that it will end in the same manner as the former Dempsey one, but things have been very much the same, up to now. Imaginative newspaper reporters, well aware of what they are able to perpetrate, in the way of lurid exaggeration, should never believe without question all that their colleagues write.

Doyen of all columnists in this country is John Junor. Apparently believing everything that he reads in papers other than his own, which I repeat he should never do, he branded Mike Tyson as being both "illiterate and inarticulate".

In point of fact, almost the very reverse is true. The champion is an avid reader, although possibly he doesn't aspire to Proust and Kafka, and with the possible exception of Ray Leonard, I would say that he responds and explains in interviews, with terms even clearer than those of the interviewer!

One great hope for the coming year is that the reporters get off his back and allow him to continue his life and chosen profession without further hassle.

* * *

Tyson didn't manage at all badly during the early months of 1988. Defending his championship in both January and March, he devastated the ageing Larry Holmes in four rounds at Atlantic City, and then travelled to Tokyo to demolish Tony Tubbs in two.

It was in the cruiserweight division that a future possible heavyweight star emerged. Evander Holyfield, already the holder of the WBA and IBF

versions of the championship, watched Carlos de Leon defend his WBC title in January against José Mario Flores, and then, in April, faced the Puerto Rican in a unification showdown. Holyfield proved to be by far the better man and forced the referee to intercede in the eighth round.

Among the light-heavyweights, little championship action was witnessed in the first months of the year. Neither "Prince" Charles Williams (IBF), nor Don Lalonde (WBC), put in any activity. Virgil Hill (WBA), alone defended his title, halting Jean-Marie Emebe in eleven rounds during April.

Of the super-middleweights, the busy Chong-Pal Park consolidated his position as WBA champion by knocking out Polly Pasieron in March. The same month, at Dusseldorf, Graciano Rocchigiani battled for Park's returned IBF belt, versus Vince Boulware, and won without too much trouble in round eight.

Both the IBF and WBA trophies at the traditional middleweight poundage were placed on the line during the first third of the year. Frank Tate came to England and brought Tony Sibson's career to a close with a ten-round knockout in February, and the continually-improving Sumbu Kalambay outpointed Mike McCallum in Italy, during March.

Over the same period, not a great deal happened among the light-middles. Gianfranco Rosi took on Duane Thomas in January, and stopped him in the seventh at Genoa. Neither Matthew Hilton, (IBF), nor Julian Jackson (WBA), went to the post, each having boxed late in 1987.

All three claimants of the welterweight crown did well. Lloyd Honeyghan had forfeited IBF recognition late the previous year, when he lost on a technical decision to Mexico's Jorge Vaca, but with the WBC crown on the line when the pair

Pictured here on the road to regaining his former WBC welterweight title, Lloyd Honeyghan (facing camera) smashes away at former conqueror, Jorge Vaca, only moments from victory in the third round

Action Images

boxed a return in March, 1988, the Brit had no trouble at all with his opponent, and knocked him out easily in three rounds to regain the title. Marlon Starling, who had surprisingly defeated Mark Breland via the knockout route, to annex the WBA belt, defended it in February against Fujio Ozaki with a points win, and then tackled Breland again in April. He retained the title, but only by the controversial verdict of a draw. The same month, Jamaica's Simon Brown boxed Tyrone Trice in France for the vacant IBF championship, and the referee stopped their contest in the fourteenth round in the former's favour.

Argentina's Juan M. Coggi, the holder of the WBA light-welterweight belt, did not defend it during the period under discussion. But both the IBF and WBC belts were up for grabs. In February, after Terry Marsh had retired under somewhat strange circumstances, James "Buddy" McGirt caused a surprise by battering Frankie Warren to defeat in twelve rounds. In March, Roger Mayweather made his first defence of the WBC championship and easily flattened Mauricio Aceves in the third round.

All three lightweight claimants were busy. Greg Haugen turned the tables on his old conqueror, IBF title-holder Vinny Pazienza, with a gruelling fifteen-round points verdict in February. Haugen was again in action two months later, and was awarded a technical decision over Miguel Santana. In March, José Luis Ramirez outpointed Pernell Whitaker in France to retain the WBC championship, and in April the popular two-fisted little Mexican idol, Julio Cesar Chavez, stopped Rodolfo Aguilar in six rounds at Las Vegas.

Azumah Nelson was extended for the full twelve rounds before gaining the verdict over Mario Martinez, who had made a challenge for the WBC super-featherweight title. Rocky Lockridge was also pushed for a full fifteen rounds when he faced Harold Knight with his IBF championship at stake, but managed to win through. Brian Mitchell, too, had to go the full route, this time over twelve rounds, before being declared the victor over WBA challenger José Rivera.

Among the feathers, Calvin Grove started the year off very well, obliging the referee to halt proceedings as early as the fourth round against Antonio Rivera, thus lifting the IBF laurels. The afore-mentioned Azumah Nelson, having had weight problems at this poundage, relinquished his WBC belt and saw his old championship go to a worthy successor: the all-conquering little Aussie, Jeff Fenech, stopped Victor Callejas in the tenth at Sydney, in March. Antonio Esparragoza, the Venezuelan WBA champion, did not box early in the year.

Jeff Fenech, like Azumah Nelson, had his own weight problems, and after he gave up his WBC version of the super-bantamweight crown to box as a full featherweight, his old title was put on the line in February, 1988, with Daniel Zaragoza and Carlos Zarate in opposite corners. The referee stopped the bout in the tenth round in Zaragoza's favour. Seung-Hoon Lee, the IBF champion, handed in his belt, preferring to make a bid for one of the more prestigious versions of the title, if and when he got the chance. Meanwhile, Julio Gervacio, the WBA title-holder, made a first defence against Bernardo Pinango and lost the championship via a twelve-round points defeat.

All three versions of the bantamweight title proper were defended early in 1988. Wilfredo Vasquez drew with Takuya Muguruma over twelve rounds in a WBA match, Kelvin Seabrooks stopped Fernando Beltran in two under the auspices of the IBF, and Miguel Lora outpointed Lucio Lopez over twelve for the WBC title.

Again, at the super-flyweight poundage, the three claimants made defences as the year began. The first of them was Thailander Kaosai Galaxy, who, in January, scored a twelve-round points win over Kongtoranee Payakarun. The following month, Indonesia's Elly Pical had to go the full fifteen rounds before defeating Raul Diaz to retain his IBF belt. But in April, Jesus Rojas took on the evergreen Gilberto Roman, and lost his WBC title after twelve rounds with the little Mexican.

Chang-Ho Choi, the South Korean IBF flyweight king, got a shock when he visited Manila and lost his crown over fifteen rounds of battling with Filipino Rolando Bohol. Sot Chitalada made his fifth successful defence of the WBC version of the title, stopping Hideaki Kamishiro in the seventh round, and Fidel Bassa decisively outpointed Ireland's Dave McAuley at Belfast, in a blistering WBA twelve-rounder.

The light-flyweight division was represented only once during the first months of the year, when Myung-Woo Yuh gained a twelve-rounds points verdict over Wilibaldo Salazar in a WBA match. Jung-Koo Chang (WBC), and Jum-Hwan Choi (IBF), not only made no early-year defences against foreign opposition, but studiously stayed well away from one another, apparently preferring merely a portion of the championship rather than face a unifying campaign, which would end with a single title-holder, but a certain South Korean one.

The tiny mini-flyweights were not lazy during this period. The WBA got into the sometimes-dubbed "straw-weight" division, by giving its blessing to a bout between Luis Gamez, of Venezuela, and Bong-Jun Kim, of South Korea. Gamez was adjudged the victor on points, and went on to stop Kenji Yokozawa in three rounds at Tokyo. Meanwhile, Hiroki Ioka, of Japan, stopped Kyung-Yung Lee, of South Korea, when the latter, having handed in his IBF belt, sought to annex the WBC one. His bid failed in the final round, when he was stopped. A couple of months later, in a bout to find a new IBF title-holder to replace Lee, Samuth Sithnaruepol, of Thailand, forced the referee to intervene in the eleventh round at Bangkok, to save Domingo "Pretty Boy" Lucas, of the Philippines.

* * *

With the close of the above summary of world championship contests from January to April, the events of the new season follow logically in the ensuing pages with month by month descriptions of major activity throughout the world.

The World Boxing Season

May 1988–April 1989, graphically highlighted month by month as viewed by O.F. Snelling, one of Britain's foremost ring observers and historians.

MAY

Lalonde Sets Up Leonard Match

The beginning of the new season found champions of all three authoritative bodies in action.

Perhaps the most colourful contest of the month saw the New York-based Canadian, Don Lalonde, making his first defence of the WBC light-heavyweight title, in opposition to Trinidad's former WBA king-pin, Leslie Stewart, before an open-air crowd at Port of Spain.

The handsome "golden boy" Lalonde, darling of the ladies for his looks, and supported strongly by many fight fans for his exciting style and power of punch, lost little time in attempting to establish his superiority. Although an inferior boxer to the West Indian, he caught his challenger with a right to the jaw in the opening round which heralded the start of things to come. It was in the second session that the champion connected forcibly with a similar blow which dropped Stewart briefly to one knee.

Although obliged to take the mandatory count of eight before resuming, the Trinidadian was not badly hurt, and he piled into the strong but cruder Canadian with a fine exhibition of boxing. By the fifth round the challenger had more than evened up the score, and he looked as if he might well surge ahead to take a points victory when Lalonde once again slung over a powerful right-hander to the head. It felled Stewart heavily, and this time he was very slow to arise.

Lalonde sensed victory, and he charged in with a fearsome two-fisted barrage. As wild and crude as this attack undoubtedly was, many of his punches got through, and to devastating effect. Stewart was virtually helpless when the referee hastily stopped the battle and declared the champion the victor.

*　*　*

The super-middleweight division, by no means universally-recognised since its introduction in 1984 by the IBF, had been dominated by the very active Chong-Pal Park almost from its inception, with the busy South Korean eventually taking over the WBA version of the championship.

The veteran Venezuelan, Fully Obelmejias, twice halted by Marvin Hagler early in the decade in brave attempts to win the middleweight crown, had not been particularly successful in recent years, and when he travelled to Suanbao, South Korea, to do battle with Park for the heavier honours, the betting odds were well in favour of the Oriental. But the Latin-American caused a considerable surprise by outpointing the champion decisively to take a well-earned unanimous points verdict, flooring Chong-Pal Park in the tenth round for good measure.

*　*　*

WBA light-welterweight champion, the Argentinian southpaw Juan M. Coggi, faced the South Korean Sang-Ho Lee in the Italian town of Roseto Degli Abruzzi. It was his first defence of the belt, and Coggi came through with flying colours.

Not a great deal of aggressive action was shown by either contestant in the opening round, but the South American was merely taking cautious stock of an opponent whose qualities were not common knowledge. Once having decided that he had little to fear from his challenger, Coggi came out for the second round and pitched into his man with a two-fisted assault. Halfway through the session Lee succumbed to the barrage and was counted out.

*　*　*

The IBF featherweight title was at stake when Calvin Grove, the champion, hitherto undefeated,

Following a successful defence of his IBF featherweight title against Myron Taylor, the champion, Calvin Grove, explains his winning formula

Peter Goldfield/USA

faced fellow American, Myron Taylor, of Philadelphia. The challenger, brother of the better-known Meldrick Taylor, was a substitute for yet another Taylor: Bernard of that ilk, who was injured during training.

Although the challenger came in at very short notice and saved the show at Atlantic City, it is doubtful if he could have put up a much better performance had he had the advantage of a more reasonable period for preparation. Although game and willing enough to carry the fight to his opponent, he was not really in the same class as Grove.

Taylor managed to do fairly well during the first half of the battle, without actually winning many of the rounds. But as the bout progressed, Grove grew more and more confident, and began to streak ahead with fast and flashy long-distance boxing. By the end of the fifteenth round there was little doubting which man would receive the verdict.

A unanimous decision on the part of the three judges not only found Calvin Grove retaining his title, but by an overwhelming margin. Taylor was credited with winning hardly a single round.

* * *

All three versions of the super-bantamweight championship were at stake during the month.

The reign of Bernardo Pinango, Venezuela's WBA title-holder, came to an end in the border town of Tijuana, Mexico, when he was outpointed in a not very exciting contest held at the district's bull ring. His adversary was Juan J. Estrada, the local challenger. The Mexican showed considerable aggression in the early rounds, but seemed to lose heart as the bout progressed, with the champion evening up the scoring during the middle sessions. The contest warmed up a little in its final stages as both men tried desperately to catch the judges' eyes, and at the final bell there was very little in it. A narrow victory in the challenger's favour, with the officials disagreeing, was nevertheless a popular decision with the partisan crowd.

Following the decision made by Seung-Hoon Lee, the South Korean holder of the IBF belt at this poundage, José Sanabria, of Venezuela, faced Moises Fuentes, from Colombia, for the vacant honours. Bucaramanga was the scene of this encounter, scheduled for fifteen rounds, but Sanabria proved to be the stronger and more dominant of the pair, and he knocked out his opponent in the fifth.

Mexico's Daniel Zaragoza, super-bantamweight king-pin according to the WBC, made the first defence of his diadem by accepting the challenge of Seung-Hoon Lee, the South Korean who had given up the IBF belt in order to contest this more prestigious version of the title.

Before a naturally partisan crowd at Youchan, the Korean staged a fine battle, with one of the judges seeing him as the victor at the close of twelve rounds. However, a second judge viewed Zaragoza as a narrow winner, while the third official scored the contest even, and a draw was declared, with the Mexican thus retaining his championship.

* * *

Two brothers winning world boxing championships is rare enough in the annals of the ring, but hitherto, no pair of identical twins had ever managed to scale the highest honours. Thailander Kaokor Galaxy, twin brother of the WBA super-flyweight champion, Kaosai Galaxy, got his name into the record books when he made his challenge in Bangkok for the same governing body's version of the bantamweight title.

In opposition to Wilfredo Vasquez, of Puerto Rico, the little Thailander came very close to ignominious defeat in the fifth round, when a fine punch from the Latin-American champion sent him to the canvas. But the challenger was on his feet in an instant and was battling back furiously to erase his opponent's advantage.

A split decision in favour of Galaxy was naturally a popular one with the onlookers, but the Vasquez camp talked of filing a complaint with the WBA against the verdict. Perhaps the fairest thing that can be said is that the fight was very closely-contested and that all three judges might well have voted for Galaxy had not Vasquez scored the clean knockdown in the fifth round.

* * *

Rolando Bohol, Filipino IBF titleholder in the flyweight division, had very little trouble in retaining his belt when he faced Cho-Woon Park, yet another of the seemingly endless parade of South Korean fighters to bear this same common name.

Boxing before his own countrymen at Manila, Bohol very nearly ended matters in the opening round, when he dropped his man to the boards. The bell intervened as the referee counted, and might well have saved the Korean from a knockout defeat, but the respite in his corner enabled him to throw off the effects of the blow and to come out willingly for the second round.

However, he was completely outclassed, and although he struggled on for the full fifteen rounds, the unanimous decision in Bohol's favour showed an overwhelming margin of points in the champion's favour when the scores were announced.

JUNE

Typhoon Tyson Blows Away Spinks

Topping a month of considerable activity at the highest level of the game was undoubtedly the long-awaited "showdown" in Atlantic City between "Iron" Mike Tyson, undisputed heavyweight champion of the world, and Michael Spinks, former holder of the IBF version of the title and twice victor over an ageing Larry Holmes.

Despite the continued disparagements in the sporting world that Spinks was really no more than a blown-up light-heavyweight and had no place at all in the same ring with so strong and formidable a man as Tyson, the two-year-long "hype" of this prospective battle made it the most lucrative and widely-watched boxing promotion of all time.

In the event, the confrontation proved to be hardly more than a fiasco. After a considerable delay before the eventual entry of the gladiators — said by some observers to have been a psychological ploy on the part of Spinks, and by others of a more cynical disposition to have been a marked reluctance on the part of the challenger to leave his quarters — the contest was all over in a matter of a minute and a half.

Spinks appeared to be in a state of shock, and ready to accept what he considered to be the inevitable. The very first blows landed by Tyson could plainly be seen to distress his adversary. Mike's first spirited charge, which forced his man back to the ropes, culminated in a paralysing smash to the body which sent Spinks to his knees on the canvas.

Once back on his feet, and facing the oncoming and murderous-looking champion, the challenger threw a wild right. "Iron" Mike had no trouble in avoiding it and simply hurled in the finisher. It caught Spinks cleanly on the jaw, deposited him heavily to the boards on to his back, and with his head beneath the ropes, the "greatest battle of all time" was over.

* * *

Two bouts, with the WBA and IBF versions of the light-heavyweight honours at stake, gave something of a line on the relative merits of the twelve stone seven claimants.

Gaining world-wide coverage on television was Virgil Hill, who defended his WBA crown against the Californian-based Ramzi Hassan at Las Vegas, on a bill sporting no less than three world title contests. Taking third place to the Hearns-Barkley and Mayweather-Brazier battles, Hill threw away the chance of a lifetime to gain a good following and a prospective fortune by turning in a lack-lustre performance which had many home observers reaching for the "off" switch on their sets. The champion won on points and fairly easily, but he was most unimpressive.

By comparison, "Prince" Charles Williams, IBF title-holder and conqueror of the rumbustious Bobby Czyz, looked very good as he made his first defence when the Frenchman, Richard Caramanolis, challenged him before an enthusiastic crowd at Annecy.

Williams very nearly finished matters in the opening round, felling his man for a compulsory count of eight. Although Caramanolis was able to continue it was evident from that moment which way the contest would go. The Frenchman was game enough, and he charged into the champion with everything he had, but Williams was by far the more talented and stronger man.

The challenger was taking a systematic drubbing, and after having been dropped twice in the eleventh round his corner wisely surrendered on his behalf.

* * *

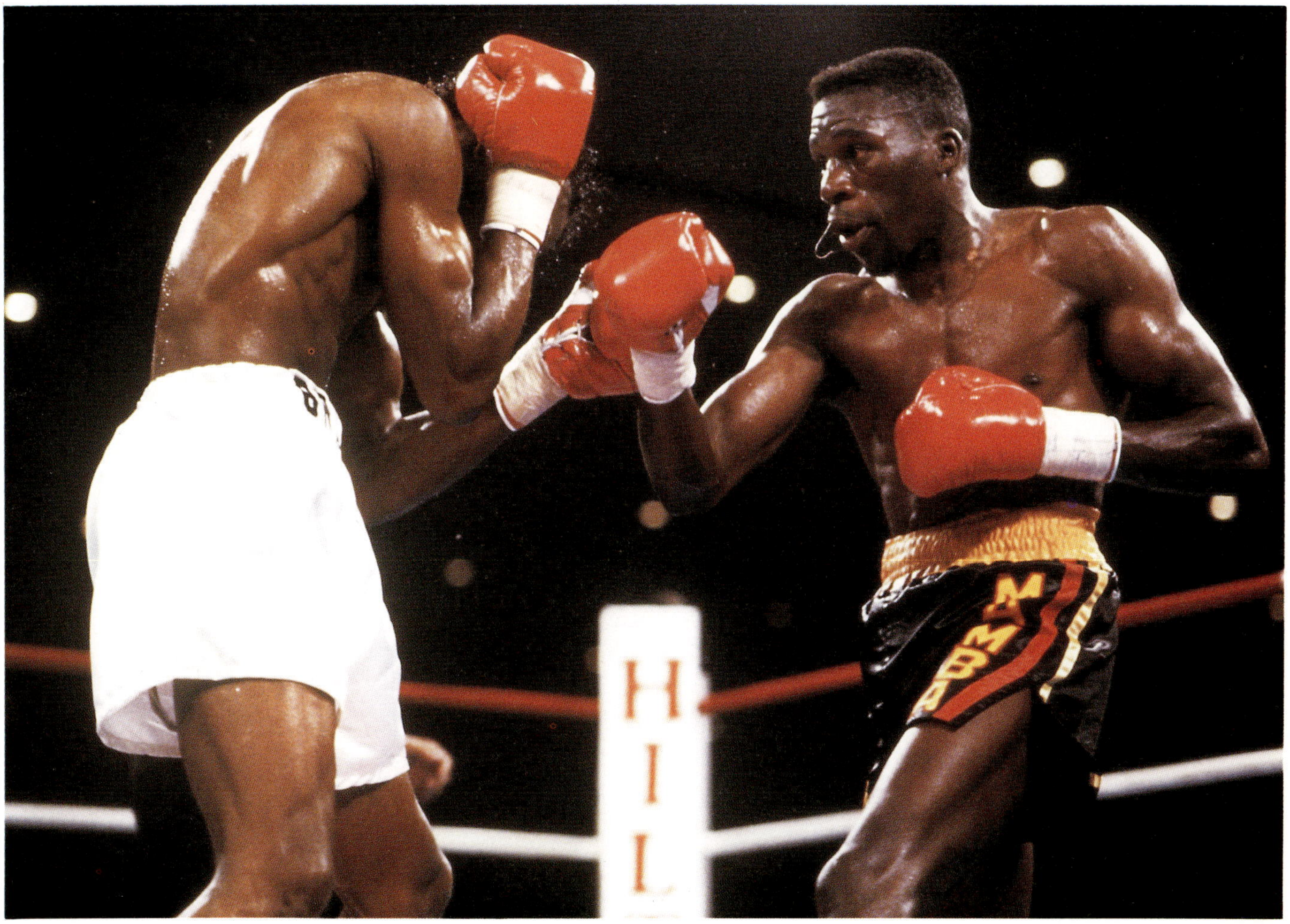

When defending his WBC light-welter title, Roger Mayweather (right), despite being an odds-on favourite, seemed fortunate to receive the decision over unfancied Harold Brazier

Tom Casino

In one of the year's great upsets, Thomas Hearns (right) lost his WBC middleweight title when he was stopped in the third round by Iran Barkley

Tom Casino

Super-middleweights were on view in Berlin when the German holder of the IBF version of the championship, Graciano Rocchigiani, made his first defence in opposition to the American challenger, Nicky Walker.

It was a gruelling battle, with plenty of blood in evidence, both fighters sustaining cuts above their eyes. But although the visitor did his utmost, and forced the fight throughout, Rocchigiani was far too good for him in every department. While the champion was unable to score a knockout, he sailed to a comfortable points win, with each of the judges favouring him by a healthy margin.

*　　　*　　　*

Among the middleweights proper, Las Vegas was the scene of one of the year's most unexpected upsets, when Thomas "Hit Man" Hearns placed his WBC eleven stone six title in jeopardy against Iran Barkley.

Riding on the crest of a wave, and basking in the adulation of being the first man ever to win world championships in four separate divisions — albeit fairly new "intermediate" weight classes being represented — Hearns entered the ring a heavy favourite. Indeed, the odds seemed quite justified as he went to work, easily out-speeding and out-scoring his clumsier adversary.

Barkley, an unabashed slugger, was made to appear almost like a novice in the first two rounds. Hearns took both sessions on points with plenty to spare, and he came out for the third in top form, giving every indication that the contest would not last very much longer.

It didn't. Barkley was cut badly above both eyes, and blood was seeping from his mouth as the champion danced around him and whipped home forceful punches with apparent ease. But suddenly, and almost in desperation, the challenger threw a right-hander. It caught Hearns on the jaw and sent him flat.

The crowd was in an uproar at this sudden turn of events, and although nobody — not even Hearns — could hear the count, he somehow staggered erect, perhaps more by instinct than design. His eyes were glazed and his spindly legs were tottery. The referee looked very closely at him before waving Barkley forward, and the crude challenger almost lost the day in a wild effort to land again on the reeling defenceless champion.

Bundled to the ropes, Hearns half-fell and was half-pushed through the strands and on to the apron of the ring. There, sitting bemused on the canvas, he was obviously in no state to continue, and the referee waved the bout over.

Also at middleweight, the Italian-based WBA

Hearns (right) has Barkley doubling up from a body punch as he swarms all over his rival, who later gained sweet revenge

Tom Casino

champion from Zaire, Sumbu Kalambay, faced the challenge of Robbie Sims, half-brother of the more famous "Marvelous" Marvin Hagler, who was at the ringside to give fraternal moral support.

Sims, a rugged southpaw who for some years had been among the forefront of contenders at this poundage, waged a hard and plucky battle, but the man from the Congo proved to be a far better champion than had first been believed. He won a clear and convincing points victory with all three judges rendering a unanimous decision.

* * *

Roger Mayweather, light-welterweight king in the eyes of the WBC, received quite a shock when he put his crown on the line against Harold Brazier, of Indiana, in a supporting contest to the Hearns-Barkley upset at Las Vegas.

While the opening rounds were rather dull, and the crowd called for more action, things hotted up considerably as the fight progressed, and a ding-dong battle ensued, with neither man being able to dominate matters completely. The judges' scoring was extremely close at the end of twelve rounds, with one official even awarding the decision to Brazier by a single point. But the other two judges saw Mayweather as having just won the contest. The onlookers were none too pleased, and it was not a popular verdict, despite the fact that the champion was a Las Vegas resident and the majority of fans wanted to see him win.

* * *

Hard-punching Azumah Nelson, of Ghana, proved that he is probably the best of the claimants to the super-featherweight crown when he staged an extremely impressive performance in Atlantic City when defending his WBC belt against the Texan southpaw, Lupe Suarez.

The champion took a little time in establishing his superiority, but once he had got the measure of a game but limited opponent, he began to turn on the heat. By the eighth round he was scoring solidly and the luckless challenger began to look a sorry sight. When Nelson came out confidently for the ninth and stretched the Texan on the canvas with a two-fisted barrage, the contest was as good as over. Although Suarez pluckily climbed erect, the referee could see that he had little fight left in him, and after completing the eight-count he called a halt to the proceedings.

* * *

In a hard battle before an appreciative audience at Los Angeles, Antonio Esparragoza, the WBA

Opposite: Despite having Hassan under pressure on several occasions, Hill (right) lacked the winning punch and had to settle for a points verdict

Christopher M. Farina

featherweight titleholder from Venezuela, came perilously close to losing to his Mexican challenger, Marcos Villasana.

The champion streaked ahead in the earlier rounds, with Villasana earning cautions for wayward punching to the body, but as the bout progressed the challenger began to make up lost ground and forged ahead himself.

A very low punch in the fifth round led the referee to halt the contest temporarily as he instructed the three judges to deduct a point from the Mexican's tally for the obvious infringement, and this proved to be the factor between winning and losing.

A split decision at the close found one judge favouring Esparragoza, with another scoring for Villasana. The third judge had matters entirely even, and a draw was declared, but had the point not been deducted in the fifth round from the Mexican's tally he would have won the contest and the title by a single point!

* * *

While South Korea dominated the light-flyweight division, boasting three claimants to the world title at this poundage, June found the fortunes of two of the three champions taking very divergent turns.

Myung-Woo Yuh was extremely lucky to hold on to his belt in Seoul after facing the Puerto Rican, José de Jesus. A spirited battle closed with the judges unable to agree upon a unanimous victor. Scoring was very close, but one official had de Jesus in front by a couple of points, and only the fact that the other two judges both felt that the champion had just nosed ahead kept the WBA light-flyweight belt in South Korea.

On the other hand, Jung-Koo Chang, defending his WBC crown for the fifteenth time, on this occasion in Tokyo, had a remarkably easy victory over Hideyuki Ohashi, of Japan. Three times the challenger was sent to the boards in the third round, but managed to last until the bell. In the seventh he was again dropped on two occasions, and when, in the eighth, Ohashi was battered to the canvas twice more the now one-sided encounter was rightfully halted to save the challenger from further punishment.

* * *

The mini-flyweight — or so-called "straw-weight" division — for the tiniest of all boxers, scaling only

Virgil Hill (left) keeps Ramzi Hassan at bay with the left lead on his way to a successful WBA light-heavyweight defence

Tom Casino

MADD

Azumah Nelson stands menacingly over his rival, Lupe Suarez, in the ninth round. When Suarez arose, the contest was halted, leaving the WBC super-feather belt still in the Ghanian's capable hands

Tom Casino

seven and a half stone, was represented at Osaka when the WBC titleholder, Japan's Horoki Ioka, made his second defence, this time versus Thailand's Napa Kiatwanchai.

Ioka was extremely lucky to hang on to his unbeaten record, for the challenger gave him a very tough time and was considered to have been aggressive and successful enough to have earned a draw.

JULY

Tate Finishes Second to Nunn

In a busy month of world title defences, outstanding in attractiveness and also in performance was the IBF battle at middleweight in Las Vegas between two old amateur rivals, Frank Tate, Olympic gold medallist at light-middleweight, and the flashy southpaw defensive wizard, Michael "Second To" Nunn.

Before turning professional, Tate had twice defeated Nunn in their three simon-pure meetings, but this time it was an entirely different matter. With both men undefeated as professionals, although Tate had not gone back, as far as his ability was concerned, Nunn had gone forward immeasurably.

Taking a leaf out of the book of the arrogant "Sugar" Ray Leonard, the Californian-based challenger taunted the champion with both words and gestures. Although boxing cagily for the most part, Nunn was not averse to mixing it with the reputedly harder-hitting Tate. He surprised everyone present by carrying the fight to his man, and he gained a useful psychological advantage with his unpredictability.

Few onlookers would have given Nunn much chance of knocking out the champion or stopping him, but at the close of round eight, by which time the challenger was well in front, he sank a vicious left deep into Tate's body and dropped him on to all fours. The bell saved him as he sought to struggle erect, and Nunn's corner remonstrated loudly that he should have been counted out.

But the minute's respite only delayed the inevitable. Tate was utterly demoralised and when his opponent pitched in for the finisher in round nine he so overwhelmed the champion that the referee quickly stepped in and brought matters to a conclusion.

* * *

At light-middleweight, that hardy old war-horse, Buster Drayton, of Philadelphia, finally came to the end of the line in a plucky but vain challenge for the WBA championship, when pitted against the Virgin Islander, powerful Julian Jackson, at Atlantic City.

Drayton's experience enabled him to weather the first two rounds, although Jackson was definitely in charge, but in the third round the champion nullified his opponent completely with a blistering attack and then connected with a terrific left hook to the jaw. Drayton dropped like the proverbial log, his head banging forcibly against the floor of the ring. As the referee began to count, the ringside doctor was up the steps and through the ropes in an instant. While, amazingly, he made an instinctive effort to climb to his feet, the fight was stopped on the medico's authority.

In the open air at San Remo, the awkward Italian WBC light-middleweight king, Gianfranco

Kelvin Seabrooks (left) lost his IBF bantamweight title to Orlando Canizales with just two minutes remaining of their fierce fifteen-rounder, when, after rising from a count, the referee came to his rescue

Tom Casino

Just as the bell rang to end the sixth round of the WBA welterweight title battle between Marlon Starling and Tomas Molinares, the challenger (left) connected with the right . . .

Tom Casino

Rosi, waged a game but fruitless battle against the "Texas Cobra", Don Curry, back once again on the world championship trail.

Although Rosi had been rather surprisingly successful in his earlier title defences, since his unorthodox manner of boxing is hardly impressive, he stood little chance against his American challenger, who dominated matters right from the start.

During the nine rounds the contest lasted, Rosi bustled and mauled continually in an effort to unsettle his adversary, but Curry was punching cleanly and accurately, and at times it appeared that the champion just couldn't stay on his feet.

Five times in all the champion either dropped or was punched to the canvas, and after the bell had signalled the close of round nine he wisely retired from a one-sided meeting.

* * *

All three versions of the welterweight championship were contested during the month, two at Atlantic City on the same bill, and the third in Jamaica. The so-called "Double Trouble" programme at the New Jersey gambling resort found both bouts ending unsatisfactorily, to say the least.

Lloyd Honeyghan defended his WBC title against the South Korean, Yung-Kil Chung, and the London-based champion seemed to be well ahead, with the fight comfortably in his charge, when, after a melée at close quarters, Honeyghan brought up a left uppercut to the body. It caught Chung in the groin, and he sank to the boards, rolling over and over in apparent agony. While the rule states that in the event of such an occurrence, the disabled man will be given five minutes to recover, on the face of things it seemed that the Korean had more than had enough, knew that he was on a hiding to nothing, and took the easy way out. His seconds retired their charge before the five minutes had elapsed.

Even more disappointing was the fight between Marlon Starling, the WBA champion, and the little-known Colombian, Tomas Molinares. Once again the titleholder appeared to have things well in hand when unexpected drama suddenly struck. As the bell rang to end the sixth round, the challenger threw a right-hander which connected forcibly with Starling's jaw and flattened him. Amid scenes of confusion, the champion lay completely *hors de combat*.

While there is no doubt at all that the final blow landed after the bell had sounded, opinions differ as to whether the punch was blatantly foul or unintentional. While the consensus was that Starling heard the bell, relaxed and dropped his defences and then took the wallop, my own opinion, after repeated viewings of the fight on video, is that Molinares started a "one-two" just as the bell sounded. The left shot out almost simultaneously with the audible clang and the right came over to the exposed jaw momentarily afterwards. Starling had no time to relax.

With both contests ending in confusion and recriminations, it was comforting to see the IBF champion, Simon Brown, establishing himself so well before a home crowd at Kingston, Jamaica. He completely outclassed the former WBC titleholder, Jorge Vaca, of Mexico, and felled him no fewer than six times before the referee mercifully brought the one-sided match to a close in the third round.

* * *

The light-welterweights were represented in New York City, but not for very long, when James "Buddy" McGirt made his initial defence of the IBF belt in opposition to Howard Davis.

The challenger, who had won the lightweight gold medal at the 1984 Olympics, and had then appeared to be almost a certainty to win a professional title, was making his third attempt at a championship, having twice failed to annex WBC honours. Coming in as a substitute for the indisposed Meldrick Taylor, Davis later claimed to have been weakened by an effort to make the weight in too short a time.

It is rather ironic that this match, announced as the last fifteen-rounder to be held in the United States — the IBF having finally bowed to pressure by intending to reduce all bouts under its auspices to twelve rounds — should be one so brief. After turning on the heat early in the opening round, McGirt continued to keep up the attack, and towards the close of the session he shot over a right to the jaw which dumped Davis heavily.

Although the former Olympic star made an effort to rise, he was completely bemused, and the referee counted him out to give the champion a one-round knockout victory.

* * *

A Sacramento crowd witnessed a bruising and gory clash for the IBF super-featherweight crown when holder Rocky Lockridge crossed gloves with his challenger, Tony Lopez.

Although the ruling body's decision to limit contests under its jurisdiction was not to take effect until September, the powers that be bowed to the wishes of the Californian authorities, who confine their championship bouts to twelve rounds. The contest travelled its full distance and a unanimous decision was rendered in favour of the Sacramento man, Tony Lopez.

Lockridge, always a dangerous fighter and punishing hitter, did not surrender his crown easily; the Californian was made to battle all the way. Although Lopez took the early rounds and began to surge ahead, the champion rallied and evened up matters as the bout progressed. In the eighth session, with a bad cut over the right eye which he had suffered earlier, he landed a heavy right to the jaw which sent Lopez to the boards.

The result shows Starling stretched out, dead to the world, leaving Molinares as the new champion, despite great confusion as to whether a foul had been committed

Tom Casino

In the second of the "Double Trouble" welter championship bouts, Lloyd Honeyghan (right), holder of the IBF version, steams into the South Korean, Yung-Kil Chung

Tom Casino

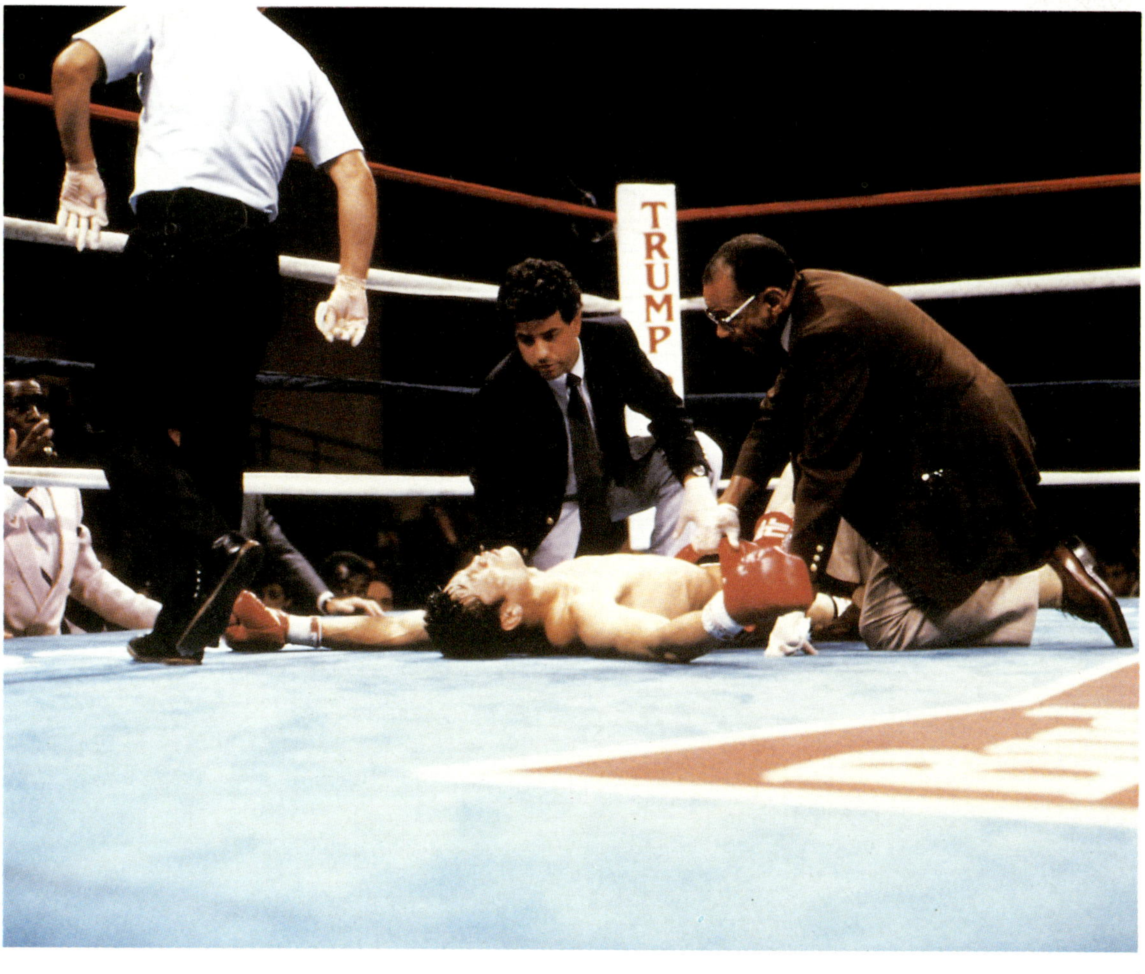

After taking a left uppercut to the groin, Chung was given five minutes to recover, but soon decided that this was a more sensible arrangement

Tom Casino

Although the challenger was up at three, the referee counted the compulsory eight before signalling both men to continue. Despite the champion's desperate efforts to finish his adversary, Lopez fought defensively until the bell and then came out the fresher of the pair as he boxed brilliantly to wipe away the temporary advantage Lockridge had scored.

Rocky was now cut again, this time under the left eye, but Lopez was not unmarked. His own right eye was severely the worse for wear.

Both men piled on the pressure in the closing rounds in order to clinch the contest, but Lopez was now by far the stronger. The verdict in his favour was enthusiastically received by the large Sacramento crowd.

*   *   *

The last bantamweight fifteen-rounder almost went its full distance and provided one of the most thrilling fights of the year when Kelvin Seabrooks put his IBF title up for grabs against the Texan challenger, Orlando Canizales, at Atlantic City.

It appeared to be all over in the opening round, when the man from Laredo dropped the champion with a heavy right, but Seabrooks came back gamely. Although he suffered considerable facial

In the last fifteen-rounder to be held in the States, "Buddy" McGirt, defending his IBF light-welterweight title, kaoyed Howard Davis in the first

Tom Casino

damage to himself, the title-holder opened a dangerous cut over his opponent's eye, but could never quite establish his superiority during the contest.

Seabrooks was floored again during a desperate rally in the final round, and although he wobbled erect and was willing enough to continue, Canizales' final attack was so furious that the battle was stopped after just a minute of the session.

The crowning of the Texan as the new champion celebrated the ascension to world championship status of yet another pair of boxing brothers. Gaby Canizales, who won the WBA bantam title in 1986, had also beaten Seabrooks early in the North Carolinan's career.

* * *

Mexico's great little super-flyweight champion, Gilberto Roman, got something of a surprise when he travelled to Kawagoe, Japan, to defend his WBC title against Yoshiyuki Uchida.

Although Roman was definitely the better man of the two, he was careless enough to relax his usually immaculate boxing in the fourth round, and found himself on the canvas taking a count. But he was not seriously hurt, and came out for the next round with the intention of finishing matters. Barely half a minute of the fifth had elapsed, and Uchida had taken two counts, when the referee stopped the fight in Roman's favour.

* * *

A glorious reign at the top sadly came to an end when the WBC's flyweight champion, Sot Chitalada, of Thailand, who had held the title since 1984, was decisively outpointed by Yong-Kang Kim at Pohang, South Korea.

Greatly weakened by desperate efforts to make the weight, Chitalada was but a mere shadow of the brilliant fighter he had once been, and could accomplish nothing effective. He was soundly beaten on points, although a spokesman from his camp suggested that the little Thailander might soon come back as a full bantamweight.

AUGUST

Fiery Fenech Down(e)s Tyrone

The heftier world champions relaxed during August. The seven championship bouts decided during the month featured featherweights, bantams, and the tinier men from the Orient.

Both the IBF and the WBC featherweight belts were placed on the line. The first defence was that of Calvin Grove, IBF king-pin, who travelled to Mexicali, Mexico, to face the challenge of local hero Jorge Paez. The second contest presented the popular little Aussie, Jeff Fenech, who opposed his foremost contender, Tyrone Downes, the Barbadian, at Melbourne, for the WBC crown.

The Grove versus Paez contest turned out to be very interesting and closely-waged, but was marred considerably by histrionics and clowning on the part of both boxers. At the close of the bout a split decision was announced. While one judge saw it as honours even, the other two had the challenger just slightly ahead. It was his final burst of aggression in the fifteenth round, sending the champion to the boards on no less than three occasions, which just turned the tide in favour of the Mexican.

Jeff Fenech had a much more comfortable time when defending his belt against the veteran Downes. The West Indian certainly tried hard enough, but he was really no match for an outstanding champion.

Fenech had a little bother in settling down during the opening rounds, but very soon established command. In the fourth he twice sent his challenger to the canvas with powerful blows which heralded the shape of things to come. Although Downes managed to last out the round, the champion had now sensed victory.

He charged into the attack at the start of the fifth and once again sent his man to the boards with a powerful right to the body. Downes stayed down for nine, but he was obviously beaten. A further attack to the body dropped him yet again, and this time the referee did not bother to continue counting. He waved the one-sided encounter over and declared Fenech the winner.

* * *

José Sanabria, the Venezuelan holder of the IBF super-bantamweight belt, made his first defence of the championship when he travelled to Capo d' Orlando to face the European eight stone six title-holder, Vincenzo Belcastro.

Although Belcastro had the reputation of being a big puncher, he found the South American just a bit too good for him. The Italian forced the fight as best he could, but Sanabria clearly won a spirited contest on points.

* * *

Both the WBA and the WBC versions of the bantamweight title were in contention during the month. The first bout took place in Los Angeles, while the second was fought out at Pusan.

Miguel "Happy" Lora, the undefeated little Colombian WBC champion, defended his honours for the seventh time, when he crossed gloves with the former holder, Albert Davila. This was the second time the pair had met for the title, and once again Lora proved to be much the better man in all departments of the game. Although he was badly cut over both eyes, the game Californian never gave up trying. But at the close of twelve rounds Lora was announced the victor by a unanimous verdict, each judge scoring him the winner by a wide margin.

At Pusan, the South Korean challenger, Sung-Il Moon, was adjudged the winner on a technical decision when he met the WBA champion, Kaokor Galaxy. The Thailander, who had made history in May by becoming one of the first of twin brothers to win world championships, was behind on points, according to all three officials, when the South Korean suffered a nasty gash over the right

Opposite: Miguel "Happy" Lora successfully put his WBC bantamweight title on the line for the seventh time, when beating Albert Davila

Christopher M. Farina

HILT

eye in the sixth round, from a clash of heads. In accordance with the rules, the bout was stopped and the verdict awarded to the challenger.

*　　*　　*

Also at Pusan, Myung-Woo Yuh, the Korean WBA light-flyweight king, did not have a great deal of trouble with Putt Ohyuthanakorn, of Thailand, when he made his ninth defence of the belt. After summing up his opponent in the early rounds, the champion piled in with both fists during the sixth session and stretched the Thailander out for the full count.

The day afterwards, at Bangkok, the very last fifteen-round IBF title bout took place when Thailander Samuth Sithnaruepol met the South Korean In-Kyu Hwang in defence of his championship. The tiny men boxed at a brisk pace over the allotted distance, with the local being returned the winner by a unanimous decision.

SEPTEMBER

McGirt's Taylor Made for Meldrick

This was another month of limited activity on the world championship scene, with only five title contests taking place, and those among men in the lighter divisions.

James "Buddy" McGirt, came in as the favourite to break Meldrick Taylor's string of victories when he put up his IBF light-welterweight belt in Atlantic City. McGirt's summary disposal of Howard Davis in the opening round back in July had the spectators on the edges of their seats and anticipating early fireworks.

But Taylor, another 1984 Olympic gold medallist, dominated the contest from the opening bell. McGirt did manage to make his presence felt in that first round, but thereafter the challenger matched the champion's almost every move both outboxing and out-fighting his big-hitting opponent.

Going into the twelfth and final round, all three judges had the young Californian well ahead on points, but Taylor did not appear to be content with this type of victory. When he streaked in with a two-fisted attack and punched the tired champion all round the ring it came as no surprise when the referee stopped the battle before the final bell to save McGirt from further unnecessary punishment.

Another world light-welterweight title contest ended with a stoppage in the last round when the WBC champion Roger Mayweather faced Rodolfo Gonzales, of Mexico.

Las Vegas-based Mayweather did not have too far to travel to Los Angeles, where a good crowd watched a spirited but one-sided encounter. Mayweather was altogether too clever for his man, and by the eighth round he was hitting Gonzales at will, and even appealed to the referee to stop the affair.

But the third man in the ring waved the pair on,

Meldrick Taylor (left) sets up an attack in pursuit of "Buddy" McGirt's IBF light-welter crown, during the early stages of their Atlantic City humdinger

Tom Casino

until in the tenth the ringside doctor briefly halted proceedings to inspect the challenger's damaged left eye. By this time all Gonzales could do at best was to last the distance, but in the twelfth round Mayweather caught him with a right-hander which sent him to the boards.

He was very unsteady as he continued the fight, and the champion's final rally was so overwhelming that the bout was stopped as Gonzales tottered round the ring.

* * *

IBF super-bantamweight champion, José Sanabria, Venezuela, made another European jaunt when he travelled to Noget-sur-Marne to meet the challenge of Frenchman Fabrice Benichou. The South American got a little more than he had expected, and was fortunate to come through with his title still intact. Even so, although Benichou was ahead on the score-cards of all three judges when the battle came to its close, it was due to bad damage incurred to his left eye as early as the second round which was the deciding factor concerning the eventual result. The injury was aggravated as the contest continued, but the Frenchman was able to match Sanabria in almost everything he attempted, and could be termed a very unlucky loser.

Going into the tenth, Benichou was already cut both above and below the eye, and a driving attack from the Venezuelan worsened the damage. With the eye now completely closed, but with the referee allowing things to continue, the plucky challenger was quite unable to produce his best and the bout was finally stopped.

* * *

Urabaya was the scene of an IBF super-flyweight championship contest when Elly Pical, the Indonesian title-holder, faced the challenge of South Korea's Chang-Ki Kim.

The fight was billed as being the first bout under the auspices of this governing body to be decided over the reduced distance of twelve rounds, rather than fifteen — although this was not strictly true — thus bringing the IBF into line with the other authoritative boards by popular demand.

In company with the Sithnareupol–Hwang mini-flyweight title bout, which had taken place just a few days before and was the very last IBF contest of fifteen rounds, this championship meeting went its full distance. Pical boxed extremely well to outpoint the Korean over the twelve sessions.

Also in the super-flyweight division, this time with the WBC title on the line, Mexico's great little box-fighter, Gilberto Roman, journeyed to Nagoya to defend his honours against the Japanese contender, Kiyoshi Hatanaka.

Roman established his undoubted superiority early in the contest, sending his man to the boards for a count in the very opening round. But the challenger was plucky, and he rose to continue the

Once again Taylor scores with the left hand as McGirt begins to lose his grip on the title. The referee stepped in to rescue "Buddy" during the twelfth and final round

Tom Casino

HILTON
I Love
You

fight. He was again dropped to the canvas by a wayward delivery which went extremely low, and the champion was rightly penalised.

However, Roman was in no real danger of losing the contest at any time, and he ran out a unanimous victor after the full twelve rounds.

OCTOBER

A Lightweight Double for Chavez

Boxing got back to its more normal activity in October, when eleven title bouts took place, and with no fewer than six of these being decided under the jurisdiction of the IBF.

At light-heavyweight, "Prince" Charles Williams, the champion, had an easy outing when he travelled to Villeneuve d'Ornon to meet the local favourite, the Frenchman Rufino Angulo. Although the challenger managed to hold his own during the opening round, Williams went to work in the second, and before the close of the session he had floored Angulo on two occasions. The Frenchman was again outclassed during the third, during which he went to the boards twice more. It came as no surprise at all when the fight was stopped in Williams' favour.

* * *

The IBF was again in charge, this time in Berlin, when the German southpaw, Graciano Rocchigiani, made the second defence of his super-middleweight crown in opposition to his American challenger, Chris Reid.

Reid came determined to make a battle of it, and he threw everything he had into a continuous attack. But the titleholder was too good and too strong for him, and by the eleventh round Rocchigiani had built up a formidable lead. It was when the German caught Reid with a fine left hook, followed by a fierce two-fisted attack, that the end became obviously apparent. Reid was almost helpless, although still on his feet, when the towel came in from his corner, signifying surrender.

* * *

When Simon Brown, the United States-based Jamaican, defended his welterweight title in Lausanne versus the Swiss-Italian Mauro Martelli, champion of Europe, the IBF was again on hand to organise matters.

Brown, who had won the title in fine style and defended it for the first time before a Jamaican crowd, proved that he would make a very good opponent for the other claimants when he won an excellent battle by outpointing Martelli over the full twelve rounds. Although he took a little time to settle down, once Brown had got the measure of his man there was no doubt which of the pair was the better of the two. After the halfway mark the champion forged ahead, and the verdict in his favour marked his game opponent's first loss since entering the professional ranks.

* * *

In a supporting bout to Chavez-Ramirez, Raul Perez (left) created a major shock when he beat the previously undefeated Miguel Lora, thus winning the Colombian's WBC bantamweight title

Christopher M. Farina

Three versions of the lightweight championship were put on the line during October. Firstly, Greg Haugen travelled to Copenhagen to defend his IBF title against the local Gert Bo Jacobsen, and the day afterwards, at Las Vegas, Julio Cesar Chavez and José Luis Ramirez clashed in a showdown to decide which of the pair would hold both the WBA and WBC world titles.

Greg Haugen was altogether too strong and forceful for the plucky but inadequate Jacobsen. Only in the opening round, when the champion was feeling his opponent out, did the Danish challenger look at all dangerous. True, he caught his man later on with a few of his much-vaunted right-handers, but they had little effect on Haugen, who grew more and more confident as the bout progressed.

By the sixth round it appeared evident that the champion was going to win, and it was now a matter of whether or not Jacobsen could last the limit without being stopped. During the eighth and ninth rounds the Dane was subjected to a very bad beating, and only his courage kept him erect.

The end came in the tenth, when Haugen scored with a sparkling one-two, his final right-hander catching Jacobsen beautifully and dumping him heavily on the boards. It looked to be a knockout victory, but somehow the challenger got to his feet before the final count, and after the referee decided that he was fit to continue and waved the fighters on, Jacobsen's corner-men wisely tossed in the towel of surrender.

The battle in the desert when the two Mexican former stable-mates, Chavez and Ramirez met, was a keen and interesting fight which looked like going all the way and then ended dramatically but unsatisfactorily.

The brilliant Chavez was, of course, widely-tipped to win this unification contest, and he soon forged ahead early in the battle, proving that the odds in his favour were justified. As cagey and as cunning as the veteran Ramirez was, he could never quite match the scintillating boxing and two-

Opposite: Roger "Black Mamba" Mayweather, the WBC light-welterweight champion, seen here in Las Vegas, made a successful defence of his title during the month, stopping Rodolfo Gonzalez in twelve rounds

Christopher M. Farina

Julio Cesar Chavez (right) two-fistedly attacks Jose Luis Ramirez, on the way to adding WBC lightweight honours to his WBC crown

Christopher M. Farina

Chavez acknowledges the cheers of the crowd

Christopher M. Farina

handed fighting of the WBA belt-holder. Although no knockdowns were scored, Chavez was well ahead on points by the penultimate round, and all Ramirez could honestly look for was the kudos of going the full distance.

But it was in this eleventh round that the pair came together with a clash of heads, and Ramirez came off second best. A very nasty vertical gash had opened up over the WBC champion's brow, and after a medical inspection the referee was ordered to stop the bout. With all three judges having Chavez ahead on points, one of them by a wide margin, he thus became both the WBA and WBC champion by a technical decision.

*   *   *

The battle at Sacramento for the IBF super-featherweight title proved to be a scorcher, and one which earned the approbation of a partisan crowd as local hero Tony Lopez defended his crown against Puerto Rico's clever and willing challenger, Juan Molina.

Lopez was making his first defence since out-pointing Rocky Lockridge in the summer, but he began the contest looking like anything but a world champion. His more aggressive opponent forced matters early on, and in the second round he dropped the title-holder to the canvas with a well-placed left hook. The Californian took the compulsory count of eight, and although he fought his way out of difficulty the battle seemed all over bar the shouting.

Molina again looked as if he might fell his man in the fifth, when he had Lopez on the verge of a knockout with a right to the jaw, which he followed up with a two-fisted barrage, but he inexplicably failed to press his advantage, and the more rugged Lopez bulled his way out of trouble.

It was the Californian's superior strength and ruggedness which pulled him from almost certain defeat to a slight advantage during the second half of the contest. By sheer drive he nullified the speedier and sharper efforts of the Puerto Rican, and after the final bell, when the decision was announced, Lopez was declared the winner by a unanimous verdict.

While Lopez was roundly cheered by his supporters, only the fact that he was the home-town boy made the decision a popular one. Impartial observers felt that Molina had done enough to earn a draw.

*   *   *

Moriguchi was the scene of an exciting clash when the Japanese challenger, Takuya Muguruma, made a brave effort to battle his way back to championship status when he faced Juan J. Estrada, of Mexico, for the WBA super-bantamweight crown.

Muguruma, who had briefly held the eight stone six belt, and had then failed in a bid to regain it, put on a few pounds in weight and now mixed it with the slightly heavier title-holder. But Estrada proved to be just too good for him, and while the Japanese almost managed to stay to the end of the contest, the bout was stopped in the eleventh round after the challenger had been overwhelmed by the Mexican's superior attack.

*   *   *

At bantamweight proper, in a supporting bout to the Chavez-Ramirez meeting at Las Vegas,

Miguel "Happy" Lora, the hitherto undefeated WBC champion, got the shock of his life when he made his eighth defence of the title, this time in opposition to the lean and lanky Raul Perez.

The first half of this rousing bout was largely in favour of the defending champion, but as the battle wore on, so the challenger began to make more of an impression, and by the closing rounds the Colombian was beginning to look desperate. Although he tried to force matters at the finish, he was met punch for punch by the Mexican, who now sensed victory. The officials' verdict in favour of Perez found two of them awarding the fight by a comfortable margin to the challenger.

* * *

The super-flyweights were represented at Seoul, when Kaosai Galaxy, of Thailand, defended his WBA belt against the South Korean challenger, Chang-Ho Choi.

Although the Korean made a brave effort, Galaxy was far too good for him, and the end came in the eighth round after the aggressive Thailander succeeded in nailing his man and putting him down for the full count.

* * *

A very interesting situation developed in the flyweight division when both the WBA and IBF titles were contested for within days of each other. Fidel Bassa, of Colombia, defended the WBA version against Ray Medel, and the Filipino, Rolando Bohol, boxed Britain's Duke McKenzie for the IBF belt.

Bassa, a familiar face to British boxing fans, had twice humbled the Belfast flyweight, Dave McAuley, and was established as a good, if not great title-holder. Placing it at stake in San Antonio, Texas, against the local favourite, Ray Medel, the champion surged ahead in the early rounds through his superior boxing. But the challenger's heavier punching eventually began to take its toll, and the later rounds were largely in favour of Medel. However, Bassa had done enough to take an unanimous decision, although the home crowd naturally did not approve.

When Duke McKenzie, with a superb, if somewhat unexciting display of clever boxing, took round after round from the visiting Filipino champion, Rolando Bohol, at Wembley, he looked like cruising to a fairly easy points victory. But going into the eleventh he surprised everybody by sending the title-holder flat on to his back with a superb combination. Although Bohol arose, the jubilant McKenzie quickly floored him again, and the referee counted the champion out as his corner threw in the towel.

With Duke McKenzie winning this version of the championship in such positive fashion, and with Bassa retaining his own share of the title with some difficulty, the lad from Croydon might well be favoured to add the WBA belt to his IBF one if the Colombian could be induced to come to the British Isles for a third time.

Britain's Duke McKenzie (left) appears to be sizing up the IBF flyweight champion, Rolando Bohol, during the early stages of their title fight. McKenzie won in the eleventh when the Filipino was counted out
Action Images

Duke McKenzie (left) and Rolando Bohol locked together, just prior to the finish
Action Images

NOVEMBER
Five-Timer Leonard

No fewer than 18 world title contests took place during November, and the month also witnessed one of the most amazing pugilistic accomplishments of all time.

The feat referred to was yet another return to the ring from "retirement" by Ray Leonard, who had, the previous year, come back again to take Marvin Hagler's WBC middleweight title and yet another enormous fortune — only calmly to relinquish the belt without defending it.

The idea of a never-too-robust welterweight, no matter how gifted, returning to action after a lengthy lay-off and then swapping punches with the most formidable eleven stone six champion of the present era seemed almost an impossibility, but "Sugar" Ray had done it and had boxed a brainy battle to gain a narrow and disputed victory. Now, at the tail-end of 1988, he was throwing his hat back into the ring and challenging "Golden Boy" Don Lalonde, holder of the WBC light-heavyweight title!

There was a certain method in Leonard's apparent madness. Hitherto, the WBC had shown scant interest in the super-middleweight division, inaugurated in 1984 for boxers between eleven and a half and twelve and a half stone, and dominated — to a large extent — by Chong-Pal Park in faraway South Korea. But now, in addition to Lalonde being induced to place his established 175 lb title at stake, further cash and kudos were ensured by making the match a *double* championship go — a WBC super-middleweight title being thrown in as well — and with the Canadian being obliged to reduce to 168 lbs, or twelve stone exactly! It was a shrewd move, and it reduced what might otherwise have been an almost insuperable barrier for a man even as remarkable as "Sugar" Ray Leonard.

The consensus of opinion was that on this occasion Leonard had bitten off more than he could chew — and to employ another cliché frequently used at the time — was going to the post just once too often. This despite the fact that Lalonde was not in the same class as his challenger as a stylish boxer. But the handsome, fair-haired Canadian had proved that he was a murderous hitter with his right fist, and Leonard more than once felt the full force of his bigger adversary's delivery in the opening rounds.

In fact, a right-hander in the fourth caught Leonard high on the head and dropped him briefly to the canvas. But he got up with no sign of having been hurt too badly, and from that moment forward he began to take the initiative.

Leonard was well ahead and scoring solidly by the ninth round, and as Lalonde began to grow erratic in the face of his challenger's sustained attack, Leonard whipped over a smashing left hook to the jaw which felled him with a bang. Lalonde scrambled erect with some difficulty, still as game as ever, and clear-headed enough to nod sporting acknowledgement to his opponent, but "Sugar" Ray had no intention of letting him off the hook, and a further barrage of blows from either fist sent his man crashing to the boards again. He was now hopelessly beaten, and the referee waved the battle over.

Ray Leonard, a previous holder of the welter, light-middleweight, and middleweight titles, now entered the record books as the first man to win five championships in separate weight divisions with his annexation of the super-middle and light-heavyweight honours! While boxing achievements have admittedly been cheapened — or at least lessened — by the introduction of various conflicting authorities and the several intermediate divisions, there is no denying this man's enormous over-all accomplishments and that at the age of well over 30 and at his natural poundage, which would perhaps be a bit over eleven stone, there is no man in the world to compare with him.

The WBA version of the light-heavyweight title was also at stake during the month when Virgil Hill delighted his hometown crowd at Bismark, North Dakota, stopping his Canadian challenger, Willie Featherstone, in ten rounds. It was a somewhat one-sided encounter, with Hill proving to be a far superior craftsman in every department. He not only won every round but cut his opponent badly and knocked him down for a long count as early as the third round. Featherstone was hopelessly beaten by the tenth, when the referee intervened as he lay slumped against the ropes.

* * *

Both the IBF and WBA middleweight titles were placed on the line during the month.

Initially, Michael Nunn met the veteran Argentinian warhorse, Juan Domingo Roldan, in the first defence of his share of the title, at Las Vegas, and he turned in a workmanlike job. Two more conflicting styles than those presented by these particular antagonists it would be hard to find, and Nunn was fully expected to back away and score jabbing points at long range, never giving the two-fisted and uncompromising challenger a chance to effect his bull-like tactics. But the champion surprisingly scored a knockdown in the opening round, and thereafter he dominated the contest, varying between fast, defensive boxing on the retreat and dogged punch-swapping at close quarters.

He was doing almost as he liked with the courageous but ineffective Roldan by the eighth round, and towards the close of the session he forced his man to the ropes and with a devastating barrage of blows sent the South American heavily to the canvas. Roldan was thoroughly beaten. He tried desperately to regain his feet, but the referee counted him out and the fight was over. The game loser, who had by now three times made his bid for the eleven-six championship, with losing battles against Marvin Hagler, Thomas Hearns, and now Michael Nunn, announced his retirement from the game almost immediately after the fight.

The second middleweight title encounter, that for the WBA belt, took place at Monte Carlo, where Sumbu Kalambay, the African-born resident of Italy, faced a New York challenger, Doug de Witt. This contest was roughly similar to the one for the IBF title, with de Witt providing most of the aggression and Kalambay all the science and point-scoring.

The champion did not take very long to establish the fact that he was the boss, and thereafter he blocked and countered his challenger's every move, and by the end of the sixth round the game New Yorker had been reduced almost to complete fistic impotence.

Although de Witt came out for the seventh round even more aggressively than he had done up to this point, Kalambay also stepped up the pace, and after setting his man up with a series of punishing jabs he switched to a left hook and felled his opponent. The plucky challenger dragged himself erect by the count of eight, but he was obviously all at sea and so unable to defend himself properly that the referee had no hesitation in calling the contest off.

* * *

The IBF light-middleweight championship was at stake in Las Vegas when aggressive and two-fisted Matthew Hilton faced up to Philadelphia's southpaw hope, Robert "Bam Bam" Hines.

From the pattern of the early rounds it looked as though it would be only a matter of time before the Canadian champion won by a sensational stoppage. His punching was far more accurate and heavier than that of his opponent, and in the second he sent Hines to the floor for a count. Again, in the third, Hilton connected with a solid right and dropped his adversary a second time.

Hines was now cut and swollen about the brows, but gave no thought at all to bowing out. By the fourth he had come back bravely into the fight, and was scoring as often and as effectively as the champion.

By the sixth round the Philadelphian was definitely on top and was looking very good. Hilton, on the other hand, was not only cut badly above the eyes himself, but was showing evidence that this might be his first losing battle in 29 contests.

As the contest progressed, so Hines got better and better, a truly surprising reversal of things, and at the final bell a sorely battered and very tired champion knew that he had been soundly trounced. The verdict of the three ringside officials was unanimous, and while in some quarters it was believed that Hilton had weakened himself in managing to reach the limit of eleven stone, no such excuse was offered for his defeat.

* * *

In a supporting bout to the Leonard-Lalonde topliner at Las Vegas, Roger Mayweather and Vinny Pazienza waged a bitter and bad-tempered battle for the WBC light-welterweight championship.

It was, for the most part, a one-sided boxing lesson, with title-holder Mayweather shooting out solid jabs and countering effectively whenever the exuberant but crude Pazienza launched an attack. The contest was marred by taunts and jibes between the two fighters, and on more than one occasion the pair continued punching well after the bell had signalled the end of a round.

Towards the end of the bout, Pazienza was cut so badly, and was being hit so much at Mayweather's will that it appeared as if the challenger would not last the distance. The champion's frequent let-ups and short periods of inactivity fortified his later statement to the effect that he had not tried to knock Pazienza out but just wanted to punish him.

At the final bell both boxers seemed reluctant to stop fighting, and Lou Duva, veteran manager of the challenger, was into the ring like a shot and rushing to separate the men. Mayweather threw a punch at Duva and broke the skin on his cheek in a disreputable melée before the referee was able to pull them apart.

The IBF light-middleweight title changed hands when the challenger, Robert Hines (right), came back after a bad start, to punch out a solid points victory over the champion, Matthew Hilton

Tom Casino

Robert Hines (left) is shown soaked by his own blood, but it is also apparent that Hilton is beginning to blow-up from his own exertions

Christopher M. Farina

In his first defence of the IBF middleweight crown, Michael Nunn (right) shoots a right to the head of the Argentinian challenger, Juan Domingo Roldan

Tom Casino

The decision of the judges was overwhelmingly, and quite justifiably, in favour of the Las Vegas-based Mayweather, but he received a very unenviable reception from a disgusted crowd, who hadn't appreciated his frequently negative tactics. While this battle presented some wonderful box-fighting, at intervals, from the champion, and a "Rocky"-like do-or-die exhibition of sheer guts and sustained aggression from his opponent, the unethical flavour of the match from start to finish, which was seen all over the world on television, did nothing at all for the reputation of the sport. This was by no means the first occasion that the volatile Lou Duva, a septuagenarian, incidentally, had acted more like a contestant than a chief second!

* * *

London's Jim McDonnell, former undefeated European featherweight champion and the victor of 24 straight professional engagements, had spent his whole career in the shadows of more glamorous British performers like Barry McGuigan, Lloyd Honeyghan, and Frank Bruno. In a ring in South London, not too far from the famous Elephant and Castle, he at last got his chance to win a world title and demand the sort of big money earned by his more publicised fellow-countrymen when he faced Brian Mitchell in a bout for the super-featherweight championship, as viewed by the WBA.

Jim made a brave attempt, but the fact soon became apparent that he was now, for the first time, boxing in an entirely different class. Mitchell, an experienced box-fighter from South Africa, who had already successfully defended his belt in such varied foreign countries as Spain, Italy, France, Panama, and Puerto Rico, was far too strong and talented for the game but ineffective McDonnell, winning clearly on points.

The champion won almost every round, and although the Londoner put everything he had into his bid for the highest honours, he was completely out-generalled from start to finish.

* * *

Two of the three versions of the traditional featherweight crown, at nine stone, were defended during the month.

First was that of the WBA, at Marsala, Italy, when Venezuelan champion Antonio Esparragoza took on his challenger, José Marmolejo, of Panama. The latter made a brave effort, but he was not in the same class as Esparragoza. The title-holder delivered both a boxing lesson and a clean knockout when he defeated his man in the eighth round.

At Melbourne, later in the month, Jeff Fenech proved for all the world to see that he ranks with the greatest fighters ever developed in Australian rings. Defending his WBC title in opposition to New Jersey's George "Go Go" Navarro, he was so far superior to his opponent that very early on in the contest the desperate challenger was resorting to grab and hug tactics in order to survive.

It was a scrambling bout, with Navarro doing his utmost to nullify Fenech's more positive work by his holding, and with the referee continually breaking the men and warning the culprit.

Three times in the fourth round the little Aussie dropped the American with powerful body punches, and in the fifth round the contest had become so one-sided that it was stopped in the title-holder's favour.

* * *

Among the super-bantamweights, two of the three claimants to the crown put their honours at stake, but with no great upsets or surprises ensuing.

At Gravelines, in Northern France, Thierry Jacob made a determined challenge for the IBF belt in the possession of Venezuela's José Sanabria, but the busy South American, who was making

Roldan is on the way to being counted out in the eighth round as a series of combination punches from Nunn send him crashing to the canvas

Tom Casino

his third defence inside four months, really had little trouble with his French opponent. Jacob was in difficulty as early as the opening round, when he was cut over the right brow, but although he fought back strongly in the second he was no match for his more skilled antagonist.

As the rounds passed, so Sanabria grew better and stronger, and by the sixth, after Jacob had slumped to the boards for a long count, the champion sent in such an overwhelming series of blows that the referee wisely stepped in and led the Frenchman to his stool.

Similarly, Daniel Zaragoza of Mexico, former holder of the bantamweight title and now the wearer of the WBC super-bantamweight belt, had no great trouble with his Italian challenger, Valerio Nati, in Forli.

Zaragoza took few chances in the opening rounds, but by the fourth he had summed his man up and came out for the fifth with the intention of finishing matters. A beautifully-executed left to the jaw early on felled Nati with a bang. Although he made a valiant effort to beat the referee's toll he was counted out while still on his knees.

* * *

The WBC claimant of the bantamweight championship did not make a defence during November, but both the WBA and IBF beltholders were in action.

South Korea's Sung-Il Moon, who had beaten Kaokor Galaxy for the WBA title in the summer, placed his honours on the line for the first time before the usual enthusiastic crowd in Seoul. His adversary was Edgar Montserrat, from Panama, and a fine contest ensued. Moon came through with flying colours when, in the seventh round, he put his challenger down for the full count.

Although Jimmy Navarro was named as the foremost challenger to champion Orlando Canizales by the IBF, his record revealed that he had not boxed seriously for almost a year. This inactivity, as much as anything else, perhaps, was responsible for a most one-sided confrontation which ended in the opening round. At San Antonio, Texas, a partisan crowd cheered on Canizales, from nearby Laredo, as he tore into his opponent from the bell in his initial defence of the title. He forced Navarro against the ropes and sent him to the boards with an immaculate left hook.

The challenger was quick to climb to his feet, but the referee insisted on giving him the eight count. He then went on the defensive, and did some clever "milling on the retreat" in order to survive, until Canizales finally stretched him prone on the boards for the full count of ten.

* * *

On an extremely attractive bill at Las Vegas, Gilberto Roman and Jesus "Sugar Baby" Rojas were quite content to be "underneath" Leonard-Lalonde and Mayweather-Pazienza in a world championship extravaganza which was televised world-wide and also packed the Caesar's Palace outdoor arena with over 13,000 onlookers.

Roman, the brilliant little Mexican box-fighter, had originally won the WBC super-flyweight crown back in 1986, and had defended it successfully against the best on six occasions before being stopped in eleven rounds by Santos Laciar. But less than a year later he came back in fine form to outpoint Jesus Rojas, who had beaten Laciar for

The South African holder of the WBA super-featherweight belt, Brian Mitchell, was just too ringwise for Jim McDonnell (left), and the Briton's title challenge was easily repelled

Action Images

"Sugar" Ray Leonard (left) meets "Golden Boy" Don Lalonde.

Tom Casino

the title in 1987. He was now putting his belt on the line against the flashy Colombian.

Although overshadowed by Ray Leonard, Don Lalonde, Roger Mayweather, and Vinny Pazienza, as far as the sensational is concerned, Gilberto Roman gave all true boxing followers a fine example of what is sometimes now referred to only cynically as the "Noble Art".

Opposing a man who had been a world champion himself, and therefore certainly no slouch, Roman both out-fought and out-boxed his man, beating him to the punch again and again, and nullifying almost every move the brave Colombian chose to make. Although Rojas came on strongly in the later rounds in a desperate effort to reverse the trend, Roman merely stepped up the pace a trifle.

The Mexican was declared the victor by a unanimous decision, with one judge having awarded only one round to a plucky but ineffective challenger.

* * *

The flyweight division marked the re-appearance of Yong-Kang Kim, of South Korea, making his first defence of the traditional eight-stone championship since defeating the WBC king-pin, Sot Chitalada. Kim established that his unexpected victory over the Thailander was no accident when, at Chungju, he took on the Filippino, Emil Romano, who boxes out of Japan, and pounded out a convincing twelve-round win.

* * *

In Manila, Jum-Hwan Choi, the South Korean holder of the IBF light-flyweight belt, got a big surprise when he travelled to the capital of the islands and took on an old opponent, Tacy Macalos, before the challenger's home crowd. Choi had outpointed the Filippino over fifteen rounds back in March, 1987, and was favoured to repeat the win. But Macalos upset the odds by not only gaining the verdict of the officials after twelve rounds, but by dropping the champion for a count in the eighth round. With this victory, the South Korean monopoly on light-flyweight matters was broken.

The WBA holder of the title of this particular weight division, South Korean Myung-Woo Yuh, faced up to the challenge of Indonesia's Bahar Udin, in Seoul. Udin made a brave try, but the champion was far too good for him, and after having summed up his opponent over the first half dozen rounds he floored his challenger for the full count in the seventh.

Opposite: The WBC super-featherweight champion, Azumah Nelson, had an easy night when he knocked out the Brazilian challenger, Sydnei dal Rovere, in the third round

Christopher M. Farina

* * *

The tiniest of all the little men, the seven stone seven mini-flyweights, were represented in Osaka when Japan's WBC title-holder, Hiroki Ioka, took on Napa Kiatwanchai, of Thailand, for the second time. They had boxed the previous June, with many onlookers feeling that Kiatwanchai had earned the decision rather than the drawn verdict that was announced. Matters had been further complicated by the suggestion that the last round had not travelled its full three minutes.

This time the challenger made no mistake, and outpointed the Japanese incumbent unmistakably over the full twelve rounds.

DECEMBER

Super Nelson Eyes McGuigan

In strong contrast to the previous month, a period of extreme activity on the world championship front, December was a very quiet few weeks. None of the heavier title-holders made defences, no doubt preferring to celebrate Christmas, and only two of the lighter men risked their laurels.

Before an enthusiastic crowd of spectators in Accra, Azumah Nelson, Ghana's pride and the WBC super-featherweight champion, made a voluntary defence of his crown against a Brazilian challenger, Sydnei dal Rovere.

Although the South American was technically only a featherweight, the WBC rules allow for a champion at a heavier poundage squeezing in an extra engagement between mandatory defences — provided his opponent is rated in the top ten in his own division and would therefore — on the face of things — provide some sort of match. Even so, this contest was something of a mis-match, and was really little more than a Ghanaian holiday.

Nelson took things very easily in the first couple of rounds, but six minutes of sparring was enough to inform him that he had little to defeat in dal Rovere. Going to work in the third he whipped over a devastating left which felled his challenger. The Brazilian just managed to crawl to his feet before the final count, but the referee continued the toll and Nelson was adjudged the victor on a count out.

* * *

Jung-Koo Chang, who had held the WBC light-flyweight belt since 1983, relinquished it voluntarily, owing to ill-health — a rather sad occurrence, perhaps, since the South Koreans had until recently been dominant in this division with all three major governing bodies. Matched for the vacated title were Soon-Jung Kang, yet another Korean, and German Torres, of Mexico, who had already made no fewer than four earlier attempts to win this championship, failing against Hilario Zapata in 1981 and on three occasions versus Jung-Koo Chang between 1983 and 1986. He was certainly the perennial contender. The little Mexican was finally rewarded for his persistence in the last month of 1988 when in Seoul he decisively outpointed Kang over the full distance of twelve rounds.

PONY
WORLD CHAMPION
WBC
AZUMAH NELSON

JANUARY

Meek John No Match for Taylor

The year 1989 began quietly, as far as championship boxing is concerned. Only four world title contests took place, one at super-middleweight, two at light-welterweight, and one junior-bantamweight bout.

With the IBF super-middleweight belt at stake, the all-action German champion, Graciano Rocchigiani, faced the challenge of Thulani "Sugar Boy" Malinga at Berlin. It was not one of the title-holder's finer performances, but he was obviously in a totally different class from his South African challenger. All three judges voted overwhelmingly for the popular Rocchigiani, with two of them awarding the German eleven of the twelve rounds. This contest marked the local favourite's third successful defence of the IBF championship, and he must be given a strong chance of defeating his WBA and WBC counterparts if pugilistic politics ever allow a top-level showdown.

* * *

The two light-welterweight clashes took place on the same day, one in Atlantic City, and the other at Vasto, in Italy.

Making his first defence of the IBF championship at ten stone, Meldrick Taylor, of Philadelphia, impressed the onlookers at the New Jersey gambling resort when he turned in a masterly performance against his challenger, John Meekins, of New York.

Although the champion looked very good, this was by no means because of any deficiences in his opponent. In fact, the game Meekins went forward all the time in a desperate effort to snatch the title, and he had Taylor cut and bleeding quite badly.

But the Philadelphian boxed beautifully, and often appeared twice as fast as his adversary. At times he was hitting Meekins almost without a return, and on several occasions had him staggering. Only one round, the third, might have been to the advantage of the challenger. By the close of the seventh he was badly cut and bruised about the right eye, and although he was keen to continue, the ringside doctor examined him and advised the referee to call a halt.

Unfortunately, the WBA defence of the light-welterweight title by Juan M. Coggi, of Argentina, was not nearly in the same class. Veteran challenger Harold Brazier, who had done so well the previous summer in a strong battle against Roger Mayweather, was not at all impressive on this occasion, while southpaw Coggi did very little, for the most part, except keep ahead in a somewhat dull bout.

One thrill was provided in round ten, when the champion threw over a left which temporarily decked Brazier. But Coggi failed to follow up the advantage and just coasted home for the next two sessions. A unanimous decision provided no dissent from a crowd who favoured the part-Italian

Defending the IBF light-welterweight title for the first time, Meldrick Taylor (left) was far too classy for the challenger, John Meekins, who was stopped at the end of the seventh round

Tom Casino

Coggi, but he certainly did not show evidence of ever becoming the undisputed king of his division.

* * *

Coming in as a substitute for the Colombian challenger, Albert Castro, at fairly short notice, South Korean Tae-Il Chang was on a hiding to nothing when he faced WBA super-flyweight champion Kaosai Galaxy, the pride of Thailand, at Bangkok. Chang proved to be no match for the title-holder, and was knocked out as early as the second round.

Once again Taylor's jab finds its way through Meekins' guard. Note the damage to Meekins' left eye

Tom Casino

FEBRUARY

Iron Mike Dents British Dreams

This month marked the eagerly-awaited return to the ring of undisputed heavyweight champion of the world, "Iron" Mike Tyson, after a multitude of accidents and traumatic occurrences in his private life.

This was the first time Tyson had put up his fists in deadly seriousness since his brief demolition job on Michael Spinks, eight months previously, but his present challenger, Britain's Frank Bruno, had been inactive for twice that length of time, his advisers preferring to have Bruno remain idle, sitting out the several postponements of this clash, rather than risk the chance of big Frank suffering a reversal in opposition to another contender.

Las Vegas was the scene of the encounter, with the event arousing only moderate enthusiasm in the United States, but with Great Britain showing tremendous excitement at the Wandsworth hero's second attempt to snatch boxing's greatest prize.

It looked as if the fight might be a replica of the Spinks contest, when in the opening seconds of the first round, Tyson charged in and caught his challenger with a right to the head which stunned him and sent him momentarily to the canvas. Although Bruno was on his feet very quickly, the referee gave him a standing count of eight before waving the pair together again.

Bruno faced Tyson's renewed attack with some vicious offensive work of his own, and the onlookers were surprised to see the challenger stagger the champion with a fine left hook to the head. For a second or two it really looked as if big Frank might pull off the upset of the century, but Mike weathered the assault. From that moment forward there was only one man in it.

Once he had got into his stride in the second round, Tyson proved what a great champion he is. Bruno had felt the power of his opponent's punches, and now showed little real aggression himself. Despite the admonitions of the referee, he continually claimed Mike with an arm round his head, as he hit with the other fist, but Tyson was not unduly inconvenienced.

At long range, the British fighter did little more than flick out his left ineffectively, and as the contest progressed, it rapidly became evident that it was only a matter of time before Bruno was badly hurt.

The end came in the fifth round, when Tyson bulled his man to the ropes and then smashed him mercilessly with lefts and rights to the face and head, almost without a return. Although Bruno stayed erect, the barrage continued, and even as his manager began to run round the ring and throw in the towel of surrender, the referee stepped in and saved Bruno in what was now a one-sided fight.

* * *

In a battle for the vacant WBC light-heavyweight title, and overshadowed by the attention paid to Bruno's challenge, veteran Dennis Andries nevertheless performed a wonderful job in stopping the Texan, Tony Willis, in the fifth round at Tucson.

Andries was far too strong and aggressive for his opponent, and he bull-dozed the unfortunate American during the early rounds. The end came in the fifth, when a fine combination of punches

Dennis Andries (right) winds up the left for another assault on the hapless American, Tony Willis. The Briton regained his old WBC light-heavyweight belt when Willis was rescued by the referee in the fifth round

Sporting Pictures (UK) Ltd

sent Willis to the boards. Although he climbed erect before the end of the count, the third man in the ring took a quick glance at his condition and waved the battle over.

Following Ted "Kid" Lewis and Lloyd Honeyghan, Andries became the third British boxer to regain a world championship.

* * *

Atlantic City witnessed one of the most dramatic pugilistic upsets of modern times: a battle waged so fiercely that already early in the full twelve months of championship events, it was hailed by the press as the fight of the year.

Iran Barkley, WBC middleweight title-holder by virtue of his stunning and unexpected defeat of Thomas Hearns, was favoured to halt the return to top class activity of the Panamanian "old man", Roberto Duran, but the ever-durable "Hands of Stone" established himself as an all-time great by pounding out a close majority decision over Barkley and becoming yet another of the few fighters to win four world titles at different weights.

After ten rounds of fairly even exchanges, the pace had not abated when the pair crossed gloves for the penultimate session. The amazing Duran stepped up the pace, and after a rapid two-fisted attack, whipped over a perfectly-timed right-hander which sent the American crashing to the canvas.

He climbed to his feet and tore back into the fray, and somehow managed to stave off a knockout defeat. Both men went at it furiously in the final round, in a do-or-die effort to pip the decision, and when the bell rang to end this furious fight, not a soul in the Convention Centre felt certain of the outcome.

Two of the three judges gave the nod to Duran by a small margin, with the eleventh-round knockdown undoubtedly being the factor which swayed them in his favour. But the closeness of the battle should take nothing at all from Duran's remarkable achievement.

Following his great win over Thomas Hearns, Iran Barkley (left) was expected to retain his WBC middleweight title against Roberto Duran. But, in one of the year's best fights, the "old man", Duran, re-wrote the form book with a thrilling points victory

Tom Casino

* * *

IBF light-middleweight kingpin Robert Hines and WBA champion Julian Jackson both put their titles at stake, as did the unpredictable Don Curry, the WBC incumbent.

"Bam Bam" Hines, who had surprisingly taken the belt from Canada's Matthew Hilton, was expected to stem the undefeated flow of Darrin "Schoolboy" van Horn's success in Atlantic City. But the youthful Southerner, with 38 wins behind him, established himself as the master, and proved himself the better man in all departments of the game. All three officials marked their cards in favour of the Kentuckian by a very comfortable margin.

Julian Jackson's defence of his own version of the title, in opposition to little-known challenger Francisco de Jesus, of Brazil, was not nearly so much a surprise occasion when the pair met at Las Vegas. The South American made a gutsy bid for the championship, but he was in far too exalted company. Jackson dropped him heavily as early as the second round, and de Jesus was obliged to take the mandatory eight-count before being allowed to resume. The challenger kept trying throughout the subsequent exchanges, but he took considerable stick from a champion who had the contest well in hand. The end came in the eighth round, when a devastating right to the temple dropped him for the full count.

The up-and-down career of the once seemingly invincible Don Curry, suffered yet another set-back when he travelled to Grenoble to defend his WBC light-middleweight championship against France's René Jacquot. The challenger, while undoubtedly being a high-ranking contender, only served to show the mediocre level of ability among most aspirants in this particular division. Curry was said to have weakened himself by training down to eleven stone — a rather familiar excuse for his defeats? The clear unanimous verdict in favour of the Frenchman stressed how far the famed "Texas Cobra" has deteriorated.

* * *

All three welterweight claimants to world honours also put their belts on the line during the month. Mark Breland (WBA), and Lloyd Honeyghan (WBC), both defended on the same day — and on the same bill, while Simon Brown (IBF), took on his challenger a fortnight later.

The "needle" match between Honeyghan and Marlon Starling occurred at Caesar's Palace, Las Vegas. With both men having pronounced an intensive dislike of the other, a close and exciting battle was envisaged by all. But the outcome was something of a let-down, although there was plenty of action during the nine rounds the meeting lasted.

On the face of things, Starling seemed the better man in all aspects of the art, but Honeyghan claimed afterwards that a fortuitous blow to the right side of his visage had affected a nerve, causing him excruciating pain. Certainly, the unusual ballooning of his cheek, early in the encounter, did much to substantiate his claim — but such accidental injuries are all in the game. It's like a fighter saying that if he hadn't been caught with a peach of a right to the chin he wouldn't have been knocked out! But Starling appeared to be on top throughout, and when Honeyghan was half-punched, half-wrestled to the canvas in the ninth session, he seemed to be more exhausted than hurt really badly. The referee's intervention, soon after he arose, was inevitable.

In startling contrast, in the same ring, was lanky Mark Breland's ridiculously easy victory over Korea's Seung-Soon Lee. A lightning-like combination of punches, almost before the sound of the bell had died away, dropped the challenger. He staggered upright in considerable confusion, and when it was apparent that he had no defence at all to Breland's second onslaught, the one-sided contest was quickly brought to a conclusion by the referee, with the first minute of the fight still having some seconds to go.

The ubiquitous appeal of professional boxing was very evident when an adventurous promoter from behind Churchill's "Iron Curtain" staged an attractive show in Budapest, signing Jamaican-born Simon Brown to defend his IBF ten stone seven championship against Jorge Maysonet, the Puerto Rican challenger at present boxing out of New York.

Although Brown was impressive with a masterly and clinical destruction of his opponent in three rounds, and the enthusiastic Hungarian crowd saw some exciting action, the bout was very one-sided, and was almost as much of a mis-match as the Breland-Lee affair. After sizing up his opponent in the first round, Brown dominated the second and then floored his man with a right cross, followed by a crisp left hook to the jaw. The plucky challenger struggled up, but he would have been levelled for the full count had not the bell intervened. He was twice decked fairly early in the third, and although game enough to continue after arising, he had little to offer. Maysonet was being punched without retaliation when the contest was stopped.

* * *

The brilliant southpaw Olympic gold medallist from Virginia, Pernell Whitaker, finally "came good", when he fulfilled his early promise and handed IBF lightweight champion, Greg Haugen, an extremely one-sided battering, before an enthusiastic and partisan local crowd at Hampton.

Although the dour and rugged Haugen went forward all the time and put up a wonderful battle, his challenger practically waltzed through the twelve rounds, with a masterly display of boxing and crisp punching, to take the title by a unanimous decision, with two of the three judges awarding him every round.

Haugen was sent to the canvas for the first time in his career in the sixth, but he battled back courageously. Whitaker appeared to get better and better as the contest progressed, and during the latter half of the fight he was doing almost as he pleased. It was an overwhelming victory, and, in the opinion of many observers, it stamped the clever Virginian as the foremost claimant to nine stone nine honours in the world.

* * *

Among the super-featherweights, it has long been a source of argument as to which practitioner at this poundage is the finest. World-wide fight fans had an opportunity to assess and revise their opinions when both the WBA and WBC claimants showed their wares during the month.

At Capo d'Orlando, the globe-trotting South African, Brian Mitchell, top dog in the view of the WBA, put up his share of the championship for the seventh time — all defences being away from home — when he crossed fists with Italy's Salvatore Bottiglieri.

At no time did Mitchell look extended. He took command of the situation from the very start, and both out-punched and out-boxed a challenger who had forsaken the nine stone division to try his luck at the heavier weight. Mitchell was well on top by the eighth round, when he launched an attack which culminated with a heavy right that sent the challenger to the canvas. It did not quite keep him down, but when he arose to face the two-fisted barrage from a far superior adversary, the bout was brought to a halt to save him from a needless battering.

The former Olympic champion, Pernell Whitaker, fulfilled his potential when he defeated Greg Haugen on points to become IBF lightweight champion. In the picture, Whitaker (right) appears to be countering Haugen's attack

Tom Casino

British supporters of the charismatic and popular Barry McGuigan, hot on the comeback trail and looking for a shot at the WBC title in this division, must have raised their eyebrows questioningly, when vouchsafed an opportunity to watch Ghana's Azumah Nelson on TV, in the chief supporting bout on the Tyson-Bruno card.

Shaping up to Mexico's Mario Martinez, who had held him to a close verdict almost exactly a year previously, Nelson really went to town. He

Right: Frank Bruno (left) was not expected to last long against Mike Tyson in his quest to become Britain's first heavyweight champion. Although stopped in the fifth, Frank performed creditably

Christopher M. Farina

Far right: Bruno leads with a solid left, but to no avail, as Tyson gets inside the jab, looking to set up yet another vicious attack

Christopher M. Farina

handed his challenger quite a pasting during the first eleven rounds, and although Martinez took everything in a very plucky manner, he was ripe for the finish in the final session. A sizzling left hook to the draw dropped him to the boards, but did not keep him down. When he struggled to his feet, intent upon lasting the contest through, Nelson launched an attack so fast and powerful that his opponent could only just stand and take everything thrown at him. This burst of half a dozen incredible punches to the head and jaw literally left the man out on his feet. He would have slumped inert had not the referee jumped forward immediately, and held him, to prevent the champion from striking again.

*   *   *

At the bantamweight poundage, in a contest for the WBA version of the championship, the South Korean title-holder, Sung-Il Moon, had a fairly easy ride when he clashed with his Japanese challenger, Chaiki Kobayashi, at Taejon.

Before an enthusiastic crowd, Moon had so far established his supremacy by the fifth round, that the bout was brought to a stop, to save an outclassed man from further punishment.

*   *   *

Singapore was the scene of a closely-contested bout for the super-flyweight title. Veteran Elly Pical, the Indonesian holder of the IBF belt, met a tough nut in the little Texan, Mike Phelps, who seldom let up for a moment over the full twelve

Bottom left: Azumah Nelson (left), the WBC super-featherweight champion, is pictured outboxing the very game Mexican, Mario Martinez. The challenger finally succumbed in the last round when he was rescued by the referee

Christopher M. Farina

Bottom right: Always on the attack, Darrin van Horn (right) well deserved his points victory over the IBF light-middles champion, Robert Hines. At the age of 21, Darrin looks sure to have a big future in the game

Tom Casino

rounds as he waged a brave battle to take the decision. There was a division of opinion among the officials, with one giving the challenger the nod, but with the other two seeing Pical as the victor. Things were close enough for the crowd to give the American a rousing ovation for his gallant try.

* * *

Southpaw Thailander Napa Kiatwanchai pounded out a convincing victory to retain his WBC mini-flyweight title in opposition to John Arief of Indonesia, at Bangkok. Two of the judges awarded the champion every one of the twelve rounds, by the wide margin of thirteen points. The third official gave the challenger the better of one session, but still awarded Kiatwanchai the fight by fifteen points! Arief could offer little more than courage, and in the latter half of the one-sided contest he was floored on three occasions.

The American southpaw, Tony de Luca (right) tries to come forward, but, picking his punches well, Duke McKenzie, the IBF flyweight champion, was always in control. McKenzie retained his title on a fourth round cut-eye stoppage

Action Images

MARCH
Lightning Nunn Strikes in One

Interesting activity among the champions continued during the month of March, when a dozen title bouts were decided.

With Evander Holyfield, undisputed king of the cruiserweight division, having returned his three belts in order to campaign among the heavyweights, eventually hoping for a big-money crack at Mike Tyson, everything was wide open again as far as the WBA, the WBC, and the IBF were concerned. First off the mark to establish a new champion was the WBA, when recognising France's Taoufik Belbouli and America's Michael Greer as the two foremost contenders.

The battle took place at Casablanca, and the Tunisian-born, naturalised Frenchman, received a fine welcome from an enthusiastic crowd. Rising to the occasion, Belbouli gave his opponent quite a pasting, almost scoring a clean knockout victory in the fourth round. Greer had difficulty in beating the count, and would almost certainly have been stopped immediately, had not the bell saved him.

Belbouli continued to dominate the contest, although Greer made it hard going for him during the next three rounds. But in the eighth, the Tunisian went into top gear and so overwhelmed his man with punches, that the bout was stopped.

France, a country which had, for so long, been bereft of any world champions at all, now boasts three claimants! Taoufik Belbouli, René Jacquot and Fabrice Benichou, make up the trio.

* * *

Bobby Czyz, the New Jersey light-heavyweight, who had looked so impressive defending the IBF title until taking an unexpected hammering from "Prince" Charles Williams, made a plucky effort to lift the WBA version of the championship from North Dakota's Virgil Hill.

Shaping up before the usual enthusiastic crowd at his home-town of Bismark, Hill gave a masterful performance against his rugged challenger for almost the whole of the fight, taking round after round with a dazzling exhibition of boxing. At only one time did Czyz look dangerous, when he clipped the champion on the jaw with a right-hander, sending Hill momentarily to one knee.

However, the referee ruled it as a slip, and although Czyz tried hard to repeat his early success, he was thoroughly beaten. The three judges awarded a unanimous decision to Virgil Hill by an extremely wide margin.

* * *

The middleweight division — always the most popular after the heavyweights — has long been dominated by really "class" fighters, of the calibre of Marvin Hagler, Ray Leonard, Thomas Hearns, and Roberto Duran. Now it looks as if another "great" has arrived to carry on the fine traditions of the division.

Sumbu Kalambay lies prostrate, the victim of a perfect left to the jaw delivered by Michael Nunn. The first round finish saw Nunn retain his IBF middleweight crown without having to raise a sweat

Christopher M. Farina

Michael Nunn, the flashy holder of the IBF portion of the championship, was fully expected to face his toughest test when crossing gloves with the Italian-based African, Sumbu Kalambay, who has been deposed by the WBA for preferring to meet Nunn rather than his foremost contender, Herol "Bomber" Graham.

In the event, this coming-together at Las Vegas turned out to be a very brief affair with an unexpected finish, leaving the crowd stunned and amazed.

Only very rarely do we truly get the one-punch victory, when a single wallop right out of the blue puts paid to happenings for the night. But southpaw Nunn, after sparring with his more-experienced adversary for the first minute or so of round one, suddenly stepped in with a perfect left to the jaw over Kalambay's guard and put him flat on his back.

The African was utterly beaten. He raised his head and looked about with glassy eyes as instinct alone forced him to try to rise. He just about staggered erect after the referee had dropped his arm for the final time, but then collapsed.

* * *

Sacramento was the scene of an exciting battle for the IBF super-featherweight title, when local hero Tony Lopez defended his belt against the man from whom he had won it the previous summer, veteran Rocky Lockridge.

The second largest crowd ever to witness a fight in Sacramento, turned out with the expectancy of seeing a repeat of the first thriller between these two, in the same ring, and they were not disappointed. But whereas in the first encounter, it was Lopez who survived a near-knockout to struggle up and fight his way back to win the contest, on this occasion it was Lockridge who narrowly avoided being stopped inside the distance.

While the challenger was always dangerous, Lopez surged ahead on points by virtue of neater and cleverer boxing, and in the third round he launched a fast combination which dumped Lockridge unceremoniously on the canvas. Rocky was obliged to take the eight-count, but fought his way out of further trouble during the round.

A clash of heads in the fifth found Lopez with a cut brow, but fortunately the wound was not severe enough to warrant a closure and the rendering of a technical decision. Although the gash bled profusely for the rest of the fight, Lockridge himself was slightly cut and badly swollen about the eyes, but was still full of fight right until the final bell.

With all three judges voting for Lopez as the victor, the verdict was a popular one, and there is little doubt that if a match could be made between the Californian and Ghana's Azumah Nelson for Sacramento, yet another record for attendance and receipts would be established.

* * *

Venezuela's popular little WBA nine-stone kingpin, Antonio Esparragoza, travelled to Kawasaki to defend the belt against his foremost challenger, the big punching Mitsuru Sugiya, of Japan.

The occasion marked the champion's fourth defence of the championship, and he came through with flying colours, overwhelming his man during most of the battle and eventually flattening him for the full count in the tenth round.

Although the Japanese appeared to be the harder puncher of the two, it was Esparragoza who connected with the really heavy artillery successfully. He sent Sugiya to the canvas for a count in the third round, and dropped him twice with right-handers to the jaw in the sixth.

For a time it appeared that the game but struggling challenger might last the full twelve rounds, but in the tenth the Venezuelan opened up with a spirited barrage and floored Sugiya for the full count.

The IBF featherweight title was also on the line during the month, when Jorge "Maromero" Paez, the flamboyant champion, defended against Pennsylvania's Calvin Grove, the man from whom he had won his belt.

The battle was held in the bull-ring at Mexicali, and a thrilling contest took place. In the previous meeting, in the same ring, Grove had looked to be a points winner until the fifteenth and final round, when he suffered three knockdowns to lose his title by a narrow decision. But on this occasion the Mexican showed far more aggression than he had done earlier, and in round ten he sent Grove to the floor with a hefty right. Although the challenger scrambled to his feet, Paez did not let him off the hook, and after dealing out considerable punishment he felled Calvin once again.

Grove beat the count a second time, but was ripe for the finisher, only to have the bell save him. But it was only a matter of postponing the inevitable: a perfect right to the jaw wilted him, and a flashing left uppercut sent him sprawling again. He tried hard to beat the referee's toll, but was just too late. In any case, the contest would have been stopped before further damage could be done.

* * *

IBF super-bantamweight champion, José Sanabria, received a shock when he made a second defence of his title against the same man, Frenchman Fabrice Benichou, at Limoges.

Although, in their earlier encounter, Benichou had built up a points lead, Sanabria's heavier punching and greater aggression had resulted in their battle being stopped. But this time the challenger did his utmost to keep out of trouble, and once again forged into the lead as the rounds progressed, by superior boxing.

Sanabria came out for the final session in desperation, and he succeeded in flooring Benichou. But he could not keep his man down, and the challenger survived until the bell. It was a split decision in favour of the Frenchman, and he was an extremely lucky man to have just snatched the verdict.

* * *

At the bantamweight poundage, Mexico met

Argentina when Raul Perez defended the WBC crown against Lucio Lopez in Los Angeles.

It was one of the goriest encounters ever seen in that district, with both men bleeding profusely from injuries caused by the clashing of heads. But after the ringside medical official inspected the cuts closely, he ruled that they were not dangerous to either man's eyesight and the bloody battle was allowed to continue.

The lanky champion was far too smart a boxer for the chunky but more aggressive challenger, and although at no time did Perez have things all his own way, he gradually built up a lead on points. Lopez put in a grandstand finish in the final round, having been sent to the boards briefly in the eleventh, but his last spurt was too late, and the Mexican was awarded a unanimous verdict.

* * *

Both the IBF and WBC flyweight titles were placed on the line during the month.

First off the mark was South Korea's Yong-Kang Kim, who travelled to Aomori, Japan, to face the home-ground challenge of Yukhito Tamakuma. It proved to be a hard battle, going the full twelve rounds, but the champion was the better man, and he earned the nod of all three judges.

A few days later, on the other side of the world, at the Royal Albert Hall in London, IBF champion Duke McKenzie made a first defence in oppostion to Tony de Luca, of the United States.

McKenzie began the contest in his usual careful and painstaking manner, and had soon solved the American's southpaw style. Little excitement was given to the fans, but a cut over the challenger's eye in the third heralded that things might not go on for very much longer. Although the action was briefly halted in the fourth round for a doctor to inspect de Luca's cut, the bout was allowed to be continued. But a succession of blows worsened the injury, and when the fight was stopped again for medical inspection, de Luca was pulled out.

* * *

Mexico's tiny WBC light-flyweight champion, German Torres, got the surprise of his life when making the first defence of his title against South Korea's Yul-Woo Lee, at Taejon. The challenger turned on the heat and sent the title-holder to the canvas for the full count in the ninth round. Thus, yet another South Korean establishes a claim to honours at this poundage.

* * *

Nico Thomas, of Indonesia, had the advantage of home ground when he challenged Thailand's IBF mini-flyweight champion, Samuth Sithnaruepol, at Jakarta. The latter's title was at stake, and a closely-waged contest ensued. It went the full twelve rounds, and following the final bell a draw was declared, thus enabling the little Thai to retain his crown.

The victory salute. Raul Perez acknowledges the cheers of the crowd after retaining his WBC bantamweight title against the tough Argentinian, Lucio Lopez

Christopher M. Farina

APRIL

Sad Fenech Forced to Bow Out

None of the heftier claimants to world championship honours were employed during the month. Heaviest of all the belt-holders seen in action were the two welterweights, Mark Breland and Simon Brown.

At Atlantic City, the very lean and lanky WBA champion, Breland, faced the challenge of Colombia's Rafael Pineda, who came into this contest with 20 successful battles behind him, and with 19 of those having been won inside the distance. But most of his career had been spent as a lightweight, and he was only really a light-welter, even now. At five feet seven, he stood seven inches shorter than Breland who, at six feet two, had an enormous height and reach advantage.

The unbeaten Pineda was willing enough, and gave the man from Brooklyn quite a bit to think about in the opening round. But once Breland had settled down and had got his left jab going, he began to dictate the way the pattern of the fight would go.

It was during the fourth round that Pineda took a blow to the face and then suddenly turned his back on Breland and walked to the ropes. The champion followed, and hooked a right over the Colombian's shoulder, to catch him on the jaw and send his gum-shield spinning. Pineda angrily retaliated with a round-house left and complained bitterly to the referee that he had been thumbed in the eye by the champion.

How this could have occurred it is difficult to see, since the gloves in use were the variety with the thumb attached, expressly designed to prevent such incidents as the challenger claimed had occurred. He returned to the fray, but seemed to have little heart left for the job. When Breland connected with another punch to the face in the following round, Pineda again turned his back on his opponent, but this time spat out his gum-shield and walked towards his corner. The referee was in no mood for further demonstrations and straightaway stopped the fight in Breland's favour.

Simon Brown drew a tougher customer in the person of Al "Bumblebee" Long, from California. They met in Washington, DC, the Jamaican-born IBF title-holder's adopted home town. It was the first world championship contest seen in the nation's capital for 30 years.

It was not one of Brown's better evenings, and he had considerable trouble with the fast-hitting challenger during the early rounds. But as the bout progressed, so the champion's superior strength and more solid punching began to prevail.

It was in the seventh round that a rapid combination of blows to the head, culminating with a left uppercut to the jaw, sent Long face downwards to the boards. For a time he did not stir, but then made an effort to beat the count. But, in this, he was unsuccessful, and Brown had chalked up his fourth successful defence of the belt.

* * *

The WBA light-welterweight championship was on the line when Argentinian title-holder Juan M. Coggi crossed gloves with his Japanese challenger, Akinobu Hiranaka, at Vasto, Italy.

The battle was a thrilling one, and more than once it seemed that it would be over before the end of the scheduled twelve rounds. The first shock of the evening came when the Japanese, who had been on the receiving end during most of the first two rounds, surprisingly felled Coggi with a beauty of a left hook to the head in the third. The Argentinian beat the count, but in came Hiranaka again, and once more he decked his man, this time with a right to the jaw.

Coggi did well to stay out of further trouble until the bell, and then, having fully recovered, set about giving his challenger a boxing lesson. He mounted up the points as the fight progressed, and although there were no further knockdowns, there was an accidental clash of heads at one stage, with the Japanese coming off second best.

He suffered a cut which bled profusely, and on

Pernell Whitaker (right), the IBF lightweight champion, stabs the southpaw jab into the face of his challenger, Louie Lomeli. The referee stopped the action in the third round after Lomeli had risen from a count

Tom Casino

two occasions the battle was halted in order that the challenger's wound could be inspected. Fortunately, the cut was not bad enough to stop the bout permanently, but both men very nearly brought about a finish in the last hectic round. Coggi shot over a left that had Hiranaka on the very verge of a knockout, but the game Oriental came back with a spirited attack which very nearly spelled curtains for the champion.

The decision, by the British referee and two female American judges, was unanimously in favour of Juan M. Coggi.

* * *

With practically the whole of the audience behind him, and cheering his every move, Pernell Whitaker made the first defence of the IBF lightweight title, since winning it from Greg Haugen. To the delight of the home-town crowd at Norfolk, Virginia, he completely outclassed his challenger, Louie Lomeli, of Chicago.

Known as a southpaw stylist rather than a rumbustious slugger with a heavy punch, the champion gave the lie to rumours that he had no stomach for a battle against an aggressive opponent. Lomeli came forward all the time, and Whitaker matched his every move. With a combination of skilful jabbing and solid hitting, he dominated his challenger almost throughout the brief set-to.

Only once, during the second round, did Lomeli look really dangerous. He connected with a hard left hook to the head and had Whitaker tottering for a moment, but the champion soon threw off the effects of the blow and came back strongly for the rest of the round.

After a masterful exhibition of boxing, Whitaker stepped in with a perfect left hook in the third round and dropped Lomeli to the boards. Although the Chicagoan climbed erect and waited impatiently for the mandatory eight count to be completed, he now stood no chance at all. The champion tore in with a furious two-fisted attack, and it came as no surprise to anyone when the referee signalled that the bout was over.

* * *

Jeff Fenech, one of the few outstanding claimants to a world championship, was all set to stake his WBC featherweight title against Antonio Esparragoza, the WBA champion, in a step towards unification, and the odds are that he would have won. But — "the best-laid plans of mice and men . . ."

The end is near. Al Long (right) is backed against the ropes under attack at the hands of the defending IBF welterweight title-holder, Simon Brown. Long was counted out in the seventh

Tom Casino

In another welterweight championship battle, Mark Breland successfully defended his WBA belt against an inept Rafael Pineda, who virtually retired himself in the fifth round

Tom Casino

In what his faction must have viewed as a sort of warm-up fight, versus Mexico's Marcos Villasana, at Melbourne, the tough, crowd-pleasing little Aussie, gained the verdict of the officials by a wide margin, but in doing so he also managed to end his career!

A fighter who had always been plagued with hand injuries all through his considerable activity, which amounted to 23 victories on the trot, and with the last eleven of these being world title fights in three different divisions, Fenech broke the knuckles of his left hand in three separate places and also damaged his right fist. But struggling on in great pain, throughout a strenuous battle, in which his opponent continued to keep coming at him, Fenech must have made up his mind about halfway through, that with continued damage to his brittle fists, it would be pointless to continue his boxing career.

Almost immediately after the fight was over, and the verdict declared, he announced his retirement from the ring. It will be interesting to see if he really meant it, or whether, with a slow recovery and relatively sound knuckles, he develops a different viewpoint. If little Jeff Fenech — arguably the best fighting man ever to have been developed in Australia — does a U-turn in a few months time he will by no means be the first man in the history of boxing to have done so.

* * *

WBA super-bantamweight king-pin, Juan J. Estrada, of Mexico, was very impressive when tackling his challenger from Venezuela, Jesus Poll, at Los Angeles.

Throughout the battle, Poll made a grand fight of it, employing speed and scintillating boxing to the full, but Estrada was the heavier puncher, and, whenever he landed cleanly, his blows definitely hurt his man. He felled the Venezuelan with a right to the head in the third round, but Poll got up and tore back into the scrap.

The champion suffered a gash over his right eye in the ninth round, but it was not bad enough to warrant a closure. By this time, Estrada had got the measure of his opponent, and in the tenth round he staggered Poll with a beautiful left hook. He followed up with a barrage, sending Poll heavily to the boards, and the end looked imminent. The challenger managed to get to his feet but was in a bad state, and the referee gave him an eight count before allowing the bout to continue.

One more burst of action, and Poll slumped to the canvas again. This time the referee called it off, although it is to the Venezuelan's credit that he pulled himself upright and made every effort to carry on.

* * *

Yokohama was the scene of a WBA super-flyweight title match, when Japan's Kenji Matsumura challenged the busy little champion from Thailand, Kaosai Galaxy.

It was Galaxy's tenth defence of the belt, and he boxed his way to a unanimous points victory in fine style. Although the champion had a little difficulty early on in fathoming things out, and overcoming his man's aggressive counters, he was the master pretty well all the way. He scored a knockdown in the tenth round, and almost scored a knockout, too. Although the Japanese survived the round and managed to stay upright until the final bell, there was no doubt at all as to which man had won.

* * *

At Barranquilla, Fidel Bassa, the Colombian holder of the WBA flyweight championship, had no great difficulty with his latest challenger, Julio Gudino, of Panama.

Setting about his opponent in the style, now familiar to his admirers, from the opening bell, Bassa decided to make his presence felt and to dominate matters. It came as no surprise when the popular little title-holder stopped Gudino in the sixth round.

With the WBA mini-flyweight championship in abeyance, South Korean Bong-Jun Kim, was matched with Colombia's Agustin Garcia, at Seoul.

The Oriental boxer was altogether too good for the South American, and won on a stoppage in round seven. He thus annexed the belt relinquished by the former champion at this poundage, Luis Gamez.

The World's Leading Fighters

Shows the complete career records of 444 leading fighters from the current international boxing scene compiled by Eric Armit. The records set out to cover all the top-rated active men in their respective divisions as at the end of April, 1989.

Results Code:

PTS	- Points
CO	- Count Out
RSC	- Referee Stopped Contest
RTD	- Retired
DIS	- Disqualified
NC	- No Contest
ND	- No Decision
TD	- Technical Decision
T DRAW	- Technical Draw

Title Bout Code:

ABU	- African Boxing Union
CON AM	- Continental American
EBU	- European Boxing Union
FECARBOX	- Central American & Carribean
IBF	- International Boxing Federation
NABF	- North American Boxing Federation
OPBF	- Orient & Pacific Boxing Federation
USBA	- United States Boxing Association
WBA	- World Boxing Association
WBC	- World Boxing Council

Mauricio Aceves
Mexico City, Mexico. *Born* 18.12.60
Lightweight

14.07.79 Mario Castelan W PTS 4 Mexico City
18.08.79 Juan Soto W RSC 3 Mexico City
10.10.79 Lupe Martinez W PTS 6 Mexico City
01.12.79 Juan Soto W RSC 2 Mexico City
16.02.80 Pedro Molina W CO 8 Mexico City
24.03.80 Pedro Molina L DIS 3 Mexico City
24.05.80 Maximo Guevara W CO 4 Guadalajara
07.06.80 Angel Mata L CO 2 Mexico City
09.10.80 Cayetano Correa W RSC 8 Mexico City
25.11.80 Armando Villalobos W CO 7 Guadalajara
20.12.80 Ricardo Peralta L RSC 6 Merida
16.12.81 Cayetano Correa DREW 10 Mexico City
.81 Chuchu Ramirez W CO 9 Mexico City
10.03.82 Rene Arredondo L PTS 10 Mexico City
03.11.82 Raul Guerrero W PTS 10 Mexico City
.06.83 Alejandro Garcia W CO 4 Acapulco
23.04.84 Jorge Mercado W RSC 5 Mexico City
14.07.84 Agustin Vincenteno W CO 2 Mexico City
08.09.84 Miguel Dominguez W PTS 10 Mexico City
27.10.84 Ricardo Peralta L CO 5 Merida
23.03.85 Herminio Delgado W RSC 9 Mexico City
21.12.85 Arturo Hernandez W RSC 5 Minatitlan
28.04.86 Eduardo Dominguez W RSC 8 Tijuana
07.08.86 Martin Morado W TD 8 Los Angeles
09.10.86 Ernie Landeros W RSC 8 Los Angeles
26.03.87 Mark Fernandez W RSC 5 Los Angeles
28.05.87 Julio Ruiz W CO 6 Los Angeles
29.08.87 Alfredo Layne W RSC 5 Los Angeles
14.12.87 Tony Contreras W PTS 10 Tijuana
24.03.88 Roger Mayweather L CO 3 Los Angeles
(*WBC L. Welterweight Title Challenge*)
21.01.89 Amancio Castro DREW 12 Monteria
(*Vacant WBO Lightweight Title*)
Summary: 31 contests, won 23, drew 2, lost 6.

Rodolfo Aguilar
Panama City, Panama. *Born* 08.05.65
Lightweight

21.05.83 Alfredo Ashley W PTS 4 Colon
17.09.83 Carlos Rodriguez W PTS 4 Panama City
15.10.83 Tomas Palacios W PTS 4 Colon
19.11.83 Daniel Melo W PTS 4 Panama City
17.12.83 Juan Perez W RSC 5 Panama City
16.04.84 Ray Best W RSC 4 Colon
28.04.84 Leroy Durant W RSC 3 Panama City
03.06.84 Jose Williams W PTS 10 Colon
25.08.84 Esquiel Mosquera W PTS 10 Colon
27.10.84 Geronimo Luquez W PTS 10 Panama City
28.12.84 Felipe Julio W CO 3 Panama City
15.02.85 Aurelio Benitez W RSC 3 Panama City
27.04.85 Enrique Ramirez W CO 4 Panama City
15.06.85 Ray Williams W RSC 7 Panama City
16.11.85 Julio Ruiz W PTS 10 Panama City
21.03.86 Ildemar Paisan L PTS 10 Caracas
20.12.86 Aquilino Asprilla W RSC 4 Panama City
14.02.87 Rafael Williams W PTS 10 Colon
31.07.87 Ismaldi Pineda W PTS 10 Panama City
15.08.87 Luis Portocarrero W RSC 5 Panama City
20.02.88 Pedro Padilla W RSC 9 Panama City
16.04.88 Julio Cesar Chavez L RSC 6 Las Vegas
(*WBA Lightweight Title Challenge*)
24.10.88 Terrence Alli W PTS 10 Los Angeles
20.03.89 Jose Rivera W PTS 10 Los Angeles
Summary: 24 contests, won 22, lost 2.

Kyung-Duk Ahn
South Korea. *Born* 21.09.62
Former Undefeated South Korean L. Welterweight Champion. Former OPBF L. Welterweight Champion

12.06.81 Wang-Soo Kim W PTS 4 Kwangju
24.07.82 Suk-Nam Woo W PTS 4 Seoul
05.02.83 Yung-Wan Kim W PTS 4 Pusan
20.02.83 Chong-Lim Suh W RSC 2 Chinju
27.03.83 Heung-Sik Shin W RSC 3 Chinju
01.05.83 In-Sun Kim W RSC 3 Chinju
05.06.83 Byung-Sun Yuh W RSC 3 Chonju
21.08.83 Kuk-Jim Lim W PTS 8 Daejon
24.09.83 Hong-Kyu Lim W CO 7 Chinju
(*South Korean L. Welterweight Title Challenge*)
04.11.83 Suh-Aeng Lee W CO 9 Chinju
(*South Korean L. Welterweight Title Defence*)
27.11.83 Hwa-Yung Song W PTS 10 Masan
(*South Korean L. Welterweight Title Defence*)
29.11.83 Daeh-Yun Oh W CO 9 Pusan
11.03.84 Joe Lim W CO 4 Chinju
08.05.84 Chong-Hak Lee W PTS 10 Chinju
(*South Korean L. Welterweight Title Defence*)
09.09.84 Tae-Wang Kang W PTS 10 Inchon
(*South Korean L. Welterweight Title Defence*)
19.01.85 Wha-Yung Song W PTS 10 Daejon
(*South Korean L. Welterweight Title Defence*)
27.04.85 Ki-Young Park W RSC 9 Ulsan
(*South Korean L. Welterweight Title Defence*)
13.07.85 Rang-Ku Park W PTS 10 Chungju
(*South Korean L. Welterweight Title Defence*)
02.10.85 Eung-Shik Kim W PTS 12 Seoul
(*OPBF L. Welterweight Title Challenge*)
03.01.86 Yodkan Donjadee W RSC 3 Chinju
(*OPBF L. Welterweight Title Defence*)
05.04.86 Allan Alegria W PTS 10 Masan
01.11.86 Sang-Ho Lee L PTS 12 Pohang
(*OPBF L. Welterweight Title Defence*)
26.04.87 Tae-Wang Kang W PTS 10 Chinju
29.08.87 Pyung-Sup Kim W PTS 10 Chinju
27.12.87 Ruben Rabago W PTS 10 Pohang
05.04.88 Boy Romero W CO 3 Jinju
22.12.88 In-Sun Kim W CO 6 Seoul
Summary: 27 contests, won 26, lost 1.

Olian (Baby O) Alexander
Huntington, USA. *Born* 17.02.60
Cruiserweight

12.10.84 Paul Madison L RSC 6 Wichita
15.12.84 James Wilder W RSC 3 Waukegan
02.04.85 Londale Freison W CO 1 Colorado Springs
14.09.85 Jim Berry W CO 3 Oklahoma City
16.11.85 Bob Wiggins W RSC 1 Oklahoma City
14.12.85 Charles Jamison W CO 2 Oklahoma City
02.08.86 Orlin Norris W PTS 4 San Jose
14.08.86 Mike Bardwell W RSC 1 Vallejo
26.09.86 David Kliewer W CO 2 Wichita
02.10.86 Mike Bardwell W PTS 4 San Jose
30.10.86 David Smith W PTS 6 San Jose
13.11.86 Mike Bardwell W RSC 2 San Jose
04.12.86 Rafael Fimbres W RSC 1 San Carlos
04.03.87 Lorenzo Boyd W CO 6 San Rafael
16.04.87 Calvin Sherman W RSC 2 San Rafael
05.06.87 Dwain Bonds W RSC 6 Pleasanton
09.07.87 Mike Gans L PTS 8 Oakland
02.10.87 Henry Hearns W RSC 8 Pleasanton
19.03.88 Eric Williams W CO 6 Pleasanton
26.10.88 Joey Parker W PTS 10 San Jose
23.11.88 Dwight Muhammad Qawi L RSC 3 Philadelphia
Summary: 21 contests, won 18, lost 3.

Bashiru Ali
Oakland, USA. *Born* Lagos, Nigeria 27.02.56
Nigerian Heavyweight Champion. Former WBC International Cruiserweight Champion. Former NABF & USBA Cruiserweight Champion

01.06.78 Junior Albers L PTS 6 Sacramento
21.06.78 Charles Terrell W PTS 6 Concord
12.07.78 Jim Ingram L PTS 6 Oakland
22.07.78 William Tavake W PTS 6 Truckee
28.07.78 Reggie Phillips L PTS 5 San Diego
06.12.78 Tony Stone W PTS 6 Stockton
27.02.79 Greg McPherson W PTS 10 San Carlos
27.03.79 Basheer Wadud W PTS 6 San Carlos
24.04.79 Greg McPherson W PTS 10 San Carlos
27.06.79 Pete McIntyre L PTS 10 Los Angeles
05.10.79 Yaqui Lopez L PTS 10 San Carlos
31.01.80 Len Provo W RSC 8 San Carlos
29.02.80 David Smith W PTS 10 San Carlos
11.04.80 Yaqui Meneses W DIS 8 San Jose
25.07.80 Jim Ingram W CO 7 San Carlos
28.08.80 Byron Campbell W RSC 5 San Carlos
16.10.80 Young Alvaro Lopez W RSC 10 San Carlos
03.12.80 Jesse Burnett W PTS 12 Anaheim
(*USBA Cruiserweight Title Challenge*)
15.02.81 Reggie Patrick W PTS 8 Atlantic City
28.02.81 Marcus Jackson W PTS 8 Atlantic City
02.10.81 Marvin Camel L PTS 12 San Francisco
(*USBA Cruiserweight Title Defence*)
12.11.81 Wilbert Albers W RSC 4 Oakland
25.02.82 Jesse Avila W RSC 4 San Jose
12.03.82 King David Smith W PTS 10 San Francisco
17.04.82 Fernando Montes W RSC 9 Mexico City
27.05.82 Greg McPherson W RSC 5 San Jose
25.08.82 Roger Braxton W PTS 10 Concord

02.10.82 Henry Hearns L RSC 2 Las Vegas
07.11.82 Mario Rosa W PTS 8 McAfee
20.11.82 Don Addison W RSC 2 Atlantic City
18.03.83 Leon Taylor L PTS 6 Atlantic City
09.06.83 Ruben Williams W PTS 10 San Jose
02.06.84 Carlos de Leon L PTS 12 Oakland
(*WBC Cruiserweight Title Challenge*)
12.09.84 Yaqui Lopez W PTS 12 Stockton
29.09.84 Michael Arms W CO 6 Anchorage
07.05.85 Young Joe Louis W CO 2 Reno
19.06.85 Anthony Davis W RSC 9 Reno
(*NABF Cruiserweight Title Challenge*)
14.08.85 Dee Dee Collier W CO 2 Reno
14.01.86 Michael Arms W PTS 10 Reno
22.04.86 Henry Tillman L RSC 1 Las Vegas
(*NABF Cruiserweight Title Defence*)
10.04.87 Tommy Richardson W PTS 12 Jacksonville
(*Vacant WBC International Cruiserweight Title*)
05.12.87 Kevin Wagstaff W CO 1 Ibadan
(*WBC International Cruiserweight Title Defence*)
.87 Mike Gans W CO 4 Lagos
08.08.88 Angelo Rottoli L PTS 12 San Pellegrino
(*WBC International Cruiserweight Title Defence*)
23.09.88 Charles Udalor W CO 5 Lagos
(*Nigerian Heavyweight Title Challenge*)
15.02.89 Anthony Witherspoon L PTS 12 Philadelphia
(*Vacant WBA Americas Cruiserweight Title*)
Summary: 46 contests, won 33, lost 13.

Terrence (Halley) Alli
Atlantic City, USA. *Born* Georgetown, Guyana 29.06.60
Former Undefeated USBA Lightweight Champion

02.12.79 Winston Goodridge W PTS 4 Georgetown
26.12.79 Walter Smith L PTS 6 Georgetown
14.01.80 Lloyd John W CO 3 Port of Spain
26.02.80 Clyde Wilson W PTS 6 Georgetown
05.03.80 Ricardo Croquer W PTS 6 Port of Spain
30.04.80 Cleophas James W PTS 6 Port of Spain
29.03.81 Cleophas James W PTS 8 Port of Spain
27.05.81 Walter Smith W PTS 6 Port of Spain
15.08.81 Michael Drayton W RSC 8 Port of Spain
28.11.81 Ismael Santana L RSC 3 Port of Spain
22.01.82 Nedric Simmons W RSC 4 Toronto
20.03.82 Rick Pappa W PTS 6 Toronto
16.04.82 Johnny Summerhays L PTS 10 Toronto
11.09.82 Norberto Velez W PTS 6 Atlantic City
07.10.82 Thomas Baker DREW 6 Atlantic City
16.12.82 Primo Ramos W RSC 2 Atlantic City
27.02.83 Edwin Luis Rivera W RSC 8 Atlantic City
02.06.83 Danny Avery W PTS 8 Atlantic City
18.06.83 Gonzalo Montellano W PTS 10 Atlantic City
05.11.83 Jerome Artis W RSC 2 Atlantic City
12.11.83 Ivan Montalvo W RSC 5 Las Vegas
05.04.84 Ezzard Charles Adams W RSC 7 Atlantic City
17.05.84 Melvin Paul W PTS 12 Atlantic City
21.06.84 John Senegal W RSC 2 Atlantic City
02.08.84 Efrain Nieves W PTS 12 Atlantic City
05.09.84 Frank Newton W RSC 3 Atlantic City
24.10.84 Victor Babilonia W PTS 10 Atlantic City
12.01.85 Harry Arroyo L RSC 11 Atlantic City
(*IBF Lightweight Title Challenge*)
04.09.85 Eduardo Valdez W PTS 10 Atlantic City
23.10.85 Erskine Wade W RSC 10 Atlantic City
27.11.85 Denny Vargas W PTS 10 Atlantic City
10.01.86 Anthony Williams W PTS 10 Atlantic City
30.03.86 Cornelius Boza-Edwards DREW 10 Las Vegas
15.08.86 Pedro Montero W DIS 2 Atlantic City
27.09.86 Miguel Santana W PTS 12 Atlantic City
(*Vacant USBA Lightweight Title*)
02.01.87 Roberto Medina W PTS 10 Atlantic City
11.03.87 Jeff Bumphus W RSC 8 Atlantic City
19.05.87 Rodney Moore W RSC 9 Atlantic City
19.07.87 Jose Luis Ramirez L PTS 12 St Tropez
(*Vacant WBC Lightweight Title*)
04.09.87 Joey Olivera W PTS 10 Las Vegas
23.12.87 Miguel Santana W PTS 10 Atlantic City
21.03.88 Darryl Tyson W PTS 10 Atlantic City
22.05.88 Jerry Page W PTS 10 Atlantic City
24.10.88 Rodolfo Aguilar L PTS 10 Los Angeles
04.03.89 David Thio W CO 9 Lyon
Summary: 45 contests, won 37, drew 2, lost 6.

Elvis Alvarez
Colombia
Latin American & WBO Flyweight Champion. Former Undefeated Colombian S. Flyweight Champion

16.09.83 Belin Bello W PTS 4 Sincelejo
29.06.84 Heriberto Malave W CO 4 Buenaventura
30.08.84 Eugenio Oviedo W RSC 3 Cartagena
22.02.85 Heriberto Malave W PTS 8 Buenaventura
01.03.85 Rodolfo Blanco L PTS 10 Barranquilla
28.03.85 Victor Tejedor W CO 4 Barranquilla
03.05.85 Jaime Diaz W RSC 5 Barranquilla
16.05.86 Toribio Riascos W PTS 10 Medellin
(*Colombian S. Flyweight Title Challenge*)
31.10.86 Alfredo Lugo W RSC 9 Monteria
(*Colombian S. Flyweight Title Defence*)
13.02.87 Israel Contreras W PTS 10 Barranquilla
31.07.87 Edgar Monserrat L PTS 10 Panama City
05.02.88 Victor Sierra L PTS 10 Medellin
21.05.88 Lincoln Salcedo W RSC 5 Bucaramanga
(*Latin American Flyweight Title Challenge*)
08.10.88 Jorge Lugo W CO 5 Bello
(*Latin American Flyweight Title Defence*)
02.12.88 Joselo Perez W PTS 8 Barranquilla
03.03.89 Miguel Mercedes W PTS 12 Medellin
(*Vacant WBO Flyweight Title*)
Summary: 16 contests, won 13, lost 3.

Dennis Andries
Hackney, England. *Born* Guyana 05.11.53
WBC L. Heavyweight Champion.
Former Undefeated British Heavyweight Champion

16.05.78 Ray Pearce W CO 2 Newport
01.06.78 Mark Seabrook W RSC 1 London
20.06.78 Bonny McKenzie L PTS 8 Southend
18.09.78 Ken Jones W PTS 6 London
31.10.78 Neville Estaban W PTS 6 Barnsley
14.11.78 Les McAteer DREW 8 Birkenhead
22.11.78 Glen McEwan W RSC 7 Stoke
04.12.78 Tom Collins W PTS 8 Southend
22.01.79 Bunny Johnson L PTS 10 Wolverhampton
30.01.79 Tom Collins W CO 6 Southend
05.04.79 Francis Hand W RSC 8 Liverpool
06.06.79 Bonny McKenzie W PTS 8 Burslem
17.09.79 Johnny Waldron W RTD 10 Mayfair
27.02.80 Bunny Johnson L PTS 15 Burslem
(*British L. Heavyweight Title Challenge*)
17.04.80 Mustafa Wasajja L PTS 8 Copenhagen
18.06.80 Chris Lawson W RSC 8 Burslem
23.03.81 Shaun Chalcraft W PTS 10 London
16.09.81 Liam Coleman W RSC 6 Burslem
12.10.81 David Pearce L RSC 7 London
23.11.81 Alek Penarski W PTS 10 Chesterfield
15.03.82 Tom Collins L PTS 15 London
(*Vacant British L. Heavyweight Title*)
10.08.82 Keith Bristol W PTS 10 London
28.02.83 Karl Canwell W CO 4 London
19.05.83 Chris Lawson W CO 4 London
22.09.83 Keith Bristol W CO 4 London
26.01.84 Tom Collins W PTS 12 London
(*British L. Heavyweight Title Challenge*)
06.04.84 Tom Collins W PTS 12 Watford
(*British L. Heavyweight Title Defence*)
10.10.84 Devon Bailey W CO 12 London
(*British L. Heavyweight Title Defence*)
23.03.85 Jose Seys W RSC 3 London
07.05.85 Jeff Meachum W CO 4 New Orleans
25.05.85 Tim Broady W RSC 5 Atlantic City
06.06.85 Marcus Dorsey W CO 3 Lafayette
11.12.85 Alex Blanchard DREW 12 London
(*EBU L. Heavyweight Title Challenge*)
13.02.86 Keith Bristol W RSC 6 London
(*British L. Heavyweight Title Defence*)
30.04.86 J. B. Williamson W PTS 12 London
(*WBC L. Heavyweight Title Challenge*)
10.09.86 Tony Sibson W RSC 9 London
(*WBC & British L. Heavyweight Title Defence*)
07.03.87 Thomas Hearns L RSC 10 Detroit
(*WBC L. Heavyweight Title Defence*)
06.10.87 Robert Folley W PTS 10 Phoenix
20.02.88 Jamie Howe W PTS 10 Detroit
22.05.88 Bobby Czyz W PTS 10 Atlantic City
10.09.88 Tony Harrison W RTD 7 Detroit
17.10.88 Paul Madison W RSC 4 Tucson
21.02.89 Tony Willis W RSC 5 Tucson
(*Vacant WBC L. Heavyweight Title*)
Summary: 43 contests, won 34, drew 2, lost 7.

Rufino Angulo
Floriac, France. *Born* 15.03.56
Former French L. Heavyweight Champion

24.11.78 Andre Genasi W RSC 6 Villeneuve
06.04.79 Rhida Hakimi W CO 2 Villeneuve
08.12.79 Daniel Hyvon W RSC 4 Paris
21.12.79 Maurice Renaud DREW 6 Agen
01.02.80 Serge Sinelnikov W PTS 6 Agen
15.02.80 Mauro da Cruz W PTS 6 Bordeaux
28.03.80 Moussa Mukandjo L RSC 5 Chaux
18.10.80 Maurice Renaud W PTS 8 Villeneuve
06.12.80 Idrissa Konate W CO 4 Villeneuve
31.01.81 Pierre Joly DREW 10 Villeneuve
10.04.81 Joel Bonnetaz W PTS 8 Villeneuve
05.06.81 Jacques Chinon L PTS 12 Villeneuve
(*French Middleweight Title Challenge*)
23.10.81 Christian d'Helft L DIS 4 Perigueux
07.11.81 Manuel Lira W PTS 8 Villeneuve
13.11.81 Cosimo Funto W RSC 6 Rome
11.12.81 Geatano Ardito L DIS 4 Florence
12.02.82 Michel Pagani L DIS 4 Calais
05.03.82 Andre Mongalema W CO 8 Paris
19.05.82 Eric Kopec W CO 6 Villeneuve
09.10.82 Yawe Davis W PTS 8 Villeneuve
04.02.83 Carl Canwell W RSC 5 Bordeaux
19.03.83 Keith Bristol W RSC 6 Villeneuve
13.06.83 Tony Mundine W CO 5 Paris
05.08.83 Bonny McKenzie W PTS 8 Nimes
08.10.83 David Conteh W DIS 4 Villeneuve
21.11.83 Rudi Koopmans L PTS 12 Paris
(*EBU L. Heavyweight Title Challenge*)
24.02.84 Mwehu Beya L PTS 8 Bordeaux
19.04.84 Mwehu Beya W PTS 8 Paris
25.05.84 Trevor Cattouse W RSC 3 Toulouse
31.10.84 Horst Lang W CO 4 Bordeaux
07.12.84 Jonjo Greene W PTS 8 Bordeaux
29.03.85 Willie Edwards L PTS 10 Bordeaux
20.12.85 Ian Lazarus W PTS 8 Bordeaux
27.01.86 Jonjo Greene W PTS 8 Paris
14.03.86 Nye Williams W PTS 8 Bordeaux
10.04.86 Yombo Araka L PTS 8 Antibes
06.12.86 Abdel Moumene W RTD 3 Gailliard
05.02.87 Jean-Noel Camara W PTS 10 Bordeaux
16.04.87 Richard Caramanolis W CO 2 Marseilles
(*French L. Heavyweight Title Challenge*)
05.10.87 Roy Saffold W DIS 6 Paris
21.11.87 Virgil Hall L PTS 12 Paris
(*WBA L. Heavyweight Title Challenge*)
13.02.88 Noel Magee DREW 8 Paris
28.03.88 Richard Caramanolis L RSC 4 Paris
(*French L. Heavyweight Title Defence*)
21.10.88 Charles Williams L RSC 3 Villeneuve d'Ornon
(*IBF L. Heavyweight Title Challenge*)
Summary: 44 contests, won 29, drew 3, lost 12.

Dennis Andries

Peter Shaw

Lupe Aquino
Chula Vista, USA. *Born* Tijuana 23.01.63
Former WBC L. Middleweight Champion. Former Undefeated NABF L. Middleweight Champion

02.04.81 Alberto Garcia W RSC 1 Los Angeles
15.05.81 Henry Drummond W PTS 4 Los Angeles
12.08.81 Rocky Cabilles W RSC 1 Las Vegas
09.09.81 Ramondo Solorzano W CO 2 Las Vegas
24.09.81 Bobby Silva W RSC 1 Las Vegas
22.10.81 Ricardo Garcia W RSC 6 Las Vegas
07.11.81 Willie McGee W CO 1 Las Vegas
17.11.81 Danny Favella W PTS 8 Phoenix
05.12.81 Barreto Hernandez W RSC 2 Las Vegas
17.12.81 Paul Gonzalez W CO 1 Phoenix
18.02.82 Andres Obregon W RSC 1 Phoenix
25.02.82 Solomon Jones W RSC 1 Las Vegas
25.03.82 Joe Moliere W PTS 8 Las Vegas
22.05.82 Eddie Nuno W PTS 8 Las Vegas
21.07.82 Clayton Hires W PTS 10 Las Vegas
07.12.82 Reinaldo Rogue W CO 2 San Diego
31.01.83 Tim Harris W PTS 10 Los Angeles
21.02.83 Rudy Hernandez L PTS 10 Los Angeles
27.05.83 Chino Bermudez W PTS 10 Los Angeles
14.06.83 Eduardo Dominguez W RSC 4 Ventura
09.08.83 David Madrid W RSC 1 Ventura
18.08.83 Victor Abraham W RSC 7 Los Angeles
10.09.83 Steve Herron W RSC 5 Atlantic City
25.11.83 Eric Martin DREW 10 Las Vegas
16.12.83 Tomas Chavez W RTD 1 Ventura
17.04.84 Marlon Starling L PTS 12 Atlantic City (*NABF and USBA Welterweight Title Challenge*)
18.06.85 Lloyd Taylor W RSC 1 Atlantic City
30.07.85 Carl Riskus W RSC 3 Atlantic City
01.11.85 David Noel W PTS 10 Port of Spain
10.10.86 Nat Dryer W RSC 5 Las Vegas
11.11.86 Diomedes Colome W CO 5 Las Vegas
09.01.87 Anthony Wiley W RSC 2 Las Vegas
06.04.87 Davey Moore W RSC 5 Las Vegas
12.07.87 Duane Thomas W PTS 12 Bordeaux (*WBC L. Middleweight Title Challenge*)
02.10.87 Gianfranco Rosi L PTS 12 Perugia (*WBC L. Middleweight Title Defence*)
03.01.88 Don Curry L PTS 12 Genoa
10.04.88 Milton McCrory W PTS 10 Atlantic City
24.06.88 Royan Hammond W PTS 12 Las Vegas (*Vacant NABF L. Middleweight Title*)
08.12.88 John D. Jackson L RTD 7 Detroit
24.04.89 James Williams W CO 1 Tijuana (*Vacant WBO L. Middleweight Title*)
Summary: 40 contests, won 34, drew 1, lost 5.

John Arief
Indonesia
WBC International M. Flyweight Champion. Former Undefeated Indonesian M. Flyweight Champion

12.07.86 Cesar Batho W PTS 4 Surabaya
07.09.86 Kid Manguni W PTS 6 Surabaya
11.10.86 Hudi L DIS 7 Malang
02.11.86 Danche W CO 2 Surabaya
07.12.86 Julius Leojan W PTS 12 Surabaya (*Indonesian M. Flyweight Title Challenge*)
25.01.87 Demi W PTS 10 Gresik
01.03.87 Susyadi W PTS 8 Gresik
01.06.87 Samuth Sithnaruepol DREW 12 Surabaya (*OPBF M. Flyweight Title Challenge*)
05.07.87 Nana Suhana W PTS 12 Gresik (*Indonesian M. Flyweight Title Defence*)
06.09.87 Ded Donjadee W PTS 10 Surabaya
31.10.87 Nico Thomas L PTS 8 Surabaya
15.12.87 John Pelor W PTS 8 Surabaya
27.12.87 Gim Suryaman L PTS 8 Surabaya
18.02.88 Gim Suryaman W PTS 12 Malang (*Indonesian M. Flyweight Title Defence*)
16.04.88 Nico Thomas W PTS 12 Malang (*Indonesian M. Flyweight Title Defence*)
15.07.88 Asawin Sordusit W RSC 12 Surabaya (*Vacant WBC International M. Flyweight Title*)
11.02.89 Napa Kiatwanchai L PTS 12 Bangkok (*WBC M. Flyweight Title Challenge*)
Summary: 17 contests, won 12, drew 1, lost 4.

Rene Arredondo
Apatzingan, Mexico. *Born* 15.06.61
Former WBC L. Welterweight Champion

15.11.79 Zorrita Gomez W CO 1 Vera Cruz
30.12.80 Arturo Millan W RSC 3 Mexico City
31.01.81 Juan Reyes W CO 3 Mexico City
18.03.81 Pablo Santiago W CO 1 Mexico City
12.06.81 Beto Ramos W CO 5 Acapulco
11.07.81 Marcelo Vega W CO 1 Mexico City
07.08.81 Carmelo Montes W RSC 5 Acapulco
09.09.81 Ubaldo Ramirez W RSC 4 Mexico City
09.10.81 Isabel Gonzalez W CO 3 Acapulco
06.11.81 Saul Montana W RSC 4 Acapulco
11.12.81 Jose Rosas W PTS 10 Acapulco
03.02.82 Sergio Cabrera W RSC 3 Mexico City
03.03.82 Luis Rivera W CO 1 Mexico City
10.03.82 Mauricio Aceves W PTS 10 Mexico City
02.04.82 Emilio Solano W CO 3 Ciudad Valles
27.04.82 Herminio Delgado W CO 3 Mexico City
22.05.82 Jose Luis Escalante W DIS 4 Mexico City
26.06.82 Juan Carlos Alvarado W RSC 6 Mexico City
11.08.82 Leoncio Ortiz W RSC 5 Mexico City
13.10.82 Leoncio Ortiz L PTS 10 Mexico City
26.11.82 Francisco Tapia W RSC 3 Mexico City
15.12.82 Jose Luis Tapia W RSC 2 Mexico City
20.02.83 Hector Rivera W RSC 4 San Juan
09.07.83 Andre Wynn W CO 1 Los Angeles
25.08.83 Carlos Hernandez W CO 1 Los Angeles
03.09.83 Leonardo Cruz W PTS 10 Los Angeles
24.09.83 Rigoberto Ruiz W RSC 6 Los Angeles
08.12.83 Dario de Jesus W RSC 4 Los Angeles
16.02.84 Pedro Roche W CO 4 Los Angeles
12.04.84 Ricardo Lomeli W RSC 2 Los Angeles
17.05.84 Claude Noel W CO 2 Los Angeles
23.06.84 Jose Angulo W RSC 4 Los Angeles
25.09.84 Efren Olivo W RSC 5 Harlingen
02.11.84 Pedro Carbajal W RSC 1 Los Angeles
19.04.85 Hector Medina W CO 1 Los Angeles
23.05.85 Hugo Hernandez W RSC 4 Los Angeles
03.07.85 Rodolfo Gonzalez L PTS 10 Los Angeles
26.09.85 Saul Julio W RSC 4 Los Angeles
20.12.85 Eduardo Valdez W RSC 2 Los Angeles
05.05.86 Lonnie Smith W RSC 5 Los Angeles (*WBC L. Welterweight Title Challenge*)
24.07.86 Tsuyoshi Hamada L CO 1 Tokyo (*WBC L. Welterweight Title Defence*)
06.11.86 Saoul Mamby W PTS 10 Los Angeles
22.07.87 Tsuyoshi Hamada W RSC 6 Tokyo (*WBC L. Welterweight Title Challenge*)
12.11.87 Roger Mayweather L RSC 6 Los Angeles (*WBC L. Welterweight Title Defence*)
23.06.88 Lalo Velasquez W CO 5 Los Angeles
15.10.88 Joe Melvin W CO 4 Oklahoma City
19.04.89 Don Caples L PTS 10 Harlingen
Summary: 47 contests, won 42, lost 5.

Miguel (Puma) Arroyo
Salta, Argentine. *Born* 10.03.62
South American Welterweight Champion. Former Argentine Welterweight Champion

10.09.82 Jose Toloza W RTD 5 Salta
01.10.82 Alberto Villalba L RTD 5 Salta
06.05.83 Jorge O. Martinez W PTS 6 Catamarca
30.09.83 Jose Comolli W RSC 7 Salta
11.10.83 Marc Villagra W PTS 8 Salta
28.10.83 Alberto Sosa W CO 8 Salta
25.11.83 Martin Duran W PTS 10 Salta
20.12.83 Martin Duran W CO 1 Salta
24.05.84 Mario Pereyra W CO 2 Salta
29.06.84 Jose L. Luduena W RSC 6 Salta
31.07.84 Jorge Pino W RSC 2 Salta
13.09.84 Hector Gonzalez W PTS 10 Salta
11.10.84 Sergio Combis W CO 1 Salta
26.10.84 Miguel Pereyra W CO 1 Salta
09.11.84 Julio Fernandez L PTS 10 Salta
21.12.84 Osmar Ochoa W PTS 12 Salta
22.03.85 Juan A. Flores W CO 3 Salta
06.04.85 Hector D. Gonzalez DREW 10 Buenos Aires
19.04.85 Enrique Coronel W RTD 7 Salta
12.07.85 Cesar Valdes W CO 8 Salta
26.07.85 Oscar Sosa W PTS 10 Salta
08.08.85 Carlos Prieto W PTS 10 Salta
27.09.85 Juan Barboza W PTS 10 Salta
15.11.85 Carlos Herrera W TD 5 Salta
18.02.86 Francisco Cardozo W CO 1 Salta
08.03.86 Ramon Abeldano W PTS 12 Buenos Aires (*Argentinian Welterweight Title Challenge*)
21.03.86 Domingo Sosa W PTS 10 Salta
25.04.86 Alberto Villalva W CO 4 Salta
30.05.86 Juan C. Ortiz W CO 1 Salta
14.06.86 Ramon Abeldano W CO 6 Buenos Aires (*South American Welterweight Title Challenge*)
11.07.86 Mario Matthysse W DIS 8 Salta
23.08.86 Antonio R. Juarez W RSC 8 Esquel (*Argentinian Welterweight Title Defence*)
15.11.86 Lorenzo Garcia L PTS 10 Buenos Aires
20.03.87 Simon Escobar L RSC 10 Villa Mercedes (*Argentinian Welterweight Title Defence*)
22.05.87 Miguel Tejeda W PTS 10 Salta
05.06.87 Carlos Herrera W CO 1 Salta
19.06.87 Simon Escobar W RTD 8 Salta (*South American Welterweight Title Defence*)
21.08.87 Jose Campos W CO 2 Salta
13.11.87 Osvaldo Diaz W CO 5 Salta
18.12.87 Cesar Perez W CO 4 Salta
12.02.88 Jose da Silva W RTD 4 Salta
07.05.88 Marcelo di Croce W RSC 4 San Antonio (*South American Welterweight Title Defence*)
14.07.88 Lorenzo Garcia DREW 10 Salta
30.09.88 Felipe Nino W CO 4 Salta
21.10.88 Lorenzo Garcia DREW 10 Salta
03.12.88 Jorge Morello W CO 9 Tartagal
29.12.88 Juan Sosa W CO 1 Salta
23.01.89 Juan Ceballos W RSC 5 Mar del Plata
03.03.89 Jose Raies W RTD 2 Salta
18.03.89 Nestor Albarracin W CO 8 Buenos Aires
06.04.89 Osmar Ochoa W PTS 10 La Rioja
Summary: 51 contests, won 44, drew 3, lost 4.

Diego Avila
Xalcoton, Mexico. *Born* 13.11.59
Bantamweight

02.08.80 Victor Montero W PTS 6 Mexico City
06.09.80 Eugenio Morgan W PTS 6 Mexico City
11.11.80 Mario Nava W PTS 8 Mexico City
10.12.80 Jose Garibo W PTS 8 Mexico City
.81 Ubaldo Rivas W PTS 8 Mexico City
01.04.81 Salvador Estrada W PTS 10 Mexico City
13.05.81 Agustin Ahutal W RSC 7 Mexico City
13.06.81 Angel Lira W CO 5 Mexico City
31.07.81 Jose L. Riestra W CO 5 San Luis Potosi
29.08.81 Albanico Dominguez W CO 7 Hermosillo
25.09.81 Macario Tovar W PTS 10 Mazatlan
20.11.81 Felipe Fernandez W PTS 10 Mexico City
01.02.82 Leonardo Valdez L RSC 9 Mexicali
19.05.82 Mario Nava DREW 10 Mexico City
03.07.82 Gilberto Roman W DIS 7 Mexico City
10.09.82 Jesus Lopez L DIS 9 Culiacan
07.11.82 Javier Marquez DREW 10 Mexicali
22.01.83 Jorge Ramirez L PTS 10 Mexico City
11.06.83 Heriberto Saavedra W PTS 10 Mexico City
13.08.83 Jorge de Jesus L DIS 10 Mexico City
23.09.83 Rodolfo Ortega DREW 10 Mexico City
26.11.83 Rodolfo Ortega W CO 7 Mexico City
27.01.84 Jesus Lopez L PTS 10 Torreon
13.03.84 Carlos de la Paz W RSC 8 Tijuana
17.07.84 Antonio Avelar L RSC 3 Tijuana
31.08.84 Mario Nava W PTS 10 Mexico City
20.10.84 Manuel Aguilar W RSC 5 Mexico City
01.12.84 Gilberto Roman L RSC 8 Mexicali
29.03.85 Cardenio Ulloa W PTS 10 Miami
07.06.85 Miguel Lora L RSC 8 Miami
08.08.85 Mario Gomez L RSC 7 Nuevo Laredo
10.11.85 Richie Sandoval L PTS 10 Pomona
19.04.86 Jorge Ramirez L PTS 12 Mexico City (*Mexican Bantamweight Title Challenge*)
07.06.86 Mario Nava W PTS 10 Mexico City
18.07.86 Raul Perez L PTS 10 Tijuana
07.10.86 Antonio Gonzalez W PTS 10 Tijuana
01.11.86 Carlos Castro W DIS 1 Merida
27.12.86 Felipe Gutierrez W PTS 10 Merida
20.02.87 Jose Valdez L PTS 10 Guasave
25.05.87 Felix Montiel L PTS 10 Los Mochis
11.09.87 German Vasquez W RSC 3 Monterrey
12.10.87 Antonio Lozada W RSC 6 Tijuana
31.10.87 Victor Rabanales W PTS 10 Mexico City
20.11.87 Juan Carazo L PTS 10 Chicago
23.01.88 Victor Rabanales W PTS 10 Mexico City
18.03.88 Roberto Rios L RSC 6 Guadalajara
25.04.88 Antonio Lozada L RSC 6 Tijuana
23.07.88 Ramon Arreola W PTS 10 Mexico City
20.08.88 Rene Rodriguez W PTS 10 Mexico City
01.10.88 Ciro Cayetano W CO 8 Mexico City
10.12.88 Dionisio Espinoza W CO 1 Mexico City
07.01.89 Victor Flores W PTS 10 Mexico City
Summary: 52 contests, won 32, drew 3, lost 17.

In-Chul Baek

Ko Hung, South Korea. *Born* 20.12.61
OPBF Middleweight Champion. Former Undefeated OPBF L. Middleweight Champion

09.05.80 Sung-Jong Park W CO 2 Seoul
08.06.80 Yung-Chil Yang W RSC 2 Seoul
25.09.80 Jong-Hyun Park W CO 1 Seoul
21.11.80 Byung-Chun Choi W CO 3 Seoul
22.11.80 Sun-Kap Choi W CO 4 Seoul
29.11.80 Jang-Ho Choi W CO 3 Seoul
07.12.80 Bok-Kyu Lim W RSC 3 Seoul
14.02.81 Yung-Sil Chung W RSC 4 Seoul
19.04.81 Hiroshi Izumiya W RSC 3 Seoul
23.06.81 Conrado Salinas W CO 2 Seoul
21.08.81 Alberto Cruz W CO 1 Daejon
11.10.81 Jin-Nam Kim W RSC 3 Daejon
25.10.81 Aquilino Nicolas W CO 2 Seoul
28.11.81 Joe Wilisco W CO 3 Seoul
27.12.81 Sung-Ho Lee W RSC 12 Seoul
(*Vacant OPBF L. Middleweight Title*)
14.02.82 Alberto Cruz W CO 1 Daejon
(*OPBF L. Middleweight Title Defence*)
21.03.82 Kenji Miyata W RSC 9 Pusan
24.04.82 Muhammad Ibrahim W RSC 3 Kwangju
(*OPBF L. Middleweight Title Defence*)
13.06.82 Michihiro Horihata W RSC 2 Pusan
(*OPBF L. Middleweight Title Defence*)
03.07.82 Antonio Reyna W CO 2 Daejon
26.09.82 Fred Galang W CO 3 Taegu
23.10.82 Yohi Ari W CO 10 Chungju
(*OPBF L. Middleweight Title Defence*)
11.12.82 Kongrag Vorchareenrat W CO 3 Seoul
(*OPBF L. Middleweight Title Defence*)
02.01.83 Romy Angeles W CO 3 Daejon
(*OPBF L. Middleweight Title Defence*)
27.02.83 Jesus Gonzalez W CO 3 Daejon
27.03.83 Chong-Ho Kim W CO 7 Chinju
(*OPBF L. Middleweight Title Defence*)
19.05.83 Sean Mannion L PTS 10 Atlantic City
10.07.83 Yohi Arai W CO 5 Daejon
(*OPBF L. Middleweight Title Defence*)
13.11.83 Satenfa Pratip W CO 3 Cheju
07.01.84 Sakaria Ve W CO 6 Daejon
24.03.84 Mike de Guzman W CO 3 Ryoisan
(*OPBF L. Middleweight Title Defence*)
23.07.84 Alberto Bapaimo W CO 4 Osan
(*OPBF L. Middleweight Title Defence*)
12.01.85 Hendris Salmon W RSC 2 Kwangju
(*OPBF L. Middleweight Title Defence*)
20.04.85 Jaeh-Yung Yuh W RSC 5 Seoul
(*OPBF L. Middleweight Title Defence*)
13.07.85 Alberto Bapaimo W CO 3 Chungju
(*OPBF L. Middleweight Title Defence*)
27.10.85 Fred Hutchings W CO 9 Pusan
15.03.86 Troy Waters W PTS 12 Seoul
(*OPBF L. Middleweight Title Defence*)
28.06.86 Sang-Do Chung W PTS 12 Pohang
(*OPBF L. Middleweight Title Defence*)
27.07.86 Chun-Hwan Noh W RSC 5 Chungju
18.10.86 Jun-Sok Hwang W PTS 12 Inchon
(*OPBF L. Middleweight Title Defence*)
15.03.87 Paul James W PTS 10 Seoul
12.07.87 Hideo Kawamoto W CO 2 Ahnyang
21.11.87 Julian Jackson L RSC 3 Las Vegas
(*Vacant WBA L. Middleweight Title*)
17.04.88 Ketut Udiyana W CO 2 Nonsan
(*Vacant OPBF Middleweight Title*)
30.07.88 Jae-Ok Kim W CO 6 Pusan
(*OPBF Middleweight Title Defence*)
22.12.88 Chong-Pal Park W RSC 9 Seoul
Summary: 46 contests, won 44, lost 2.

Paul Banke

Pomona, USA. *Born* 01.03.64
S. Bantamweight

02.08.85 Elmer Mejia W RSC 2 Phoenix
24.08.85 Mike Perez W RSC 2 Phoenix
17.11.85 Mike Rodella W RSC 2 Coachella
20.11.85 Juvenal Molina W PTS 4 Los Angeles
07.02.86 Arturo Lozado W PTS 6 Pomona
13.06.86 Ralph Gutierrez W PTS 4 Las Vegas
25.07.86 Ralph Gutierrez W PTS 4 Las Vegas
05.08.86 Pete Solarez L PTS 5 Las Vegas
20.04.87 Andre Smith L PTS 8 Santa Monica
28.05.87 Willie Garcia W RSC 2 Los Angeles
12.06.87 Tony Talley W RSC 6 Riverside
15.07.87 Hector Lizarraga W PTS 10 Riverside
13.08.87 Jesus Poll L RSC 7 Los Angeles
11.12.87 Ramon Rico W PTS 10 San Jose
07.03.88 Lucilo Nolasco W PTS 10 Los Angeles
09.05.88 Alberto Mercado W RSC 3 Los Angeles
13.07.88 Robert Shannon W PTS 10 Los Angeles
13.09.88 Carlos Romero W RSC 11 Los Angeles
09.01.89 Ramiro Adame W RSC 6 Los Angeles
Summary: 19 contests, won 16, lost 3.

Iran (The Blade) Barkley

New York, USA. *Born* 09.05.60
Former WBC Middleweight Champion. Former Undefeated Con. Am. Middleweight Champion

09.12.82 Larry Jordan W RSC 2 Atlantic City
06.01.83 Bruce Starling W CO 1 Atlantic City
29.01.83 Dominique Williams W RSC 1 Atlantic City
18.02.83 Don Franklin W PTS 4 Atlantic City
31.03.83 Osley Silas L PTS 6 Atlantic City
18.06.83 Jose Torres W PTS 6 Atlantic City
18.08.83 Frankie Minton W RSC 5 Atlantic City
05.12.83 Marciano Bernardi W RSC 1 Atlantic City
06.01.84 Robbie Sims L RSC 6 Atlantic City
05.07.84 Esteban Pizzaro W PTS 8 Atlantic City
23.08.84 John Ford W RSC 4 Atlantic City
01.11.84 Ed Hall L PTS 8 Atlantic City
21.02.85 Osley Silas W RSC 6 Atlantic City
26.04.85 Norberto Sabater W RSC 2 New York
24.05.85 Randy Smith W PTS 10 New York
11.07.85 Carlos Betancourt W RSC 1 New York
08.08.85 Bill Lee W RSC 3 New York
29.08.85 Norberto Sabater W CO 2 New York
01.11.85 Wilford Scypion W CO 8 New York
06.12.85 Mike Tinley W PTS 12 New York
(*Vacant Con. Am. Middleweight Title*)
19.06.86 Tony Harrison W RSC 3 New York
(*Con. Am. Middleweight Title Defence*)
24.07.86 Bastante Blanco W RTD 3 New York
17.10.86 James Kinchen W PTS 10 Detroit
20.02.87 Stacy McSwain W PTS 10 Atlantic City
03.04.87 Jorge Amparo W PTS 10 Las Vegas
23.10.87 Sumbu Kalambay L PTS 15 Livorno
(*Vacant WBA Middleweight Title*)
29.01.88 Sanderline Williams W PTS 10 Atlantic City
06.03.88 Michael Olajide W RSC 5 New York
06.06.88 Thomas Hearns W RSC 3 Las Vegas
(*WBC Middleweight Title Challenge*)
24.02.89 Roberto Duran L PTS 12 Atlantic City
(*WBC Middleweight Title Defence*)
Summary: 30 contests, won 25, lost 5

Fidel Bassa

Magdalena, Colombia. *Born* 18.12.62
WBA Flyweight Champion. Former Undefeated Fecarbox & Colombian Flyweight Champion

23.12.83 Emilio Tamarillo W CO 2 Barranquilla
27.01.84 Juan Gomez W PTS 4 Barranquilla
11.05.84 Jairo Bedoya W CO 2 Barranquilla
10.06.84 Bernardo Ceballos W RSC 1 Barranquilla
31.08.84 Felipe Medrano W CO 5 Barranquilla
21.09.84 Eugenio Oviedo W CO 2 Cartagena
01.03.85 Jorge Lugo W CO 4 Barranquilla
(*Colombian Flyweight Title Challenge*)
29.03.85 Rafael Julio W RSC 3 Barranquilla
(*Colombian Flyweight Title Defence*)
04.05.85 Antonio Mitre W RSC 4 Barranquilla
21.06.85 Leonardo Paredes W RTD 6 Cartagena
(*Fecarbox Flyweight Title Challenge*)
30.08.85 Victor Tejedor W CO 1 Barranquilla
28.09.85 Ernesto Sanchez W PTS 10 Barranquilla
31.01.86 Victor Sierra W PTS 10 Cartagena
14.03.86 Jose Castillo W RSC 2 Bogota
30.04.86 Manuel Sallago W RSC 8 Barranquilla
17.10.86 Pedro Nieves W CO 1 Barranquilla
13.02.87 Hilario Zapata W PTS 15 Barranquilla
(*WBA Flyweight Title Challenge*)
25.04.87 Dave McAuley W CO 13 Belfast
(*WBA Flyweight Title Defence*)
15.08.87 Hilario Zapata DREW 15 Panama City
(*WBA Flyweight Title Defence*)
18.12.87 Felix Marty W PTS 12 Cartagena
(*WBA Flyweight Title Defence*)
26.03.88 Dave McAuley W PTS 12 Belfast
(*WBA Flyweight Title Defence*)
02.10.88 Raymond Medel W PTS 12 San Antonio
(*WBA Flyweight Title Defence*)
15.04.89 Julio Gudino W RSC 6 Barranquilla
(*WBA Flyweight Title Defence*)
Summary: 23 contests, won 22, drew 1.

Jackie Beard

Jackson, USA. *Born* 10.09.61
Former Undefeated NABF Featherweight Champion

25.04.81 Reyes Polanco W CO 2 Phoenix
11.06.81 Gilbert Favella W CO 2 Detroit
26.06.81 Dave Green W CO 1 Nashville
29.09.81 Robert Anderson W PTS 8 Phoenix
13.10.81 Mike Rodriguez W RSC 2 Phoenix

Iran Barkley (right) fells the once-great Thomas Hearns to win the WBC middleweight title in June, 1988

Tom Casino

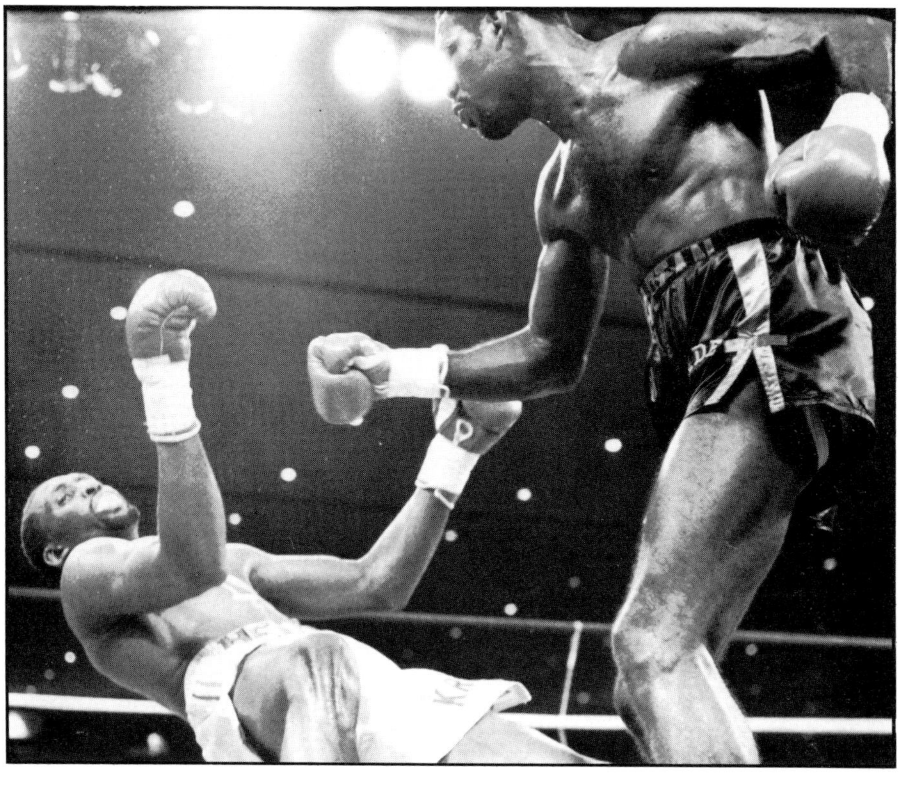

29.10.81 Jeff Long W CO 1 Plainfield
19.11.81 Sylvester Kennon W PTS 8 Detroit
03.12.81 Al Fowler W PTS 10 Jackson
17.12.81 Rafael Rodriguez W RSC 2 Phoenix
23.01.82 Manuel Santos W RSC 6 Detroit
11.02.82 Carlos Santana W RSC 2 Jackson
28.02.82 Reyes Gonzalez W RSC 5 Las Vegas
01.05.82 Jose Caba L PTS 10 Miami
22.06.82 Nicky Perez W RSC 7 Phoenix
(*NABF Featherweight Title Challenge*)
27.08.82 Joe Mayes W CO 2 Detroit
15.09.82 Ruben Moreno W RSC 6 New York
20.02.83 Bernabe Montanez W PTS 10 San Juan
25.04.83 Victor Flores W PTS 10 Chicago
15.07.83 Margarito Marquez W PTS 12 Las Vegas
(*NABF Featherweight Title Defence*)
19.11.83 Paul de Vorce W PTS 12 Las Vegas
(*NABF Featherweight Title Defence*)
18.01.84 Carlos Flores W RSC 5 Corpus Christi
31.05.84 Ray Garza W RSC 1 Detroit
18.07.84 Refugio Rogas W PTS 12 Las Vegas
(*NABF Featherweight Title Defence*)
27.10.84 Carlos Albuerne W PTS 10 Jackson
20.12.84 Paul Graham W PTS 10 Chicago
31.01.85 Paul Graham W RSC 6 Detroit
09.05.85 Anthony English W PTS 10 Atlantic City
15.02.86 Nedric Simmons W RSC 4 Montreal
10.07.86 Johnny de la Rosa L PTS 12 New York
(*Con. Am. S. Featherweight Title Challenge*)
08.01.87 Dennis Cruz L RTD 7 New York
18.06.87 Richie Otero W PTS 8 New York
09.07.87 Donnie Parker W RSC 9 New York
17.09.87 Angel Hernandez W RSC 4 New York
05.02.88 Ray Doughty W CO 1 Atlantic City
14.04.88 Pedro Montero W RSC 5 New York
09.06.88 Margarito Marquez W PTS 10 Lewiston
27.10.88 Eddie Pollard W PTS 10 New York
Summary: 37 contests, won 34, lost 3.

Taoufik Belbouli
France. *Born* Mauritania, 10.12.54
WBA Cruiserweight Champion. Former Undefeated French Heavyweight Champion

25.11.82 Primo Ruberti W RSC 2 Marseilles
10.02.83 Fred Voltine W RSC 4 Marseilles
30.06.83 Maurice Gomis W PTS 8 Aix
12.11.83 Marco Vitaglione W PTS 8 Tunis
10.12.83 N. Alsea W RSC 3 Noumea
27.01.84 Damien Marignan W CO 2 Aix
02.02.84 Ali Lukusa W CO 2 Marseilles
17.03.84 Dragomir Popovic W RSC 1 Tunis
19.04.84 Marco Vitaglione W DIS 3 Aix
06.07.84 Achene Reffas W RSC 8 Marseilles
05.09.84 Benchabak W CO 7 Tunis
29.03.85 Safir Digibele W RSC 4 Aix
01.06.85 Yawe Davis L PTS 8 Paris
18.04.86 Damien Marignan W RSC 3 Marseilles
(*Vacant French Heavyweight Title*)
15.05.86 Mbuyanga Kalombo W CO 4 Paris
12.09.86 Louis Pergaud W CO 4 Aix
03.04.87 Mbuyanga Kalombo W RSC 9 Nimes
12.05.87 James Dixon W PTS 8 Le Mans
08.06.87 Arturo Arvizu W CO 1 Merignac
19.07.87 Peter Mulindwa W CO 1 Merignac
15.08.87 Ricky Spain W RSC 8 St Tropez
08.10.87 Marvin Camel W RSC 3 Paris
03.03.88 Lionel Byarm W CO 7 Casablanca
15.05.88 Terry Mims W CO 5 Casablanca
13.08.88 Lorenzo Boyd W RSC 2 Deauville
10.10.88 Roy Saffold W RSC 4 Nogent
06.03.89 Jack Johnson W RSC 1 Nogent
25.03.89 Michael Greer W RSC 8 Casablanca
(*Vacant WBA Cruiserweight Title*)
Summary: 28 contests, won 27, lost 1.

Vincenzo Belcastro
Fuscaldo, Italy. *Born* 02.02.61
EBU Bantamweight Champion. Former Italian Bantamweight Champion

29.12.84 Claudio Tanda W PTS 6 Casoria
27.04.85 German Nunez W PTS 6 Avellino
17.05.85 Alessandro de Santis L PTS 6 Marotta
04.06.85 Alessandro de Santis DREW 6 Genoa
13.09.85 Alessandro de Santis W PTS 6 Marotta
29.10.85 Thierry Jacob L PTS 6 Paris
26.12.85 Raso Tigan W RTD 2 Pavia
21.03.86 Jean-Paul Guillard W PTS 6 Pavia
08.05.86 Makaya Kotey W PTS 4 Salerno
02.08.86 Makaya Kotey W PTS 6 Postiglione
11.10.86 Maurizio Lupino W PTS 12 Cefalu
(*Italian Bantamweight Title Challenge*)
06.12.86 Maurizio Lupino W DIS 7 Lamezia
(*Italian Bantamweight Title Defence*)
27.02.87 Alessandro de Santis DREW 12 Villariccio
(*Italian Bantamweight Title Defence*)
02.06.87 Antontio Picardi L PTS 12 Casoria
(*Italian Bantamweight Title Defence*)
07.11.87 Ley Umba Sengi W PTS 8 Salerno
08.01.88 Bofungo Eymono W PTS 6 Casoria
05.03.88 Ley Umba Sengi W PTS 6 Pesaro
13.04.88 Fabrice Benichou W CO 3 Busalia
(*EBU Bantamweight Title Challenge*)
01.06.88 Lorenzo Pacheco W RSC 9 Campione
(*EBU Bantamweight Title Defence*)
21.08.88 Jose Sanabria L PTS 12 Capo d'Orlando
(*IBF S. Bantamweight Title Challenge*)
02.11.88 Billy Hardy W PTS 12 Paola
(*EBU Bantamweight Title Defence*)
10.02.89 Antonio Picardi W PTS 8 Capo d'Orlando
Summary: 22 contests, won 16, drew 2, lost 4.

Jesse Benavides
Corpus Christi, USA. *Born* 03.11.63
USBA S. Bantamweight Champion

27.09.84 Tommy Valdez W CO 1 Corpus Christi
14.11.84 Ray Espinoza W CO 2 Detroit
31.01.85 Bobby Adams W RSC 3 Detroit
08.02.85 Agustin Soberanes W PTS 4 Stateline
31.03.85 Adolfo Lopez W PTS 6 Laughlin
21.05.85 Rogelio Leanos W RSC 7 Corpus Christi
10.07.85 Pedro Rodriguez W PTS 8 Corpus Christi
25.09.85 Eddie Gonzales W RSC 2 Corpus Christi
24.10.85 Eddie Petty W RSC 3 Detroit
13.12.85 Juan Armienta W RSC 1 San Antonio
10.02.86 Eugenio Morgan W RSC 3 Laughlin
11.05.86 Gerardo Velasquez W CO 1 Corpus Christi
15.06.86 Alvaro Rosquero W CO 2 Corpus Christi
28.07.86 Tony Escobar W RSC 6 Phoenix
23.08.86 David Johnson W PTS 10 Corpus Christi
10.03.87 John Boyd W RSC 10 Corpus Christi
29.05.87 Hector Cortez W CO 5 Detroit
15.08.87 Arturo Tebaqui W RSC 3 San Antonio
25.09.87 Hugo Partida W RSC 4 Tucson
31.10.87 Mike Moreno W CO 4 Phoenix
20.11.87 Greg Richardson W PTS 12 Atlantic City
(*Vacant USBA S. Bantamweight Title*)
29.05.88 James Pipps W CO 2 Houston
(*USBA S. Bantamweight Title Defence*)
28.07.88 Pedro Decima L RSC 3 Las Vegas
02.10.88 Richard Abila W PTS 10 San Antonio
23.11.88 Diego Briones W RSC 4 Tucson
15.12.88 Jeff Hannah W CO 3 Tucson
28.04.89 Danny Garcia W RSC 9 Tucson
(*USBA S. Bantamweight Title Defence*)
Summary: 27 contests, won 26, lost 1.

Jesse Benavides
Peter Goldfield/USA

Rodrigo Benech
Montevideo, Uruguay. *Born* 22.10.57
South American L. Heavyweight Champion

23.01.87 Antonio Galvan W PTS 6 Mar del Plata
21.03.87 Miguel Robledo W RSC 1 Buenos Aires
04.04.87 Antonio Galvan W CO 2 General Roca
24.04.87 Julio Lamela W CO 3 Cipolletti
21.05.87 Roberto Villalba W PTS 8 Montevideo
04.07.87 Yawe Davis L RTD 1 Ribera
09.10.87 Albert Barragan W CO 1 Montevideo
08.01.88 Jose Galvan W CO 1 Brandsen
28.01.88 Anibal Romero W RTD 4 Montevideo
30.03.88 Juan Barrera W CO 1 Paysandu
07.05.88 Mwehu Beya L PTS 8 Abruzzi
08.07.88 Sergio Merani L PTS 10 Paysandu
05.08.88 Miguel Steimbach W RSC 2 Puerto Madryn
06.10.88 Alberto Ubelart W CO 7 Montevideo
26.11.88 Jorge Salgado W CO 7 Paysandu
(*South American L. Heavyweight Title Challenge*)
21.01.89 Paul Muyodi W RSC 2 Vasto
25.03.89 Roberto Villalka W PTS 10 Buenos Aires
29.04.89 Paul Muyodi L RSC 6 Vasto
Summary: 18 contests, won 14, lost 4.

Eduardo Benevent
Buenos Aires, Argentine. *Born* 15.05.62
South American L. Welterweight Champion. Argentinian Welterweight Champion

10.07.82 Daniel Roldan W PTS 6 Buenos Aires
13.10.82 Martin Duran W PTS 8 Mendoza
11.12.82 Marcelo Villagra W PTS 6 Beunos Aries
28.01.83 Silvano Melgarejo W PTS 8 General Pintos
18.02.83 Jorge Zaccardi W RSC 6 Vedia
11.03.83 Carlos Fallone W PTS 10 Lincoln
15.04.83 Oscar Ballesteros W PTS 10 Vedia
14.05.83 Carlos Lobos W RSC 2 Buenos Aires
01.07.83 Silvano Melgarejo W PTS 10 Los Toldos
23.07.83 Sergio Loyola W PTS 10 Lincoln
30.09.83 Jorge Pereyra W CO 2 Lincoln
14.10.83 Raul Gonzalez W RSC 1 Mendoza
04.11.83 Luis Rodriguez W PTS 10 Vedia
26.11.83 Raul Colombo W PTS 10 Vedia
02.12.83 Raul Gonzalez W CO 2 General Pintos
18.02.84 Jose Funes W PTS 10 Lincoln
14.12.84 Julio Aguilera W RSC 6 Vedia
16.03.85 Ramon Colado DREW 10 Lincoln
18.05.85 Osvaldo Cabral W TD 6 Vedia
01.06.85 Osvaldo Cabral L PTS 10 Vedia
20.07.85 Sergio Brites W PTS 10 Lincoln
20.09.85 Sergio Combis L PTS 10 Rosario
22.03.86 Ricardo Espinosa W PTS 10 Rojas
11.04.86 Jorge Tejeda L PTS 10 Jose Carlos Paz
19.07.86 Adolfo Arce Rossi W PTS 10 Lincoln
19.09.86 Ramon Collado L PTS 10 Olavarria
13.12.86 Jose Magarinos W PTS 10 Lincoln
13.02.87 Hector Vilte L PTS 10 Salta
04.04.87 Hugo Hernandez L PTS 10 Buenos Aires
20.06.87 Hugo Hernandez L RSC 2 Buenos Aires
14.08.87 Hugo Luero W PTS 10 Rio Gallegos
12.09.87 Juan Ortiz W PTS 10 Lincoln
02.04.88 Hugo Hernandez L PTS 12 Lincoln
(*Argentinian L. Welterweight Title Challenge*)
12.11.88 Raul Bianco W PTS 12 Lincoln
17.12.88 Jose Saldivia W PTS 12 Lincoln
(*Vacant Argentinian Welterweight Title*)
18.03.89 Oscar Benavidez W PTS 12 Lincoln
(*Vacant South American L. Welterweight Title*)
Summary: 36 contests, won 27, drew 1, lost 8.

Fabrice Benichou
France. *Born* Madrid, 05.04.65
IBF S. Bantamweight Champion. Former EBU Bantamweight Champion

19.07.84 Claudio Tanda W PTS 6 Pistoia
07.08.84 Corrado Infanti W PTS 6 Follonica
05.10.84 Jose Chacon L PTS 6 Barinas
15.06.85 Ernesto Ford L PTS 6 Panama City
19.07.85 Gerardo Rodriguez W PTS Colon
16.11.85 Humberto Moreno W RSC 3 Panama City
08.02.86 Jesse Williams W RSC 7 Miami
09.05.86 Abdel Diane W RSC 4 Sassari
04.07.86 Jalleline Mastouri W PTS 6 Porlezza
15.09.86 Fernando Beltran L PTS 8 Paris

03.11.86 Juan Muriel W PTS 8 Paris
28.11.86 Rocky Otero W PTS 8 Toulon
31.01.87 Kelvin Smart W RSC 1 Montpelier
06.02.87 Rocky Lawlor W RSC 1 Antibes
13.02.87 Moussa Sangare L RSC 6 Villeurbanne
14.03.87 Jean Paul Guillard W RSC 3 St Nazaire
27.04.87 James Tolliver W CO 1 Paris
25.06.87 Shane Silvester W RSC 3 Paris
06.07.87 Haidar Nourredine L RSC 3 Differdange
05.10.87 Vicente Fernandez W RTD 1 Paris
21.11.87 Sonny Long W PTS 8 Paris
30.01.88 Thierry Jacob W CO 9 Calais
(*Vacant EBU Bantamweight Title*)
13.04.88 Vincenzo Belcastro L CO 3 Busalia
(*EBU Bantamweight Title Defence*)
06.06.88 Efren Chavez W PTS 8 Las Vegas
24.06.88 Alberto Contreras W RTD 3 Las Vegas
26.09.88 Jose Sanabria L RSC 10 Noget sur Marne
(*IBF S. Bantamweight Title Challenge*)
07.11.88 Ray Armand L PTS 8 Paris
21.11.88 Miguel Pequeno W PTS 8 Amiens
09.12.88 Isidoro Medina W CO 2 Rodez
20.01.89 Jose Gallegos W PTS 8 Limoges
10.03.89 Jose Sanabria W PTS 12 Limoges
(*IBF S. Bantamweight Title Challenge*)
Summary: 31 contests, won 23, lost 8.

Nigel Benn
West Ham, England. *Born* 22.01.64
Commonwealth Middleweight Champion

28.01.87 Graeme Ahmed W RSC 2 Croydon
04.03.87 Kevin Roper W RSC 1 Basildon
22.04.87 Bob Niewenhuizen W RSC 1 London
09.05.87 Winston Burnett W RSC 4 London
17.06.87 Reggie Marks W RSC 1 London
01.07.87 Leon Morris W CO 1 London
09.08.87 Eddie Smith W CO 1 Windsor
16.09.87 Winston Burnett W RSC 3 London
13.10.87 Russell Barker W RSC 1 Windsor
03.11.87 Ronnie Yeo W RSC 1 London
24.11.87 Ian Chantler W CO 1 Wisbech
02.12.87 Reggie Miller W CO 7 London
27.01.88 Fermin Chirinos W CO 2 London
07.02.88 Byron Prince W RSC 2 Stafford
24.02.88 Greg Taylor W RSC 2 Aberavon
14.03.88 Darren Hobson W CO 1 Norwich
20.04.88 Abdul Amoru Sanda W RSC 2 London
(*Vacant Commonwealth Middleweight Title*)
28.05.88 Tim Williams W RSC 2 London
26.10.88 Anthony Logan W CO 2 London
(*Commonwealth Middleweight Title Defence*)
10.12.88 David Noel W RSC 1 London
(*Commonwealth Middleweight Title Defence*)
08.02.89 Mike Chilambe W CO 1 London
(*Commonwealth Middleweight Title Defence*)
28.03.89 Mbayo Wa Mbayo W CO 2 Glasgow
Summary: 22 contests, won 22.

Trevor (The Preacher) Berbick
Miami, USA. *Born* Jamaica 01.08.53
Former WBC Heavyweight Champion. Former Undefeated Canadian, Commonwealth & USBA Heavyweight Champion

20.11.76 Wayne Martin W RSC 5 Shediac
07.12.76 Bobby Halpern W RSC 3 Halifax
09.01.77 Ace Lucas W CO 2 New Glasgow
25.01.77 Joe Maye W RSC 7 Halifax
18.08.77 William Moore W CO 4 Halifax
08.09.77 Eddie Owens W RSC 5 Halifax
08.12.77 Eugene Green W PTS 10 Halifax
28.06.78 Horst Geisler W RSC 1 Halifax
01.08.78 Tony Moore W RSC 5 Halifax
12.09.78 Greg Johnson W RSC 4 Halifax
08.10.78 Greg Sorrentino W RTD 7 Halifax
03.04.79 Bernardo Mercado L CO 1 Halifax
26.05.79 Earl McLeay W CO 7 Glace Bay
(*Vacant Canadian Heavyweight Title*)
14.06.79 Leroy Caldwell DREW 10 Winnipeg
11.12.79 Ngozika Ekwelum W RSC 4 Halifax
11.03.80 Johnny Warr W PTS 10 Halifax
20.06.80 John Tate W CO 9 Montreal
27.08.80 Ron Rousselle W CO 1 Edmonton
(*Canadian Heavyweight Title Defence*)

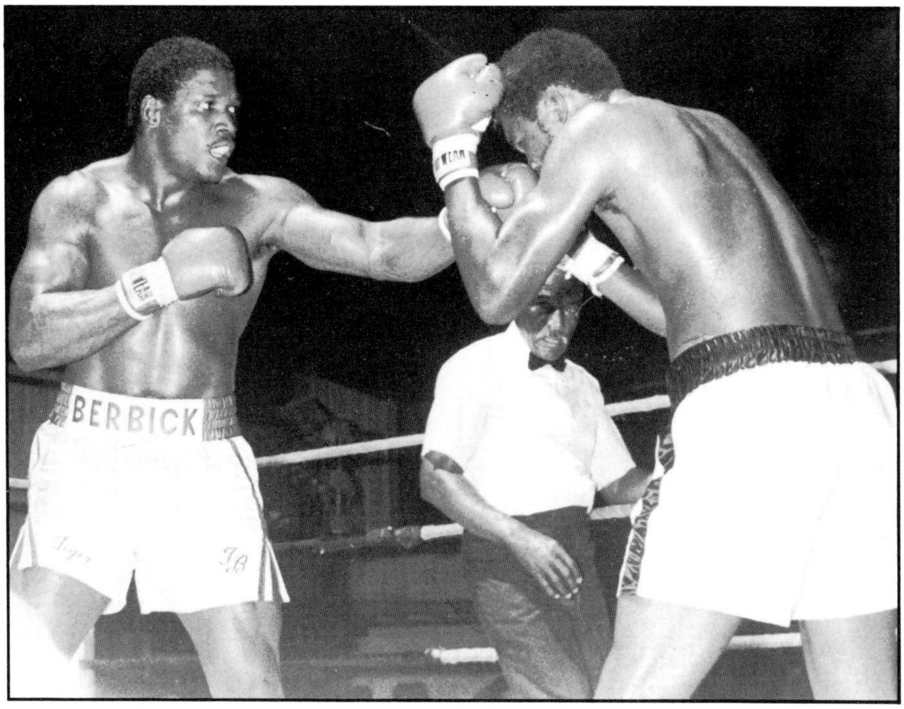

Trevor Berbick (left), seen outjabbing Ernie Barr during his Commonwealth heavyweight title defence in September, 1984

Andrew Seymour

11.11.80 Chuck Findlay W CO 1 Halifax
(*Canadian Heavyweight Title Defence*)
31.01.81 Chuck Gardner W RSC 4 Kingston
11.04.81 Larry Holmes L PTS 15 Las Vegas
(*WBC Heavyweight Title Challenge*)
21.07.81 Conroy Nelson W RSC 2 Halifax
(*Canadian Heavyweight Title Defence & Vacant Commonwealth Heavyweight Title*)
11.12.81 Muhammad Ali W PTS 10 Nassau
05.03.82 Gordie Racette W RSC 11 Nandimo
(*Commonwealth & Canadian Heavyweight Title Defence*)
24.04.82 Leroy Caldwell W PTS 10 Las Vegas
11.06.82 Greg Page W PTS 10 Las Vegas
02.10.82 Renaldo Snipes L PTS 10 Atlantic City
28.05.83 S.T. Gordon L PTS 10 Las Vegas
09.09.83 Ken Lakusta W CO 10 Edmonton
(*Commonwealth & Canadian Heavyweight Title Defence*)
19.02.84 Mike Cohen W CO 4 Tampa
13.03.84 Mark Lee W PTS 10 London
01.09.84 Ernie Barr W RSC 4 Nassau
(*Commonwealth Heavyweight Title Defence*)
28.11.84 Walter Santemore W PTS 10 Atlantic City
15.06.85 David Bey W RSC 11 Las Vegas
(*USBA Heavyweight Title Defence*
10.08.85 Mitchell Green W PTS 12 Las Vegas
(*USBA Heavyweight Title Defence*)
17.01.86 Mike Perkins W RSC 10 Atlanta
22.03.86 Pinklon Thomas W PTS 12 Las Vegas
(*WBC Heavyweight Title Challenge*)
22.11.86 Mike Tyson L RSC 2 Las Vegas
(*WBC Heavyweight Title Defence*)
31.07.87 Art Terry W RSC 5 Fort Myers
29.10.87 Lorenzo Boyd W RSC 3 Sunrise
24.11.87 Robert Evans W PTS 10 Halifax
27.06.88 Carl Williams L PTS 12 Atlantic City
(*USBA Heavyweight Title Challenge*)
20.09.88 O.T. Davis W CO 3 Oklahoma City
25.02.89 James Douglas L PTS 10 Las Vegas
Summary: 44 contests, won 36, drew 1, lost 7.

Mwehu Beya
Italy. *Born* Zaire, 30.09.56
Italian L. Heavyweight Champion

05.01.83 Giovani Marchesini W RTD 4 Ischia
24.02.83 Tshiamala Kalenga L PTS 6 Bologna
22.04.83 Walter Borghesi W RTD 1 San Remo
11.06.83 Slobodan Kacar L RSC 3 Pesaro
29.12.83 Butangi Nzolameso W PTS 6 Capo d'Orlando
24.02.84 Rufino Angulo W PTS 8 Bordeaux
19.04.84 Rufino Angulo L PTS 8 Paris
26.10.84 Sugar Boy Malinga L RSC 6 Johannesburg
22.06.85 Miguel Martin W RSC 3 Biarritz
23.05.86 Kalongo Bolemi W PTS 6 Ferrara
31.10.86 Juan Barrero W PTS 6 Abano
29.11.86 Juan Barrero DREW 6 Rovigo
19.12.86 Juan Barrero W RSC 3 Ancona
01.05.87 Enrico Scacchia DREW 10 Martigny
23.07.87 Alex Blanchard L RSC 7 Paris
13.02.88 Alfredo Cacciatore W RSC 7 Azzano
(*Vacant Italian L. Heavyweight Title*)
07.05.88 Rodrigo Benech W PTS 8 Abruzzi
31.07.88 Mike Quattara W PTS 8 Livorno
14.09.88 Nestor Giovannini L PTS 12 Scheggia
(*WBC International L. Heavyweight Title Challenge*)
19.11.88 Mauro Galvano DREW 12 Gragnano
(*Italian L. Heavyweight Title Defence*)
Summary: 20 contests, won 11, drew 3, lost 6.

Tyrell Biggs

Tom Casino

Tyrell Biggs
Philadelphia, USA. *Born* 22.12.60
Heavyweight

15.11.84 Mike Evans W PTS 6 New York
20.04.85 Mike Perkins W RSC 1 Corpus Christi
17.05.85 Grady Daniels W RSC 2 Stateline
13.07.85 Eddie Richardson W RSC 3 Atlantic City
29.08.85 Sterling Benjamin W RSC 7 Atlanta
19.11.85 Danny Sutton W RSC 7 Metairie
21.12.85 Tony Anthony W CO 1 Virginia Beach
25.01.86 James Tillis W PTS 8 Lancaster
23.03.86 Jeff Sims W PTS 10 Reno
14.08.86 Rod Smith W RSC 6 New York
14.09.86 Percell Davis W PTS 10 Atlantic City
29.10.86 Robert Evans W RSC 5 London
12.12.86 Renaldo Snipes W PTS 10 New York
07.03.87 David Bey W RSC 6 Las Vegas
31.07.87 Lorenzo Boyd W RSC 3 Corpus Christi
16.10.87 Mike Tyson L RSC 7 Atlantic City
(*World Heavyweight Title Challenge*)
29.10.88 Francesco Damiani L RSC 5 Milan
Summary: 17 contests, won 15, lost 2.

Levi Billups
San Diego, USA. *Born* 18.05.60
Heavyweight

25.07.86 Orlin Norris L RSC 1 San Diego
22.10.86 Tony Crawford W CO 2 Universal City
30.10.86 Isaac King W CO 1 Irvine
11.11.86 Zeke Thompson W CO 1 Long Beach
14.11.86 Clinton Bonds L PTS 6 Universal City
10.12.86 Mike Gans W PTS 6 Long Beach
09.02.87 Mike White L RSC 5 Long Beach
02.04.87 Terry Anderson W RSC 5 Stockton
18.05.87 Mike Hunter W PTS 8 Los Angeles
22.08.87 Bob Quarry W PTS 8 Sagamihara
17.12.87 Roger Troupe W RSC 3 Los Angeles
27.01.88 David Slaughter W RSC 1 San Diego
03.02.88 Oscar Holman W PTS 6 Riverside
16.03.88 Everett Martin W PTS 6 Riverside
20.04.88 Rod Stockton W PTS 10 Riverside
18.05.88 Bret Hughes W CO 2 Riverside
30.06.88 Mike White W RSC 5 Irvine
27.02.89 Lionel Washington L RSC 8 Reseda
Summary: 18 contests, won 14, lost 4.

Ari (Cobra) Blanca
Masbate, Philippines. *Born* 17.11.62
Philippines S. Flyweight Champion. Former Philippines Bantamweight Champion

19.07.83 Boy Cua W CO 3 Manila
11.09.83 Joe Asperos W RSC 1 Pasay
01.10.83 Bobby Castillo W RSC 1 Tayuman
14.10.83 Bobby Pinos W PTS 4 Pasay
26.11.83 John Matienza L PTS 6 Quezon
10.03.84 Bon Hermo W RSC 3 San Pedro
21.03.84 Young Arganda W RSC 2 Sucat
25.04.84 Wilson Rigo W PTS 8 San Pedro
25.05.84 Rod Mollen W RSC 7 San Pedro
30.06.84 Guiller de Gala W RSC 4 San Pedro
29.07.84 Bobby Pinos W PTS 10 Pasay
01.09.84 Joe Guevarra W PTS 10 Manila
30.10.84 Abel Magracia W PTS 10 Manila
15.12.84 Joe Hiyas W PTS 10 San Pedro
15.03.85 Ernie Cataluna W RSC 10 Manila
(*Philippines Bantamweight Title Challenge*)
20.06.85 Ernie Cataluna L PTS 10 Manila
(*Philippines Bantamweight Title Defence*)
25.08.85 Amri Sanusi W PTS 10 Jakarta
09.10.85 Tito Gregorio W RSC 1 Manila
22.12.85 Rudy Palicua W RSC 6 Sucat
31.03.86 Willy Bernadas W RSC 10 Paranaque
25.06.86 Luis Espinosa L PTS 10 Paranaque
16.07.86 Jun Resma W PTS 10 Manila
30.08.86 Loremer Pontino L PTS 10 Santos City
22.11.86 Ric Barimbad W PTS 10 Tagum
28.09.87 Jun Edwards W PTS 10 Los Banos
30.10.87 Billy Endrina W PTS 10 San Pablo
25.11.87 Billy Endrina W PTS 10 Paranaque
16.01.88 Al Mariano W PTS 10 Manila
15.04.88 Joseph Ladipe W PTS 10 Quezon
07.05.88 Ruben de la Cruz W PTS 10 Tagum
25.06.88 Joseph Ladipe W PTS 10 Tagum
02.09.88 Romy Navarrete W PTS 10 Quezon
19.11.88 Dadoy Andujar W PTS 10 Davao
23.12.88 Rolando Bohol T DRAW 2 Manila
28.01.89 Edel Geronimo W PTS 12 Davao
(*Philippines S. Flyweight Title Challenge*)
Summary: 35 contests, won 30, drew 1, lost 4.

Alex Blanchard
Amsterdam, Holland. *Born* Surinam 03.01.58
Dutch L. Heavyweight Champion. Former EBU L. Heavyweight Champion. Former Undefeated Benelux L. Heavyweight Champion

08.01.79 Klaus Hein W CO 4 Rotterdam
07.03.79 Rainer Gutekunst W RTD 3 Rotterdam
26.03.79 Sonny Kamunga W PTS 6 Groningen
28.05.79 Jean-Luc Lami W CO 2 Amsterdam
05.11.79 Etienne Bayadikilla W RSC 4 Rotterdam
26.11.79 Josef Kossman W RTD 1 Rotterdam
28.01.80 Mike McCoy W CO 2 Rotterdam
31.03.80 Oscar Angus W RSC 2 Rotterdam
28.04.80 Billy Lauder W CO 4 Amsterdam
19.05.80 Michel Chapier W RSC 6 Rotterdam
13.06.80 Gregory Marshall W CO 2 Lubeck
01.09.80 Franz Dorfer W RSC 3 Rotterdam
29.09.80 Bonny McKenzie W PTS 8 Rotterdam
20.10.80 Michel Pagani W CO 1 Rotterdam
03.03.81 Jose Lozano W PTS 8 Rotterdam
15.03.81 Earl Edwards W RSC 4 The Hague
07.09.81 Doug Demming W RSC 6 Rotterdam
05.10.81 Andre Mongalema W RSC 5 Rotterdam
02.11.81 Ennio Cometti W RSC 6 Rotterdam
24.05.82 Rudy Robles W CO 6 Rotterdam
06.09.82 Hendrik Seys W RSC 2 Rotterdam
(*Benelux L. Heavyweight Title Challenge*)
15.11.82 Rudi Koopmans L RSC 8 Rotterdam
(*EBU L. Heavyweight Title Challenge*)
18.06.83 Jose Seys W RSC 10 Izegem
(*Benelux L. Heavyweight Title Defence*)
17.10.83 James Churn W CO 4 The Hague
18.11.83 Sergio Bosio W CO 3 Middlekerke
28.05.84 Richard Caramanolis W RSC 6 Amsterdam
(*EBU L. Heavyweight Title Challenge*)
15.09.84 Manfred Jassman W RTD 4 Dortmund
(*EBU L. Heavyweight Title Defence*)
11.02.85 Jerry Reddick W CO 2 Amsterdam
22.04.85 Richard Caramanolis DREW 12 Rotterdam
(*EBU L. Heavyweight Title Defence*)
11.12.85 Dennis Andries DREW 12 London
(*EBU L. Heavyweight Title Defence*)
26.03.86 Tarmo Uusivirta DREW 10 Amsterdam
03.10.86 Ralf Rocchigiani W PTS 12 Berlin
(*EBU L. Heavyweight Title Defence*)
01.12.86 Tom Collins W PTS 10 Arnhem
23.07.87 Mwehu Beya W RSC 7 Paris
15.08.87 Enrico Scacchia W RSC 9 Berne
(*EBU L. Heavyweight Title Defence*)
11.11.87 Tom Collins L CO 2 Wembley
(*EBU L. Heavyweight Title Defence*)
14.03.88 James Shavers W RSC 8 Arnhem
07.10.88 Agamil Yilderim W CO 5 Berlin
07.11.88 Johnny Held W RSC 6 Rotterdam
(*Vacant Dutch L. Heavyweight Title*)
15.12.88 Tarmo Uusivirta DREW 12 Helsinki
Summary: 40 contests, won 34, drew 4, lost 2.

Rodolfo Blanco
Colombia
Former Undefeated Colombian L. Flyweight Champion

05.03.82 Jose Iriarte L PTS 4 Cartagena
20.03.82 Urbano Saltarin W CO 2 San Onofre
17.04.82 Arnold Velasquez L PTS 4 Cartagena
11.03.83 Manuel Ariza L PTS 4 Sincelejo
16.06.83 Jaime Paternina W PTS 6 Sincelejo
30.07.83 Manuel Julio W RSC 5 Sincelejo
16.09.83 Nelson Polanco W PTS 8 Sincelejo
11.03.84 Leonardo Paredes W PTS 10 Barranquilla
27.07.84 Agustin Garcia L PTS 10 Cartagena
(*Colombian L. Flyweight Title Challenge*)
01.03.85 Elvis Alvarez W PTS 8 Barranquilla
21.03.85 Jose Iriarte W CO 3 Barranquilla
21.06.85 Arnold Velasquez W CO 5 Barranquilla
30.08.85 Alfredo Cardales W RSC 5 Barranquilla
27.09.85 Benedicto Murillo DREW 10 Barranquilla
18.10.85 Joselo Perez W RSC 4 Cartagena
31.01.86 Agustin Garcia W PTS 10 Cartagena
(*Colombian L. Flyweight Title Challenge*)
20.03.86 Felix Berrios W CO 2 Barranquilla
30.04.86 Hermogenes Murillo W PTS 10 Barranquilla
21.06.86 Rafael Julio W PTS 8 San Onofre
04.04.87 Alfredo Gomez W RSC 3 San Andres
19.06.87 Rafael Ramos W RSC 3 Barranquilla
20.09.87 Myung-Woo Yuh L CO 8 Inchon
(*WBA L. Flyweight Title Challenge*)
04.03.88 Jose Iriarte W RSC 2 Santa Marta
25.03.88 Eduardo Tunon W CO 2 Barranquilla
15.07.88 Felix Marty W RSC 6 Barranquilla
28.11.88 Betulio Gonzalez W RSC 8 Maracaibo
08.04.89 Alfredo Cardales W RSC 3 Bucaramanga
Summary: 27 contests, won 21, drew 1, lost 5.

Maurice Blocker
Peter Goldfield/USA

Maurice (Thin Man) Blocker
Washington DC, USA. *Born* 15.05.63
Former Undefeated NABF Welterweight Champion

16.02.82 Leon Gardner W RSC 2 Atlantic City
09.03.82 Calvin Hardnett W RSC 1 Atlantic City
29.03.82 Charles Triplett W RSC 1 Atlantic City
13.04.82 Cliff Lee W RSC 6 Atlantic City
27.04.82 Mike Ross W PTS 4 Atlantic City
23.05.82 Tony Reed W RSC 1 Atlantic City
22.06.82 Larry Fleming W RSC 4 Atlantic City
02.11.82 Leo Davis W RSC 1 Atlantic City
30.11.82 Jerome Artis W PTS 8 Atlantic City
11.01.83 Roberto Hernandez W PTS 10 Atlantic City
03.03.83 Don Morgan W PTS 10 Atlantic City
03.04.83 Mao de la Rosa W CO 1 Atlantic City
05.07.83 Danny Paul W PTS 10 Atlantic City
22.10.83 Ernest Jackson W PTS 10 Atlantic City
27.12.83 Mike Mayon W RSC 4 Atlantic City
24.01.84 Terrence Holmes W RSC 7 Atlantic City
02.06.84 Robert Adams W PTS 10 Washington
10.07.84 Clayton Hires W PTS 10 Atlantic City
07.05.85 Ricardo Bryant W PTS 10 Atlantic City
23.07.85 Pedro Vilella W PTS 12 Washington
(*NABF Welterweight Title Challenge*)
07.12.85 Efren Olivo W CO 1 Washington
21.03.86 Leland Hart W PTS 10 Washington
26.07.86 Juan A. Villa W RSC 8 Washington
21.02.87 Adam George W RSC 2 Atlantic City
18.04.87 Lloyd Honeyghan L PTS 12 London
(*WBC Welterweight Title Challenge*)
27.06.88 Orlando Orozco W RTD 5 Atlantic City
10.11.88 Ruben Villaman W CO 3 Las Vegas
Summary: 27 contests, won 26, lost 1.

Craig Bodzianowski
Chicago, USA. *Born* 07.02.61
WBA Americas Cruiserweight Champion

16.10.81 Lawrence Lopresto W CO 1 Chicago
24.01.83 Dave Townsend W RSC 2 Chicago
07.03.83 Bob Obey W RSC 5 Chicago
20.03.83 Dick Scott W CO 3 Chicago
22.05.83 Jessie Hicks W PTS 6 Chicago
28.07.83 James Churn W RSC 5 Chicago
22.08.83 Leonard Brandon W CO 2 Chicago
07.11.83 Vernon Bridges W RSC 3 Chicago

01.12.83 John Words W CO 1 Chicago
20.12.83 Ron Draper W CO 1 Chicago
03.02.84 James Dixon W RSC 8 Chicago
04.04.84 Frank Draper W RSC 1 Chicago
09.05.84 Frank Sargent W PTS 10 Chicago
14.12.85 Frank Sargent W CO 2 Chicago
06.04.86 Ric Enis W CO 3 Chicago
10.08.86 Steve Mormino W PTS 8 Chicago
16.12.86 Bob Hitz W RSC 3 Alsip
12.04.87 Alfonso Ratliff L PTS 10 Chicago
30.08.87 Otis Bates W CO 1 Chicago
13.11.87 Al Houck W CO 2 Chicago
28.02.88 Earl Lewis W PTS 8 Chicago
12.05.88 Alfonso Ratliff L PTS 10 Harvey
23.11.88 Dawud Shaw W RTD 6 Philadelphia
07.12.88 Andre Crowder DREW 8 Harvey
15.02.89 Andre Crowder W RSC 2 Philadelphia
18.04.89 Anthony Witherspoon W PTS 12 Scranton
(*WBA Americas Cruiserweight Title Challenge*)
Summary: 26 contests, won 23, drew 1, lost 2.

Rolando Bohol
Himalayan, Philippines. *Born* 25.12.66
Former IBF Flyweight Champion

18.01.84 Bert Baco DREW 4 Paranaque
29.02.84 Ely Tabucol W RSC 2 Paranaque
21.03.84 Moirby Evasco W PTS 4 Paranaque
04.04.84 Ruben Portugues W PTS 4 Paranaque
02.05.84 Danny Duran W PTS 6 Paranaque
30.05.84 Bert Baco W PTS 6 Paranaque
11.07.84 John Calanogan W PTS 6 Paranaque
01.08.84 Jun Villacerna W RSC 2 Sucat
26.08.84 Junior Capino W PTS 8 Paranaque
17.10.84 Joel Advincula W PTS 8 Paranaque
14.11.84 Ric Bajelot DREW 8 Paranaque
16.01.85 John Calanogan W PTS 8 Paranaque
06.03.85 Cecilio Tutor W PTS 10 Paranaque
19.04.85 Henry Balina W PTS 10 Paranaque
03.07.85 Dommy Ursua W PTS 10 Paranaque
29.09.85 Dadoy Andujar L PTS 10 Santos City
30.10.85 Paul Torres W PTS 10 Paranaque
05.02.86 Titino Dignos W PTS 10 Paranaque
16.04.86 Ric Santiago W RSC 7 Paranaque
05.07.86 Rey Cogonon W PTS 10 Manila
20.07.86 Chun Huh L PTS 10 Sokcho
10.09.86 Allan Makitoki W PTS 10 Paranaque
15.11.86 Manasseh Base W PTS 10 Paranaque
20.02.87 Faustino Simbajon W PTS 10 Paranaque
18.05.87 Ademar Amad W PTS 10 Manila
30.08.87 Rod Naiconi W PTS 10 Paranaque
16.01.88 Chang-Ho Choi W PTS 15 Manila
(*IBF Flyweight Title Challenge*)
06.05.88 Cho-Woon Park W PTS 15 Manila
(*IBF Flyweight Title Defence*)
05.10.88 Duke McKenzie L CO 11 Wembley
(*IBF Flyweight Title Defence*)
23.12.88 Ari Blanca T DRAW 2 Manila
18.02.89 Saksamuth Singsamang W RSC 2 Manila
Summary: 31 contests, won 25, drew 3, lost 3.

Salvatore Bottiglieri
Naples, Italy. *Born* 30.01.60
WBC International Featherweight Champion. Former Undefeated Italian Featherweight Champion

11.02.82 Antonio Pocai W RSC 2 Naples
19.02.82 Eloi da Sylva W PTS 6 Naples
11.04.82 David Mahmutovic W CO 1 Ischia
14.05.82 Luciano Frasca W RTD 2 Naples
29.05.82 Andrea Ricci W PTS 4 Milan
08.08.82 Antonio Franca W RTD 4 Camerota
06.10.82 Museta Bingunia DREW 6 Gragnano
29.12.82 Jofre II W PTS 8 Amalfi
24.02.83 Andrea Ricci W PTS 6 Bologna
19.03.83 Luis de la Sagra W RSC 4 Naples
24.04.83 Carlo Compiani W RTD 1 San Remo
24.07.83 Luciano Frasca L DIS 1 Rome
21.09.83 Jose Luis Vicho L PTS 8 Caserta
22.10.83 Pasquale Mazza W PTS 8 St Vincent
03.03.84 Salvatore Melluzzo W RSC 10 Riva Garda
(*Italian Featherweight Title Challenge*)
10.06.84 Pasquale Mazza W PTS 12 San Giuseppe
(*Italian Featherweight Title Defence*)
28.09.84 Salvatore Melluzzo W RSC 12 Vietri
(*Italian Featherweight Title Defence*)
27.03.85 Joseph Sekisambu W PTS 6 Nocera
06.07.85 Santiago Machin W PTS 6 Lerici
31.10.85 Joseph Sekisambu W PTS 8 Viterbo
08.02.86 Vicente Jorge W PTS 8 Eboli
19.07.86 Jim McDonnell L PTS 12 Wembley
(*EBU Featherweight Title Challenge*)
06.09.86 Ley Umba Sengi W PTS 6 Naples
21.11.86 Carlo Quintano W PTS 12 Campione
(*Vacant Italian Featherweight Title*)
22.03.87 Osmar Avila W RSC 7 Ischia
(*Vacant WBC International Featherweight Title*)
15.07.87 Alvaro Bohorquez W PTS 12 Capo d'Orlando
(*WBC International Featherweight Title Defence*)
09.04.88 Alvaro Bohorquez W PTS 12 Casigno
(*WBC International Featherweight Title Defence*)
27.08.88 Tony Miller W PTS 12 Castagneto
(*WBC International Featherweight Title Defence*)
22.11.88 Johnny B. Good W RSC 2 San Pellegrino
27.12.88 Julio Garcia W RTD 2 San Pellegrino
10.02.89 Brian Mitchell L RSC 8 Capo d'Orlando
(*WBA S. Featherweight Title Challenge*)
Summary: 31 contests, won 26, drew 1, lost 4.

Kamel Bou Ali
Somrane, Tunisia. *Born* 06.12.58
WBC International S. Featherweight Champion

05.12.77 Angelo Emili W PTS 4 Bologna
13.07.79 Daniel Passeyrand W RSC 3 Valence
23.02.81 Pasquale Mazza DREW 6 Rome
09.03.81 Michel Siracusa W RSC 5 Rome
07.05.82 Hugo Carrizo W RSC 1 Bologna
02.06.82 Richard Saka W RSC 1 Chianciano
04.08.82 Tanio II W RSC 5 Rimini
08.10.82 Simadilu Lubaki W RSC 3 Rimini
17.03.83 Sammy Meck W RSC 6 Capo d'Orlando
05.11.83 Isidoro Cabeza W PTS 10 Tunis
13.01.84 Marcial Santiago W PTS 8 Riva del Garda
22.02.84 Roberto Pineiro W RSC 6 Milan
17.03.84 Robert Mullins W CO 2 Tunis
13.04.84 Hector Cortes W DIS 10 Milan
12.06.84 Angel Mendiola W RSC 4 Anchorage
29.07.84 Roberto Castanon W RSC 2 Milan
05.09.84 Victor Acosta W PTS 10 Tunis
17.11.84 Alfredo Layne W DIS 6 Riva del Garda
27.01.85 Rocky Lockridge L RSC 6 Riva del Garda
(*WBA S. Featherweight Title Challenge*)
13.12.85 Trevor Evelyn W RSC 5 Cesena
01.03.86 Paul Graham W CO 6 Tunis
28.11.86 Carlos Rodriguez W CO 2 Abano Terme
19.12.86 Sam Johnson W DIS 3 Ancona
30.12.86 Kamel Djadda W PTS 8 Cagliari
13.03.87 Idabeth Rojas W RSC 2 Forli
11.04.87 Ray Doughty W RSC 6 Bologna
22.05.87 Jose Vasquez W RTD 5 Jesi
24.07.87 Troy Davis W RSC 1 Silvi Marina
25.09.87 Richie Fowler W RSC 2 Quarto St Eleno
28.11.87 Luis Rodriguez W CO 2 Oristano
11.12.87 Gil Maldonado W CO 3 Livorno
27.02.88 Julio Gonzalez W CO 1 San Juan
10.04.88 Rafael Gandarilla W PTS 8 Iglesias
22.04.88 Jose Mosqueda W DIS 3 Milan
31.08.88 Robert Dickie W RSC 6 Stoke
(*WBC International S. Featherweight Title Challenge*)
22.11.88 Jesus Quinones W CO 2 Milan
18.02.89 Jose Luis Cruz W RSC 2 Pieve Emanuele
14.04.89 Manuel Billalba W PTS 12 Cagliari
(*WBC International S. Featherweight Title Defence*)
Summary: 38 contests, won 36, drew 1, lost 1.

Donovan Boucher
Toronto, Canada. *Born* Jamaica 1962
Canadian Welterweight Champion

15.08.85 Zest Holmes W PTS 6 Sarnia
19.09.85 Marco Carella W CO 1 Toronto
16.11.85 John Shepherd W PTS 6 Reno
19.12.85 Terry Francis W PTS 6 Ottowa
10.02.86 Ray Green W CO 1 Toronto
27.03.86 Benoit Boudreau W PTS 6 Dartmouth
08.06.86 Jim Sudberry W PTS 6 Toronto
25.08.86 Cortez Treadwell W PTS 6 Toronto
30.09.86 Gerry Meekison W PTS 8 Halifax
10.11.86 Chris Clarke L PTS 10 Halifax
27.01.87 Ira Hathaway W PTS 6 Toronto
10.02.87 Dennis Sigouin W PTS 10 Montreal
16.03.87 Robin Smith W RSC 4 Toronto
22.04.87 Jacques de Blois W RSC 2 Toronto
30.04.87 Arnie Wells W RSC 6 Detroit
07.07.87 Danny Winters W CO 7 Halifax
(*Vacant Canadian Welterweight Title*)
19.11.87 Wayne Gordon W RSC 11 Windsor
(*Canadian Welterweight Title Defence*)
25.03.88 Shawn O'Sullivan W RSC 2 Toronto
(*Canadian Welterweight Title Defence*)
12.08.88 Ali Saalam W RTD 1 New York
27.09.88 Pat McWilliams W RSC 7 Halifax
(*Canadian Welterweight Title Defence*)
23.01.89 Paul Jones W DIS 6 Toronto
Summary: 21 contests, won 20, lost 1.

Steve Boyle
Glasgow, Scotland. *Born* 28.11.62
British & WBC International Lightweight Champion

19.05.83 Shaun Dooney W RSC 3 Sunderland
06.06.83 Frankie Lake W RTD 3 London
13.06.83 Mike McKenzie W PTS 6 Glasgow
19.09.83 Craig Walsh W PTS 6 Glasgow
17.10.83 Johnny Grant W PTS 6 London
28.11.83 Robert Lloyd L PTS 6 Rhyl
07.12.83 Gary Lucas DREW 6 Stoke
27.02.84 Willie Wilson W RSC 3 Nottingham
26.03.84 Rocky Mensah DREW 8 Glasgow
11.06.84 Dave Haggarty W RSC 1 Glasgow
17.09.84 Gary Williams W CO 2 Glasgow
19.11.84 Jimmy Bunclark W RSC 2 Glasgow
21.01.85 Rory Burke W RSC 3 Glasgow
25.03.85 Peter Eubanks W PTS 8 Glasgow
03.06.85 Dave Savage W RSC 7 Glasgow
16.09.85 Junaido Musah W CO 4 Glasgow
14.10.85 Stanley Jones W CO 1 Glasgow
24.02.86 Mickey Baker W RSC 2 Glasgow
24.05.86 Tony Willis L RSC 9 Manchester
(*British Lightweight Title Challenge*)
11.12.86 Simon Eubanks W RSC 6 Livingston
03.03.87 Mike Durvan W PTS 10 Livingston
21.09.87 Billy Buchanan W RSC 7 Glasgow
16.11.87 Muhammad Lovelock W PTS 8 Glasgow
24.02.88 Alex Dickson W CO 2 Glasgow
(*British Lightweight Title Challenge*)
19.04.88 Mark Brannon W RSC 4 Glasgow
01.11.88 Joey Jacobs W CO 8 Glasgow
(*British Lightweight Title Defence*)
30.01.89 Pedro Gutierrez W PTS 12 Glasgow
(*Vacant WBC International Lightweight Title*)
Summary: 27 contests, won 23, drew 2, lost 2.

Jorge Bracamonte
Villa Maria, Argentine. *Born* 18.05.62
Welterweight

25.02.83 Julio Paladino W PTS 6 General Deheza
12.03.83 Mario Fernandez W PTS 6 Buenos Aires
31.03.83 Julio Cortez W PTS 6 Villa Maria
20.05.83 Hugo Oliva W RTD 3 Villa Maria
17.06.83 Victor Campos W PTS 8 Villa Maria
26.08.83 Julio Aguilera W CO 2 Tancacha
30.09.83 Victor Campos W RTD 3 Cordoba
18.05.84 Hector Vilte W PTS 10 Villa Maria
22.06.84 Manuel Della Devola W RSC 10 Villa Maria
16.08.84 Hector Ruiz W PTS 12 Villa Maria
16.11.84 Hector Ruiz W CO 6 Cordoba
12.12.84 Hugo Benitez W RTD 7 Villa Maria
06.06.86 Rolando Soria W PTS 10 Las Varillas
11.07.86 Alberto Villalba W PTS 10 Villa Maria
19.09.86 Domingo Sosa W PTS 10 Villa Maria
14.11.86 Alberto Villalba W PTS 10 Villa Maria
02.04.88 Luis Quiroga W PTS 8 San Luis
22.04.88 Carlos Corzo W RTD 4 Juan B. Alberdi
13.05.88 Sergio Combis W CO 1 Marcos Juarez
25.06.88 Jorge Tejeda W PTS 10 Buenos Aires
09.07.88 Juan Ortiz W PTS 10 Buenos Aires
03.09.88 Hugo Luero L CO 9 Buenos Airies
14.12.88 Hugo Luero W PTS 10 Villa Maria
10.03.89 Hugo Hernandez W RSC 9 Mar del Plata
01.04.89 Hugo Luero W PTS 10 Buenos Aires
Summary: 25 contests, won 24, lost 1.

Livingstone Bramble

New Jersey, USA. *Born* 03.03.60
Former WBA Lightweight Champion

16.10.80 Jesus Serrano W RSC 1 Totowa
04.12.80 Bruce Williams DREW 4 Atlantic City
19.01.81 Jesus Serrano W PTS 6 Atlantic City
18.03.81 Jorge Nina W DIS 2 Totowa
16.04.81 Andre Jimenez W CO 2 Totowa
21.05.81 John Byrd W RSC 4 Totowa
04.06.81 Ken Bogner W RSC 7 Atlantic City
20.08.81 Quadir Hart W RSC 1 Totowa
31.08.81 Anthony Fletcher L PTS 8 Atlantic City
08.10.81 Alejandro Arias W PTS 8 Totowa
19.01.82 Jerome Artis W PTS 10 Atlantic City
19.04.82 Emilio Diaz W RSC 1 Atlantic City
03.07.82 Manuel Madera W RSC 4 Totowa
22.08.82 Miguel Meza W RSC 4 McAfee
27.10.82 James Busceme W PTS 10 Atlantic City
22.01.83 Romeo Sandoval W RSC 9 Atlantic City
23.02.83 Teddy Hatfield W RSC 7 Totowa
26.04.83 Gaetan Hart W PTS 10 Atlantic City
13.09.83 Juan Hernandez W RSC 5 Atlantic City
23.11.83 Tom Crowley W RSC 5 Atlantic City
15.12.83 Lorenzo Guzman W CO 2 Totowa
22.01.84 Rafael Williams W PTS 10 Atlantic City
01.06.84 Ray Mancini W RSC 14 Buffalo
(*WBA Lightweight Title Challenge*)
24.10.84 Edwin Curet W PTS 10 Atlantic City
16.02.85 Ray Mancini W PTS 15 Reno
(*WBA Lightweight Title Defence*)
16.02.86 Tyrone Cranley W RSC 13 Reno
(*WBA Lightweight Title Defence*)
26.09.86 Edwin Rosario L CO 2 Miami
(*WBA Lightweight Title Defence*)
03.04.87 Fred Pendleton DREW 10 Atlantic City
15.06.87 John Kalbhenn W RSC 5 Atlantic City
30.03.88 Edwin Curet W RSC 8 Atlantic City
10.07.88 Fred Pendleton L RSC 10 Atlantic City
(*Vacant USBA Lightweight Title*)
21.02.89 Bryant Paden W PTS 10 Atlantic City
Summary: 32 contests, won 27, drew 2, lost 3.

Harold Brazier

South Bend, USA. *Born* 22.10.55
NABF L. Welterweight Champion

18.05.82 Lester Groves W PTS 6 Memphis
24.06.82 Tim Hall W RSC 3 Indianapolis
08.07.82 Chris Mazzola L PTS 4 Atlantic City
17.07.82 Joe Silverberg W PTS 6 Frankfort
20.08.82 Tom Tarantino W RSC 4 Chicago
25.08.82 Mike Essett W PTS 4 Indianapolis
11.09.82 Billy Collins L PTS 6 Atlantic City
20.09.82 Dave Martin W RSC 8 Toronto
28.09.82 Pete Podgurski W PTS 6 Merrillville
13.10.82 Emil Gottardo W RSC 3 Chicago
08.11.82 Toby Tyler W RSC 4 St Paul
04.02.83 Gil Miconda W RSC 3 Meridan
11.02.83 Brian Anderson W PTS 6 Winnipeg
03.03.83 Jeff Gettemey W RSC 3 Hammond
16.03.83 Cesar Guzman W PTS 6 Atlantic City
14.05.83 Ken Saale W RSC 4 St Ann
21.06.83 Mario Cusson L PTS 8 Montreal
25.07.83 Andre Martinez W CO 2 St Paul
06.08.83 Kel Robin L PTS 8 Tampa
24.10.83 Lloyd Honeyghan L PTS 10 London
28.11.83 Brian Baronet L PTS 10 Durban
10.01.84 Tom Lally W CO 3 Highland
07.02.84 Grover Washington W PTS 6 Highland
13.03.84 Tony Taylor W CO 5 Highland
10.04.84 Curtis Gholston W PTS 6 Highland
08.05.84 Kent Acuff W RSC 4 Highland
16.05.84 Tony Taylor W PTS 6 Fort Wayne
12.06.84 Henry Mobley W PTS 6 Highland
13.07.84 Ken Larson W RSC 2 Michigan City
24.07.84 Kenny Heflin W PTS 10 Birmingham
21.08.84 Santos Rodriguez W RSC 2 South Bend
13.12.84 Anthony Travis W CO 1 Merrillville
11.01.85 Mike Essett W PTS 10 Hammond
11.03.85 Ron Chambers W PTS 10 South Bend
20.03.85 Charlie Brown W RSC 8 Lake Tahoe
16.04.85 Mike Willis W RSC 1 Highland
10.06.85 Danny Miller W CO 6 South Bend
25.06.85 Roosevelt Jones W CO 6 Birmingham
17.10.85 Joey Ruiz W PTS 10 Merrillville
01.11.85 Rocky Trampler W CO 4 Louisville
09.02.86 Ken Snider W RSC 5 Indianapolis
11.05.86 Meldrick Taylor L PTS 10 Corpus Christi
27.06.86 Ozzie O'Neal W RSC 10 French Lick
01.08.86 Willie McIntosh W CO 3 Laporte
05.09.86 John Meekins T DRAW 2 Atlantic City
(*Vacant NABF L. Welterweight Title*)
31.10.86 Brian Baronet W RSC 10 Atlantic City
(*Vacant NABF L. Welterweight Title*)
24.01.87 Bobby Brown W CO 6 Springfield
09.02.87 Ray Myers W CO 2 Bowling Green
24.02.87 John Meekins W PTS 12 Atlantic City
(*NABF L. Welterweight Title Defence*)
14.03.87 Jimmy Baker W RTD 6 Columbus
31.03.87 Billy Willis W CO 3 Richmond
17.04.87 Roosevelt Jones W RSC 4 Springfield
16.05.87 Jose Martinez W RSC 4 Hammond
12.06.87 Donnie Marshall W CO 5 Lincoln
09.07.87 Willie Barnes W RSC 8 Louisville
28.07.87 Leroy Jones W RSC 6 Lexington
31.07.87 Dave Reynolds W PTS 8 Fort Knox
26.09.87 Jorge Acosta W RSC 5 Lowell
05.11.87 Rafael Sanchez W CO 2 Indianapolis
05.12.87 Ray Sparks W CO 3 Davenport
28.01.88 Willie Ray W RSC 4 Omaha
04.03.88 Robin Blake W RSC 9 Las Vegas
(*NABF L. Welterweight Title Defence*)
12.04.88 Billy Moore W CO 2 Springfield
06.06.88 Roger Mayweather L PTS 12 Las Vegas
(*WBC L. Welterweight Title Challenge*)
05.07.88 Darryl Bryant W RSC 6 Oklahoma City
20.07.88 Herminio Morales W RSC 4 South Bend
02.09.88 John Rafuse W PTS 12 South Bend
(*NABF L. Welterweight Title Defence*)
04.10.88 Jerry Brown W RSC 7 Oklahoma City
18.11.88 Willard Johnson W RSC 6 Louisville
21.01.89 Juan M. Coggi L PTS 12 Vasto
(*WBA L. Welterweight Title Challenge*)
Summary: 70 contests, won 60, drew 1, lost 9.

Harold Brazier (left) shown successfully defending his NABF light-welterweight title against "Rocking" Robin Blake, March, 1988.

Christopher M. Farina

Mark Breland

Brooklyn, USA. *Born* 11.05.63
WBA Welterweight Champion

15.11.84 Dwight Williams W PTS 6 New York
05.01.85 Marlon Palmer W PTS 6 Atlantic City
06.04.85 Steve Little W PTS 6 San Angelo
17.05.85 Vince Dunfee W RSC 2 Stateline
19.06.85 Dario de Jesus W RSC 2 Totowa
20.07.85 Don Shiver W RSC 1 Norfolk
18.10.85 Donald Gwinn W RSC 2 New York
21.12.85 Hedgemon Robertson W PTS 8 Virginia Beach
25.01.86 Troy Wortham W PTS 10 Lancaster
02.03.86 Richard Aguirre W CO 1 Lancaster
12.04.86 Darryl Anthony W RSC Totowa
15.05.86 Ricardo Avendano W CO 1 New York
21.06.86 John Munduga W CO 6 Atlantic City
14.09.86 Reggie Miller W RSC 2 Atlantic City
15.10.86 Ralph Twinning W RSC 2 Columbia
13.11.86 Orlando Orozco W RSC 2 New York
06.02.87 Harold Volbrecht W CO 7 Atlantic City
(*Vacant WBA Welterweight Title*)
10.07.87 Juan Rondon W PTS 10 Santa Margherita
22.08.87 Marlon Starling L CO 11 Columbia
(*WBA Welterweight Title Defence*)
05.12.87 Javier Suazo W PTS 10 Atlantic City
05.02.88 Juan Alonzo Villa W RSC 3 Atlantic CIty
16.04.88 Marlon Starling DREW 12 Las Vegas
(*WBA Welterweight Title Challenge*)
11.08.88 Pablo Baez W CO 1 Chicago
07.10.88 Ozzie O'Neal W RSC 1 Detroit
05.02.89 Seung-Soon Lee W RSC 1 Las Vegas
(*Vacant WBA Welterweight Title*)
22.04.89 Rafael Pineda W RSC 5 Atlantic City
(*WBA Welterweight Title Defence*)
Summary: 26 contests, won 24, drew 1, lost 1.

Glenwood (The Beast) Brown

Plainfield, USA. *Born* 25.07.67
WBA Americas Welterweight Champion

19.06.86 Bob Harris W RSC 4 New York
11.07.86 Dennis Wade W RSC 1 Stevensonville
28.08.86 Hilario Mercedes W PTS 4 New York
20.09.86 James Byrd W RSC 1 Philadelphia
25.10.86 Billy Mitchum W RSC 1 Arlington
13.11.86 Donald Gwynn W CO 2 New York
26.11.86 Victor Davis W PTS 6 Atlantic City
29.01.87 Antoine Lark W RSC 3 New York
12.03.87 Joe Johnson W RSC 4 New York
23.04.87 Hilario Mercedes W CO 4 New York
04.06.87 Kent Acuff W RSC 2 New York
07.07.87 Jeff Graves W RSC 1 New York
20.08.87 Kevin Austin W CO 3 New York
01.10.87 Rasheed Ali W PTS 8 New York
17.12.87 Joe Edens W RSC 2 New York
04.02.88 Ken Releford W RSC 6 New York
06.03.88 Keheven Johnson W CO 2 New York
14.04.88 Orlando Orozco W PTS 10 New York
27.06.88 Saoul Mamby L PTS 10 New York
28.09.88 Ariel Conde W RSC 4 Detroit
10.11.88 Juan Rondon W CO 2 New York
17.01.89 Lester Yarborough W PTS 10 Detroit
09.02.89 Saoul Mamby W PTS 12 New York
(*Vacant WBA Americas Welterweight Title*)
13.04.89 Mike English W RSC 1 New York
Summary: 24 contests, won 23, lost 1.

Simon Brown

Peter Goldfield/USA

Simon Brown
Washington, DC, USA. *Born* Jamaica 15.08.63
IBF Welterweight Champion

16.02.82 Rick Williams W PTS 4 Atlantic City
02.03.82 Vito Maselli W PTS 6 Atlantic City
10.04.82 Willie White W RSC 2 Atlantic City
27.04.82 Cookie James W RSC 5 Atlantic City
22.06.82 Cliff Lee W RSC 2 Atlantic City
18.07.82 Gene Ellington W RSC 1 Atlantic City
03.08.82 Carlos Santana W RSC 3 Atlantic City
23.08.82 Sergio Bautista W RSC 7 Atlantic City
05.10.82 George Burton W RSC 6 Atlantic City
09.11.82 Allen Braswell W CO 1 Atlantic City
14.12.82 Ruby Ortiz W CO 1 Washington
25.01.83 Ricardo Bryant W RSC 7 Atlantic City
15.03.83 Tom Moody W RSC 3 Atlantic City
26.04.83 Pete Seward W RSC 8 Atlantic City
04.06.83 Domingo Ayala W RSC 1 Atlantic City
01.11.83 Darryl Penn W PTS 10 Atlantic City
13.12.83 Robert Adams W PTS 10 Atlantic City
02.06.84 Clayton Hires W PTS 10 Washington
17.07.84 Jerome Johnson W PTS 10 Atlantic City
30.04.85 Martin Rojas W RSC 8 Atlantic City
23.07.85 Randy Mitchum W RSC 1 Washington
22.11.85 Marlon Starling L PTS 12 Atlantic City
(*USBA Welterweight Title Challenge*)
21.03.86 Kevin Howard W RSC 7 Washington
08.06.86 Shawn O'Sullivan W RSC 3 Toronto
25.09.87 Dexter Smith W RSC 6 Kingston
23.04.88 Tyrone Trice W RSC 14 Berck sur Mer
(*Vacant IBF Welterweight Title*)
16.07.88 Jorge Vaca W RSC 3 Kingston
(*IBF Welterweight Title Defence*)
14.10.88 Mauro Martelli W PTS 12 Lausanne
(*IBF Welterweight Title Defence*)
18.02.89 Jorge Maysonet W RSC 3 Budapest
(*IBF Welterweight Title Defence*)
27.04.89 Al Long W CO 7 Washington
(*IBF Welterweight Title Defence*)
Summary: 30 contests, won 29, lost 1.

Frank Bruno
Wandsworth, England. *Born* 16.11.61
Former Undefeated EBU Heavyweight Champion

17.03.82 Lupe Guerra W CO 1 London
30.03.82 Harvey Steichen W RSC 2 Wembley
20.04.82 Tom Stevenson W CO 1 London
04.05.82 Ron Gibbs W RSC 4 Wembley
01.06.82 Tony Moore W RSC 2 London
14.09.82 George Scott W RSC 1 Wembley
23.10.82 Ali Lukusa W CO 2 Berlin
09.11.82 Rudi Gauwe W CO 2 London
23.11.82 George Butzbach W RTD 1 Wembley
07.12.82 Gilberto Acuna W RSC 1 London
18.01.83 Stewart Lithgo W RTD 4 London
08.02.83 Peter Mulendwa W CO 3 London
01.03.83 Winston Allen W RSC 2 London
05.04.83 Eddie Neilson W RSC 3 London
03.05.83 Scott Ledoux W RSC 3 Wembley
31.05.83 Barry Funches W RSC 5 London
09.07.83 Mike Jameson W CO 2 Chicago
27.09.83 Bill Sharkey W CO 1 Wembley
11.10.83 Floyd Cummings W RSC 7 London
06.12.83 Walter Santemore W CO 4 London
13.03.84 Juan Figueroa W CO 1 Wembley
13.05.84 James Smith L CO 10 Wembley
25.09.84 Ken Lakusta W CO 2 Wembley
06.11.84 Jeff Jordan W RSC 3 London
27.11.84 Phil Brown W PTS 10 Wembley
26.03.85 Lucien Rodriguez W RSC 1 Wembley
01.10.85 Anders Eklund W CO 4 Wembley
(*EBU Heavyweight Title Challenge*)
04.12.85 Larry Frazier W CO 2 London
04.03.86 Gerrie Coetzee W CO 1 Wembley
19.07.86 Tim Witherspoon L RSC 11 Wembley
(*WBA Heavyweight Title Challenge*)
24.03.87 James Tillis W RSC 5 Wembley
27.06.87 Chuck Gardner W CO 1 Cannes
30.08.87 Reggie Gross W RSC 8 Marbella
24.10.87 Joe Bugner W RSC 8 London
25.02.89 Mike Tyson L RSC 5 Las Vegas
(*WBC Heavyweight Title Challenge*)
Summary: 35 contests, won 32, lost 3.

Anthony Byrd
Pomona, USA. *Born* 27.10.62
WBA Americas S. Middleweight Champion

10.02.86 Ruben Blackwell W PTS 4 Los Angeles
17.03.86 Gilbert Baptist L PTS 4 Los Angeles
20.05.86 Milton Bush W CO 1 Los Angeles
12.06.86 Martin Love W CO 2 Los Angeles
13.08.86 John Roy W RSC 6 Los Angeles
30.09.86 Ricky Locke W PTS 4 Reseda
18.05.87 Willie Wilson T DRAW 4 Los Angeles
17.03.88 Willie Wilson W RSC 7 San Diego
16.05.88 Marcos Geraldo W RSC 4 Tijuana
01.07.88 Juan Hernandez W RSC 4 Del Mar
18.08.88 Tim Williams W PTS San Diego
15.11.88 Kenny Snow W PTS 10 San Diego
13.02.89 Mike Peak W PTS 12 Los Angeles
(*Vacant WBA Americas S. Middleweight Title*)
Summary: 13 contests, won 11, drew 1, lost 1.

Efren Calamati
Arezzo, Italy
Italian & EBU L. Welterweight Champion

06.07.85 Andrea Ricci W RSC 4 Lerici
15.09.85 Faical Naifer W PTS 6 Arezzo
25.10.85 Saadil Mechiche W PTS 8 Genoa
08.02.86 Franco Callegari W PTS 6 Eboli
18.04.86 Abdel Arrow W RTD 3 Arezzo
14.06.86 Mokhtar Fridhar W CO 4 Praiano
02.07.86 Mwilambwe Tshikala W PTS 6 Agnone
26.07.86 Abdel Arrow W PTS 6 Castagneto
26.09.86 Abdel Chaboune W RSC 2 Arezzo
21.11.86 Jean-Luc Sautreau W RSC 2 Arezzo
10.01.87 Mwilambwe Tshikala W RSC 3 Agrigento
11.03.87 Angelo Quintavalle W RSC 4 Cosenza
21.03.87 Faical Naifer W PTS 8 Ischia
25.04.87 Abdul Kareem W CO 5 Acciaroli
22.05.87 Abdel Marbi W PTS 8 Arezzo
04.07.87 Bruno Simili W RSC 4 Arezzo
02.10.87 Fernand Blanco W PTS 8 Perugia
31.10.87 Belaid Khaldi W DIS 4 Azzano
20.11.87 Jose Maillot W PTS 8 Zingonia
28.02.88 Alain Leon Bamba W DIS 3 Trecase
02.07.88 Salvatore Nardino W RSC 5 Arezzo
(*Italian L. Welterweight Title Challenge*)
04.12.88 Raffaele Paoletti W RSC 3 San Pellegrino
25.01.89 Tusikoleta Nkalankete W PTS 12 Arezzo
(*EBU L. Welterweight Title Challenge*)
27.04.89 Madjid Mahdjoub W PTS 12 Arezzo
(*EBU L. Welterweight Title Defence*)
Summary: 24 contests, won 24.

Victor (Luvy) Callejas
Guaynabo, Puerto Rico. *Born* 12.11.60
Former Undefeated WBA S. Bantamweight Champion

18.02.79 Jose Parrilla L PTS 4 San Juan
20.04.79 Jose Parrilla W PTS 6 St Croix
04.08.79 Wilt Jones W CO 1 St Martin
26.11.79 Albert Pagan W CO 3 St Martin
20.09.80 Noel Rivera W CO 2 San Juan
08.11.80 Pedro Garcia W RSC 2 Detroit
03.12.80 Ralph Ortiz W CO 1 St Martin
02.05.81 Milton Torres W RSC 2 Ponce
02.10.81 Victor Bultron W CO 4 Arroyo
21.11.81 Lazaro Fabian W RSC 3 San Juan
10.12.81 Juan Pimentel W CO 2 San Juan
31.03.82 Elvin Gonzalez W RSC 2 Rio Piedras
20.05.82 Carlos Alcibar W CO 3 San Juan
12.06.82 Felix Sagredo W CO 2 Miami
13.11.82 Vicente Garza W RSC 4 San Juan
15.12.82 Neil Rubio W RSC 3 Chicago
19.01.83 Manuel Santos W CO 2 San Juan
16.03.83 Jose Ortiz T DRAW 2 San Juan
07.05.83 Juan Bazan W CO 3 Guaynabo
15.02.84 Bernardo Checa W RSC 3 San Juan
26.05.84 Loris Stecca W RSC 8 Guaynabo
(*WBA S. Bantamweight Title Challenge*)
02.02.85 Seung-Hoon Lee W PTS 15 San Juan
(*WBA S. Bantamweight Title Defence*)
08.11.85 Loris Stecca W RTD 6 Rimini
(*WBA S. Bantamweight Title Defence*)
27.03.87 Cleo Garcia W PTS 10 San Juan
22.11.87 Pedro Nolasco W CO 1 Las Vegas
07.03.88 Jeff Fenech L RSC 10 Sydney
(*Vacant WBC Featherweight Title*)
12.04.89 Juan Torres W RSC 7 Belfast
Summary: 27 contests, won 24, drew 1, lost 2.

Hector (Macho) Camacho
New York, USA. *Born* Bayamon, Puerto Rico 24.05.62
WBO L. Welterweight Champion. Former Undefeated WBC & NABF Lightweight Champion. Former Undefeated WBC & NABF S. Featherweight Champion

12.09.80 David Brown W PTS 4 New York
12.12.80 Benny Llanos W CO 1 New York
12.03.81 Herman Ingram W PTS 6 New York
27.03.81 Robert Johnson W CO 1 New York
24.04.81 Jerry Strickland W RSC 2 New York
02.05.81 Tomas Diaz W PTS 6 New York
16.05.81 Kato Ali W RSC 7 Kiamesha Lake
25.06.81 Marcial Santiago W PTS 8 New York
24.07.81 Jose Figueroa W CO 1 New York
16.09.81 Robert Mullins W RSC 6 New York
05.11.81 Tony Murray W PTS 10 New York
11.12.81 Blaine Dickson W PTS 12 New York
(*NABF S. Featherweight Title Challenge*)
15.02.82 Jorge Nina W PTS 8 New York
31.03.82 Rafael Lopez W RSC 3 New York
21.05.82 Refugio Rojas W RSC 1 New York
(*NABF S. Featherweight Title Defence*)
11.07.82 Louie Loi W RSC 7 New York
28.08.82 Johnny Sato W CO 4 Atlantic City
30.10.82 Melvin Paul W PTS 10 Atlantic City
20.11.82 Greg Coverson W PTS 10 Las Vegas
12.02.83 John Montes W CO 1 Anchorage
03.04.83 Irleis Perez W PTS 10 Phoenix
07.08.83 Rafael Limon W RSC 5 San Juan
(*Vacant WBC S. Featherweight Title*)
18.11.83 Rafael Solis W CO 5 San Juan
(*WBC S. Featherweight Title Defence*)
20.05.84 Rafael Williams W RSC 7 Corpus Christi
19.01.85 Louie Burke W RSC 5 Atlantic City
29.04.85 Roque Montoya W PTS 12 Buffalo
(*Vacant NABF Lightweight Title*)
10.08.85 Jose Luis Ramirez W PTS 12 Las Vegas
(*WBC Lightweight Title Challenge*)
18.12.85 Freddie Roach W PTS 10 Sacramento
13.06.86 Edwin Rosario W PTS 12 New York
(*WBC Lightweight Title Defence*)
26.09.86 Cornelius Boza-Edwards W PTS 12 Miami
(*WBC Lightweight Title Defence*)
02.05.87 Howard Davis W PTS 10 Atlantic City
25.06.88 Reyes Cruz W PTS 10 Atlantic City
22.10.88 Rick Souce W RSC 4 Bayamon
06.03.89 Ray Mancini W PTS 12 Reno
(*Vacant WBO L. Welterweight Title*)
Summary: 34 contests, won 34.

Gaby Canizales
Laredo, USA. *Born* 01.05.60
Former WBA & USBA Bantamweight Champion

30.04.79 Jose Perez W CO 1 Monclova
07.05.79 Juanio Bernal W CO 1 Monclova
06.06.80 Polin Flores W CO 1 Laredo
15.06.80 Jose Salas W CO 2 Laredo
02.09.80 Miguel Meza W CO 2 Laredo
13.09.80 Oscar Gomez W CO 6 San Antonio

14.10.80 Memo Velazquez W CO 1 Laredo
05.12.80 Miguel Medina W CO 6 Corpus Christi
10.03.81 Cecilio Ostos W CO 1 Laredo
05.05.81 Mario Nava L PTS 10 Laredo
14.05.81 Calvin Sheppard W PTS 10 Dallas
15.06.81 Elias de Leon W CO 2 Laredo
27.06.81 Jorge Cruz W CO 1 Laredo
01.09.81 Francisco Bejines W RSC 2 Laredo
31.10.81 Mario Gomez W RSC 10 Laredo
02.12.81 Mario Nava W PTS 10 Laredo
11.02.81 Ed Bonilla W CO 2 Laredo
10.03.82 Juan Castellanos W PTS 12 Laredo
22.04.82 Ramon Guillen W CO 5 Laredo
16.05.82 Ricardo Varela W PTS 10 San Antonio
24.06.82 Diego Rosario W RSC 5 Atlantic City
(*Vacant USBA Bantamweight Title*)
01.08.82 Jose Torres W PTS 10 San Antonio
22.09.82 Franco Torregoza W CO 10 Atlantic City
(*USBA Bantamweight Title Defence*)
19.10.82 Jose L. Soto W CO 2 Laredo
23.11.82 Gustavo Martinez W CO 3 Laredo
13.03.83 Jeff Chandler L PTS 15 Atlantic City
(*WBA Bantamweight Title Challenge*)
13.05.83 Ron Cisneros W RSC 10 Laredo
(*USBA Bantamweight Title Defence*)
19.10.83 Norberto Castellanos W RSC 1 Laredo
12.11.83 James Pipps W RSC 6 Beaumont
(*USBA Bantamweight Title Defence*)
07.02.84 Pedro Rodriguez W RSC 3 Houston
06.06.84 Javier Diaz W CO 2 San Antonio
25.08.84 Kelvin Seabrooks W PTS 12 Laredo
(*USBA Bantamweight Title Defence*)
30.01.85 Jeff Whaley W PTS 10 Atlantic City
22.05.85 Troy Townsend W RSC 10 Atlantic City
10.03.86 Richard Sandoval W RSC 7 Las Vegas
(*WBA Bantamweight Title Challenge*)
04.06.86 Bernardo Pinango L PTS 15 East Rutherford
(*WBA Bantamweight Title Defence*)
11.12.86 Armando Morales W CO 2 Houston
30.01.87 Mauro Diaz W PTS 10 San Antonio
29.03.87 Mike Moreno W RSC 3 Tucson
05.05.87 Julio Blanco W PTS 10 San Antonio
06.07.87 Raul Perez L RSC 9 Tijuana
18.09.87 Alejandro Valenzuela W CO 3 Phoenix
27.11.87 Louis Curtis W PTS 12 Atlantic City
(*Vacant USBA Bantamweight Title*)
25.03.88 Kenny Mitchell L PTS 12 Houston
(*USBA Bantamweight Title Defence*)
03.06.88 Julio Blanco W CO 7 Tucson
21.07.88 Lucilo Nolasco W PTS 10 Tucson
17.10.88 Alex Valenzuela W PTS 10 Tucson
15.12.88 Carlos Castro W CO 3 Tucson
22.04.89 Tony Pruitt W RSC 1 Detroit
Summary: 49 contests, won 44, lost 5.

Gaby Canizales

Peter Goldfield/USA

Orlando Canizales
Laredo, USA. *Born* 25.11.65
IBF Bantamweight Champion. Former Undefeated USBA S. Flyweight Champion. Former Undefeated NABF Flyweight Champion.

25.08.84 Juan Perez W RSC 2 Laredo
09.11.84 Rey Euresti W CO 1 San Antonio
05.03.85 Rogelio Leanos DREW 4 Houston
09.04.85 John Camaro W RSC 1 Houston
09.05.85 Nelson Garcia W RSC 1 Houston
26.07.85 Manuel Sago W RSC 2 Atlantic City
09.10.85 Roland Luna W RSC 1 Houston
18.10.85 Armando Quiroz W PTS 6 Laredo
20.11.85 Steve Whetstone W RSC 3 Houston
12.12.85 Jorge Fuentes W RSC 5 Houston
12.03.86 Timo Villaneuva W RSC 2 Houston
06.05.86 Javier Diaz W PTS 10 San Antonio
20.07.86 Paul Gonzales L PTS 12 Stateline
(*NABF Flyweight Title Challenge*)
27.09.86 Juan Garcia W CO 1 Victoria
11.12.86 Jorge Vazquez W CO 2 Houston
30.01.87 Prudencio Cardona W RSC 6 San Antonio
20.02.87 Javier Lucas W RSC 9 San Jose
03.06.87 Alonzo Gonzalez W PTS 10 San Jose
25.09.87 Jose Olivares W CO 4 San Antonio
12.11.87 Armando Velasco W RSC 4 Houston
(*Vacant NABF Flyweight title*)
15.04.88 Louis Curtis W RSC 2 Atlantic City
(*Vacant USBA S. Flyweight Title*)
09.07.88 Kelvin Seabrooks W RSC 15 Atlantic City
(*IBF Bantamweight Title Challenge*)
29.11.88 Jimmy Navarro W CO 1 San Antonio
(*IBF Bantamweight Title Defence*)
Summary: 23 contests, won 21, drew 1, lost 1.

Don Caples
Houston, USA. *Born* 1967
L. Welterweight

06.07.84 Alex Guerrero W RSC 4 Houston
17.08.84 Eloy Santos W PTS 4 Houston
13.09.84 Pedro Adames DREW 6 Houston
16.01.85 Fred Batista W PTS 6 Lafayette
26.02.85 Mario Salazar W RSC 7 Corpus Christi
10.04.85 Larry Highsmith W PTS 8 Atlantic City
09.05.85 Carlos Garcia W PTS 6 Houston
17.07.85 Ricky Aviles W RSC 3 Houston
07.08.85 Pedro Barbosa W PTS 6 Houston
04.09.85 Jimmy Jackson W PTS 8 Atlantic City
30.10.85 Darryl Savoy W PTS 10 Las Vegas
18.12.85 Tony English L RSC 10 Atlantic City
12.02.86 Mario Salazar W RSC 5 Houston
12.03.86 Andy Minsker W PTS 10 Las Vegas
16.07.86 Darryl Savoy W PTS 10 Galveston
11.09.86 Vicente Velasco W RTD 9 Houston
11.12.86 Kenny Baysmore L RSC 2 Houston
(*USBA S. Featherweight Title Challenge*)
12.02.87 Harold Warren W PTS 8 Houston
23.06.87 Sylvester Kennon L RSC 1 Houston
29.05.88 Tomas Gonzalez W PTS 8 Houston
19.04.89 Rene Arredondo W PTS 10 Harlingen
Summary: 21 contests, won 17, drew 1, lost 3.

Richard Caramanolis
Marseilles, France. *Born* 07.03.58
French L. Heavyweight Champion. Former EBU L. Heavyweight Champion

29.02.80 Bojan Sverzina W PTS 6 Marseilles
21.03.80 Darko Barakovic W CO 1 Montpellier
18.04.80 Gabriel Lazzari W PTS 6 Paris
09.05.80 Bruno Arati W RSC 6 Marseilles
06.06.80 Jose Centa W RTD 3 Marseilles
04.10.80 Boyd Farrar W RTD 7 Marseilles
28.11.80 Maurice Trepant W PTS 8 Marseilles
30.01.81 Robert Desnouck W PTS 8 Marseilles
27.02.81 Ibelo Moano W PTS 8 Marseilles
03.04.81 Robert Powell W CO 1 Marseilles
21.04.81 Bonny McKenzie W PTS 8 Marseilles
19.06.81 Carlton Benoit W PTS 8 Marseilles
10.10.81 Trevor Cattouse W CO 2 Marseilles
23.10.81 Gino Freo W CO 5 Marseilles
11.12.81 Avenamar Peralta W CO 9 Marseilles
21.01.82 Alek Penarski W CO 1 Paris
19.02.82 John Cox W RTD 7 Marseilles
05.03.82 Pierre Kabassu W PTS 10 Nice
02.04.82 Eric Kopec W RSC 4 Marseilles
08.10.82 Dave Conteh W PTS 10 Marseilles
04.12.82 Fred Serres W PTS 10 Marseilles
10.02.83 Hocine Tafer W CO 6 Marseilles
(*French L. Heavyweight Title Challenge*)
29.04.83 Manuel Lira W CO 1 Aix
19.05.83 Cordwell Hylton W CO 4 Paris
10.10.83 Vedat Akova W RSC 5 Paris
02.02.84 Rudi Koopmans W RTD 8 Marseilles
(*EBU L. Heavyweight Title Challenge*)
28.05.84 Alex Blanchard L RSC 6 Amsterdam
(*EBU L. Heavyweight Title Defence*)
12.10.84 Sergio Bosio W RSC 2 Antibes
22.04.85 Alex Blanchard DREW 12 Rotterdam
(*EBU L. Heavyweight Title Challenge*)
14.07.85 Arthel Lawhorne DREW 7 Monte Carlo
21.02.86 Stuart Robinson W RTD 4 Marseilles
18.04.86 Pierre Kabassu W RTD 6 Marseilles
(*French L. Heavyweight Title Defence*)
30.05.86 Jean-Max Delnard W RSC 5 Avignon
(*French L. Heavyweight Title Defence*)
20.12.86 Lennie Howard W RSC 1 St Ouen
31.01.87 Jose Seys W RSC 4 Montpelier
16.04.87 Rufino Angulo L CO 2 Marseilles
(*French L. Heavyweight Title Defence*)
22.05.87 Jerry Brown W CO 1 La Seyne
21.11.87 Terry Walker W RSC 3 Paris
28.03.88 Rufino Angulo W RSC 4 Paris
(*French L. Heavyweight Title Challenge*)
10.06.88 Charles Williams L RTD 11 Annecy
(*IBF L. Heavyweight Title Challenge*)
03.10.88 Jose Seys W PTS 8 Paris
19.11.88 Lahcen Hamdi W RSC 2 Chateau Thierry
23.01.89 Abner Blackstock W RSC 6 Paris
10.03.89 Eric Nicoletta L RTD 8 Sete
Summary: 44 contests, won 38, drew 2, lost 4.

Juan Carazo
Caguas, Puerto Rico. *Born* 1964
S. Bantamweight

17.03.84 Marcos Claudia W RSC 2 San Juan
23.06.84 Israel Santiago W RSC 3 San Juan
08.12.84 Martin Lantigua W CO 1 San Juan
02.02.85 Julio Guerrero W PTS 8 Hato Rey
28.02.85 Jose Pena W CO 3 Santo Domingo
23.03.85 Fernando Mateo W CO 1 Santiago
18.11.85 Julio Osoro W RSC 2 Caguas
21.12.85 Edwin Calix W CO 2 Caguas
03.05.86 Tom Elston W RSC 5 Guaynabo
30.05.86 Jesus Bastardo W PTS 10 Curacao
12.09.86 Luis Navarro W RSC 3 Chicago
28.11.86 Jesus Bastardo W RSC 6 Curacao
14.03.87 Wilfredo Vasquez L CO 1 San Juan
30.07.87 William Ramos W PTS 10 San Juan
11.08.87 Jose Luis Vegagil W RSC 3 Chicago
20.11.87 Diego Avila W PTS 10 Chicago
09.04.88 Tim Silva W RSC 6 Las Vegas
13.05.88 Vincente Arias W CO 5 San Juan
08.10.88 Santos Laciar W PTS 12 Caguas
Summary: 19 contests, won 18, lost 1.

Candelario (Changuito) Carmona
La Poza, Mexico. *Born* 02.02.59
Bantamweight

.79 Vicente Perez W PTS 6 Acapulco
.79 Juan Veloz L PTS 6 Acapulco
08.02.80 Esteban Perez W PTS 8 Acapulco
02.05.80 Rafael Morales W PTS 10 Acapulco
11.07.80 Popeye Mendoza W RSC 6 Acapulco
29.05.81 Julio Avendano W PTS 10 Acapulco
04.09.81 Jacob Gutierrez W CO 1 Acapulco
03.10.81 Ed Valdespino W CO 1 Acapulco
05.03.82 Emilio Sosa W CO 1 Acapulco
20.06.82 Chong-Kwan Chun W CO 6 Seoul
27.08.82 Martin Flores W CO 1 Acapulco
09.10.82 Jesus Becerra W RSC 6 Mexico City
19.11.82 Puma Fuentes W CO 6 Salina Cruz
11.12.82 Ed Acosta W PTS 10 Merida
04.05.83 Raul Dominguez W RSC 2 Mexico City
11.06.83 Tomas Chavez W CO 2 Chicago
25.06.83 Javier Davila L CO 2 Mexico City
25.09.83 Al Rivera W CO 2 Acapulco
05.11.83 Jorge Ortega W RSC 4 Acapulco
31.03.84 Javier Guerrero W RSC 9 Mexico City
26.05.84 Rafael Alonso L RSC 6 Mexico City
11.08.84 Dan Guillen W RSC 8 Mexico City
23.11.84 Adrian Cortez W CO 4 Zihuatanejo
28.12.84 Delfino Carranza W CO 3 Zihuatanejo
08.02.85 Gabriel Ocampo W CO 2 Acapulco
06.04.85 Carlos Segura W RTD 6 Zihuatanejo
24.08.85 Rodolfo Flores W CO 3 Mexico City

06.09.85 Jose Valdez W RSC 9 Los Mochis
19.10.85 Bobby Ruiz W RSC 5 Mexico City
13.12.85 Gil Morales W RSC 2 Salina Cruz
21.02.86 Mario Nava W RSC 6 Acapulco
28.03.86 Sargent Morales W CO 4 Zihuatanejo
28.06.86 Javier Roman W CO 2 Marquelia
14.07.86 Estardo Kuri W CO 2 Salina Cruz
16.08.86 Lupe Torres W CO 6 Manzanillo
15.09.86 Joel Patron W PTS 10 Tijuana
15.02.87 Jorge Ramirez L PTS 12 Mexicali
(Mexican Bantamweight Title Challenge)
29.05.87 Jose Valdez L PTS 10 Guasave
24.07.87 Fernie Morales W PTS 10 Juarez
29.08.87 Gato Flores W PTS 10 Guasave
30.10.87 Fernie Morales L PTS 10 Juarez
06.02.88 Roman Jimenez W CO 7 Puebla
25.03.88 Santiago Caballero W PTS 10 Acapulco
11.06.88 Julio Pliego W CO 6 Lazaro Cardenas
06.08.88 Fernando Varguez DREW 10 Merida
08.10.88 Carlos Salinas W RSC 4 Mexico City
31.03.89 Elpidio Molina W RSC 8 Minatitlan
Summary: 47 contests, won 40, drew 1, lost 6.

Renaldo (Little Red) Carter
Detroit, USA. *Born* 25.08.68
S. Bantamweight

30.09.86 Sherman Dixon W RSC 3 Detroit
28.10.86 Aaron Sheckles W PTS 4 Detroit
06.01.87 Bill Fuller W CO 1 Detroit
27.01.87 Kim Johnson W RSC 2 Detroit
24.02.87 Walter Gallman W RSC 1 Detroit
31.03.87 Nick Wagner W RSC 2 Detroit
28.04.87 Jorge Lujan W CO 1 Detroit
30.05.87 John Johnson W PTS 6 Las Vegas
01.08.87 David Natera W PTS 6 Las Vegas
18.08.87 Louie Coronado W PTS 6 Detroit
29.09.87 Randy Garlindo W RSC 1 Detroit
16.10.87 Juan Camaro W RSC 2 Atlantic City
21.11.87 Steve Guzman W PTS 8 Las Vegas
28.01.88 Tim Silva W PTS 10 Detroit
23.02.88 Jorge Vasquez W RSC 4 Detroit
30.03.88 Ryan Fore W RSC 2 Detroit
27.04.88 Jeff Hanna W PTS 10 Detroit
25.05.88 Mario Lozano W CO 4 Detroit
27.07.88 Tony Martinez W RSC 9 Detroit
28.09.88 Edgar Garcia W PTS 10 Detroit
29.10.88 Danny Garcia L RSC 2 Las Vegas
Summary: 21 contests, won 20, lost 1.

Stefano Cassi
Bergamo, Italy. *Born* 06.06.62
Italian Lightweight Champion

28.01.86 Bofunga Eymono W PTS 6 Bergamo
30.05.86 Baldomero Tienda W CO 2 Abano
19.09.86 Comiss Guebhouli W CO 2 Lerici
01.11.86 Fathi Kaabi W CO 3 Calatina
29.11.86 Benito Murillo W RSC 4 Abbiategrasso
02.02.87 Andre Blanco W RSC 2 Cinisello
20.03.87 Claudio Bicai W RSC 5 Empoli
16.05.87 Tahar Ayari W PTS 6 Bergamo
29.06.87 Fathi Kaabi W RTD 4 Abbiategrasso
24.07.87 Andre Blanco W RTD 3 Silvi Marina
09.10.87 Fathi Kaabi W RTD 4 Aosta
21.11.87 Mwilambwe Tshikala W RSC 5 Trezzano
11.12.87 Yvon Tatula W PTS 6 Livorno
29.01.88 Faical Naifer W PTS 6 Rimini
22.04.88 Fernando Blanco W RSC 7 Milan
04.06.88 Fernando Blanco W CO 3 Cagliari
14.07.88 Mario Salazar W RSC 2 Milan
17.11.88 Faical Naifer W PTS 8 Novara
20.01.89 Alfredo Raininger W RSC 8 Pozzano
(Vacant Italian Lightweight Title)
10.03.89 Alain Leon Bamba W RSC 5 Bergamo
Summary: 20 contests, won 20.

Alberto Castro
San Bernardo, Colombia. *Born* 20.04.63
Latin American Flyweight Champion

05.11.82 Rafael Soto W CO 2 Sincelejo
25.04.83 Antonio Solano W CO 6 Sincelejo
18.06.83 Jorge Lugo W PTS 8 Sincelejo
30.07.83 Manuel Ariza W RSC 5 Sincelejo
16.09.83 Juan Polo Perez W PTS 10 Sincelejo
04.11.83 Alex Miranda W RSC 8 Sincelejo
23.12.83 Juan Polo Perez W PTS 10 Monteria
17.02.84 Pedro Padilla W CO 5 Sincelejo
04.03.84 Uriel Londono W RSC 8 Sincelejo
11.04.84 Nestor Obregon W RSC 4 Sincelejo
(Latin American Flyweight Title Challenge)
07.07.84 Betulio Gonzalez W PTS 12 Maracaibo
(Latin American Flyweight Title Defence)
10.10.84 Hilario Zapata L PTS 10 Isla Margarita
15.12.84 Ernesto Sanchez W PTS 10 Colon
30.03.85 Juan Disla W CO 3 Colon
03.08.85 Ernesto Sanchez W PTS 12 Panama City
(Latin American Flyweight Title Defence)
27.09.85 Francisco Alvarez DREW 10 Barranquilla
12.04.86 Jorge Rivas W CO 2 David
28.06.86 Juan Herrera W RSC 6 Colon
13.09.86 Hilario Zapata L PTS 15 Panama City
(WBA Flyweight Title Challenge)
20.12.86 Edgar Monserrat W RSC 8 Panama City
17.10.87 Alejandro Pastrana W RSC 5 Sincelejo
30.04.88 Eudo Bermudez W RSC 4 Cartagena
13.08.88 Manuel Sayago W RSC 9 Caragena
Summary: 23 contests, won 20, drew 1, lost 2.

Armando Castro
Mexico City, Mexico
Former Mexican S. Flyweight Champion

13.10.84 Antonio Escamilla W PTS 4 Mexico City
11.05.85 Esteban Ayala L DIS 1 Mexico City
20.07.85 Martin Villaneuva W PTS 4 Mexico City
20.09.85 Domingo Dominguez W RSC 2 Mexico City
10.10.85 Jesse Martinez W RSC 2 Nuevo Laredo
23.11.85 Fernando Hernandez W PTS 6 Mexico City
14.05.86 Pablo Gomez W RSC 1 Mexico City
17.05.86 Eduardo Ramirez L PTS 6 Mexico City
26.07.86 Aquilino Lopez W CO 4 Mexico City
12.11.86 Raul Quiroga W PTS 10 Mexico City
06.12.86 Oscar Ortiz W RSC 7 Mexico City
19.12.86 Ismael Benitez W CO 4 Acapulco
18.02.87 Oscar Ortiz W RSC 5 Mexico City
28.03.87 Fernando Varguez L PTS 10 Merida
17.04.87 Francisco Gonzalez L PTS Cancun
11.07.87 Carlos de la Paz W RSC 1 Mexico City
08.08.87 Mijailo Hernandez W RSC 5 Mexico City
03.10.87 Victor Rabanales L RSC 1 Mexico City
14.11.87 Artemio Ruiz W CO 4 Mexico City
19.12.87 Jimmy Fernandez W RSC 5 Mexico City
(Mexican S. Flyweight Title Challenge)
13.02.88 Jose Montiel W RSC 4 Mexico City
(Mexican S. Flyweight Title Defence)
30.04.88 Sergio Cornejo W RSC 3 Mexico City
(Mexican S. Flyweight Title Defence)
10.07.88 Jose Montiel L PTS 12 Los Mochis
(Mexican S. Flyweight Title Defence)
14.10.88 Jose Montiel L RTD 9 Los Mochis
(Mexican S. Flyweight Title Challenge)
03.03.89 Betillo Ochoa W PTS 10 Jalapa
Summary: 25 contests, won 18, lost 7.

Jorge (Locomotora) Castro
Puerto Deseado, Argentine. *Born* 18.08.67
Light-Middleweight

14.02.87 Patricio Carachi W CO 1 Caleta Oliva
14.03.87 Jorge Morello DREW 6 Caleta Oliva
10.04.87 Roberto Martinez W PTS 6 Rivadavia
07.05.87 Alberto Alvarado W CO 2 Rivadavia
05.06.87 Sergio Machuca W CO 1 Rivadavia
03.07.87 Carlso Almada W RTD 3 Caleta Oliva
09.08.87 Jorge Morello DREW 10 Caleta Oliva
13.09.87 Luis Sanchez W CO 2 Caleta Oliva
24.09.87 Antonio Juarez W PTS 10 Rivadavia
09.10.87 Sergio Combis W PTS 10 Rivadavia
13.11.87 Jorge Pino W PTS 10 Rivadavia
11.12.87 Jose Alvarado W CO 3 Rivadavia
23.12.87 Sergio Ronconi W PTS 10 Rivadavia
15.01.88 Hugo Lucro W DIS 8 Caleta Oliva
19.02.88 Pedro Ruiz W CO 3 Catamarca
04.03.88 Cesar Perez W CO 1 Rivadavia
18.03.88 Hugo Lucro W RTD 7 Rivadavia
09.04.88 Domingo Sosa W CO 1 Caleta Oliva
13.05.88 Ramon Ramos W CO 1 Rivadavia
17.06.88 Carlos Prieto W CO 7 Rivadavia
02.07.88 Carlos Pastran W CO 2 Rivadavia
17.07.88 Robinson Zamora W CO 2 Rio Gallegos
30.07.88 Ramon Abeldano W PTS 10 Buenos Aires
10.09.88 Antonio Juarez W PTS 10 Caleta Oliva
24.09.88 Fernando Ernesto W CO 2 Buenos Aires
08.10.88 Ramon Abeldano W CO 1 Rivadavia
22.10.88 Ramon Alegre W CO 4 Buenos Aires
08.11.88 Alphonso Bailey W CO 5 Monte Carlo
22.11.88 Jean-Pierre Iniami W CO 4 San Pellegrino
10.12.88 Juan Ortiz W RSC 2 Buenos Aires
23.12.88 Mario Matthysse W CO 7 Trelew
23.01.89 Osvaldo Diaz W CO 1 Mar del Plata
04.02.89 Jose Toloza W RTD 4 Villa Carlos Paz
27.02.89 Lorenzo Garcia W PTS 10 Mar del Plata
10.03.89 Jorge Martinez W CO 4 La Rioja
20.03.89 Ernest Sena W PTS 10 Mendoza
15.04.89 Hugo Marinangeli W CO 4 Rivadavia
Summary: 37 contests, won 35, drew 2.

Jung-Koo (The Hawk) Chang
Pusan, South Korea. *Born* 04.02.63
Former Undefeated WBC L. Flyweight Champion

17.11.80 Jong-Yul Suh W CO 3 Seoul
19.11.80 Jin-Hyong Park W CO 3 Seoul
22.11.80 Eu-Kwan Lee W PTS 4 Seoul
23.11.80 Ho-Chol Pyun W PTS 4 Seoul
29.11.80 Hi-Sup Shin W PTS 4 Seoul
09.12.80 Nam-Keun Kang W PTS 6 Seoul
11.01.81 Jin-Hyong Park W CO 2 Pusan
23.01.81 Chang-Pyo Hong W PTS 8 Pusan
29.03.81 Yo-Dong Kim W PTS 6 Pusan
25.04.81 Michael Bulka W PTS 10 Pusan
07.06.81 Oscar Bolivar W PTS 10 Daejon
04.09.81 Rod Esmero W PTS 10 Pusan
11.10.81 Leonardo Paredes W CO 6 Daejon
18.11.81 Chut Thairungriang W CO 2 Pusan
26.12.81 Alfonso Lopez W CO 3 Seoul
10.02.82 Jong-Kwan Chung W RSC 6 Taegu
04.04.82 Luk-Odd Phitiporn W CO 5 Pusan
06.06.82 Amado Ursua W PTS 10 Seoul
18.09.82 Hilario Zapata L PTS 15 Chonju
(WBC L. Flyweight Title Challenge)
05.12.82 Rodrigo Saonoy W PTS 10 Chungju
06.02.83 Tito Abella W CO 2 Chungju
26.03.83 Hilario Zapata W RSC 3 Daejon
(WBC L. Flyweight Title Challenge)
11.06.83 Masaharu Iha W RSC 2 Taegu
(WBC L. Flyweight Title Defence)
10.09.83 German Torres W PTS 12 Daejon
(WBC L. Flyweight Title Defence)
31.03.84 Sot Chitalada W PTS 12 Pusan
(WBC L. Flyweight Title Defence)
18.08.84 Katsuo Tokashiki W RSC 9 Pohang
(WBC L. Flyweight Title Defence)
15.12.84 Tadashi Kuramochi W PTS 12 Pusan
(WBC L. Flyweight Title Defence)
27.04.85 German Torres W PTS 12 Ulsan
(WBC L. Flyweight Title Defence)
03.08.85 Francisco Montiel W PTS 12 Seoul
(WBC L. Flyweight Title Defence)
10.11.85 Jorge Cano W PTS 12 Daejon
(WBC L. Flyweight Title Defence)
13.04.86 German Torres W PTS 12 Kwangju
(WBC L. Flyweight Title Defence)
13.09.86 Francisco Montiel W PTS 12 Seoul
(WBC L. Flyweight Title Defence)
14.12.86 Hideyuki Ohashi W RSC 5 Inchon
(WBC L. Flyweight Title Defence)
19.04.87 Efren Pinto W RSC 6 Seoul
(WBC L. Flyweight Title Defence)
28.06.87 Agustin Garcia W RSC 10 Seoul
(WBC L. Flyweight Title Defence)
13.12.87 Isidro Perez W PTS 12 Seoul
(WBC L. Flyweight Title Defence)
27.06.88 Hideyuki Ohashi W RSC 8 Tokyo
(WBC L. Flyweight Title Defence)
Summary: 37 contests, won 36, lost 1.

Tae-Il Chang
South Korea. *Born* 10.04.65
Former Undefeated OPBF S. Flyweight Champion.
Former IBF & South Korean S. Flyweight Champion

18.10.81 Byung-Kyu Lee DREW 4 Seoul
08.11.81 Rae-Ki Ahn W PTS 4 Seoul
06.12.81 Jae-Min Shin W PTS 6 Seoul
14.02.82 Yong-Bon Yun W CO 1 Seoul
20.03.82 Yun-Sik Chae W PTS 6 Seoul
28.03.82 Jae-Sung Uhm L PTS 6 Seoul
18.09.83 Sang-Suk Bang W PTS 6 Seoul
23.10.83 Chung-Dae Lee W PTS 6 Seoul
04.12.83 Won-Keun Chae W PTS 6 Seoul
25.12.83 Joong-Suk Kwon W PTS 8 Seoul
12.02.84 Hoi-Yul Yang W PTS 8 Seoul
08.04.84 Chang-Kyun Oh W PTS 8 Seoul
13.05.84 Yun-Kuk Lee W PTS 8 Seoul
13.07.84 Masaharu Inami W CO 9 Yokohama

09.09.84 Ok-Kyun Yuh W RSC 9 Seoul
(*South Korean S. Flyweight Title Challenge*)
03.11.84 Seung-Hyun Bang L PTS 10 Seoul
(*South Korean S. Flyweight Title Defence*)
24.03.85 Byung-Yum Choi W CO 2 Mokpo
01.06.85 Edel Geronimo W PTS 12 Inchon
(*Vacant OPBF S. Flyweight Title*)
01.03.86 Sa-Yung Kim W PTS 10 Mokpo
12.04.86 Jang-Kyun Oh W CO 3 Yungchun
31.05.86 Wongso Indrajit W CO 5 Seoul
03.08.86 Nongberd Napathaya W CO 3 Seoul
17.10.86 Ruben de la Cruz W CO 7 Suwon
15.02.87 Hi-Suk Kim W RSC 5 Buju
17.05.87 Soon-Chun Kwan W PTS 15 Pusan
(*Vacant IBF S. Flyweight Title*)
17.10.87 Elly Pical L PTS 15 Jakarta
(*IBF S. Flyweight Title Defence*)
24.01.88 Byong-Kwan Chung W PTS 12 Chungbok
(*OPBF S. Flyweight Title Challenge*)
26.03.88 Yossi Amnifu W PTS 12 Namhae
(*OPBF S. Flyweight Title Defence*)
22.05.88 Kazuto Kurahachai W CO 6 Tagawa
(*OPBF S. Flyweight Title Defence*)
24.07.88 Seung-Kwan Lee W RSC 7 Pohang
(*OPBF S. Flyweight Title Defence*)
15.01.89 Kaosai Galaxy L CO 2 Bangkok
(*WBA S. Flyweight Title Challenge*)
Summary: 31 contests, won 26, drew 1, lost 4.

Eric Chavez
Talisay, Philippines. *Born* 09.04.62
M. Flyweight

08.05.85 Jun Gavero DREW 4 Leyte
01.06.85 Luis Pelamo W CO 3 Cebu
25.08.85 Con Con Duran DREW 4 Samar
07.09.85 Danilo Staton W PTS 4 Mandaue
03.10.85 Danilo Staton W PTS 4 Lapu
09.11.85 Con Con Duran TD 2 Cebu
03.12.85 Edgar Capino W PTS 4 Quezon City
07.12.85 Leopoldo Bangsoyao W PTS 4 Benguet
26.01.86 Darrel Tuazon W PTS 6 Benguet
22.02.86 Bernie Bernardo W PTS 6 Manila
01.03.86 Joel Revilla W PTS 6 Manila
16.05.86 Gil Lugban W PTS 8 Pasay
30.05.86 Danny Duran W PTS 8 Mandaluyong
12.06.86 Romy Austria W PTS 8 San Fernando
09.07.86 Arsenio Perez W PTS 10 Olongapo
27.09.86 Ric Santiago W PTS 10 Mandaluyong
29.10.86 Jun Altarejos W TD 4 Paranaque
11.12.86 Nick Dalisay DREW 10 Manila
27.12.86 Robert Palarit W PTS 10 Quezon City
28.02.87 Bahar Udin W CO 5 Jakarta
28.04.87 Mikio Uchida W RSC 5 Nagoya
30.08.87 Edwin Inocencio W RSC 2 Balanga
24.10.87 Romy Austria W PTS 10 Balanga
12.12.87 Mario Alguin W PTS 10 Quezon City
19.08.88 Dommy Ursua W RSC 1 Quezon City
10.11.88 Romy Austria W RSC 3 Manila
16.12.88 Elson Duran W RSC 5 Manila
Summary: 27 contests, won 23, drew 4.

Julio Cesar Chavez
Ciudad Obregon, Mexico. *Born* 12.07.62
WBC & WBA Lightweight Champion. Former Undefeated WBC S. Featherweight Champion

05.02.80 Andres Felix W CO 6 Culiacan
08.04.80 Ramon Flores W CO 3 Navojoa
20.05.80 Roberto Garcia W CO 6 Guaymas
18.07.80 Tito Geraldo W PTS 6 Guamuchil
05.09.80 Miguel Cebrero W PTS 10 Culiacan
22.09.80 Jesus Lara W PTS 10 Culiacan
13.10.80 Jesus Martinez W CO 1 Culiacan
26.11.80 Andres Felix W CO 2 Culiacan
15.12.80 Roberto Flores W CO 3 Culiacan
02.02.81 Julio Gaxiola W RSC 4 Tijuana
03.04.81 Miguel Ruiz W CO 1 Culiacan
08.05.81 Eduardo Acosta W CO 2 Culiacan
05.06.81 Victor Games W CO 1 Culiacan
26.06.81 Fidel Navarro W CO 1 Culiacan
10.07.81 Bobby Dominguez W CO 3 Culiacan
27.07.81 Daniel Martinez W RSC 1 Tijuana
07.08.81 Jesus Lara W RSC 2 Culiacan
31.08.81 Daniel Felizardo W CO 3 Tijuana
25.09.81 Jorge Ramirez W CO 2 Culiacan
19.10.81 Jose Medina W CO 6 Tijuana
18.12.81 Manuel Vasquez W RSC 7 Culiacan
12.01.82 Ramon Lucas W CO 1 Tijuana

Julio Cesar Chavez
Christopher M. Farina

29.01.82 Jesus Garcia W RSC 2 Guamuchil
04.02.82 Ramon Peraza W CO 1 Tijuana
19.02.82 Carlos Bryant W CO 2 Culiacan
11.03.82 Johnny Jensen W CO 3 Tijuana
26.04.82 Ben Abarca W PTS 10 Mexicali
08.05.82 Juan C. Alvarado W CO 3 Culiacan
19.07.82 Gustavo Salgado W CO 2 Tijuana
20.08.82 Santos Rodriguez W RSC 8 Culiacan
28.09.82 Jose Resendez W RSC 6 Tijuana
23.10.82 Jerry Lewis W RSC 5 Tijuana
11.12.82 Jerry Lewis W DIS 6 Sacramento
04.03.83 Otoniel Lopez W CO 5 Ensenada
04.04.83 Ernesto Herrera W CO 2 Tijuana
01.05.83 Javier Fragoso W CO 4 San Juan
15.06.83 Romeo Sandoval W RSC 2 Los Angeles
16.07.83 Ben Abarca W RSC 5 Culiacan
01.09.83 Adrian Arreola W PTS 10 Los Angeles
30.12.83 Armando Flores W RSC 3 Mazatlan
04.05.84 Ramon Avitia W CO 6 Culiacan
13.07.84 Delfino Martinez W CO 3 Hermosillo
13.09.84 Mario Martinez W RSC 8 Los Angeles
(*Vacant WBC S. Featherweight Title*)
01.01.85 Manny Hernandez W RSC 3 Mexico City
19.04.85 Ruben Castillo W RSC 6 Los Angeles
(*WBC S. Featherweight Title Defence*)
07.07.85 Roger Mayweather W RSC 2 Las Vegas
(*WBC S. Featherweight Title Defence*)
22.09.85 Dwight Pratchett W PTS 12 Las Vegas
(*WBC S. Featherweight Title Defence*)
19.12.85 Jeff Bumphus W TD 5 Los Angeles
22.03.86 Roberto Collins W CO 2 Las Vegas
15.05.86 Faustino Barrios W RSC 5 Paris
(*WBC S. Featherweight Title Defence*)
13.06.86 Refugio Rojas W RSC 7 New York
(*WBC S. Featherweight Title Defence*)
03.08.86 Rocky Lockridge W PTS 12 Monte Carlo
(*WBC S. Featherweight Title Defence*)
12.12.86 Juan Laporte W PTS 12 New York
(*WBC S. Featherweight Title Defence*)
18.04.87 Francisco Tomas Cruz W RSC 3 Nimes
(*WBC S. Featherweight Title Defence*)
21.08.87 Danilo Cabrera W PTS 12 Tijuana
(*WBC S. Featherweight Title Defence*)
21.11.87 Edwin Rosario W RSC 11 Las Vegas
(*WBA Lightweight Title Challenge*)
05.03.88 Nicky Perez W RSC 3 Tijuana
16.04.88 Rodolfo Aguilar W RSC 6 Las Vegas
(*WBA Lightweight Title Defence*)
04.06.88 Rafael Limon W RSC 7 Mazatlan
01.08.88 Vernon Buchanan W RSC 3 Los Angeles
29.10.88 Jose Luis Ramirez W TD 11 Las Vegas
(*WBC Lightweight Title Challenge & WBA Lightweight Title Defence*)
Summary: 61 contests, won 61.

Yun-Un Chin
Chunnam, South Korea. *Born* 11.07.67
Flyweight

01.06.85 Won-Ho Lee W CO 1 Inchon
29.06.85 In-Kwang Kang W CO 3 Seoul
13.12.85 In-Kwang Kang W PTS 6 Taegu
31.05.86 Hyun-Jong Yuh W PTS 6 Buchon
26.07.86 Jong-Ku Lee W CO 1 Osan
17.10.86 Byung-Kap Kim W PTS 8 Suwon
22.02.87 Nam-Chul Kim W PTS 8 Seoul
18.04.87 Hi-Chul Kim W RSC 2 Jumchon
14.06.87 Jae-Ki Lee W RSC 2 Bukok
04.07.87 Petchainat Donjadee W PTS 10 Masan
30.08.87 No-Song Chae W RSC 2 Kumi
31.10.87 Yeunyong Sithprasong W PTS 10 Jochiwon
10.01.88 Romeo Opriasa W PTS 10 Pusan
09.04.88 Seung-Yap Kang W RSC 1 Jinju
05.06.88 Yong-Ki Chi W RSC 4 Ulsan
21.08.88 Chan-Woo Yang W RSC 7 Seoul
04.12.88 Dae-Chul Chun W CO 2 Kwangju
01.03.89 Jesus Rojas W PTS 10 Seoul
Summary: 18 contests, won 18.

Sot Chitalada
Thailand. *Born* 24.05.62
Former WBC Flyweight Champion

05.12.82 Srithunchai Sithsanae W CO 2 Bangkok
23.01.83 Suriya Pratumvadee W PTS 6 Bangkok
18.12.83 Niphonyuth Sakadam W CO 3 Bangkok
30.01.84 Jownaranoi Chomkatha W CO 2 Bangkok
31.03.84 Jung-Koo Chang L PTS 12 Pusan
(*WBC L. Flyweight Title Challenge*)
05.06.84 Wick Tengam W RSC 6 Bangkok
02.07.84 Rudy Palicua W RSC 7 Bangkok
08.10.84 Gabriel Bernal W PTS 12 Bangkok
(*WBC Flyweight Title Challenge*)
20.02.85 Charlie Magri W RTD 4 London
(*WBC Flyweight Title Defence*)
22.06.85 Gabriel Bernal DREW 12 Bangkok
(*WBC Flyweight Title Defence*)
22.02.86 Freddie Castillo W PTS 12 Kuwait
(*WBC Flyweight Title Defence*)
30.08.86 Moon-Jim Choi W RSC 9 Bangkok
12.10.86 Narkalart Kiatsontaya W CO 2 Bangkok
10.12.86 Gabriel Bernal W PTS 12 Bangkok
(*WBC Flyweight Title Defence*)
05.09.87 Rae-Ki Ahn W CO 4 Bangkok
(*WBC Flyweight Title Defence*)
31.01.88 Hideaki Kamishiro W RSC 7 Osaka
(*WBC Flyweight Title Defence*)
23.07.88 Yong-Kang Kim L PTS 12 Pohang
(*WBC Flyweight Title Defence*)

30.12.88 Nelson Cabig W RSC 9 Bangkok
28.02.89 Boy Selda W RSC 6 Bangkok
Summary: 20 contests, won 17, drew 1, lost 2.

Chang-Ho Choi

South Korea. *Born* 10.02.64
Former IBF Flyweight Champion. Former Undefeated South Korean Flyweight Champion

01.12.82 Chang-Yung Chung L PTS 4 Seoul
13.07.85 Hwang-Sik Wang W RSC 3 Chungju
22.09.85 Chun-Chi Hyun W PTS 4 Chungju
05.12.85 Ki-Bong Lee W RSC 1 Seoul
08.12.85 Ki-Sang Kim W PTS 4 Seoul
10.12.85 Byung-Nam Park W RSC 3 Seoul
12.01.86 Yung-Hyon Kang W CO 2 Seoul
22.02.86 Chung-Dong Kim W RSC 3 Daejon
13.04.86 Ro-Seung Choi W CO 1 Kwangju
18.05.86 Ha-Sik Lim L PTS 8 Taegu
29.06.86 Chung-Seop Chun W RSC 6 Seoul
02.08.86 Bok-Kyu Choi W RSC 1 Inchon
18.10.86 Chu-Shik Cho W RSC 5 Inchon
14.12.86 Sung-Dae Park W RSC 2 Inchon
22.02.87 Heun-Kuk Chae W PTS 10 Inchon
(*Vacant South Korean Flyweight Title*)
05.09.87 Dodie Penalosa W CO 11 Manila
(*IBF Flyweight Title Challenge*)
16.01.88 Rolando Bohol L PTS 15 Manila
(*IBF Flyweight Title Defence*)
06.08.88 Yung-Woo Chang W CO 4 Jumchon
09.10.88 Kaosai Galaxy L CO 8 Seoul
(*WBA S. Flyweight Title Challenge*)
Summary: 19 contests, won 15, lost 4.

Jum-Hwan Choi

Pusan, South Korea. *Born* 09.06.63
Former IBF L. Flyweight Champion

13.03.83 Chong-Don Kim W PTS 6 Seoul
03.04.83 Sung-Kyu Kim W PTS 6 Seoul
17.04.83 Yong-Soo Kim W PTS 6 Seoul
08.05.83 Won-Soo Chung W PTS 6 Seoul
29.05.83 Hyung-Soo Choi W PTS 6 Seoul
12.06.83 Byung-Dae Yuh W PTS 6 Seoul
10.07.83 Ha-Sik Lim W PTS 8 Seoul
14.08.83 Sung-Kwan Chun W PTS 8 Seoul
23.10.83 Chang-Yung Chang W PTS 10 Seoul
25.12.83 Ha-Sik Lim W PTS 10 Seoul
13.05.84 Jung-Hyun Kim W CO 2 Seoul
15.07.84 Kyung-Jae Chang W PTS 10 Pohang
16.11.84 Dodie Penalosa L PTS 15 Manila
(*IBF L. Flyweight Title Challenge*)
30.03.85 Kyung-Jae Chang W PTS 10 Suwon
23.01.86 Yung-Il Choi W PTS 10 Seoul
07.12.86 Cho-Woon Park W PTS 15 Pusan
(*Vacant IBF L. Flyweight Title*)
29.03.87 Tacy Macalos W PTS 15 Seoul
(*IBF L. Flyweight Title Defence*)
05.07.87 Toshihiko Matsuta W RSC 4 Seoul
(*IBF L. Flyweight Title Defence*)
09.08.87 Azadin Anhar W RSC 3 Jakarta
(*IBF L. Flyweight Title Defence*)
30.01.88 Rolando Pascua W PTS 10 Masan
05.11.88 Tacy Macalos L PTS 12 Manila
(*IBF L. Flyweight Title Defence*)
Summary: 21 Contests, won 19, lost 2.

Chil-Sung Chun

Sinan, South Korea. *Born* 07.07.61
Lightweight

01.03.86 Chong-Ha Chin W CO 3 Mokpo
28.06.86 Oh-Yong Kim W CO 2 Kunsan
26.07.86 Thungberm Lukmatulee W CO 3 Osan
17.10.86 Lulu Villaverde W PTS 10 Hongchun
17.01.87 Ayuthaya Sithphakamron W CO 1 Hongchun
04.03.87 Louis Ilago W CO 8 Chunchon
14.06.87 Darryl Tyson W PTS 10 Bukok
30.08.87 Yoshimitsu Azato W TD 4 Kumi
08.10.87 Rico Velasquez L RTD 4 Los Angeles
20.12.87 Juhari W PTS 10 Pyongtaek
26.03.88 Leo Sabanal W RSC 3 Seoul
05.06.88 Samon Donjadee W CO 3 Ulsan
27.11.88 Superboy Eakvat W RSC 4 Seoul
19.02.89 Lulu Villaverde W CO 3 Taejon
30.04.89 Rafael Limon W PTS 10 Jinju
Summary: 15 contests, won 14, lost 1.

Bi-Won Chung

South Korea. *Born* 15.01.60
Former IBF Flyweight Champion. Former South Korean L. Flyweight Champion

28.02.82 Soon-Jae Lee W PTS 4 Seoul
28.03.82 Byung-Hwa Chung W RSC 2 Seoul
26.04.82 Keun-Pil Chung W RSC 2 Seoul
21.05.82 Ki-Man Yuh W PTS 4 Seoul
23.05.82 Kang-Hwan Kim W PTS 4 Seoul
24.05.82 Chul Hyun W PTS 4 Seoul
05.06.82 Chong-Bong Choi W PTS 4 Seoul
31.07.82 Ki-Yung Kim W PTS 6 Seoul
31.10.82 Yun-Ree Moon DREW 6 Seoul
22.01.83 Keum-Sup Han W PTS 8 Seoul
19.02.83 Tatsuya Sugi W RTD 5 Seoul
03.04.83 Soon-Yun Mah DREW 10 Seoul
06.05.83 Soon-Yun Mah W CO 8 Seoul
(*South Korean L. Flyweight Title Challenge*)
26.07.83 Jae-Hong Kim L PTS 10 Seoul
(*South Korean L. Flyweight Title Defence*)
29.03.84 Sung-Kyu Kim W PTS 10 Seoul
27.05.84 Myung-Woo Yuh L PTS 10 Seoul
09.07.84 German Torres L PTS 10 Seoul
08.09.84 Dosa Kim L PTS 10 Seoul
08.12.84 Soon-Jung Kang W PTS 10 Chinju
16.02.85 Keum-Sup Han W PTS 10 Seoul
14.04.85 Soon-Jung Kang W PTS 10 Pohang
25.05.85 Benjie Miole W PTS 10 Buhan
20.10.85 Boy Samson W CO 2 Nonsan
28.12.85 Oh-Kong Son W PTS 10 Suwon
27.04.86 Chong-Kwan Chung W PTS Pusan
(*IBF Flyweight Title Challenge*)
02.08.86 Hi-Sup Shin L RSC 15 Inchon
(*IBF Flyweight Title Defence*)
20.12.86 Rolando Protacio W RSC 5 Seoul
14.03.87 Ronnie Vallescas W CO 3 Chunchon
27.06.87 Downrung Technicutaradit W PTS 10 Chochiwon
13.09.87 Chung-Sup Chun W CO 4 Jinju
20.12.87 Ritchai Lukmingkwan W RSC 8 Pyungtaek
21.02.88 Den Chuwatana W PTS 10 Seoul
05.06.88 Min-Woong Suh W PTS 10 Ulsan
02.09.88 Dodie Penalosa L PTS 10 Manila
29.01.89 Yung-Ki Chung W CO 7 Pohang
Summary: 35 contests, won 27, drew 2, lost 6.

Hi-Yun Chung

South Korea
OPBF S. Bantamweight Champion. Former Undefeated South Korean S. Flyweight & S. Bantamweight Champion

02.12.81 Hyo-Myung Yuh L PTS 4 Seoul
21.02.82 Sun-Bin Lim W PTS 4 Seoul
07.03.82 Yun Young W PTS 4 Seoul
23.05.82 Choon-Sung Yuh W PTS 4 Seoul
25.05.82 Cha-Suk Oh W PTS 4 Seoul
05.06.82 Rang-Soo Park W PTS 4 Seoul
31.07.82 Yun-Kap Choi W PTS 6 Seoul
19.10.82 Chong-Hyuk Lim W PTS 6 Seoul
27.11.82 Yuerk Choo W PTS 8 Seoul
26.12.82 Ok-Kyun Yuh W PTS 10 Seoul
(*South Korean S. Flyweight Title Challenge*)
27.02.83 Jae-Myung Choi DREW 10 Seoul
(*South Korean S. Flyweight Title Defence*)
06.05.83 Diego de Villa W CO 8 Seoul
26.06.83 Joo-Do Chun L PTS 10 Seoul
(*South Korean S. Flyweight Title Defence*)
03.09.83 Ho-Chung Kim W PTS 8 Seoul
26.11.83 Baek-Man Lee W PTS 10 Seoul
05.02.84 Kyu-Chan Cho W PTS 10 Seoul
(*South Korean S. Flyweight Title Challenge*)
25.03.84 Hyung-Sik Lim DREW 10 Seoul
(*South Korean S. Flyweight Title Defence*)
19.05.84 Elly Pical L TD 4 Seoul
(*OPBF S. Flyweight Title Challenge*)
29.11.85 Tae-Yul Suh W CO 4 Chungju
18.01.86 Yung-Kil Choi W PTS 8 Seoul
14.06.86 Hong-Kyu Yang W CO 2 Inchon
17.08.86 Kyu-Chang Cho DREW 10 Seoul
07.11.86 Hun-Yung Park W PTS 10 Seoul
(*South Korean S. Bantamweight Title Challenge*)
27.12.86 Jung-Man Park W PTS 10 Taeju
(*South Korean S. Bantamweight Title Defence*)
24.03.87 Prayoonsak Muangsurin W TD 7 Samutprakarn
(*OPBF S. Bantamweight Title Challenge*)
16.05.87 Joe Hiyas L PTS 12 Manila
(*Vacant WBC International S. Bantamweight Title*)
18.07.87 Flash Emmanuel W TD 6 Boeun
(*OPBF S. Bantamweight Title Defence*)
24.10.87 Takashi Shuto W CO 5 Joungsun
(*OPBF S. Bantamweight Title Defence*)
13.02.88 Chung-Woo Park DREW 12 Seoul
(*OPBF S. Bantamweight Title Defence*)
17.07.88 Chae-Dong Lim W PTS 10 Seoul
11.02.89 Yung-Duk Park W CO 2 Jongju
(*OPBF S. Bantamweight Title Defence*)
Summary: 31 contests, won 23, drew 4, lost 4.

Soon-Yong Chung

Kyungki-do, South Korea. *Born* 03.04.65
Former OPBF L. Flyweight Champion. Former Undefeated South Korean L. Flyweight Champion

12.06.83 Sang-Ku Han W PTS 4 Seoul
31.07.83 Seung-Hyun Kwak W PTS 4 Seoul
03.09.83 Jin-Sin Lee W RSC 3 Seoul
25.09.83 Uk-Ki Cho W RSC 2 Seoul
23.10.83 Ji-Ok Kim W PTS 4 Seoul
10.12.83 Chang-Ho Chun W PTS 4 Seoul
12.12.83 Kyung-Tae Chun W PTS 4 Seoul
14.12.83 Hong-Ki Lee W PTS 4 Seoul
16.12.83 Sung-Jae Kim W PTS 6 Seoul
07.01.84 Cho-Woon Park L PTS 4 Seoul
08.03.87 Hyun-Chong Yuh W PTS 8 Seoul
17.05.87 Dae-Chul Chun W PTS 8 Pusan
13.06.87 Chung-Yul Son DREW 8 Chungju
30.08.87 Myung-Kyu Lee W PTS 10 Kumi
21.11.87 Min-Woong Suh DREW 10 Uijungbu
23.04.88 Chang-Woo Hong W RSC 2 Buchun
(*South Korean L. Flyweight Title Challenge*)
14.08.88 Sonny Vidal W RSC 9 Seoul
(*Vacant OPBF L. Flyweight Title*)
12.11.88 Azadin Anhar W RSC 1 Chungju
(*OPBF L. Flyweight Title Defence*)
29.01.89 Thanjai Donjaedee W CO 5 Pohang
(*OPBF L. Flyweight Title Defence*)
16.04.89 Den Chuwatana L PTS 12 Pohang
(*OPBF L. Flyweight Title Defence*)
Summary: 20 contests, won 16, drew 2, lost 2.

Yung-Kil Chung

South Korea. *Born* 08.09.63
Former Undefeated South Korean & OPBF Welterweight Champion

26.12.81 Ki-Nak Jung W PTS 4 Seoul
14.02.82 Jae-Hyung Lim W PTS 4 Daejon
15.04.82 Seung-Ho Kim DREW 6 Ulsan
19.06.82 Dong-Uwn Shin L PTS 8 Seoul
04.09.82 Hwa-Young Song DREW 4 Taegu
10.12.82 Byung-Soon Yuh W RSC 5 Chungju
05.02.83 Yung-Man Park W PTS 8 Daejon
21.05.83 Dong-Bok Lee W RSC 2 Seoul
17.06.83 Seung-Soon Lee L PTS 10 Seoul
(*South Korean Welterweight Title Challenge*)
03.09.83 Ki-Hae Song W RSC 5 Seoul
13.11.83 Chong-Won Park W RSC 5 Juju
05.02.84 Seung-Soon Lee L PTS 10 Seoul
(*South Korean Welterweight Title Challenge*)
21.03.84 Chong-Won Park W CO 6 Pusan
19.05.84 Tae-Wang Kang W PTS 10 Daejon
18.11.84 Jae-Young Park W CO 4 Daejon
(*Vacant South Korean Welterweight Title*)
19.01.85 Kang-Chul Choi W RSC 5 Taegu
(*South Korean Welterweight Title Defence*)
14.04.85 Young-Bae Lee W PTS 10 Pohang
(*South Korean Welterweight Title Defence*)
17.07.85 Kyung-Shik Park W RSC 7 Masan
(*South Korean Welterweight Title Defence*)
27.10.85 Joo-Kwan Chung W PTS 10 Pusan
(*South Korean Welterweight Title Defence*)
29.11.85 Young-Bae Lee W CO 10 Chungju
(*South Korean Welterweight Title Defence*)
16.02.86 Kyung-Shik Park W CO 6 Ulsan
(*South Korean Welterweight Title Defence*)
27.04.86 Kang-Chul Choi W CO 4 Pusan
(*South Korean Welterweight Title Defence*)
27.07.86 Youg-Chul Park W RSC 6 Hongchun
(*South Korean Welterweight Title Defence*)

18.10.86 In-Son Kim W CO 7 Inchon
(South Korean Welterweight Title Defence)
31.01.87 Noli Deguia W CO 1 Sungjung
29.03.87 Seung-Soon Lee W PTS 12 Wonju
(OPBF Welterweight Title Challenge)
13.06.87 Francisco Ferrer W PTS 12 Chungju
(OPBF Welterweight Title Defence)
23.08.87 Noboyuki Tabata W RSC 9 Jumchon
(OPBF Welterweight Title Defence)
14.11.87 Arman Pecar W CO 4 Seoul
(OPBF Welterweight Title Defence)
12.03.88 Rolando Ferrer W CO 3 Samchunpo
29.07.88 Lloyd Honeghan L RSC 5 Atlantic City
(WBC Welterweight Title Challenge)
15.01.89 Francisco Ferrer W RSC 10 Seoul
Summary: 32 contests, won 26, drew 2, lost 4.

Den Chuwatana
Thailand
OPBF L. Flyweight Champion & Former Undefeated Thai L. Flyweight Champion

30.09.87 Petchchainart Donjaedee W PTS 6 Bangkok
05.11.87 Kwanchai Sorpoonpit W PTS 6 Bangkok
21.02.88 Bi-Won Chung L PTS 10 Seoul
27.04.88 Yoen Yong Sithprasong W PTS 6 Bangkok
13.10.88 Sakchai Kiatsontaya W CO 2 Bangkok
18.12.88 Mai Thornburifarm W RSC 2 Bangkok
(Vacant Thai L. Flyweight Title)
16.02.89 Thepitak Sornuchanart W CO 6 Bangkok
16.04.89 Soon-Yong Chung W PTS 12 Pohang
(OPBF L. Flyweight Title Challenge)
Summary: 8 contests, won 7, lost 1.

Richard Clarke

Richard (Shrimpy) Clarke
Jamaica. *Born* 20.04.63
Con. Am. & WBC International Flyweight Champion. Former Undefeated Commonwealth & Fecarbox Flyweight Champion

31.01.81 Alejandro Perez W PTS 6 Kingston
18.05.81 Alejandro Perez W PTS 6 Kingston
16.09.81 Norman Tomlinson W CO 4 Kingston
01.12.81 Jim Bowens W CO 1 Kingston
30.01.82 William Santos W CO 4 Kingston
26.03.82 Pascual Polanco W PTS 6 Kingtson
18.12.82 Juan Bisono L PTS 8 Haiti
26.04.83 Juan Bisono L PTS 8 Haiti
01.12.84 Vicente Arias W PTS 6 Haiti
04.05.85 Alfonso Lopez W PTS 10 Haiti
24.08.85 Kid Macumba W RTD 11 Haiti
(Vacant Fecarbox Flyweight Title)
13.11.85 Bernardo Diaz W PTS 10 Kingston
26.04.86 Wayne Mulholland W CO 4 Kingston
(Vacant Commonwealth Flyweight Title)
04.10.86 Amado Ursua W PTS 10 Kingston
05.12.86 Juan Herrera W PTS 12 Kingston
(Vacant Con. Am. Flyweight Title)
01.05.87 Jimmy Fernandez W PTS 12 Kingston
(Vacant WBC International Flyweight Title)
25.09.87 Prudencio Cardona W PTS 10 Kingston
03.12.87 Julio Gudino W PTS 12 Kingston
(WBC International Flyweight Title Defence)
16.07.88 Abraham Garcia W RSC 3 Kingston
23.02.89 Roy Thompson W PTS 10 Kingston
28.04.89 Rosendo Gonzalez W RSC 7 Kingston
Summary: 21 contests, won 19, lost 2.

Pat Clinton
Croy, Scotland. *Born* 04.04.64
British Flyweight Champion

10.10.85 Gordon Stobie W PTS 6 Alfreton
11.11.85 Tony Rahman W PTS 6 Glasgow
24.02.86 Tony Rahman W PTS 6 Glasgow
29.04.86 Des Gargano W PTS 6 Manchester
09.06.86 George Bailey W CO 2 Glasgow
20.10.86 Ginger Staples W RSC 2 Glasgow
17.11.86 Gypsy Johnny W RSC 5 Glasgow
19.01.87 Sean Casey W CO 6 Glasgow
16.02.87 Des Gargano W PTS 6 Glasgow
14.04.87 Jose Manuel Diaz W RSC 8 Cumbernauld
19.05.87 Miguel Pequeno W CO 4 Cumbernauld
22.09.87 Joe Kelly W RSC 2 London
09.03.88 Joe Kelly W PTS 12 London
(Vacant British Flyweight Title)
16.02.89 Eyup Can L PTS 12 Copenhagen
(Vacant EBU Flyweight Title)
Summary: 14 contests, won 13, lost 1.

Pierre Coetzer
Pretoria, South Africa. *Born* 12.06.61
South African Heavyweight Champion

05.02.83 Isaac Ndlamlege W RSC 1 Johannesburg
14.03.83 Caifas Masondo W CO 2 Durban
23.04.83 Jerry Shezi W PTS 6 Johannesburg
11.06.83 Louis Hendriks W RSC 5 Johannesburg
04.07.83 Ron Ellis W CO 4 Durban
03.09.83 Steve Gee W PTS 8 Johannesburg
28.01.84 Billy Thomas W RSC 5 Johannesburg
31.03.84 Felipe Rodriguez W RSC 2 Johannesburg
18.05.84 Leroy Caldwell W PTS 8 Johannesburg
16.07.84 Bernard Benton L PTS 10 Durban
22.09.84 Bennie Knoetze W CO 3 Johannesburg
(Vacant South African Heavyweight Title)
25.03.85 Mark Lee W PTS 10 Durban
13.05.85 Rick Sekorski W PTS 10 Johannesburg
08.07.85 David Jaco W CO 6 Johannesburg
07.09.85 Dion Simpson W RSC 8 Johannesburg
30.09.85 Larry Frazier W PTS 10 Johannesburg
19.02.86 Young Joe Louis W RSC Johannesburg
02.04.86 Franco Thomas W CO 2 Durban
14.05.86 K. P.Porter W RSC 6 Johannesburg
27.09.86 Luis Lozano W CO 1 Sun City
08.03.87 Chris Jacobs W CO 2 Johannesburg
30.08.87 Alfredo Evangelista W PTS 10 Johannesburg
28.09.87 Bernard Benton W CO 1 Johannesburg
06.03.88 Ossie Ocasio L PTS 19 Cape Town
15.08.88 Tim Anderson W RSC 2 Durban
20.09.88 Manuel de Almeida W RSC 4 Johannesburg
26.11.88 Ossie Ocasio W PTS 10 Johannesburg
11.02.89 Mike White W CO 8 Johannesburg
18.03.89 James Pritchard W RSC 8 Johannesburg
Summary: 29 contests, won 27, lost 2.

Juan M. (Latigo) Coggi
Rosario, Argentine. *Born* 19.12.61
WBA L. Welterweight Champion. Former Undefeated Argentinian L. Welterweight Champion

02.04.82 Horacio Valdez W CO 4 La Plata
07.05.82 Viterman Sanchez W PTS 6 La Plata
11.06.82 Ramon Gramasco W CO 2 Brandsen
10.09.82 Felipe Baez W RSC 6 Brandsen
22.10.82 Rogelio Florentin W CO 2 Brandsen
12.11.82 Carlos Fallone W RSC 4 Brandsen
10.12.82 Roberto Villalobos W PTS 8 Brandsen
11.02.83 Osvaldo Cobros W CO 1 Brandsen
08.04.83 Carlos Fallone W CO 7 J C Paz
18.05.83 Apolinario Romero W PTS 10 Buenos Aires
15.06.83 Sergio Brites W CO 2 Buenos Aires
14.10.83 Anibal Ozuna W PTS 10 La Plata
09.11.83 Apolinario Romero W PTS 10 Buenos Aires
07.12.83 Anibal Ozuna W CO 2 Buenos Aires
23.12.83 Romulo Ibarra W PTS 10 Brandsen
10.02.84 Marcelo Villagra W PTS 10 Las Flores
09.03.84 Ricardo Espinoza W PTS 10 Mar del Plata
23.06.84 Ricardo Espinoza W RSC 2 Buenos Aires
10.08.84 Pedro A. Gutierrez W CO 1 La Plata
01.09.84 Ramon Collado W PTS 10 Buenos Aires
11.11.84 Marcelo Villagra W PTS 10 San Juan
22.02.85 Miguel Pereyra W PTS 10 Mar del Plata
09.03.85 Adolfo Rossi L PTS 10 Buenos Aires
11.05.85 Ramon Jara W CO 7 Buenos Aires
20.06.85 Ramon Collado DREW 10 Las Flores
03.08.85 Miguel Pereyra W RTD 7 Buenos Aires
31.08.85 Oscar Sosa W RTD 7 Rojas
26.10.85 Ruben Verdun W TD 7 Rojas
07.03.86 Sergio Brites W CO 5 Mar del Plata
05.04.86 Edecio Molina W PTS 10 Buenos Aires
14.06.86 Jose Saldivia W CO 2 Santa Maria
19.07.86 Ramon Collado DREW 10 La Plata
25.10.86 Hugo Hernandez W CO 3 Buenos Aires
(Argentinian L. Welterweight Title Challenge)
04.04.87 Jose Magarinos W CO 5 General Roca
04.07.87 Patrizio Oliva W CO 3 Ribera
(WBA L. Welterweight Title Challenge)
19.02.88 Mario Araya W CO 6 Catamarca
07.05.88 Sang-Ho Lee W CO 2 Roseto
(WBA L. Welterweight Title Defence)
12.08.88 Osvaldo Maldonado W RTD 6 Trelew
14.10.88 Jorge Tejeda W PTS 10 Guernica
02.12.88 Jorge Tejeda W PTS 10 Mar del Plata
21.01.89 Harold Brazier W PTS 12 Vasto
(WBA L. Welterweight Title Defence)
25.02.89 Raul Bianco W CO 2 Villa Carlos Paz
29.04.89 Akinobu Hiranaka W PTS 12 Vasto
(WBA L. Welterweight Title Defence)
Summary: 43 contests, won 40, drew 2, lost 1.

Juan M. Coggi

George Collins
Camberley, England. *Born* 07.10.67
Welterweight

20.02.85 Bobby Welburn W RSC 2 London
24.04.85 Andy Roberts W RSC 3 London
11.05.85 Lee Woolis W PTS 4 Hastings
28.05.85 Tim Gladwish W RSC 2 London
18.09.85 Ray Price W PTS 4 London
12.10.85 Vince Stewart W RSC 5 Birmingham
26.10.85 Andre Kimbu W PTS 6 Monte Carlo
21.11.85 Mickey Bird W RSC 5 Huddersfield
05.12.85 Geoff Pegler W CO 1 Digbeth
22.01.86 Andres Uribe W RSC 1 London
20.02.86 Mark Davey W RSC 5 Halifax
19.03.86 Hector Perez CO 1 London
01.04.86 George Kerr W PTS 8 Leeds
30.04.86 Lenny Gloster W PTS 8 London
28.05.86 Dennis Sigouin W PTS 8 London
10.09.86 Mark Brawood W PTS 8 London
09.10.86 Teddy Johnson W CO 1 Croydon
04.11.86 Del Bryan W RSC 4 Oldham
27.01.87 Ariel Conde W RSC 2 Glasgow
04.03.87 Carlos Hernandez W CO 1 Basildon
22.04.87 Thomas Garcia W RSC 5 London
09.05.87 Tony Brown W RSC 5 London
17.06.87 Don Vanarva W CO 2 London
01.07.87 Ray Coleman W RSC 5 London
09.08.87 Jimmy Thornton W RSC 1 Windsor
22.09.87 Larry Nichols W RSC 2 London
13.10.87 Kehevan Johnson W CO 2 Windsor
02.12.87 Frankie Lake W RSC 1 London
12.01.88 Luciano Fernandez W RSC 1 Cardiff
09.02.88 Ian Chantler W PTS 8 London
12.04.88 Sammy Floyd W PTS 8 Cardiff
25.06.88 Jamie Ollenburger W RSC 6 Luton
07.09.88 Juan Rondon W RSC 5 Reading
14.12.88 Chris Blake W PTS 8 London
31.01.89 Frankie Davis W PTS 8 Reading
05.04.89 Gary Jacobs L PTS 12 London
(Commonwealth & WBC International Welterweight Title Challenge)
Summary: 36 contests, won 35, lost 1.

Steve Collins
Brockton, USA. *Born* Ireland 21.07.64
Irish Middleweight Champion

24.10.86 Julio Mercado W RSC 3 Lowell
26.11.86 Mike Bonislawski W PTS 4 Dorchester
20.12.86 Dick Hollaway W RSC 2 Dorchester
10.10.87 Jim Holmes W CO 1 Attleboro
29.10.87 Harold Souther W PTS 8 Lowell
20.11.87 Mike Williams W PTS 6 Atlantic City
09.12.87 Benny Simms W PTS 8 Atlantic City
18.03.88 Sammy Storey W PTS 10 Boston
(Irish Middleweight Title Challenge)
26.05.88 Lester Yarbrough W PTS 10 Boston
30.07.88 Mike Dale W PTS 8 Brockton
22.10.88 Muhammad Shabbaz W RTD 3 Salem
10.12.88 Jesse Lanton W PTS 10 Salem
07.02.89 Paul McPeek W RSC 9 Atlantic City
Summary: 13 contests, won 13.

Tom Collins
Leeds, England. *Born* Curacao 01.07.55
British L. Heavyweight Champion. Former EBU L. Heavyweight Champion

17.01.77 Ginger McIntyre W RSC 2 Birmingham
16.05.77 Mick Dolan W PTS 6 Manchester
01.06.77 Johnny Cox W CO 3 Dudley
23.11.77 George Gray W RSC 3 Stoke
19.01.78 Clint Jones W RSC 3 London
21.03.78 Joe Jackson W PTS 8 Luton
09.05.78 Harald Skog L PTS 8 Oslo
17.07.78 Karl Canwell L RSC 6 London
28.11.78 Carlton Benoit W CO 1 Sheffield
04.12.78 Dennis Andries L PTS 8 Southend
30.01.79 Dennis Andries L CO 6 Southend
22.10.79 Danny Lawford W RSC 7 Nottingham
28.11.79 Eddie Smith W PTS 8 Solihull
25.02.80 Greg Evans W RSC 1 Bradford
15.04.80 Chris Lawson W RSC 4 Blackpool
04.12.80 Mustafa Wasajja L PTS 8 Randers
09.03.81 Karl Canwell W PTS 10 Bradford
15.03.82 Dennis Andries W PTS 15 London
(Vacant British L. Heavyweight Title)
26.05.82 Trevor Cattouse W CO 4 Leeds
(British L. Heavyweight Title Defence)
07.10.82 John Odhiambo L RSC 5 Copenhagen
09.03.83 Antonio Harris W RSC 6 Solihull
(British L. Heavyweight Title Defence)
09.04.83 Alex Sua W PTS 12 Auckland
17.12.83 Leslie Stewart L PTS 10 Trinidad
26.01.84 Dennis Andries L PTS 12 London
(British L. Heavyweight Title Defence)
06.04.84 Dennis Andries L PTS 12 Watford
(British L. Heavyweight Title Challenge)
21.09.84 Alek Penarski L PTS 8 Alfreton
24.01.85 Jonjo Greene W RSC 7 Manchester
30.03.85 Chisanda Mutti L PTS 10 Dortmund
18.04.85 Andy Straughn L CO 1 Halifax
14.10.85 Harry Cowap W CO 4 London
29.11.85 Ralf Rocchigiani L PTS 8 Frankfurt
20.12.85 Pierre Kabassu DREW 8 Forbach
01.04.86 Winston Burnett W PTS 8 Leeds
19.04.86 Yawe Davis W CO 3 San Remo
01.12.86 Alex Blanchard L PTS 10 Arnhem
11.03.87 John Moody W RSC 10 London
(Vacant British L. Heavyweight Title)
11.11.87 Alex Blanchard W CO 2 Usk
(EBU L. Heavyweight Title Challenge)
11.05.88 Mark Kaylor W CO 9 Wembley
(EBU L. Heavyweight Title Defence)
07.09.88 Pedro van Raamsdonk L RSC 7 Reading
(EBU L. Heavyweight Title Defence)
22.03.89 Tony Wilson W RSC 2 Reading
(British L. Heavyweight Title Challenge)
Summary: 40 contests, won 24, drew 1, lost 15.

Diomedes Colome
Dominican Republic. *Born* 03.05.65
Welterweight

23.12.82 David Rosen W PTS 4 Las Vegas
20.01.83 Tony Montgomery L PTS 4 Los Angeles
24.02.83 Frank White W PTS 4 Los Angeles
24.03.83 Javier Ruiz W CO 2 Los Angeles
03.04.83 Roberto Leyva W CO 2 Phoenix
21.04.83 Raul Nava W RSC 1 Las Vegas
10.05.83 Mike Castro W CO 2 Phoenix
18.06.83 Howard Smith W CO 2 San Carlos
28.07.83 Eddie Wright W RTD 2 Las Vegas
07.08.83 Dexter Smith W PTS 8 Las Vegas
22.12.83 Jesse Ruiz W RSC 5 Las Vegas
20.01.84 Ken Releford W RSC 3 Las Vegas
03.02.84 Reggie Miller W PTS 10 Las Vegas
30.03.84 Gary Baca W RSC 7 Las Vegas
12.06.84 Eric Martin L PTS 12 Las Vegas
09.08.84 Eric Martin W PTS 12 Las Vegas
11.10.84 Clayton Hires W PTS 10 Las Vegas
24.01.85 Anthony Thomas W PTS 8 Las Vegas
08.07.85 Kel Robins W RSC 5 Los Angeles
15.10.85 Derrick Kelly W PTS 10 Los Angeles
17.12.85 Manning Galloway L PTS 12 Los Angeles
11.11.86 Lupe Aquino L CO 5 Las Vegas
16.09.87 Floyd Peavy W RSC 6 Los Angeles
24.11.87 Charles Nwokolo W PTS 10 Los Angeles
02.09.88 Erik Hernandez W PTS 10 Las Vegas
Summary: 25 contests, won 21, lost 4.

Ruben Condori
Salta, Argentine. *Born* 18.03.60
Former Undefeated Argentinian S. Flyweight Champion. Former Argentinian Flyweight Champion. Former Undefeated South American Flyweight Champion

03.06.77 Damian Roman W RSC 3 Salta
05.08.77 Jose Lopez W PTS 6 Salta
19.08.77 Luis Gomez W PTS 6 Salta
02.09.77 Raul Anchanga W CO 1 Salta
23.09.77 Ramon Galarce W PTS 6 Salta
25.11.77 Jose Lopez DREW 8 Salta
17.02.78 Hectori Patri DREW 6 Salta
03.03.78 Roberto Sosa W RTD 4 Salta
07.04.78 Carlos Cortes W PTS 6 Salta
12.05.78 Jose Gutierrez W RSC 3 Salta
07.07.78 Cisco Altamirano W PTS 10 Salta
01.09.78 Luis Gomez W RSC 6 Salta
20.10.78 Jorge Mansilla W RSC 6 Salta
23.03.79 Ric Gomez W PTS 10 Salta
11.05.79 Jose Narvaez L PTS 10 La Rioja
02.06.79 Marino Suarez L PTS 10 General Pico
27.07.79 Domingo Aragon DREW 10 Rosario
28.09.79 Enrique Navarro W CO 3 Salta
19.10.79 Adrian Roman L TD 7 Cordoba
16.11.79 Hector Velasquez W PTS 10 Salta
07.12.79 Jose Ibiris W PTS 10 Salta
28.12.79 Jose Ibiris W PTS 10 Salta
18.01.80 Raul Perez W PTS 10 Salta
29.02.80 Rodolfo Rodriguez W PTS 10 Salta
28.03.80 Santos Laciar DREW 10 Cordoba
19.04.80 Adrian Roman DREW 10 Buenos Aires
16.05.80 Domingo Aragon W PTS 10 Salta
06.06.80 Jorge O. Aguilar W PTS 10 Salta
01.08.80 Miguel Lazarte W PTS 10 Salta
05.09.80 Paulo Ribeiro W PTS 10 Salta
24.10.80 Hector Barreto W PTS 10 Salta
12.12.80 Erik Vanegas W CO 4 San Pedro
15.01.81 Hector Patri T DRAW 3 Salta
18.02.81 Miguel Lazarte W PTS 10 Salta
27.02.81 Jorge Chavarria W PTS 10 Salta
16.04.81 Alfonso Lopez DREW 10 Salta
15.05.81 Felix Colman W PTS 10 Salta
04.09.81 Juan Rios W RSC 8 Salta
18.09.81 Santos Laciar DREW 10 Cordoba
09.10.81 Adrian Roman W PTS 12 Salta
(Vacant Argentinian Flyweight Title)
06.11.81 Miguel Lazarte W PTS 10 Salta
19.02.82 Adrian Roman L PTS 10 Cordoba
23.04.82 Miguel Lazarte W PTS 10 Salta
21.05.82 Domingo Aragon W PTS 10 Salta
10.09.82 Adrian Roman L RSC 7 Salta
(Argentinian Flyweight Title Defence)
17.12.82 Ramon Albers L PTS 10 Concordia
03.02.83 Felix Colman W PTS 10 Posadas
14.03.83 Welile Nkosinkulu L PTS 10 Cape Town
20.05.83 Ramon Albers W PTS 10 Salta
19.06.83 Alberto Pacheco W PTS 10 Salta
30.06.83 Jaime Miranda W PTS 12 Salta
(Vacant South American Flyweight Title)
07.10.83 Alberto Pacheco DREW 10 Reconquista
30.12.83 Adrian Roman W PTS 12 Salta
(South American Flyweight Title Defence)
10.02.84 Ramon Rodriguez W RTD 8 Jujuy
16.03.84 Adrian Roman L PTS 12 Cordoba
(Argentinian Flyweight Title Challenge)
18.04.84 Ramon Albers DREW 10 Concordia
31.08.84 Hector Fernandez W RSC 6 Salta
09.10.84 Jose Cufre W PTS 10 Salta
17.01.85 Raul Perez W RSC 6 Salta
05.02.85 Jaime Loyola W PTS 10 Salta
08.03.85 Adrian Roman W PTS 10 Salta
29.03.85 Armando Romero W PTS 10 Salta
17.05.85 Gustavo Ballas L PTS 10 Villa Maria
14.06.85 Ramon Albers W PTS 10 Salta
05.07.85 Jose Cufre W CO 10 Salta
09.08.85 Jose Cufre L PTS 10 Villa Maria
04.10.85 Alberto Pacheco W PTS 10 Salta
22.11.85 Jose Narvaez W PTS 10 Salta
13.12.85 Lucio Lopez W PTS 10 Salta
12.02.86 Juan Ivalo W RSC 7 Salta
14.03.86 Memo Manrique W RTD 5 Salta
11.04.86 Gustavo Ballas W PTS 12 Salta
(Argentinian S. Flyweight Title Challenge)
16.05.86 Hector Patri W PTS 10 Salta
18.07.86 Gilberto Roman L PTS 12 Salta
(WBC S. Flyweight Title Challenge)
04.10.86 Lucio Lopez L PTS 10 Buenos Aries
08.11.86 Lucio Lopez DREW 10 Corrientes
06.12.86 Gustavo Ballas L PTS 12 Buenos Aires
(South American S. Flyweight Title Challenge)
14.02.87 Luis Ocampo W RSC 11 Posadas
(Argentinian S. Flyweight Title Defence)
03.04.87 Guillermo Manrique W RTD 6 Salta
15.05.87 Jose Badilla W PTS 10 Salta
13.06.87 Gustavo Ballas W PTS 10 Buenos Aires
04.09.87 Francisco Quiroz W PTS 10 Salta
04.12.87 Juan Cortes W PTS 10 Salta
23.01.88 Oscar Vergara W CO 3 Salta
29.04.88 Nelson Urlich W RTD 7 Tartagal
01.07.88 Carlos Salazar W PTS 10 Tartagal
27.08.88 Nelson Urlich W RTD 3 La Paz
06.10.88 Juan Garcia W CO 4 Villazon
02.12.88 Lucio Lopez W PTS 10 Salta
23.12.88 Juan Cortes DREW 10 Salta
11.02.89 Adrian Roman L PTS 10 Villa Carlos Paz
Summary: 91 contests, won 65, drew 12, lost 14.

Israel Contreras
Guiria Venezuela. *Born* 27.12.60
Venezuelan & WBO Bantamweight Champion

17.07.81 Marcelino Gonzalez W CO 1 La Victoria
23.08.81 Henry Mejias W RSC 2 Valencia
19.10.81 Orlando Reyes W PTS 4 Caracas
23.11.81 Jose Villegas W RSC 4 Valencia
15.12.81 Manuel Gonzalez W RSC 1 Carupano
24.04.82 Jose Vasquez W RSC 3 Cumana
05.07.82 Francisco Quiroz W PTS 10 Caracas
09.08.82 Jose Noguera W RSC 4 Porlamar
27.09.82 Magno Carmona W PTS 10 Barquisimeto
08.11.82 Dok-Yuk Chan W RSC 6 Caracas
29.11.82 Dorismel Zuniga W CO 1 Caracas
31.01.83 Jun Resma W PTS 10 Caracas
28.02.83 Jorge Mayorga W CO 1 Barquisimeto
16.05.83 Magno Carmona W CO 6 Caracas
28.11.83 Bernardo Diaz W PTS 10 Caracas
13.02.84 Jesus Bisono W CO 1 Caracas
27.05.84 Valerio Zea W RSC 3 Maracaibo
18.08.84 Jose Chacon DREW 10 Panama City
02.02.85 William Ramos W RSC 1 Hato Rey
30.03.85 Felix Marquez W CO 1 Aruba
29.06.85 Hector Martinez W PTS 10 Curacao
28.09.85 Jesus Flores W CO 1 Margarita
31.01.86 Juan Muriel W RSC 1 Turmedo
22.02.86 Freddy Pitalua W CO 2 Caracas
22.03.86 Miguel Perez W RSC 1 Macuto
01.11.86 Kaosai Galaxy L CO 5 Curacao
(WBA S. Flyweight Title Challenge)
13.02.87 Elvis Alvarez L PTS 10 Barranquilla
08.08.87 Oscar Bolivar W PTS 10 Caracas
18.09.87 Ali Camacho W PTS 12 Caraballera
(Vacant Venezuelan Bantamweight Title)
09.05.88 Oscar Bolivar W PTS 10 Curacao
29.07.88 Edwin Rangel W CO 2 La Guaira
09.09.88 Eduardo Valdez W RSC 1 Monteria
08.10.88 Franciso Quiroz W RSC 1 Maiquetia
03.02.89 Maurizio Lupino W CO 1 Caracas
(Vacant WBO Bantamweight Title)
Summary: 34 contests, won 31, drew 1, lost 2.

(Smokin') Bert Cooper
Philadelphia, USA. *Born* 10.01.66
Former NABF Cruiserweight Champion

11.09.84 Dennis Caldwell W CO 1 Altantic City
30.10.84 Mark Young W CO 2 Altantic City
24.11.84 Ian Priest W RSC 1 Gateshead
23.02.85 Alvin Fuggs W CO 1 Atlantic City
18.04.85 Lorenzo Boyd W CO 1 Monroe
09.05.85 Jim Jones W CO 1 Atlantic City
20.05.85 Larry Givens W RSC 3 Reno

Bert Cooper (left) on the way to stopping Tony Fulilangi, March, 1988

Christopher M. Farina

03.08.85 Tim Davenport W RSC 1 Scranton
09.10.85 Ray Davison W PTS 6 Atlantic City
11.12.85 Cedric Parsons W CO 1 Altantic City
31.01.86 Reggie Gross L RSC 8 Atlantic City
18.04.86 Oscar Holman W RSC 10 Atlantic City
15.06.86 Henry Tillman W PTS 12 Atlantic City (*NABF Cruiserweight Title Challenge*)
26.08.86 Tyrone Booze W PTS 12 Stateline (*NABF Cruiserweight Title Defence*)
10.10.86 Spencer Chavis W CO 3 Las Vegas ((*NABF Cruiserweight Title Defence*)
02.12.86 Carlos Hernandez W RSC 8 Atlantic City
14.02.87 Willie de Wit W RSC 2 Regina
21.06.87 Carl Williams L RTD 7 Atlantic City (*Vacant USBA Heavyweight Title*)
20.11.87 Andre McCall W RSC 6 Atlantic City (*NABF Cruiserweight Title Defence*)
04.12.87 Tim Bullock W RSC 3 Altantic City
19.03.88 Tony Fulilangi W RSC 4 Las Vegas (*NABF Cruiserweight Title Defence*)
01.06.88 Everett Martin L PTS 10 Atlantic City
27.09.88 Tony Morrison W RSC 9 Halifax (*NABF Cruiserweight Title Defence*)
15.02.89 Nate Miller L RTD 6 Philadelphia (*NABF Cruiserweight Title Defence*)
Summary: 24 contests, won 20, lost 4.

Renato Cornett
New South Wales, Australia. *Born* 12.06.65
Australian S. Featherweight Champion

11.07.86 Bobby Mastro W PTS 8 Edensor Park
01.08.86 Larry Valesini W RSC 2 Dapto
29.08.86 Graeme Jeffries W PTS 10 Edensor Park
18.09.86 Brian Roberts W PTS 10 Homebush
05.02.87 Craig Pevy W PTS 8 Sydney
06.03.87 Percy Israel W PTS 10 Sydney
04.07.87 Steve Assang W CO 4 Seven Hills
07.08.87 Brian Roberts W PTS 10 Blacktown
06.09.87 Gary Clark W CO 2 Fitzroy
19.12.87 Kirk Blair W PTS 10 Edensor Park
12.02.88 Gary Milanes W CO 4 Sydney
28.05.88 Tony Miller W PTS 12 Sydney (*Australian S. Featherweight Title Challenge*)
24.09.88 Geron Porras W TD 5 Parramatta
08.02.89 Benji Marquez W PTS 10 Canberra
05.04.89 Bruno Rabanales DREW 10 Rooty Hill
Summary: 15 contests, won 14, drew 1.

Alberto Cortes
Alta Gracia, Argentine. *Born* 24.09.63
Latin American & Argentinian Lightweight Champion

04.11.83 Victor Casas W RSC 6 Cordoba
18.11.83 Jose Flores W CO 2 Cordoba
02.12.83 Carlos Guayanes W CO 2 Cordoba
23.12.83 Angel Colmenares W CO 3 Alta Gracia
23.03.84 Fidel Rivera W PTS 8 Cordoba
13.04.84 Claudia Alvarez W CO 2 Cordoba
18.05.84 Silverio Villalba W RTD 3 Alta Gracia
08.06.84 Hector Vilte W PTS 10 Cordoba
15.09.84 Carlos Pereyra W PTS 8 Cordoba
19.04.85 Pedro Quiroga W RTD 5 Rio
10.05.85 Norberto Reyna W CO 1 La Rioja
24.05.85 Mario Araya W PTS 10 La Rioja
05.07.85 Juan Maltes W CO 2 La Rioja
19.07.85 Apolinario Romero W RTD 9 La Rioja
09.08.85 Luis Aseguin W RTD 2 Rio Cuarto

Alberto Cortes

06.09.85 Marcelo Romero W PTS 10 La Rioja
20.09.85 Ernesto Rivero W CO 2 Alta Gracia
04.10.85 Hugo Fernandez W PTS 10 Carmen
25.10.85 Sergio Loyola W CO 2 La Rioja
20.12.85 Mario Araya W PTS 10 La Rioja
09.05.86 Ric Espinosa W PTS 10 Cordoba
06.06.86 Miguel Pereyra W PTS 10 Cordoba
19.06.86 Alfredo Chavez W PTS 10 La Rioja
01.08.86 Edecio Molina W RTD 6 Cordoba
30.08.86 Mario Vizcaya W RTD 4 Cordoba
16.10.86 Fernando da Costa W PTS 10 La Rioja
23.12.86 Jorge Gonzalez W PTS 10 La Rioja
12.02.87 Mario Araya W PTS 10 La Rioja
08.05.87 Alberto Vico W PTS 10 Alta Gracia
04.09.87 Oscar Benavidez W CO 4 La Rioja (*Latin American Lightweight Title Challenge*)
16.10.87 Luis A. Soto W CO 3 La Rioja (*Argentinian Lightweight Title Challenge*)
13.02.88 Jorge Gonzalez W CO 4 Alta Gracia (*Latin American Lightweight Title Defence*)
11.03.88 Miguel Pereyra W PTS 10 Cordoba
22.04.88 Pedro Miranda W CO 3 Cordoba
07.05.88 Miguel Ramirez W RTD 3 Alta Gracia
08.07.88 Julio Melone W RTD 7 Cordoba
06.08.88 Jesus Romero W DIS 9 Buenos Aires (*Argentinian Lightweight Title Defence*)
10.09.88 Geronimo Luquez W PTS 12 Cordoba (*Latin American Lightweight Title Defence*)
15.10.88 Mario Fernandez W PTS 10 Buenos Aires
18.11.88 Nicasio Caceres W PTS 10 Cordoba
17.12.88 Geronimo Luquez W PTS 12 Alta Gracia (*Latin American Lightweight Title Defence*)
23.01.89 Marc Armand W DIS 7 Paris
Summary: 42 contests, won 42.

Hugo Corti
Puerto San Martin, Argentine. *Born* 03.06.63
Argentinian Middleweight Champion

23.08.85 Alberto Heredia W PTS 6 San Nicolas
11.10.85 Francisco Cardozo W RTD 3 Puerto San Martin
09.11.85 Alberto Heredia W RSC 2 Buenos Aires
10.01.86 Daniel Gonzalez W CO 5 Villa Galvez
28.02.86 Juan Ceballos W RTD 8 Bouquet
14.03.86 Ed Contreras W PTS 10 Rosario
11.04.86 Nestor Albarracin W PTS 10 Rosario
05.07.86 Carlos Schultz W PTS 10 San Lorenzo
01.08.86 Vicente Silva W PTS 10 Rosario
05.09.86 Lhis Marquez W PTS 10 Reconquista
07.11.86 Bautista Romero W CO 3 San Genaro
05.12.86 Hugo Vera W RSC 6 Reconquista
14.03.87 Dario Matteoni L PTS 12 Buenos Aires (*Argentinian Middleweight Title Challenge*)
31.07.87 Roberto Ruiz W PTS 10 Buenos Aires
11.12.87 Ed Contreras W PTS 12 Rosario
07.05.88 Dario Matteoni W DIS 6 Boulogne (*Argentinian Middleweight Title Challenge*)
10.09.88 Julio Ravallo W PTS 10 Buenos Aires
17.02.89 Hugo Corro W CO 4 Mar del Plata
28.04.89 Lou Carfaro W RSC 6 Perth
Summary: 19 contests, won 18, lost 1.

Steve (Super Kid) Cruz
Fort Worth, USA. *Born* 02.11.63
Former WBA Featherweight Champion.
Con. Am. Featherweight Champion

29.10.81 Pascual Aranda W CO 1 Fort Worth
02.12.81 Homero Gonzalez W RSC 1 Laredo
15.12.81 Ricky Cortez W CO 1 Lubbock
15.01.82 Jesse Sierra W RSC 5 Fort Worth
13.02.82 Ali Akar W CO 2 Beaumont
26.02.82 Juan Barbosa W RSC 1 San Antonio
10.03.82 Richard Fowler W RSC 2 Lake Charles
09.04.82 Carlos Flores W PTS 8 Fort Worth
26.06.82 Andy Rodriguez W CO 2 Fort Worth
14.07.82 Ed Richardson W RSC 1 Fort Worth
01.08.82 Javier Barajas W PTS 8 San Antonio
22.10.82 Nicky Perez W PTS 10 Fort Worth
15.07.83 Rey Garza W PTS 8 Fort Worth
28.07.83 Jose Resendez W PTS 8 Fort Worth
25.08.83 Salvadore Ugalde W PTS 8 Las Vegas
13.10.83 Angel Hernandez W RSC 1 Dallas
09.11.83 Nicky Perez W PTS 10 Las Vegas
20.01.84 Dana Roston W PTS 10 Las Vegas

Don Curry

Peter Goldfield/USA

21.02.84 Victor Acosta W PTS 10 Dallas
29.03.84 Leonardo Valdez L RSC 1 Las Vegas
16.06.84 Salvador Ugalde W PTS 10 Fort Worth
15.12.84 Jesus Lopez W CO 10 Fort Worth
28.05.85 Jerome Brooks W RSC 3 Fort Worth
22.06.85 Juan Veloz W PTS 10 Atlantic City
04.12.85 Tommy Cordova W RSC 9 Las Vegas
07.02.86 Rocky Garcia W PTS 10 Las Vegas
23.06.86 Barry McGuigan W PTS 15 Las Vegas
(WBA Featherweight Title Challenge)
21.11.86 Roger Arevalo W PTS 10 Fort Worth
06.03.87 Antonio Esparragoza L RSC 12 Fort Worth
(WBA Featherweight Title Defence)
16.08.87 Rogelio Lopez W RSC 6 Fort Worth
18.12.87 Jeff Franklin L PTS 10 Las Vegas
14.06.88 Alfredo Rangel W CO 5 New Orleans
(Vacant Con. Am Featherweight Title)
12.08.88 Fred Adams W CO 4 Pasadena
(Con Am. Featherweight Title Defence)
30.09.88 Amos Cowart W RSC 1 Winter Haven
09.12.88 Martin Galvan W RSC 7 El Paso
Summary: 35 contests, won 32, lost 3.

Don (Lone Star Cobra) Curry
Fort Worth, USA. *Born* 07.09.61
Former WBC L. Middleweight Champion. Former Undefeated USBA L. Middleweight Champion. Former World Welterweight Champion. Former Undefeated NABF & USBA Welterweight Champion

26.12.80 Marty Tinco W CO 1 Las Vegas
16.01.81 Juan Ramirez W RSC 2 San Antonio
26.02.81 Jerry Reyes W RSC 2 Las Vegas
26.03.81 Rigoberto Lopez W RSC 2 Las Vegas
23.04.81 Danny Favela W RSC 5 Fort Worth
28.05.81 Joe Moliere W RSC 1 Las Vegas
02.07.81 Eddie Campbell W RSC 6 Atlantic City
22.08.81 Eddie Casper W CO 1 Las Vegas
29.10.81 Vernon Lewis W RSC 1 Fort Worth
26.11.81 Curtis Ramsey W PTS 10 Las Vegas
10.03.82 Mike Senegal W RSC 10 Lake Charles
04.05.82 Bruce Finch W RSC 4 Las Vegas
(NABF Welterweight Title Challenge)
15.06.82 Jake Torrance W DIS 4 Nashville
10.07.82 Adolfo Viruet W PTS 10 Atlantic City
23.10.82 Marlon Starling W PTS 12 Atlantic City
(NABF Welterweight Title Defence & USBA Welterweight Title Challenge)
13.02.83 Jun-Sok Hwang W PTS 15 Fort Worth
(Vacant WBA Welterweight Title)
03.09.83 Roger Stafford W RSC 1 Marsala
(WBA Welterweight Title Defence)
04.02.84 Marlon Starling W PTS 15 Atlantic City
(WBA Welterweight Title Defence & Vacant IBF Welterweight Title)
21.04.84 Elio Diaz W RTD 7 Fort Worth
(WBA & IBF Welterweight Title Defence)
22.09.84 Nino la Rocca W RSC 6 Monte Carlo
(WBA & IBF Welterweight Title Defence)
19.01.85 Colin Jones W RSC 4 Birmingham
(WBA & IBF Welterweight Title Defence)
30.03.85 James Green W RSC 2 Dallas
22.06.85 Pablo Baez W RSC 6 Atlantic City
06.12.85 Milton McCrory W CO 2 Las Vegas
(WBA Welterweight Title Defence & WBC Welterweight Title Challenge)
09.03.86 Eduardo Rodriguez W CO 2 Fort Worth
(WBA Welterweight Title Defence)
27.09.86 Lloyd Honeyghan L RTD 6 Atlantic City
(World Welterweight Title Defence)
07.02.87 Tony Montgomery W DIS 5 Las Vegas
(Vacant USBA L. Middleweight Title)
04.04.87 Carlos Santos W DIS 5 Las Vegas
(USBA L. Middleweight Title Defence)
18.07.87 Mike McCallum L CO 5 Las Vegas
(WBA L. Middleweight Title Challenge)
08.12.87 Rigoberto Lopez W RSC 4 Reseda
03.01.88 Lupe Aquino W PTS 12 Genoa
08.07.88 Gianfranco Rosi W RTD 9 San Remo
(WBC L. Middleweight Title Challenge)
03.01.89 Mike Sacchetti W RSC 5 New Orleans
11.02.89 Rene Jacquot L PTS 12 Grenoble
(WBC L. Middleweight Title Defence)
Summary: 34 contests, won 31, lost 3.

Bobby Czyz (left) left-hooks Leslie Stewart. Bobby won on points in October, 1988, to line up another world title shot

Tom Casino

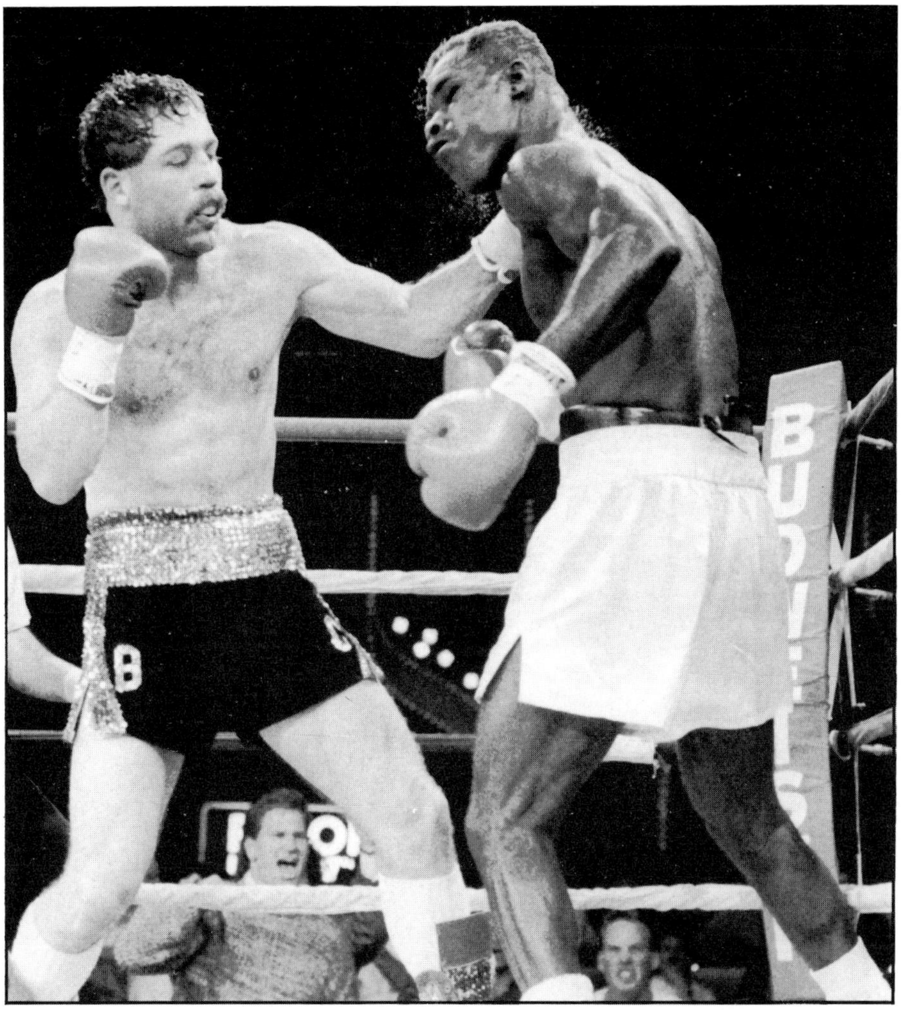

Eric (The Whip) Curry
Detroit, USA. *Born* 17.09.65
Cruiserweight

17.06.82 Ozzie Masters W CO 1 Detroit
05.08.82 Lee Lamphere L PTS 4 Detroit
16.09.82 Bill Hollis W PTS 4 Windsor
28.10.82 Nekoda Leftenant W RSC 1 Oak Park
23.11.83 Leonard Brandon W CO 2 Russellville
08.12.83 Bill Hollis W PTS 4 Detroit
21.12.83 Clarence Johnson W RSC 1 Detroit
07.03.84 Kelly Kroy W RSC 3 Russellville
10.03.84 Bill Hollis W PTS 4 Detroit
10.05.84 Brian Simmons W RSC 5 Allen Park
30.04.85 Danny Smearer W CO 3 Halifax
20.05.86 Dee Collier W PTS 10 Los Angeles
10.07.86 Larry Alexander L PTS 10 Los Angeles
31.03.87 Nick Kendrick W CO 4 Detroit
28.04.87 Ivy Brown W PTS 6 Detroit
11.06.87 John Barbier W RSC 4 Detroit
24.08.87 Mickey Pryor W RSC 5 Louisville
29.09.87 Woody Clark W PTS 10 Detroit
28.01.88 Richard Mason W PTS 10 Detroit
25.05.88 Curtis Isaac W PTS 10 Detroit
23.07.88 Eric Williams W RSC 2 Dearborn
26.10.88 Aaron Brown W RSC 2 Detroit
Summary: 22 contests, won 20, lost 2.

Bobby (Chappie) Czyz
Wanaque, USA. *Born* 20.02.62
Former IBF L. Heavyweight Champion

24.04.80 Hank Whitmore W RSC 1 Totowa
08.05.80 Jamal Abubkarr W PTS 4 Atlantic City
22.05.80 Dalton Swift W RSC 2 Totowa
19.06.80 Ronald Cousins W RSC 1 Totowa
17.07.80 Bruce Strauss W RSC 5 Totowa
21.08.80 Leo Martinez W PTS 8 Totowa
18.09.80 Johnny Davis W RSC 1 Totowa
16.10.80 Tommy Merola W RSC 2 Totowa
18.12.80 Skipper Jones W RSC 7 Totowa
08.02.81 Danny Long W RSC 5 Great Gorge
22.02.81 Teddy Mann W PTS 8 Atlantic City
21.05.81 Oscar Albarado W RSC 3 Totowa
18.06.81 Reggie Jones W RTD 7 Totowa
26.07.81 Rick Noggle W RSC 7 Tampa
08.10.81 Dan Snyder W RSC 2 Totowa
12.11.81 Elisha Obed W DIS 6 East Rutherford
17.01.82 Robbie Sims W PTS 10 Atlantic City
23.05.82 Bob Coolidge W RSC 4 Atlantic City
03.07.82 Manuel Melon W RSC 2 Totowa
25.09.82 Chris Linson W RSC 2 McAfee
20.11.82 Mustafa Hamsho L PTS 10 Atlantic City
09.09.83 Bert Lee W RSC 2 Las Vegas
25.10.83 Bill Medei W RSC 4 Atlantic City
15.02.84 Jim Baker W RSC 1 Totowa
30.05.84 Mark Frazie W PTS 10 Atlantic City
25.10.84 Marvin Mack W PTS 10 Totowa
18.01.85 Tim Broady W RSC 4 Houston
09.05.85 Mike Fisher W PTS 10 West Orange
26.07.85 Murray Sutherland W PTS 10 Atlantic City
06.09.86 Slobodan Kacar W RSC 5 Las Vegas
(IBF L. Heavyweight Title Challenge)
26.12.86 David Sears W RSC 1 West Orange
(IBF L. Heavyweight Title Defence)
21.02.87 Willie Edwards W CO 2 Atlantic City
(IBF L. Heavyweight Title Defence)
03.05.87 Jim MacDonald W RSC 6 Atlantic City
((IBF L. Heavyweight Title Defence)
29.10.87 Charles Williams L RTD 9 Las Vegas
((IBF L. Heavyweight Title Defence)
22.05.88 Dennis Andries L PTS 10 Atlantic City
25.10.88 Leslie Stewart W PTS 10 Atlantic City
27.12.88 Mike Devito W CO 7 Fort Myers
04.03.89 Virgil Hill L PTS 12 Bismark
(WBA L. Heavyweight Title Challenge)
Summary: 38 contests, won 34, lost 4.

Sidnei dal Rovere
Sao Paulo, Brazil. *Born* 20.03.59
South American & Brazilian Featherweight Champion

04.01.85 Domingos Zigrini W RSC 3 Rio de Janeiro
23.01.85 Carlos Henrique W PTS 6 Rio de Janeiro
05.05.85 Hercilio Mesias W PTS 8 Sao Paulo

26.05.85 Alejandro Carvacho W RTD 3 Sao Paulo
29.10.85 Jose de Paula W PTS 12 Sao Paulo
(*Brazilian Featherweight Title Challenge*)
17.11.85 Jaime Loyola W PTS 8 Sao Paulo
20.04.86 Ercilio Mesias W RTD 5 Sao Paulo
22.02.87 Jorge Ojeda W PTS 10 Sao Paulo
18.04.87 Bruno Jacob W CO 6 Nimes
31.05.87 Faustino Ponce W RSC 2 Curitiba
09.08.87 Neris de Guardia W RTD 3 Sao Paulo
11.10.87 Ruben Ponce W DIS 9 Araraquara
23.01.88 Luis Ocampo W PTS 10 Asuncion
11.03.88 Alfredo Benavidez W PTS 10 Salvador
10.06.88 Miguel Francia W TD 6 Salvador
(*Vacant South American Featherweight Title*)
14.08.88 Ernesto Quintana W RSC 6 Londrina
(*South American Featherweight Title Defence*)
07.11.88 Juan Noriega W CO 7 Sao Paulo
10.12.88 Azumah Nelson L CO 3 Accra
(*WBC S. Featherweight Title Challenge*)
Summary: 18 contests, won 17, lost 1.

Francesco Damiani
Italy. *Born* 04.10.58
EBU & WBC International Heavyweight Champion

05.01.85 Allou Gobe W RSC 3 Perugia
08.03.85 Georg Butzbach W RSC 2 Modena
20.04.85 Dragomir Popovic W RSC 6 Ceriale
17.05.85 Larry Robertson W RSC 1 Stateline
29.06.85 Walter Santemore W PTS 6 Bellaria
13.07.85 Ricky Keller W RSC 1 Atlantic City
28.09.85 Felipe Rodriguez W RSC 5 Sassari
31.01.86 Bobby Crabtree W CO 6 Abbiategrasso
14.02.86 Tom Trimm W RSC 2 Milan
02.04.86 Mike Perkins W RSC 5 Totowa
30.05.86 Danny Sutton W RSC 7 Abano Terme
04.07.86 Donnie Long W RSC 2 Porlezza
19.09.86 Rick Sekorski W PTS 10 Lerici
14.11.86 K. P. Porter W RSC 5 San Giuseppe
19.12.86 Rod Smith W RSC 2 Ancona
14.02.87 Eddie Gregg W RSC 1 Lucca
(*Vacant WBC International Heavyweight Title*)
11.04.87 James Broad W PTS 10 Bologna
11.07.87 Eddie Richardson W PTS 10 Corsica
09.10.87 Anders Eklund W RSC 6 Aosta
(*WBC International Heavyweight Title Defence & EBU Heavyweight Title Challenge*)
22.01.88 Dorcey Gaymon W RSC 4 Atlantic City
22.04.88 John Emmen W RSC 3 Milan
(*EBU Heavyweight Title Defence*)
29.10.88 Tyrell Biggs W RSC 5 Milan
17.12.88 Manfred Jassman W CO 3 Sassari
(*EBU Heavyweight Title Defence*)
Summary: 23 contests, won 23.

Robert Daniels
Miami, USA. *Born* 1967
Cruiserweight

04.03.84 James Roper W CO 1 Miami
04.05.84 Jose Marino W CO 1 Homestead
12.06.84 Eric Holley L PTS 4 Miami
23.06.84 Brooks Gorton W RSC 2 West Palm Beach
31.07.84 Randy Armstrong W RSC 2 Miami
24.10.84 Larry Sanchez W CO 2 Fort Lauderdale
24.08.85 Ed Sharkey W RSC 1 Miami
27.09.85 Mike de Angelo W RSC 2 Miami
25.10.85 Milton Owens W CO 5 Miami
28.02.87 Norris Ford W RSC 1 Miami
16.05.87 Ernie Simmons W RSC 6 Miami
15.01.88 Ron Gadson W RSC 1 Miami
22.04.88 Jack Johnson W CO 4 Hialeah
30.07.88 Jerome Brown W CO 2 Miami
29.10.88 Rod Stockton W CO 6 Las Vegas
16.12.88 Bruce Johnson W CO 2 Miami
31.01.89 Bobby Thomas W RSC 5 Fort Lauderdale
Summary: 17 contests, won 16, lost 1.

Ebo Danquah
Ghana
ABU Flyweight Champion. Former WBC International L. Flyweight Champion.
Former Undefeated ABU L. Flyweight Champion

29.06.85 Nana Yaw Konadu DREW 6 Accra
05.10.85 Gabriel Kuphey W PTS 6 Accra
22.02.86 Attah Yeboah W PTS 6 Accra
28.06.86 Muschen Bailey W PTS 8 Accra
26.07.86 Gabriel Kuphey W PTS 8 Accra
30.08.86 George Foreman DREW 8 Accra
25.10.86 Kikongo Karrim W RTD 4 Accra
14.02.87 Ankara Lopez W CO 3 Accra
30.05.87 James Njoroge W CO 5 Accra
(*Vacant ABU L. Flyweight Title*)
12.09.87 Little Baguio W PTS 12 Accra
(*WBC International L. Flyweight Title Challenge*)
13.07.88 Giampiero Pinna W RSC 7 Santa Marinelli
(*WBC International L. Flyweight Title Defence*)
06.08.88 Stainless Tony W RSC 6 Accra
15.10.88 Giampiero Pinna L PTS 12 Montesarchio
(*WBC International L. Flyweight Title Defence*)
26.11.88 Jimmy Young W CO 3 Accra
(*Vacant ABU Flyweight Title*)
Summary: 14 contests, won 11, drew 2, lost 1.

Jose (Rocky) da Silva
Pernambuco, Brazil. *Born* 30.12.61
South American & Brazilian Middleweight Champion

17.08.86 Pedro Ferraro W CO 3 Sao Paulo
10.04.87 Fernando Ernesto W RTD 9 Sao Paulo
(*Vacant Brazilian Middleweight Title*)
04.07.87 Enrique Coronel W PTS 10 Porto Alegre
01.11.87 Mauro Cruz W RSC 5 Sao Paulo
(*Brazilian Middleweight Title Defence*)
28.11.87 Reginald Santos W PTS 10 Salvador
(*Brazilian Middleweight Title Defence*)
20.12.87 Juan Lopez W CO 6 Rio de Janeiro
14.03.88 Carlos Velazquez W CO 2 Porto Alegre
14.08.88 Perfecto Bobadilla W PTS 12 Londrina
(*Vacant South American Middleweight Title*)
21.01.89 Dario Matteoni L CO 5 Punta del Este
Summary: 9 contests, won 8, lost 1.

Albert Davila
Pomona, USA. *Born* 10.08.54
Former Undefeated NABF Bantamweight Champion.
Former Undefeated WBC Bantamweight Champion

01.03.73 Carlos Villareal W PTS 4 Los Angeles
15.03.73 Tomas Heurta W PTS 4 Los Angeles
06.04.73 Ruben Mozqueda W CO 5 San Bernardino
28.04.73 Tomas Heurta W PTS 5 Los Angeles
31.05.73 Jose Marquecho W PTS 6 Los Angeles
05.07.73 Alberto Cabanig W PTS 6 Los Angeles
23.08.73 Baby Corona W PTS 6 Los Angeles
04.10.73 Juan Lopez W PTS 6 Los Angeles
13.12.73 Juan Lopez W CO 2 Los Angeles
31.01.74 Teo Cubillas W PTS 10 Los Angeles
21.03.74 Mario Rogelio W RSC 7 Los Angeles
24.05.74 Rudy Gonzalez W RSC 7 Los Angeles
13.06.74 Tanny Amancio W PTS 10 Los Angeles
25.07.74 Cecil Escobido L PTS 10 Los Angeles
12.12.74 Bonnie Necessario W PTS 10 Los Angeles
10.04.75 Jose del Rio W RSC 5 Los Angeles
21.05.75 Raul Pacheco W PTS 10 Las Vegas
05.07.75 Eliseo Cosme L PTS 10 Los Angeles
04.12.75 Seco Luna W PTS 10 Los Angeles
25.02.76 Lupe Pintor W PTS 10 Los Angeles
28.04.76 Raul Tirado L PTS 10 Los Angeles
19.06.76 Jose Rosa W PTS 10 Los Angeles
19.07.76 Wilfredo Gomez L RSC 9 San Juan
28.08.76 Cubano Hernandez W PTS 10 Los Angeles
19.11.76 Jose Medina W RSC 3 Los Angeles
28.04.77 Carlos Alcivar W PTS 10 Los Angeles
09.06.77 Frankie Duarte W RSC 5 Los Angeles
07.07.77 Manuel Vasquez W PTS 10 Los Angeles
25.08.77 Alberto Cabanig W CO 10 Los Angeles
17.11.77 Rodolfo Martinez W CO 7 Los Angeles
25.02.78 Carlos Zarate L RSC 8 Los Angeles
(*WBC Bantamweight Title Challenge*)
04.05.78 Ramon Aguinaga W CO 4 Los Angeles
08.06.78 Manny Vasquez W CO 6 Los Angeles
15.09.78 Jorge Lujan L PTS 15 New Orleans
(*WBA Bantamweight Title Challenge*)
07.12.78 Mario Castro W CO 7 Los Angeles
15.02.79 Ricardo Varela W PTS 10 Los Angeles
12.04.79 Patricio Nunez W RSC 9 Los Angeles
31.05.79 Frank Granados W PTS 10 Los Angeles
12.07.79 Eddie Logan W PTS 10 Los Angeles
25.09.79 Jose Resendez W PTS 10 Los Angeles
14.12.79 Jose Resendez W PTS 10 San Bernardino
02.02.80 Manuel Ruelas W CO 4 Phoenix
12.04.80 Melvin Johnson W CO 2 Tucson
21.06.80 Richie Rozelle W RSC 2 Las Vegas
17.07.80 Miguel Flores W CO 4 Los Angeles
13.09.80 Terry Pizzaro W CO 6 San Antonio
19.12.80 Lupe Pintor L PTS 15 Las Vegas
(*WBC Bantamweight Title Challenge*)
26.01.82 Enrique Castro W RSC 9 Los Angeles
05.03.82 Javier Flores W PTS 10 Las Vegas
29.04.82 Franco Torregoza W PTS 10 Los Angeles
03.06.82 Hwan-Seul Chul W RSC 2 Los Angeles
18.09.82 Silvestre Guerrero ND 2 Los Angeles
18.11.82 Alberto Sandoval W PTS 10 Los Angeles
29.04.83 Artemio Ruiz W RSC 3 Los Angeles
01.09.83 Kiko Bejines W CO 12 Los Angeles
(*Vacant WBC Bantamweight Title*)
17.11.83 Julio Rodriguez W PTS 10 Los Angeles
26.05.84 Enrique Sanchez W RSC 11 Miami
(*WBC Bantamweight Title Defence*)
07.11.85 Eleonico Mercedes W RSC 6 Los Angeles
05.05.86 Francis Childs W RSC 9 Los Angeles
03.07.86 Mike Moreno W PTS 10 San Jose
15.11.86 Miguel Lora L PTS 12 Barranquilla
(*WBC Bantamweight Title Challenge*)
23.03.87 Edel Geronimo W PTS 10 Irvine
22.06.87 Frankie Duarte L RSC 10 Los Angeles
(*NABF Bantamweight Title Challenge*)
03.11.87 Juan J. Estrada W TD 3 Los Angeles
21.04.88 Gilberto Contreras W PTS 12 Los Angeles
(*Vacant NABF Bantamweight Title*)
01.08.88 Miguel Lora L PTS 12 Los Angeles
(*WBC Bantamweight Title Challenge*)
Summary: 66 contests, won 55, lost 10, no decision 1.

Aaron Davis

Aaron Davis
New York, USA. *Born* 07.04.67
Con. Am. Welterweight Champion

15.05.86 Juan Torres W PTS 6 New York
10.07.86 Keith Martin W CO 6 New York
28.08.86 Terry Young W PTS 6 New York
07.11.86 Jean-Pierre Calvez W RTD 2 Paris
13.12.86 Abdel Arik W PTS 6 Paris
29.01.87 Martin Kearney W RSC 4 New York
26.03.87 James Johnson W RSC 2 Atlantic City
27.04.87 Joel Brival W PTS 8 Paris
07.05.87 James Sudberry W RSC 4 New York
06.06.87 Mbayo Wa Mbayo W PTS 8 St Nazaire
23.07.87 Marvin McDowell W RSC 4 New York
03.09.87 Warren Nelson W PTS 8 New York
12.11.87 Brian Nitz W RSC 4 New York
21.12.87 Boubekeur Cherif W RTD 5 Paris
24.02.88 Jesus Velez W RTD 2 New York
18.04.88 Judas Clottey W PTS 8 Paris
16.06.88 Tyrone Moore W RTD 8 New York
31.07.88 Sammy Floyd W RSC 7 New York
19.09.88 Daniel Bicchieray W PTS 8 Corbiel
27.10.88 Horace Shufford W PTS 10 New York
30.11.88 Larry Nichols W RTD 4 Detroit
09.02.89 Jose de Lima W DIS 4 New York
13.04.89 Luis Santana W PTS 12 New York
(*Vacant Con. Am. Welterweight Title*)
Summary: 23 contests, won 23.

Howard Davis
Glen Cove, USA. *Born* 14.02.56
L. Welterweight

15.01.77 Jose Resto W PTS 6 Las Vegas
20.03.77 Ricky Craney W RSC 3 Louisville
11.05.77 Carlos Gonzalez W PTS 6 New York
17.07.77 Dom Monaco W RSC 8 Miami
13.09.77 Turi Pineda W RSC 4 Los Angeles
04.02.78 Jose Fernandez W PTS 8 Las Vegas
13.05.78 Larry Stanton W PTS 10 Orlando
09.07.78 Norman Goins W PTS 10 Indianapolis
04.11.78 Luis Davila W PTS 10 Atlantic City
21.04.79 Carlo Usai W CO 3 New York
17.06.79 Jose Hernandez W CO 7 San Antonio
14.09.79 Maurice Watkins W PTS 10 Houston
23.02.80 Vilomar Fernandez W PTS 12 Atlantic City
07.06.80 Jim Watt L PTS 15 Glasgow
(*WBC Lightweight Title Challenge*)
06.12.80 Johnny Lira W PTS 10 Lake Tahoe
26.06.81 Larry Stanton W RSC 8 Hauppauge
16.04.82 Angel Cruz W PTS 10 New York
03.06.82 Julio Valdez W PTS 10 Atlantic City
22.07.82 Tony Collins W RTD 4 Atlantic City
26.08.82 James Martinez W RSC 5 Atlantic City
16.10.82 Cocoa Sanchez W PTS 10 Atlantic City
12.11.82 Claude Noel W PTS 10 Miami
27.02.83 Tony Baltazar W PTS 10 Atlantic City
10.04.83 George Feeney W PTS 10 San Remo
18.06.83 Greg Coverson W RSC 8 Atlantic City
03.03.84 Connie Swift W RSC 8 Atlantic City
16.05.84 Darrell Stovall W RSC 2 Las Vegas
23.06.84 Edwin Rosario L PTS 12 San Juan
(*WBC Lightweight Title Challenge*)
15.12.84 Bobby Johnson W PTS 10 Uniondale
16.10.85 Sammy Matos W RSC 4 New Brunswick
28.02.86 Joe Manley L PTS 10 Atlantic City
16.08.86 Meldrick Taylor DREW 10 Atlantic City
27.02.87 Othal Dixon W PTS 10 Atlantic City
02.05.87 Hector Camacho L PTS 10 Atlantic City
21.01.88 Ali Karim Muhammad W RSC 9 New York
15.03.88 Shelton Leblanc W PTS 10 New York
28.04.88 Ron Johnson W PTS 8 Dorchester
31.07.88 James McGirt L CO 1 New York
(*IBF L. Welterweight Title Challenge*)
Summary: 38 contests, won 32, drew 1, lost 5.

Dwight Davison
Detroit, USA. *Born* 18.03.55
Middleweight

11.06.77 Warren Coaston W CO 1 Detroit
01.07.77 Malcolm Brown W RSC 3 Detroit
09.08.77 Marvin Sanders W RSC 5 Las Vegas
15.11.77 Ruben Rascon W PTS 6 Phoenix
26.11.77 Sammy Long W CO 2 Columbus
10.12.77 Gary Coates W PTS 6 Grand Rapids
16.03.78 Ali Muhammad W PTS 6 Kalamazoo
21.04.78 Murray Sutherland W CO 4 Livonia
17.05.78 Shane Bosley W CO 2 Flint
23.06.78 Rod Coupe W CO 1 Detroit
18.07.78 Andres Ramirez W CO 5 Phoenix

Dwight Davison

Peter Goldfield/USA

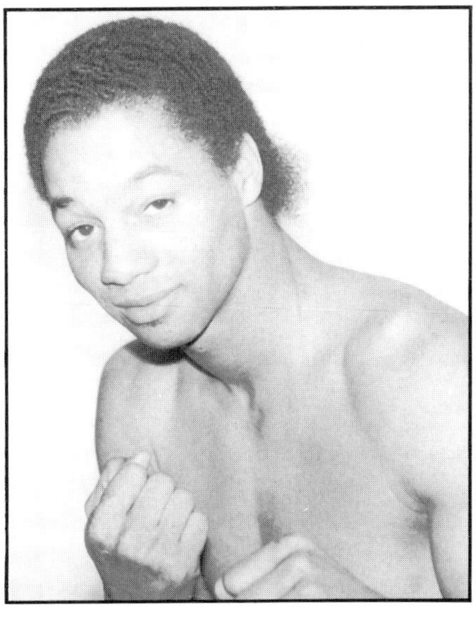

20.07.78 Mike West W CO 1 Detroit
25.08.78 Tony Brooks W PTS 8 Houston
09.09.78 Lloyd Richardson W RSC 8 Detroit
26.10.78 Ralph Moncrief W PTS 8 Detroit
09.11.78 Al Campbell W CO 1 Detroit
09.12.78 Jeff Morgan W CO 3 Detroit
25.01.79 Ben Sanchez W RSC 2 Detroit
09.02.79 Bob Patterson W CO 3 Detroit
24.05.79 Tommy Hannah W RSC 9 Detroit
15.09.79 Keith Broom W CO 3 Detroit
15.11.79 Willie Monroe W PTS 10 Detroit
13.01.80 Simon Smith W CO 1 Las Vegas
24.01.80 Doug Demmings W RSC 5 Detroit
22.02.80 Jaime Thomas W RSC 6 Detroit
23.05.80 Sugar Ray Seales W RSC 10 Clarkston
08.08.80 Curtis Parker W PTS 10 Las Vegas
07.02.81 Cliff Wills W CO 8 Atlantic City
11.04.81 Robbie Epps L PTS 10 Las Vegas
12.06.81 Angel Castro W CO 1 Detroit
08.08.81 Wilford Scypion W PTS 10 Kiamesha Lake
14.11.81 Lamont Lovelady W RSC 8 Cleveland
21.02.82 Tony Sibson L PTS 12 Birmingham
15.12.82 Steve Williams W RSC 7 Chicago
20.04.83 Frank Medina W CO 2 San Jose
13.08.83 Lindell Holmes W RSC 8 Las Vegas
09.03.84 Charles la Cour W RSC 4 Las Vegas
17.10.84 Ernie Rabotte W PTS 10 Reno
16.02.85 Irwin Hines W CO 5 Kingston
31.01.86 Charlie Boston L PTS 8 Atlantic City
24.03.87 Sanderline Williams L PTS 10 Cleveland
06.10.87 Carlos Tite W RSC 5 Phoenix
25.03.88 Ron Daniels W RSC 3 Detroit
28.05.88 Philip Morefield W PTS 10 Detroit
08.12.88 Willie Wilson DREW 10 Detroit
28.04.89 Oscar Pena W RSC 4 Tucson
Summary: 46 contests, won 41, drew 1, lost 4.

Pedro Decima
Tucuman, Argentine. *Born* 10.03.64
Former Undefeated Argentine S. Bantamweight Champion

17.11.84 Diego Ferrero W RSC 4 Buenos Aires
01.03.85 Gustavo Villarruel W PTS 6 Mar del Plata
06.04.85 Elvio Ramirez W RSC 5 Buenos Aires
04.05.85 Ramon Maciel W RSC 2 Buenos Aires
07.06.85 Armando Cancio W RTD 7 San Miguel
07.08.85 Daniel Aguero W CO 2 Buenos Aires
23.08.85 Cesar Villarruel W PTS 10 Olavarria
18.09.85 Miguel Francia W CO 3 Buenos Aires
04.10.85 Raul Gomez W CO 10 Mar del Plata
15.11.85 Jose A. Gomez W CO 3 Mar del Plata
13.12.85 Julio Ramirez W CO 7 Mar del Plata
14.02.86 Pascual Sosa W PTS 10 Mar del Plata
19.07.86 Ramon Soria W CO 2 Mar del Plata
19.09.86 Raul Gomez W PTS 10 Mar del Plata
14.11.86 Ramon Soria L PTS 10 Mendoza
16.01.87 Ramon Dominguez W RTD 3 Mar del Plata
(*Argentinian S. Bantamweight Title Challenge*)
15.08.87 Raul Gomez W PTS 10 Buenos Aires
03.10.87 Carlos Laciar W RTD 8 Buenos Aires
(*Argentinian S. Bantamweight Title Defence*)
27.05.88 Allan Makitoki W RSC 2 Las Vegas
28.07.88 Jesse Benavides W RSC 3 Las Vegas
16.09.88 Louie Espinosa L RSC 8 Las Vegas
09.12.88 Robert Shannon W RSC 4 Las Vegas
17.01.89 Julian Solis W PTS 10 Las Vegas
10.03.89 Tony Pruitt W RSC 1 Miami
Summary: 24 contests, won 22, lost 2.

Francisco (Chiquinho) de Jesus
Brazil. *Born* 09.05.56
Brazilian & Con. Am. L. Middleweight Champion. Former South American L. Middleweight Champion

04.11.80 Joaquin Albino W DIS 6 Sao Paulo
18.11.80 Dioni Ferreira W CO 3 Sao Paulo
02.12.80 Crispin de Oliveira W RTD 5 Sao Paulo
30.01.81 Edson Lima W PTS 10 Sao Paulo
13.03.81 Diogenes Pacheco W PTS 10 Sao Paulo
14.04.81 Joao Tavares W PTS 10 Sao Paulo
19.06.81 Mario Martiliano W PTS 12 Sao Paulo
(*Vacant Brazilian L. Middleweight Title*)
31.07.81 Daniel Arreola W PTS 10 Sao Paulo
24.09.81 Mario Martiliano W RSC 9 Sao Paulo
(*Brazilian L. Middleweight Title Defence*)
05.02.82 Mario Martiliano W PTS 12 Sao Paulo
(*Brazilian L. Middleweight Title Defence*)

Francisco de Jesus

Peter Goldfield/USA

13.05.82 Ismael Santos W RTD 3 Asuncion
27.08.82 Juan Peralta W PTS 10 Sao Paulo
12.10.82 Walter Gomez W PTS 12 Sao Paulo
(*South American L. Middleweight Title Challenge*)
19.12.82 Pedro Flores W RTD 6 Sao Paulo
19.03.83 Alberto Herrera W RTD 2 Sao Paulo
14.05.83 Miguel Angel Curbelo W PTS 10 Santo Andre
12.11.83 Joao Tavares W RSC 9 Rio de Janeiro
(*South American L. Middleweight Title Defence*)
21.02.84 Mario Maldonado W PTS 10 Atlantic City
17.05.84 Patricio Diaz W PTS 12 Sao Paulo
(*South American L. Middleweight Title Defence*)
23.10.84 Ernest Jackson W PTS 10 Atlantic City
22.01.85 Matthew Hilton L PTS 10 Montreal
26.05.85 Luis Flores Teran W RTD 5 Sao Paulo
06.10.85 Fernando Ernesto W PTS 12 Sao Paulo
(*Brazilian L. Middleweight Title Defence*)
17.11.85 Julio Sanchez W PTS 10 Sao Paulo
30.04.86 Ramon Ramos L PTS 12 Banfield
(*South American L. Middleweight Title Defence*)
18.10.87 Leonel Riberio W PTS 12 Araraquara
(*Brazilian L. Middleweight Title Defence*)
25.08.88 Matt Farrago W RSC 8 New York
(*Vacant Con. Am. L. Middleweight Title*)
25.02.89 Julian Jackson L CO 8 Las Vegas
(*WBA L. Middleweight Title Challenge*)
Summary: 28 contests, won 25, lost 3.

Jose (Caguista) de Jesus
Puerto Rico. *Born* 1963
Former Undefeated Con. Am. L. Flyweight Champion

23.10.81 Luis Fuentes W PTS 6 Arroyo
21.11.81 Edwin de Jesus W RSC 1 Arroyo
10.12.81 Jose Latimer W CO 2 San Juan
12.02.82 Hector Cruz W RSC 5 Aguadilla
20.05.82 Luis Fuentes W PTS 6 San Juan
13.11.82 Eugenio Paulino W RSC 2 San Juan
15.12.82 Fidel Gonzalez W CO 1 Chicago
19.01.83 Jose R. Ortiz W RSC 2 San Juan
20.02.83 Edwin de Jesus W PTS 8 San Juan
07.05.83 Max Villlanueva W CO 1 Guaynabo
28.06.83 Giovanni Ramirez W CO 2 Guaynabo
18.06.83 Orlando Maestre W CO 2 San Juan
(*Vacant Con. Am. L. Flyweight Title*)
19.11.83 Julio Tejeda W RSC 3 San Juan
05.05.84 Benedicto Murillo W RSC 7 Guaynabo
02.02.85 Bernardo Diaz T DRAW 7 San Juan
30.03.85 Mveleli Luzihpho W CO 3 Sun City
09.03.86 Myung-Woo Yuh L PTS 15 Suwon
(*WBA L. Flyweight Title Challenge*)
02.08.86 Pedro Feliciano W PTS 10 San Juan
25.04.87 Jose Ruiz W PTS 10 San Juan
06.06.87 Jorge Ortiz W RSC 2 San Juan
28.11.87 Victor Cruz W RSC 4 San Juan
02.04.88 Ramon Pichardo W RSC 3 San Juan
12.06.88 Myung-Woo Yuh L PTS 12 Seoul
(*WBA L. Flyweight Title Challenge*)
Summary: 23 contests, won 20, drew 1, lost 2.

Fred Delgado
Puerto Rico. *Born* 29.10.63
L. Heavyweight

17.02.84 Tom Doughty W RSC 2 Miami
02.03.84 Arnold Neal W RSC 3 Miami
17.04.84 Dennis Gonzalez W CO 1 Miami
15.05.84 Dwayne Reed W CO 1 Miami
28.08.84 Kelvin McKinney W RSC 1 Miami
15.12.84 Larry Sanchez W RSC 1 Miami
08.02.86 Joe Lewis W RSC 1 Miami
11.07.86 Bill Hollis W RSC 1 Miami
01.08.86 Chris Wells W RSC 2 Miami
23.08.86 Bobby Lloyd W CO 3 Miami
16.10.87 Butch Hall DREW 4 Atlantic City
21.11.87 Paul Madison W PTS 4 Las Vegas
22.01.88 Don Crudup W CO 1 Atlantic City
13.05.88 Junior Edmonds W RSC 5 San Juan
22.10.88 Dave Putter W CO 2 Bayamon
07.12.88 Aaron Green W RSC 2 Miami
15.02.89 Bert Gravley W RSC 8 Philadelphia
22.04.89 Michael Moorer L RSC 1 Detroit
(*WBO L. Heavyweight Title Challenge*)
Summary: 18 contests, won 16, drew 1, lost 1.

Francesco dell 'Aquila
Campobello, Italy. *Born* 27.11.65
Italian Middleweight Champion

28.12.86 Musangu Ngeleka W PTS 6 Capo d'Orlando
27.03.87 Inino Bolamba W PTS 6 Vezzano
18.04.87 Hassen Jalni W PTS 6 Beausoleil
02.06.87 Inino Bolamba W PTS 6 Casoria
15.07.87 Bechir Chaarane W PTS 6 Capo d'Orlando
07.10.87 Kabunda Kamanga W CO 4 San Giuseppe
31.10.87 Michele Renna W PTS 6 Azzano
20.11.87 Abder Laachira W PTS 6 Zingonia
03.01.88 Denys Cronin W RSC 2 Genoa
27.01.88 Sam Huston W RSC 2 Genoa
19.03.88 Angelo Liquori W RSC 3 Latina
(*Vacant Italian Middleweight Title*)
13.04.88 Paul Tchoue DREW 8 Busalia
21.05.88 Roberto Manoni W RTD 5 San Mango
(*Italian Middleweight Title Defence*)
08.07.88 Fidel O'Toole W DIS 3 San Remo
21.08.88 William Clayton W CO 3 Capo d'Orlando
14.09.88 Perfecto Bobadilla W CO 2 Scheggia
29.10.88 Jose Rosemain W PTS 8 San Giuseppe
14.12.88 Jean-Noel Camara W RSC 2 San Pellegrino
13.01.89 Akim Zeroual DREW 8 San Pellegrino
17.02.89 Jean-Pierre Iniama W PTS 8 San Pellegrino
Summary: 20 contests, won 18, drew 2.

Tony (Bazooka) de Luca
San Diego, USA. *Born* 08.07.62
Flyweight

24.06.83 Alberto Garcia W PTS 4 Santa Rosa
15.09.83 Jose Hernandez W PTS 4 San Rafael
28.03.85 Alberto Garcia W PTS 4 San Diego
27.06.85 Jose Morales W CO 2 San Diego
18.07.85 Rufino Lugo DREW 6 San Diego
15.08.85 Alberto Hernandez T DRAW 4 San Diego
17.10.85 Manuel Martinez W RSC 1 San Diego
21.11.85 Eduardo Pacheco W RSC 5 San Diego
11.01.86 Mauro Diaz L RSC 5 Big Bear City
17.04.86 Oscar Aguilar W CO 2 San Diego
25.07.86 Jose Hernandez W RSC 5 San Diego
26.03.87 Jose Quirino W PTS 8 San Diego
21.05.87 Abraham Garcia W PTS 10 San Diego
19.08.87 Efren Pinto W PTS 10 San Diego
19.11.87 Jose M. Diaz W PTS 10 San Diego
18.02.88 Katsumi Komiyama T DRAW 2 San Diego
08.05.88 Odwa Mdeleni W PTS 10 East London
22.09.88 Abraham Garcia W PTS 10 San Diego
08.03.89 Duke McKenzie L RSC 4 London
(*IBF Flyweight Title Challenge*)
Summary: 19 contests, won 14, drew 3, lost 2.

Giovanni de Marco
Alvignano, Italy. *Born* 11.12.60
WBC International L. Middleweight Champion.
Former Italian Middleweight Champion

03.04.82 Walter Borghesi W RSC 2 Piedemonte
28.05.82 Mario Loreni W RSC 3 Empoli
11.06.82 Hosanna Mobana W RSC 2 Lucca
07.08.82 Mauricio Hernandez da Cruz W PTS 6 Vairano
08.10.82 Mabobo Kamunga W PTS 6 Florence
18.12.82 Butangi Nbolameso W RSC 2 Piedemonte
12.03.83 Waluenga Nkongo W RSC 4 Piedemonte
15.04.83 Christian Chesini W RSC 7 Florence
11.06.83 Giovanni Cannizzo W CO 4 Piedemonte
16.07.83 Paul Muyodi W DIS 3 Messina
21.09.83 Mayele Mabele W PTS 6 Caserta
12.12.83 Robert Dormoy W RSC 2 Piedemonte
28.12.83 Folly Muyanga W PTS 6 Campobasso
16.03.84 Butangi Nbolameso W PTS 8 Viterbo
07.06.84 Mayele Mabele W PTS 8 Vieste
21.11.84 Tony Britton W RSC 5 Lucca
04.01.85 Aldo Buzzetti W RTD 5 Lucca
(*Italian Middleweight Title Challenge*)
29.03.85 Mosimo Maeleke W PTS 8 Rome
05.06.85 Edmondo Buttiglione DREW 12 Lucca
(*Italian Middleweight Title Defence*)
26.09.85 Sumbu Kalambay L PTS 12 Caserta
(*Italian Middleweight Title Defence*)
19.04.86 Giovanni Martorina W PTS 8 San Remo
03.09.86 Sumbu Kalambay L RTD 11 Silvo
(*Italian Middleweight Title Challenge*)
17.04.87 Mabobo Kamunga W PTS 8 Caserta
28.06.87 Inino Wa Bolamba W PTS 8 San Nicola
01.08.87 Nazario Mariotti W PTS 8 Asiago
02.12.87 Ramon Abeldano W PTS 12 San Giuseppe
(*WBC International L. Middleweight Title Challenge*)
07.05.88 Ian Chantler W PTS 6 Roseto
08.07.88 Tyrone McKnight W PTS 6 San Remo
24.08.88 Felipe Carvallo W PTS 12 San Nicola
(*WBC International L. Middleweight Title Defence*)
30.11.88 Kitenge Wa Kitenge W PTS 8 Chiavaria
Summary: 30 contests, won 27, drew 1, lost 2.

Doug de Witt
Peter Goldfield/USA

Doug (Cobra) de Witt
Youngstown, USA. *Born* 13.08.61
WBO Middleweight Champion. Former Undefeated USBA Middleweight Champion

28.03.80 Peter Pennello W PTS 4 Tarrytown
14.05.80 Charles Hecker W CO 3 White Plains
11.06.80 Calvin Clark W PTS 4 White Plains
17.09.80 Larry Davis W PTS 6 White Plains
15.10.80 Terry Duncan W PTS 6 White Plains
17.12.80 Derrick Doughty W CO 1 White Plains
21.01.81 Larry Davis W PTS 6 White Plains
18.02.81 Pop Nance W PTS 8 White Plains
08.03.81 Ben Serrano L PTS 8 Atlantic City
24.04.81 Kevin Cheatham W CO 1 White Plains
25.06.81 Lenny Villers W RSC 8 Tarrytown
09.10.81 Danny McAloon W RSC 3 White Plains
24.11.81 Tony Suero DREW 8 White Plains
22.12.81 Charles Hecker W RSC 5 Atlantic City
04.02.82 Danny Long W PTS 8 Atlantic City
04.03.82 Bill Medei W RSC 1 Atlantic City
21.03.82 Ben Serrano DREW 8 Atlantic City
04.08.82 Mike Hyman W RSC 6 White Plains
02.10.82 Billy Page W CO 1 Atlantic City
20.10.82 Teddy Mann W RSC 5 White Plains
03.12.82 Larry Rayford W RSC 6 New Orleans
16.02.83 Vernon Reed W CO 1 East Rutherford
09.08.83 Kane Starling W RSC 8 White Plains
09.09.83 Hector Rosario W RSC 4 White Plains
13.01.84 Fred Boynton W RTD 5 White Plains
17.02.84 Mike Tinley W PTS 12 Atlantic City
19.04.84 Rico Hoye W PTS 10 Atlantic City
04.10.84 Jimmy Sykes W RSC 1 Atlantic City
08.03.85 Don Lee DREW 10 Atlantic City
30.08.85 Robbie Sims L PTS 10 Atlantic City
18.01.86 Louis Rivera W RSC 7 Atlantic City
06.05.86 Charlie Boston W PTS 10 Atlantic City
13.07.86 Milton McCrory L PTS 10 Las Vegas
17.10.86 Thomas Hearns L PTS 12 Detroit
(*NABF Middleweight Title Challenge*)
20.02.87 Jose Quinones L RSC 3 Atlantic City
18.08.87 Lenny Lapaglia W PTS 10 Atlantic City
06.11.87 Tony Thornton W PTS 13 Atlantic City
(*Vacant USBA Middleweight Title*)
29.01.88 Ron Essett DREW 10 Atlantic City
19.08.88 Alberto Gonzalez W CO 6 Atlantic City
08.11.88 Sumbu Kalambay L RSC 7 Monte Carlo
(*WBA Middleweight Title Challenge*)
18.04.89 Robbie Sims W PTS 12 Atlantic City
(*Vacant WBO Middleweight Title*)
Summary: 41 contests, won 31, drew 4, lost 6.

Claudemir Dias
Brazil
Brazilian Flyweight Champion

04.01.85 Pedro Domingos W CO 2 Rio de Janeiro
02.03.85 Francisco Gonzalez W PTS 6 Rio de Janeiro
04.04.85 Renaldo Bacaroglo W RTD 4 Rio de Janeiro
11.05.85 Valdir Lobo W RSC 5 Sao Paulo
06.07.85 Paulo Ribeiro W RTD 6 Sao Paulo
(*Brazilian Flyweight Title Challenge*)
07.09.85 Guillen Acevedo W PTS 10 Sao Paulo
29.11.85 Paulo Ribeiro W CO 7 Sao Paulo
(*Brazilian Flyweight Title Defence*)
09.03.86 Carlos Mayorca W PTS 10 Sao Paulo
05.04.86 Jose Badilla W RTD 8 Sao Paulo
18.05.86 Julio Olivera W RTD 2 Sao Paulo
26.07.86 Crispin Alvarez W RTD 3 Sao Paulo
17.08.86 Julio Gudino W PTS 10 Sao Paulo
05.10.86 Jesus Bastardo W PTS 10 Sao Paulo
06.12.86 Hilario Zapata L PTS 15 Saldavor
(*WBA Flyweight Title Challenge*)
15.12.87 Carlos Mayorca W PTS 10 Salvador
08.04.88 Roberto Santos W PTS 10 Salvador
(*Brazilian Flyweight Title Defence*)
10.06.88 Carlos Mayorca W PTS 10 Salvador
17.12.88 Wilson Goncalves W RTD 5 Belem
(*Brazilian Flyweight Title Defence*)
Summary: 18 contests, won 17, lost 1.

Jorge Urbina Diaz
Patzcuaro, Mexico. *Born* 02.01.66
S. Bantamweight

23.04.82 Sergio Jimenez W CO 4 Guadalajara
21.05.82 Antonio Ramos W CO 3 Guadalajara
26.06.82 Raul Martinez W RSC 2 Guadalajara
20.01.83 Luis Fernando W CO 5 Uruapan
04.02.83 Alejandro Sosa W PTS 10 Colima
17.02.83 Jesus Mayorga W PTS 10 Guadalajara
11.03.83 Javier Hernandez L RSC 2 Mexico City
13.05.83 Ricardo Gonzalez W CO 4 Guadalajara
03.06.83 Mario Rivera W RSC 1 Guadalajara
05.08.83 Roberto Ramos W CO 5 Guadalajara
16.09.83 Lupe Torres W PTS 10 Guadalajara
12.11.83 Damian Hernandez W RSC 7 Mexico City
16.12.83 Roberto Martinez W CO 2 Guadalajara
13.01.84 Oscar Guzman W CO 3 Guadalajara
17.02.84 Jesus Mayorga W PTS 10 Guadalajara
06.04.84 Julio Duendano W RSC 5 Guadalajara
11.05.84 Fidel Martinez DREW 10 Guadalajara
08.06.84 Jose Valdez W RSC 8 Guadalajara
13.07.84 Felipe Fernandez W RSC 6 Guadalajara
23.08.84 Carlos de la Paz L CO 2 Guadalajara
02.11.84 Lupe Torres W CO 4 Guadalajara
19.01.85 Hilario Manjarrez W CO 4 Mexico City
01.03.85 Javier Hernandez L RSC 4 Zihuatanejo
30.03.85 Angel Faz W CO 2 Monterrey
17.05.85 Enrique Ursua W RSC 7 Guadalajara
06.07.85 Jose Pineda L PTS 10 Ciudad Valles
06.09.85 Jorge "Topito" Ramirez L PTS 10 Monterrey
18.10.85 Martin Garcia W PTS 10 Guadalajara
10.02.86 Paul Lucas DREW 8 Los Angeles
05.04.86 Jaime Garza L RSC 3 Palm Springs
05.06.86 Gaby Gutierrez W RSC 7 Sacramento
03.07.86 Eddie Rodriguez W PTS 8 San Jose

13.08.86 Darryl Thigpen W RSC 6 Los Angeles
04.09.86 Alex Madrid W RSC 1 San Jose
02.10.86 Adrian Arreola W PTS 10 San Jose
13.11.86 Hector Cortez W PTS 12 San Jose
11.12.86 Tony Montoya W RSC 5 San Jose
12.02.87 Jorge Rodriguez W PTS 10 San Jose
05.04.87 Seung-Hoon Lee L CO 10 Seoul
(*IBF S. Bantamweight Title Challenge*)
07.08.87 Harold Petty W PTS 10 San Jose
28.03.88 Jorge "Schoolboy" Ramirez L RSC 5 Los Angeles
13.06.88 Mike Moreno W CO 6 Fresno
Summary: 42 contests, won 32, drew 2, lost 8.

Policarpo Diaz
Palomeras, Spain. *Born* 21.11.66
EBU & Spanish Lightweight Champion

15.03.86 Miguel Rodriguez W PTS 4 Madrid
05.04.86 Jimmy Cruz W RTD 4 Madrid
16.05.86 Tony Granados W CO 3 Rubi
24.05.86 Juan Alonso W PTS 6 Madrid
06.06.86 Jesus Bezanilla W CO 4 Madrid
13.06.86 Angel Rodriguez W PTS 6 Barcelona
05.07.86 Jose Hernando W PTS 10 Burgos
(*Spanish Lightweight Title Challenge*)
24.07.86 Carlos Rodriguez W PTS 8 Villafranca
23.08.86 Angel Rodriguez W RTD 4 Almeria
(*Spanish Lightweight Title Defence*)
12.09.86 Jose Guervos W RSC 5 Melilla
01.11.86 Emilio Molero W CO 2 Villalba
12.12.86 Rafael Munoz W RTD 6 Madrid
(*Spanish Lightweight Title Defence*)
07.03.87 Salvador del Pino W RTD 3 Madrid
(*Spanish Lightweight Title Defence*)
11.07.87 Jose Hernando W CO 9 Madrid
(*Spanish Lightweight Title Defence*)
31.07.87 Eddy Molina W PTS 8 Madrid
14.08.87 Lofti Ben Sayel W RSC 3 Madrid
16.10.87 Fernando Blanco W PTS 8 Madrid
23.10.87 Eddy Molina W PTS 8 Madrid
21.11.87 Jose Arenas W CO 3 Valencia
(*Spanish Lightweight Title Defence*)
05.02.88 Roland Leclercq W CO 2 Madrid
19.05.88 Konrad Mittermeier W CO 2 Madrid
11.07.88 Madjid Mahdjoub W RSC 3 Madrid
30.11.88 Luca de Lorenzi W CO 5 Chiavaria
(*Vacant EBU Lightweight Title*)
23.02.89 Alain Simoes W PTS 12 Madrid
(*EBU Lightweight Title Defence*)
Summary: 24 contests, won 24.

Michael (Dynamite) Dokes
Akron, USA. *Born* 10.08.58
Former WBA & Con. Am. Heavyweight Champion.
Former Undefeated NABF Heavyweight Champion

15.10.76 Al Byrd W RSC 4 Los Angeles
14.01.77 Sergio Rodriguez W RSC 2 Pensacola
29.01.77 Dave Wilson W PTS 4 Miami
06.03.77 Charlie Jordan W RSC 4 Marion
10.04.77 Ed Turner W PTS 6 Miami
03.03.78 George Holden W CO 3 Curacao
25.03.78 Abdul Khan W PTS 8 Las Vegas
29.04.78 Dan Johnson W PTS 6 Los Angeles
26.09.78 Terry Mims W PTS 8 Miami
27.10.78 Eugene Green W PTS 8 New York
08.12.78 Ira Martin W RSC 8 New York
23.03.79 Wendell Bailey W PTS 10 Las Vegas
12.05.79 Greg Sorrentino W RSC 3 Las Vegas
20.07.79 Willie McIntyre W CO 2 Miami
28.09.79 Jimmy Young W PTS 10 Las Vegas
13.01.80 Earl Tripp W RSC 1 Las Vegas
10.02.80 Lucien Rodriguez W PTS 10 Miami
19.04.80 Ossie Ocasio DREW 10 San Juan
28.06.80 Ossie Ocasio W RSC 1 San Juan
02.10.80 Tom Fischer W CO 7 Las Vegas
22.03.81 Randy Cobb W PTS 10 Las Vegas
12.06.81 John L.Gardner W CO 4 Detroit
09.08.81 Harry Terrell W CO 1 Cleveland
06.11.81 George Chaplin W PTS 10 Pittsburgh
30.01.82 Lynn Ball W RSC 1 Las Vegas
(*Vacant NABF Heavyweight Title*)
20.03.82 Franco Thomas W RSC 5 Atlantic City
(*NABF Heavyweight Title Defence*)
10.12.82 Mike Weaver W RSC 1 Las Vegas
(*WBA Heavyweight Title Challenge*)
20.05.83 Mike Weaver DREW 15 Las Vegas
(*WBA Heavyweight Title Defence*)
23.09.83 Gerrie Coetzee L CO 10 Richfield
(*WBA Heavyweight Title Defence*)

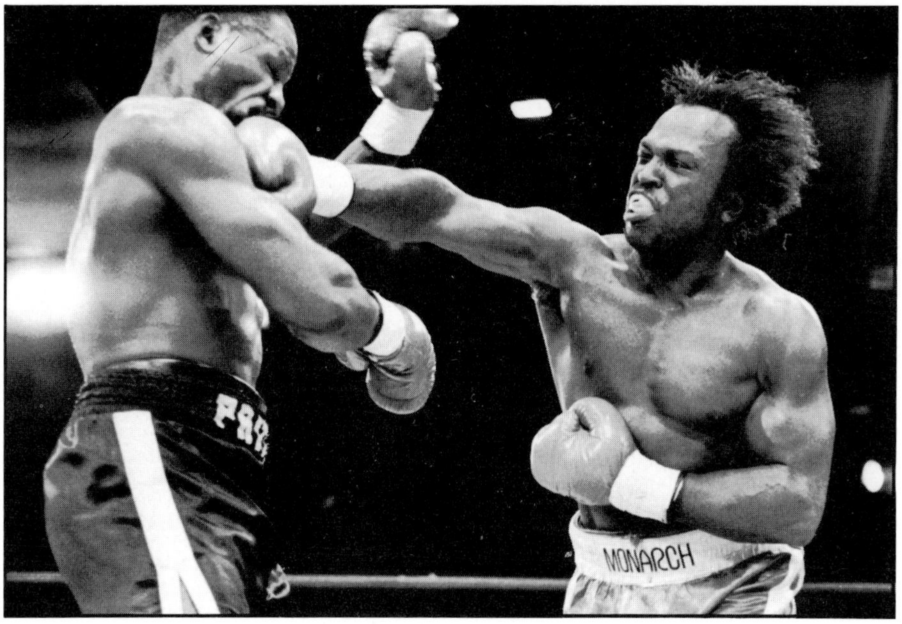

Michael Dokes (right) stuns James Pritchard moments before stopping him in April, 1988

31.08.84 Mike Jameson W PTS 10 Las Vegas
16.02.85 Young Joe Louis W CO 2 Kingston
15.03.85 Randy Cobb W TD 4 Las Vegas
(*Vacant Con. Am. Heavyweight Title*)
17.12.87 K. P. Porter W RSC 5 New York
22.01.88 Ken Lakusta W RSC 7 Atlantic City
24.02.88 Eddie Richardson W RSC 10 New York
28.04.88 James Pritchard W RSC 7 New York
27.06.88 Andy Stokes W RSC 1 New York
28.07.88 Manuel de Almedia W RTD 4 New York
27.10.88 Curtis Isaac W CO 4 New York
09.12.88 Rick Sekorski W PTS 12 Atlantic City
(*Con. Am. Heavyweight Title Defence*)
11.03.89 Evander Holyfield L RSC 10 Las Vegas
(*Con. Am. Heavyweight Title Defence*)
Summary: 41 contests, won 37, drew 2, lost 2.

Luiz Dorea
Bahia, Brazil. *Born* 07.03.65
WBC International L. Welterweight Champion

07.12.86 Francisco Mesquita DREW 6 Salvador
07.02.87 Ignacio Silva W PTS 6 Bahia
14.08.87 Jesse Maciel W CO 10 Salvador
08.10.87 Alfredo Ayala W PTS 10 Salvador
26.02.88 Tony Jones W PTS 12 Bahia
(*WBC International L. Welterweight Title Challenge*)
10.06.88 Domingo Guzman W CO 6 Bahia
10.03.89 Alejandro Balsamo W PTS 10 Salvador
Summary: 7 contests, won 6, drew 1.

James (Buster) Douglas
Ohio, USA. *Born* 07.04.60
Heavyweight

31.05.81 Dan Banks W CO 3 Columbus
23.07.81 Michael Lear W PTS 4 Columbus
27.09.81 Mike Rodgers W CO 3 Columbus
14.10.81 Tommy Stevenson W RSC 5 Indianapolis
23.10.81 Johnny Clark W PTS 4 Toledo
06.11.81 David Bey L RSC 3 Pittsburgh
23.12.81 Donny Johnson W RSC 3 Canton
23.01.82 Hubert Adams W CO 1 McConnelsville
14.02.82 Don Townsend W PTS 6 Erie
16.02.82 Marvin Earle W CO 2 Kalamazoo
25.03.82 Rick Enis W PTS 6 Indianapolis
24.04.82 Mel Daniels W RSC 4 Johnstown
16.10.82 Steffen Tangstad DREW 8 Chicago
20.11.82 Tim Johnson W CO 1 Columbus
09.03.83 Jesse Clark W CO 2 Niles
29.03.83 Leroy Diggs W CO 7 Atlantic City
16.04.83 Jesse Clark W RSC 2 Muskegon
29.04.83 Henry Porter W CO 2 Atlantic City
05.07.83 Dave Johnson W PTS 10 Atlantic City
28.09.83 Eugene Cato W RSC 1 Atlantic City
17.12.83 Mike White L RSC 9 Atlantic City
09.07.84 Dave Starkey NC 1 Columbus
09.11.84 Randy Cobb W PTS 10 Las Vegas
27.03.85 Dion Simpson W RSC 1 Atlantic City
09.05.85 Jesse Ferguson L PTS 10 Atlantic City
17.01.86 Greg Page W PTS 10 Atlanta
19.04.86 Dave Jaco W PTS 10 Las Vegas
06.09.86 Dee Collier W PTS 10 Las Vegas
30.05.87 Tony Tucker L RSC 10 Las Vegas
(*Vacant IBF Heavyweight Title*)
19.11.87 Donnie Long W CO 2 Columbus
24.02.88 Percell Davis W RSC 10 Daluth
16.04.88 Jerry Halstead W RSC 9 Las Vegas
27.06.88 Mike Williams W RSC 7 Atlantic City
25.02.89 Trevor Berbick W PTS 10 Las Vegas
Summary: 34 contests, won 28, drew 1, lost 4, no contest 1.

Tyrone Downes
Barbados. *Born* 1958
Former Undefeated Barbados & Commonwealth Featherweight Champion. Former Undefeated Barbados & Fecarbox Lightweight Champion

12.02.75 Bruce Scanterbury W PTS 6 Bridgetown
20.03.75 Bruce Scanterbury W PTS 8 Bridgetown
11.04.75 Malcolm Beckles W PTS 10 Bridgetown
24.05.76 Silford Ashley W PTS 10 Bridgetown
04.06.76 Silford Ashley W PTS 10 Bridgetown
23.06.77 Norman Yearwood W PTS 10 Bridgetown
21.07.77 Norman Yearwood W PTS 15 Bridgetown
(*Barbados Featherweight Title Challenge*)
03.01.78 Hurricane Jackson W PTS 15 Bridgetown
(*Barbados Lightweight Title Challenge*)
04.03.79 Azor Agosto W PTS 10 Bridgetown
20.03.79 Malcolm Beckles W PTS 10 Bridgetown
15.06.80 Miguel Morales L RSC 6 Port of Spain
12.08.80 Fitzroy Davidson L PTS 10 Port of Spain
20.03.81 Jesus Flores L PTS 10 Port of Spain
29.01.82 Julius Martin W PTS 8 Port of Spain
04.06.82 Ismael Santana W RSC 10 Port of Spain
27.08.82 Roberto Pineiro W PTS 10 Port of Spain
22.02.83 Nelson Cruz W RSC 5 Port of Spain
19.08.83 Geronimo Luquez W PTS 12 Port of Spain
(*Vacant Fecarbox Lightweight Title*)
02.12.83 Luis Rivera W RSC 5 Port of Spain
16.12.83 David Capo W RSC 7 Port of Spain
16.03.84 Denzil Surall W RSC 5 Port of Spain
17.05.84 Marcos Villasana L RSC 4 Los Angeles
27.10.84 Aurelio Benitez W PTS 10 Port of Spain
01.03.85 Terry Kemp W RSC 3 Port of Spain
10.05.85 Florentino Garcia W RSC 2 Fort Lauderdale
11.06.85 Bernard Taylor L PTS 10 Atlantic City
03.08.85 Alberto Parra W PTS 10 Port of Spain
01.11.85 Hector Cortes W RSC 3 Port of Spain
28.02.86 Snake Mandeya W PTS 12 Port of Spain
(*Vacant Commonwealth Featherweight Title*)
04.10.86 Edwin Pintor W PTS 10 Bridgetown
16.03.87 Roger Arevalo W PTS 10 Los Angeles
23.05.87 Ray Akwaye W RTD 5 Port of Spain
(*Commonwealth Featherweight Title Defence*)

02.10.87 Felix Guzman W CO 2 Port of Spain
12.08.88 Jeff Fenech L RSC 5 Melbourne
(*WBC Featherweight Title Challege*)
01.12.88 William Gonzalez W CO 8 Port of Spain
31.03.89 Wilfredo Navas W RSC 2 Port of Spain
Summary: 36 contests, won 30, lost 6.

Buster (Demon) Drayton
Philadelphia, USA. *Born* 02.03.53
Former IBF L. Middleweight Champion

09.11.78 Charles Carey DREW 4 Virginia Beach
14.12.78 Jesse Carter W PTS 6 Virginia Beach
31.05.79 Frank Moore W CO 1 Virginia Beach
03.07.79 Bob Saxton W CO 1 Atlantic City
30.08.79 Jesse Carter W CO 6 Virginia Beach
20.09.79 Julius Spell W PTS 4 Virginia Beach
18.10.79 Cliff Smith W RSC 1 Philadelphia
09.08.80 Bill Harrington W RSC 2 Atlantic City
01.10.80 Curtis Taylor ND 8 Atlantic City
06.11.80 Kevin Perry L RSC 3 Atlantic City
24.01.81 Dan Snyder W CO 4 Philadelphia
07.02.81 Mark Holmes L PTS 6 Atlantic City
14.06.81 Mario Maldonado L PTS 8 Atlantic City
25.07.81 Tyrone Demby W PTS 6 Atlantic City
23.12.81 D. C. Walker W CO 2 Providence
17.01.82 Dan Snyder W PTS 8 Atlantic City
07.03.82 Lindell Holmes L PTS 10 Atlantic City
29.04.82 Duane Thomas W RSC 7 Atlantic City
31.07.82 Bruce Johnson W RSC 9 Atlantic City
31.10.82 Sumbu Kalambay L PTS 8 San Remo
05.02.83 Bushy Bester L PTS 10 Johannesburg
12.04.83 Dave Plowden W PTS 8 Charleston
12.05.83 Clint Jackson W RSC 2 Bristol
09.06.83 Patrizio Diaz W PTS 10 Atlantic City
01.09.83 Mario Maldonado L PTS 10 Atlantic City
01.10.83 Fred Hutchings L PTS 10 Stockton
28.01.84 Greg Clark W RSC 2 Johannesburg
11.04.84 Jimmy Cable W CO 1 London
13.05.84 Mark Kaylor W RSC 7 Wembley
25.06.84 Gary Coates W CO 4 Atlantic City
26.09.84 Terry Holmes W RTD 2 Atlantic City
28.11.84 Tony Harrison W RSC 10 Atlantic City
13.02.85 Thomas Smith W PTS 10 Atlantic City
14.04.85 James Kinchen L PTS 10 London
10.06.85 Dennis Johnson W RSC 10 Metairie
14.09.85 John Jarvis W RSC 6 Atlantic City
22.01.86 Bruce Jackson W CO 5 Atlantic City
04.04.86 Sammy Leonard W RSC 4 Atlantic City
04.06.86 Carlos Santos W PTS 15 East Rutherford
(*Vacant IBF L. Middleweight Title*)
20.06.86 Benito Fernandez W RSC 5 Paris
24.08.86 Davey Moore W RSC 10 Juan les Pins
(*IBF L. Middleweight Title Defence*)
28.02.87 Juan A. Villa W CO 2 Vincennes
27.03.87 Said Skouma W RTD 10 Cannes
(*IBF L. Middleweight Title Defence*)
27.06.87 Matthew Hilton L PTS 15 Montreal
(*IBF L. Middleweight Title Defence*)
05.12.87 Leroy Jones W CO 4 Davenport
30.07.88 Julian Jackson L RSC 3 Atlantic City
(*WBA L. Middleweight Title Challenge*)
27.03.89 Terry Norris L PTS 12 Las Vegas
(*NABF L. Middleweight Title Challenge*)
Summary: 47 contests, won 33, drew 1, lost 12, no decision 1.

Frankie Duarte
Venice, USA. *Born* 03.09.54
Former Undefeated NABF Bantamweight Champion

16.08.73 Tony Ramos W CO 1 Los Angeles
27.09.73 Baby Corona W RSC 3 Los Angeles
18.10.73 Manny Gonzalez W PTS 4 Los Angeles
25.10.73 Juan Lopez W RSC 4 Los Angeles
15.11.73 Joaquin Heredia W CO 2 Los Angeles
02.01.74 Johnny Meza W RSC 1 Las Vegas
10.01.74 Gaspar Montejo W CO 3 Los Angeles
26.01.74 Jorge Rodriguez W RSC 2 Tucson
07.02.74 Pedro Torres W CO 3 Los Angeles
12.02.74 Jorge de la Rosa W RSC 1 Sacramento
21.03.74 Frank Granados W RSC 5 Los Angeles
24.05.74 Tetsuru Kawakami W PTS 10 Los Angeles
11.07.74 Rufino Hernandez W RSC 3 Los Angeles
29.08.74 Antonio Garcia W CO 5 Los Angeles
26.09.74 Tanny Amancio W RSC 5 Los Angeles
04.11.74 Cecil Escobido W RSC 2 Honolulu
03.12.74 Joe Guevara L PTS 12 Sacramento
13.03.75 Jorge Altamirano W PTS 10 Los Angeles
24.04.75 Famosito Gomez W PTS 10 Los Angeles
29.05.75 Famosito Gomez L PTS 10 Los Angeles
20.09.75 Jose Rosa W CO 6 Los Angeles
15.10.75 Al Diaz W PTS 10 Honolulu
08.01.76 Seco Luna W PTS 10 Los Angeles
13.02.76 Santiago Hernandez W CO 4 San Bernardino
17.06.76 Francisco Cruz W RSC 8 Los Angeles
11.05.76 Ernie Graf W RSC 6 Honolulu
27.06.76 Jose Cazares W RSC 4 Tijuana
11.11.76 Alfonso Gutierrez W RSC 5 Los Angeles
09.12.76 Martin Buchanan W RSC 4 Los Angeles
14.04.77 Jorge Carrasco W CO 9 Los Angeles
09.06.77 Albert Davila L RSC 5 Los Angeles
12.02.78 Chamaco Lopez W RSC 9 Mexicali
25.02.78 Danny O'Campo W RSC 9 Los Angeles
29.08.78 Peter King W PTS 10 Pico Rivera
22.02.79 Francisco Flores W PTS 12 Los Angeles
19.06.79 Rolando Navarrete L PTS 10 Honolulu
24.02.81 Neptali Alamag L PTS 10 Honolulu
30.05.84 Louis Hernandez W CO 7 Reseda
20.07.84 David Rojas W RSC 4 Culver City
20.11.84 Carlos Canchola W PTS 10 Reseda
10.04.85 Richie Sandoval L PTS 10 Sacramento
24.09.85 Ron Cisneros W RSC 7 Los Angeles
29.10.85 Fred Jackson T DRAW 2 Reseda
28.01.86 Pedro Gonzalez W RSC 1 Reseda
17.03.86 Mike Moreno W PTS 10 Los Angeles
20.05.86 George Garcia W RSC 6 Los Angeles
10.07.86 Jesus Salud W RSC 9 Los Angeles
(*Vacant NABF Bantamweight Title*)
30.09.86 Jose Torres W RSC 9 Reseda
03.02.87 Bernardo Pinango L PTS 15 Los Angeles
(*WBA Bantamweight Title Challenge*)
22.06.87 Albert Davila W RSC 10 Los Angeles
(*NABF Bantamweight Title Defence*)
29.06.88 Ron Cisneros W RSC 7 Reseda
27.09.88 Miguel Juarez W PTS 10 Reseda
Summary: 52 contests, won 44, drew 1, lost 7.

Johnny (Super D) Duplessis
New Orleans, USA. *Born* 04.08.66
Former Undefeated Con. Am. Lightweight Champion

25.09.84 Willie Covington W RSC 2 Metairie
11.10.84 James Seals W PTS 4 Morgan City
16.10.84 Ken Pryor W RSC 4 Pasadena
20.11.84 Elton Sneez W CO 2 Metairie
04.12.84 Marvin Freeman W CO 1 St Bernard
16.01.85 Ray Smith W CO 2 Lafayette
21.02.85 Tony Guerrero W PTS 4 Morgan City
04.03.85 Jerome Brooks W RSC 5 Metairie
18.04.85 Tony Guerrero W RSC 3 Monroe
07.05.85 Darren Neal W RSC 4 Metairie
10.06.85 James Sanders W RSC 4 Metairie
11.07.85 Jim Martin W PTS 6 Morgan City
30.07.85 Victor McCray W CO 2 Metairie
06.09.85 Reuben Moran W CO 1 Terrytown
17.09.85 Norris Steiner W RSC 4 Metairie
15.10.85 Reese Smith W PTS 6 Metairie
26.11.85 Darryl Jacobs W PTS 6 Atlantic City
06.03.86 Joey Soler W PTS 8 Metairie
06.05.86 Joe Celestine W RSC 3 Metairie
01.07.86 Earl Sabber W RSC 3 New Orleans
26.08.86 Mark Lassien W CO 2 Metairie
11.12.86 Edwin Curet W PTS 10 Metairie
09.03.87 Nelson Bolanos W RSC 6 New Orleans
(*Con. Am. Lightweight Title Challenge*)
30.06.87 Robert Dixon W RSC 5 Metairie
25.08.87 Anthony Williams W PTS 10 Atlantic City
16.12.87 Sergio Aguirre W PTS 10 New Orleans
16.04.88 Herminio Morales W RSC 2 Las Vegas
12.06.88 Louie Lomeli L PTS 10 Villa Park
22.09.88 Felix Dubray W CO 7 New Orleans
10.11.88 Harold Romero W RSC 7 Buras
03.01.89 Tunde Foster W RSC 9 New Orleans
11.03.89 Miguel Medina W CO 4 Las Vegas
Summary: 32 contests, won 31, lost 1.

Johnny du Plooy
Johannesburg, South Africa. *Born* 27.09.64
Heavyweight

27.04.85 Serfonis Naile W RSC 1 Johannesburg
10.07.85 Blessing Mbyasa W CO 1 Durban
07.09.85 Howard Mpepsi W RSC 5 Johannesburg
18.12.85 Hansie van den Berg W CO 3 Cape Town
19.02.86 Linus Wallette W RSC 1 Johannesburg
02.04.86 Ron Ellis W RSC 2 Durban
14.05.86 Stanley Ross W PTS 8 Johannesburg
01.09.86 Mike Jameson W PTS 10 Durban

Johnny du Plooy

Peter Goldfield/USA

07.10.86 Young Joe Louis W RTD 4 Durban
30.10.86 Steve Zouski W RSC 4 Hartford
22.11.86 David Jaco W CO 2 Johannesburg
07.02.87 K. P. Porter W CO 6 Sun City
27.04.87 David Bey W CO 9 Johannesburg
24.06.87 James Tillis W RSC 10 Johannesburg
27.07.87 Tyrone Booze W CO 2 Johannesburg
12.09.87 Bennie Knoetze W CO 1 Johannesburg
31.10.87 Rickey Parkey W RSC 10 Sun City
28.11.87 Mike Weaver L RTD 6 Johannesburg
27.02.88 James Broad W CO 4 Johannesburg
30.04.88 Mike Weaver W CO 2 Sun City
02.07.88 James Pritchard DREW 10 Sun City
12.08.88 Renaldo Snipes L RSC 7 Milwaukee
22.10.88 James Pritchard W RSC 10 Sun City
18.12.88 Everett Martin W CO 7 Orlando
25.02.89 Mike Rouse W PTS 10 Sun City
Summary: 25 contests, won 22, drew 1, lost 2.

Roberto (Hands of Stone) Duran
Guarare, Panama. *Born* 16.05.51
WBC Middleweight Champion. Former Undefeated World Lightweight Champion. Former WBC Welterweight Champion. Former Undefeated WBA L. Middleweight Champion

08.03.67 Carlos Mendoza W PTS 4 Colon
04.04.67 Manuel Jimenez W CO 1 Colon
14.05.67 Juan Gondola W CO 1 Colon
30.05.67 Eduardo Morales W CO 1 Panama City
10.08.67 Enrique Jacobo W CO 1 Panama City
12.01.68 Cesar de Leon W CO 2 Panama City
20.06.68 Eduardo Morales W CO 1 Panama City
25.08.68 Leroy Cargill W CO 1 Panama City
07.12.68 Carlos Howard W CO 1 Panama City
19.01.69 Alberto Brands W RSC 4 Panama City
01.02.69 Eduardo Fruto W PTS 8 Panama City
18.05.69 Jacinto Garcia W RSC 4 Panama City
22.06.69 Adolfo Osses W RSC 7 Panama City
16.07.69 Serafin Garcia W RSC 5 Panama City
23.11.69 Luis Patino W CO 8 Panama City
05.04.70 Felipe Torres W PTS 10 Mexico City
16.05.70 Ernesto Marcel W RSC 10 Panama City
10.07.70 Clemente Mucino W CO 6 Colon
05.09.70 Marvin Castanedas W CO 1 Panama City
18.10.70 Nacho Castanedas W RSC 3 Panama City
09.01.71 Jose Angel Herrera W RSC 6 Monterrey
06.03.71 Jose Acosta W CO 1 Panama City
29.05.71 Lloyd Marshall W CO 6 Panama City
18.07.71 Fermin Soto W RSC 3 Monterrey
13.09.71 Benny Henertas W CO 1 New York
16.10.71 Hiroshi Kobayashi W CO 7 Panama City
15.01.72 Angel Robinson Garcia W PTS 10 Panama City
10.03.72 Francisco Munoz W RSC 1 Panama City
26.06.72 Ken Buchanan W RSC 13 New York
(*WBA Lightweight Title Challenge*)
02.09.72 Greg Potter W CO 1 Panama City
29.10.72 Lupe Ramirez W CO 1 Panama City
17.11.72 Esteban de Jesus L PTS 10 New York
20.01.73 Jimmy Robertson W CO 5 Panama City
(*WBA Lightweight Title Defence*)
22.02.73 Juan Medina W RSC 7 Los Angeles
17.03.73 Javier Ayala W PTS 10 Los Angeles
14.04.73 Gerardo Ferrat W CO 2 Panama City

02.06.73 Hector Thompson W RSC 8 Panama City
(WBA Lightweight Title Defence)
04.08.73 Doc McClendon W PTS 10 San Juan
08.09.73 Guts Ishimatsu W RSC 10 Panama City
(WBA Lightweight Title Defence)
01.12.73 Tony Garcia W CO 2 Santiago
21.01.74 Leonard Taverez W RSC 4 Paris
16.02.74 Armando Mendoza W RSC 3 Panama City
16.03.74 Esteban de Jesus W RSC 11 Panama City
(WBA Lightweight Title Defence)
06.07.74 Flash Gallego W RSC 5 Panama City
02.09.74 Hector Matta W PTS 10 San Juan
31.10.74 Jose Vasquez W CO 2 San Jose
16.11.74 Adalberto Vanegas W CO 1 Panama City
21.12.74 Masataka Takayama W RSC 1 San Jose
(WBA Lightweight Title Defence)
15.02.75 Andres Salgado W CO 1 Panama City
02.03.75 Ray Lampkin W CO 14 Panama City
(WBA Lightweight Title Defence)
03.06.75 Jose Peterson W RSC 1 Miami
02.08.75 Pedro Mendoza W CO 1 Managua
13.09.75 Alirio Acuna W CO 3 Chitre
30.09.75 Edwin Viruet W PTS 10 Uniondale
14.12.75 Leonico Ortiz W CO 15 San Juan
(WBA Lightweight Title Defence)
04.05.76 Saoul Mamby W PTS 10 Miami
22.05.76 Lou Bizzarro W CO 14 Erie
(WBA Lightweight Title Defence)
31.07.76 Emiliano Villa W RSC 7 Panama City
15.10.76 Alvaro Rojas W CO 11 Los Angeles
(WBA Lightweight Title Defence)
29.01.77 Vilomar Fernandez W CO 13 Miami
(WBA Lightweight Title Defence)
16.05.77 Javier Muniz W PTS 10 Landover
06.08.77 Bernardo Diaz W CO 1 Panama City
17.09.77 Edwin Viruet W PTS 15 Philadelphia
(WBA Lightweight Title Defence)
21.01.78 Esteban de Jesus W CO 12 Las Vegas
(WBA Lightweight Title Defence. WBC Lightweight Title Challenge)
27.04.78 Adolph Viruet W PTS 10 New York
01.09.78 Ezequiel Obando W CO 2 Panama City
08.12.78 Monroe Brooks W RSC 8 New York
08.04.79 Jimmy Heair W PTS 10 Las Vegas
22.06.79 Carlos Palomino W PTS 10 New York
28.09.79 Zeferino Gonzalez W PTS 10 Las Vegas
13.01.80 Josef Nsubuga W RSC 4 Las Vegas
24.02.80 Wellington Wheatley W RSC 7 Las Vegas
20.06.80 Ray Leonard W PTS 15 Montreal
(WBC Welterweight Title Challenge)
25.11.80 Ray Leonard L RTD 8 New Orleans
(WBC Welterweight Title Defence)
09.08.81 Nino Gonzalez W PTS 10 Cleveland
26.09.81 Luigi Minchillo W PTS 10 Las Vegas
30.01.82 Wilfred Benitez L PTS 15 Las Vegas
(WBC L. Middleweight Title Challenge)
04.09.82 Kirkland Laing L PTS 10 Detroit
12.11.82 Jimmy Batten W PTS 10 Miami
29.01.83 Pipino Cuevas W RSC 4 Los Angeles
16.06.83 Davey Moore W RSC 8 New York
(WBA L. Middleweight Title Challenge)

Roberto Duran

Peter Goldfield/USA

10.11.83 Marvin Hagler L PTS 15 Las Vegas
(World Middleweight Title Challenge)
15.06.84 Thomas Hearns L CO 2 Las Vegas
(WBC L. Middleweight Title Challenge)
31.01.86 Manuel Zambrano W CO 2 Panama
18.04.86 Jorge Suero W CO 2 Panama
23.06.86 Robbie Sims L PTS 10 Las Vegas
16.05.87 Victor Claudio W PTS 10 Miami
12.09.87 Juan C. Gimenez W PTS 10 Miami
05.02.87 Ricky Stackhouse W PTS 10 Atlantic City
14.04.88 Paul Thorn W RSC 6 Atlantic City
01.10.88 Jeff Lanas W PTS 10 Chicago
24.02.89 Iran Barkley W PTS 12 Atlantic City
(WBC Middleweight Title Challenge)

Summary: 92 contests, won 85, lost 7.

Anders (Tiny) Eklund

Sweden. *Born* 22.12.57
WBA Americas Heavyweight Champion. Former EBU Heavyweight Champion

07.10.82 Damien Marignan W PTS 4 Copenhagen
05.11.82 Theo Josephs W PTS 4 Copenhagen
02.12.82 Ricky James W RSC 3 Randers
11.02.83 Terry O'Connor W PTS 4 Copenhagen
08.04.83 Felipe Rodriguez W PTS 6 Copenhagen
14.09.83 Paddy Finn W RSC 1 London
06.10.83 Guido Trane DREW 6 Copenhagen
13.10.83 Noel Quarless L RSC 1 London
17.12.83 Steve Gee W RSC 5 Mariehamn
13.01.84 Joe Bugner L PTS 10 Randers
05.10.84 Rocky Burton W CO 1 Randers
27.10.84 Rudi Gauwe W RSC 6 Mariehamn
09.11.84 Dorcey Gaymon W RSC 8 Copenhagen
09.03.85 Steffen Tangstad W RSC 4 Copenhagen
(EBU Heavyweight Title Challenge)
01.10.85 Frank Bruno L CO 4 Wembley
(EBU Heavyweight Title Defence)
18.04.86 Glenn McCrory W PTS 8 Randers
03.10.86 Tony Foster W CO 2 Copenhagen
17.10.86 Jesse Ferguson W PTS 10 Copenhagen
27.02.87 Stefano Vassallo W PTS 8 Randers
28.03.87 Alfredo Evangelista W CO 7 Copenhagen
(EBU Heavyweight Title Challenge)
09.10.87 Francesco Damiani L RSC 6 Aosta
(EBU Heavyweight Title Defence & WBC International Heavyweight Title Challenge)
12.12.88 Ricky Kellar W RSC 3 Helsinki
16.03.89 Phil Brown W PTS 12 Reno
(Vacant WBA Americas Heavyweight Title)

Summary: 23 contests, won 18, drew 1, lost 4.

Carlos Elliott

Japan. *Born* Alabama, USA 29.04.62
OPBF L. Middleweight Champion. Former Undefeated Japanese L. Middleweight Champion

04.03.83 Masahashi Yoshida W CO 2 Tokyo
21.06.83 Nobo Chisaka W CO 2 Hachinohe
02.09.83 Won-Ki Chung W CO 4 Tokyo
19.11.83 Chung-Jae Hwang W CO 2 Daejon
03.02.84 Young Dela Cruz W CO 1 Tokyo
05.04.84 Byung-Sun Yuh W CO 5 Tokyo
30.07.84 Junya Kushikino L CO 6 Tokyo
(Japanese Welterweight Title Challenge)
11.10.84 Ki-Keum Son W CO 3 Tokyo
10.01.85 Ki-Young Park W RSC 5 Tokyo
20.07.85 Mugen Kawasaka W CO 2 Hachinohe
(Japanese L. Middleweight Title Challenge)
07.11.85 Mitsuo Hatano W RSC 8 Tokyo
(Japanese L. Middleweight Title Defence)
09.01.86 Noboru Kawaguchi W RSC 1 Tokyo
(Japanese L. Middleweight Title Defence)
24.03.86 Mitsuo Hatano W RSC 5 Tokyo
(Japanese L. Middleweight Title Defence)
24.07.86 Tony Stockey W CO 1 Tokyo
02.12.86 Rolando Aldemir W RSC 5 Tokyo
02.04.87 Jae-Hyung Yuh W RSC 9 Tokyo
(Vacant OPBF L. Middleweight Title)
22.07.87 Francisco Ferrer W PTS 8 Tokyo
28.11.87 San-Do-Chung W PTS 12 Hachinohe
(OPBF L. Middleweight Title Defence)
21.03.88 Renato Angulo W RSC 5 Tokyo
02.07.88 Francisco Lisboa L PTS 12 Palembang
(OPBF L. Middleweight Title Defence)
06.10.88 Rex Cabusa W RSC 2 Tokyo
01.12.88 Francisco Lisboa W CO 11 Tokyo
(OPBF L. Middleweight Title Challenge)
15.04.89 Archie Garcia W RSC 3 Tokyo

Summary: 23 contests, won 21, lost 2.

Carlos Elliott scores another kayo win

Lester Ellis
Melbourne, Australia. *Born* England 15.03.65
Australian L. Welterweight Champion. Former Commonwealth L. Welterweight Champion. Former IBF S. Featherweight Champion. Former Undefeated Commonwealth S. Featherweight Champion. Former Undefeated Australian Lightweight Champion

24.04.83 Ben Lappori W RSC 4 Preston
25.06.83 Roy Hughes W RSC 2 Heidelberg
06.10.83 Brian Roberts W PTS 8 Tottenham
17.11.83 Gary Williams W CO 2 Tottenham
01.12.83 Charlie Andrews W RSC 2 Shepperton
15.12.83 Kirk Blair W RSC 5 Tottenham
13.02.84 Jeff Smith W RSC 8 Melbourne
09.03.84 Dennis Talbot W RSC 3 Melbourne
20.05.84 Norm Stevens W RSC 6 Heidelberg
30.05.84 Lindsay Roberts W CO 1 Melbourne
04.07.84 Richard Fowler W RSC 10 Melbourne
14.09.84 Steve Sammy Sims W PTS 10 Melbourne
18.10.84 Kyoshi Sasaki W PTS 10 Melbourne
16.11.84 John Sichula W PTS 12 Melbourne
(*Commonwealth S. Featherweight Title Challenge*)
15.02.85 Hwan-Kil-Yuh W PTS 15 Melbourne
(*IBF S. Featherweight Title Challenge*)
26.04.85 Rod Sequenan W CO 13 Melbourne
(*IBF S. Featherweight Title Defence*)
12.07.85 Barry Michael L PTS 15 Melbourne
(*IBF S. Featherweight Title Defence*)
04.11.85 Conrad Maez W RSC 2 Brisbane
02.12.85 Marvin Garris W PTS 10 Sidney
16.12.85 John Sichula L RSC 4 Melbourne
27.03.86 Rafael Solis W RSC 8 Melbourne
13.06.86 Idabeth Rojas W PTS 10 Adelaide
09.10.86 Tony Miller W PTS 10 Melbourne
13.03.87 Ernesto Espana W PTS 10 Melbourne
30.04.87 Dale Artango W RTD 6 Melbourne
(*Australian Lightweight Title Challenge*)
18.06.87 Babu Gounder W RSC 2 Melbourne
28.08.87 Tommy Cordova W RSC 10 Melbourne
12.02.88 Jun Tito W CO 3 Sydney
16.03.88 Pat Leglise W RTD 5 Brisbane
(*Australian L. Welterweight Title Challenge*)
20.04.88 Rod Sequenan W CO 1 Brisbane
13.07.88 Iwao Otomo W PTS 10 Brisbane
05.08.88 Tony Laing W PTS 12 Adelaide
(*Commonwealth L. Welterweight Title Challenge*)
13.10.88 Robert Harkin W RSC 4 Melbourne
(*Commonwealth L. Welterweight Title Defence*)
21.03.89 Steve Larrimore L RSC 11 Perth
(*Commonwealth L. Welterweight Title Defence*)
Summary: 34 contests, won 31, lost 3.

Jean-Marie Emebe
France. *Born* Cameroons 17.08.55
L. Heavyweight. Former Undefeated ABU Middleweight Champion

03.07.76 Idrissa Konate W CO 5 Douala
14.08.76 Yene Dieudonne W CO 4 Douala
16.11.76 Manuel Lira W CO 3 Paris
21.05.77 Jean Grandjean W RSC 2 Douala
27.07.77 Abrahim Yovoutousso W CO 5 Douala
05.11.77 Billy Savage W CO 4 Lagos
(*ABU Middleweight Title Challenge*)
11.05.78 Joe Wilson W CO 5 Togo
06.10.78 Jose Hernandez W CO 7 Douala
02.03.79 Jacques Chinon W PTS 8 Douala
07.04.79 Jose Lozano W RTD 8 Douala
05.05.79 Idrissa Konate W RSC 3 Yaounde
09.11.79 Richard Ofuso W CO 1 Dakar
(*ABU Middleweight Title Defence*)
06.01.80 Jose Lozano L DIS 4 Libreville
19.03.81 Agamil Yilderim W RSC 9 Paris
21.05.81 Mel Dennis W RSC 3 Paris
07.11.81 Phil Keating W RSC 5 Noumea
14.12.81 Fred Reed W RSC 4 Paris
30.01.82 Bruce Strauss W CO 3 Yaounde
21.03.82 Ralph Moncrief W PTS 10 Atlantic City
14.12.82 William Brigham W RSC 2 Pasadena
18.02.83 Bob Patterson W RSC 9 New York
27.05.83 Murray Sutherland L RSC 9 Providence
10.02.84 Mauricio da Cruz W CO 1 Abidjan
06.04.86 John Davis W PTS 10 Abidjan
06.05.85 Jose Seys W RSC 3 Grenoble
13.12.85 Jonjo Greene W PTS 10 Antibes
20.09.96 Marvin Johnson L RSC 13 Indianapolis
(*WBA L. Heavyweight Title Challenge*)
20.12.86 Tony Golden W CO 4 Yaounde
24.04.87 Jose Seys L DIS 4 Abidjan
03.04.88 Virgil Hill L RSC 11 Bismark
(*WBA L. Heavyweight Title Challenge*)
13.03.89 Dawud Shaw W RSC 3 Paris
Summary: 31 contests, won 26, lost 5.

Antonio Esparragoza
Venezuela. *Born* 02.09.59
WBA Featherweight Champion

24.02.81 Antony Wasa W RSC 2 Cumana
01.10.81 Ramon Bolivar W RSC 2 Maracay
31.10.81 Luis Solorzano W RSC 2 Maracay
25.01.82 David Siso W CO 2 Barquisimeto
01.02.82 Angel Torres L RSC 6 Caracas
10.05.82 Francisco Leta W RSC 5 Cumana
24.05.82 Alejandro Garcia W RSC 2 Cumana
21.06.82 Tito Roque W RSC 2 Cumana
26.07.82 Angel Torres W RSC 9 Cumana
04.10.82 Bernardo Pinango DREW 10 Caracas
06.11.82 Fred Pitalua W RSC 4 Caracas
19.02.83 Antonio Rodriguez W RSC 3 Cumana
26.03.83 Jose Mosqueda W RSC 7 Catia
13.05.83 Alberto Parra W RSC 3 Margarita
01.10.83 Fabio Mosquera W CO 3 Caracas
16.12.83 Ruben Veliz W RSC 3 Ciudad Bolivar
15.05.84 Jose de Jesus W RSC 5 Aruba
07.07.84 Eduardo Laguna W RSC 4 Maracaibo
11.08.84 Jose Guerrero W PTS 10 Aruba
10.10.84 Bernardo Checa DREW 10 Isla Margarita
02.02.85 Jeff Roberts W RSC 7 San Juan
23.02.85 Jose Rivera W RSC 2 Santo Domingo
04.05.85 Johnny de la Rosa W RSC 2 Aruba
17.02.86 Jose Ortiz W CO 2 Turmero
22.03.86 Bernardo Checa W CO 2 Caracas
19.05.86 Nelson Rodriguez DREW 10 San Juan
16.01.86 Octavio Quinonen W RSC 3 Phoenix
06.03.87 Steve Cruz W RSC 12 Fort Worth
(*WBA Featherweight Title Challenge*)
26.07.87 Pascual Aranda W CO 10 Houston
(*WBA Featherweight Title Defence*)
23.06.88 Marcos Villasana DREW 12 Los Angeles
(*WBA Featherweight Title Defence*)
05.11.88 Jose Marmolejo W CO 8 Marsala
(*WBA Featherweight Title Defence*)
25.03.89 Mitsuru Sugiya W CO 10 Kawasaki
(*WBA Featherweight Title Defence*)
Summary: 32 contests, won 27, drew 4, lost1.

Louie Espinosa
Phoenix, USA. *Born* 12.05.62
Former WBA & NABF S. Bantamweight Champion

23.11.82 Adan Uribe W RSC 3 Phoenix
14.12.82 Ashby Dancy W RSC 3 Tucson
11.02.83 Leonard Ayala W CO 2 Phoenix
01.03.83 Felipe de Jesus W RSC 7 Phoenix
03.04.83 Ron Gary W PTS 6 Phoenix
10.05.83 Hector Sifuentes W PTS 6 Phoenix
27.06.83 Jose Resendez W PTS 6 Phoenix
09.09.83 Manny Juarez W RSC 5 Las Vegas
25.10.83 Dana Roston L PTS 10 Las Vegas
14.01.84 Arnold White W CO 1 Reno
15.06.84 Dwight Pratchett W PTS 8 Las Vegas
11.09.84 Ed Richardson W RSC 4 Lafayette
28.11.84 Elvin Gonzalez W RSC 5 Atlantic City
14.12.84 Raul Albaladejo W PTS 8 New York
16.02.85 Juan Romero W RSC 5 Reno
19.07.85 Troy Townsend W RSC 8 Poughkeepsie
03.08.85 Ron Gary W RSC 6 Phoenix
24.08.85 Felipe Olivar W RSC 4 Phoenix
03.10.85 Jesse Sierra W RSC 4 Austin
30.01.86 Angel Valle W CO 2 Los Angeles
01.05.86 Carmelo Negron W RSC 4 New York
12.08.86 Jerry Davis W RSC 1 Ashland
16.01.87 Tommy Valoy W RSC 4 Phoenix
(*Vacant WBA S. Bantamweight Title*)
16.05.87 Capri Lipkins W CO 8 San Juan
15.07.87 Manuel Vilchez W RSC 15 Phoenix
(*WBA S. Bantamweight Title Defence*)
15.08.87 Mike Ayala W CO 9 San Antonio
(*WBA S. Bantamweight Title Defence*)
28.11.87 Julio Gervacio L PTS 12 San Juan
(*WBA S. Bantamweight Title Defence*)
28.01.88 Refugio Rojas W RSC 8 Tucson
29.03.88 Tony Cisneros W RSC 3 Edmonton
08.04.88 Jerome Coffee W RSC 5 Las Vegas
(*Vacant NABF S. Bantamweight Title*)
10.05.88 Francisco Pena W CO 2 Phoenix
27.05.88 Jesus Poll L PTS 12 Las Vegas
(*NABF S. Bantamweight Title Defence*)
10.09.88 Tony Montoya W RSC 6 Guadalupe
16.09.88 Pedro Decima W RSC 8 Las Vegas
04.02.89 Alejandro Garcia W CO 3 Phoenix
04.04.89 Adam Garcia W RSC 7 Phoenix
Summary: 36 contests, won 33, lost 3.

Luis (Luisito) Espinosa
Manila, Philippines. *Born* 26.06.68
Bantamweight

25.05.84 Vladimir Raffy W PTS 4 San Pedro
29.07.84 Ric Santiago W PTS 4 Pasay City
17.08.84 Ariel Samson L PTS 6 Tayuman
15.09.84 Manuel Corpus W RSC 3 Pasay City
22.09.84 Danny Duran W RSC 2 Pasay City
16.11.84 Titing Dignos W PTS 6 Quezon City
22.03.85 Romy Austria W PTS 10 Pasay City
29.05.85 Roger Pilapil W PTS 10 Paranaque
19.07.85 Romy Navarrete W PTS 10 Pasig
06.12.85 Jun Resma L PTS 10 Paranaque
02.02.86 Dadoy Andujar L PTS 10 Santos City
22.03.86 Robinson Cabuaso W PTS 10 Quezon City
25.06.86 Ari Blanca W PTS 10 Paranaque
08.11.86 Bong-Ho Lee W PTS 10 Manila
07.02.87 Ruben de la Cruz W RSC 9 Davao
16.05.87 Roger Pilapil W RSC 3 Manila
05.09.87 Dadoy Andujar W PTS 10 Quezon City
27.09.87 Loremer Pontino W CO 3 Tagum
14.03.88 Juan J. Estrada L RSC 10 Tijuana
(*WBC International Bantamweight Title Challenge*)
20.05.88 Ron Cisneros W PTS 10 San Francisco
23.07.88 Mauro Diaz W CO 2 San Francisco
04.12.88 Yung-Chun Min L PTS 10 Kwangju
18.02.89 Somboon Yos W CO 2 Manila
Summary: 23 contests, won 18, lost 5.

Ron Essett

Peter Goldfield/USA

Ron (The Dragon) Essett
Indianapolis, USA. *Born* 19.02.63
NABF Middleweight Champion

31.10.84 Carl Dixon W RSC 3 Atlantic City
24.11.84 Shawn Ayers W RSC 5 Stateline
23.01.85 Ken Heflin W CO 1 Indianapolis
29.05.85 Gary Jones W CO 2 Merrillville
16.07.85 Jesse Abrams W RSC 3 Indianapolis
17.10.85 Kris Golanski W RSC 4 Merrillville
20.11.85 Victor Claudio W PTS 8 Atlantic City
04.12.85 Jesse Abrams W RSC 2 Indianapolis
09.02.86 Steve Gamble W PTS 10 Indianapolis
15.05.86 Joe McKnight W RSC 4 Merrillville
27.06.86 Charles Campbell L PTS 8 French Lick
14.09.86 Dale Jackson L CO 10 Atlantic City
13.12.86 Gary Thomas W PTS 6 Martinsville
03.06.87 Osley Silas W RSC 7 Baltimore
23.10.87 Dave Tiberi W PTS 8 Atlantic City
29.01.88 Doug deWitt DREW 10 Atlantic City
18.04.88 Akim Zeroual W RTD 4 Paris
14.06.88 Dwight Hunter W PTS 8 Baltimore
19.07.88 Chester Jackson W RSC 2 Indianapolis
18.10.88 Sanderline Williams W PTS 13 Cleveland
(*Vacant NABF Middleweight Title*)
13.12.88 Juan C. Gimenez DREW 8 Baltard
02.03.89 Juan Elizondo W RSC 1 Baltimore
Summary: 22 contests, won 18, drew 2, lost 2.

Juan J. (Dinamita) Estrada
Tijuana, Mexico. *Born* 28.11.63
WBA S. Bantamweight Champion. Former Undefeated WBC International Bantamweight Champion

07.08.83 Victor Cuevas W CO 1 Tijuana
30.08.83 Jaime Fraile W CO 1 Tijuana
26.09.83 Jorge de Alba W CO 1 Tijuana
29.10.83 Jose L. Maytorena W CO 1 Tijuana
28.11.83 Fausto Mendoza W CO 1 Tijuana
19.12.83 Jose Alvarado W CO 1 Ensenada
05.03.84 Bonny Millan W CO 1 Tijuana
27.03.84 Jiquilpan Canedo L RSC 8 Tijuana
29.05.84 Lupe Rubin W CO 2 Tijuana
03.07.84 Jiquilpan Canedo W RSC 6 Tijuana
14.08.84 Alvino Aguilar W CO 2 Tijuana
01.10.84 Ubaldo Gonzalez W RSC 4 Tijuana
19.11.84 Angel Felix W RSC 3 Tijuana
10.12.84 Alberto Martinez L PTS 10 Tijuana
11.02.85 Julio Valle W RSC 9 Tijuana
08.03.85 Pedro Rodriguez W RSC 10 Tijuana
14.03.85 Martin Dominguez W CO 2 Ensenada
22.04.85 Felipe Mojica W CO 6 Tijuana
16.05.85 Ron Cisneros W PTS 10 Los Angeles
11.06.85 Jose Cazeres W RSC 2 Tijuana
27.07.85 Tony Escobar W PTS 10 Ensenada
26.09.85 Ramon Jimenez W CO 4 Tijuana
14.10.85 Manuel Aguilar L RSC 2 Tijuana
06.12.85 Manuel Aguilar W RSC 9 Tijuana
17.03.86 Alejandro Flores W CO 5 Tijuana
25.04.86 Lupe Torres W RSC 8 Tijuana
16.06.86 Jorge Ramirez L PTS 12 Tijuana (*Mexican Bantamweight Title Challenge*)
06.09.86 Lucio Lopez L PTS 10 Buenos Aires
27.10.86 Rodolfo Ortega W CO 6 Tijuana
08.12.86 Koetha Tanaka W RSC 4 Tijuana
03.02.87 Edel Geronimo W PTS 10 Los Angeles
20.03.87 Miguel Cota W RSC 4 Mexicali
18.05.87 Jose L. Cruz W CO 3 Tijuana
22.06.87 Azael Moran W CO 2 Tijuana
10.09.87 Lucilo Nolasco L RTD 7 Los Angeles
03.11.87 Albert Davila L TD 3 Los Angeles
07.12.87 Raul Valdez W TD 10 Tijuana (*WBC International Bantamweight Title Challenge*)
14.03.88 Luis Espinosa W RSC 10 Tijuana (*WBC International Bantamweight Title Defence*)
28.05.88 Bernardo Pinango W PTS 12 Tijuana (*WBA S. Bantamweight Title Challenge*)
15.10.88 Takuya Muguruma W RSC 11 Moriguchi (*WBA S. Bantamweight Title Defence*)
04.04.89 Jesus Poll W RSC 10 Los Angeles (*WBA S. Bantamweight Title Defence*)
Summary: 41 contests, won 34, lost 7.

Chris Eubank
Brighton, England. *Born* 08.08.66
Middleweight

03.10.85 Tim Brown W PTS 4 Atlantic City
07.11.85 Kenny Cannida W PTS 4 Atlantic City
08.01.86 Mike Bragwell W PTS 4 Atlantic City
25.02.86 Eric Holland W PTS 4 Atlantic City
25.03.87 James Canty W PTS 4 Atlantic City
15.02.88 Darren Parker W RSC 1 Copthorne
07.03.88 Winston Burnett W PTS 6 Hove
26.04.88 Michael Justin W RSC 5 Hove
04.05.88 Greg George W RSC 5 Wembley
18.05.88 Steve Aquilina W RSC 4 Portsmouth
31.01.89 Simon Collins W RSC 4 London
08.02.89 Anthony Logan W PTS 8 London
01.03.89 Franki Moro W PTS 8 London
Summary: 13 contests, won 13.

Mike Evans
Illinois, USA. *Born* 1960
Heavyweight

02.06.83 Dee Dee Collier W PTS 4 Los Angeles
04.08.83 Frank Garcia DREW 4 Los Angeles
26.08.83 Ricky Reese L RSC 1 Los Angeles
02.06.84 Larry Roberson W PTS 6 Chicago
11.08.84 Jim Peat W RSC 3 Woodstock
15.11.84 Tyrell Biggs L PTS 6 New York
29.05.85 Don Townsend W RSC 4 Merrillville
28.06.85 Larry Roberson W RSC 1 Hammond
08.08.85 Wesley Smith W PTS 6 Chicago
21.09.85 Jessie Hicks W RSC 5 Chicago
20.11.85 Frank Draper W RSC 3 Erie
12.12.85 Dave Slaughter W RSC 7 Chicago
13.12.86 Mike Cohen W RSC 5 Bethlehem
30.05.87 Oscar Holman W PTS 8 Las Vegas
30.06.87 Jack Johnson W RSC 1 Detroit
01.08.87 Steve Zouski W PTS 8 Las Vegas
11.02.88 Steve Zouski W PTS 10 Chicago
21.05.88 David Jaco W RSC 8 Gary
07.12.88 Joey Christjohn W RSC 3 Harvey
09.03.89 Rod Stockton W CO 4 Redondo Beach
20.04.89 Tony Tubbs L PTS 10 Redondo Beach
Summary: 21 contests, won 17, drew 1, lost 3.

Willie Featherstone
Toronto, Canada. *Born* 14.05.59
Canadian L. Heavyweight Champion. Former Commonwealth L. Heavyweight Champion

17.01.78 Murray Sutherland W RSC 3 Toronto
03.04.78 Al Bell W CO 1 Toronto
11.07.78 Harry White W RSC 1 Toronto
05.02.79 Tyrone Freeman W PTS 8 Hull
18.12.79 Bob Lalonde W CO 1 Montreal
27.01.80 Jo Jo Dent W RSC 2 Montreal
12.02.80 Elisha Obed L PTS 8 Montreal
25.03.80 Marciano Bernardi DREW 10 Montreal
27.01.81 Bill Hollis W RSC 4 Toronto
02.06.81 Wes Rowe W PTS 8 Toronto
10.12.81 Doug Demmings L PTS 10 Winnipeg
22.06.84 Tony Curovic W PTS 8 Toronto
11.12.84 Bill Hollis W CO 1 Toronto
14.02.85 Frankie Minton W PTS 8 Toronto
31.05.85 Tim Long W RSC 3 Toronto
03.12.85 Darryl Spain W CO 5 Toronto
01.04.86 Jerry Harris W PTS 8 Toronto
14.06.86 Danny Lindstrom L PTS 8 Edmonton
18.08.86 Roddy MacDonald W RTD 5 Toronto (*Canadian L. Heavyweight Title Challenge*)
14.03.87 Roddy MacDonald W PTS 12 Sydney (*Canadian L. Heavyweight Title Defence*)
12.09.87 Enoch Chama W PTS 12 Sydney (*Vacant Commonwealth L. Heavyweight Title*)
08.12.87 Danny Lindstrom W PTS 12 Toronto (*Commonwealth and Canadian L. Heavyweight Title Defence*)
27.05.88 Dave Fidler W RSC 9 Port Hawkesbury (*Commonwealth & Canadian L. Heavyweight Title Defence*)
11.11.88 Virgil Hill L RSC 10 Bismark (*WBA L. Heavyweight Title Challenge*)
21.04.89 Guy Waters L PTS 12 Sydney (*Commonwealth L. Heavyweight Title Defence*)
Summary: 25 contests, won 19, drew 1, lost 5.

Jeff Fenech
Sydney, Australia. *Born* 28.05.64
Former WBC & Australian Featherweight Champion. Former Undefeated WBC S. Bantamweight Champion. Former Undefeated IBF Bantamweight Champion. Former Undefeated Australian S. Flyweight Champion

12.10.84 Bobby Williams W RSC 2 Marrickville
26.10.84 Percy Israel W RSC 7 Marrickville
30.11.84 Junior Thompson W RSC 3 Marrickville (*Vacant Australian S. Flyweight Title*)
15.12.84 Iliesa Manila W RSC 2 Suva
01.02.85 Wayne Mulholland W RSC 5 Dapto
04.03.85 Rolly Navarro W RSC 4 Sydney
26.04.85 Satoshi Shingaki W RSC 9 Sydney (*IBF Bantamweight Title Challenge*)
14.06.85 John Matienza W RSC 6 Sydney
26.07.85 John Farrell W CO 9 Brisbane
23.08.85 Satoshi Shingaki W CO 3 Sydney (*IBF Bantamweight Title Defence*)
04.11.85 Kenny Butts W RTD 2 Brisbane
02.12.85 Jerome Coffee W PTS 15 Sydney (*IBF Bantamweight Title Defence*)
11.04.86 Daniel Zaragoza W PTS 10 Sydney
18.07.86 Steve McCrory W RSC 14 Sydney (*IBF Bantamweight Title Defence*)
03.04.87 Tony Miller W PTS 12 Melbourne (*Australian Featherweight Title Challenge*)
08.05.87 Samart Payakarun W RSC 4 Sydney (*WBC S. Bantamweight Title Challenge*)
10.07.87 Greg Richardson W RTD 5 Sydney (*WBC S. Bantamweight Title Defence*)
16.10.87 Carlos Zarate W TD 4 Sydney (*WBC S. Bantamweight Title Defence*)
11.12.87 Osmar Avila W CO 1 Sydney
07.03.88 Victor Callejas W RSC 10 Sydney (*Vacant WBC Featherweight Title*)
12.08.88 Tyrone Downes W RSC 5 Melbourne (*WBC Featherweight Title Defence*)
30.11.88 George Navarro W RSC 5 Melbourne (*WBC Featherweight Title Defence*)
08.04.89 Marcos Villasana W PTS 12 Melbourne (*WBC Featherweight Title Defence*)
Summary: 23 contests, won 23.

Antoine Fernandez
Montbeliard, France. *Born* 02.04.65
Welterweight

12.09.86 Fred Costa W RTD 3 Paris
25.10.86 Pascal Lorcy W RTD 8 St Nazaire
03.11.86 Abder Souhihi W RTD 3 Paris
08.12.86 Brahim Messaoudi W PTS 10 Paris
06.02.87 Francesco Galli W CO 2 Antibes
28.02.87 Jean-Marie Touati DREW 12 Vincennes (*French Welterweight Title Challenge*)
16.04.87 Mike English W CO 1 Marseilles
30.04.87 Memo Rojas W CO 1 Nice
15.05.87 Ron Perkins W CO 3 Geneva
08.06.87 Harlein Holden W CO 2 Merignac
25.06.87 Luciano Navarra W PTS 8 Geneva
19.07.87 Simon Eubanks W PTS 8 St Tropez
08.10.87 Eduardo Brinoles W RSC 5 Paris
06.11.87 Lennie Gloster W RSC 2 Antibes
27.12.87 Donald Gwynn W CO 3 Martigny
04.03.88 Mauro Martelli L PTS 12 Geneva (*EBU Welterweight Title Challenge*)
15.05.88 Walter Cowans W CO 5 Casablanca
26.05.88 Juan Estrada W RSC 5 Vincennes
26.06.88 Sergio Aguirre W RTD 4 Grande Synthe
11.09.88 Ricky Randall W RSC 4 Lille
26.09.88 Mark Donwell W RSC 4 Noget sur Marne
08.10.88 Anthony Travis W PTS 8 Franconville
14.10.88 Mike Essett W RSC 6 Lausanne
04.11.88 Keheven Johnson W RSC 2 Annecy
21.11.88 Mike Essett W CO 5 Amiens
22.12.88 Tomas Garcia W PTS 8 Paris
28.01.89 Ken Foreman W RSC 5 Franconville
13.02.89 Eric Martin W PTS 10 Nogent
10.04.89 Alejandro Robles W RSC 4 Baltard
Summary: 29 contests, won 27, drew 1, lost 1.

Ernesto Ford
Colon, Panama. *Born* 06.11.65
Latin American S. Flyweight Champion

14.12.84 Martin Barcenas W CO 2 Colon
19.01.85 German Henriquez W RSC 1 Colon
01.03.85 Jose Cepeda W CO 3 Colon
30.03.85 Felipe Lam W CO 2 Colon
27.04.85 Gilberto Barcenas W PTS 4 Colon
15.06.85 Fabrice Benichou W PTS 6 Panama City
01.11.85 Luis Chanis W PTS 6 Colon
29.03.86 Ernesto Sanchez W PTS 8 Colon
31.05.86 Jose Chacon W PTS 10 Colon
13.09.86 Edgar Monserrat L PTS 10 Panama City
21.02.87 Rafael Montero W RSC 4 Panama City
20.06.87 Alex Miranda W RSC 7 Colon
17.10.87 Luis Chanis W PTS 10 Colon
20.02.88 Oscar Bolivar W RSC 9 Panama City
16.07.88 Jairo Martinez W PTS 10 Colon
06.08.88 Jesus Bastardo W RSC 2 Colon
17.09.88 Alfredo Lugo W RSC 3 Colon (*Latin American S. Flyweight Title Challenge*)
28.04.89 Jose Castillo W RSC 5 Panama City
Summary: 18 contests, won 17, lost 1.

George Foreman
Marshall, USA. *Born* 22.01.48
Former World Heavyweight Champion

23.06.69 Don Waldheim W RSC 3 New York
01.07.69 Fred Askew W CO 1 Houston
14.07.69 Sylvester Dulaire W RSC 1 Washington
18.08.69 Chuck Wepner W RSC 3 New York
18.09.69 John Carroll W CO 1 Seattle
23.09.69 Cookie Wallace W CO 2 Houston
07.10.69 Vernon Clay W CO 2 Houston
31.10.69 Roberto Davila W PTS 8 New York
05.11.69 Leo Peterson W CO 4 Scranton
18.11.69 Max Martinez W CO 2 Houston
06.12.69 Bob Hazleton W CO 1 Las Vegas
16.12.69 Levi Forte W PTS 10 Miami
18.12.69 Gary Wiler W CO 1 Seattle

George Foreman

Christopher M. Farina

06.01.70 Charlie Polite W CO 4 Houston
26.01.70 Jack O'Halloran W CO 5 New York
16.02.70 Greg Peralta W PTS 10 New York
31.03.70 Rufus Brassell W CO 1 Houston
17.04.70 James J. Woody W RSC 3 New York
29.04.70 Aaron Eastling W CO 4 Cleveland
16.05.70 George Johnson W RSC 7 Los Angeles
20.07.70 Roger Russell W CO 1 Philadelphia
04.08.70 George Chuvalo W RSC 3 New York
03.11.70 Lou Bailey W CO Oklahoma City
18.11.70 Boone Kirkman W RSC 2 New York
19.12.70 Mel Turnbow W RSC 1 Seattle
08.02.71 Charlie Boston W CO 1 St Paul
03.04.71 Stanford Harris W CO 2 Lake Geneva
10.05.71 Greg Peralta W RSC 10 Oakland
14.09.71 Vic Scott W RSC 1 El Paso
21.09.71 Leroy Caldwell W CO 3 Beaumont
07.10.71 Ollie Wilson W CO 2 San Antonio
29.10.71 Luis Pires W RSC 4 New York
29.02.72 Murphy Goodwin W CO 2 Austin
07.03.72 Clarence Boone W CO 2 Beaumont
10.04.72 Ted Gullick W CO 2 Los Angeles
11.05.72 Miguel Paez W CO 2 Oakland
10.10.72 Terry Sorrells W CO 2 Salt Lake City
22.01.73 Joe Frazier W RSC 2 Kingston
(*World Heavyweight Title Challenge*)
01.09.73 Joe Roman W CO 1 Tokyo
(*World Heavyweight Title Defence*)
26.03.74 Ken Norton W RSC 2 Caracas
(*World Heavyweight Title Defence*)
30.10.74 Muhammad Ali L CO 8 Kinshasa
(*World Heavyweight Title Defence*)
24.01.76 Ron Lyle W CO 5 Las Vegas
15.06.76 Joe Frazier W RSC 5 New York
14.08.76 Scott le Doux W CO 3 Utica
15.10.76 Dino Dennis W RSC 4 Los Angeles
22.01.77 Pedro Agosta W CO 4 Pensacola
17.03.77 Jimmy Young L PTS 12 San Juan
09.03.87 Steve Zouski W RSC 4 Sacramento
09.07.87 Charlie Hostetter W CO 3 Oakland
15.09.87 Bobby Crabtree W RSC 6 Springfield
21.11.87 Tim Anderson W RSC 4 Orlando
18.12.87 Rick Sekorski W RSC 3 Las Vegas
23.01.88 Tom Trimm W CO 1 Orlando
05.02.88 Guido Trane W RSC 5 Las Vegas
19.03.88 Dwight Muhammad Qawi W RSC 7 Las Vegas
21.05.88 Frank Williams W RSC 3 Anchorage
26.06.88 Carlos Hernandez W RSC 4 Atlantic City
25.08.88 Ladislao Mijangos W RSC 2 Fort Myers
10.09.88 Bobby Hitz W CO 1 Detroit
27.10.88 Tony Fulilangi W RSC 2 Marshall
28.12.88 David Jaco W RSC 1 Bakersfield
26.01.89 Mark Young W RSC 7 Rochester
16.02.89 Manuel de Almeida W RSC 3 Orlando
30.04.89 J. B. Williamson W RSC 5 Galveston
Summary: 64 contests, won 62, lost 2.

Tunde (The Doctor) Foster
New York, USA. *Born* England 09.11.65
WBA Americas Lightweight Champion

10.12.85 Dennis Wade W CO 1 Atlantic City
14.01.86 Jorge Sanchez W RSC 3 Atlantic City
17.04.86 Darryl Loving W RSC 1 New York
05.06.86 James Woodhouse W PTS 6 New York
10.07.86 Calvin Hardy W RSC 1 New York
28.08.86 Danny Parker W RSC 5 New York
09.10.86 Richie Otero W RSC 5 New York
13.11.86 Tim Davies W CO 2 New York
11.12.86 Ron Washington W CO 2 New York
08.01.87 Sebastian Wilburn W PTS 6 New York
12.03.87 Derrick McGuire W PTS 8 New York
04.06.87 Lamont Buchanan W RSC 2 New York
20.08.87 Chris Silvas W RSC 2 New York
10.10.87 Sam Ray Taylor W PTS 8 Las Vegas
06.03.88 Bryant Paden DREW 8 New York
28.04.88 Pedro Pablo Torres W RSC 4 New York
02.06.88 Jerry Smith W RSC 2 New York
24.06.88 Anthony English W PTS 8 Atlantic City
11.08.88 Juan Nunez W RSC 6 New York
08.09.88 Lupe Hernandez W RSC 5 New York
10.11.88 Darren McGrew W PTS 10 New York
03.01.89 Johnny Duplessis L RSC 9 New Orleans
13.04.89 Johnny de la Rosa W RSC 10 New York
(*Vacant WBA Americas Lightweight Title*)
Summary: 23 contests, won 21, drew 1, lost 1.

Tunde Foster

Peter Goldfield/USA

Miguel Francia
Buenos Aires, Argentine. *Born* 19.09.61
Argentinian Featherweight Champion

18.11.83 Eduardo Bagala W PTS 6 Tres Arroyos
24.03.84 Eduardo Bagala W TD 5 Buenos Aires
02.06.84 Eduardo Bagala W PTS 6 Buenos Aires
21.07.84 Fidel Avila L RSC 5 Buenos Aires
01.09.84 Antonio Aguirre W RSC 3 Buenos Aires
06.10.84 Jorge Fernandez W PTS 8 Buenos Aires
16.03.85 Julio Ramirez W PTS 8 Buenos Aires
12.04.85 Luis Rodriguez W PTS 10 Rosario
07.06.85 Julio Ramirez L PTS 10 San Nicolas
02.08.85 Carlos Velazquez DREW 10 Caleta Oliva
30.08.85 Esteban Bustos DREW 10 Salta
18.09.85 Pedro Decima L CO 3 Buenos Aires
14.12.85 Osmar Avila L RSC 8 Lincoln
14.03.86 Carlos Velazquez W PTS 10 Rivadavia
06.06.86 Ramon Dominguez W DIS 10 Rosario
07.11.86 Osmar Avila L PTS 12 Mar del Plata
25.07.87 Jose Mario Lopez W PTS 12 Buenos Aires
(*Argentinian Featherweight Title Challenge*)
09.10.87 Ruben Astorga W PTS 10 Montevideo
18.12.87 Fidel Avila W PTS 10 Temperley
02.03.88 Ruben Astorga W PTS 10 Buenos Aires
06.05.88 Raul Gomez W PTS 10 Montevideo
10.06.88 Sidnei dal Rovere L TD 6 Salvador
(*Vacant South American Featherweight Title*)
23.07.88 Marcelo Luna W PTS 10 Buenos Aires
08.09.88 Jose Fernandez W RTD 7 Venado Tuerto
14.10.88 Hugo Ramirez W TD 5 Laboulaye
02.12.88 Juan Astorga W RSC 9 Tapiales
16.12.88 Fidel Avila W CO 10 Rio Grande
18.03.89 Claudio Martinet DREW 10 Buenos Aires
Summary: 28 contests, won 19, drew 3, lost 6.

Jeff Frankin
Las Vegas, USA. *Born* 30.09.62
Former USBA Featherweight Champion

29.09.83 Roberto Cantu W PTS 6 Las Vegas
25.10.83 Manny Juarez W PTS 6 Las Vegas
22.12.83 Tito Arazte W RSC 3 Las Vegas
20.01.84 David Vela W PTS 4 Las Vegas
03.02.84 John Rivera W RTD 3 Las Vegas
11.10.84 Candid Partida W PTS 6 Las Vegas
13.12.84 Roy Muniz W PTS 4 Stateline
24.05.85 Andy Minsker L PTS 6 Las Vegas
25.09.85 Evelio Perez DREW 6 Las Vegas
30.03.86 Gus Lopez W RSC 4 Las Vegas
22.04.86 Danny Garcia W PTS 6 Las Vegas
23.06.86 Evelio Perez W PTS 4 Las Vegas
13.07.86 Don Porter W RSC 3 Las Vegas
25.07.86 Lupe Gutierrez L PTS 8 Las Vegas
17.10.86 Sylvester Kennon W CO 4 Bismark
11.11.86 Alex Vega W CO 1 Las Vegas
26.12.86 Mark Perea W PTS 8 Las Vegas
05.03.87 Adam Garcia W RSC 4 Las Vegas
20.03.87 Jesus Poll DREW 8 Las Vegas
18.07.87 Adam Garcia W PTS 10 Las Vegas
09.10.87 Tracy Patterson W PTS 10 Las Vegas
18.12.87 Steve Cruz W PTS 10 Las Vegas
05.02.88 Bernard Taylor DREW 12 Las Vegas
(*NABF Featherweight Title Challenge*)
08.04.88 Aaron Lopez W PTS 12 Las Vegas
(*Vacant USBA Featherweight Title*)
26.07.88 Hugo Anguiano W PTS 10 Reseda
15.10.88 Miguel Medina W RSC 6 Bakersfield
06.03.89 Lupe Gutierrez L PTS 12 Reno
(*USBA Featherweight Title Defence*)
Summary: 27 contests, won 21, drew 3, lost 3.

Moises Fuentes
Bucaramanga, Colombia
Former Colombian S. Bantamweight Champion

11.03.83 Jorge Acosta W PTS 4 Barranquilla
29.10.83 Augusto Borge W CO 5 Bucaramanga
26.11.83 Kadid Prada W CO 3 Bucaramanga
30.04.84 Gustavo Dixon W CO 6 Bucaramanga
09.03.85 Juan Estupinan W PTS 8 Bucaramanga
27.04.85 Jesus Espitia W RSC 5 Bucaramanga
17.08.85 Mario Livingstone W CO 5 Bucaramanga
(*Colombian S. Bantamweight Title Challenge*)
05.10.85 Ezequiel Hernandez W PTS 10 Bucaramanga
30.11.85 Marcelino Gelez W CO 6 Bucaramanga
(*Colombian S. Bantamweight Title Defence*)
22.03.86 Ezequiel Hernandez W PTS 10 Bucaramanga
(*Colombian S. Bantamweight Title Defence*)
09.05.86 Manuel Salgado W PTS 10 San Vincente
(*Colombian S. Bantamweight Title Defence*)
03.10.86 Alejandro Galvis W RSC 5 Bucaramanga
(*Colombian S. Bantamweight Title Defence*)
08.11.86 Jaime Castellon W RSC 7 Bucaramanga
(*Colombian S. Bantamweight Title Defence*)
13.03.87 Joaquin Caraballo W CO 6 Bucaramanga
(*Colombian S. Bantamweight Title Defence*)
03.04.87 Alvaro Narvaez W PTS 10 Bucaramanga
(*Colombian S. Bantamweight Title Defence*)
15.05.87 Luis Mendoza L PTS 10 Cartagena
(*Colombian S. Bantamweight Title Defence*)
02.08.87 Francisco Arroyo W PTS 10 Barranquilla
19.12.87 Gabreil Narvaez W PTS 8 Bucaramanga
05.02.88 Robinson Garcia W PTS Medellin
21.05.88 Jose Sanabria L CO 5 Bucaramanga
(*Vacant IBF S. Bantamweight Title*)
07.10.88 Jose Burgos W PTS 8 Bello
01.04.89 Antonio Morelos W CO 3 Bucaramanga
Summary: 22 contests, won 20, lost 2.

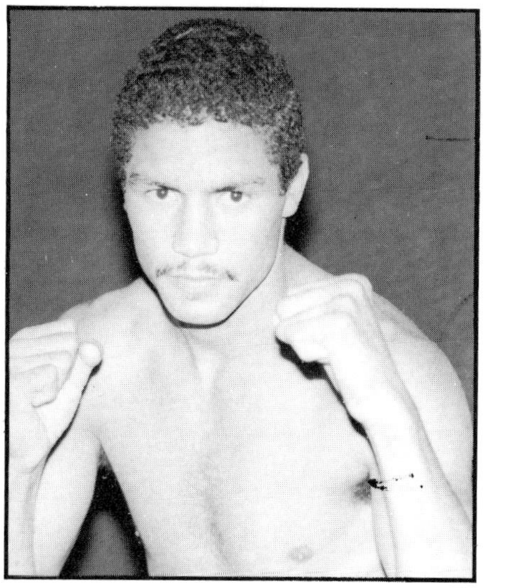

Sammy Fuentes

Peter Goldfield/USA

Sammy Fuentes
Loiza, Puerto Rico. *Born* 18.02.64
Lightweight

20.11.82 Victor Aponte W RSC 3 Arguadilla
12.02.83 Roberto Ortiz W PTS 4 Canovanas
24.03.83 Victor Fontanez W RSC 2 Trujillo
16.04.83 Edwin Rodriguez W RSC 2 Trujillo
18.08.83 Juan Nazario L RSC 5 Trujillo

11.11.83 Angus Alleyne W CO 1 Port of Spain
16.12.83 Fitzroy Davidson L DIS 7 Port of Spain
01.09.84 Roberto Lopez W CO 2 Carolina
21.02.85 Jocko King W PTS 6 Atlantic City
25.03.85 Cirilo Morell W CO 2 New York
19.06.85 Othal Dixon W PTS 10 Atlantic City
09.10.85 Harry Arroyo W RSC 7 Atlantic City
13.11.85 Roberto Juarez W RSC 8 Las Vegas
10.01.86 Ali Karim Muhammad W RSC 8 Atlantic City
14.02.86 Marvin Garris W RSC 5 Atlantic City
06.04.86 Frankie Warren L PTS 10 Corpus Christi
30.05.86 Frankie Randall L RSC 2 Atlantic City
28.11.86 Roger Mayweather L RSC 9 Atlantic City (*Vacant Con. Am. Lightweight Title*)
18.04.87 Jerome Spottville W RSC 1 San Juan
25.06.87 Nick Parker W RSC 6 San Juan
09.12.87 Tony Martin W CO 5 Atlantic City
12.02.88 Fred Pendleton L RSC 1 Atlantic City
05.10.88 Vince Releford W RSC 2 Los Angeles
09.01.89 Santos Cardona W RSC 2 Los Angeles
28.02.89 John Montes W RSC 7 Los Angeles
Summary: 25 contests, won 19, lost 6.

Kaokor Galaxy
Petchaboon, Thailand. *Born* 15.05.59
Former WBA Bantamweight Champion. Former Undefeated Thai Bantamweight Champion

09.10.85 Kwanarong Savadivaree W CO 3 Bangkok
30.10.85 Kiat Kiatsonthaya W CO 4 Bangkok
27.11.85 Rakchai Kiatsontaya W PTS 6 Bangkok
08.01.86 Mansor Jitpatana W CO 4 Bangkok
19.02.86 Panchai Kiatsontaya W PTS 6 Bangkok
26.03.86 Nakalart Kiatsontaya W PTS 6 Bangkok
11.06.86 Rakchai Kiatsontaya W CO 5 Bangkok
09.07.86 Kwan Sisamnuay W CO 4 Bangkok (*Vacant Thai Bantamweight Title*)
13.08.86 Nakalart Kiatsontaya W CO 5 Bangkok
25.09.86 Singnoi Singkrungtorn W CO 5 Bangkok (*Thai Bantamweight Title Defence*)
14.01.87 Keiichi Ozaki W PTS 10 Bangkok
05.04.87 Yon-Man Cha W RSC 6 Bangkok
07.05.87 Ben Capaggan W RSC 2 Bangkok
25.06.87 Tony Pruitt W RSC 8 Bangkok
06.09.87 Russell Finn W RSC 3 Bangkok
12.10.87 Constancio Dangla W CO 4 Bangkok
14.12.87 Do-Buk Cha W CO 2 Bangkok
09.05.88 Wilfredo Vasquez W PTS 12 Bangkok (*WBA Bantamweight Title Challenge*)
14.08.88 Sung-Il Moon L TD 6 Pusan (*WBA Bantamweight Title Defence*)
12.09.88 John Matienza W RSC 3 Bangkok
09.11.88 Jorge Rodriguez W CO 8 Bangkok
15.01.89 Hun-Kuk Cha W CO 3 Bangkok
19.02.89 Noel Cornelio W CO 3 Bangkok
24.04.89 Speedy Kikuchi W CO 3 Bangkok
Summary: 24 contests, won 23, lost 1.

Kaosai Galaxy
Petchaboon, Thailand. *Born* 15.05.59
WBA S. Flyweight Champion. Former Undefeated Thai Bantamweight Champion

17.12.80 Pukk Srithum W CO 5 Bangkok
31.12.80 Prasong Sithkempetch W CO 3 Bangkok
26.01.81 Prasong Sithkempetch W CO 1 Bangkok
13.05.81 Terdsakdi Pornthavee W CO 3 Bangkok
10.06.81 Tanee Singchaowang W CO 1 Bangkok
24.06.81 Phichitsuk Kor-u-Sayarm W PTS 6 Bangkok
29.07.81 Sakda Saksuree L PTS 10 Bangkok (*Thai Bantamweight Title Challenge*)
29.08.81 Monsak Muangsurin W RSC 3 Bangkok
10.09.81 Sakda Saksuree W CO 6 Bangkok
14.10.81 Tsuguyuki Toma W CO 4 Bangkok
25.01.82 Sak Chorsirirat W CO 7 Bangkok (*Thai Bantamweight Title Challenge*)
10.03.82 Katsuyuki Ohashi W CO 7 Bangkok
14.04.82 Yu-Ok Joo W RSC 4 Bangkok
24.05.82 Ali Formentera W RSC 5 Bangkok
14.07.82 Agus Suyanto W RSC 4 Bangkok
26.08.82 Adan Uribe W CO 4 Bangkok
13.10.82 Willie Jensen W CO 2 Bangkok
27.11.82 Mun-Kyun Joo W RSC 4 Nakorn
24.12.82 Marciano Sekiyama W CO 4 Bangkok
23.02.83 Jose Luis Soto W CO 2 Bangkok
10.05.83 Luis Ibanez W CO 3 Bangkok
30.06.83 Montsayarm Mahacha W RSC 3 Bangkok
03.08.83 Chang-Yung Park W PTS 10 Bangkok
12.10.83 Gil Ragas W RSC 7 Bangkok
13.12.83 Noritetsu Kato W RTD 4 Bangkok
14.03.84 Sung-Um Jae W PTS 10 Bangkok
11.07.84 Val de Vera W RSC 7 Bangkok
02.09.84 Yun-Lee Moon W RSC 2 Bangkok
21.11.84 Eusebio Espinal W CO 6 Bangkok (*Vacant WBA S. Flyweight Title*)
06.03.85 Dong-Chun Lee W CO 7 Bangkok (*WBA S. Flyweight Title Defence*)
17.07.85 Rafael Orono W RSC 5 Bangkok (*WBA S. Flyweight Title Defence*)
23.12.85 Edgar Monserrat W RSC 2 Bangkok (*WBA S. Flyweight Title Defence*)
01.11.86 Israel Contreras W CO 5 Curacao (*WBA S. Flyweight Title Defence*)
28.02.87 Elly Pical W CO 14 Jakarta (*WBA S. Flyweight Title Defence*)
25.06.87 Joung-Sup Chun W CO 3 Bangkok
12.10.87 Byong-Kwan Chun W RSC 3 Bangkok (*WBA S. Flyweight Title Defence*)
26.01.88 Kongtoranee Payakarun W PTS 12 Bangkok (*WBA S. Flyweight Title Defence*)
09.05.88 Kap-Sup Song W RSC 7 Bangkok
17.09.88 Jun Llano W CO 3 Bangkok
09.10.88 Chang-Ho Choi W CO 8 Seoul (*WBA S. Flyweight Title Defence*)
15.01.89 Tae-Il Chang W CO 2 Bangkok (*WBA S. Flyweight Title Defence*)
08.04.89 Kenji Matsumura W PTS 12 Yokohama (*WBA S. Flyweight Title Defence*)
Summary: 42 contests, won 41, lost 1.

Manning (The Spoiler) Galloway
Columbus, USA. *Born* 27.04.60
USBA Welterweight Champion

06.12.78 Gene Ellington W PTS 6 Cleveland
24.01.79 Mel Hauser W PTS 6 Cleveland
27.04.79 Mike Blunt L PTS 6 Dayton
09.05.79 Calvin Straughter W PTS 6 Columbus
17.05.79 Forrest Winchester L PTS 6 Columbus
28.06.79 Phil Beattie W CO 2 Columbus
01.08.79 Calvin Sraughter W PTS 4 Columbus
30.09.79 Larry McCall W PTS 8 Canton
01.12.79 Woody Harris W PTS 6 Detroit
28.12.79 Greg Netter W PTS 12 Columbus
09.02.80 Dale Gordon W PTS 6 Clarksburg
01.03.80 Tony Taylor W PTS 10 Columbus
29.03.80 W.C. Honnycut L PTS 6 Detroit
16.05.80 Curtis Taylor L CO 2 Lexington
30.05.80 Danny Paul L PTS 6 Wyandotte
04.10.80 Don Morgan W PTS 10 Morristown
09.01.81 Willie Rodriguez L PTS 12 Columbus
02.04.81 Bruce Johnson W PTS 8 Tampa
26.04.81 Tap Harris W PTS 10 Canton
10.09.81 Jerome Kinney W PTS 10 Detroit
23.01.82 Greg Netter W PTS 8 McConnellsville
05.03.82 Wendell Rutledge W RSC 2 Johnstown
16.04.82 Roy Gumbs DREW 10 Toronto
16.07.82 Lloyd Taylor W PTS 8 Washington
05.09.82 Charlie Weir L CO 7 Johannesburg
14.10.82 Dennis Fain W PTS 12 Akron
23.10.82 Calvin Porter L PTS 8 Lancaster
04.02.83 Dennis Fain W PTS 10 Akron
03.04.83 Darnell Knox W PTS 10 Akron
08.10.83 Nino la Rocca L PTS 8 St Vincent
02.12.83 Kenny Snow W PTS 10 Tampa
19.12.83 Greg Netter W PTS 8 Columbus
06.02.84 Forrest Pitts W CO 8 Columbus
12.03.84 Greg Harper W CO 6 Columbus
30.04.84 Sam Gervin W RSC 8 Columbus
21.05.84 Earl Caldwell W PTS 8 Columbus
09.07.84 Alonso Cates W PTS 8 Columbus
18.10.84 Earl Caldwell W RSC 4 Akron
04.04.85 Lloyd Taylor W PTS 10 Washington
13.07.85 Sammy Brooks W PTS 10 Oklahoma City
20.08.85 Al Long W PTS 10 Los Angeles
21.11.85 Jerome Kinney W PTS 10 Los Angeles
17.12.85 Diomedes Colome W PTS 12 Los Angeles
20.05.86 Al Hamza W PTS 10 Chicago
25.06.86 Luis Santana L TD 8 Los Angeles
27.04.87 Charles Nwokolo L PTS 12 Los Angeles
21.09.87 Pete Seward W PTS 6 Akron
14.01.88 Oscar Pena W PTS 8 Houston
04.05.88 Tony Releford W RSC 7 Houston
06.07.88 Rollin Williams W PTS 12 Houston (*USBA Welterweight Title Challenge*)
05.12.88 Charles Hollis W PTS 10 Tyler
23.01.89 Said Skouma W PTS 10 Paris
31.03.89 Eric Hernandez W PTS 12 Las Vegas (*USBA Welterweight Title Defence*)
Summary: 53 contests, won 41, drew 1, lost 11.

Mauro Galvano
Fiumicino, Italy. *Born* 30.03.64
S. Middleweight

26.02.86 Gabriele Lazzari W RSC 4 Cosenza
19.04.86 Joseph Kassongo W PTS 6 San Remo
08.05.86 Ndomingiedi Lusikina W PTS 4 Salerno
04.10.86 Klayina Awouitoh W PTS 6 Turin
24.10.86 Biagio Vallefuoco DREW 6 Carrara
25.07.87 Ngomingiedi Lusikina W PTS 6 Ostia
31.10.87 Michel Moukory W RSC 4 Alzano
27.03.88 Ngomingiedi Lusikina W PTS 6 Crotone
21.05.88 Moba Salay W PTS 6 San Mango
31.07.88 Abdel Moustafa W PTS 8 Livorno
14.09.88 Julio Gonzalez W PTS 8 Scheggia
19.11.88 Mwehu Beya DREW 12 Gragnano (*Italian L. Heavyweight Title Challenge*)
25.01.89 Kevin Roper W RSC 5 Arezzo
Summary: 13 contests, won 11, drew 2.

Agustin (Baby) Garcia
Colombia
Former Colombian L. Flyweight Champion

28.06.80 Jairo Bedoya W PTS 6 Cartagena
22.08.80 John Jaramillo W PTS 8 Maicao
22.11.80 Rodolfo Rodriguez L RSC 3 Maracaibo
30.01.81 Felipe Medrano W CO 2 Cartagena (*Vacant Colombian L. Flyweight Title*)
27.03.81 Orlando Maestre DREW 12 Barranquilla (*Colombian L. Flyweight Title Defence*)
06.07.82 Reinaldo Becerra L PTS 12 Caracas (*Con. Am. L. Flyweight Title Challenge*)
22.08.81 Nelson Polanco W CO 10 Apartado (*Colombian L. Flyweight Title Defence*)
19.06.82 Homer Meza L RSC 8 Cartagena
27.08.82 Felipe Medrano W PTS 12 Maicao (*Colombian L. Flyweight Title Defence*)
27.11.82 Agustin Higirino L RSC 3 Santa Marta
12.05.83 Uriel Londono W PTS 10 Cerete (*Colombian L. Flyweight Title Defence*)
18.06.83 Nelson Polanco W PTS 10 Cartagena (*Colombian L. Flyweight Title Defence*)
20.08.83 Jose Iriarte W PTS 10 Cartagena (*Columbian L. Flyweight Title Defence*)
18.02.84 Jorge Lugo W PTS 8 Cartagena
14.04.84 Alfredo Gomez W PTS 10 Cartagena
27.07.84 Rodolfo Blanco W PTS 10 Cartagena (*Colombian L. Flyweight Title Defence*)
21.09.84 Juan Gomez W RSC 3 Cartagena
06.10.84 Bernardo Gonzalez W PTS 8 Cartagena
29.03.85 Prudencio Cardona W PTS 10 Cartagena
03.05.85 Victor Sierra W PTS 10 Cartagena
21.06.85 Santos Hoo W PTS 10 Cartagena
20.07.85 Francisco Quiroz W PTS 10 Cartagena
18.10.85 Benedicto Murillo DREW 10 Cartagena
31.01.86 Rodolfo Blanco L PTS 10 Cartagena (*Colombian L. Flyweight Title Defence*)
08.08.86 Rafael Julio DREW 8 Santa Marta
12.09.86 Manuel Julio W RSC 2 Cartagena
31.10.86 Ruben Veraga W PTS 6 Monteria
21.12.86 Alfredo Cardales W RSC 4 Cartagena
13.02.87 Jose Castillo W CO 5 Barranquilla
13.03.87 Arnold Velasquez W PTS 8 Cartagena
03.04.87 Jose Iriarte W PTS 8 Barranquilla
28.06.87 Jung-Koo Chang L RSC 10 Seoul (*WBC L. Flyweight Title Challenge*)
11.09.87 Manuel Julio W PTS 10 Barranquilla
30.10.87 Felipe Medrano W CO 3 Cartagena
19.02.88 Luis Salazar W CO 5 Cartagena
04.03.88 Bernardo Ceballos W RTD 2 Santa Marta
25.03.88 Orlando Maestre W PTS 10 Barranquilla
18.11.88 Alfredo Cardales W PTS 8 Barranquilla
16.04.89 Bong-Jun Kim L RSC 7 Seoul (*Vacant WBA M. Flyweight Title*)
Summary: 39 contests, won 29, drew 3, lost 7.

Luis Gabriel Garcia
Venezuela
Latin American Welterweight Champion

20.04.85 Danilo Villalobos W PTS 4 Margarita
08.06.85 Alexander Jimenez W RSC 1 Caracas
15.07.85 Jose Guzman W RSC 5 Maracaibo
27.07.85 Ali Garrido W CO 2 Margarita
02.11.85 Danilo Tronconi W RSC 1 Maracaibo
17.02.86 Benito Martinez W RSC 1 Turmero
08.08.87 Errol Williams W CO 1 Caraballera
18.09.87 Antonio Guerra W CO 3 Caraballera
29.11.87 Wayne Harris W PTS 10 Georgetown
16.05.88 Dario Liriano W RSC 4 Santo Domingo

06.08.88 Rogelio Cousins W RSC 2 Colon
17.09.88 Erick Perea W RSC 5 Colon
(*Vacant Latin American Welterweight Title*)
14.01.89 Mateo Valdez W RSC 7 Turmero
28.04.89 Rigoberto Ramos W RSC 6 Panama City
Summary: 14 contests, won 14.

Loreto Garza
Sacramento, USA. *Born* 23.05.62
Con. Am. L. Welterweight Champion

01.02.83 Don Canada W CO 2 Sacramento
05.04.83 James Sowell W CO 2 Sacramento
21.06.83 Francisco Estrella W CO 1 Sacramento
21.10.83 Howard Smith W RSC 4 Sacramento
25.10.83 Jose Resendez W CO 3 Sacramento
15.11.83 Francisco Tomas Cruz L RSC 4 Sacramento
06.03.84 Peter Cunningham W PTS 6 Sacramento
03.04.84 Jerry Lewis W RSC 3 Sacramento
03.07.84 Mario Castro W RSC 2 Sacramento
18.06.85 Ernie Landeros DREW 6 Sacramento
15.08.85 Rene Hedman W RSC 1 Sacramento
23.02.86 Chauncey Hayes W PTS 8 Richmond
05.06.86 Erwin Brown W RSC 3 Sacramento
20.07.86 Roberto Garcia W RSC 2 Stateline
27.09.86 Roberto Garcia W CO 7 Stateline
09.03.87 Mucio Nava W CO 1 Sacramento
21.05.87 Willie Montana W RSC 6 Sacramento
01.07.87 Gary Williams W RSC 1 Sacramento
01.09.87 Amy Pacana W RSC 2 Sacramento
25.09.87 Javier Juarez W RSC 1 Sacramento
12.02.88 Charlie "Choo Choo" Brown W RSC 4 Sacramento
22.04.88 Harry Arroyo W RSC 1 Sacramento
(*Con. Am. L. Welterweight Title Challenge*)
23.07.88 Stewart Baynes W RSC 9 Sacramento
25.01.89 Joe Manley W CO 7 Sacramento
05.03.89 Manuel Nery W RSC 2 Sacramento
Summary: 25 contests, won 23, drew 1, lost 1.

Gino (Young Willie Pep) Gelormino
New York, USA. *Born* 05.09.60
Con. Am. S. Featherweight Champion

23.04.81 Reg Hill W PTS 4 New York
28.05.81 Joe Barmah W RSC 1 New York
17.07.81 Quadia Hart W RSC 1 New York
09.01.82 Ramon Lopez W RSC 6 New York
08.02.82 Mark Cerenzia W RSC 4 New York
26.02.82 Julio de Jesus W PTS 6 New York
15.03.82 Tim Mark W RSC 1 New York
12.04.82 Jaime Renta W RSC 3 New York
15.06.82 Jose Ortiz W PTS 8 New York
16.07.82 Mujahid Muhammad W RSC 3 New York
26.08.82 Sylvester Price W RSC 6 Atlantic City
16.10.82 Edwin Rivera W PTS 8 Atlantic City
19.11.82 Jim Magnifico W RSC 3 New York
25.02.83 Tony Trys W RSC 6 New York
22.04.83 Joe Mayes W RSC 2 New York
05.05.83 Sylvester Kennon L CO 5 Atlantic City
02.03.84 Frank Mackey W RSC 6 New York
14.12.84 Twist Welcome W RSC 4 New York
08.03.85 Tomas Diaz W PTS 10 New York
19.04.85 Teo Centeneo W RSC 1 Long Beach
01.11.85 Elijah Muhammad W PTS 10 New York
23.04.87 Richie Otero W PTS 8 New York
18.06.87 Donnie Parker W PTS 8 New York
24.02.88 Norman Bates W RSC 6 New York
25.03.88 Gary Stallworth W RSC 5 New York
02.06.88 Mike Grow W RSC 12 New York
(*Vacant Con. Am. S. Featherweight Title*)
25.08.88 Angel Hernandez W RSC 5 New York
(*Con. Am. S. Featherweight Title Defence*)
12.01.89 Darrin McGrew W RSC 2 New York
16.03.89 Manuel Rodriguez W CO 1 New York
21.04.89 Dana Roston W RSC 7 New York
Summary: 30 contests, won 29, lost 1.

Julio Gervacio
La Romana, Dominican Republic. *Born* 17.10.67
Former WBA S. Bantamweight Champion

21.12.85 Felix Llanos W CO 1 Caguas
05.03.86 Jose Vega DREW 4 Aguadilla
03.05.86 Wilfredo Lanza W CO 2 Guaynabo
30.05.86 Jesus Poll DREW 6 Curacao
22.06.86 Pedro Arroyo W RSC 3 San Juan
05.07.86 Javier Arce W CO 1 San Juan
06.09.86 Jose Rivera W RSC 1 San Juan
04.10.86 Atilano Quinones W PTS 6 San Juan
08.11.86 Jesus Filomeno W RSC 3 San Juan
06.12.86 Edwin Salgado W PTS 8 San Juan
10.01.87 Jorge Ortiz W RSC 3 San Juan
21.02.87 Jaime Polo W CO 2 San Juan
19.03.87 Manuel Miranda W RSC 2 San Juan
16.05.87 Rafael Forte W CO 2 San Juan
06.06.87 Jeff Hanna W RSC 4 San Juan
08.08.87 Carlos Flores W RSC 5 San Juan
03.09.87 Ramon Cruz W RSC 10 San Juan
28.11.87 Louie Espinosa W PTS 12 San Juan
(*WBA S. Bantamweight Title Challenge*)
27.02.88 Bernado Pinango L PTS 12 San Juan
(*WBA S. Bantamweight Title Defence*)
02.04.88 Paul Mingo W CO 2 San Juan
11.07.88 Angel Vargas W RSC 5 San Juan
06.10.88 Chris Diaz W RSC 5 Guaynabo
03.11.88 Santos Cruz W RSC 8 Trujillo Alto
29.04.89 Kenny Mitchell L PTS 12 San Juan
(*Vacant WBO S. Bantamweight Title*)
Summary: 24 contests, won 20, drew 2, lost 2.

Juan C. (Puma) Gimenez
Asuncion, Paraguay. *Born* 20.12.60
WBC International Middleweight Champion. Former South American L. Heavyweight Champion

02.07.82 Delfin Olivera W RSC 2 Asuncion
06.08.82 Clarismundo Silva W CO 4 Asuncion
17.09.82 Helmut Ulka W CO 6 Asuncion
14.10.82 Freddie Brown W PTS 10 Asuncion
04.02.83 Andres Olmedo W PTS 10 Asuncion
12.07.83 Luis Vega W RSC 4 Asuncion
12.08.83 Andres Olmedo W PTS 10 Asuncion
28.09.83 Alfredo Morales W CO 1 Asuncion
13.11.83 Jose Maria Flores W CO 1 Asuncion
(*Vacant South American L. Heavyweight Title*)
13.01.84 Juan Leiva W PTS 10 Asuncion
25.02.84 Jorge Servin W RTD 4 Asuncion
(*South American L. Heavyweight Title Defence*)
06.04.84 Jorge Salgado DREW 12 Asuncion
(*South American L. Heavyweight Title Defence*)
09.06.84 Cesar Romero L PTS 10 Buenos Aires
02.08.84 Juan Leiva W RTD 4 Posadas
08.09.84 Victor Robledo L PTS 12 Buenos Aires
(*South American L. Heavyweight Title Defence*)
14.12.84 Jorge Salgado W RSC 10 Asuncion
15.02.85 Ed Contreras W PTS 10 Asuncion
20.04.85 Roberto Ruiz W RSC 7 Buenos Aires
17.05.85 Enrique Coronel W PTS 10 Asuncion
04.08.85 Joao Tavares W CO 4 Asuncion
26.09.85 Antonio Caro W RTD 4 Asuncion
11.10.85 Enrique Coronel W CO 5 Obera
25.11.85 Osmar Ochoa W PTS 10 Asuncion
07.06.86 Carlos Herrera W CO 3 Buenos Aires
13.09.86 Juan Domingo Roldan L PTS 10 Buenos Aires
15.11.86 Pompilio Salgado DREW 10 Barranquilla
20.02.87 Mauro F. Cruz W RTD 8 Asuncion
20.03.87 Julio Gonzalez W PTS 10 Asuncion
08.05.87 Enrique Coronel W PTS 10 Asuncion
29.05.87 Hugo Vera W RSC 10 Asuncion
12.09.87 Roberto Duran L PTS 10 Miami
23.10.87 Jimmy Smith W CO 1 Miami
23.01.88 Jorge Amparo W PTS 12 Asuncion
(*WBC International Middleweight Title Challenge*)
22.03.88 Horacio Silva W PTS 10 Asuncion
04.08.88 Claudio Pereira W CO 5 Asuncion
08.10.88 Ralph Smiley W PTS 8 Franconville
14.11.88 Ralph Smiley W PTS 10 Noget
13.12.88 Ron Essett DREW 8 Baltard
25.03.89 Harvey Hester W CO 7 Casablanca
Summary: 39 contests, won 32, drew 3, lost 4.

Nestor Giovannini
Rafaela, Argentine. *Born* 07.02.61
WBC International L. Heavyweight Champion. Former Argentinian L. Heavyweight Champion

06.07.84 Mario Melo L PTS 6 Morteros
25.08.84 Miguel Mosna W PTS 6 Buenos Aires
06.10.84 Anibal Romero W PTS 6 Buenos Aires
03.11.84 Mario Melo W PTS 6 Buenos Aires
08.12.84 Miguel Mosna W PTS 8 Buenos Aires
22.03.85 Daniel Guibaudo W CO 5 Rafaela
11.04.85 Anibal Romero W PTS 10 Rafaela
18.05.85 Mario Melo L RSC 5 Buenos Aires
25.07.85 Juan Leiva W RTD 1 Rafaela
23.08.85 Anibal Romero W PTS 10 San Vicente
13.09.85 Victor Robledo W PTS 10 Rafaela
05.10.85 Sergio Merani DREW 8 Buenos Aires
21.11.85 Juan Rodriguez W PTS 10 Rafaela
20.12.85 Juan Fernandez W PTS 12 Rafaela
11.04.86 Miguel Cea W RSC 7 Rafaela
04.07.86 Pedro Ferraro W CO 8 Rafaela
23.08.86 Jorge Salgado W TD 11 Buenos Aires
(*Argentinian L. Heavyweight Title Challenge*)

Gino Gelormino walks away after stopping Angel Hernandez, August, 1988

13.11.86 Anibal Romero W PTS 10 Rafaela
12.12.86 Jorge Salgado DREW 12 Rafaela
(*South American L. Heavyweight Title Challenge*)
06.02.87 Clarismundo Silva W PTS 10 Rafaela
13.03.87 Eduardo Contreras W PTS 12 Rafaela
(*Argentinian L. Heavyweight Title Defence*)
09.06.87 Miguel Steinbach W PTS 10 Rafaela
10.07.87 Miguel Maldonado W RTD 7 Tandil
21.08.87 Angel Caro W PTS 10 Rafaela
25.09.87 Angel Caro W RTD 3 Resistencia
09.10.87 Nestor Albarracin W CO 4 Ceres
13.11.87 Eduardo Contreras W PTS 10 Rosario
12.12.87 Jorge Salgado L PTS 12 Ushuaia
(*Argentinian L. Heavyweight Title Defence*)
31.03.88 Noe Cruciani W CO 1 Spoleto
(*WBC International L. Heavyweight Title Challenge*)
14.09.88 Mwehu Beya W PTS 12 Scheggia
(*WBC International L. Heavyweight Title Defence*)
29.11.88 Mabobo Kamunga W PTS 8 San Pellegrino
17.03.89 Victor Robledo W PTS 10 Rafaela
Summary: 32 contests, won 27, drew 2, lost 3.

Rolando (Bad News) Gomez
Corpus Christi, USA. *Born* 10.06.65
Con. Am. S. Flyweight Champion

26.02.85 Raymond Medel W PTS 4 Corpus Christi
19.03.85 Ruben Flores W CO 1 Corpus Christi
09.04.85 Joel Elizondo W RSC 3 Corpus Christi
21.05.85 Jorge Fuentes W RSC 2 Corpus Christi
10.07.85 Luciano Reyes W RSC 2 Corpus Christi
17.12.85 Bobby de la Rosa W CO 4 Robstown
17.02.86 Ramiro Adams L PTS 8 Robstown
06.04.86 Tony Perez W RSC 4 Corpus Christi
15.06.86 Miguel Meza W CO 6 Corpus Christi
20.07.86 Tim Silva W PTS 6 Corpus Christi
23.08.86 Lee Cargle W PTS 6 Corpus Christi
20.11.86 Gilberto Villacana W RSC 4 Corpus Christi
10.03.87 Tim Silva W RSC 7 Corpus Christi
15.07.87 Jorge Samano W PTS 8 Phoenix
15.08.87 Eddie Rangel W RSC 5 San Antonio
04.11.87 Gilberto Contreras W PTS 12 Corpus Christi
(*Vacant Con. Am. S. Flyweight Title*)
14.02.88 Javier Diaz W RSC 9 Corpus Christi
09.08.88 Domicio Espinosa W RSC 6 Corpus Christi
12.09.88 Mike Ayala W PTS 10 Corpus Christi
30.11.88 Ramon Solis W PTS 10 Corpus Christi
13.02.89 Kenny Mitchell L PTS 12 Los Angeles
(*USBA Bantamweight Title Challenge*)
Summary: 21 contests, won 19, lost 2.

Paul Gonzales
Pecos, USA. *Born* 18.04.64
Former Undefeated NABF Flyweight Champion

10.08.85 Jose Torres W PTS 6 Reseda
05.12.85 Joey Roach W PTS 8 Hollywood
02.02.86 Alonzo Gonzales W PTS 12 Hollywood
(*NABF Flyweight Title Challenge*)
17.04.86 Javier Barajas W PTS 10 Bakersfield
20.07.86 Orlando Canizales W PTS 12 Stateline
(*NABF Flyweight Title Defence*)
07.07.87 Lucilo Nolasco W PTS 10 Los Angeles
18.10.87 Ron Cisneros W PTS 10 Stateline
23.05.88 Jorge Ortega W PTS 10 Irvine
17.06.88 Raymond Medel L PTS 12 San Antonio
(*USBA Flyweight Title Challenge*)
25.07.88 Javier Diaz W PTS 10 Irvine
25.01.89 Abe Garcia W RSC 5 Sacramento
Summary: 11 contests, won 10, lost 1.

David Gonzalez
Houston, USA. *Born* 1967
L. Welterweight

12.06.85 Isidro Trujano W RSC 3 Houston
17.07.85 Rogelio Leanos W CO 2 Houston
07.08.85 Steve McKyer W PTS 4 Houston
27.08.85 Gilford Darton W RSC 2 Houston
11.09.85 Ed Parker L CO 3 Houston
12.11.85 Ed Gonzalez W RSC 3 Houston
02.12.85 Jose Gonzalez W PTS 4 Virginia Beach
01.03.86 Fred Miller W CO 4 Beaumont
24.04.86 Ray Nino W CO 2 Houston
29.05.86 Ed Parker W PTS 8 Houston
20.07.86 Mario Salazar W RSC 3 Houston
14.11.86 Gustavo Martinez W RSC 3 San Antonio
15.03.87 Jerry Venzor W CO 5 San Antonio
15.04.87 Ernie Landeros DREW 10 Oakland
19.06.87 Nick Alfaro W RSC 2 Oakland
19.08.87 Joey Olivera W PTS 10 Oakland
05.10.87 Martin Quiroz W RSC 4 Santa Clara
26.02.88 Felix Gonzalez W RSC 10 Santa Clara
01.04.88 Dwayne Swift W RSC 8 Santa Clara
19.08.88 Ricarddo Velasquez W RSC 8 San Jose
30.09.88 Cedric Powell W RSC 5 Santa Clara
29.10.88 Antonio Gonzalez W PTS 10 Las Vegas
15.02.89 Antonio Gonzalez W CO 4 Oakland
29.03.89 Howard Stewart W PTS 10 Oakland
Summary: 24 contests, won 22, drew 1, lost 1.

Humberto (Chiquita) Gonzalez
Netzahualcoyotl, Mexico. *Born* 22.03.67
Former Undefeated Mexican L. Flyweight Champion

01.09.84 Jorge Ortega W PTS 4 Mexico City
19.12.84 Narciso Perez W RSC 1 Mexico City
20.02.85 Carmelo Perez W RSC 1 Mexico City
20.04.85 Francisco Villa Gomez W RSC 1 Mexico City
08.06.85 Martin Alvarez W RSC 2 Mexico City
27.07.85 Otilio Gallegos W RSC 2 Mexico City
07.09.85 Eduardo Ramirez W CO 4 Mexico City
09.11.85 Javier Alvarez W RSC 1 Mexico City
14.12.85 Carlos Rezago W CO 5 Mexico City
15.03.86 Martin Perez W RSC 2 Mexico City
22.05.86 Sergio Medina W CO 3 Neza
18.06.86 Alcie Hernandez W RSC 2 Mexico City
08.10.86 Agustin Macias W RSC 4 Mexico City
06.12.86 Jorge Gutierrez W RSC 5 Mexico City
22.02.87 Javier Alonso W CO 1 Acapulco
09.05.87 Ruben Padilla W RSC 7 Mexico City
13.06.87 Santiago Mendez W RSC 8 Mexico City
25.07.87 Jose M. Diaz W CO 2 Mexico City
26.09.87 Jorge Cano W PTS 12 Cancun
(*Mexican L. Flyweight Title Challenge*)
05.03.88 Jose L. Zepeda W CO 6 Tijuana
04.06.88 Javier Varguez W RSC 5 Mexico City
(*Mexican L. Flyweight Title Defence*)
22.10.88 Jorge Rivera W CO 4 Cozumel
Summary: 22 contests, won 22.

Rodolfo (Gato) Gonzalez
Mexico City, Mexico. *Born* 02.07.59
L. Welterweight

21.10.78 Manuel Ferrer W RSC 5 Mexico City
23.12.78 Jose Tolosa W CO 1 Mazatlan
10.02.79 Juan Hernandez W RSC 4 Merida
16.03.79 Chucho Saucedo W CO 3 Mazatlan
26.05.79 Lupe Perez W RSC 6 Merida
07.07.79 Rafael Rojas W RSC 3 Mazatlan
22.07.79 Jose Escalante W CO 4 San Luis Potosi
25.08.79 Juan Elizondo W CO 6 Tijuana
06.10.79 Humberto Caicedo W CO 1 McAllen
10.11.79 Salvador Torres W CO 1 Guadalajara
08.12.79 Curtis Ramsey W RSC 2 Los Angeles
16.02.80 Alfredo Pitalua W RSC 10 Mexico City
02.04.80 Nacho Jiminez W CO 3 Los Angeles
03.07.80 Modesto Concepcion W CO 2 Los Angeles
26.07.80 Herman Montes T DRAW 3 Los Angeles
04.10.80 Celso Limon W PTS 10 Guadalajara
16.12.80 Norman Goins W RSC 1 Los Angeles
16.03.81 Vilomar Fernandez W RSC 2 Los Angeles
13.06.81 Andy Ganigan W PTS 10 Los Angeles
25.07.81 Tai-Jin Moon W PTS 10 Los Angeles
12.09.81 Claude Noel L PTS 15 Atlantic City
(*Vacant WBA Lightweight Title*)
09.09.82 Robert Turner W CO 1 Fort Worth
02.10.82 Vicente Mijares L RSC 9 Torreon
11.12.82 Cayetano Correa L PTS 10 Mexico City
11.05.83 Carlos Villacana W RSC 4 Corpus Christi
24.06.83 Daniel Felizardo W RSC 2 Fort Worth
26.07.83 James Martinez W PTS 10 Houston
19.08.83 Agustin Estrada W PTS 10 Juarez
22.10.83 Bennie Abarca W PTS 10 Tijuana
27.01.84 Vicente Mijares L PTS 10 Torreon
01.03.84 Roberto Collins W RSC 3 Los Angeles
31.05.84 Roque Montoya W TD 8 Los Angeles
12.07.84 See-Kwon Lee W CO 1 Los Angeles
14.12.84 Javier Barcenas W RSC 1 Acapulco
18.02.85 Jose Luis Castillo W CO 4 Tijuana
29.03.85 Juan Cruces W RSC 3 Miami
23.05.85 Darrell Cottrell W CO 5 Los Angeles
03.07.85 Rene Arredondo W PTS 10 Los Angeles
26.09.85 Luis Urraca W RSC 5 Los Angeles
20.11.85 Lorenzo Garcia W PTS 10 Los Angeles
25.02.86 Rollin Williams W PTS 4 Los Angeles
03.03.86 Jamey Ollenberger W PTS 10 Sacramento
15.08.86 Jorge Hernandez W PTS 10 Guadalajara
10.01.87 Patrizio Oliva L PTS 15 Agrigento
(*WBA L. Welterweight Title Challenge*)
25.07.87 Rigoberto Lopez W CO 6 Mexico City
09.10.87 Ronnie Shields L PTS 10 Los Angeles
22.12.87 Roberto Collins W CO 2 Obregon
01.07.88 Jorge Morales W CO 1 Mexico City
22.09.88 Roger Mayweather L RSC 12 Los Angeles
(*WBC L. Welterweight Title Challenge*)
Summary: 49 contests, won 41, drew 1, lost 7.

Herol Graham
Sheffield, England. *Born* 13.09.59
British Middleweight Champion. Former EBU Middleweight Champion. Former Undefeated British, Commonwealth & EBU L. Middleweight Champion

28.11.78 Vivian Waite W PTS 6 Sheffield
04.12.78 Curtis Marsh W RTD 1 Southend
22.01.79 Jimmy Roberts W RSC 2 Bradford
12.02.79 Dave Southwell W PTS 8 Reading
28.02.79 Dave Southwell W PTS 8 Burslem
27.03.79 George Walker W PTS 8 Southend
27.04.79 Mac Nicholson W PTS 8 Newcastle
16.05.79 Gordon George W PTS 8 Sheffield
26.09.79 Lloyd James W PTS 8 Sheffield
27.10.79 Billy Ahearne W RSC 3 Barnsley
27.11.79 Errol McKenzie W PTS 8 Sheffield
12.02.80 Glen McEwan W PTS 8 Sheffield
22.04.80 George Danahar W PTS 8 Sheffield
09.09.80 Joey Mack W PTS 8 Sheffield
30.10.80 Larry Mayes W RSC 4 Liverpool
22.01.81 Lancelot Innes W PTS 10 Liverpool
24.03.81 Pat Thomas W PTS 15 Sheffield
(*British L. Middleweight Title Challenge*)
17.06.81 Prince Rodney W RSC 1 Sheffield
25.11.81 Kenny Bristol W PTS 15 Sheffield
(*Commonwealth L. Middleweight Title Challenge*)
24.02.82 Chris Christian W RSC 9 Sheffield
(*British & Commonwealth L. Middleweight Title Defence*)
22.04.82 Fred Coranson W PTS 10 Liverpool
30.09.82 Hunter Clay W PTS 15 Lagos
(*Commonwealth L. Middleweight Title Defence*)
15.03.83 Tony Nelson W RTD 5 Wembley
23.05.83 Clemente Tshinza W CO 2 Sheffield
(*Vacant EBU L. Middleweight Title*)
11.10.83 Carlos Betancourt W CO 1 London
09.12.83 Germain le Maitre W RSC 8 St Nazaire
(*EBU L. Middleweight Title Defence*)
22.07.84 Lindell Holmes W RSC 5 Sheffield
25.09.84 Irwin Hines W CO 2 Wembley

Herol Graham

Derek Rowe (Photos) Ltd

16.10.84 Jose Seys W RSC 6 London
26.11.84 Liam Coleman W RSC 3 Sheffield
06.03.85 Jose Rosemain W CO 5 London
24.04.85 Jimmy Price W CO 1 London
(*Vacant British Middleweight Title*)
16.10.85 Roberto Ruiz W RSC 2 London
03.12.85 Sanderline Williams W PTS 10 Belfast
05.02.86 Ayub Kalule W RSC 10 Sheffield
(*EBU Middleweight Title Challenge*)
23.06.86 Ernie Rabotte W RSC 1 Las Vegas
04.11.86 Mark Kaylor W RTD 8 Wembley
(*EBU Middleweight Title Defence*)
17.01.87 Charlie Boston W RTD 7 Belfast
26.05.87 Sumbu Kalambay L PTS 12 Wembley
(*EBU Middleweight Title Defence*)
05.12.87 Ricky Stackhouse W RSC 8 Doncaster
08.06.88 James Cook W RSC 5 Sheffield
(*Vacant British Middleweight Title*)
23.11.88 Johny Melfah W RSC 5 London
(*British Middleweight Title Defence*)

Summary: 42 contests, won 41, lost 1.

Uriah Grant
Jamaica. *Born* 1961
L. Heavyweight

22.06.84 Rogelio Bolanos W RSC 3 Palm Beach
07.12.84 Henry Tillman L RSC 2 Houston
10.05.85 Keith Allen W RSC 5 Fort Lauderdale
23.07.85 Fred Jenkins W RTD 1 Miami
17.10.85 Ricky Womack L PTS 6 Merrillville
25.10.85 James Sisco W RSC 2 Miami
26.11.85 Gary Clarke W CO 4 Miami
26.12.85 Dean Moore W RSC 6 Miami
31.01.86 Reg Neal W CO 1 Miami
21.02.86 Matt Saad Muhammad W PTS 10 Fort Lauderdale
06.05.86 Leslie Stewart L PTS 8 Atlantic City
28.08.86 Grover Robinson W RSC 7 Los Angeles
19.10.86 Abdul Muhammad W RSC 1 Fort Pierce
18.11.86 Arthel Lawhorne W RSC 10 Los Angeles
19.12.86 Manuel Murillo W RSC 6 Miami
22.01.87 Robert Folley W RTD 4 Los Angeles
09.04.87 Ramzi Hassan L PTS 12 Los Angeles
08.08.87 Abdul Muhammad W CO 1 Sunrise
23.10.87 Eric Holly W RSC 5 Miami
28.11.87 Louis Coleman W CO 1 New Haven
24.09.88 Joe Lasisi L PTS 10 Las Vegas

Summary: 21 contests, won 16, lost 5.

Michael Greer
Memphis, USA. *Born* 09.09.55
Former Undefeated Con. Am. Cruiserweight Champion

22.04.80 Steve Mormino W PTS 4 Memphis
13.05.80 Phil Brown DREW 6 Memphis
01.07.80 John Pinney W CO 6 Memphis
26.07.80 George Goforth W PTS 8 Jenkins
09.09.80 Art Pruitt W RSC 6 Memphis
27.09.80 George Goforth W CO 5 Jenkins
08.02.81 Ed Turner W RSC 5 Sedalia
04.04.81 Fred Miller W CO 2 Owensboro
22.04.81 Willie Goodman W PTS 6 Birmingham
26.06.81 Tony James W RSC 1 Blythville
13.10.81 Henry Porter W PTS 8 Memphis
24.11.81 James Dixon W PTS 10 Memphis
16.02.82 Demetrius Edwards W PTS 10 Memphis
07.04.82 Charles Bryant W CO 2 Nashville
18.05.82 Tom Stevenson L CO 1 Memphis
18.07.82 Charles Allen W CO 1 Pensacola
17.08.82 Larry Strogen W RSC 4 Memphis
22.10.82 Carl Williams L RSC 3 New York
08.01.83 Henry Porter DREW 8 St Ann
16.02.83 Jeff Sims L RSC 3 East Rutherford
28.04.83 Otis Bates W PTS 12 Little Rock
24.09.83 Pinklon Thomas L RSC 5 Totowa
06.12.83 Keith Allen W PTS 6 Memphis
24.01.84 Larry Jones W RSC 1 Memphis
03.02.84 Dick Scott DREW 6 Memphis
10.09.84 Mike Rollins W CO 2 Helena
22.11.84 Pisai Finai W RSC 3 St Paul
22.01.85 Nick Smith W CO 1 Memphis
27.02.85 Dwight Muhammad Qawi L PTS 10 Atlantic City
13.03.85 Andy Stokes W PTS 8 Las Vegas
03.09.85 Rick Willis W RSC 5 Memphis
05.11.85 Keith Allen W RSC 8 Memphis
07.01.86 Paul Madison W PTS 10 Memphis
04.03.86 Willard Dumas W CO 1 Memphis
03.06.86 Alan Whitfield W CO 3 Memphis
10.08.86 Carlos de Leon L RSC 8 Giardini Naxos
(*WBC Cruiserweight Title Challenge*)
07.10.86 Lupe Guerra W CO 4 Memphis
08.11.86 David Harvey W CO 2 Greenville
02.12.86 David Kliewer W RSC 3 Memphis
03.03.87 Aaron Brown W RSC 6 Memphis
21.05.87 Johnny Davis W PTS 12 Memphis
(*Vacant Con. Am. Cruiserweight Title*)
01.09.87 Curtis Isaac W PTS 12 Memphis
(*Con. Am. Cruiserweight Title Defence*)
05.01.88 Keith Allen W RSC 4 Memphis
02.02.88 Pat Strachan W PTS 12 Memphis
(*Con. Am. Cruiserweight Title Defence*)
05.07.88 Rick Enis W CO 9 Memphis
28.09.88 Rick Enis W CO 8 Tel Aviv
(*Con. Am. Cruiserweight Title Defence*)
25.03.89 Taoufik Belbouli L RSC 8 Casablanca
(*Vacant WBA Cruiserweight Title*)

Summary: 47 contests, won 37, drew 3, lost 7.

Calvin (Silky) Grove
Coatsville, USA. *Born* 05.08.62
Former IBF Featherweight Champion. Former Unbeaten USBA Featherweight Champion

03.06.82 Mike Davis W CO 2 Conshohocken
13.06.82 Greg Turner W RSC 1 Atlantic City
19.07.82 Jose Abru W RSC 2 Atlantic City
04.08.82 Sylvester Kennon W PTS 6 Atlantic City
22.09.82 Rick Stinnie W CO 1 Atlantic City
27.10.82 Leon Drummond W CO 2 Atlantic City
24.11.82 Tony Rutledge W PTS 6 Atlantic City
13.01.83 Ray Evans W PTS 6 Atlantic City
12.03.83 Jose Figueroa W PTS 6 Atlantic City
15.06.83 Santos Cruz W PTS 8 Atlantic City
17.07.83 Juan Figueroa W PTS 8 Atlantic City
22.09.83 Vic del Rio W RSC 3 Atlantic City
23.11.83 William Martinez W RSC 3 Atlantic City
17.01.84 Harrison Azari W RSC 1 Philadelphia
06.03.84 Sylvester Price W RSC 4 Atlantic City
07.04.84 Pedro Montero W PTS 10 Atlantic City
21.05.84 Satos Moreno W PTS 10 Atlantic City
21.08.84 Margarito Marquez W RSC 5 Atlantic City
13.12.84 Pascual Aranda W RSC 3 Atlantic City
04.02.84 Kelvin Seabrooks W PTS 10 Atlantic City
24.04.85 Idabeth Rojas W PTS 10 Atlantic City
28.06.85 Irving Mitchell W PTS 12 Atlantic City
(*USBA Featherweight Title Challenge*)
19.09.85 Paul Devorce W PTS 10 Atlantic City
25.10.85 Dana Roston W PTS 12 Atlantic City
(*USBA Featherweight Title Defence*)
16.02.86 Jeff Roberts W PTS 10 Troy
03.05.86 Pepe Vazquez W PTS 10 Glens Falls
(*USBA Featherweight Title Defence*)
04.09.86 Billy White W RSC 6 Atlantic City
(*USBA Featherweight Title Defence*)
28.11.86 Aristides Acevedo W PTS 10 Atlantic City
26.03.87 Angel Hernandez W PTS 10 Atlantic City
10.09.87 Tony Cisneros W PTS 10 Houston
12.11.87 Capri Lipkins W PTS 8 Houston
23.01.88 Antonio Rivera W RSC 4 Gamaches
(*IBF Featherweight Title Challenge*)
17.05.88 Myron Taylor W PTS 15 Atlantic City
(*IBF Featherweight Title Defence*)
04.08.88 Jorge Paez L PTS 15 Mexicali
(*IBF Featherweight Title Defence*)
10.11.88 Jesse Williams W CO 6 Stateline
30.03.89 Jorge Paez L CO 11 Mexicali
(*IBF Featherweight Title Challenge*)

Summary: 36 contests, won 34, lost 2.

Julio Gudino
Panama
Panamanian Flyweight Champion

19.07.80 Leonardo Paredes L PTS 4 Santiago
31.01.81 Ariel Moreno W PTS 4 Panama City
08.08.81 Leonardo Paredes L PTS 6 Colon
03.10.81 Javier Bultron L PTS 6 Chitre
01.11.81 Bernardino Moreno L PTS 6 Panama City
19.05.82 Benedicto Murillo L PTS 8 Panama City
29.05.82 Javier Bultron W PTS 6 Panama City
19.06.82 Carlos Orobio W PTS 6 Panama City
24.07.82 Benito Vargas W PTS 8 Chorerra
27.11.82 Felipe Lam W CO 8 Panama City
04.03.83 Virgilio Chifundo L PTS 6 Panama City
19.11.83 Benedicto Murillo L PTS 8 Panama City
29.06.84 Gilberto Barcenas W PTS 6 Panama City
01.09.84 Enrique Sanchez L RSC 5 Panama City
06.07.85 Alex Miranda W PTS 10 Panama City
16.11.85 Cesar Polanco W PTS 10 Panama City
28.02.86 Alex Miranda W RSC 3 Colon
17.08.86 Claudemir Dias L PTS 10 Sao Paulo
17.10.87 Eduard Tunon W RSC 10 Colon
(*Panamanian Flyweight Title Challenge*)
03.12.87 Richard Clarke L PTS 12 Kingston
(*WBC International Flyweight Title Challenge*)
02.12.88 Hilario Zapata W PTS 10 Panama City
15.04.89 Fidel Bassa L RSC 6 Barranquilla
(*WBA Flyweight Title Challenge*)

Summary: 22 contests, won 11, lost 11.

Lupe Gutierrez
San Jose, USA. *Born* 13.12.63
USBA Featherweight Champion

30.01.85 Lucilio Nolasco W RSC 3 San Jose
21.02.85 Enrique Castillo W PTS 5 San Jose
11.04.85 Juan Cantu L CO 1 San Jose
21.06.85 Ralph Gudino W CO 4 Visalia
12.07.85 Herman Guillen W CO 4 Santa Clara
27.08.88 Juan Armienta W CO 1 Santa Clara
13.09.85 Darryl Thigpen W RSC 4 San Jose
29.10.85 Hector Lizarraga W CO 2 Stockton
05.12.85 Lamart Baker W RSC 3 San Jose
18.12.85 Heriberto Chavez W RSC 1 San Jose
20.02.86 Henry Lugo W PTS 8 San Jose
02.07.86 Lorenzo Garcia W RSC 2 San Jose
25.07.86 Jeff Franklin W PTS 8 Las Vegas
15.10.86 Denzil Surall W RSC 2 Turlock
13.11.86 J.T. Walker W PTS 10 San Jose
25.03.88 Willie Davis W RSC 4 San Jose
05.05.88 Ricardo Torres W CO 6 San Jose
17.06.88 Ramon Rico W CO 1 Las Vegas
05.08.88 Richie Fowler W RSC 2 San Jose
09.09.88 Rosendo Alonzo W RSC 2 Modesto
12.11.88 Allan Makitoki L CO 8 Stockton
06.03.89 Jeff Franklin W PTS 12 Reno
(*USBA Featherweight Title Challenge*)

Summary: 22 contests, won 20, lost 2.

Pedro Gutierrez
San Andres, Argentine. *Born* 22.10.55
Former Argentinian S. Featherweight Champion

16.04.77 Ramon Villalba W PTS 6 Buenos Aires
02.07.77 Ramon Villalba W PTS 6 Buenos Aires
27.08.77 Emilio Diaz W PTS 6 Buenos Aires
29.10.77 Julio Sandoval W RTD 4 Buenos Aires
10.12.77 Adolfo Felice W PTS 8 Buenos Aires
01.04.78 Eduardo Valenzuela W PTS 8 Buenos Aires
14.04.78 Nestor Gundin DREW 6 San Pedro
20.05.78 Lorenzo Garcia W RSC 5 Buenos Aires
15.07.78 Adolfo Felice W PTS 8 Buenos Aires
04.11.78 Armando Perez T DRAW 6 Alvear
22.12.78 Lorenzo Garcia L PTS 10 San Pedro
12.04.79 Gustavo Martinez L PTS 10 Tucuman
31.05.79 Orlando Lucero W PTS 10 Villa Carlos Paz
22.06.79 Demetrio Ibarra W PTS 10 Baradero
10.08.79 Carlos Sanchez W PTS 10 Puerto Madryn
23.11.79 Hipolito Nunez DREW 10 San Salvador
21.12.79 Carlos Sanchez W PTS 10 Trelew
05.04.80 Juan Carranza W CO 9 Mar del Plata
18.04.80 Hipolito Nunez DREW 10 Salta
16.05.80 Daniel Murua L PTS 10 Bolivar
14.06.80 Lorenzo Garcia L PTS 10 Baradero
19.07.80 Juan Alvarez W PTS 10 San Nicolas
13.09.80 Juan Carranza W PTS 10 General Cabrera
11.10.80 Faustino Barrios W PTS 10 Buenos Aires
22.11.80 Faustino Barrios L PTS 10 Buenos Aires
05.05.81 Faustino Barrios W PTS 10 San Nicolas
08.05.81 Victor Escobar DREW 10 Rio Gallegos
03.07.81 Carlos Olivera DREW 10 Mar del Plata
11.09.81 Carlos Sanchez L PTS 10 Trelew
31.10.81 Eduardo Prieto L PTS 10 Iquique
13.08.82 Carlos Olivera L TD 9 Mar del Plata
06.11.82 Jose Manrique W PTS 10 Montevideo
03.12.82 Mario Vizcaya W CO 7 Rio Cuarto
17.12.82 Hipolito Nunez DREW 10 Salta
08.04.83 Luis Soto W PTS 10 Catamarca
12.05.83 Luis Soto L PTS 10 Catamarca
27.07.83 Ruben Stamuli W RSC 4 Buenos Aires
20.08.83 Carlos Olivera W PTS 10 Mar del Plata
07.10.83 Fernando Sosa W PTS 10 Mar del Plata
05.11.83 Luis Zarate DREW 10 Mar del Plata
09.12.83 Ruben Stamulis W RTD 9 Mar del Plata
02.03.84 Hipolito Nunez W PTS 10 Mar del Plata
23.03.84 Norberto Reyna W CO 2 San Juan
13.04.84 Hipolito Nunez W RSC 9 Mar del Plata
12.05.84 Fernando Sosa L PTS 10 Buenos Aires
07.07.84 Faustino Barrios L PTS 10 Buenos Aires
25.08.84 Carlos Olivera W RSC 10 Buenos Aires

12.10.84 Alberto Aragon W PTS 12 Buenos Aires
11.01.85 Faustino Barrios W PTS 12 Mar del Plata (*Argentinian S. Featherweight Title Challenge*)
24.03.85 Francisco Tomas Cruz L PTS 12 Sao Paulo
10.05.85 Hipolito Nunez DREW 10 Salta
14.06.85 Raul Bianco W CO 6 Rio Cuarto
06.07.85 Daniel Murua W PTS 10 Rojas
09.08.85 Hipolito Nunez DREW 10 Tucuman
25.09.85 Faustino Barrios W PTS 10 Buenos Aires
08.11.85 Alberto Cejas W RSC 9 Mar del Plata
19.12.85 Jose Villareal W RSC 9 Tucuman
31.01.86 Ramon Soria W RSC 10 Mar del Plata
22.03.86 Faustino Barrios L PTS 12 Buenos Aires (*Argentinian S. Featherweight Title Defence*)
08.08.86 Julio Melone W PTS 10 Cordoba
05.09.86 Abraham Valenzuela W PTS 10 San Luis
21.11.86 Ricardo Espinosa W PTS 10 San Luis
15.12.86 Ramon Soria L PTS 10 San Luis
11.04.87 Jorge Pompe W PTS 10 Rojas
15.05.87 Raul Bianco W PTS 10 Rio Cuarto
31.07.87 Jose Ricardo Gil W RSC 10 Parana
11.09.87 Raul Rosas W CO 2 Villa Mercedes
04.12.87 Julio Miranda L PTS 12 San Salvador (*Argentinian S. Featherweight Title Challenge*)
13.05.88 Ricardo Espinoza W PTS 10 Necochea
04.06.88 Eduardo Galan W PTS 10 Buenos Aires
09.09.88 Reynaldo Cadena W PTS 10 Laboulaye
29.10.88 Geronimo Luquez W PTS 10 Buenos Aires
30.01.89 Steve Boyle L PTS 12 Glasgow (*Vacant WBC International Lightweight Title*)
17.03.89 Juan Palacio W RTD 4 Laboulaye
Summary: 74 contests, won 48, drew 10, lost 16.

Jeff Harding
Australia. *Born* 05.02.65
OPBF L. Heavyweight Champion

07.11.86 Tommy Roberts W CO 4 Marrickville
05.02.87 Emmanuel Otti W RTD 5 Sydney
19.06.87 Matereti Valu W RSC 2 Blacktown
24.07.87 John Taupau W RSC 2 Sydney
25.09.87 Luke Joel W RSC 2 Cronulla
11.12.87 Moses Villa W CO 2 Sydney
16.03.88 Apollo Sweet W PTS 10 Mount Pritchard
28.04.88 Doug Sam W RTD 5 Sydney (*OPBF Light-Heavyweight Title Challenge*)
06.06.88 Jorge Salgado W RSC 5 Moore Park
18.07.88 Don Lee W RTD 8 Sydney
05.09.88 Dean Moore W RSC 8 Sydney
07.12.88 Carlos Antunes W RSC 9 Tweeds Head
01.03.89 Art Jimmerson W PTS 10 Cardiff
Summary: 13 contests, won 13.

Ramzi Hassan
California, USA. *Born* Palestine 07.12.62
L. Heavyweight

01.09.82 Nova Garcia W PTS 4 Merrillville
16.10.82 Clarence Osby W PTS 4 Chicago
17.11.82 Anton Hibbler W PTS 4 Hammond
03.01.83 Gary Jones W PTS 4 Chicago
07.02.83 Kirk Bell W CO 1 Chicago
07.03.83 James Churn W PTS 6 Chicago
20.03.83 John Cox W PTS 4 Chicago
28.04.83 Clarence Osby L PTS 6 Hammond
20.06.83 Francis Sargent W RSC 1 Chicago
13.10.83 Jimmy Bills W PTS 6 San Jose
04.11.83 Larry Musgrove W PTS 6 San Jose
23.02.84 Larry Musgrove W PTS 6 San Jose
11.08.84 Eddie Bell W PTS 4 Woodstock
22.09.84 Jerry Harris W PTS 4 Arlington Heights
02.11.84 Jim Wilder W PTS 6 Chicago
20.12.84 James Churn W PTS 6 Chicago
25.02.85 Roy Saffold W CO 4 Chicago
22.03.85 Al Rankin W PTS 8 Hammond
28.06.85 Steve Alread W CO 1 Hammond
08.08.85 Slobodan Kacar L PTS 10 Chicago
19.06.86 Danny Blake W PTS 8 San Diego
28.08.86 Jerry Okorodudu W PTS 10 Los Angeles
03.12.86 Kelvin Kelly W PTS 10 Los Angeles
23.02.87 Jeff Lampkin W PTS 10 Los Angeles
09.04.87 Uriah Grant W PTS 12 Los Angeles
16.06.87 Jimmy Bills W PTS 10 Reno
30.06.87 Glenn Kennedy W PTS 12 Los Angeles
24.11.87 Tony Willis L RSC 12 Los Angeles (*Vacant USBA L. Heavyweight Title*)
06.06.88 Virgil Hill L PTS 12 Las Vegas (*WBA L. Heavyweight Title Challenge*)
03.12.88 Michael Moorer L RSC 5 Cleveland
Summary: 30 contests, won 25, lost 5.

Kiyoshi Hatanaka
Aichi, Japan. *Born* 07.03.67
Former Undefeated Japanese S. Flyweight Champion

27.11.84 Harelya Yamauchi W CO 1 Nagoya
05.02.85 Chuji Sanuki W RSC 1 Osaka
29.04.85 Shigehito Hayashe W CO 1 Osaka
26.06.85 Shuichi Sakakibara W CO 1 Nagoya
28.07.85 Shinpei Sato W CO 1 Okazaki
08.10.85 Takuji Hijiri W PTS 4 Nagoya
30.11.85 Akio Kawamata W PTS 6 Hamamatsu
04.03.86 Hiromitsu Tatsuki W CO 1 Osaka
09.05.86 Takashi Hirata W PTS 8 Nagoya
14.07.86 Tadashi Maruo W PTS 10 Tokyo
18.10.86 Masaki Sono W CO 2 Nagoya
23.02.87 Tadashi Maruo W RSC 3 Tokyo (*Japanese S. Flyweight Title Challenge*)
10.07.87 Terukai Miyasato W PTS 10 Nagoya (*Japanese S. Flyweight Title Defence*)
29.10.87 Surasith Meeprasert W CO 1 Nagoya
26.02.88 Constancio Dangla W CO 3 Nagoya
03.09.88 Gilberto Roman L PTS 12 Nagoya (*WBC S. Flyweight Title Challenge*)
24.01.89 Dong-Chun Lee W PTS 10 Tokyo
Summary: 17 contests, won 16, lost 1.

Greg (Mutt) Haugen
Auburn, USA. *Born* 31.08.60
Former IBF Lightweight Champion. Former Undefeated NABF Lightweight Champion

04.11.82 Noel Arriesgado W PTS 8 Anchorage
04.12.82 Noel Arriesgado W RSC 7 Anchorage
13.01.83 Joe Perez W PTS 10 Seattle
23.02.83 Max Cervantes W RSC 4 Seattle
29.03.83 Larry Yazee W RSC 2 Seattle
26.04.83 Chuck Peralta W PTS 10 Seattle
12.07.83 Roosevelt Booth W PTS 4 Miami
20.09.83 Ted Michaeliszyn W PTS 6 Las Vegas
27.09.84 Tony Villa W RSC 2 Las Vegas
07.02.85 Ted Michaeliszyn W RSC 7 Seattle
07.03.85 Juan del Toro T DRAW 1 Seattle
17.07.85 Jeff Bumphus W PTS 8 Atlantic City
22.08.85 Freddie Roach W RSC 7 Las Vegas
06.11.85 Chris Calvin W RSC 6 Las Vegas
06.01.86 Charlie Brown W RSC 1 Las Vegas
16.02.86 Juan Alvarado W RSC 9 Reno
26.03.86 Ken Willis W PTS 10 Las Vegas
24.05.86 Edwin Curet W PTS 12 Las Vegas (*Vacant NABF Lightweight Title*)
19.08.86 Ernie Landeros W PTS 10 Las Vegas
05.12.86 Jimmy Paul W PTS 15 Las Vegas (*IBF Lighweight Title Challenge*)
07.06.87 Vinny Pazienza L PTS 15 Providence (*IBF Lightweight Title Defence*)
16.12.87 Derrick McGuire W RSC 6 Las Vegas
06.02.88 Vinny Pazienza W PTS 15 Atlantic City (*IBF Lightweight Title Challenge*)
11.04.88 Miguel Santana W TD 11 Tacoma (*IBF Lightweight Title Defence*)
28.10.88 Gert Bo Jacobsen W RTD 10 Copenhagen (*IBF Lightweight Title Defence*)
18.02.89 Pernell Whitaker L PTS 12 Hampton (*IBF Lightweight Title Defence*)
Summary: 26 contests, won 23, drew 1, lost 2.

Floyd Havard
Swansea, Wales. *Born* 16.10.65
British S. Featherweight Champion

30.11.85 Dean Bramhald W RSC 3 Cardiff
22.01.86 Sugar Gibiliru W PTS 6 London
20.02.86 Dean Bramhald W PTS 6 Halifax
10.03.86 Russell Jones W PTS 8 Cardiff
28.04.86 Tony McLaggon W CO 2 Cardiff
24.05.86 Sugar Gibiliru W PTS 8 Manchester
20.09.86 George Jones W RSC 4 Hemel Hempstead
25.10.86 Joe Duffy W RSC 3 Stevenage
29.11.86 Marvin P. Gray W RSC 2 London
14.03.87 Nigel Senior W RSC 5 London
14.04.87 Ray Newby W RSC 7 Cumbernauld
28.04.87 Hector Clottey W RSC 5 Halifax
19.05.87 Kid Sumali W RTD 2 Cumbernauld
22.09.87 Frank Loukil W RSC 4 London
11.11.87 Cedric Powell W PTS 8 Usk
12.01.88 Mario Salazar W RSC 2 Cardiff
24.02.88 Richard Fowler W RSC 1 Aberavon
20.04.88 Benji Marques W PTS 8 London
18.05.88 Pat Cowdell W RSC 8 Aberavon (*British S. Featherweight Title Challenge*)
15.11.88 John Kalbhenn W PTS 10 Norwich
11.04.89 Idabeth Rojas W PTS 10 Aberavon
Summary: 21 contests, won 21.

Magne Havnaa
Oslo, Norway. *Born* 16.09.63
Cruiserweight

03.10.86 Johnny Nelson W PTS 4 Copenhagen
17.10.86 Eddy Vandenhouwele W PTS 4 Randers
21.11.86 Abner Blackstock W RSC 6 Copenhagen
06.02.87 Mike Quealy W RTD 3 Herning

Greg Haugen

Christopher M. Farina

28.03.87 Stewart Lithgo W RSC 5 Copenhagen
02.10.87 Andy Gerrard W PTS 8 Copenhagen
09.10.87 Alfonso Ratliff W PTS 8 Skive
12.02.88 Roy Smith W CO 4 Elsinore
12.05.88 Yves Monsieur W PTS 8 Copenhagen
28.10.88 John Williams W RTD 4 Copenhagen
08.12.88 John Westgarth W PTS 8 Copenhagen
16.02.89 Dave Muhammed W RSC 6 Copenhagen
27.04.89 Lennie Howard W RTD 3 Skive
Summary: 14 contests, won 14.

Thomas (Hit Man) Hearns
Detroit, USA. *Born* 18.10.58
WBO S. Middleweight Champion. Former WBC Middleweight Champion. Former Undefeated WBC L. Heavyweight Champion. Former WBA Welterweight Champion. Former Undefeated USBA Welterweight Champion. Former Undefeated WBC L. Middleweight Champion. Former Undefeated NABF Middleweight Champion

25.11.77 Jerome Hill W CO 2 Detroit
07.12.77 Jerry Strickland W CO 3 Mount Clemens
16.12.77 Willie Wren W RSC 3 Detroit
29.01.78 Anthony House W CO 2 Detroit
10.02.78 Robert Adams W CO 3 Detroit
17.02.78 Billy Goodwin W RSC 2 Saginaw
17.03.78 Ray Fields W RSC 2 Detroit
31.03.78 Tyrone Phelps W CO 3 Saginaw
08.06.78 Jimmy Rothwell W CO 1 Detroit
20.07.78 Raul Aguirre W CO 2 Detroit
03.08.78 Eddie Marcelle W CO 2 Detroit
07.09.78 Bruce Finch W CO 3 Detroit
26.10.78 Pedro Rojas W RSC 1 Detroit
09.12.78 Rudy Barro W CO 4 Detroit
13.01.79 Clyde Gray W RSC 10 Detroit
31.01.79 Sammy Ruckard W RSC 8 Detroit
03.03.79 Segundo Murillo W RSC 8 Detroit
03.04.79 Alfonso Hayman W PTS 10 Philadelphia
20.05.79 Harold Weston W RTD 6 Las Vegas
28.06.79 Bruce Curry W CO 3 Detroit
23.08.79 Mao de la Rosa W RSC 2 Detroit
22.09.79 Jose Figueroa W CO 3 Los Angeles
18.10.79 Saensak Muangsurin W RSC 3 Detroit
30.11.79 Mike Colbert W PTS 10 New Orleans
03.02.80 Jim Richard W CO 3 Las Vegas
02.03.80 Angel Espada W RSC 4 Detroit
(*Vacant USBA Welterweight Title*)
31.03.80 Santiago Valdez W RSC 1 Las Vegas
03.05.80 Eddie Gazo W CO 1 Detroit
02.08.80 Pipino Cuevas W RSC 2 Detroit
(*WBA Welterweight Title Challenge*)
06.12.80 Luis Primera W CO 6 Detroit
(*WBA Welterweight Title Defence*)
25.04.81 Randy Shields W RSC 12 Phoenix
(*WBA Welterweight Title Defence*)
25.06.81 Pablo Baez W RSC 4 Houston
(*WBA Welterweight Title Defence*)
16.09.81 Ray Leonard L RSC 14 Las Vegas
(*WBA Welterweight Title Defence & WBC Welterweight Title Challenge*)
11.12.81 Ernie Singletary W PTS 10 Nassau
27.02.82 Marcos Geraldo W CO 1 Las Vegas
25.07.82 Jeff McCracken W RSC 8 Detroit
03.12.82 Wilfred Benitez W PTS 15 New Orleans
(*WBC L. Middleweight Title Challenge*)
10.07.83 Murray Sutherland W PTS 10 Atlantic City
11.02.84 Luigi Minchillo W PTS 12 Detroit
(*WBC L. Middleweight Title Defence*)
15.06.84 Roberto Duran W CO 2 Las Vegas
(*WBC L. Middleweight Title Defence*)
15.09.84 Fred Hutchings W RSC 3 Saginaw
(*WBC L. Middleweight Title Defence*)
15.04.85 Marvin Hagler L RSC 3 Las Vegas
(*World Middleweight Title Challenge*)
10.03.86 James Shuler W CO 1 Las Vegas
(*NABF Middleweight Title Challenge*)
23.06.86 Mark Medal W RSC 8 Las Vegas
(*WBC L. Middleweight Title Defence*)
17.10.86 Doug de Witt W PTS 12 Detroit
(*NABF Middleweight Title Defence*)
07.03.87 Dennis Andries W RSC 10 Detroit
(*WBC L. Heavyweight Title Challenge*)
29.10.87 Juan Domingo Roldan W CO 4 Las Vegas
(*Vacant WBC Middleweight Title*)
06.06.88 Iran Barkley L RSC 3 Las Vegas
(*WBC Middleweight Title Defence*)
04.11.88 James Kinchen W PTS 12 Las Vegas
(*Vacant WBO S. Middleweight Title*)
Summary: 49 contests, won 46, lost 3.

Genaro Hernandez
Los Angeles, USA. *Born* 10.05.66
S. Featherweight

27.09.84 Dino Ramirez W PTS 4 Los Angeles
17.11.84 Martin Escobar W PTS 4 Los Angeles
24.06.85 Dino Ramirez W PTS 6 Irvine
29.10.85 Randy Archuleta W PTS 6 Stockton
12.12.85 Jose Maytorena W RSC 1 Bakersfield
17.02.86 Pablo Montana W RSC 2 Phoenix
24.02.86 Terry Baldwin W RSC 2 Irvine
31.03.86 Larry Villareal W PTS 6 Irvine
28.04.86 Jorge Valdez W RSC 3 Irvine
21.07.86 Terry Baldwin W RSC 7 Irvine
12.09.86 Lupe Miranda W PTS 10 Las Vegas
12.12.86 J. L. Ivey W PTS 10 Las Vegas
31.08.87 Kenny Wyatt W PTS 10 Irvine
25.04.88 Juan Vega W RSC 9 Irvine
25.07.88 Jose Mosqueda W PTS 10 Irvine
22.11.88 Refugio Rojas W CO 6 Los Angeles
Summary: 16 contests, won 16.

Virgil (Sugar) Hill
Williston, USA. *Born* 18.01.64
WBA L. Heavyweight Champion. Former Undefeated Con. Am. L. Heavyweight Champion

15.11.84 Arthur Wright W RSC 2 New York
05.01.85 John Tyrrell W RSC 1 Atlantic City
16.02.85 Dave Vedder W PTS 6 Reno
13.07.85 Dawud Shaw W PTS 6 Atlantic City
22.01.86 Fred Jordan W RSC 4 Atlantic City
02.03.86 James Williamson W RSC 6 Lancaster
30.04.86 Abdul Hakim W RSC 4 Atlantic City
30.06.86 Santiago Valdez W RSC 1 Everett
10.07.86 Mike Sedillo W PTS 8 Los Angeles
02.08.86 Willie Mayberry W RSC 1 Detroit
14.08.86 Marcus Dorsey W RSC 2 Lynnwood
04.10.86 Wayne Caplette W CO 1 Williston
17.10.86 Eric Winbush W PTS 10 Bismark
11.12.86 Clarence Osby W PTS 12 New York
(*Vacant Con. Am. L. Heavyweight Title*)
03.03.87 James Williams W CO 4 Fargo
01.05.87 Marvin Camel W CO 1 Grand Forks
13.06.87 Marcos Geraldo W RSC 2 Lake Tahoe
22.07.87 Junior Edmond W PTS 10 Minot
05.09.87 Leslie Stewart W RSC 4 Atlantic City
(*WBA L. Heavyweight Title Challenge*)
21.11.87 Rufino Angulo W PTS 12 Paris
(*WBA L. Heavyweight Title Defence*)
03.04.88 Jean-Marie Emebe W RSC 11 Bismark
(*WBA L. Heavyweight Title Defence*)
06.06.88 Ramzi Hassan W PTS 12 Las Vegas
(*WBA L. Heavyweight Title Defence*)
11.11.88 Willie Featherstone W RSC 10 Bismark
(*WBA L. Heavyweight Title Defence*)
04.03.89 Bobby Czyz W PTS 12 Bismark
(*WBA L. Heavyweight Title Defence*)
Summary: 24 contests, won 24.

Thomas Hearns (left) wins the WBO middleweight title when outpointing James Kinchen, November, 1988

Tom Casino

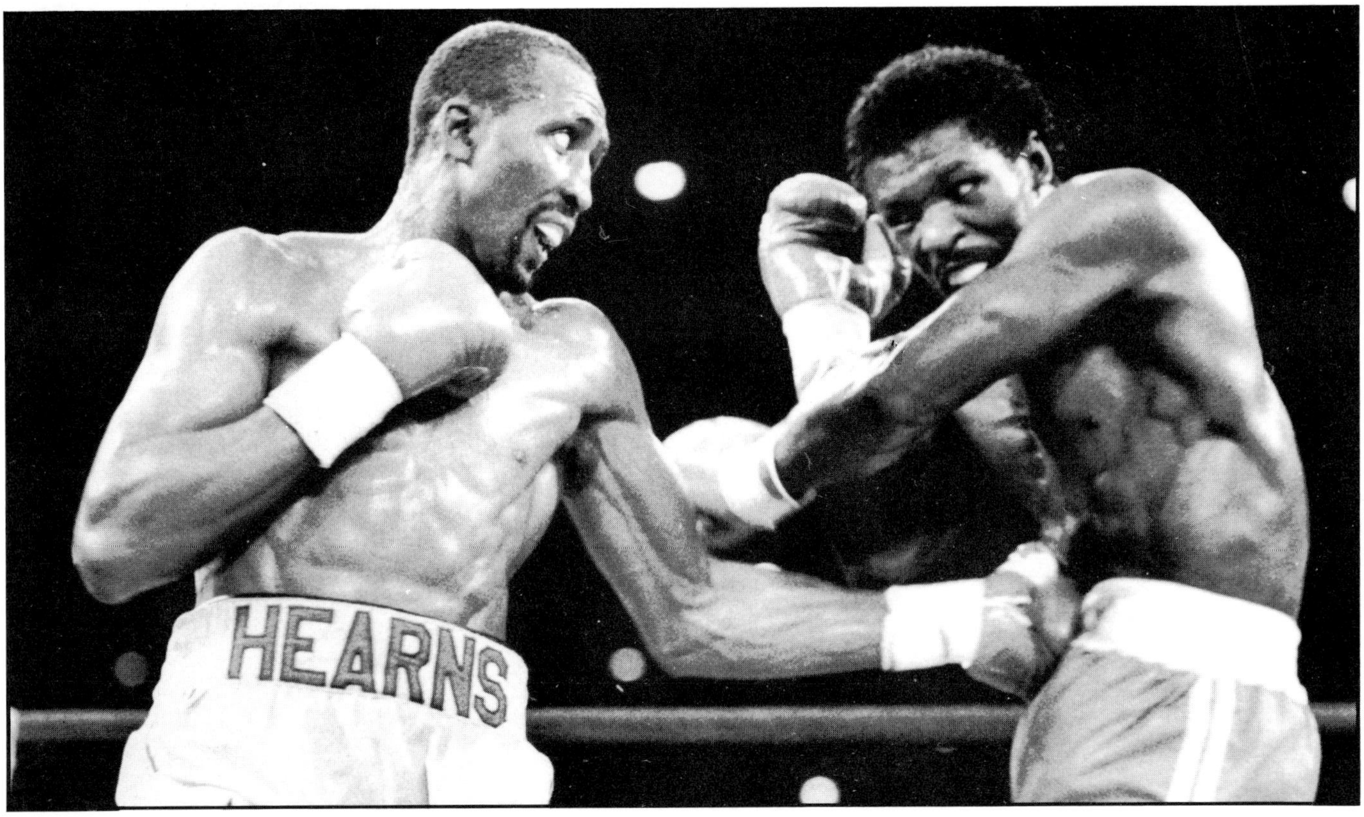

Dave Hilton
Montreal, Canada. *Born* 09.12.63
Middleweight. Former Undefeated Con. Am. & Canadian Welterweight Champion

10.02.81 Noel Torres W RSC 2 Montreal
10.03.81 Kevin Coffee W CO 1 Montreal
14.06.81 Denis Brisson W PTS 4 Montreal
26.06.81 Eddie Ortiz W CO 2 Halifax
29.09.81 Brian Anderson W PTS 4 Montreal
03.11.81 Daniel Gagnon W RSC 4 Montreal
15.12.81 Ray Rosa W RSC 1 Montreal
04.03.82 Henry Rosa W CO 1 Montreal
22.06.82 Daniel Gagnon W PTS 6 Montreal
21.09.82 Bobby Green W CO 1 Montreal
19.10.82 Tim Elliott W CO 2 Montreal
12.11.82 Jean-Paul Petrin W CO 6 Montreal
14.12.82 Mike Blunt W RSC 1 Montreal
25.01.83 Bob Harvey W RSC 3 Montreal
15.02.83 Sam Gervins W PTS 8 Montreal
21.06.83 Pedro Acosta W CO 2 Montreal
29.07.83 Bruce Strauss W CO 3 Cornwall
04.12.83 Mario Cusson T DRAW 3 Montreal
(*Canadian Welterweight Title Challenge*)
25.03.84 Mario Cusson W RSC 1 Montreal
(*Canadian Welterweight Title Challenge*)
10.07.84 Dennis Sigouin W RSC 10 Montreal
(*Vacant Con. Am. Welterweight Title & Canadian Welterweight Title Defence*)
11.12.84 Pete Padilla W RSC 2 Montreal
(*Con. Am. Welterweight Title Defence*)
22.01.85 Sammy Horne W RSC 3 Montreal
15.03.85 Dennis Fain W RSC 2 Las Vegas
29.04.85 Roberto Hernandez W CO 9 Buffalo
06.06.85 Dennis Horne W RSC 2 Las Vegas
(*Con. Am. Welterweight Title Defence*)
22.01.88 Hector Rosario DREW 10 Atlantic City
29.09.88 Ron Amundsen W PTS 10 Atlantic City
14.03.89 Steve Little W PTS 10 Atlantic City
Summary: 28 contests, won 26, drew 2.

Matthew Hilton

Christopher M. Farina

Matthew Hilton
Montreal, Canada. *Born* 27.12.65
Former IBF L. Middleweight Champion

25.01.83 Denis Brisson W RSC 2 Montreal
15.02.83 Adrian Green W RSC 3 Montreal
29.03.83 Frank Minnigan W PTS 4 Montreal
26.04.83 Jacques Deblois W PTS 4 Montreal
24.05.83 Mike Essett W PTS 6 Montreal
21.06.83 Clint Harris W CO 4 Montreal
29.07.83 Harold France W CO 3 Cornwall
23.08.83 Frank Mackay W RSC 1 Laval
10.11.83 Hardy Jones W RSC 6 Montreal
04.12.83 Eddie Hollett W RSC 5 Montreal
30.04.84 Reggie Ford W CO 1 Quebec
01.06.84 Nino Gonzalez W RSC 7 Montreal
10.07.84 Ron Thermidor W RSC 2 Montreal
14.10.84 Sam Gervins W PTS 10 Montreal
11.12.84 Bill Bradley W RTD 3 Montreal
22.01.85 Francisco de Jesus W PTS 10 Montreal
29.04.85 Roberto Hernandez W CO 9 Buffalo
06.09.85 Lopez McGee W RSC 4 Miami
20.10.85 Vito Antuofermo W RTD 4 Montreal
15.02.86 Wilfred Benitez W CO 9 Montreal
19.04.86 Bruce Jackson W RTD 5 Las Vegas
20.05.86 Robert McCorvey W RSC 1 New York
13.06.86 Cheto Ramos W PTS 10 New York
22.11.86 Frank Owens W RSC 2 Las Vegas
12.12.86 Bill Clayton W RSC 2 New York
29.04.87 Muhammad Eltassi W RSC 2 Montreal
27.06.87 Buster Drayton W PTS 15 Montreal
(*IBF L. Middleweight Title Challenge*)
16.10.87 Jack Callahan W RTD 2 Atlantic City
(*IBF L. Middleweight Title Defence*)
29.07.88 Paul Whittaker W RSC 4 Las Vegas
04.11.88 Robert Hines L PTS 12 Las Vegas
(*IBF L. Middleweight Title Defence*)
Summary: 30 contests, won 29, lost 1.

Robert (Bam Bam) Hines
Philadelphia, USA. *Born* 28.03.61
Former IBF L. Middleweight Champion. Former Undefeated USBA L. Middleweight Champion

08.03.81 Joe Robinson W PTS 4 Atlantic City
30.07.81 Ira Robinson W CO 2 Philadelphia
17.09.81 Jose Green W RSC 2 Atlantic City
07.11.81 Rocky Balboa W RSC 1 Las Vegas
22.12.81 Ted White W PTS 6 Atlantic City
02.03.82 Larry Fleming W PTS 6 Atlantic City
24.06.82 Billy Hodge W CO 1 Atlantic City
19.07.82 Sammy Rookard W RSC 1 Atlantic City
25.09.82 Thomas Mays W RSC 4 McAfee
17.10.82 Louie Mateo W RSC 4 Atlantic City
12.11.82 Richard House W CO 2 Atlantic City
19.02.83 J. J. Cottrell W PTS 8 Las Vegas
26.05.83 Ed Campbell W RSC 3 Atlantic City
14.07.83 Jake Torrance W PTS 8 Totowa
17.09.83 Lanny Edmonds W RSC 7 Atlantic City
22.01.83 Ramon Abeldano W RSC 7 Atlantic City
30.05.84 Dennis Fain W RSC 2 Atlantic City
27.06.84 Ricardo Bryant L RSC 7 Atlantic City
08.04.85 Kevin Howard W PTS 10 Atlantic City
01.07.85 James Green DREW 10 Atlantic City
31.03.87 Ismael Negron W RSC 7 Philadelphia
01.06.87 Anthony Wiley W RSC 6 Philadelphia
18.08.87 Don Bowers NC 2 Philadelphia
23.10.87 Tony Montgomery W RSC 10 Atlantic City
(*Vacant USBA L. Middleweight Title*)
21.04.88 Steve Little W PTS 12 Atlantic City
(*USBA L. Middleweight Title Defence*)
16.08.88 Jose de Lima W RSC 3 Philadelphia
04.11.88 Matthew Hilton W PTS 12 Las Vegas
(*IBF L. Middleweight Title Challenge*)
05.02.89 Darrin van Horn L PTS 12 Atlantic City
(*IBF L. Middleweight Title Defence*)
Summary: 28 contests, won 24, drew 1, lost 2, no contest 1.

Gary Hinton
Philadelphia, USA. *Born* 29.08.56
Former IBF L. Welterweight Champion. Former Undefeated USBA & Con. Am. L. Welterweight Champion

24.01.78 Billy Jones W PTS 4 Philadelphia
06.06.78 Daryl Guyton W CO 3 Philadelphia
21.09.78 Craig Jones W PTS 4 Philadelphia
24.10.78 Chuck Jones W RSC 2 Philadelphia
23.01.79 Mike Ross W PTS 6 Philadelphia
10.04.79 Lou Daniels W CO 2 Philadelphia
16.07.79 Jorge Nina W PTS 6 Philadelphia
14.11.79 Jerry Graham W PTS 6 Philadelphia
05.06.80 Ron Green W PTS 8 Atlantic City
03.07.80 Charles Brown L PTS 10 Atlantic City
01.10.80 Ernie Jackson DREW 8 Atlantic City
12.11.80 Jerry Graham W PTS 8 Philadelphia
05.02.81 Orlando Montalvo W CO 3 Atlantic City
17.06.81 Wyatt Simpkins W PTS 8 Philadelphia
30.07.81 Victor Mangual W PTS 8 Philadelphia
02.09.81 Teddy Hatfield W RSC 3 Philadelphia
14.11.81 Curtis Harris L PTS 10 Atlantic City
22.12.81 Victor Mangual W RSC 4 Atlantic City
15.04.82 Luis Mejias W CO 7 Atlantic City
24.11.82 Sam Gervins W PTS 8 Atlantic City
13.02.83 Jose Renta W CO 2 Atlantic City
14.03.83 Clemente Rojas W RSC 5 Atlantic City
31.08.83 Steve Mitchell W CO 5 Atlantic City
17.12.83 Felix Reyes W PTS 10 Atlantic City
26.03.84 Jerome Kinney W PTS 12 Atlantic City
(*USBA L. Welterweight Title Challenge*)
11.07.84 Brett Lally W PTS 12 Atlantic City
(*USBA L. Welterweight Title Defence*)
02.03.85 Aaron Pryor L PTS 15 Atlantic City
(*IBF L. Welterweight Title Challenge*)
23.08.85 Joe Manley DREW 12 Atlantic City
(*USBA L. Welterweight Title Defence*)
05.11.85 Darryl Fuller W PTS 12 Atlantic City
(*Con. Am. L. Welterweight Title Challenge*)
26.04.86 Antonio Reyes Cruz W PTS 15 Lucca
(*Vacant IBF L. Welterweight Title*)
30.10.86 Joe Manley L CO 10 Hartford
(*IBF L. Welterweight Title Defence*)
05.05.88 Frank Montgomery W PTS 10 Atlantic City
07.07.88 Dexter Smith W PTS 10 Tampa
20.10.88 Juan Alonzo Villa W RSC 4 Philadelphia
23.02.89 Joe Walker W PTS 10 Detroit
Summary: 35 contests, won 29, drew 2, lost 4.

Akinobu Hiranaka
Okinawa, Japan. *Born* 14.11.63
Former Undefeated Japanese L. Welterweight Champion

24.03.85 Kazumi Yokoi W CO 1 Naha
30.06.85 Naomi Fuji W RSC 4 Osaka
02.10.85 Thai Suracharern W CO 2 Okinawa
09.01.86 Masahiro Tanabu W CO 6 Tokyo
(*Japanese L. Welterweight Title Challenge*)
06.04.86 Teruhide Nishida W CO 1 Okinawa
01.05.86 Masahiro Tanabu W CO 5 Tokyo
(*Japanese L. Welterweight Title Defence*)
17.08.86 Makoto Ito W CO 2 Tokyo
(*Japanese L. Welterweight Title Defence*)
14.12.86 Nilo Alamag W RSC 7 Okinawa
15.03.87 Yoshifumi Kitajima W PTS 10 Okinawa
(*Japanese L. Welterweight Title Defence*)
16.06.87 Archie Garcia W RSC 5 Tokyo
11.08.87 Naoki Ito W CO 1 Tokyo
(*Japanese L. Welterweight Title Defence*)
13.10.87 Tetsuya Manaka W RSC 8 Tokyo
(*Japanese L. Welterweight Title Defence*)
26.01.88 Eiji Kikusaki W CO 2 Tokyo
(*Japanese L. Welterweight Title Defence*)
24.04.88 Tadanobu Miura W RSC 1 Okinawa
(*Japanese L. Welterweight Title Defence*)
31.05.88 Seiji Nagasawa W CO 1 Tokyo
(*Japanese L. Welterweight Title Defence*)
21.07.88 Tricky Kawaguchi W RSC 5 Kitakyushu
(*Japanese L. Welterweight Title Defence*)
07.03.89 Yoshihiro Yamamoto W PTS 10 Tokyo
29.04.89 Juan M. Coggi L PTS 12 Vasto
(*WBA L. Welterweight Title Challenge*)
Summary: 18 contests, won 17, lost 1.

Paul Hodkinson

Paul Hodkinson
Liverpool, England. *Born* 14.09.65
British & EBU Featherweight Champion

19.07.86 Mark Champney W CO 2 Wembley
17.09.86 Phil Lashley W RSC 2 London
29.09.86 Les Remikie W RTD 4 London
29.10.86 Craig Windsor W CO 2 Belfast
17.01.87 Steve Sammy Sims W CO 5 Belfast
26.02.87 Kamel Djadda W RSC 4 London
25.04.87 Russell Jones W RSC 6 Belfast
31.07.87 Tomas Arguelles DREW 8 Panama City

19.10.87 Tomas Arguelles W CO 6 Belfast
03.12.87 Marcus Smith W RSC 7 Belfast
27.01.88 Richie Foster W RSC 3 Belfast
18.05.88 Peter Harris W RSC 12 Aberavon
(*British Featherweight Title Challenge*)
14.12.88 Kevin Taylor W RSC 2 Kirkby
(*British Featherweight Title Defence*)
18.01.89 Johnny Carter W CO 1 London
12.04.89 Raymond Armand W RSC 2 Belfast
(*Vacant EBU Featherweight Title*)
Summary: 15 contests, won 14, drew 1.

Lindell Holmes
Detroit, USA. *Born* 10.10.58
USBA S. Middleweight Champion

15.11.79 Rodney Coupe W RSC 1 Detroit
07.02.80 Dave Roberts W CO 3 Wyandotte
02.03.80 Cliff Askew W CO 1 Detroit
03.05.80 Willie Torres W RSC 6 Detroit
17.07.80 Vern Cunningham W CO 4 Maumee
10.09.80 Benny Mitchell W CO 3 Detroit
18.10.80 George Madison W RSC 3 Toledo
02.12.80 Sammy Floyd W CO 4 Toledo
12.12.80 Gary Thomas W CO 4 Detroit
31.01.81 Fermin Guzman W CO 8 Philadelphia
12.04.81 Carlton Swift W PTS 8 Atlantic City
28.05.81 Jimmy Waire W RSC 8 Phoenix
13.08.81 Danny Alexander W CO 3 Detroit
13.10.81 Rudy Robles W RSC 8 Phoenix
14.11.81 Irwin Hines L CO 3 Atlantic City
07.03.82 Buster Drayton W PTS 10 Atlantic City
24.07.82 Leslie Gardner W CO 4 Detroit
27.08.82 Jamie Thomas W RSC 4 Detroit
10.07.83 Alonzo Cutchin W RTD 2 Atlantic City
13.08.83 Dwight Davison L RSC 8 Las Vegas
21.03.84 Roy Gumbs W CO 7 London
12.04.84 Ricky Davis W CO 1 Ann Arbor
15.05.84 Leroy Hester W RSC 6 Atlantic City
22.07.84 Herol Graham L RSC 5 Sheffield
09.11.84 Ayub Kalule L PTS 10 Copenhagen
20.12.84 Billy Robertson W RSC 12 Los Angeles
13.02.85 Andre Cooper W RSC 7 Atlantic City
16.05.85 Danny Miller W CO 2 Winnipeg
29.06.85 Sanderline Williams W RSC 9 Atlantic City
15.10.85 Luis Rivera W RSC 8 Los Angeles
17.12.85 Jack Padia W RSC 6 Los Angeles
25.02.86 Murray Sutherland W RSC 3 Detroit
(*USBA S. Middleweight Title Challenge*)
17.03.86 Brian Miller W CO 9 Los Angeles
11.04.86 Matt Lewis W RSC 7 Los Angeles
06.07.86 Chong-Pal Park T DRAW 2 Chungju
(*IBF S. Middleweight Title Challenge*)
28.10.86 Sammy Floyd W RSC 4 Detroit
03.02.87 Lamont Kirkland W RTD 9 Los Angeles
(*USBA S. Middleweight Title Defence*)
11.03.87 Ron Malek W CO 3 Toledo
03.05.87 Chong-Pal Park L PTS 15 Inchon
(*IBF S. Middleweight Title Challenge*)
16.09.87 Jorge Amparo W PTS 12 Los Angeles
(*USBA S. Middleweight Title Defence*)
12.03.88 Lottie Mwale W CO 8 Dusseldorf
09.05.88 Steve Darnell W RSC 2 Los Angeles
(*USBA S. Middleweight Title Defence*)
26.06.88 Ralph Ward W PTS 8 Atlantic City
25.08.88 Ricky Stackhouse W RSC 1 Fort Myers
25.11.88 Phillip Morefield W RSC 6 Detroit
31.01.89 Fermin Chirino W PTS 10 Atlantic City
Summary: 46 contests, won 40, drew 1, lost 5.

Evander (The Real Deal) Holyfield
Atmore, USA. *Born* 19.10.62
Con. Am. Heavyweight Champion. Former Undefeated World Cruiserweight Champion

15.11.84 Lyonel Byarm W PTS 6 New York
20.01.85 Eric Winbush W PTS 6 Atlantic City
13.03.85 Fred Brown W RSC 1 Norfolk
20.04.85 Mark Rivera W RSC 2 Corpus Christi
20.07.85 Tyrone Booze W PTS 8 Norfolk
29.08.85 Rick Myers W RTD 1 Atlanta
30.10.85 Jeff Meachum W RSC 5 Atlantic City
06.12.85 Anthony Davis W RSC 4 Virginia Beach
01.03.86 Chisanda Mutti W RSC 3 Lancaster
06.04.86 Jesse Shelby W RSC 3 Corpus Christi
28.05.86 Terry Mims W RSC 5 Metairie
12.07.86 Dwight Muhammad Qawi W PTS 15 Atlanta
(*WBA Cruiserweight Title Challenge*)
10.12.86 Mike Brothers W RSC 3 Paris
14.02.87 Henry Tillman W RSC 7 Reno
(*WBA Cruiserweight Title Defence*)

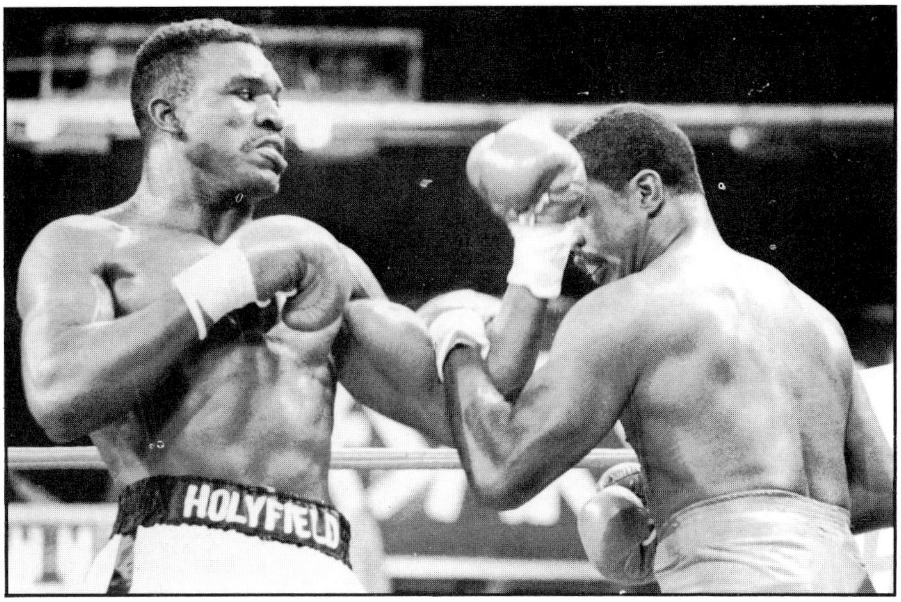

Evander Holyfield (left) united the world cruiserweight title when defeating Carlos de Leon in April, 1988

Christopher M. Farina

15.05.87 Rickey Parkey W RSC 3 Las Vegas
(*IBF Cruiserweight Title Challenge*)
15.08.87 Ossie Ocasio W RSC 11 St Tropez
(*WBA & IBF Cruiserweight Title Defence*)
05.12.87 Dwight Muhammad Qawi W CO 4 Atlantic City
(*IBF Cruiserweight Title Defence*)
09.04.88 Carlos de Leon W RSC 8 Las Vegas
(*WBA & IBF Cruiserweight Title Defence. WBC Cruiserweight Title Challenge*)
16.07.88 James Tillis W RTD 5 Lake Tahoe
09.12.88 Pinklon Thomas W RTD 7 Atlantic City
11.03.89 Michael Dokes W RSC 10 Las Vegas
(*Con. Am. Heavyweight Title Challenge*)
Summary: 21 contests, won 21.

Lloyd Honeyghan
Bermondsey, England. *Born* Jamaica 22.04.60
Former WBC Welterweight Champion. Former Undefeated British, Commonwealth, EBU & WBA/IBF Welterweight Champion

08.12.80 Mike Sullivan W PTS 6 London
20.01.81 Dai Davies W RSC 5 London
10.02.81 Dave Sullivan W PTS 6 London
16.11.81 Dave Finigan W RSC 1 London
24.11.81 Alan Cooper W RSC 4 Wembley
25.01.82 Dave Finigan W CO 2 London
09.02.82 Granville Allen W RSC 5 London
02.03.82 Tommy McCallum W PTS 6 London
15.03.82 Derek McKenzie W RSC 3 London
23.03.82 Dave Sullivan W RSC 3 London
18.05.82 Kostas Petrou W PTS 8 London
22.09.82 Kid Murray W RSC 3 London
22.11.82 Frank McCord W CO 1 London
18.01.83 Lloyd Hibbert W PTS 10 London
01.03.83 Sid Smith W CO 4 London
05.04.83 Cliff Gilpin W PTS 12 London
(*Vacant British Welterweight Title*)
09.07.83 Kevin Austin W RSC 10 Chicago
24.10.83 Harold Brazier W PTS 10 London
06.12.83 Cliff Gilpin W PTS 12 London
(*British Welterweight Title Defence*)
05.06.84 Roberto Mendez W PTS 8 London
05.01.85 Gianfranco Rosi W CO 3 Perugia
(*EBU Welterweight Title Challenge*)
12.02.85 R. W. Smith W RTD 6 London
06.03.85 Roger Stafford W RSC 9 London
30.08.85 Danny Paul W PTS 10 Atlantic City
01.10.85 Ralph Twinning W RSC 4 Wembley
27.11.85 Sylvester Mittee W RSC 8 London
(*EBU Welterweight Title Defence, British & Commonwealth Welterweight Title Challenge*)
20.05.86 Horace Shufford W RSC 8 Wembley
27.09.86 Don Curry W RTD 6 Atlantic City
(*World Welterweight Title Challenge*)
22.02.87 Johnny Bumphus W RSC 2 Wembley
(*IBF Welterweight Title Defence*)
18.04.87 Maurice Blocker W PTS 12 London
(*WBC Welterweight Title Defence*)
30.08.87 Gene Hatcher W RSC 1 Marbella
(*WBC Welterweight Title Defence*)
28.10.87 Jorge Vaca L TD 8 Wembley
(*WBC Welterweight Title Defence*)
29.03.88 Jorge Vaca W CO 3 Wembley
(*WBC Welterweight Title Challenge*)
29.07.88 Yung-Kil Chung W RSC 5 Atlantic City
(*WBC Welterweight Title Defence*)
05.02.89 Marlon Starling L RSC 9 Las Vegas
(*WBC Welterweight Title Defence*)
Summary: 35 contests, won 33, lost 2.

Courtney (Dangerous) Hooper
Detroit, USA. *Born* 24.10.62
L. Welterweight

31.01.85 Harold Kimbro W PTS 4 Detroit
21.02.85 Zest Holmes W RSC 1 Detroit
06.06.85 Roger Brown W CO 3 Detroit
25.09.85 Harold Warren W PTS 6 Corpus Christi
21.11.85 Dick Greene W CO 1 Detroit
10.02.86 Carl Williams W RSC 3 Laughlin
27.02.86 Bobby Vann W RSC 3 Detroit
24.04.86 Joey Soler W PTS 8 Detroit
10.06.86 Terry Butler W RSC 4 Detroit
10.07.86 Charles Baez L PTS 6 New York
15.08.86 Kearns Ibarra W RSC 1 Detroit
10.10.86 Aurelio Martinez W CO 1 Las Vegas
17.10.86 Jerome Spotsville W RSC 2 Detroit
05.12.86 Stewart Baynes W RSC 1 Las Vegas
16.01.87 Joe Baker W CO 5 Detroit
30.06.87 Joe Edens W RSC 3 Detroit
18.08.87 Richard Fowler W RSC 4 Detroit
29.09.87 Dwayne Primm W PTS 8 Detroit
28.01.88 Ron Johnson W RSC 6 Detroit
30.03.88 Ford Jennings W RSC 1 Detroit
23.07.88 Phil Rosas W PTS 10 Dearborn
28.09.88 Billy Parks W PTS 8 Detroit
26.10.88 C. J. Duffy W PTS 10 Detroit
30.11.88 Howard Stewart W PTS 12 Detroit
Summary: 24 contests, won 23, lost 1.

Mark Horikoshi
USA. *Born* 16.11.61
Former Japanese S. Bantamweight Champion

12.07.84 Kenji Ikeda W RSC 1 Tokyo
06.09.84 Toru Kosuga W RSC 1 Tokyo
09.11.84 Jun Sato W PTS 4 Tokyo
21.12.84 Toshio Hashiguchi W RSC 1 Tokyo
16.02.85 Kenji Kimura W RSC 4 Tokyo
09.05.85 Masahide Ikehara W CO 4 Tokyo
20.07.85 Takashi Okamoto W PTS 8 Hachinohe
03.04.86 Kenji Iizumi L RSC 7 Tokyo
24.07.86 Mitsuo Imazato W CO 6 Tokyo
02.10.86 Toshimitsu Ano W PTS 10 Tokyo

16.01.87 Yoshiyuki Nomaguchi W RSC 5 Kochi (*Vacant Japanese S. Bantamweight Title Defence*)
25.03.87 Kimio Saotome W CO 3 Hachinohe (*Japanese S. Bantamweight Title Defence*)
02.07.87 Rambo Taira W CO 2 Tokyo (*Japanese S. Bantamweight Title Defence*)
07.10.87 Eiji Yakushiji W CO 6 Hiroshima (*Japanese S. Bantamweight Title Defence*)
24.01.88 Takeo Takahashi W RSC 3 Tokyo (*Japanese S. Bantamweight Title Defence*)
21.03.88 Flash Emmanuel W PTS 10 Tokyo
23.07.88 Hisao Ishido W RSC 5 Yamadamachi (*Japanese S. Bantamweight Title Defence*)
06.10.88 Atsushi Oyakawa W RSC 5 Osaka (*Japanese S. Bantamweight Title Defence*)
23.01.89 Naoto Takahashi L CO 9 Tokyo (*Japanese S. Bantamweight Title Defence*)
Summary: 19 contests, won 17, lost 2.

Cassius Clay Horne
Phoenix, USA. *Born* 30.11.67
L. Welterweight

31.05.84 Ted Michaeliszyn L RSC 4 Las Vegas
12.04.85 Ron Labatta W CO 2 Pueblo
22.04.85 Stacy Grant W RSC 1 Los Angeles
07.05.85 Chancey Hayes W CO 5 Richmond
15.08.85 Drafton Bunch L PTS 6 San Diego
13.01.86 Ron Villa W CO 3 Phoenix
25.01.86 Frank Morales W CO 1 Nogales
10.02.86 Rudy Cruz W CO 1 Laughlin
17.02.86 Derrick Hudson W CO 4 Phoenix
28.02.86 Roosevelt Jones W RSC 2 Laughlin
17.03.86 Jimmy Flores W CO 2 Phoenix
15.04.86 Hector Rodriguez W CO 1 San Antonio
05.05.86 Pedro Rocha W RSC 5 Phoenix
23.05.86 Art Lizarraga W CO 2 Las Vegas
06.06.86 Ruben Moreno W RSC 1 Phoenix
11.07.86 Stewart Baynes W RSC 4 Las Vegas
25.08.86 Ricky Lehman W RSC 7 Phoenix
24.09.86 Rosenberg Rosas W PTS 5 Las Vegas
01.11.86 Roque Montoya W CO 1 Phoenix
15.12.86 Rosenberg Rosas W PTS 10 Phoenix
23.03.87 Darryl Cottrell W RSC 2 Phoenix
04.04.87 Robert Guy L PTS 8 Las Vegas
11.05.87 Sergio Zambrano W RSC 1 Phoenix
22.06.87 Ronnie Shields DREW 10 Phoenix
08.02.88 Don Payne W CO 1 Phoenix
10.05.88 Floyd Peavy W CO 7 Phoenix
22.11.88 Joe Alexander L RSC 6 Las Vegas
Summary: 27 contests, won 22, drew 1, lost 4.

Louis Howard
St Louis, USA. *Born* 28.08.62
Welterweight

09.11.84 Victor Hernandez W PTS 6 Las Vegas
19.12.84 Jaime Fernandez W RSC 1 Las Vegas
16.01.85 David White W RSC 1 Las Vegas
15.03.85 Martin Hernandez W CO 1 Las Vegas
29.04.85 Dwight Williams W RSC 2 Buffalo
15.06.85 Chuck Peralta W RSC 3 Las Vegas
10.08.85 Rafael Gomez W RSC 3 Las Vegas
20.10.85 Dennis Benjamin W RSC 4 Montreal
19.09.86 Robert Brooks W CO 1 Chicago
07.03.87 Mark French W RSC 2 Detroit
21.09.87 Wardle Langston L PTS 8 Akron
18.11.87 Rodney Tatum W RSC 1 Youngstown
05.03.88 Charles Hollis W RSC 3 Sulphur Springs
25.03.88 Gary Coates W PTS 6 Detroit
09.06.88 Wardle Langston W RSC 2 Bridgeton
11.08.88 Genaro Castro W PTS 8 New York
29.09.88 Luis Santana DREW 12 St Louis (*NABF Welterweight Title Challenge*)
14.03.89 Derrick Rolon L RSC 3 Atlantic City
Summary: 18 contests, won 15, drew 1, lost 2.

Wongso Indrajit
Indonesia
WBC International Bantamweight Champion. Former Indonesian S. Flyweight Champion. Former Undefeated Indonesian Bantamweight Champion

.82 Liang L PTS 4 Malang
.82 Slamet Mukin L PTS 4 Surabaya
.82 Sabung W RSC 2 Surabaya
.82 Mohammed Idansah DREW 4 Surabaya
.82 Kid Firoles W PTS 4 Malang
.82 Yusup W RSC 3 Surabaya
.82 Moningko W PTS 12 Surabaya (*Vacant Indonesian S. Flyweight Title*)
08.05.83 Munadi W PTS 8 Surabaya
11.07.83 Tubagus Jaya W PTS 10 Bali
07.08.83 Moningko W CO 4 Surabaya
11.09.83 Yibon W PTS 10 Surabaya
11.12.83 Elly Pical L PTS 12 Surabaya (*Indonesian S. Flyweight Title Defence*)
12.02.84 Bob Williams W PTS 10 Surabaya
25.03.84 Tubagus Jaya W RSC 2 Malang
16.06.84 Kyu-Chan Cho L PTS 10 Surabaya
05.08.84 Doddy Pabalibun W PTS 12 Surabaya (*Vacant Indonesian S. Flyweight Title*)
14.10.84 Prayoonsak Muangsurin W PTS 10 Jakarta
17.02.85 Jun Simbajon L RSC 6 Surabaya
29.07.85 Nixon Gabriel W PTS 10 Surabaya
03.08.85 Amri Sanusi W PTS 10 Balikpapan
25.08.85 Little Holmes W RSC 4 Jakarta (*Indonesian S. Flyweight Title Defence*)
12.10.85 Edel Geronimo W PTS 10 Jakarta
26.01.86 Edward Apay L RSC 10 Surabaya
18.05.86 Pelni Rompies W PTS 12 Surabaya (*Indonesian S. Flyweight Title Defence*)
31.05.86 Tae-Il Chang L CO 5 Seoul
19.07.86 Little Holmes W PTS 12 Bengkulu (*Indonesian S. Flyweight Title Defence*)
14.09.86 Edward Apay DREW 10 Malang
11.10.86 Charlie Brown W CO 1 Malang
03.11.86 Yani Hagler DREW 10 Malang
22.11.86 Yudi Prianto W PTS 12 Bali (*Indonesian S. Flyweight Title Defence*)
25.01.87 Young W RSC 6 Gresik (*Indonesian S. Flyweight Title Defence*)
26.04.87 Byung-Kwan Chung L PTS 12 Jinju (*OPBF S. Flyweight Title Challenge*)
04.07.87 Yossy Amnifu L PTS 12 Pakanburu (*Indonesian S. Flyweight Title Defence*)
31.10.87 Ryantoha W PTS 8 Surabaya
16.01.88 Little Holmes DREW 8 Padang
18.06.88 Wim Sapulete W RSC 3 Surabaya (*Indonesian Bantamweight Title Challenge*)
04.09.88 Dae-Yong Park W RSC 10 Surabaya
26.11.88 Edel Geronimo W PTS 12 Padang (*Vacant WBC International Bantamweight Title*)
27.12.88 Thamin Sithseemok W CO 6 Surabaya
27.03.89 Chucherd Eaussampan W PTS 10 Surabaya
Summary: 40 contests, won 27, drew 4, lost 9.

Hiroki Ioka
Sakai City, Japan. *Born* 08.01.69
Former WBC M. Flyweight Champion. Former Undefeated Japanese M. Flyweight Champion

23.01.86 Yukio Yorimochi W CO 3 Tokyo
10.02.86 Hiroshi Udo W CO 2 Kochi City
05.03.86 Osamu Ueumoto W CO 2 Osaka
13.09.86 Masao Kasai W PTS 4 Matsumoto
07.10.86 Yoshihide Tobo W RSC 2 Osaka
22.02.87 Hisashi Nakatomi W RTD 1 Tokyo
28.04.87 Akira Kiyono W PTS 8 Osaka
08.07.87 Kenji Ono W PTS 10 Osaka (*Japanese M. Flyweight Title Challenge*)
18.10.87 Mai Thornburifarm W PTS 12 Osaka (*Vacant WBC M. Flyweight Title*)
31.01.88 Kyung-Yung Lee W RSC 12 Osaka (*WBC M. Flyweight Title Defence*)
05.06.88 Napa Kiatwanchai DREW 12 Osaka (*WBC M. Flyweight Title Defence*)
13.11.88 Napa Kiatwanchai L PTS 12 Osaka (*WBC M. Flyweight Title Defence*)
08.02.89 Hidekazu Kakehashi W CO 2 Osaka
Summary: 13 contests, won 11, drew 1, lost 1.

Naoki Ito
Japan
OPBF L. Welterweight Champion

05.04.85 Tetsuya Sato W CO 2 Tokyo
07.05.85 Shinichi Yoshinuma W PTS 4 Tokyo
05.08.85 Yoshifumi Kitajima W PTS 4 Tokyo
11.11.85 Shinichi Yoshinuma W PTS 4 Tokyo
21.12.85 Yoichi Isome W PTS 6 Tokyo
04.03.86 Hironobu Ogiso L RSC 4 Osaka
11.08.86 Minoru Nagata W CO 2 Tokyo
06.11.86 Hironobu Ogiso W PTS 10 Tokyo
23.03.87 Eiji Kikuzaki L RSC 2 Tokyo
18.05.87 Mon Desoloc W RSC 7 Tokyo
11.08.87 Akinobu Hiranaka L CO 1 Tokyo (*Japanese L. Welterweight Title Challenge*)
26.01.88 Nilo Acido W RTD 8 Tokyo
18.04.88 Yoshiaki Tajima W PTS 10 Tokyo
15.08.88 Mugen Kawasaka W CO 2 Tokyo
04.12.88 Kang Chul W RSC 9 Kwang-Ju (*OPBF L. Welterweight Title Challenge*)
17.04.89 Sung-Woon Song W DIS 5 Tokyo (*OPBF L. Welterweight Title Defence*)
Summary: 16 contests, won 13, lost 3.

John D. Jackson
Stanford, USA. *Born* 17.05.63
WBO L. Middleweight champion

11.03.84 Kim Brady W RSC 1 Atlantic City
11.04.84 Keith Todd W RSC 3 Scranton
10.05.84 Bob Thomas W PTS 6 Philadelphia
26.06.84 Louis Owens W PTS 4 Atlantic City
17.10.84 Felipe Montellano W PTS 6 Atlantic City
20.03.85 Gary Tibbs W CO 4 Atlantic City
13.06.85 Billy Ray Joe W RSC 1 Atlantic City
18.07.85 Robert Thomas W PTS 8 Philadephia
04.09.85 Vince Mays W RSC 5 Atlantic City
25.02.86 Orlando Montalvo W CO 2 Atlantic City
14.06.86 Mike Castronova W RSC 1 Shillington
31.07.86 Milton Leaks W PTS 8 Atlantic City
28.10.86 Tony Ojo W RSC 3 Pennsauken
25.11.86 John B. Walker W RSC 1 Atlantic City
13.01.87 Sidney Outlaw W RSC 6 Philadelphia
21.07.87 Davey Moore W PTS 10 Atlantic City
07.10.88 Cheto Ramos W RSC 4 Detroit
08.12.88 Lupe Aquino W RTD 7 Detroit (*Vacant WBO L. Middleweight Title*)
22.04.89 Steve Little W RSC 8 Detroit (*WBO L. Middleweight Title Defence*)
Summary: 19 contests, won 19.

John D. Jackson

Peter Goldfield/USA

Julian Jackson
St Thomas, Virgin Islands. *Born* 12.09.60
WBA L. Middleweight Champion. Former Undefeated Con. Am. L. Middleweight Champion

12.02.81 Inocencio Carmona W PTS 6 San Juan
05.03.81 Rafael Ayala W RSC 1 Trujillo Alto
09.04.81 Marcelino Flores W CO 2 San Juan
16.05.81 Reyes Escalera W RSC 3 St Thomas
15.08.81 Edwin Rodriguez W RSC 1 San Juan
26.09.81 Dario d'Asa W CO 3 Miami
20.03.82 Billy Page W PTS 6 Atlantic City
06.06.82 Al Cook W CO 2 Miami
18.08.82 Miguel Sepulveda W RSC 3 San Juan
17.11.82 Mack Heimbaugh W RSC 4 St Joseph
19.01.83 Domenic Fox W CO 2 San Juan
06.03.83 Jake Torrance W RSC 5 Atlantic City
18.05.83 Renaldo Rogue W RSC 1 Las Vegas
25.06.83 David Plowden W RSC 3 San Juan
15.10.83 Jeff Nelson W RSC 3 Miami
20.01.84 Carlton Brown W RSC 1 New York
17.03.84 Eddie Gazo W CO 2 Hato Rey
16.05.84 J. J. Cottrell W RSC 5 Las Vegas
20.06.84 Ron Warrior W CO 3 San Juan (*Vacant Con. Am. L. Middleweight Title*)
15.08.84 Curtis Ramsey W RSC 12 Las Vegas (*Con. Am. L. Middleweight Title Defence*)

03.11.84 Santos Solis W RSC 8 San Juan
21.11.84 Tim Harris W RSC 8 Las Vegas
(*Con. Am. L. Middleweight Title Defence*)
12.07.85 Rafael Corona W RSC 3 Santa Clara
10.08.85 Jose Padilla W RSC 3 Las Vegas
15.11.85 Raul Hernandez W RSC 1 Miami
28.02.86 Lopez McGee W CO 2 St Thomas
22.03.86 Mark Allman W RSC 1 Las Vegas
19.04.86 Pancho del Toro W CO 2 Las Vegas
20.05.86 Derrick Drane W RSC 2 New York
23.08.86 Mike McCallum L RSC 2 Miami
(*WBA L. Middleweight Title Challenge*)
19.12.86 Khalif Shabazz W CO 1 Virgin Islands
24.04.87 Milton Leaks W CO 1 Hartford
(*Vacant Con. Am. L. Middleweight Title*)
21.11.87 In-Chul Baek W RSC 3 Las Vegas
(*Vacant WBA L. Middleweight Title*)
16.04.88 Reggie Barnes W CO 1 Las Vegas
25.06.88 Efrain Olivo W CO 1 Atlantic City
30.07.88 Buster Drayton W RSC 3 Atlantic City
(*WBA L. Middleweight Title Defence*)
25.02.89 Francisco de Jesus W CO 8 Las Vegas
(*WBA L. Middleweight Title Defence*)
Summary: 37 contests, won 36, lost 1.

Tyrone (Harlem Butcher) Jackson
New York, USA. *Born* 23.10.60
Former Undefeated Con. Am. S. Featherweight Champion

04.06.81 Glenn Richardson W RSC 4 New York
25.06.81 Gilbert de Jesus W RSC 2 New York
08.08.81 Vergon Hill W PTS 4 New York
03.09.81 Jose Espada W RSC 3 Atlantic City
12.09.81 Cheo Ortiz W CO 3 New York
25.09.81 Glenn Guy W CO 1 New York
05.11.81 Darryl Graham W RSC 3 Atlantic City
05.02.82 Emilio Rodriguez W RSC 1 New York
26.02.82 Cheo Ortiz W PTS 6 New York
24.04.82 Fernando Ortiz W CO 2 Atlantic City
07.11.82 Robert Mullins W CO 3 New York
19.11.82 Jeff Roberts W PTS 8 New York
26.03.83 Tim Daniels W RSC 5 New York
01.05.83 Felix Cortes W CO 1 Atlantic City
28.05.83 Victor Acosta W PTS 10 New York
28.09.83 Willy Martinez W RSC 4 New York
13.12.83 Elvin Gonzalez W RSC 5 Atlantic City
17.04.84 Clarence Hudson W RSC 4 Atlantic City
08.03.85 Felix Thereaux W RSC 3 New York
10.05.85 Juan Torres W CO 2 New York
28.06.85 Paul de Vorce W PTS 12 New York
19.09.85 Rosendo Alonso W CO 1 New York
(*Con. Am. S. Featherweight Title Challenge*)
16.02.86 Ki-Yung Chung L RTD 6 Ulsan
(*IBF Featherweight Title Challenge*)
12.02.87 Mario Salazar W CO 2 New York
23.04.87 Floyd Favors W RSC 10 New York
(*Con. Am. S. Featherweight Title Defence*)
03.09.87 Wilmer Ruiz W CO 6 New York
(*Con. Am. S. Featherweight Title Defence*)
29.10.87 Darryl Savoy W RSC 2 New York
(*Con. Am. S. Featherweight Title Defence*)
24.02.88 Robinson Sanchez W RSC 3 New York
25.08.88 Mark Hammon W RSC 8 New York
15.12.88 Gustavo Martinez W RSC 1 New York
16.02.89 Phil Charleston W RSC 4 Detroit
Summary: 31 contests, won 30, lost 1.

Thierry Jacob
Calais, France. *Born* 08.03.65
French Bantamweight Champion

29.10.85 Vincenzo Belcastro W PTS 6 Paris
09.11.85 Eloi Kiroffo W RSC 2 Lille
14.12.85 Jean-Paul Guillard W RTD 1 Calais
08.02.86 Eloi Kiroffo W RSC 2 Lille
08.03.86 Francisco Garcia W CO 4 Calais
17.03.86 German Nunez W CO 1 Paris
05.04.86 Kevin Downer W CO 5 Boulogne
26.04.86 Mohamed Bouras W RTD 3 Calais
10.05.86 Freddy Cruz W PTS 8 Gravelines
30.05.86 Jean Chartier W RSC 3 Grande Synthe
12.09.86 Blas Canovas W RSC 4 Paris
04.10.86 Kelvin Smart W PTS 8 Calais
27.10.86 Bobby McDermott W RSC 3 Paris
29.11.86 Manuel Carrasco W RSC 2 Calais
24.01.87 Alain Limarola W RSC 5 Calais
(*French Bantamweight Title Challenge*)
18.04.87 Ezequiel Hernandez W PTS 8 Calais
23.05.87 Sammy Ruiz W RSC 4 Calais
04.07.87 Kelvin Seabrooks L CO 9 Calais
(*IBF Bantamweight Title Challenge*)
03.10.87 Juan Castellanos W PTS 8 Gravelines
14.11.87 Ricky West W CO 2 Calais
30.01.88 Fabrice Benichou L CO 9 Calais
(*Vacant EBU Bantamweight Title*)
10.09.88 Graham O'Malley W PTS 8 Grande Synthe
24.09.88 Isidro Medina W CO 2 Berck
21.10.88 Miguel Pequeno W CO 2 Calais
11.11.88 Jose Sanabria L RSC 6 Gravelines
(*IBF S. Bantamweight Title Challenge*)
02.04.89 Haidar Nourredine W DIS 3 Armentieres
10.04.89 Jose Soto W PTS 8 Nogent
Summary: 27 contests, won 24, lost 3.

Gary Jacobs
Glasgow, Scotland. *Born* 10.12.65
WBC International & Commonwealth Welterweight Champion

20.05.85 John Conlan W PTS 6 Glasgow
03.06.85 Nigel Burke W PTS 6 Glasgow
12.08.85 Mike McKenzie W PTS 6 Glasgow
07.10.85 Albert Buchanan W PTS 6 Cambuslang
11.11.85 Tyrell Wilson W CO 5 Glasgow
02.12.85 Dave Heaver W PTS 6 Glasgow
10.02.86 Courtney Phillips W RSC 5 Glasgow
10.03.86 Alistair Laurie W PTS 8 Glasgow
14.04.86 Billy Cairns W PTS 8 Glasgow
24.06.86 Dave Douglas L PTS 10 Glasgow
15.09.86 Jeff Decker W RSC 3 Glasgow
20.10.86 Kelvin Mortimer W RSC 5 Glasgow
27.01.87 Dave Douglas W PTS 10 Glasgow
24.02.87 Gary Williams W CO 7 Glasgow
06.04.87 Robert Armstrong W RTD 5 Glasgow
19.05.87 Gary Williams W RSC 3 Cumbernauld
08.06.87 Tommy McCallum W RSC 5 Glasgow
26.11.87 Jeff Decker W PTS 8 London
24.02.88 Del Bryan W PTS 10 Glasgow
19.04.88 Wilf Gentzen W PTS 12 Glasgow
(*Commonwealth Welterweight Title Challenge*)
06.06.88 Juan Alonzo Villa W RSC 5 London
16.09.88 Javier Suazo W CO 10 Las Vegas
(*Vacant WBC International Welterweight Title*)
29.11.88 Richard Rova W CO 4 London
(*Commonwealth Welterweight Title Defence*)
14.02.89 Rocky Kelly W RTD 7 London
(*Commonwealth & WBC International Welterweight Title Defence*)
05.04.89 George Collins W PTS 12 London
(*Commonwealth & WBC International Welterweight Title Defence*)
Summary: 25 contests, won 24, lost 1.

Gary Jacobs

Gert Bo Jacobsen
Oestrup, Denmark. *Born* 18.12.61
Former Undefeated WBC International & EBU Lightweight Champion

07.10.82 Chris McCallum W CO 1 Copenhagen
05.11.82 Gilbert Heluin W PTS 6 Copenhagen
02.12.82 Benito Murillo W PTS 4 Randers
11.02.83 Eddie Morgan W RSC 3 Copenhagen
08.04.83 Hugo Carrizo W PTS 6 Copenhagen
06.10.83 Gary Lucas W CO 4 Copenhagen
01.12.83 Aldo di Benedetto W CO 2 Copenhagen
13.01.84 Charles Jurietti W RSC 1 Randers
18.02.84 Jose Luis Vicho W PTS 8 Copenhagen
05.10.84 Jesus Matilla W RSC 3 Randers
09.11.84 Vicente Jorge W PTS 8 Copenhagen
08.03.85 Jose Ortiz W CO 2 Copenhagen
20.06.85 Claude Lancastre W RSC 4 Copenhagen
01.11.85 Jose Garcia W RSC 2 Copenhagen
07.12.85 Nelson Trujillo W RSC 10 Copenhagen
10.01.86 Rene Weller W RSC 8 Randers
(*EBU Lightweight Title Challenge*)
18.04.86 Alfredo Raininger W PTS 12 Randers
(*EBU Lightweight Title Defence*)
17.10.86 Fernando Blanco W PTS 12 Randers
(*EBU Lightweight Title Defence*)
06.02.87 Joey Joynson W CO 1 Herning
27.02.87 Jose A. Hernandez W PTS 12 Randers
(*EBU Lightweight Title Defence*)
28.03.87 Felipe Julio W RSC 5 Copenhagen
(*Vacant WBC International Lightweight Title*)
08.06.87 Alain Simoes W RSC 8 Merignac
(*EBU Lightweight Title Defence*)
02.10.87 Claudio Nitti W RSC 4 Copenhagen
(*EBU Lightweight Title Defence*)
15.01.88 Herbie Bivalacqua W CO 4 Skive
05.02.88 Joey Medina W RSC 6 Atlantic City
12.05.88 Marvin Garris W PTS 8 Copenhagen
28.10.88 Greg Haugen L RTD 10 Copenhagen
(*IBF Lightweight Title Challenge*)
Summary: 27 contests, won 26, lost 1.

Rene Jacquot
Toul, France
WBC L. Middleweight Champion. Former Undefeated French & EBU L. Middleweight Champion

30.10.83 Richard Bankeu W PTS 6 Strasbourg
07.01.84 Stephane Walter L PTS 6 Besancon
13.02.84 Patrick Grisot W PTS 6 Paris
20.02.84 Jean-Pierre Calvez W PTS 6 Paris
27.02.84 Victor Santoncini L PTS 6 Paris
28.04.84 Alphonse Matoubella L PTS 6 St Malo
26.10.84 Thierry Pierluigi W RSC 4 Echirolles
30.11.84 Felix di Ciocco L PTS 6 Grenoble
22.12.84 Angelo Liquori W RSC 6 Muggio
05.01.85 Salvatore Pisani W PTS 6 Voiron
22.03.85 Abdelkader Souhihi L RTD 5 Nice
07.06.85 Andrea Scardigli L PTS 6 Scandicci
29.06.85 Luciano Bruno L PTS 6 Bellaria
26.10.85 Hugues Samo W RSC 6 Grenoble
06.12.85 Helier Custos W PTS 8 Echirolles
25.01.86 Rafael Salamone W PTS 8 Grenoble
28.02.86 Yvon Segor L PTS 10 Pointe a Pitre
(*French L. Middleweight Title Challenge*)
16.05.86 Giovanni Chirra W PTS 8 Mulhouse
27.06.86 Nino la Rocca W DIS 3 Modena
03.10.86 Mauro Martelli L PTS 10 Geneva
06.12.86 Jean-Yves Piperol W RTD 5 Pointe a Pitre
23.01.87 Jean-Paul Roux W PTS 10 Echirolles
10.04.87 Yvon Segor W RSC 7 Echirolles
(*French L. Middleweight Title Challenge*)
23.06.87 Joel Brival W PTS 8 Paris
03.10.87 Serge Meyers W RTD 3 Echirolles
09.10.87 John van Elteren W RSC 5 Morges
05.12.87 Miodrag Perunovic W RTD 6 Gaillard
29.01.88 Luigi Minchillo W RSC 4 Rimini
(*Vacant EBU L. Middleweight Title*)
09.04.88 Eric Taton W RSC 12 Echirolles
(*EBU L. Middleweight Title Defence*)
29.06.88 Erwin Heiber W RTD 11 Hamburg
(*EBU L. Middleweight Title Defence*)
08.10.88 Romolo Casamonica W PTS 12 Rome
(*EBU L. Middleweight Title Defence*)
11.02.89 Don Curry W PTS 12 Grenoble
(*WBC L. Middleweight Title Challenge*)
Summary: 32 contests, won 23, lost 9.

Mark Janssen
Brisbane, Australia. *Born* 28.10.64
Australian Middleweight Champion

31.05.82 Ted Hopkins W PTS 4 Brisbane
06.06.83 Ronald Doo W RTD 2 Brisbane
15.07.83 Ted Hopkins W PTS 6 Boondall
29.08.83 Scott Withers W PTS 6 Brisbane
12.09.83 Tita Halpin W RSC 2 Mansfield
10.02.84 Al Hallett W CO 2 Urangan
19.03.84 John Siriotis W RSC 4 Brisbane

02.04.84 Peter Batty W PTS 10 Mansfield
01.06.84 Dave Sarago W PTS 10 Brisbane
20.03.85 Leroy King W RSC 10 Brisbane
01.04.85 Dave Sarago W CO 7 Brisbane
14.10.85 Roy Alexander W RSC 4 Mansfield
17.03.86 Sakaria Ve W PTS 10 Brisbane
21.04.86 Alvaro Madrid W CO 7 Brisbane
07.07.86 Craig Parsons W RSC 8 Brisbane
04.08.86 Paul James W PTS 12 Brisbane
(*Vacant Australian Middleweight Title*)
08.12.86 Paul James W RSC 7 Brisbane
(*Australian Middleweight Title Defence*)
24.06.88 Joe Nitiva W PTS 12 Sydney
(*Australian Middleweight Title Defence*)
12.08.88 Ralph Smiley W PTS 8 Melbourne
Summary: 19 contests, won 19.

Arthur Jimmerson
St Louis, USA. *Born* 04.08.63
L. Heavyweight

25.04.85 Sal Trujillo W CO 1 San Diego
27.06.85 Manuel Leyva W CO 1 San Diego
18.07.85 Bob Williams W CO 2 San Diego
27.09.85 Jay Murphy W CO 3 Phoenix
02.11.85 Danny Blake W PTS 8 San Francisco
10.02.86 Glenn Kennedy L PTS 6 Los Angeles
19.06.86 Manuel Murillo L RSC 7 San Diego
23.01.88 Jim Moore W PTS 6 St Louis
05.03.88 Assim Rizzag W CO 3 St Louis
19.05.88 Danny Thomas W PTS 6 Saginaw
04.06.88 Lopez McGee W PTS 10 St Louis
14.07.88 Lenny Lapaglia W RSC 6 New York
27.09.88 Jerry Okorodudu W PTS 10 St Louis
29.10.88 Bill Lee W PTS 10 St Louis
01.03.89 Jeff Harding L PTS 10 Cardiff
Summary: 15 contests, won 12, lost 3.

Mike Johnson
Ann Arbor, USA
L. Welterweight

27.01.84 Santos Rodriguez W CO 1 Ypsilanti
01.06.84 Paul Farley W RSC 1 Ann Arbor
09.11.84 Zest Holmes W RSC 4 Russellsville
28.02.85 Dwayne Galloway W CO 2 Ann Arbor
23.11.85 Don Terrell W RSC 2 Peoria
17.01.86 Joe Travis W PTS 6 Peoria
01.03.86 Nate Stewart W PTS 6 Peoria
15.05.86 Norman Brooks W PTS 6 Merrillville
15.08.86 Howard Stewart L PTS 6 Atlantic City
13.12.86 Zack Bensalah W RSC 2 Ypsilanti
21.03.87 Anthony Travis W PTS 6 Chicago
25.04.87 Robert Brooks W RSC 5 Chicago
30.06.87 Richard Burden DREW 10 Detroit
14.08.87 Ed Richardson W RSC 8 Tupelo
13.11.87 Tony Coleman W PTS 8 Jackson
29.04.88 Billy Parks W RSC 8 Detroit
28.05.88 Donald Payne W RSC 1 Detroit
17.06.88 Engels Pedroza W RSC 9 Las Vegas
06.08.88 Martin Quiroz DREW 10 Las Vegas
08.10.88 Robert Guy W PTS 10 Las Vegas
10.12.88 Vince Releford W RSC 9 Las Vegas
04.02.89 Eduardo Valdez W PTS 10 Detroit
Summary: 22 contests, won 19, drew 2, lost 1.

Anthony (Baby Face) Jones
Detroit, USA. *Born* 10.07.68
Lightweight

08.02.85 Roy Huntley W PTS 4 Ann Arbor
26.04.85 Forrest Lee W PTS 4 Saline
19.12.85 Leo Simmons W PTS 4 Detroit
28.02.86 Gene Traylor W RSC 2 Laughlin
26.03.86 Stuart Baynes W PTS 4 Las Vegas
24.04.86 Carl Heinz W RSC 2 Detroit
15.07.86 John Senegal W RSC 3 Clarkston
12.08.86 Richard Burden W PTS 6 Detroit
17.10.86 Mike Warren W RSC 3 Detroit
12.12.86 Keith Potts W PTS 6 Las Vegas
16.01.87 Roger Brown W PTS 6 Detroit
27.02.87 Alex Byrd W RSC 1 Detroit
06.04.87 Frankie Davis DREW 8 Las Vegas
14.07.87 Shawn Spinda W CO 1 Detroit
14.08.87 Walter Cowans W PTS 6 Detroit
20.11.87 Efrain Nievas W RSC 2 Detroit
20.02.88 Rudy Fuentes W RSC 3 Detroit
23.04.88 Martin Quiroz L RSC 4 Las Vegas
04.06.88 Dana Roston W RSC 9 Las Vegas
02.09.88 Primo Ramos W PTS 10 Las Vegas
30.10.88 Leo Martinez W CO 7 Pheonix
22.11.88 Irleis Perez W RSC 6 Las Vegas
Summary: 22 contests, won 20, drew 1, lost 1.

Sumbu Kalambay
Italy. *Born* Zaire 10.04.56
Former Undefeated WBA, EBU & Italian Middleweight Champion

10.10.80 Esperno Postl W RSC 7 Wolkersdorf
24.10.80 Luigi Marini W RSC 6 Ancona
05.12.80 Aldo Buzzetti L PTS 8 Piacenza
08.01.81 Stephane Ferrara DREW 6 Paris
05.02.81 Christian d'Helft W PTS 8 Paris
09.03.81 Cosimo Carbone W RSC 3 Rome
20.03.81 Giovanni Martorina W PTS 6 Ancona
17.04.81 Damiano Lassandro W RSC 8 Pesaro
15.05.81 Christian d'Helft W RTD 1 Pesaro
25.05.81 Giovanni Martorina W RSC 1 Milan
27.06.81 Christian d'Helft W RSC 3 Pesaro
25.09.81 Jose Duran W RSC 4 Pesaro
23.10.81 Sonny Kamunga W CO 7 Pesaro
13.11.81 Michel Pagani W CO 2 Rome
11.12.81 Jose Lozano W PTS 8 Milan
26.12.81 Gabriele Lazzari W RSC 6 Bologna
05.02.82 Steve Williams W RSC 2 Bologna
02.04.82 Costello King W RSC 2 Milan
29.05.82 Jose Quinones W CO 2 Milan
01.09.82 Joe Ouru W DIS 1 Ischia
31.10.82 Buster Drayton W PTS 8 San Remo
10.12.82 Salvatore Perez W RSC 2 Pesaro
22.12.82 Stacey McSwain W PTS 8 St Vincent
24.02.83 Bruce Johnson W RTD 6 Bologna
10.04.83 Wilson Bell W CO 1 San Remo
24.07.83 Jimmy Sykes W PTS 8 Rome
03.09.83 Guy Kennedy W RSC 6 Marsala
13.10.83 James Williams W CO 1 Pesaro
29.10.83 Ralph Moncrief W PTS 10 San Remo
09.12.83 Irwin Hines W RSC 8 Fano
19.02.84 Al Styles W RSC 2 Capo d'Orlando
13.04.84 Allen Alexander W PTS 8 Pesaro
07.07.84 Rico Hoye W PTS 8 Perugia
22.09.84 Tony Cerda W PTS 8 Monte Carlo
10.12.84 Clinton Jackson W PTS 8 Paris
08.03.85 Tony Harrison W RSC 4 Piagge
06.04.85 Duane Thomas L PTS 10 Atlantic City
27.04.85 Jose Duarte W PTS 8 Avelino
14.07.85 Don Bowers W PTS 8 Monte Carlo
26.09.85 Giovanni de Marco W PTS 12 Caserta
(*Italian Middleweight Title Challenge*)
19.12.85 Ayub Kalule L PTS 12 Ancona
(*EBU Middleweight Title Challenge*)
15.03.86 Cliff Gilpin W PTS 8 Monte Carlo
03.09.86 Giovanni de Marco W RTD 11 Silvio Marina
(*Italian Middleweight Title Defence*)
13.12.86 Cecil Pettigrew W PTS 8 Ragusa
21.03.87 Bastante Blanco W RTD 5 Ischia
26.05.87 Herol Graham W PTS 12 Wembley
(*EBU Middleweight Title Challenge*)
23.10.87 Iran Barkley W PTS 15 Livorno
(*Vacant WBA Middleweight Title*)
05.03.88 Mike McCallum W PTS 12 Pesaro
(*WBA Middleweight Title Defence*)
12.06.88 Robbie Sims W PTS 12 Ravenna
(*WBA Middleweight Title Defence*)
08.11.88 Doug de Witt W RSC 7 Monte Carlo
(*WBA Middleweight Title Defence*)
25.03.89 Michael Nunn L CO 1 Las Vegas
(*IBF Middleweight Title Challenge*)
Summary: 51 contests, won 46, drew 1, lost 4.

Soon-Jung Kang
South Korea. *Born* 15.01.62
South Korean Flyweight Champion

18.11.80 Jun-Woo Lee W PTS 4 Seoul
19.11.80 Sam-Joo Sun L PTS 4 Seoul
23.01.81 San-Moon Lee W PTS 4 Pusan
25.04.81 Jae-Huan Cho W PTS 4 Pusan
06.05.81 Yau-Kyang How W PTS 4 Seoul
09.05.81 Ki-Ho Shin L PTS 4 Seoul
29.07.81 Jung-Sok Park W PTS 4 Pusan
23.08.81 Ki-Joung Kim W PTS 6 Pusan
25.09.81 Yun-Ho Park W PTS 4 Pusan
18.11.81 Ok-Shik Kim W PTS 4 Pusan
10.02.82 Sang-Moon Lee W PTS 8 Taegu
26.06.82 Dong-Chun Lee W PTS 10 Seoul
04.09.82 Juanito Abraca W PTS 10 Taegu
09.10.82 Chan-Soo Chung W PTS 10 Seoul
(*Vacant South Korean Flyweight Title*)
02.01.83 Youn-Ri Moon W PTS 10 Daejon
26.02.83 Ki-Ho Shin W PTS 10 Seoul
(*South Korean Flyweight Title Defence*)
21.03.83 German Torres L PTS 10 Tokyo
02.04.83 Prudencio Cardona DREW 10 Seoul
17.07.83 Noel Tibay W PTS 10 Chinju
29.10.83 Sang-Moon Lee W PTS 10 Daejon
24.12.83 Chang-Young Chang W RSC 8 Seoul
26.02.84 Yun-Ho Park W PTS 10 Namhae
26.05.84 Do-Sa Kim W PTS 10 Wonju
08.12.84 Bi-Won Chung L PTS 10 Chinju
14.04.85 Bi-Won Chung L PTS 10 Pohang
22.09.85 Titing Dignos W PTS 10 Chungju
24.11.85 Houn-Kuk Chae L PTS 10 Seoul
(*Vacant South Korean Flyweight Title*)
21.02.86 Dodie Penalosa L PTS 10 Manila
27.04.86 In-Soo Kim W PTS 8 Pusan
01.06.86 Houn-Kuk Chae W PTS 10 Inchon
(*South Korean Flyweight Title Challenge*)
30.08.86 Suk-Bong Kim W PTS 10 Osan
(*South Korean Flyweight Title Defence*)

Mike Johnson (right) spoilt the form book, when stopping Engels Pedroza in June, 1988

Christopher M. Farina

14.12.86 Han-Bong Kang W RSC 4 Inchon
(*South Korean Flyweight Title Defence*)
01.03.87 Tanomsak Singboebae L PTS 12 Bangkok
(*OPBF Flyweight Title Challenge*)
26.04.87 Moon-Jin Choi W PTS 10 Chinju
(*South Korean Flyweight Title Defence*)
28.06.87 Houn-Kuk Chae W PTS 10 Inchon
(*South Korean Flyweight Title Defence*)
09.10.87 Duk-Hyun Kim W RSC 5 Anyang
(*South Korean Flyweight Title Defence*)
24.01.88 Trifon Torralba W RSC 4 Seoul
11.12.88 German Torres L PTS 12 Seoul
(*Vacant WBC L. Flyweight Title*)
Summary: 38 contests, won 28, drew 1, lost 9.

Derrick (Hurricane) Kelly
Gary, USA. *Born* 03.01.61
NABF Welterweight Champion. Former Con. Am. Welterweight Champion

22.04.83 Rodolfo Villegas W RSC 2 Los Angeles
06.05.83 Johnny Gonzales W PTS 6 Los Angeles
10.06.83 Greg Starks W CO 2 Los Angeles
17.06.83 Bob Manous W PTS 4 Los Angeles
01.07.83 Joe Molier W RSC 1 Los Angeles
13.07.83 Al Long W PTS 8 Ventura
11.08.83 Juan Veloz W CO 6 Los Angeles
15.09.83 Marcos Jacobo W PTS 6 Los Angeles
06.10.83 Bertram Buchanan W PTS 6 Los Angeles
21.05.84 Felipe Canela W PTS 10 Los Angeles
27.09.84 Tomas Perez W PTS 10 Los Angeles
20.12.84 Felipe Canela DREW 10 Los Angeles
21.02.85 Glen Corbus W RSC 6 Los Angeles
10.06.85 Roberto Mendez W RSC 7 Los Angeles
20.08.85 Nelson Ortiz W PTS 10 Los Angeles
15.10.85 Diomedes Colome L PTS 10 Los Angeles
08.04.87 Tomas Perez W PTS 12 Los Angeles
18.05.87 Lorenzo Guzman W RSC 6 Los Angeles
15.07.87 Al Long DREW 12 Riverside
13.08.87 Terry Norris W PTS 10 Los Angeles
01.10.87 Anthony Pearson W PTS 10 Los Angeles
03.11.87 Luis Santana W PTS 10 Los Angeles
07.03.88 Felipe Canela W PTS 12 Los Angeles
26.05.88 Charles Nwokolo W PTS 12 Los Angeles
(*Vacant Con. Am. Welterweight Title*)
30.01.89 Luis Santana W PTS 12 Los Angeles
(*NABF Welterweight Title Challenge*)
20.03.89 Derwin Richards W RSC 8 Los Angeles
(*NABF Welterweight Title Defence*)
Summary: 26 contests, won 23, drew 2, lost 1.

Napa Kiatwanchai
Thailand
WBC M. Flyweight Champion. Former Undefeated WBC International M. Flyweight Champion

07.08.87 Chomepichit Kiattawachai W PTS 6 Bangkok
29.09.87 Sukhum Sisfakamroan W CO 2 Bangkok
03.11.87 Sianchai Kiatsontaya W CO 1 Bangkok
21.11.87 Chomeyut Sissrimoke W RSC 5 Bangkok
26.01.88 Nico Thomas W PTS 12 Jakarta
(*Vacant WBC International M. Flyweight Title*)
16.04.88 Gim Suryaman W PTS 12 Jakarta
(*WBC International M. Flyweight Title Defence*)
05.06.88 Hiroki Ioka DREW 12 Osaka
(*WBC M. Flyweight Title Challenge*)
04.09.88 Thanjai Donjadee W RSC 4 Bangkok
13.11.88 Hiroki Ioka W PTS 12 Osaka
(*WBC M. Flyweight Title Challenge*)
11.02.89 John Arief W PTS 12 Bangkok
(*WBC M. Flyweight Title Defence*)
Summary: 10 contests, won 9, drew 1.

Bong-Jun Kim
Chon-nam, South Korea. *Born* 13.05.64
WBA M. Flyweight Champion

23.07.83 Yang-Chon Oh W PTS 4 Seoul
10.12.83 Byung-Kap Kim W PTS 4 Seoul
12.12.83 Sang-Duk Kim W PTS 4 Seoul
14.12.83 Sung-Jae Kim L RSC 3 Seoul
12.02.84 Kyu-Sik Cho DREW 4 Seoul
06.04.84 Kyu-Sik Cho W PTS 4 Seoul
17.06.84 Kyung-Jae Chang L PTS 6 Seoul
28.10.84 Il-Wan Kim W PTS 6 Seoul
24.11.84 Byung-Kwan Chung DREW 8 Gunsan
16.02.85 Chun Huh L RSC 3 Seoul
27.04.85 Byung-Man Kim W PTS 8 Seoul
20.10.85 Chang-Yung Chang W RSC 2 Nonsan
11.01.86 Yung-Sang Lee W RSC 4 Seoul
20.03.86 Hideyuki Ohashi W PTS 10 Tokyo
28.06.86 Sung-Kyu Kim W PTS 10 Kunsan
25.10.86 Ha-Shik Kim L PTS 10 Eijungbu
(*South Korean L. Flyweight Title Challenge*)
20.12.86 Dok-Hyon Kim W RSC 3 Buchon
24.01.87 Seung-Yup Kang W PTS 10 Eijungbu
14.03.87 Chung-Bok Park W RSC 4 Chunchon
14.06.87 Eul-Chol Chung DREW 10 Bukok
13.09.87 Hi-Jung Noh W CO 3 Jinju
10.01.88 Luis Gamez L PTS 12 Pusan
(*Vacant WBA M. Flyweight Title*)
09.04.88 Nana Suhana W PTS 10 Jinju
29.10.88 Sung-Kon Lee W CO 1 Ansan
29.01.89 Armando Tenoria W RSC 2 Pohang
16.04.89 Agustin Garcia W RSC 7 Seoul
(*Vacant WBA M. Flyweight Title*)
Summary: 26 contests, won 18, drew 3, lost 5.

Bong-Jun Kim

Yong-Kang Kim
Hwasoon-Kun, South Korea. *Born* 03.01.65
WBC Flyweight Champion. Former Undefeated South Korean & OPBF L. Flyweight Champion

06.04.85 Byung-Sik Bae W RSC 4 Taegu
01.06.85 Jun-Won Kang W PTS 4 Inchon
29.06.85 Yung-Suk Ahn W RSC 4 Seoul
17.08.85 Hyung-Man Lee W PTS 4 Buchon
20.10.85 Noh-Yun Hwan W CO 2 Nonsan
23.11.85 Ke-Yun Chung W PTS 8 Inchon
12.04.86 Sung-Kyu Kim W PTS 8 Yungchun
28.06.86 Su-Yung Lee W CO 2 Kunsan
26.07.86 Eul-Chul Jung W PTS 8 Osan
17.10.86 Han-Bong Kang W CO 7 Suwon
17.01.87 Ha-Sik Lim W PTS 10 Hongchun
(*South Korean L. Flyweight Title Challenge*)
08.03.87 Sung-Kyu Kim W PTS 10 Seoul
30.05.87 William Belan W CO 1 Osan
12.07.87 Jorge Cano W PTS 10 Buchon
11.12.87 Putt Ohyuthanakorn W RSC 10 Kwangju
(*Vacant OPBF L. Flyweight Title*)
20.02.88 Sonny Vidal W PTS 12 Kimpo
(*OPBF L. Flyweight Title Defence*)
23.07.88 Sot Chitalada W PTS 12 Pohang
(*WBC Flyweight Title Challenge*)
13.11.88 Emil Romano W PTS 12 Chungju
(*WBC Flyweight Title Defence*)
05.03.89 Yukhito Tamakuma W PTS 12 Aomori
(*WBC Flyweight Title Defence*)
Summary: 19 contests, won 19.

James (The Heat) Kinchen
San Diego, USA. *Born* 01.03.57
Former Undefeated NABF S. Middleweight Champion. Former Undefeated USBA Middleweight Champion

08.08.80 Daniel Marks W CO 1 Dallas
23.09.80 Larry Rayford W CO 3 New Orleans
22.01.81 Henry Drummond W PTS 4 Las Vegas
28.01.81 Fred Garcia W CO 2 San Diego
18.02.81 Danny Kirk W RSC 1 Las Vegas
25.03.81 Jimmy Owens W PTS 6 Las Vegas
15.04.81 Larry Myers W RSC 2 Las Vegas
01.05.81 Mike Hutchinson W CO 2 San Diego
03.06.81 Eddie Casper W CO 2 Las Vegas
12.06.81 James Williams W CO 2 San Diego
17.06.81 Rueben Rascone W RSC 1 Las Vegas
08.07.81 Darryl Womack W CO 2 Las Vegas
29.07.81 Juan Rivas W RSC 2 Las Vegas
21.08.81 Everett Conklin DREW 8 Las Vegas
30.09.81 Everett Conklin W CO 6 Las Vegas
04.11.81 Ron Brown W CO 6 Las Vegas
25.11.81 Jesse Avila W RSC 6 Las Vegas
13.01.82 Marvis Sanders W CO 10 Las Vegas
17.02.82 Rudy Robles W PTS 10 Las Vegas
27.03.82 Leroy Green W RSC 9 Atlantic City
23.05.82 Alejos Rodriguez W CO 4 Las Vegas
27.08.82 Joe Gonsalves W CO 5 San Jose
05.09.82 Odell Hadley W PTS 10 St Joseph
30.09.82 Tommy Howard W RSC 10 San Diego
31.10.82 Ralph Moncrief W PTS 10 McAfee
20.01.83 Mike Clark W PTS 10 San Diego
07.04.83 Ernesto Caballero W RSC 8 San Diego
19.05.83 Fred Reed W RSC 1 San Diego
28.05.83 Felton Marshall W RSC 9 Las Vegas
16.07.83 Jose Mireles W CO 1 Dallas
13.08.83 Juan Diaz W RSC 2 Las Vegas
19.11.83 Murray Sutherland W PTS 10 St Joseph
26.02.84 Al Rankin W RSC 3 Beaumont
25.04.84 Erwin Williams W CO 9 San Jose
26.09.84 Jorge Amparo DREW 10 Atlantic City
24.11.84 Alex Ramos W RSC 9 Stateline
(*USBA Middleweight Title Challenge*)
16.02.85 James Shuler L PTS 12 Atlantic City
(*NABF Middleweight Title Challenge*)
14.04.85 Buster Drayton W PTS 10 London
30.07.85 Frankie Minton W RSC 9 Atlantic City
11.07.86 Frankie Minton W CO 7 Las Vegas
17.10.86 Iran Barkley L PTS 10 Detroit
06.04.87 Juan Domingo Roldan L RSC 9 Las Vegas
18.06.87 Randy Smith W PTS 10 San Diego
25.08.87 Larry Musgrove L TD 3 Reseda
19.11.87 Milford Kemp W PTS 10 San Diego
27.01.88 Tim Williams W PTS 12 San Diego
26.02.88 Antonio Adame W CO 2 Tijuana
17.03.88 Ricky Locke W CO 3 San Diego
02.05.88 James Williams W CO 4 Tijuana
19.05.88 Juan Hernandez W PTS 10 San Diego
13.10.88 Marvin Mack W PTS 12 Stateline
(*Vacant NABF S. Middleweight Title*)
04.11.88 Thomas Hearns L PTS 12 Las Vegas
(*Vacant WBO S. Middleweight Title*)
31.03.89 Christophe Tiozzo L PTS 10 Paris
Summary: 53 contests, won 45, drew 2, lost 6.

James Kinchen

Christopher M. Farina

Muangchai Kitikasem
Thailand.
L. Flyweight

10.06.88 Bahar Udin W PTS 10 Bangkok
06.09.88 Hisao Nayuki W CO 1 Bangkok
18.11.88 Seung-Yup Kang W CO 2 Bangkok
27.12.88 Kwanchai Sorpernpit W RSC 5 Bangkok
03.02.89 Eddie Balunana W CO 4 Bangkok
Summary: 5 contests, won 5.

Chaiki Kobayashi
Japan
Bantamweight

06.03.83 Y. Inoguchi L RSC 4 Tokyo
31.07.84 H. Takamutsu W PTS 4 Tokyo
27.12.84 H. Tsutsuhiro L PTS 4 Tokyo
05.03.85 A. Uehara W PTS 4 Tokyo
05.08.85 H. Kanaya L PTS 4 Tokyo
03.10.85 M. Naito W PTS 4 Tokyo
18.11.85 T. Seto W PTS 4 Tokyo
25.02.86 Shigemitsu Koike W PTS 6 Tokyo
15.04.86 S. Yonesaka W PTS 6 Tokyo
13.09.86 E. Goku W CO 6 Matsumoto
15.12.86 Makoto Sawamura W RSC 10 Tokyo
27.04.87 Koheita Tanaka W PTS 10 Tokyo
20.07.87 Hisao Iishido W RSC 10 Tokyo
03.10.87 Naoto Takahashi W PTS 10 Tokyo
01.12.87 Joe Ladipe W PTS 10 Tokyo
18.04.88 Leopard Ari W PTS 10 Tokyo
20.06.88 Tae-Sang Chun W RSC 9 Tokyo
19.02.89 Sung-Il Moon L RSC 5 Taejon
(*WBA Bantamweight Title Challenge*)
Summary: 18 contests, won 14, lost 4.

Katsumi Komiyama
Aichi, Japan. *Born* 18.08.65
L. Flyweight

12.02.85 Makisuke Nishimura DREW 4 Osaka
28.04.85 Hideaki Suda W PTS 4 Osaka
30.06.85 Makisuke Nishimura W PTS 4 Osaka
10.08.85 Eiji Moriya W PTS 4 Osaka
14.09.85 Tatsuya Yamada W PTS 6 Osaka
23.10.85 Yasuo Yogi DREW 6 Kitakyushu
30.11.85 Akitoshi Kato W RSC 2 Hamamatsu
04.03.86 Takeo Onishi W PTS 6 Osaka
08.06.86 Hideo Yamasako W RSC 2 Osaka
14.09.86 Missile Kudo W PTS 10 Osaka
17.11.86 Tomohiro Kiyuna L PTS 10 Tokyo
12.04.87 Hiroyuki Miyata DREW 10 Tokyo
16.06.87 Hiroyuki Miyata L PTS 10 Tokyo
16.09.87 Rogelio Martinez W PTS 5 Long Beach
18.11.87 Rogelio Martinez W PTS 8 Long Beach
18.02.88 Tony de Luca T DRAW 2 San Diego
10.04.88 Mahalap Singchatchaval W CO 5 Osaka
02.07.88 Putt Ohyuthanakorn W PTS 10 Osaka
06.10.88 Roger de Rama DREW 10 Osaka
12.02.89 Myung-Woo Yuh L RSC 10 Chungji
(*WBA L. Flyweight Title Challenge*)
Summary: 20 contests, won 12, drew 5, lost 3.

Nana Yaw Konadu
Ghana
WBC International S. Flyweight Champion. Former Undefeated Commonwealth & ABU Flyweight Champion

25.05.85 George Freeman W PTS 6 Accra
29.06.85 Ebo Danquah DREW 6 Accra
07.12.85 Flash Conteh W CO 1 Accra
08.03.86 Joe Power W CO 3 Sunyani
27.06.86 Osei Owusu W CO 2 Kumasi
30.08.86 Ramon Agyare W RSC 6 Accra
25.10.86 Ray Amoo W CO 3 Accra
13.12.86 Steve Muchoki W CO 12 Accra
(*ABU Flyweight Title Challenge*)
28.08.87 Ramon Pichardo W RSC 2 Las Vegas
10.10.87 Albert Musankabala W CO 6 Accra
(*Vacant Commonwealth Flyweight Title*)
23.12.87 Pat Nkwo W CO 2 Accra
13.06.88 Adamu Mohammad W RSC 7 Accra
09.10.88 Rufus Poison W CO 3 Accra
10.12.88 Muke Mukenge W CO 1 Accra
11.03.89 Cesar Polanco W PTS 12 Accra
(*WBC International S. Flyweight Title Defence*)
Summary: 14 contests, won 13, drew 1.

Santos (Falucho) Laciar
Huinca Renanco, Argentine. *Born* 31.01.59
Former WBC S. Flyweight Champion. Former Undefeated WBA, South American & Argentinian Flyweight Champion

03.12.76 Carlos Maliene W CO 4 Huinca Renanco
13.01.77 Angel Pereyra W RTD 4 Huinca Renanco
05.02.77 Amado Chavez W RTD 5 Realico
25.02.77 Jose Flores W CO 4 Huinca Renanco
26.03.77 Alejandro Olguin DREW 10 Luiggi
22.04.77 Alberto Martin W PTD 10 Huinca Renanco
07.05.77 Jose Izquierdo W PTS 10 Realico
18.06.77 Jose Zarate W CO 1 Huinca Renanco
08.07.77 Jose Ibiris DREW 10 Huinca Renanco
09.09.77 Carlos Sosa W PTS 12 Villa Maria
30.09.77 Manuel Quinteros W RTD 8 Huinca Renanco
22.10.77 Carlos Reyes Sosa W RTD 6 Villa Carlos
04.11.77 Jose Izquierdo W PTS 10 Huinca Renanco
17.12.77 Enrique Navarro W RTD 6 Realico
13.01.78 Luis Gerez W PTS 10 Huinca Renanco
10.02.78 Jose Ibiris W PTS 10 Huinca Renanco
14.04.78 Ramon Soria DREW 10 Huinca Renanco
19.05.78 Carlos Aguero W PTS 10 Huinca Renanco
02.06.78 Reynaldo Romero W PTS 10 Huinca Renanco
08.07.78 Hector Barreto W PTS 10 Huinca Renanco
06.09.78 Jose Izquierdo W PTS 10 Villa Carlos
20.09.78 Jose Luis Lopez W RTD 4 Villa Carlos
06.10.78 Luis Gerez DREW 10 Villa Maria
21.10.78 Angel Fernandez W PTS 10 Buenos Aires
09.11.78 Felipe Rojas W CO 5 Villa Carlos
01.12.78 Ramon Soria L PTS 10 Mendoza
14.12.78 Raul Perez W PTS 10 Villa Carlos
26.01.79 Jose Ibiris W PTS 10 Villa Carlos
14.02.79 Juan Rios W PTS 10 Villa Carlos
16.03.79 Raul Perez L PTS 10 Huinca Renanco
11.04.79 Gilberto Lopez W PTS 10 Villa Carlos
26.04.79 Jose Flores W RSC 7 Villa Carlos
25.05.79 Raul Perez L PTS 10 Villa Carlos
22.06.79 Juan Espindola W PTS 10 Cordoba
02.08.79 Miguel Lazarte DREW 10 Villa Carlos
06.09.79 Luis Gomez W PTS 10 Villa Carlos
12.10.79 Hector Velasquez W PTS 10 Villa Carlos
03.11.79 Gustavo Ballas L PTS 10 Buenos Aires
07.12.79 Federico Condori W PTS 10 Buenos Aires
27.02.80 Miguel Lazarte W PTS 12 Villa Carlos
(*Vacant Argentinian Flyweight Title*)
28.03.80 Ruben Condori DREW 10 Cordoba
18.04.80 Domingo Aragon W PTS 10 Cordoba
09.05.80 Juan Brizuela W PTS 10 Cordoba
06.06.80 Adrian Roman W CO 3 Cordoba
23.07.80 Miguel Velez W RTD 6 Villa Carlos
30.08.80 Jaime Miranda T DRAW 8 Santiago
(*South American Flyweight Title Challenge*)
06.11.80 Federico Condori W PTS 10 Huinca Renanco
22.11.80 Jaime Miranda W PTS 12 Villa Carlos
(*South American Flyweight Title Challenge*)
08.12.80 Charlie Magri L PTS 10 London
30.01.81 Jose de la Cruz W CO 8 Mar del Plata
28.03.81 Peter Mathebula W RSC 7 Soweto
(*WBA Flyweight Title Challenge*)
08.05.81 Miguel Lazarte W PTS 10 Cordoba
06.06.81 Luis Ibarra L PTS 15 Buenos Aires
(*WBA Flyweight Title Defence*)
22.08.81 Rodolfo Rodriguez DREW 10 Buenos Aires
04.09.81 Santos Aragon W PTS 10 Morteros
18.09.81 Ruben Condori DREW 10 Cordoba
02.10.81 Miguel Lazarte W PTS 10 Tucuman
07.11.81 Rodolfo Rodriguez DREW 10 Buenos Aires
01.05.82 Juan Herrera W RSC 13 Merida
(*WBA Flyweight Title Challenge*)
11.06.82 Domingo Aragon W PTS 10 Huinca Renanco
08.07.82 Ruben Paniagua W PTS 10 Cordoba
22.07.82 Jose Gomez W PTS 10 Villa Carlos
14.08.82 Betulio Gonzalez W PTS 15 Maracaibo
(*WBA Flyweight Title Defence*)
09.10.82 Ramon Albers W RTD 5 Morteros
05.11.82 Steve Muchoki W RSC 13 Copenhagen
(*WBA Flyweight Title Defence*)
18.12.82 Rodolfo Rodriguez W PTS 10 Buenos Aires
04.03.83 Ramon Neri W CO 9 Cordoba
(*WBA Flyweight Title Defence*)
05.05.83 Shuichi Hozumi W RSC 2 Shizuoka
(*WBA Flyweight Title Defence*)
17.07.83 Hi-Sup Shin W CO 1 Cheju
(*WBA Flyweight Title Defence*)
16.12.83 Juan Cortes W PTS 10 Cordoba
28.01.84 Juan Herrera W PTS 15 Marsala
(*WBA Flyweight Title Defence*)
15.09.84 Prudencio Cardona W CO 10 Cordoba
(*WBA Flyweight Title Defence*)
08.12.84 Hilario Zapata W PTS 15 Buenos Aires
(*WBA Flyweight Title Defence*)
06.05.85 Antoine Montero W PTS 15 Grenoble
(*WBA Flyweight Title Defence*)
07.06.86 Jaime Miranda W PTS 10 Rio Tercero
17.07.86 Alberto Pacheco W CO 8 Santa Fe
30.08.86 Gilberto Roman DREW 12 Cordoba
(*WBC S. Flyweight Title Challenge*)
24.10.86 Jose Narvaez W PTS 10 Concepcion
08.11.86 Oscar Bolivar W PTS 10 Buenos Aires
30.01.87 Hector Patri W PTS 10 Mar del Plata
05.03.87 Jose Narvaez W PTS 10 La Rioja
21.03.87 Isaias Carvacho W CO 4 Esquel
03.04.87 Alejandro Vazquez W CO 2 Trelew
16.05.87 Gilberto Roman W RSC 11 Reims
(*WBC S. Flyweight Title Challenge*)
08.08.87 Jesus Rojas L PTS 12 Miami
(*WBC S. Flyweight Title Defence*)
10.12.87 Jose Narvaez W PTS 10 Bahia Blanca
17.02.88 Juan Ivalo W RTD 6 Mar del Plata
05.03.88 Bernardo Mendoza W CO 3 Buenos Aires
02.04.88 Jose Narvaez W PTS 10 San Luis
15.04.88 Ricardo Escobar W PTS Pico Truncado
07.05.88 Luis Ocampo W RTD 6 Buenos Aires
10.06.88 Ricardo Escobar W PTS 10 Viedma
24.06.88 Alejandro Castano W RSC 5 Justinia Posse
08.10.88 Juan Carazo L PTS 12 Caguas
17.01.89 Raul Ojeda ND 1 Villa Carlos Paz
18.02.89 Jesus Moreno W CO 3 Villa Carlos Paz
06.04.89 Hugo Gomez W PTS 10 Villa Carlos Paz
Summary: 97 contests, won 77, drew 11, lost 8, no decision 1.

Kirkland Laing

Peter Goldfield/USA

Kirkland Laing
Nottingham, England. *Born* Jamaica 20.06.54
British Welterweight Champion

14.04.75 Joe Hannaford W CO 2 Nottingham
12.05.75 Liam White W PTS 8 Nottingham
29.09.75 Derek Simpson W PTS 8 Nottingham
25.11.75 Oscar Angus W PTS 6 London
19.01.76 Terry Schofield W PTS 8 Nottingham
12.03.76 Charlie Cooper W PTS 8 Southend
13.04.76 Mike Manley W PTS 8 Southend
17.05.76 John Laine W RSC 3 Nottingham
22.09.76 Harry Watson W RSC 5 London
11.10.76 Jim Moore W RSC 2 Nottingham
22.11.76 Jim Montague W DIS 7 Birmingham
11.01.77 John Smith W PTS 10 Wolverhampton
08.03.77 Peter Morris DREW 10 Wolverhampton
16.11.77 Peter Morris W RSC 5 Solihull
27.09.78 Achille Mitchell W PTS 12 Solihull
04.04.79 Henry Rhiney W RSC 10 Birmingham
(*British Welterweight Title Challenge*)
06.11.79 Des Morrison W PTS 8 London
22.01.80 Salvo Nuciforo W RSC 6 London
19.02.80 Colin Ward W RSC 5 London
01.04.80 Colin Jones L RSC 9 Wembley
(*British Welterweight Title Defence*)
08.05.80 George Walker W PTS 8 Solihull
03.06.80 Curtis Taylor W RSC 7 London
26.11.80 Joey Singleton W PTS 12 Solihull
28.04.81 Colin Jones L RSC 9 London
(*British Welterweight Title Challenge*)
18.11.81 Cliff Gilpin W PTS 12 Solihull
09.02.82 Reg Ford L PTS 10 London
05.05.82 Joey Mack W CO 7 Solihull
04.09.82 Roberto Duran W PTS 10 Detroit
10.09.83 Fred Hutchings L CO 10 Atlantic City
27.11.84 Darwin Brewster W RSC 7 Wembley
12.02.85 Mosimo Maeleke W PTS 10 London
14.03.85 Wo Lamani Wo W RSC 6 Leicester
16.06.85 Franki Moro W PTS 8 London

05.07.85 Brian Janssen L RTD 5 Brisbane
16.05.86 Mike Picciotti W PTS 10 Atlantic City
17.09.86 Harry Theodossiadis W RSC 4 London
14.03.87 Sylvester Mittee W RSC 5 London
(*Vacant British Welterweight Title*)
26.05.87 Marvin McDowell W RSC 1 Wembley
26.11.87 Rocky Kelly W RSC 5 London
(*British Welterweight Title Defence*)
29.03.88 Sammy Floyd W PTS 8 Wembley
15.04.89 Nino la Rocca L PTS 12 Vasto
(*Vacant EBU Welterweight Title*)
Summary: 41 contests, won 34, drew 1, lost 6.

Don (Golden Boy) Lalonde
Winnipeg, Canada. *Born* 12.03.60
Former WBC L. Heavyweight Champion. Former Undefeated Con. Am & Canadian L. Heavyweight Champion

24.04.80 Kenny Nichol W CO 2 Winnipeg
16.09.80 Edmond Esquirol W PTS 4 Winnipeg
12.11.80 Muhammad Smith W CO 1 Winnipeg
20.01.81 Jim Green W RSC 3 Winnipeg
10.10.81 Wilbert Johnson W RSC 2 Winnipeg
03.11.81 Jean-Claude le Clair W RSC 2 Montreal
10.12.81 Akbar Abdullah W PTS 8 Winnipeg
06.03.81 Wilbert Johnson L PTS 6 Winnipeg
12.02.82 Randy Jackson W CO 2 Winnipeg
29.06.82 Ken Johnson W CO 2 Winnipeg
22.08.82 Akbar Abdullah W RSC 2 Ramsey
30.09.82 Jimmy Baker W RSC 8 Toronto
07.10.82 Frank Albert W RSC 2 Winnipeg
15.11.82 Don Hirtle W PTS 8 Toronto
04.07.82 Rod MacDonald W RSC 9 Waterloo
(*Canadian L. Heavyweight Title Challenge*)
25.11.83 Akbar Abdullah W CO 3 Vancouver
11.02.84 Jim Gradson W CO 1 Winnipeg
(*Canadian L. Heavyweight Title Defence*)
28.06.84 Carlos Tite W RSC 2 Merrillville
08.09.84 Don Hirtle W RSC 6 Winnipeg
(*Canadian L. Heavyweight Title Defence*)
26.04.85 John Jones W RSC 3 Hammond
16.05.85 Willie Edwards L RSC 9 Winnipeg
(*NABF L. Heavyweight Title Challenge*)
29.08.85 Jamie Howe W PTS 10 Wheeling
21.01.86 Ron Crawford W CO 2 Oklahoma
08.02.86 Roberto Rodriguez W CO 2 Oklahoma
06.04.86 Joe Brewer W CO 3 West Orange
30.04.86 Lenny Edwards W RSC 3 Cleveland
12.08.86 Fred Walters W RSC 1 Ashland
28.08.86 Terry Walker W RSC 6 New York
30.09.86 Charles Henderson W RSC 8 Detroit
06.11.86 Ben Fernandez W RSC 9 Winnipeg
07.05.87 Mustafa Hamsho W PTS 12 New York
(*Vacant Con. Am. L. Heavyweight Title*)
27.11.87 Eddie Davis W RSC 2 Port of Spain
(*Vacant WBC L. Heavyweight Title*)
29.05.88 Leslie Stewart W RSC 5 Port of Spain
(*WBC L. Heavyweight Title Defence*)
07.11.88 Ray Leonard L RSC 9 Las Vegas
(*WBC L. Heavyweight Title Defence & Vacant WBC S. Middleweight Title*)
Summary: 34 contests, won 31, lost 3.

Jeff Lampkin
Youngstown, USA. *Born* 1961
USBA Cruiserweight Champion

11.06.80 Jimmy Hearn W CO 1 Struthers
20.08.80 John Beveridge W CO 1 Warren
09.09.80 Wes Rowe W RSC 3 Warren
24.09.80 Earl Caldwell W CO 1 Struthers
28.10.80 Eddie Temple W CO 1 Warren
09.12.80 Willie Crawford W RSC 4 Warren
16.12.80 Stan Scott W RSC 3 Cleveland
20.01.81 Randy Jackson W CO 1 Niles
17.03.81 Darnell Hayes W CO 2 Niles
28.06.81 Ernie Whitmore W CO 3 Canton
19.07.81 Sylvester Wilder W RSC 1 Warren
15.08.81 Darnell Hayes W CO 2 Erie
29.10.81 Charles Williams W RSC 6 Warren
22.02.82 Phil Brown W CO 4 Youngstown
17.03.82 Mike Hardin W RSC 5 Niles
28.04.82 Fred Brown W CO 4 Warren
11.06.82 Willie Edwards L PTS 10 Las Vegas
27.08.82 Al Bolden W PTS 10 Pittsburgh
30.11.82 Willie Starling L PTS 10 Atlantic City
30.12.82 Frank Payne W RSC 3 Pittsburgh
22.01.83 Leo Rogers W RSC 3 Atlantic City
07.03.83 Rod Green W PTS 10 Chicago
13.04.83 Richie Kates L PTS 10 Atlantic City
14.06.83 Stan Ross W CO 1 Atlantic City
12.07.83 John Davis L PTS 10 Atlantic City
14.12.83 Fully Obelmejias L PTS 8 Loano
11.01.84 Anthony Witherspoon L PTS 10 Atlantic City
24.01.84 Arthel Lawhorne W RSC 6 Niles
06.03.84 Willie Crawford W RSC 4 Niles
26.05.84 Chisanda Mutti DREW 8 Dusseldorf
20.11.84 Jerome Clouden L PTS 10 Metairie
11.06.85 Jack Johnson W PTS 10 Atlantic City
06.08.85 Cedric Parsons L PTS 10 Atlantic City
03.12.85 Charles Williams L PTS 10 Atlantic City
24.01.86 Tim Broady W RSC 7 Atlantic City
11.03.86 Danny Blake W PTS 8 Niles
11.09.86 Paul Madison W RSC 5 Los Angeles
22.01.87 Jesse Shelby W PTS 10 Los Angeles
23.02.87 Ramzi Hassan L PTS 10 Los Angeles
23.06.87 Sherman Griffin L PTS 12 Houston
(*Vacant USBA Cruiserweight Title*)
05.12.87 Lottie Mwale L PTS 10 Dusseldorf
09.04.88 Patrick Lumumba L PTS 8 Las Vegas
02.07.88 Freddie Rafferty W CO 6 Sun City
17.11.88 Alfonso Ratliff W RSC 5 Atlantic City
(*USBA Cruiserweight Title Challenge*)
14.02.89 Wali Muhammad W RSC 10 Atlantic City
(*USBA Cruiserweight Title Defence*)
Summary: 45 contests, won 31, drew 1, lost 13.

Don Lalonde (left) shown in winning action against Mustafa Hamsho in New York, May, 1987

Tom Casino

Juan Laporte
Guayama, Puerto Rico. *Born* 24.11.59
NABF S. Featherweight Champion. Former WBC Featherweight Champion. Former Undefeated USBA Featherweight Champion

29.10.77 John Green W CO 1 Hamilton
11.11.77 Jerry Strickland W PTS 4 Cincinnati
15.12.77 Charlie Buggs W CO 3 Hamilton
02.03.78 Santos Cruz W PTS 4 New York
27.05.78 Jose Rodriguez L PTS 6 Los Angeles
26.07.78 Ray Viruet W PTS 6 New York
15.12.78 David Capo W PTS 8 New York
27.04.79 Lazaro Fabian W CO 1 New York
14.06.79 Jose Figueroa W CO 5 New York
16.08.79 Wardell Williams W RSC 2 Kansas City
22.08.79 Andres Torres W RSC 6 New York
19.09.78 Joe Rivera W PTS 8 New York
25.01.80 Jean Lapointe W RSC 7 New York
18.04.80 David Capo W PTS 10 New York
20.06.80 Fel Clemente W RSC 10 New York
13.09.80 Mano Morua W PTS 10 San Antonio
13.12.80 Salvador Sanchez L PTS 15 El Paso
(*WBC Featherweight Title Challenge*)
06.03.81 Roberto Bido W RSC 9 San Juan
10.04.81 Francisco Ortiz W RSC 6 New York
22.08.81 Rocky Lockridge W CO 2 Las Vegas
(*USBA Featherweight Title Challenge*)
11.12.81 Edwin Rivera W PTS 10 New York
24.01.82 Eusebio Pedroza L PTS 15 Atlantic City
(*WBA Featherweight Title Challenge*)
28.05.82 Alberto Collazo W RTD 6 New York
(*USBA Featherweight Title Defence*)
21.07.82 Edwin Rivera W PTS 10 New York
15.09.82 Mario Miranda W RTD 10 New York
(*Vacant WBC Featherweight Title*)
20.02.83 Ruben Castillo W PTS 12 San Juan
(*WBC Featherweight Title Defence*)
25.06.83 Johnny de la Rosa W PTS 12 San Juan
(*WBC Featherweight Title Defence*)
05.11.83 Gerald Hayes L PTS 10 Atlantic City
31.03.84 Wilfredo Gomez L PTS 12 San Juan
(*WBC Featherweight Title Defence*)
14.11.84 Dwight Pratchett W PTS 10 New York
23.02.85 Barry McGuigan L PTS 10 Belfast
03.04.86 Vinnie Costello W PTS 10 New York
25.09.86 Jimmy Magnifico W RSC 3 New York
12.12.86 Julio Cesar Chavez L PTS 12 New York
(*WBC S. Featherweight Title Challenge*)
23.04.87 Rafael Gandarilla W PTS 10 New York
04.06.87 Jocko King W RSC 2 New York
05.07.87 Lupe Suarez L PTS 10 Las Vegas
22.04.88 Robert Anderson W RTD 8 New York
27.05.88 Sylvester Kennon W RSC 3 New York
11.07.88 Alejandro Garcia W CO 1 San Juan
13.08.88 Nicky Perez W RSC 12 Tucson
(*NABF S. Featherweight Title Challenge*)
27.10.88 Lupe Miranda W PTS 10 Tucson
29.04.89 Juan Molina L PTS 12 San Juan
(*Vacant WBO S. Featherweight Title*)
Summary: 43 contests, won 34, lost 9.

Nino la Rocca
Italy. *Born* 05.04.59
EBU Welterweight Champion

14.09.78 Jean Paul Coppyn W RSC 1 Paris
30.12.78 Moussa Dambia W CO 3 Bamako
26.03.79 Claude Lancastre W RSC 6 Paris
05.05.79 Tidjani Assis W CO 1 Bamako
14.11.79 Giuseppe Minotti W RTD 3 Gualdo
24.01.80 Sammy Rookard W CO 3 Genoa
06.02.80 Sinclair Christie W PTS 8 Falconara
29.02.80 Don Morgan W CO 4 Rome
28.03.80 Kachama Musassa W PTS 8 Rome
11.04.80 Robert Gambini W RSC 2 Naples
02.05.80 Floyd Pearson W RSC 2 Rome
30.05.80 Larry McCall W RSC 5 Rome
21.06.80 Johnny Davis W CO 2 Bamako
27.06.80 Nelson Gomez W CO 5 Palermo
09.07.80 Tony Martey W CO 6 Bellaria
27.07.80 Billy Waith W RSC 3 Pietra Ligure
20.08.80 Claudio Pereira W RSC 7 Cerveteri
30.08.80 Benedicto Santos W RTD 4 Bamako
31.10.80 Ralph Twinning W RSC 5 Rome
04.12.80 Santiago Valdez W RTD 5 Rome
19.12.80 Frank Medina W RTD 6 Latina
29.01.80 Tyrone Wren W RSC 2 Rome
20.02.81 Francisco Gomez W CO 4 Naples
06.03.81 Yvon Segor W RSC 4 Milan
23.03.81 Vicenzo Ungaro W RTD 2 Rome
24.04.81 George Walker W CO 2 Milan
09.05.81 Claudio Pereira W PTS 8 Cremona
23.05.81 Fred Coranson W RSC 4 San Remo
04.06.81 Pete Seward W PTS 8 New York
31.07.81 Curtis Taylor W RSC 8 Velletri
14.08.81 Claudio Pereira W RSC 3 Ischia
22.10.81 Michael Senegal W PTS 8 Turin
13.11.81 Pat Thomas W RSC 4 Rome
26.11.81 Claudel Longmire W CO 1 Turin
11.12.81 Jimmy Heair W RSC 1 Milan
26.12.81 Michael Herron W RTD 6 Bologna
05.02.82 Darryl Penn W RTD 6 Bologna
02.04.82 Manuel de la Rosa W CO 6 Milan
29.05.82 Clemente Tshinza W PTS 10 Milan
18.06.82 Homer Jackson W CO 1 Naples
01.08.82 Steve Gregory W RSC 3 Carrara
22.08.82 Wo Lomami Wo W CO 2 Praia
05.09.82 Tim Harris W PTS 10 Marsala
30.10.82 Curtis Ramsey W PTS 8 San Remo
22.12.82 Danny Paul W PTS 10 St Vincent
06.02.83 Jose Hernandez W CO 1 St Vincent
10.04.83 Bobby Joe Young W RSC 8 San Remo
24.04.83 Robert Sawyer W CO 5 San Remo
22.05.83 Marvin Jenkins W RSC 1 Loano
03.07.83 Sabiyala Diavilla W PTS 8 Acciaroli
24.07.83 Pete Ranzany W PTS 10 Rome
15.09.83 Jerry Cheatham W PTS 10 New York
08.10.83 Manning Galloway W PTS 8 St Vincent
30.10.83 Harold Volbrecht W PTS 10 San Remo
29.12.83 Jake Torrance W CO 1 Capo d'Orlando
28.01.84 Tim Harris W RSC 5 Marsala
18.02.84 Gilles Elbilia L RSC 6 Capo d'Orlando
(*EBU Welterweight Title Challenge*)
30.03.84 Felipe Canela W PTS 10 Las Vegas
14.07.84 Juan Elizondo W CO 1 Monte Carlo
22.09.84 Don Curry L RSC 6 Monte Carlo
(*WBA & IBF Welterweight Title Challenge*)
27.02.85 Jerome Kinney L RSC 3 San Marino
27.06.86 Rene Jacquot L DIS 3 Modena
10.08.86 Lomani Musungu W PTS 8 Giardini
28.03.87 Mike Peoples W PTS 8 Camaiore
10.04.87 Inino Wa Bolamba W PTS 8 Latina
06.05.87 Mike Castranova W RSC 2 Lucca
23.10.87 Boubecker Cherif W RSC 4 Livorno
02.12.87 Abdel Arik W CO 1 San Giuseppe
19.12.87 Brahim Messaoudi W CO 3 Capo d'Orlando
13.04.88 Hassan Maghraoui W RTD 3 Busalla
01.06.88 Judas Clottey W CO 6 Campione
30.07.88 David Taylor W PTS 10 Livorno
27.08.88 Isias Monteiro W RSC 3 Castagneto
02.11.88 Ken Foreman W RSC 6 Paola
15.11.88 Martin Quiroz W CO 4 San Pellegrino
21.01.89 Angel Hernandez W RTD 7 Vasto
15.04.89 Kirkland Laing W PTS 12 Vasto
(*Vacant EBU Welterweight Title*)
Summary: 77 contests, won 73, lost 4.

Steve (The Heat) Larrimore
Bahamas. *Born* 14.02.63
Commonwealth L. Welterweight Champion & Con. Am. Lightweight Champion

03.11.84 Carlos Rivera W RSC 3 Nassau
22.12.84 Keith Jackson W PTS 8 Nassau
29.03.85 Arthur Clarke W PTS 10 Nassau
26.06.85 Cornelius Drane W RSC 6 Miami
09.08.85 Tony Cunningham W RSC 4 Nassau
08.09.85 Juan Arroyo W RSC 4 Nassau
19.12.86 Irleis Perez L PTS 10 Miami
31.01.87 Easy Boy Lakes W RSC 2 Nassau
15.03.87 Jaime Polo W RSC 3 Miami
08.08.87 Joe Alexander W RSC 8 Sunrise
30.01.88 Alfredo Layne W PTS 10 Nassau
16.03.88 Fred Pendleton L RSC 4 Atlantic City
23.11.88 Arvel Campbell W RSC 2 St Paul
31.01.89 Michael Benjamin W PTS 12 Nassau
(*Con. Am. Lightweight Title Challenge*)
21.03.89 Lester Ellis W RSC 11 Perth
(*Commonwealth L. Welterweight Title Challenge*)
Summary: 15 contests, won 13, lost 2.

Joe Lasisi
Lagos, Nigeria. *Born* 28.10.59
ABU L. Heavyweight Champion. Former Undefeated Nigerian & West African L. Heavyweight Champion

05.05.83 E. Osaige W CO 1 Kaduna
20.11.83 O. Johua W CO 1 Kaduna
06.04.88 Owo Blow W CO 2 Lagos
26.07.85 Jerry Okorodudu W RSC 8 Lagos
(*Vacant Nigerian L. Heavyweight Title*)
04.10.85 Sunny Emovon W RSC 1 Lagos
(*Nigerian L. Heavyweight Title Defence*)
23.11.85 Bilia Yusuf W RSC 7 Kwara
(*Nigerian L. Heavyweight Title Defence*)
06.12.85 George Mensah W RSC 2 Lagos
(*Vacant West African L. Heavyweight Title*)
07.02.86 Napoleon Abbey W CO 2 Lagos
25.04.86 Lottie Mwale W CO 8 Lagos
(*ABU L. Heavyweight Title Challenge*)
15.09.86 Ray Akwaye W CO 8 Lagos
12.06.87 Sanni Muhammad W CO 2 Lagos
28.10.87 Sergio Merani W RSC 2 Las Vegas
05.02.88 Jimmy Bills W PTS 8 Las Vegas
03.04.88 Jesse Abrams W RSC 2 Bismark
27.05.88 Jesse Shelby W RSC 1 Las Vegas
29.07.88 Mike Sedillo W RTD 8 Las Vegas
26.08.88 Joe Allotey W RTD 2 Lagos
(*ABU L. Heavyweight Title Defence*)
24.09.88 Uriah Grant W PTS 10 Las Vegas
11.11.88 Danny Lindstrom W RSC 6 Bismark
16.12.88 Jerry Okorodudu W RSC 8 Las Vegas
Summary: 20 contests, won 20.

Joe Lasisi

Christopher M. Farina

Racheed Lawal
Denmark. *Born* Sierra Leone 04.12.65
EBU S. Featherweight Champion

03.10.86 John Townsley W PTS 4 Copenhagen
17.10.86 Ivan Atencio W PTS 4 Randers
21.11.86 Steve Sims W PTS 6 Copenhagen
13.12.86 Jose Arenas W CO 4 Copenhagen
06.02.87 Roberto Castanon W PTS 8 Herning
27.02.87 Marco Gallo W CO 6 Randers
28.03.87 Jose Maillot W PTS 8 Copenhagen
02.10.87 Jose Hernando W PTS 8 Copenhagen
12.02.88 Nedrie Simmons W CO 2 Elsinore
12.05.88 Tony Pep W PTS 8 Copenhagen
08.12.88 Lars Lund Jensen W CO 12 Copenhagen
(*EBU S. Featherweight Title Challenge*)
17.03.89 John Doherty W RSC 4 Braedstrup
(*EBU S. Featherweight Title Defence*)
27.04.89 Mike Whalley W CO 3 Braedstrup
(*EBU S. Featherweight Title Defence*)
Summary: 13 contests, won 13.

(Dangerous) Don Lee
Gary, USA. *Born* 02.10.60
NABF S. Middleweight Champion

13.06.81 Billy Evans W CO 1 Gary
07.07.81 Bill Doyle W CO 2 Fort Worth
28.07.81 Joe Humphrey W CO 4 Houston
05.08.81 Garland Tripton W CO 3 Dayton
21.11.81 Willie Alexander W CO 1 Milwaukee
29.01.82 Carl Crowley W RSC 2 Milwaukee
14.02.82 Robert Powell W CO 3 Milwaukee
22.06.82 Johnny Gonzalez W CO 1 Houston
30.06.82 Dale Spain W RSC 3 Omaha
24.07.82 Karl Vinson W CO 4 Houston
26.08.82 Hollis Shaw W RSC 5 Gary
22.09.82 Ernie Dunbar W CO 2 Houston
24.10.82 Leroy Hester W RSC 8 Tampa
15.12.82 Artie McCloud L RSC 1 Chicago
03.03.83 Jessie Abrams W RSC 2 Hammond

06.05.83 Milton Owens W RSC 1 Tampa
03.07.83 Guy Kennedy DREW 10 Tampa
26.08.83 Norris McKinney W CO 1 Irving
30.09.83 Akbar Ali W RSC 2 Milwaukee
11.11.83 Lamont Hopkins W CO 1 Milwaukee
19.11.83 Johnny Heard W CO 4 Hammond
15.01.84 Tony Sibson W RSC 8 Atlantic City
01.04.84 Fred Reed W RSC 3 Milwaukee
12.10.84 Danny Blake W PTS 10 Gary
08.03.85 Doug de Witt DREW 10 Atlantic City
20.11.85 Martin Pierce W RSC 2 Atlantic City
09.03.86 Ray Ray Gray W RSC 8 Las Vegas
25.11.86 Bruce Jackson W RSC 4 Tyler
01.02.87 Michael Olajide L RSC 9 Atlantic City
24.08.87 James Wilder W PTS 8 Highland
13.11.87 Randy Smith W PTS 10 Chicago
03.02.88 Michael Watson L RSC 5 Wembley
18.07.88 Jeff Harding L RTD 8 Sydney
23.11.88 Jordan Keepers W RSC 2 St Paul
16.12.88 Terry Jackson W RSC 2 Louisville
10.02.89 Morris Virgil W RSC 2 Wauwatsoa
14.04.89 Sanderline Williams W PTS 12 Milwaukee
(Vacant NABF S. Middleweight Title)
Summary: 37 contests, won 31, drew 2, lost 4.

Kyung-Yung Lee
Poongki, South Korea. *Born* 04.12.66
Former Undefeated IBF M. Flyweight Champion

04.12.85 Yung-Jae Chung W RSC 3 Seoul
05.12.85 Jae-Hak Chun W PTS 4 Seoul
08.12.85 Jung-Ho Kang W PTS 4 Seoul
10.12.85 Hi-Jung No W PTS 6 Seoul
12.01.86 Dong-Pil Yang W PTS 6 Seoul
31.05.86 Il-Wan Kim W CO 5 Buchon
29.06.86 No-Sung Choi W PTS 6 Seoul
03.08.86 Byung-Sik Bae W PTS 8 Seoul
16.11.86 Sung-Kyu Kim W PTS 10 Seoul
14.03.87 Byung-Nam Park W CO 1 Chunchon
14.06.87 Masaharu Kawakami W CO 2 Bujok
(Vacant IBF M. Flyweight Title)
31.01.88 Hiroki Ioka L RSC 12 Osaka
(WBC M. Flyweight Title Challenge)
30.04.88 Nico Thomas W CO 4 Ulsan
24.07.88 Hi-Chung Noh W PTS 10 Pohang
29.10.88 Sang-Sik Chung W CO 2 Ansan
Summary: 15 contests, won 14, lost 1.

Sang-Ho Lee
Hyunju, South Korea. *Born* 27.10.61
Former Undefeated OPBF L. Welterweight Champion

17.02.80 Jang-Soo Nam W CO 3 Seoul
16.03.80 Hyun-Bae Lee W RSC 2 Seoul
27.04.80 Sang-Hi Kim W RSC 1 Seoul
29.06.80 Jong-Jin Choi W CO 1 Seoul
20.07.80 Young-Hon Chung W PTS 4 Seoul
15.10.80 Kyu-Sang Lee W CO 2 Seoul
19.11.80 Hi-Seoul Chung W PTS 4 Seoul
21.11.80 Kil-Young Hyang W PTS 4 Seoul
23.11.80 Kyung-Chol Choi W RSC 2 Seoul
29.11.80 Il-Kwon Chun W RSC 2 Seoul
07.12.80 Jung-Yul Lim W CO 5 Seoul
15.02.81 Doni Soriano W RSC 5 Seoul
22.02.81 Kazunori Shiratori W RSC 5 Seoul
19.04.81 Nobuyuki Chisaka W CO 1 Seoul
31.05.81 Mar Simbajon W CO 4 Seoul
12.06.81 Tadeo Ishido W CO 5 Wonju
30.08.81 Romeo Olivetti W CO 3 Seoul
01.10.81 Kazumi Nakao W RSC 3 Seoul
14.11.81 Fernand Gloria W PTS 10 Wonju
23.01.82 Takashi Sugimoto W RSC 3 Seoul
07.03.82 Romeo Olivetti W RSC 3 Wonju
22.05.82 Gar Atayde W CO 3 Seoul
13.06.82 Arcadje Singiomthong W CO 8 Pusan
17.07.82 Peter Berrigan W CO 3 Chungju
11.11.82 Ruben Rabago W PTS 10 Seoul
12.12.82 Hammer Itoi W CO 6 Masan
20.02.83 Joe Lim W RSC 8 Chinju
23.04.83 Tatsuya Moriyasu W CO 5 Seoul
18.06.83 Cisco Ferrer W CO 4 Pusan
03.08.83 Dario Melida W RSC 2 Wonju
25.09.83 Shoji Okishima W CO 10 Wonju
29.10.83 Allen Alegria L CO 3 Chinju
14.01.84 Kanakorn Tapoothai W RSC 6 Seoul
10.03.84 Max Boy Toyogon W CO 1 Seoul
14.04.84 Allen Alegria W DIS 7 Inchun
08.09.84 Ryu Otsuki W CO 4 Seoul
02.12.84 Dowthong Chuvatana W CO 6 Seoul
02.03.85 Juan Rondon W PTS 10 Seoul
02.06.85 Thai Suracharern W CO 4 Suwon
07.09.85 Ryo Asaka W CO 7 Inchon
16.11.85 Nubuyuki Tabata W CO 10 Sungnam
01.02.86 Katsuvori Hokama W RSC 2 Uejoungbu
10.05.86 Pat Leglise W RSC 9 Pusan
01.11.86 Kyung-Duk Ahn W PTS 12 Pohang
(OPBF L. Welterweight Title Challenge)
02.05.87 Yodwan Sornam W RSC 4 Daejon
12.09.87 Pastor Arcaya W CO 4 Sanchunpo
(OPBF L. Welterweight Title Defence)
21.11.87 Yoshifumi Kiatjima W RSC 7 Jaechin
05.03.88 Seijo Nagasawa W RSC 8 Taegu
07.05.88 Juan M. Coggi L CO 2 Roseto
(WBA L. Welterweight Title Challenge)
Summary: 49 contests, won 47, lost 2.

Seung-Hoon Lee
Chunbok, South Korea. *Born* 26.07.60
Former Undefeated IBF S. Bantamweight Champion. Former Undefeated South Korean Flyweight Champion

30.07.77 Jong-Sung Park W PTS 4 Seoul
30.09.77 Young-Shik Moon W RSC 1 Seoul
06.11.77 Hwan-Jin Kim L PTS 4 Seoul
20.12.77 Young-Shik Chung W PTS 6 Seoul
25.02.78 Jong-Man Kim W RSC 2 Seoul
03.10.78 Jong-Oh Kim W PTS 8 Seoul
20.12.78 Young-Hwan Kim W PTS 10 Seoul
(South Korean Flyweight Title Challenge)
10.02.79 Sor Vorasingh L PTS 12 Bangkok
07.04.79 Peter Siscon W PTS 10 Pusan
15.05.79 Prudencio Cardona W PTS 10 Seoul
29.09.79 Rene Enriquez W PTS 10 Seoul
11.11.79 Chungcherng Borkorsor W PTS 10 Seoul
30.11.79 Jose Tito W PTS 10 Seoul
02.02.80 Rafael Orono L PTS 15 Caracas
(WBC S. Flyweight Title Challenge)
09.05.80 Sung-Jun Kim W PTS 10 Seoul
19.07.80 Freddie Ebon W PTS 10 Pusan
28.09.80 Tsuguyuki Toma W RSC 7 Pusan
16.11.80 Flash Jagdon W CO 7 Pusan
22.02.81 Carlos Alcibar W PTS 10 Pusan
31.07.81 Neptali Alamag W PTS 10 Pusan
22.09.81 Sakad Saksuree W CO 6 Seoul
25.10.81 Suvan Muansgurin W PTS 10 Taegu
31.01.82 Hitoshi Ohashi W CO 1 Pusan
04.04.82 Arcades Sing-Jom Thong W CO 8 Pusan
03.06.82 Lupe Pintor L RSC 11 Los Angeles
(WBC Bantamweight Title Challenge)
13.11.82 Poker Pelegrino W RSC 9 Seoul
23.01.83 Manachai Sorvatana W CO 2 Daejon
21.03.83 Ricardo Cardona W CO 6 Masan
07.05.83 Martin Hernandez W CO 4 Seoul
18.06.83 Efren Guineta W CO 4 Taegu
21.08.83 Poker Pelegrino W RSC 7 Taegu
09.10.83 Renato Paulino W PTS 10 Taegu
18.12.83 Morsak Muangsurin W CO 1 Daejon
04.02.84 Morris Pastor W CO 2 Seoul
01.04.84 Kid Sumaila W PTS 10 Yosu
09.09.84 Ernie Sanico W RSC 4 Inchon
15.12.84 Dajvarin Hollywood W PTS 10 Pusan
02.02.85 Victor Callejas L PTS 15 San Juan
(WBA S. Bantamweight Title Challenge)
22.06.85 Pablo Pepito W PTS 10 Seoul
19.10.85 Flash Rockman W CO 1 Pohang
25.01.86 Rudy Casicas L RSC 8 Daejon
24.05.86 Majie Bona W RSC 6 Sunchon
13.09.86 Little Bangoyan W PTS 10 Daejon
18.01.87 Prayurasak Muangsurin W CO 9 Pohang
(Vacant IBF S. Bantamweight Title)
05.04.87 Jorge Urbina Diaz W CO 10 Seoul
(IBF S. Bantamweight Title Defence)
19.07.87 Lion Collins W CO 5 Pohang
(IBF S. Bantamweight Title Defence)
27.12.87 Jose Sanabria W PTS 15 Pohang
(IBF S. Bantamweight Title Defence)
20.03.88 Julian Solis W PTS 10 Ulsan
29.05.88 Daniel Zaragoza DREW 12 Youchan
(WBC S. Bantamweight Title Challenge)
27.02.89 Noree Jockygym W RSC 6 Youchan
Summary: 50 contests, won 43, drew 1, lost 6.

Seung-Soon Lee
South Korea
Former OPBF Welterweight Champion. Former Undefeated South Korean Welterweight Champion

21.11.79 Hyong-Dok Choi L PTS 4 Seoul
03.02.80 Young-Ki Yuh W PTS 4 Seoul
21.06.80 Myung-Ki Lee W RSC 1 Seoul
24.09.80 Hyon-Sok Lee W RSC 3 Seoul
17.10.80 Che-Kwon Yuh W CO 1 Seoul
18.11.80 Che-Il Yang W RSC 2 Seoul
21.11.80 Dae-Woo Han W PTS 4 Seoul
23.11.80 Sok-Sun Lim W RSC 3 Seoul
30.11.80 Mu-Sok Hwang W PTS 4 Seoul
07.12.80 Daek-Chang Chong W RSC 3 Seoul
15.03.81 Sok-Sun Lim W RSC 3 Seoul
26.04.81 Soo-Hyung Yuh W RSC 2 Taegu
16.08.81 Joe Lim W PTS 10 Seoul
27.09.81 Leo Casino W RSC 4 Seoul
21.02.82 Koru Jokker W RSC 7 Seoul
21.08.82 Yung-Sop Seo W RSC 6 Seoul
18.01.83 Jae-Yong Park W CO 7 Seoul
(South Korean Welterweight Title Challenge)
17.06.83 Yung-Kil Chung W PTS 10 Seoul
(South Korean Welterweight Title Defence)
04.09.83 Chung-Won Park W CO 9 Seoul
(South Korean Welterweight Title Defence)
05.02.84 Yung-Kil Chung W PTS 10 Seoul
(South Korean Welterweight Title Defence)
25.03.84 Mar Simbajon W CO 5 Seoul
17.06.84 Keun-Soo Park W RSC 1 Seoul
12.07.84 Sergio Sanchez W RSC 3 Los Angeles
23.09.84 Nilo Acido W RSC 4 Seoul
04.01.85 Lito Vazquez W CO 4 Seoul
24.03.85 Willie Makitoki W RSC 2 Seoul
07.07.85 Sil Sarana W CO 3 Seoul
27.10.85 Fernando Gloria W PTS 10 Seoul
14.02.86 Petch Petcharern W CO 2 Seoul
09.08.86 Dionisio Castillo W CO 4 Seoul
15.02.87 Yung-Sok Hwang W RSC 6 Wonju
(OPBF Welterweight Title Challenge)
29.03.87 Yung-Kil Chung L PTS 12 Wonju
(OPBF Welterweight Title Defence)
01.08.87 Boy Romero W CO 4 Suwon
24.04.88 Francisco Ferrer W PTS 10 Seoul
05.02.89 Mark Breland L RSC 1 Las Vegas
(Vacant WBA Welterweight Title)
Summary: 35 contests, won 32, lost 3.

Yul-Woo Lee
South Korea
WBC L.Flyweight Champion

13.07.85 Dong-Pil Yeom W PTS 4 Chungju
05.12.85 Ros-Eong Choi W PTS 4 Seoul
08.12.85 Sang-Chun Lee W PTS 4 Seoul
10.12.85 Chong-Hwa Park W CO 2 Seoul
28.06.86 Chun-Byun Kim W RSC 5 Pohang
21.07.86 Chan-Yub Chun W CO 2 Hongchun
30.08.86 Sang-Hyon Kim W PTS 10 Pohang
01.11.86 Keun-Soo Choi W PTS 10 Pohang
18.01.87 Sang-Hyun Han W PTS 10 Pohang
19.04.87 Romy Navarrete W CO 7 Inchon
28.06.87 Julio Gudino W PTS 10 Inchon
14.11.87 Arnulfo Melencion W RSC 4 Seoul
13.12.87 Amado Ursua W CO 5 Daejon
20.03.88 Duk-Hyun Kim W CO 7 Ulson
29.05.88 Miguel Mercedes L PTS 10 Youchon
09.10.88 Houn-Kuk Chae W CO 3 Seoul
22.12.88 Roger de Rama W RSC 3 Seoul
19.03.89 German Torres W CO 9 Taejon
(WBC L. Flyweight Title Challenge)
Summary: 18 contests, won 17, lost 1.

Yul-Woo Lee

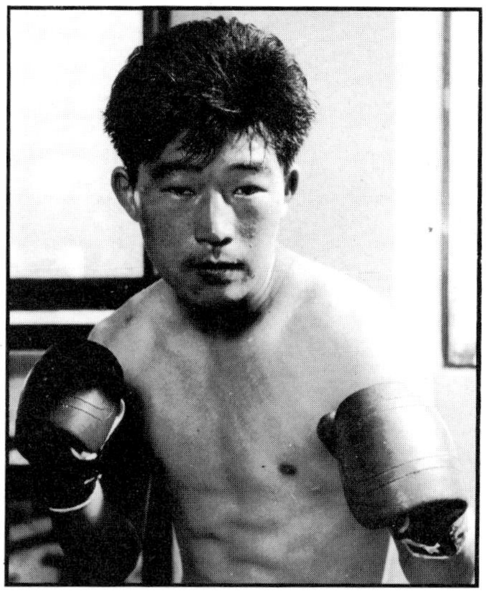

Jan Lefeber
Rotterdam, Holland. *Born* 19.05.61
EBU L. Heavyweight Champion. Former Undefeated Benelux Middleweight Champion

07.03.83 Sinisa Popovich W DIS 5 Rotterdam
25.04.83 Jean Santoncini W PTS 6 Rotterdam
13.06.83 Jose Bastient W RSC 2 Rotterdam
19.09.83 Lahcen Hamdi W PTS 6 Rotterdam
05.11.83 Graciano Rocchigiani L PTS 4 Mannheim
14.11.83 Mustapha Yazidi W PTS 6 Rotterdam
22.10.84 Ahcene Reffas W RSC 6 Rotterdam
11.02.85 Ruediger Bitterling W PTS 6 Amsterdam
25.03.85 Frankie Decaestecker L PTS 10 Rotterdam (*Benelux Middleweight Title Challenge*)
22.04.85 Claudio Bosio DREW 8 Rotterdam
29.04.85 Esperno Postl W RSC 4 Gronigen
06.05.85 Philippe Seys W PTS 8 Rotterdam
14.10.85 John van Elteren W CO 5 Scheidam (*Benelux Middleweight Title Challenge*)
08.11.85 Andreas Prox W RSC 6 Dusseldorf
24.02.86 Claudio Bosio W CO 1 Sheidam (*Benelux Middleweight Title Defence*)
26.03.86 James Cook W CO 3 Amsterdam
06.05.86 Maurice Bufi W PTS 10 Rotterdam (*Benelux Middleweight Title Defence*)
15.09.86 Carlton Warren L RSC 6 Scheidam
07.02.87 Yves Monsieur W PTS 8 Brussels
09.03.87 Lahcen Hamdi W PTS 8 Rotterdam
28.03.88 Serge Bolivard W PTS 8 Rotterdam
30.05.88 Oliver Kemayou W PTS 8 Rotterdam
29.07.88 Ralf Rocchigiani L PTS 8 Timmendorf
07.11.88 Pedro van Raamsdonk W PTS 12 Rotterdam (*EBU L. Heavyweight Title Challenge*)
09.04.89 Ralf Rocchigiani DREW 12 Berlin (*EBU L. Heavyweight Title Defence*)
Summary: 25 contests, won 19, drew 2, lost 4.

Jan Lefeber

Genaro Leon
Culiacan, Mexico. *Born* 10.08.60
L. Welterweight

28.09.84 Ramon Cardoza W CO 2 Culiacan
10.11.84 Jose Millan W RSC 9 Culiacan
23.11.84 Fidencio Cebreros W CO 2 Mazatlan
21.12.84 Gil Canchola W CO 7 Culiacan
10.03.85 Jose Lopez W CO 2 Tijuana
29.03.85 Daniel Contreras W CO 2 La Paz
09.05.85 Aaron Brown W CO 1 Los Angeles
17.05.85 Lalo Galindo W CO 1 San Luis Potosi
29.07.85 Jose Alejo W CO 2 Tijuana
13.09.85 Ray Morales W CO 7 Juarez
23.11.85 Joel Sots W CO 1 Guamuchil
08.12.85 Ruben Villaman L CO 5 Mazatlan
22.02.86 Mario Olmedo W PTS 10 Mexico City
21.03.86 Jose Bueno W CO 1 Hermosillo
03.05.86 Sergio Aguirre W RSC 1 Mexico City
15.05.86 Jaime Montano W CO 1 Obregon
29.08.86 Sergio Aguirre W RSC 4 Naucalpan
03.10.86 Patrick Boon W PTS 6 La Rochelle
25.10.86 Carlos Prieto W DIS 7 Paris
07.11.86 Rafael Paoletti W RTD 3 Bordeaux
06.02.87 Yaqui Hernandez W RSC 2 Hermosillo
09.03.87 Richard Munoz W CO 4 Tijuana
14.04.87 Jaime Castorena W CO 4 Tijuana
29.05.87 Ariel Conde W CO 1 La Paz
17.07.87 Ruben Villaman W CO 1 Hermosillo
08.10.87 Frankie Lane W CO 1 Paris
06.11.87 Joel Brival W CO 4 Antibes
06.02.88 David Taylor L RSC 1 Paris
04.06.88 Ramon Cardenas W CO 2 Mazatlan
23.07.88 Charlie Brown W CO 2 Tijuana
22.09.88 Charles Nwokolo W PTS 10 Los Angeles
09.03.89 Agustin Caballero W CO 4 Los Angeles
Summary: 32 contests, won 30, lost 2.

(Sugar) Ray Leonard
Palmer Park, USA. *Born* 17.05.56
WBC S. Middleweight Champion. Former Undefeated WBC Middleweight Champion. Former Undefeated World & NABF Welterweight Champion. Former Undefeated WBA L. Middleweight Champion. Former Undefeated WBC L. Heavyweight Champion

05.02.77 Luis Vega W PTS 6 Baltimore
14.05.77 Willie Rodriguez W PTS 6 Baltimore
10.06.77 Vinnie de Barros W RSC 3 Hartford
24.09.77 Frank Santore W RSC 5 Baltimore
05.11.77 Augustine Estrada W RSC 6 Las Vegas
17.12.77 Hector Diaz W CO 2 Washington
04.02.78 Rocky Ramon W PTS 8 Baltimore
01.03.78 Art McKnight W RSC 7 Dayon
19.03.78 Javier Muniz W CO 1 New Haven
13.04.78 Bobby Haymon W RSC 3 Landover
13.05.78 Randy Milton W RSC 8 Utica
03.06.78 Rafael Rodriguez W PTS 10 Baltimore
18.07.78 Dick Eklund W PTS 10 Boston
09.09.78 Floyd Mayweather W RSC 10 Providence
06.10.78 Randy Shields W PTS 10 Baltimore
03.11.78 Bernardo Prada W PTS 10 Portland
09.12.78 Armando Muniz W RTD 6 Springfield
11.01.79 Johnny Gant W RSC 8 Landover
11.02.79 Fernand Marcotte W RSC 8 Miami
24.03.79 Daniel Gonzales W CO 1 Tucson
21.04.79 Adolfo Viruet W PTS 10 Las Vegas
20.05.79 Marcos Geraldo W PTS 10 Baton Rouge
24.06.79 Tony Chiaverini W RTD 4 Las Vegas
12.08.79 Pete Ranzany W RSC 4 Las Vegas (*NABF Welterweight Title Challenge*)
28.09.79 Andy Price W CO 1 Las Vegas (*NABF Welterweight Title Defence*)
30.11.79 Wilfred Benitez W RSC 15 Las Vegas (*WBC Welterweight Title Challenge*)
31.03.80 Dave Green W CO 4 Landover (*WBC Welterweight Title Defence*)
20.06.80 Roberto Duran L PTS 15 Montreal (*WBC Welterweight Title Defence*)
25.11.80 Roberto Duran W RTD 8 New Orleans (*WBC Welterweight Title Challenge*)
28.03.81 Larry Bonds W RSC 10 Syracuse (*WBC Welterweight Title Defence*)
25.06.81 Ayub Kalule W RSC 9 Houston (*WBA L. Middleweight Title Challenge*)
16.09.81 Thomas Hearns W RSC 14 Las Vegas (*WBC Welterweight Title Defence & WBA Welterweight Title Challenge*)
15.02.82 Bruce Finch W RSC 3 Reno (*World Welterweight Title Defence*)
11.05.84 Kevin Howard W RSC 9 Worcester
06.04.87 Marvin Hagler W PTS 12 Las Vegas (*WBC Middleweight Title Challenge*)
07.11.88 Don Lalonde W RSC 9 Las Vegas (*WBC L. Heavyweight Title Challenge & Vacant WBC S. Middleweight Title*)
Summary: 36 contests, won 35, lost 1.

Karama Leota
Salt Lake City, USA.
Middleweight

07.02.87 Mark Cox L PTS 4 Reno
07.03.87 Cliff Hutchinson W CO 2 Reno
25.04.87 Chris Lange W CO 1 Reno
16.06.87 Carl Owens W RSC 2 Reno
03.07.87 Doug Holiman W CO 1 Gardnerville
15.08.87 Ricky Locke W PTS 6 Reno
25.11.87 John Roy W RSC 3 Las Vegas
18.12.87 James Williams W RTD 2 Las Vegas
06.02.88 Gilbert Valenzuela W PTS 6 Las Vegas
19.02.88 Alvaro Granillo W CO 1 Las Vegas
05.03.88 Fernando Garcia W CO 2 Carson City
08.04.88 Hector Jaiman W PTS 6 Las Vegas
07.05.88 Allan Harper W RSC 3 Monterey
28.05.88 German Mendoza W RSC 2 Incline Village
02.07.88 Jerome Kelly W CO 2 Gardnerville
15.07.88 James Waire W PTS 8 Stateline
23.08.88 Lester Yarbrough W RSC 4 Stateline
01.11.88 Herman Cavesuela W RSC 8 Monterey
17.01.89 Knox Brown W PTS 10 Las Vegas
28.02.89 Danny Winters W RSC 5 Las Vegas
02.05.89 Jessie Flores W PTS 10 Stateline
Summary: 21 contests, won 20, lost 1.

Rocky Lockridge
Tacoma, USA. *Born* 30.01.59
Former IBF & WBA S. Featherweight Champion. Former USBA Featherweight Champion

09.08.78 Tony Reed W RSC 2 Seattle
05.10.78 Jose Lara W PTS 6 Seattle
14.11.78 Tony Hernandez W RSC 1 Totowa
13.03.79 Melvin Bethea W CO 1 Totowa
17.04.79 Melvin Boynton W RSC 2 Totowa
27.04.79 Francisco Maldonado W CO 2 Newark
31.05.79 Ronnie Green W CO 1 Philadelphia
18.09.79 Gerald Hayes W PTS 12 East Rutherford
30.10.79 Jose Ortiz W CO 2 Totowa
08.01.80 Sammy Goss W RSC 5 Totowa
19.02.80 Fel Clemente W RSC 7 Totowa (*Vacant USBA Featherweight Title*)
08.03.80 Richard Rozelle W CO 2 McAfee
01.04.80 Joey Mayes W RSC 2 Totowa
19.06.80 Marcial Santiago W RSC 3 Totowa
13.07.80 Alfonso Evans W RSC 5 McAfee
21.08.80 Livio Nolasco W RSC 4 Totowa
04.10.80 Eusebio Pedroza L PTS 15 McAfee (*WBA Featherweight Title Challenge*)
18.12.80 Benny Marquez W RSC 3 Totowa
22.01.81 Ernesto Gonzalez W CO 1 Totowa
06.04.81 Edwin Rivera W PTS 12 Atlantic City
21.05.81 Sergio Reyes W RSC 3 Totowa
22.08.81 Juan Laporte L CO 2 Las Vegas (*USBA Featherweight Title Defence*)
12.11.81 Refugio Rojas W PTS 10 East Rutherford
10.12.81 Tony Tris W PTS 10 Totowa
14.03.82 Jose Resendez W RSC 5 Atlantic City
10.04.82 Robert Mullins W RSC 5 Atlantic City
23.05.82 Jose Nieto W RSC 8 Atlantic City
24.06.82 Daniel Felizardo W CO 2 Atlantic City
22.08.82 Miguel Hernandez W RSC 3 McAfee
25.09.82 Angel Lira W RSC 6 McAfee
24.11.82 Alberto Collazo W RSC 9 Atlantic City
24.04.83 Eusebio Pedroza L PTS 15 Liguma (*WBA Featherweight Title Challenge*)
14.07.83 Danny Cruz W RSC 1 Totowa
09.09.83 Cornelius Boza-Edwards W PTS 10 Las Vegas
23.11.83 Jeff Goodwin W RSC 3 Atlantic City
26.02.84 Roger Mayweather W CO 1 Beaumont (*WBA S. Featherweight Title Challenge*)
12.06.84 Tae-Jin Moon W RSC 11 Anchorage (*WBA S. Featherweight Title Defence*)
29.07.84 Julio Llerena W CO 6 Milan
27.01.85 Kamel Bou Ali W RSC 6 Riva del Garda (*WBA S. Featherweight Title Defence*)
19.05.85 Wilfredo Gomez L PTS 15 San Juan (*WBA S. Featherweight Title Defence*)
18.12.85 Fernando Segura W RSC 4 Atlantic City
12.03.86 Efrain Nieves W RSC 3 Atlantic City
03.08.86 Julio Cesar Chavez L PTS 12 Monte Carlo (*WBC S. Featherweight Title Challenge*)
22.10.86 Felipe Orozco W RSC 10 Atlantic City
24.05.87 Dennis Cruz W CO 7 Corpus Christi
09.08.87 Barry Michael W RTD 8 Windsor (*IBF S. Featherweight Title Challenge*)
25.10.87 Johnny de la Rosa W RSC 10 Tucson (*IBF S. Featherweight Title Defence*)
02.04.88 Harold Knight W PTS 15 Atlantic City (*IBF S. Featherweight Title Defence*)
27.07.88 Tony Lopez L PTS 12 Sacramento (*IBF S. Featherweight Title Defence*)
05.03.89 Tony Lopez L PTS 12 Sacramento (*IBF S. Featherweight Title Challenge*)
Summary: 50 contests, won 43, lost 7.

Louie Lomeli
Ocotian, Mexico. *Born* 20.12.65
Lightweight

08.08.85 Kent Acuff W RSC 3 Chicago
22.08.85 Joe Smith W CO 1 Chicago
21.09.85 Alfonso Sosa W RSC 1 Chicago
11.10.85 Roy Huntley W CO 1 Chicago
19.10.85 Walter Cowans W PTS 4 Chicago
23.11.85 Robert Brooks W RSC 4 Chicago
12.12.85 Walter Cowans W RSC 4 Chicago
18.01.86 Jerry Massey W RSC 2 Chicago
22.02.86 Angel Rodriguez W RSC 6 Chicago

22.03.86 Don Williams W RSC 1 Chicago
17.05.86 Nate Stewart W RSC 7 Chicago
25.07.86 Victor Aponte W PTS 10 Chicago
05.12.86 Walter Cowans W CO 1 Chicago
21.03.87 Sebastian Wilburn W RSC 1 Chicago
24.04.87 Jeff Bumphus W PTS 8 Davenport
31.07.87 Richard Campbell W RSC 2 Villa Park
03.09.87 Eddie Ruiz W CO 1 San Juan
20.11.87 Herminio Morales W RSC 6 Villa Park
05.01.88 Ray James W RSC 2 Lexington
06.02.88 Sal Cenicola W CO 2 Atlantic City
12.05.88 Billy White W RSC 3 Harvey
12.06.88 Johnny Duplessis W PTS 10 Villa Park
25.08.88 Shawn Spinda W RSC 3 Chicago
17.01.89 Henry Mobley W RSC 9 Chicago
30.04.89 Pernell Whitaker L RSC 3 Norfolk
(*IBF Lightweight Title Challenge*)
Summary: 25 contests, won 24, lost 1.

Louie Lomeli

Peter Goldfield/USA

Daniel Londas
Forte de France, Martinique. *Born* 17.05.54
French S. Featherweight Champion

28.11.80 Rene Kowalski W RSC 4 Reims
06.12.80 Patrick Drelon W RSC 4 Epernay
20.12.80 Abdel Kerzazi W PTS 6 Reims
05.02.81 Slaedine Gardachi W RSC 2 Paris
26.02.81 Antonio Secci W RSC 3 Paris
07.03.81 Daniel Passeyrand W RSC 3 Reims
14.03.81 George Sutton W PTS 6 Noget Sur Marne
04.04.81 Orlando Ramos W PTS 6 Fort de France
09.05.81 Angel Monstavo W CO 3 Fort de France
12.09.81 Harold Bernard W PTS 8 Fort de France
03.10.81 Elmer Sutington W RSC 4 Fort de France
17.10.81 Gerard Jacob W PTS 8 Reims
31.10.81 Vernon Penprase W PTS 8 Chalons
05.02.82 Maldo Maldonado W PTS 8 Fort de France
05.03.82 Mohammed Boundka W CO 4 Paris
27.03.82 Roberto Bido W PTS 8 Fort de France
26.04.82 Francis Bailleua W CO 2 Paris
(*French S. Featherweight Title Challenge*)
29.05.82 Alain Lefiol W RSC 8 Fort de France
(*French S. Featherweight Title Defence*)
07.06.82 Carlos Hernandez W PTS 8 Paris
06.11.82 Roberto Castanon L RTD 9 Leon
(*EBU S. Featherweight Title Challenge*)
28.12.82 Michel Siracusa L PTS 8 Aix
25.03.82 Carlos Foldes W PTS 8 Paris
07.05.83 Francis Tripp W RSC 9 Pontarlier
(*French S. Featherweight Title Defence*)
13.07.83 Nelson Cruz Tamariz W PTS 10 Fort de France
10.10.83 Sammy Meck W PTS 8 Paris
18.11.83 Michel Siracusa L RSC 10 Reims
(*French S. Featherweight Title Defence*)
14.01.84 Vicente Macias W PTS 8 Epernay
03.02.84 Farid Gallouze W RSC 4 Chalons
14.04.84 Amalio Galan W PTS 8 Epernay
26.05.84 Rene Weller L PTS 12 Dusseldorf
(*EBU Lightweight Title Challenge*)
14.12.84 Francis Tripp W RSC 4 Fort de France
26.01.85 Jose Maillot W RSC 4 Valence
22.03.85 Michel Siracusa W PTS 10 Reims
(*French S. Featherweight Title Challenge*)
26.04.85 Steve Griffith W RSC 8 Thionville
06.05.85 Carlos Laciar W PTS 8 Grenoble
15.06.85 Paul Tiziwana W CO 4 Reims
27.10.85 Sammy Meck W PTS 10 Rouen
12.12.85 Vicente Jorge W PTS 8 Reims
25.01.86 Hugo Carrizo W PTS 8 Rouen
21.02.86 Jose Garcia W RSC 8 Paris
28.04.86 Maurice Vivies W PTS 10 St Ouen
(*French S. Featherweight Title Defence*)
04.07.86 Fosa Coadrado W CO 1 Fort de France
12.09.86 Carlos Rodriguez W PTS 8 Paris
27.10.86 Paul Downie W CO 2 Paris
20.12.86 Jean-Marc Renard DREW 12 St Ouen
(*EBU S. Featherweight Title Challenge*)
16.05.87 Salvatore Curcetti L RSC 1 Reims
(*Vacant EBU S. Featherweight Title*)
04.07.87 Sammy Meck W PTS 10 Calais
(*French S. Featherweight Title Defence*)
03.10.87 Brian Mitchell L PTS 15 Gravelines
(*WBA S. Featherweight Title Challenge*)
09.01.88 Joe Alexander W PTS 8 Abidjan
05.02.88 Orlando Fernandez W PTS 8 Point a Pitre
11.03.88 Brian Roche W DIS 5 Paris
16.05.88 Sammy Meck W PTS 10 Levallois
(*French S. Featherweight Title Defence*)
07.10.88 Nigel Senior W PTS 8 Bordeaux
23.01.89 Dingan Thobela L PTS 10 Johannesburg
11.02.89 Gary Maxwell W CO 5 Chateau Thierry
Summary: 55 contests, won 47, drew 1, lost 7.

Al (Bumblebee) Long
Los Angeles, USA. *Born* 11.05.62
Welterweight

13.04.82 Leland Hart W PTS 6 Sacramento
23.07.82 Rod Stevens W PTS 4 Culver City
08.12.82 Johnny Gonzalez W PTS 6 Ventura
09.02.83 Jose Morado W RSC 2 Ventura
11.03.83 Romeo Bellis W RSC 2 Culver City
23.04.83 Roberto Veta W RSC 3 Culver City
27.05.83 Juan J. Ramirez W RSC 5 Culver City
28.06.83 Jose Serna W RSC 1 Culver City
13.07.83 Derrick Kelly L PTS 8 Ventura
02.08.83 Ignacio Acosta W RSC 1 Culver City
02.09.83 Glen Corbus W PTS 8 San Jose
01.11.83 J.D. Williams W RSC 4 Reseda
30.11.83 Joe Moliere W RSC 6 Reseda
07.05.84 Dennis Mulholland W PTS 10 Bakersfield
12.07.84 Jorge Vaca L PTS 10 Los Angeles
07.11.84 Billy Smith W RSC 1 Los Angeles
09.01.85 Robert Sawyer W PTS 10 Los Angeles
10.06.85 Mike Hutchinson W RSC 9 Los Angeles
27.07.85 Shawn O'Sullivan L PTS 8 Calgary
20.08.85 Manning Galloway L PTS 10 Los Angeles
29.10.85 Kenny Lopez W PTS 10 Stockton
27.05.86 Felipe Canela L RSC 8 Irvine
04.09.86 Felipe Canela L PTS 10 San Jose
05.02.87 Francisco Armenta W RSC 2 Riverside
19.03.87 David Gutierrez DREW 10 Riverside
23.04.87 Davidson Andeh W RTD 1 Riverside
12.06.87 Russell Mitchell W PTS 12 Riverside
15.07.87 Derrick Kelly DREW 12 Riverside
16.10.87 Al Hamza Ufo W PTS 10 Atlantic City
03.02.88 Alex Ramos W PTS 12 Riverside
22.04.88 Russell Mitchell DREW 12 Paso Robles
27.04.89 Simon Brown L CO 7 Washington
(*IBF Welterweight Title Challenge*)
Summary: 32 contests, won 22, drew 3, lost 7.

Hector Lopez
Los Angeles, USA. *Born* Mexico 01.02.67
Featherweight

01.01.85 Roberto Solis W PTS 6 Mexico City
05.03.85 Norman Moya W PTS 6 Houston
22.07.85 Moises Martinez W CO 3 Tijuana
07.08.85 Beto Gonzalez W RSC 1 Carson City
09.09.85 Ernesto Ramirez W CO 1 Tijuana
10.11.85 Joe Perez W PTS 8 Pomona
20.12.85 Felipe Olivar W CO 2 Los Angeles
25.02.86 Juan A. Lopez W PTS 10 Los Angeles
26.03.86 Frank Fazio W PTS 8 Las Vegas
13.06.86 Francisco Segura W PTS 10 Las Vegas
15.08.86 George Navarro L PTS 12 Atlantic City
09.10.86 Bruno Rabanales W PTS 10 Los Angeles
23.02.87 Refugio Rojas W PTS 10 Los Angeles
27.04.87 Bernard Taylor W RSC 9 Los Angeles
05.06.87 Leonardo Valdez W PTS 10 Los Angeles
01.10.87 George Navarro W TD 2 Los Angeles
07.05.88 Oscar Bejines W CO 9 Los Angeles
23.06.88 Maurice Beltran W RSC 9 Los Angeles
30.01.89 Rogelio Lopez W PTS 10 Los Angeles
Summary: 19 contests, won 18, lost 1.

Lucio (Metralleta) Lopez
Mercedes, Argentine. *Born* 29.03.62
South American & Argentinian Bantamweight Champion

12.03.83 Julio Juarez W RSC 1 Buenos Aires
07.05.83 Raul Gomez W PTS 6 Buenos Aires
23.09.83 Christian Diaz W CO 2 Campana
15.10.83 Hipolito Caucota W PTS 8 Buenos Aires
09.12.83 Juan Scoles W CO 4 Santa Rosa
08.02.84 Domingo Alberto W RSC 3 Montevideo
23.03.84 Jose Narvaez W CO 3 Renanco
26.05.84 Jaime Loyola W CO 8 Buenos Aires
30.06.84 Cesar Villarruel W PTS 10 Buenos Aires
22.09.84 Luis Gerez W CO 8 Buenos Aires
11.01.85 Jose Gomez W CO 4 Mercedes
15.03.85 Jose Narvaez W CO 1 Corrientes
(*Argentinian Bantamweight Title Challenge*)
19.04.85 Luis Gerez W CO 2 Corrientes
11.05.85 Valdevino Monteiro W RTD 6 Mercedes
08.06.85 Gustavo Ballas W RTD 5 Buenos Aires
12.07.85 Jaime Miranda W RTD 6 Corrientes
20.09.85 Carlos Alves W CO 6 Corrientes
(*Vacant South American Bantamweight Title*)
15.11.85 Juan Ivalo W RTD 9 Mercedes
(*Argentinian Bantamweight Title Defence*)
13.12.85 Ruben Condori L PTS 10 Salta
21.03.86 Valdevino Monteiro W CO 1 Goya
24.05.86 Edgar Roman W PTS 10 Buenos Aires
06.09.86 Juan J. Estrada W PTS 10 Buenos Aires
04.10.86 Ruben Condori W PTS 10 Buenos Aires
08.11.86 Ruben Condori DREW 10 Corrientes
12.12.86 Juan Cortes W CO 7 Corrientes
(*Argentinian Bantamweight Title Defence*)
02.05.87 Raul Gomez W PTS 10 Puerto Madryn
21.08.87 Jorge Ramirez W RTD 7 Corrientes
19.09.87 Enrique Sanchez W PTS 10 Buenos Aires
18.12.87 Alejandro Montes W CO 6 Corrientes
(*South American Bantamweight Title Defence*)
30.04.88 Miguel Lora L PTS 12 Cartagena
(*WBC Bantamweight Title Challenge*)
01.10.88 Ruben Astorga W RSC 5 Buenos Aires
02.12.88 Ruben Condori L PTS 10 Salta
09.03.89 Raul Perez L PTS 12 Los Angeles
(*WBC Bantamweight Title Challenge*)
Summary: 33 contests, won 28, drew 1, lost 4.

Tony Lopez
Sacramento, USA. *Born* 24.02.63
IBF S. Featherweight Champion

03.05.83 Juan Rodriguez W RSC 1 Sacramento
04.06.83 Ed Acosta W CO 1 Sacramento
28.06.83 Joe Cruz W CO 4 Sacramento
12.07.83 Gerald Issack W PTS 6 Sacramento
09.08.83 Leo Benitez W PTS 4 Sacramento
01.11.83 Juan Rivera W CO 1 Sacramento
15.11.83 Ruben Perales W RSC 1 Sacramento
29.11.83 Juan Torres W RSC 4 Sacramento
06.03.84 Memo Rojas W CO 2 Sacramento
03.04.84 Sam Espinosa W RSC 4 Sacramento
03.08.84 Tim Brooks W PTS 6 Reno
02.04.85 Mario Bautista W RSC 4 Sacramento
18.06.85 J. T. Walker W RSC 4 Sacramento
15.08.85 Baby de la Rosa W RSC 3 Sacramento
04.10.85 Roman Almaguer W RSC 3 Sacramento
18.12.85 Adam Garcia W PTS 10 Sacramento
03.03.86 Roberto Cantu W PTS 10 Sacramento
05.06.86 Arnel Arrozal W CO 2 Sacramento
20.07.86 Tim Brooks W PTS 10 Stateline
26.08.86 Cesar Zepeda W RSC 4 Stateline
27.09.86 Remington Garcia W RSC 4 Lake Tahoe
07.11.86 Roberto Cantu W RSC 3 Stateline
05.12.86 Heriberto Chavez W CO 2 Stateline
15.02.87 Tommy Cordova W PTS 10 Sacramento
21.05.87 Pedro Nolasco W PTS 10 Sacramento
01.07.87 Pedro Nolasco W RSC 8 Sacramento
01.09.87 Ramon Rico L DIS 7 Sacramento
25.09.87 Ramon Rico W CO 2 Sacramento
16.12.87 Gerardo Velasquez W RSC 3 Sacramento
25.03.88 Tony Pep W RSC 3 Sacramento

27.07.88 Rocky Lockridge W PTS 12 Sacramento
(*IBF S. Featherweight Title Challenge*)
27.10.88 Juan Molina W PTS 12 Sacramento
(*IBF S. Featherweight Title Defence*)
05.03.89 Rocky Lockridge W PTS 12 Sacramento
(*IBF S. Featherweight Title Defence*)
Summary: 33 contests, won 32, lost 1.

Miguel (Happy) Lora
Monteria, Colombia. *Born* 12.04.61
Former WBC Bantamweight Champion. Former Undefeated Fecarbox & Colombian S. Flyweight Champion. Former Undefeated Con. Am. Bantamweight Champion

27.07.79 Wilfredo Ruiz W PTS 6 Monteria
19.10.79 Alfredo Gomez W CO 1 Monteria
30.11.79 Tomas Maza W CO 1 Monteria
28.03.80 Justo Jorge W RSC 3 Monteria
12.06.80 Julio Soto Solano W PTS 12 Monteria
(*Fecarbox S. Flyweight Title Challenge*)
14.08.80 Orlando Tejedor W CO 1 Bogota
31.10.80 Juan Alvarez W PTS 10 Monteria
03.12.80 Arnoldo Sarmiento W RSC 3 Monteria
28.11.81 Carlos Arturo Osorio W PTS 10 Cerete
18.12.81 Luis Tapias W RSC 3 Monteria
26.02.82 Delimiro Cassiani W RSC 7 Monteria
30.07.82 Charles Maussa W RSC 7 Monteria
17.09.82 Miguel Perez W PTS 12 Monteria
(*Colombian S. Flyweight Title Challenge*)
12.05.83 Ruben Palacios W PTS 12 Cerete
(*Con. Am. Bantamweight Title Challenge*)
30.07.83 Jose Salazar W CO 3 Sincelejo
18.09.83 Pedro Romero W PTS 12 Cerete
(*Con. Am. Bantamweight Title Defence*)
17.12.83 Juan Diaz W RSC 5 Monteria
18.02.84 Edwin Rangel W PTS 10 Cartagena
03.07.84 Juan Torres W PTS 10 Miami
25.11.84 Jose Chacon W PTS 10 Monteria
10.05.85 Ramon Nery W CO 2 Miami
07.06.85 Diego Avila W RSC 8 Miami
09.08.85 Daniel Zaragoza W PTS 12 Miami
(*WBC Bantamweight Title Challenge*)
08.02.86 Wilfredo Vasquez W PTS 12 Miami
(*WBC Bantamweight Title Defence*)
23.08.86 Enrique Sanchez W RSC 6 Miami
(*WBC Bantamweight Title Defence*)
15.11.86 Albert Davila W PTS 12 Barranquilla
(*WBC Bantamweight Title Defence*)
25.07.87 Antonio Avelar W RSC 4 Miami
(*WBC Bantamweight Title Defence*)
27.11.87 Ray Minus W PTS 12 Miami
(*WBC Bantamweight Title Defence*)
30.04.88 Lucio Lopez W PTS 12 Cartagena
(*WBC Bantamweight Title Defence*)
01.08.88 Albert Davila W PTS 12 Los Angeles
(*WBC Bantamweight Title Defence*)
29.10.88 Raul Perez L PTS 12 Las Vegas
(*WBC Bantamweight Title Defence*)
Summary: 31 contests, won 30, lost 1.

Domingo (Pretty Boy) Lucas
Bulacan, Philippines. *Born* 20.12.65
Philippines M. Flyweight Champion

11.11.83 Alex de la Flor W PTS 4 Manila
18.02.84 Felipe Brazil W PTS 4 Malabon
31.03.84 Mohammad Raffi W CO 3 Malabon
27.04.84 Leonardo Saonoy W CO 1 Manila
27.07.84 Danny Duran W PTS 6 Manila
31.08.84 Felipe Brazil W PTS 6 Manila
08.03.85 Steve Ponan W RSC 7 Malabon
01.06.85 Lou Morabe W PTS 8 Malabon
27.07.85 Roberto Palarit W PTS 10 Malabon
30.08.85 Tito Abella W PTS 10 Novaliches
26.10.85 Ed Hemo W PTS 10 Manila
20.12.85 Rex Rapizo T DRAW 3 Manila
21.02.86 Robert Palarit W TD 8 Pasig
05.07.86 Jun Altarejos W PTS 10 Pasig
08.11.86 Jun Afable W PTS 12 Manila
(*Philippines M. Flyweight Title Challenge*)
06.03.87 Boy Selda W TD 4 Manila
03.07.87 Boy Selda W RSC 9 Malabon
28.10.87 Rizaldy Ocampo W RSC 6 Paranaque
(*Philippines M. Flyweight Title Defence*)
24.03.88 Samuth Sithnaruepol L RSC 11 Bangkok
(*Vacant IBF M. Flyweight Title*)
10.06.88 Sang-Hyun Han W RSC 7 Quezon City
01.09.88 Visuna Kiatsontaya W RSC 2 Manila
22.10.88 Boy Dignos W PTS 12 Manila
(*Philippines M. Flyweight Title Defence*)
16.12.88 Myung-Kon Lee W RSC 7 Manila
Summary: 23 contests, won 21, drew 1, lost 1.

Javier Lucas
Tenexpa, Mexico. *Born* 30.11.60
NABF Flyweight Champion

22.12.79 Beto Colon W PTS 8 Acapulco
11.01.80 Rafael Guerra W RSC 2 Acapulco
01.02.80 Salvador Roque W RSC 3 Acapulco
21.03.80 Ben Velasquez W CO 1 Acapulco
23.05.80 Pedro Herrera W PTS 10 Acapulco
04.07.80 Mario Nava W CO 3 Acapulco
31.08.80 Jesus Becerra W CO 5 Acapulco
31.10.80 Leo Castellanos W PTS 10 Acapulco
27.02.81 Candido Tellez W RSC 8 Acapulco
24.04.81 Freddie Castillo L PTS 10 Acapulco
26.09.81 Freddie Castillo L PTS 10 Merida
29.01.82 Victor Diaz W CO 8 Acapulco
26.02.82 Jose Segovia W CO 1 Acapulco
23.04.82 Luis Aguilar W RSC 7 Acapulco
26.06.82 Tony Escobar W RSC 7 Mexico City
14.08.82 Gabriel Bernal L CO 5 Mexico City
23.10.82 Jorge M. Vera W CO 1 Mexico City
05.03.83 Rafael Alonso W PTS 10 Mexico City
15.04.83 Elfego Lopez W CO 4 Acapulco
02.06.83 Jimmy Fernandez W RSC 4 Mexico City
10.02.84 Adrian Cortez W RSC 2 Zihuatanejo
31.03.84 Arturo Mujica W RSC 4 Acapulco
01.06.84 Marco A. Benitez W PTS 10 Acapulco
12.10.84 Jose Gallegos W PTS 10 Acapulco
16.11.84 Enrique Aguilar W CO 2 Acapulco
22.06.85 Juan Herrera W RSC 10 Merida
31.01.86 Hilario Zapata L PTS 15 Panama City
(*WBA Flyweight Title Challenge*)
25.07.86 Martin Cardenas W CO 2 Tijuana
30.10.86 Azadin Anhar W CO 4 Torreon
19.12.86 Abner Arauza W CO 1 Acapulco
20.02.87 Orlando Canizales L RSC 9 San Jose
14.07.87 Artemio Ruiz W CO 2 Acapulco
19.09.87 Pedro Rabago W RSC 3 Obregon
28.11.87 Gonzalo Villalobros W PTS 10 Mexico City
25.03.88 Victor Alanis W RSC 6 Acapulco
04.06.88 Ernesto Matta W CO 2 Mazatlan
23.07.88 Juan Herrera W RSC 3 Tijuana
04.10.88 Joey Olivo W CO 1 Tijuana
(*NABF Flyweight Title Challenge*)
17.12.88 Sam Jones W RTD 2 Tijuana
Summary: 39 contests, won 34, lost 5.

Isaias Lucero
La Paz, Mexico
Mexican L. Heavyweight Champion

30.01.87 Javier Pena W CO 1 La Paz
13.03.87 Roque Renteria W CO 3 La Paz
15.05.87 Solomon Orduno W CO 1 La Paz
19.06.87 Ric Alcaraz W CO 1 La Paz
26.07.87 Ernesto Escalante W CO 2 La Paz
28.08.87 Antonio Adame W CO 1 La Paz
19.09.87 Martin Martinez W RSC 3 La Paz
02.10.87 Luciano Sandoval W PTS 10 La Paz
13.11.87 Eusebio Noriega W CO 3 La Paz
26.02.88 Juan Hernandez W PTS 12 La Paz
(*Mexican L. Heavyweight Title Challenge*)
01.05.88 Lorenzo Benitez W CO 4 La Paz
(*Mexican L. Heavyweight Title Defence*)
03.06.88 Manuel Treviso W RSC 7 La Paz
(*Mexican L. Heavyweight Title Defence*)
15.07.88 David Cabrera W CO 7 La Paz
(*Mexican L. Heavyweight Title Defence*)
16.12.88 Juan Hernandez W RSC 10 La Paz
(*Mexican L. Heavyweight Title Defence*)
Summary: 14 contests, won 14.

Mike (The Body Snatcher) McCallum
Jamaica. *Born* 07.12.56
Former Undefeated WBA L. Middleweight Champion

19.02.81 Rigoberto Lopez W RSC 4 Las Vegas
03.03.81 Rocky Fabrizio W RSC 1 Tampa
20.03.81 Ricky Sheppard W RSC 5 Tampa
02.04.81 Shelvy Wikerson W RSC 5 Tampa
24.04.81 Dan Chapman W RSC 4 New York
30.04.81 Charles Smith W RSC 5 Tampa
10.06.81 Freddy Creech W RSC 3 Tampa
19.07.81 Bruce Strauss W RSC 2 Youngstown
27.08.81 Turko Roque W RTD 3 Tampa
08.09.81 Ed Harris W CO 1 Tampa
08.10.81 Jimmy Heair W RSC 2 Tampa
22.01.82 Greg Young W RSC 5 New York
26.03.82 Gilberto Almonte W RSC 1 Kingston
30.04.82 Reggie Ford W CO 4 New York
11.06.82 Kevin Perry W PTS 10 New York
22.10.82 Carlos Betancourt W RSC 3 New York
13.11.82 Ayub Kalule W RSC 7 Atlantic City
26.04.83 Tony Suero W RSC 3 Atlantic City
31.08.83 Jose Vallejo W CO 5 Atlantic City
25.10.83 Manuel Jimenez W PTS 10 Atlantic City
10.03.84 Hasim Razzak W CO 1 Detroit
19.10.84 Sean Mannion W PTS 15 New York
(*Vacant WBA L. Middleweight Title*)
01.12.84 Luigi Minchillo W RSC 14 Milan
(*WBA L. Middleweight Title Defence*)
15.06.85 Marcos Martinez W RSC 2 Las Vegas
28.07.85 David Braxton W RSC 8 Miami
(*WBA L. Middleweight Title Defence*)
02.05.86 James Shavers W RSC 6 Atlantic City
23.08.86 Julian Jackson W RSC 2 Miami
(*WBA L. Middleweight Title Defence*)
15.09.86 Irwin Hines W RSC 3 Paris
25.10.86 Said Skouma W CO 9 Paris
(*WBA L. Middleweight Title Defence*)
21.03.87 Leroy Hester W CO 1 Kingston
19.04.87 Milton McCrory W RSC 10 Phoenix
(*WBA L. Middleweight Title Defence*)
18.07.87 Don Curry W CO 5 Las Vegas
(*WBA L. Middleweight Title Defence*)
05.03.88 Sumbu Kalambay L PTS 12 Pesaro
(*WBA Middleweight Title Challenge*)
27.06.88 David McCluskey W RSC 2 New York
22.12.88 Randy Smith W PTS 8 Paris
09.01.89 Ralph Moncrief W PTS 10 Noget sur Marne
Summary: 36 contests, won 35, lost 1.

Glenn McCrory
Annfield Plain, England. *Born* 23.09.64
Commonwealth Cruiserweight Champion. Former Undefeated British Cruiserweight Champion

06.02.84 Barry Ellis W RSC 1 London
22.02.84 Denroy Bryan W PTS 6 London
21.03.84 Steve Abadom W PTS 6 London
30.04.84 Frank Robinson W PTS 6 London
09.05.84 Frank Robinson W RSC 4 London
13.06.84 Andrew Gerrard W PTS 6 Aberavon
06.09.84 Andrew Gerrard W PTS 8 Gateshead
27.10.84 Tony Velasco W PTS 8 Gateshead
24.11.84 Mike Perkins W PTS 8 Gateshead
19.01.85 Nate Robinson W RSC 2 Birmingham
20.02.85 Alex Williamson W PTS 8 London
27.03.85 Gypsy Carman W PTS 8 Gateshead
28.05.85 Alphonso Forbes W CO 1 London
03.09.85 John Westgarth L CO 4 Gateshead
10.12.85 Roy Skeldon W PTS 8 Gateshead
09.04.86 Rudi Pika L PTS 8 London
18.04.86 Anders Eklund L PTS 8 Randers
17.06.86 Dave Garside L RSC 7 Blackpool
07.10.86 Hughroy Currie L RSC 2 Oldham
25.11.86 Joe Adams W PTS 6 Louisville
08.01.87 Calvin Sherman W CO 1 Houston
05.02.87 Danny Lawford W PTS 8 Newcastle
18.02.87 Barry Ellis W PTS 8 London

Glenn McCrory

Derek Rowe (Photos) Ltd

31.03.87 Andy Straughn W RSC 10 Oldham
04.09.87 Chisanda Mutti W PTS 12 Gateshead
(*Commonwealth Cruiserweight Title Challenge*)
21.01.88 Tee Jay W PTS 12 London
(*British Cruiserweight Title Challenge, Commonwealth Cruiserweight Title Defence*)
22.04.88 Lou Gent W RTD 8 Gateshead
(*British & Commonwealth Cruiserweight Title Defence*)
01.11.88 Ron Warrior W CO 4 Oklahoma City
15.11.88 Lorenzo Boyd W CO 2 Metairie
28.02.89 Steve Mormino W PTS 10 Marton
Summary: 30 contests, won 25, lost 5.

Steve McCrory
Detroit, USA. *Born* 13.04.64
Con. Am. S. Bantamweight Champion

19.10.84 Jeff Hanna W RSC 4 New York
14.11.84 Eddie Rangel W RSC 2 Detroit
04.12.84 Sonny Long W PTS 6 Atlantic City
29.01.85 Vidal Padilla W PTS 6 Phoenix
09.03.85 Louis Gomis DREW 6 Paris
18.04.85 Kenny Butts W PTS 8 Atlantic City
26.05.85 Kerry Allen W PTS 6 Miami
25.07.85 Donnie Parker W PTS 6 Birmingham
15.08.85 Luigi Camputaro W PTS 6 Atlantic City
17.11.85 Lee Cargle W PTS 8 Laughlin
03.12.85 Manuel Martinez W CO 1 Las Vegas
12.03.86 Ralph Gutierrez W PTS 10 Las Vegas
18.07.86 Jeff Fenech L RSC 14 Sydney
(*IBF Bantamweight Title Challenge*)
08.11.86 Jose Sanabria L RSC 5 Stateline
24.02.87 James Tolliver W RSC 5 Detroit
21.03.87 Chris Diaz W PTS 10 Detroit
28.04.87 Ramon Guillen W CO 2 Detroit
19.05.87 Jorge Rodriguez W PTS 10 Detroit
11.06.87 Mike Moreno W PTS 12 Detroit
(*Vacant Con. Am. S. Bantamweight Title*)
18.08.87 Jose Torres W RSC 2 Detroit
27.10.87 Jorge Rodriguez W PTS 10 Detroit
17.11.87 Tony Montoya W CO 7 Detroit
23.02.88 Omar Garcia W RSC 5 Detroit
30.03.88 Julio Blanco W RSC 5 Detroit
23.04.88 Idelfonso Bernal W RSC 2 Detroit
25.05.88 Jose Ramirez W PTS 12 Detroit
(*Con. Am. S. Bantamweight Title Defence*)
23.07.88 Francisco Segura W PTS 10 Detroit
29.09.88 Juan Muriel W PTS 10 New York
17.01.89 Diego Briones W PTS 10 Detroit
16.02.89 Mark Hammon W RSC 6 Detroit
Summary: 30 contests, won 27, drew 1, lost 2.

Seamus McDonagh

Peter Goldfield/USA

Seamus McDonagh
Kiltimagh, Ireland. *Born* 03.12.62
Cruiserweight

10.12.85 Kevin Denson W RSC 2 Atlantic City
22.01.86 Dan Prescott W RSC 3 Atlantic City
15.02.86 Tony Tricker W PTS 4 Dublin
23.06.86 Andre Hayes W RSC 2 New York
24.07.86 Darrell Rister W CO 1 New York
25.09.86 Rocky Cunningham W CO 1 New York
17.10.86 Odell Jones W PTS 6 New York
13.11.86 Gary Coccioletti W RSC 6 New York
29.01.87 Gary Coccioletti W RSC 2 New York
15.04.87 Billy Saunders DREW 8 New York
06.08.87 Willie Barnes W PTS 6 New York
29.10.87 Jack Basting W CO 2 New York
17.03.88 Ray Gonzalez W RSC 7 New York
12.05.88 Mike Peak L PTS 10 New York
14.07.88 Vince Hopper W PTS 10 New York
29.09.88 Greg Gorrell W RSC 2 New York
15.12.88 Tim Tomashek W RSC 1 New York
17.02.89 Don Smith W CO 1 New York
Summary: 18 contests, won 16, drew 1, lost 1.

Jim McDonnell
Stepney, England. *Born* 12.09.60
Former Undefeated EBU Featherweight Champion

22.03.83 Phil Duke W PTS 6 London
05.04.83 Willie Wilson W RSC 3 London
26.04.83 Ray Plant W RSC 3 London
04.10.83 Steve Pollard W RSC 5 London
06.12.83 Alex Irvine W PTS 8 London
23.01.84 Willie Wilson W CO 2 London
06.02.84 Gerry Beard W PTS 8 London
02.04.84 Gerry Beard W PTS 8 London
01.05.84 Keith Foreman W PTS 8 London
13.05.84 Rory Burke W PTS 8 Wembley
13.11.84 Steve Pollard W RSC 6 London
18.01.85 Pat Doherty W PTS 10 London
06.03.85 Haidar Nourredine W RSC 1 London
26.03.85 Clyde Ruan W PTS 10 Wembley
01.10.85 Jeff Roberts W PTS 8 Wembley
05.11.85 Jose Luis Vicho W CO 4 Wembley
(*Vacant EBU Featherweight Title*)
07.05.86 Ruben Palacios W RSC 7 London
19.07.86 Salvatore Bottiglierri W PTS 12 Wembley
(*EBU Featherweight Title Defence*)
04.11.86 Troy Davis W PTS 10 Wembley
24.03.87 Ricky Clements W RSC 5 Wembley
15.05.87 Samuel O'Near W RSC 1 Geneva
25.02.88 Rafael Gandarilla W PTS 10 London
29.03.88 Joel Segura W CO 7 Wembley
04.05.88 Angel Hernandez W PTS 10 Wembley
02.11.88 Brian Mitchell L PTS 12 London
(*WBA S. Featherweight Title Challenge*)
10.03.89 Benji Marquez W PTS 10 Brentwood
Summary: 26 contests, won 25, lost 1.

James (Buddy) McGirt
New York, USA. *Born* 17.01.64
Former IBF L. Welterweight Champion. Former Undefeated Con. Am. L. Welterweight Champion

13.03.82 Lamont Haithcoach DREW 4 Bergen
22.05.82 Michael Palms W RSC 3 Atlantic City
21.09.82 Mike Evans W RSC 1 Bergen
30.09.82 Ray Rivera W CO 1 Totowa
30.12.82 Dave Bolden W CO 5 Bergen
16.02.83 Cesar Guzman W PTS 6 East Rutherford
21.04.83 Tom Dietz W RSC 3 Newark
26.05.83 Darnell Smith W RSC 1 Newark
06.09.83 Les Toney W RSC 1 Atlantic City
30.09.83 Larry Fleming W CO 3 New York
09.12.83 Richard Hernandez W RSC 7 New York
17.02.84 Felix Nance W RSC 2 New York
30.03.84 Jake Torrance W RSC 6 New York
25.05.84 Pete Padilla W RSC 10 New York
12.07.84 Manuel Toribio W CO 3 New York
15.12.84 Felix Nance W RSC 9 Uniondale
08.03.85 Michael Blunt W CO 1 Scranton
24.05.85 Allen Braswell W PTS 10 New York
11.07.85 Ralph Twinning W RSC 1 New York
29.08.85 Willie Rodriguez W RSC 7 New York
04.10.85 Jose Alejandro W RSC 7 New York
21.12.85 Sugar Boy Nando W RSC 5 Miami
(*Vacant Con. Am. L. Welterweight Title*)
21.02.86 Joey Ferrell W PTS 10 Atlantic City
10.03.86 Dave Odem W RSC 1 Uniondale
11.04.86 Kelly Koble W RSC 4 Los Angeles
20.05.86 Ricky Young W RSC 10 New York
23.06.86 Rudy Fuentes W RSC 8 New York
20.07.86 Frankie Warren L PTS 10 Corpus Christi
25.09.86 Saoul Mamby W PTS 10 New York
06.01.87 Joe Edens W RSC 1 Detroit
29.01.87 Eric Martin W PTS 10 New York
24.04.87 Vince Releford W RSC 2 Albany
(*Con. Am. L. Welterweight Title Defence*)
18.06.87 Sergio Aguirre W RSC 2 New York
06.08.87 Roger Brown W RSC 5 New York
01.10.87 Eduardo Lugo W RSC 3 New York
17.12.87 John Senegal W RSC 1 New York
14.02.88 Frankie Warren W RSC 12 Corpus Christi
(*Vacant IBF L. Welterweight Title*)
31.07.88 Howard Davis W CO 1 New York
(*IBF L. Welterweight Title Defence*)
03.09.88 Meldrick Taylor L RSC 12 Atlantic City
(*IBF L. Welterweight Title Defence*)
12.01.89 Manuel de Leon W RSC 6 New York
17.02.89 Willie Taylor W PTS 10 New York
16.03.89 Edwin Curet W PTS 10 New York
Summary: 42 contests, won 39, drew 1, lost 2.

Barry McGuigan
Clones, Ireland. *Born* 28.02.61
Former WBA Featherweight Champion. Former Undefeated British & EBU Featherweight Champion

10.05.81 Selvin Bell W RSC 2 Dublin
20.06.81 Gary Lucas W RSC 4 Wembley
03.08.81 Peter Eubank L PTS 8 Brighton
22.09.81 Jean-Marc Renard W PTS 8 Belfast
26.10.81 Terry Pizzaro W RSC 4 Belfast
08.12.81 Peter Eubanks W RSC 8 Belfast
27.01.82 Luis de la Sagra W PTS 8 Belfast
08.02.82 Ian Murray W RSC 3 London
23.02.82 Angel Oliver W RSC 3 Belfast
23.03.82 Angelo Licata W RTD 2 Belfast
22.04.82 Gary Lucas W CO 1 Enniskillen
14.06.82 Young Ali W CO 6 London
05.10.82 Jimmy Duncan W RTD 4 Belfast
09.11.82 Paul Huggins W RSC 5 Belfast

James McGirt (left) shown winning the vacant IBF light-welterweight title against Frankie Warren, February, 1988

Tom Casino

12.04.83 Vernon Penprase W RSC 2 Belfast
(Vacant British Featherweight Title)
22.05.83 Sammy Meck W RSC 6 Navan
09.07.83 Lavon McGowan W CO 1 Chicago
05.10.83 Ruben Herasme W CO 2 Belfast
16.11.83 Valerio Nati W CO 6 Belfast
(Vacant EBU Featherweight Title)
25.01.84 Charm Chiteule W RSC 10 Belfast
04.04.84 Jose Caba W RSC 7 Belfast
05.06.84 Esteban Eguia W CO 3 London
(EBU Featherweight Title Defence)
30.06.84 Paul de Vorce W RSC 5 Belfast
13.10.84 Felipe Orozco W CO 2 Belfast
19.12.84 Clyde Ruan W CO 4 Belfast
(British & EBU Featherweight Title Defence)
23.02.85 Juan Laporte W PTS 10 Belfast
26.03.85 Farid Gallouze W RTD 2 Wembley
(EBU Featherweight Title Defence)
08.06.85 Eusebio Pedroza W PTS 15 London
(WBA Featherweight Title Challenge)
28.09.85 Bernard Taylor W RTD 8 Belfast
(WBA Featherweight Title Defence)
15.02.86 Danilo Cabrera W RSC 14 Dublin
(WBA Featherweight Title Defence)
23.06.86 Steve Cruz L PTS 15 Las Vegas
(WBA Featherweight Title Defence)
20.04.88 Nicky Perez W RSC 4 London
25.06.88 Francisco Tomas Cruz W RSC 4 Luton
01.12.88 Julio Miranda W RSC 8 London
Summary: 34 contests, won 32, lost 2.

Clinton McKenzie

Derek Rowe (Photos) Ltd

Clinton McKenzie
Croydon, England. *Born* 15.09.55
Former Undefeated British L. Welterweight Champion. Former EBU L. Welterweight Champion

26.10.76 Jimmy King W PTS 8 London
15.11.76 Barton McAllister W PTS 8 London
01.02.77 George McGurk W PTS 8 London
14.02.77 Harry Watson W RTD London
21.03.77 Colin Power L CO 2 London
18.04.77 Al Stewart W RTD 3 London
07.05.77 Fernand Roelandts W PTS 8 Antwerp
10.06.77 Messaoud Bouchachiba W PTS 8 Ghent
05.09.77 Johnny Pincham L PTS 8 London
10.10.77 Kevin Davies W PTS 8 London
03.11.77 Erkki Meronen W RTD 4 Randers
16.01.78 Chris Davies W PTS 12 Nottingham
02.03.78 Mike Everett W PTS 10 Oslo
23.05.78 Chris Walker W PTS 8 London
11.10.78 Jim Montague W RSC 10 Belfast
(Vacant British L. Welterweight Title)
15.12.78 Tony Marty W PTS 8 London
06.02.79 Colin Power L PTS 15 Wembley
(British L. Welterweight Title Defence)
25.02.79 Bruce Curry L PTS 10 Las Vegas
30.04.79 Des Morrison W PTS 12 London
11.09.79 Colin Power W PTS 15 Wembley
(British L. Welterweight Title Challenge)
10.12.79 Roger Guest W PTS 8 London
19.02.80 Roger Guest W PTS 8 London
01.04.80 George Feeney W PTS 10 Wembley
17.04.80 George Peacock W RSC 3 London
12.06.80 Hans-Henrik Palm L PTS 8 Randers
04.07.80 Obisia Nwankpa L PTS 15 Lagos
(Vacant Commonwealth L. Welterweight Title)
27.08.80 Giuseppe Martinese L RTD 10 Senegalia
(Vacant EBU L. Welterweight Title)
06.01.81 Des Morrison W RSC 14 London
(British L. Welterweight Title Defence)
31.03.81 Sylvester Mittee W PTS 15 Wembley
(British L. Welterweight Title Defence)
13.10.81 Antonio Guinaldo W PTS 12 London
(EBU L. Welterweight Title Challenge)
19.02.82 Steve Early W RSC 4 London
(British L. Welterweight Title Defence)
01.06.82 Ernie Bing L DIS 1 London
12.10.82 Robert Gambini L DIS 2 London
(EBU L. Welterweight Title Defence)
09.11.82 Luciano Navarra W RSC 5 London
23.11.82 Memo Arreola W RSC 3 Wembley
08.04.83 Alan Lamb W PTS 12 Liverpool
(British L. Welterweight Title Defence)
26.09.83 Tommy McCallum W CO 4 London
15.01.84 Sammy Young W RSC 7 Atlantic City
30.04.84 Brett Lally W PTS 10 London
19.09.84 Terry Marsh L PTS 12 London
(British L. Welterweight Title Defence)
07.09.85 Lloyd Christie W PTS 10 Isle of Man
04.12.85 Tony Laing L PTS 10 London
06.03.86 Tony Adams W RSC 7 Manchester
07.05.86 Tony Laing L PTS 12 London
(Vacant British L. Welterweight Title)
20.09.86 Tony McKenzie L RSC 3 Hemel Hempstead
(Vacant British L. Welterweight Title)
10.03.88 Chris Blake W PTS 8 Croydon
26.04.88 Ensley Bingham W PTS 8 London
10.12.88 Mike Durvan W PTS 10 London
24.01.89 Lloyd Christie W PTS 12 Kings Heath
(British L. Welterweight Title Challenge)
Summary: 49 contests, won 36, lost 13.

Duke McKenzie
Croydon, England. *Born* 05.05.63
IBF Flyweight Champion. Former Undefeated British & EBU Flyweight Champion

23.11.82 Charlie Brown W RSC 1 Wembley
24.01.83 Andy King W RSC 2 London
27.02.83 Dave Pearson W RSC 1 Las Vegas
03.03.83 Gregorio Hernandez W RSC 3 Los Angeles
19.03.83 Lupe Sanchez W CO 2 Reno
18.10.83 Jerry Davis W RSC 3 Atlantic City
22.11.83 Alain Limarola W PTS 6 Wembley
15.01.84 David Capo W PTS 4 Atlantic City
23.05.84 Gary Roberts W CO 1 London
06.03.85 Julio Guerrero W PTS 8 London
05.06.85 Danny Flynn W RSC 4 London
(Vacant British Flyweight Title)
16.10.85 Orlando Maestre W PTS 8 London
19.02.86 Sonny Long W PTS 10 London
20.05.86 Charlie Magri W RTD 5 Wembley
(British Flyweight Title Defence & EBU Flyweight Title Challenge)
19.11.86 Lee Cargie W PTS 10 Atlantic City
17.12.86 Piero Pinna W PTS 12 Acqui Terme
(EBU Flyweight Title Defence)
24.03.87 Jose Manuel Diaz W PTS 8 Wembley
02.12.87 Juan Herrera W PTS 10 Wembley
09.03.88 Agapito Gomez W CO 2 Wembley
(EBU Flyweight Title Defence)
04.05.88 Jose Gallegos W PTS 10 Wembley
05.10.88 Rolando Bohol W CO 11 Wembley
(IBF Flyweight Title Challenge)
30.11.88 Artemio Ruiz W PTS 10 London
08.03.89 Tony de Luca W RSC 4 London
(IBF Flyweight Title Defence)
Summary: 23 contests, won 23.

Tacy Macalos
San Juan, Philippines. *Born* 28.10.65
IBF L. Flyweight Champion. Former Philippines L. Flyweight Champion

17.02.84 Ariel Samson L PTS 4 Manila
07.03.84 Sonny Altarejos DREW 4 Paranaque
24.03.84 Sammy Baculong DREW 4 Baguio
28.04.84 Ramon Lupasi W PTS 4 Cavite
26.05.84 Sammy Baculong W PTS 4 Baguio
15.06.84 John Calanogan L PTS 4 Manila
18.07.84 Julius Olegaric W PTS 6 Paranaque
01.09.84 Sonny Altarejos DREW 6 Manila
21.09.84 Elmer de Galla W PTS 6 Muntinlupa
13.10.84 Bert Chan W PTS 6 Baguio
04.11.84 Junior Capino W PTS 8 Manila
04.01.85 Joel Advincula W PTS 8 Cavite
30.03.85 Danny Duran W RSC 6 Quezon City
12.05.85 Steve Ponan W PTS 8 Quezon City
29.05.85 Tito Abella W PTS 10 Paranaque
31.08.85 Ed Adame W RSC 5 Paranaque
12.10.85 Lou Marabe W PTS 10 Angeles
02.12.85 Ariel Samson W PTS 10 Pasay
15.03.86 Rolando Protacio W PTS 10 Santos City
16.05.86 Junior Baylon W PTS 10 Angeles
16.07.86 Titing Dignos W RSC 4 Manila
30.10.86 Little Baguio W RSC 8 Olongapo
(Philippines L. Flyweight Title Challenge)
24.01.87 Ronnie Vallescas W PTS 10 Quezon City
29.03.87 Jum-Hwan Choi L PTS 15 Seoul
(IBF L. Flyweight Title Challenge)
04.07.87 Sonny Vidal L RSC 8 Manila
(Philippines L. Flyweight Title Defence)
30.09.87 Leopard Ari W RSC 3 Paranaque
19.12.87 Ranulfo Melencion W RSC 2 Manila
27.03.88 Cesar de la Cruz W RSC 5 Valencia
15.04.88 Rittichai Lukmingkwan W RSC 4 Quezon City
30.07.88 Thanjai Donjaedee W CO 3 Manila
05.11.88 Jum-Hwan Choi W PTS 12 Manila
(IBF L. Flyweight Title Challenge)
04.03.89 Seung-Yap Kang W RSC 4 Manila
Summary: 32 contests, won 25, drew 3, lost 4.

Thulani (Sugar Boy) Malinga
Natal, South Africa. *Born* 11.12.59
Former South African L. Heavyweight Champion. Former Undefeated South African Middleweight Champion

08.08.81 Victor Zulu W RSC 1 Durban
12.09.81 Cyprian Shandu W PTS 4 Durban
30.11.81 Werdie Jacobs W CO 3 Durban
17.04.82 Patrick Tshabalala L PTS 6 Ermelo
05.06.82 Morris Mohloai W PTS 6 Ladysmith
28.08.82 Graham Mdingi W RSC 2 Ladysmith
13.09.82 Shadrack Sithole W CO 2 Pietermaritzburg
04.10.82 David Kalako W PTS 6 Durban
07.02.83 Samson Mohloai W PTS 12 Durban
(Vacant South African Middleweight Title)
27.02.84 John Dlamini W CO 4 Pietermaritzburg
01.05.84 Prince Tukane W PTS 8 Durban
15.06.84 Michael Motsoane W PTS 12 Johannesburg
(South African Middleweight Title Defence)
26.10.84 Mwehu Beya W RSC 6 Johannesburg
15.03.85 Gavin Stirrup W RSC 2 Johannesburg
20.04.85 Robert Madi W RSC 8 Durban
22.06.85 Frankie Decaestecker W RSC 6 Rustenburg
27.07.85 Piet de Bruin W PTS 8 Sun City
14.12.85 Kosie van Vuuren W RSC 11 Durban
(South African Middleweight Title Defence)
08.03.86 Piet de Bruin W RSC 8 Johannesburg
(South African Middleweight Title Defence)
28.06.86 Greg Clark W PTS 12 Johannesburg
(South African Middleweight Title Defence)
19.10.86 Sakkie Horn W PTS 12 Johannesburg
(South African L. Heavyweight Title Challenge)
15.12.86 Fred Rafferty W PTS 12 Durban
(South African L. Heavyweight Title Defence)
09.05.87 Sakki Horn L PTS 12 Pietersburg
(South African L. Heavyweight Title Defence)
18.10.87 Prince Tukane W RSC 6 East London
01.02.88 Harry Cowap W PTS 10 Johannesburg
07.03.88 Jim MacDonald W PTS 10 Orkney
18.07.88 Larry Musgrove W PTS 10 Durban
27.01.89 Graciano Rocchigiani L PTS 12 Berlin
(IBF S. Middleweight Title Challenge)
11.03.89 Mike Peak W PTS 10 Springs
Summary: 29 contests, won 26, lost 3.

Jose Marmolejo
Puerto Pina, Panama. *Born* 12.07.62
Latin American Featherweight Champion

30.04.82 Mario Acosta W PTS 4 Panama City
19.06.82 Juan Perez W PTS 4 Colon
21.08.82 Anibal Moreno W PTS 4 Panama City
20.11.82 Ruben Almillategui W PTS 4 Panama City
21.05.83 Virgilio Barrera L PTS 8 Colon
02.07.83 Jose Meneses L RSC 5 Colon

16.12.83 Humberto Mejias W RSC 3 Panama City
18.02.84 Carlos Pino W PTS 10 Panama City
29.06.84 Francisco Fernandez W PTS 10 Panama City
(*Latin American Featherweight Title Challenge*)
27.10.84 Javier Brown W PTS 10 Panama City
15.12.84 Pedro Gonzalez W RSC 5 Colon
(*Latin American Featherweight Title Defence*)
30.03.85 Hermogenes Prado W CO 3 Colon
03.08.85 Virgilio Barrera W CO 1 Panama City
(*Latin American Featherweight Title Defence*)
14.12.85 Jorge Lujan W PTS 12 Panama City
(*Latin American Featherweight Title Defence*)
18.03.86 Emilio Aponte W RSC 3 Chiriqui
09.08.86 Ernesto Quintana W CO 7 Panama City
13.09.86 Jose Meneses W CO 3 Panama City
21.02.87 Felipe Angulo W PTS 10 Panama City
05.11.88 Antonio Esparragoza L CO 8 Marsala
(*WBA Featherweight Title Challenge*)
Summary: 19 contests, won 16, lost 3.

Mauro Martelli
Lausanne, Switzerland. *Born* 16.04.65
Former Undefeated EBU Welterweight Champion

16.11.84 George Ssonko W PTS 6 Chavannes
26.12.84 Lifetu Basila W CO 3 Berne
26.01.85 Thierry Pierluigi W RSC 2 Chavannes
22.02.85 Bacha Ben Amar W PTS 6 Chavannes
26.03.85 Mohamed Zeroual W PTS 6 Geneva
30.04.85 Karim Ouattara W PTS 6 Geneva
07.06.85 Kid Bello W PTS 8 Lausanne
06.07.85 Idelfonso Martinez W RSC 4 Ascona
29.08.85 Mickey Lerwill W PTS 6 Geneva
18.10.85 Ngindola Engote W PTS 6 Lausanne
02.11.85 Patrick Grisot W PTS 6 Villeneuve
30.11.85 Domenico Ricci W PTS 6 Geneva
29.12.85 Robert Dormoy W RSC 6 Chavannes
09.03.86 Frankie Decaestecker W RTD 5 Chavannes
01.04.86 Rafael Fuentes W RTD 4 Geneva
26.04.86 Abdel Souihi W PTS 8 Berne
30.05.86 Joaquin Velasquez W PTS 5 Geneva
05.07.86 Cliff Gilpin W PTS 8 Ecubens
05.09.86 Franki Moro W PTS 8 Crissier
03.10.86 Rene Jacquot W PTS 10 Geneva
27.10.86 Yvon Segor W RSC 7 Geneva
26.11.86 Pietro Ciarla W CO 7 Martigny
28.12.86 Nazario Mariotti W RSC 8 Chavannes
29.01.87 Martin Camara W PTS 8 Crans Montana
28.02.87 John van Elteren W PTS 8 Lausanne
01.05.87 Kid Taylor W RSC 5 Bulle
15.05.87 Juan Rondon W PTS 8 Geneva
26.06.87 Alfonso Redondo W PTS 12 Geneva
(*EBU Welterweight Title Challenge*)
09.10.87 Erwin Heiber W PTS 12 Morges
(*EBU Welterweight Title Defence*)
27.12.87 Jean-Marie Touati W PTS 12 Martigny
(*EBU Welterweight Title Defence*)
04.03.88 Antoine Fernandez W PTS 12 Geneva
(*EBU Welterweight Title Defence*)
23.04.88 Steve Mitchell W PTS 8 Berck sur Mer
04.06.88 Efisio Galici W PTS 12 Cagliari
(*EBU Welterweight Title Defence*)
14.10.88 Simon Brown L PTS 12 Lausanne
(*IBF Welterweight Title Challenge*)
Summary: 34 contests, won 33, lost 1.

Gerardo Martinez
San Jose, USA. *Born* 18.11.65
NABF Bantamweight Champion

05.12.85 Manuel Medina W PTS 4 San Jose
16.01.86 Rafael Rocha W PTS 4 San Jose
06.03.86 Nick Garcia W PTS 4 San Jose
10.04.86 Hilario Aguilar W PTS 4 San Jose
03.07.86 Bernie Mack W RSC 1 San Jose
13.11.86 Javier Lara W PTS 6 San Jose
11.12.86 Francisco Arevalo W PTS 6 San Jose
20.05.87 Pedro Flores W RSC 4 Oakland
03.06.87 Jesse Alviar W RSC 5 San Jose
10.07.87 Margarito Arreola W PTS 6 Santa Clara
07.08.87 Carlos Manzano W PTS 8 San Jose
28.08.87 Hector Diaz W PTS 10 Santa Clara
05.10.87 Francisco Arevalo W RSC 4 Santa Clara
18.11.87 Jose Luis Gutierrez W CO 1 Oakland
26.02.88 Edel Bernal W RSC 1 Santa Clara
01.04.88 Hector Diaz W RSC 4 Santa Clara
15.07.88 Tim Silva W RTD 6 San Jose
19.08.88 Ron Cisneros W RSC 4 San Jose
30.09.88 Jesus Muniz W RSC 1 Santa Clara
04.11.88 Alberto Martinez W PTS 12 San Francisco
(*Vacant NABF Bantamweight Title*)
10.03.89 Mario Lozano W CO 2 Santa Clara
Summary: 21 contests, won 21.

Mario (Azabache) Martinez
Guadalajara, Mexico. *Born* 15.08.65
S. Featherweight

22.02.80 Juan Cejas W CO 1 Guadalajara
07.03.80 Guillermo Jimenez W RSC 6 Guadalajara
28.03.80 J. Carlos Rubio W CO 1 Guadalajara
06.06.80 Enrique Hernandez W CO 1 Guadalajara
22.06.80 J. Luis Villamar W PTS 10 Guadalajara
11.07.80 Arturo Hernandez W CO 7 Guadalajara
15.08.80 Javier Olmos W PTS 10 Guadalajara
12.09.80 Juan Cordero W PTS 10 Guadalajara
24.10.80 Chamaco Flores W RSC 3 Guadalajara
21.11.80 Arturo Hernandez W RSC 1 Guadalajara
05.12.80 Javier Muniz W PTS 10 Guadalajara
30.01.81 Alfredo Martinez W CO 3 Guadalajara
06.02.81 Tony Escobar W PTS 10 Guadalajara
27.03.81 Lobo Aguilar DREW 10 Vallarta
25.04.81 Felipe Hernandez W PTS 10 Mexico City
06.06.81 Rosendo Alonso L PTS 10 Guadalajara
04.09.81 Jorge Vera W CO 2 Guadalajara
13.11.81 Martin Garcia W RSC 8 Guadalajara
05.02.82 Ambrosio Luna W CO 1 Guadalajara
25.03.82 Artemio Ramirez W PTS 10 Guadalajara
30.04.82 Ubaldo Rivas W PTS 10 Guadalajara
06.08.82 Memo Mayorga W CO 10 Guadalajara
15.11.82 Arturo Hernandez DREW 10 Guadalajara
14.01.83 Gerardo Pena W PTS 10 Guadalajara
11.02.83 Gus Dominguez W PTS 10 Guadalajara
15.04.83 Mauro Gutierrez W PTS 10 Guadalajara
21.05.83 Boni Flores W RSC 6 Mexico City
09.07.83 Miguel Alvarez W PTS 10 Mexico City
02.09.83 Norberto Cabrera W PTS 10 Hermosillo
29.10.83 Justo Garcia W PTS 10 Guadalajara
16.12.83 Ad Zapata W RSC 1 Mazatlan
28.01.84 Rafael Gandarilla W RSC 7 Guadalajara
05.03.84 Kazuo Tanaka W CO 2 Tijuana
26.04.84 Ray Brooks W CO 2 Los Angeles
17.05.84 Roberto Castanon W RSC 6 Los Angeles
23.06.84 Rolando Navarrete W RSC 5 Los Angeles
13.09.84 Julio Cesar Chavez L RSC 8 Los Angeles
(*Vacant WBC S. Featherweight Title*)
17.01.85 Martin Morado W RSC 6 Los Angeles
07.03.85 Frank Newton W PTS 10 Los Angeles
02.05.85 Adrian Arreola W PTS 10 Los Angeles
06.07.85 Miguel Alvarez W RSC 6 Mexicali
15.08.85 Rod Sequenan W PTS 10 Los Angeles
07.11.85 Roger Mayweather L PTS 10 Los Angeles
30.01.86 Leonardo Valdez W RSC 10 Los Angeles
25.05.86 Ramon Marchena W RSC 7 Tijuana
03.07.86 Dana Roston W RSC 7 Los Angeles
12.09.86 Angel Garcia W RSC 6 Chicago
06.02.87 Jimmy Jackson W RSC 3 Los Angeles
09.07.87 Darrell Savoy W RSC 3 Los Angeles
21.08.87 Jorge Gomez W RSC 10 Tijuana
12.11.87 Jose Mosqueda W PTS 10 Los Angeles
29.02.88 Azumah Nelson L PTS 12 Los Angeles
(*Vacant WBC S. Feathereweight Title*)
05.09.88 Betillo Gutierrez W PTS 10 Tijuana
25.02.89 Azumah Nelson L RSC 12 Las Vegas
(*WBC S. Featherweight Title Challenge*)
Summary: 54 contests, won 47, drew 2, lost 5.

Gary Mason
Wandsworth, England. *Born* Jamaica 15.12.62
British Heavyweight Champion

16.10.84 Al Malcom W CO 1 London
14.12.84 Al Malcolm W RSC 2 Wembley
18.01.85 Frank Robinson W RSC 1 London
06.03.85 Luc Goosens W CO 1 London
05.11.85 Steve Gee W RSC 5 Wembley
04.12.85 Steve Gee W RSC 5 London
19.02.86 Denroy Bryan W CO 1 London
04.03.86 Charles Hostetter W RSC 1 Wembley
09.04.86 Louis Pergaud W RTD 4 London
24.04.86 Maurice Gomis W RSC 3 London
20.05.86 Ivy Brown W CO 2 Wembley
19.07.86 Mark Young W CO 5 Wembley
17.09.86 Lorenzo Boyd W CO 2 London
04.11.86 Donny Long W CO 1 Wembley
26.11.86 Oscar Holman W PTS 8 Wolverhampton
22.02.87 Rod Smith W RSC 1 Wembley
24.03.87 Richard Scott W RSC 1 Wembley
18.04.87 Woody Clark W RSC 2 London
26.05.87 Billy Joe Thomas W RSC 2 Wembley
30.08.87 Eddie Richardson W RSC 7 Marbella
25.09.87 Andre van den Oetalaar W CO 2 Southend
24.10.87 Andrew Gerrard W RSC 6 London
03.12.87 Sam Scaff W RSC 2 Southend
03.02.88 Alfonso Ratliff W RSC 6 Wembley
09.03.88 Rickey Parkey W RSC 1 Wembley
13.04.88 Manuel Clay Almedia W RSC 7 London
24.10.88 David Jaco W RSC 4 Windsor
30.11.88 James Tillis W RSC 5 London
18.01.89 Hughroy Currie W CO 4 London
(*Vacant British Heavyweight Title*)
29.03.89 Terry Armstrong W CO 3 Wembley
Summary: 30 contests, won 30.

Walter Masseroni
San Isidro, Argentine. *Born* 28.09.63
Argentinian Heavyweight Champion

16.06.84 Miguel Mosna L PTS 6 Buenos Aires
04.04.86 Jorge Dascola L PTS 8 Rio Tercero
16.05.86 Jorge Dascola L PTS 10 Cordoba
03.07.86 Anibal Perez W PTS 10 Beccar
11.09.87 Julio Lamela W RTD 3 Beccar
23.12.87 Daniel Guibaudo W CO 3 Carupa
22.04.88 Jorge Cambiasso W CO 3 Beccar
(*Argentinian Heavyweight Title Challenge*)
03.06.88 Juan Farias W CO 2 Beccar
12.08.88 Raul Venturelli W CO 1 Beccar
(*Argentinian Heavyweight Title Defence*)
14.10.88 Daniel Guibaudo W CO 3 Beccar
12.12.88 Jose Augusto dos Santos W CO 1 Buenos Aires
21.01.89 Mauricio Villegas W PTS 10 Punta del Este
Summary: 12 contests, won 9, lost 3.

Walter Masseroni

Kenji Matsumura
Takasago, Japan. *Born* 15.02.60
OPBF Flyweight Champion

23.07.85 Shigenobu Nakasama W PTS 6 Takamatsu
29.10.85 Yukinari Oshiro W RSC 3 Osaka
23.01.86 Kentoku Nakama L PTS 10 Tokyo
22.03.86 Masaru Yoshimoto W RSC 9 Himeji
20.05.86 Francisco Montiel L PTS 10 Sendai
25.10.86 Hitoshi Taniuchi W RSC 9 Osaka
23.12.86 Putt Ohyuthanakorn W CO 2 Kakogawa
03.05.87 Tanomsak Singboebae W PTS 12 Kakogawa
(*OPBF Flyweight Title Challenge*)
14.09.87 Elysser Bautista W PTS 12 Himeji
(*OPBF Flyweight Title Defence*)
11.02.88 Cho-Woon Park W PTS 12 Himeji
(*OPBF Flyweight Title Defence*)
26.06.88 Yosuke Matsuoka DREW 10 Himeji
17.10.88 Akio Kawamata W CO 2 Tokyo
(*OPBF Flyweight Title Defence*)
08.04.89 Kaosai Galaxy L PTS 12 Yokohama
(*WBA S. Flyweight Title Challenge*)
Summary: 13 contests, won 9, drew 1, lost 3.

Dario Matteoni
Tigre, Argentine. *Born* 31.08.60
Former Argentinian Middleweight Champion

09.12.83 Eusebio Suarez W CO 5 Vedia
24.03.84 Hector Quintero W RSC 4 Wheelwright
13.04.84 Juan Ledesma W CO 2 Vedia
04.05.84 Hector Lescano W RSC 2 Junin
17.05.84 Juan Ripani DREW 10 Venado Tuerto
22.06.84 Juan Ledesma W RTD 3 Rufino
14.09.84 Carlos Bazan W CO 3 Rio Tercero
09.11.84 Luis Sosa W PTS 10 Calchin
03.05.85 Geronimo Ramirez W RTD 3 Resistencia
20.07.85 Eduardo Contreras W PTS 10 Buenos Aires
26.10.85 Patricio Diaz W RTD 4 Buenos Aires
27.12.85 Carlos Schulz W CO 4 San Salvador
07.02.86 Miguel Maldonado W RTD 5 Mar del Plata
(*Vacant Argentinian Middleweight Title*)
23.05.86 Roberto Iluffi W CO 2 San Juan
22.08.86 Eduardo Contreras W PTS 10 Don Torcuato
22.11.86 Angelo Caro W CO 2 Baradero
(*Argentinian Middleweight Title Defence*)
14.03.87 Hugo Corti W PTS 12 Buenos Aires
(*Argentinian Middleweight Title Defence*)
27.04.87 Ralph Smiley W PTS 10 Paris
07.05.88 Hugo Corti L DIS 6 Boulogne
(*Argentinian Middleweight Title Defence*)
14.10.88 Antonio Galvan W CO 2 Beccar
12.12.88 Julio Gonzales W CO 3 Buenos Aires
21.01.89 Jose da Silva W CO 5 Punta del Este
Summary: 22 contests, won 20, drew 1, lost 1.

Jorge Maysonet
Catano, Puerto Rico. *Born* 13.02.64
Welterweight

06.10.84 Danny Garcia W RSC 4 Carolina
01.12.84 Juan Lebron W RSC 1 Catano
31.01.85 Elvin Pena W RSC 1 Santiago
09.03.85 Carlos Velez W RSC 3 Catano
22.06.85 Cesar Pinales W RSC 1 Catano
25.07.85 Jose Alejandro L PTS 4 New York
05.10.85 Hector Santiago W CO 2 Guaynabo
01.03.86 Cesar Pinales W CO 2 Barceloneta
07.06.86 Jose Tejeda W RSC 8 San Juan
02.08.86 Charles Baez W RSC 1 San Juan
06.09.86 Cirilo Morel W RSC 2 San Juan
21.02.87 Joe Alexander W RSC 9 San Juan
25.04.87 Danny Garcia L RSC 3 San Juan
08.08.87 Ivan Montalvo W CO 5 San Juan
03.09.87 Jose Benitez W RSC 5 San Juan
25.03.88 Mohammed Kawoya W RTD 6 New York
28.04.88 Hugh Kearney W RSC 1 Philadelphia
16.06.88 Milton Leaks W CO 1 Philadelphia
15.09.88 Sammy Rivera W RSC 5 Philadelphia
06.12.88 Khalif Shabazz W RSC 4 Philadelphia
18.02.89 Simon Brown L RSC 3 Budapest
(*IBF Welterweight Title Challenge*)
Summary: 21 contests, won 18, lost 3.

Jorge Maysonet

Peter Goldfield/USA

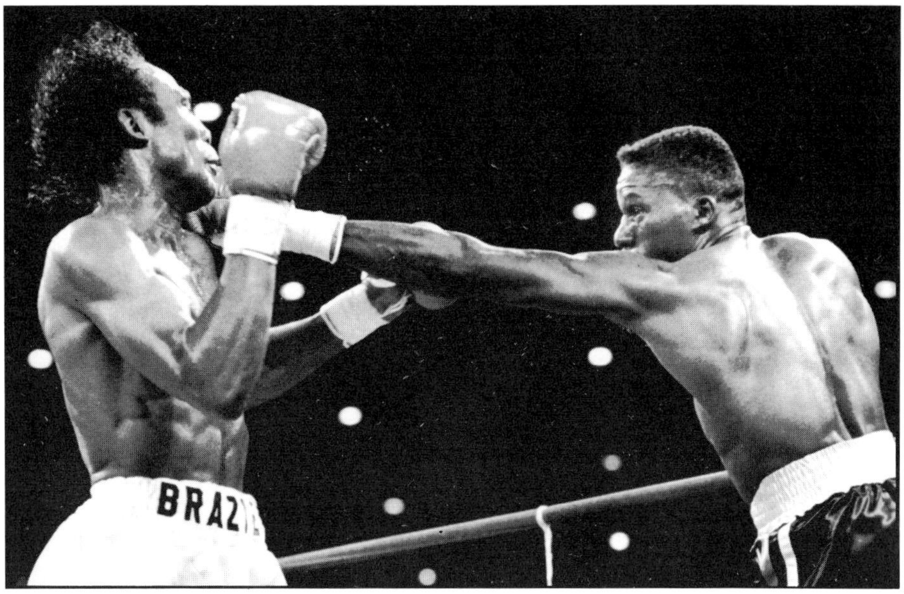

Roger Mayweather (right) outscores Harold Brazier, June, 1988

Tom Casino

Roger (Black Mamba) Mayweather
Grand Rapids, USA. *Born* 24.04.61
WBC L. Welterweight Champion. Former Undefeated Con. Am. Lightweight Champion. Former WBA S. Featherweight Champion. Former Undefeated USBA S. Featherweight Champion

29.07.81 Andrew Ruiz W RSC 1 Las Vegas
05.08.81 Jaime Nava W PTS 8 Las Vegas
24.09.81 Javier Benitez W RSC 5 Las Vegas
21.10.81 Juan Hernandez W PTS 6 Las Vegas
07.11.81 Vinnie Hines W RSC 2 Las Vegas
14.11.81 Adrian Arreola W RSC 6 Las Vegas
24.01.82 Roberto Garcia W RSC 3 Las Vegas
03.04.82 Jimmy Blevins W PTS 10 Las Vegas
27.05.82 Kelvin Lampkin W PTS 10 Las Vegas
29.07.82 Carlton Sparrow W CO 4 Las Vegas
18.08.82 Arturo Leon W PTS 10 Las Vegas
29.09.82 Frankie Moultrie W RSC 9 Las Vegas
23.10.82 Ruben Munoz W PTS 12 Atlantic City
(*USBA S. Featherweight Title Challenge*)
17.11.82 Elmer Suttington W RSC 2 St Joseph
19.01.83 Sam Serrano W CO 8 San Juan
(*WBA S. Featherweight Title Challenge*)
20.04.83 Jorge Alvarado W RSC 8 San Jose
(*WBA S. Featherweight Title Defence*)
17.08.83 Benedicto Villablanca W CO 1 Las Vegas
(*WBA S. Featherweight Title Defence*)
26.02.84 Rocky Lockridge L CO 1 Beaumont
(*WBA S. Featherweight Title Defence*)
08.07.84 Tony Baltazar L PTS 10 Los Angeles
22.09.84 Efren Nieves W PTS 10 Grand Rapids
21.11.84 Martin Quiroz W RSC 3 Las Vegas
28.02.85 Billy White W RSC 5 Las Vegas
12.05.85 Kenny Baysmore W RSC 3 Tyler
(*USBA S. Featherweight Title Challenge*)
07.07.85 Julio Cesar Chavez L RSC 2 Las Vegas
(*WBC S. Featherweight Title Challenge*)
07.11.85 Mario Martinez W PTS 10 Los Angeles
15.01.86 Walter Sims W PTS 10 Las Vegas
12.03.86 Fred Pendleton L RSC 6 Las Vegas
03.07.86 Oscar Bejinez W RTD 8 Los Angeles
07.08.86 Sergio Zambrano W RTD 6 Los Angeles
28.11.86 Sammy Fuentes W RSC 9 Atlantic City
(*Vacant Con. Am. Lightweight Title*)
28.03.87 Pernell Whitaker L PTS Norfolk
(*Vacant NABF Lightweight Title*)
14.05.87 Frankie Davis W RSC 4 Las Vegas
14.07.87 Mitchell Julien W RSC 3 Las Vegas
12.11.87 Rene Arredondo W RSC 6 Los Angeles
(*WBC L. Welterweight Title Challenge*)
05.01.88 Marvin Garris W RSC 7 Las Vegas
24.03.88 Mauricio Aceves W CO 3 Los Angeles
(*WBC L. Welterweight Title Defence*)
06.06.88 Harold Brazier W PTS 12 Las Vegas
(*WBC L. Welterweight Title Defence*)
22.09.88 Rodolfo Gonzalez W RSC 12 Los Angeles
(*WBC L. Welterweight Title Defence*)
07.11.88 Vinny Pazienza W PTS 12 Las Vegas
(*WBC L. Welterweight Title Defence*)
Summary: 39 contests, won 34, lost 5.

Raymond Medel
San Antonio, USA. *Born* 27.09.67
USBA S. Flyweight Champion. Former Undefeated USBA Flyweight Champion.

11.12.84 Ruben Flores W CO 1 San Antonio
06.02.85 Leo Alvarado W PTS 4 San Antonio
26.02.85 Rolando Gomez L PTS 4 Corpus Christi
09.04.85 Nelson Garcia W PTS 4 San Antonio
27.06.85 Juan Diaz W PTS 8 San Antonio
10.09.85 Polo Saucedo W RSC 5 San Antonio
25.09.85 John Vasquez W PTS 6 Corpus Christi
12.12.85 Gabriel Bernal L PTS 10 Houston
03.04.86 Mike Phelps L PTS 12 Beaumont
24.06.86 Armando Velasco W PTS 10 San Antonio
16.09.86 Azadin Anhar W PTS 10 San Antonio
08.02.87 Henry Brent W RSC 8 San Antonio
(*USBA Flyweight Title Challenge*)
01.05.87 Richard Abila W PTS 10 San Antonio
19.07.87 Obed Munoz W CO 5 San Antonio
10.11.87 Homero Aguilar W RSC 10 San Antonio
(*USBA Flyweight Title Defence*)
10.04.88 Pop Robinson W PTS 8 Atlantic City
17.06.88 Paul Gonzales W PTS 12 San Antonio
(*USBA Flyweight Title Defence*)
02.10.88 Fidel Bassa L PTS 12 San Antonio
(*WBA Flyweight Title Challenge*)
23.11.88 Mauro Diaz W PTS 12 Tucson
(*Vacant USBA S. Flyweight Title*)
28.04.89 Simon Contreras W RSC 2 Tucson
Summary: 20 contests, won 16, lost 4.

John Meekins
New York, USA. *Born* 19.05.65
L. Welterweight

19.10.84 Carlos Ruiz W RSC 1 New York
14.11.84 Murray Frazier W CO 3 Atlantic City
27.12.84 Melvin Richardson W RSC 3 Atlantic City
14.02.85 John Rafuse W RSC 6 Atlantic City
07.03.85 Roger Brown W RSC 3 Atlantic City
02.05.85 Jose Alejandro W CO 3 Atlantic City
05.06.85 Ozzie O'Neal W RSC 7 Atlantic City
15.08.85 Sammy Young W RSC 3 Atlantic City
18.09.85 Joey Ferrell W PTS 10 Atlantic City
11.12.85 Martin Quiroz T DRAW 1 Atlantic City
24.01.86 Juan Santana W PTS 10 Atlantic City
21.03.86 Grant Walters W RTD 6 Atlantic City
01.08.86 Davey Montana W RSC 1 Atlantic City
05.09.86 Harold Brazier T DRAW 2 Atlantic City
(*Vacant NABF L. Welterweight Title*)
09.12.86 George Leach W RSC 5 Atlantic City
24.02.87 Harold Brazier L PTS 12 Atlantic City
(*NABF L. Welterweight Title Challenge*)
17.04.87 Sergio Aguirre W RSC 3 Atlantic City
23.06.87 Robert Guy W PTS 10 Atlantic City
18.09.87 Howard Stewart W CO 9 Atlantic City
15.01.88 Othal Dixon W RSC 2 Atlantic City
19.05.88 Mike Mungin W PTS 10 Atlantic City
05.08.88 Mohammed Kawoya W RSC 3 Atlantic City

11.10.88 Saoul Mamby W PTS 10 Atlantic City
21.01.89 Meldrick Taylor L RSC 7 Atlantic City
(IBF L. Welterweight Title Challenge)
Summary: 24 contests, won 20, drew 2, lost 2.

Mario Melo
General Piran, Argentine. *Born* 11.02.62
Argentinian L. Heavyweight Champion

16.06.84 Carlos Galli W RTD 4 General Madariaga
06.07.84 Nestor Giovannini W PTS 6 Morteros
03.11.84 Nestor Giovannini L PTS 6 Buenos Aires
22.02.85 Ramon Geremias W CO 2 Pinamar
18.05.85 Nestor Giovannini W RSC 5 Buenos Aires
08.06.85 Miguel Mosna W RSC 2 Buenos Aires
08.07.85 Mario Campos W CO 1 General Madariaga
10.08.85 Sergio Merani L PTS 10 General Madariaga
16.11.85 Miguel Mosna L RTD 8 General Madariaga
20.09.86 Luis Alvarado W CO 2 Pico Truncado
07.01.87 Daniel Gonzalez W CO 2 Mar de Ajo
20.02.87 Joao Tavares W RSC 2 Mar de Ajo
15.05.87 Alberto Barragan W CO 1 Concepcion
21.06.87 Paul Muyodi L CO 3 Spoleto
07.11.87 Angel Caro W RTD 2 General Madariaga
05.12.87 Juan Rodriguez W CO 1 General Piran
27.02.88 Ed Contreras W RTD 4 Pinamar
26.03.88 Sergio Merani W CO 9 General Madariaga
05.08.88 Miguel Mosna W CO 3 Pica Truncado
(Vacant Argentinian L. Heavyweight Title)
17.09.88 Anibal Perez W CO 1 General Madariaga
08.04.89 Daniel Guibaudo W DIS 4 De Mayo
Summary: 21 contests, won 17, lost 4.

Santiago Mendez
Yucatan, Mexico. *Born* 28.07.63
M. Flyweight

18.06.80 Jorge Rejon DREW 4 Izamal
12.01.81 Francisco Cancha W PTS 4 Izamal
02.05.81 Huracan Sandoval W RSC 4 Quintana Roo
20.06.81 Freddy Santos W PTS 4 Cozumel
18.07.81 Jesus Rivera W PTS 4 Cozumel
12.09.81 Juan Cano W RSC 8 Cozumel
14.11.81 Carlos Medina W PTS 8 Cozumel
19.12.81 Javier Alonso W PTS 6 Merida
20.01.82 Fernando Varguez W RSC 7 Merida
17.02.82 Javier Alonso W RSC 5 Merida
21.04.82 Valerio Olivares W CO 10 Merida
02.06.82 Baby Luis L RSC 10 Merida
04.08.82 Rodolfo Alvarado W RSC 10 Merida
11.09.82 Javier Varguez L PTS 10 Cancun
28.11.82 Pastor Brito W PTS 10 Cancun
16.12.82 Rosendo Ake W PTS 10 Merida
08.04.83 Carlos Reyes W CO 10 Chetumal
25.06.83 Baby Luis L PTS 12 Merida
13.08.83 Rodolfo Alvarado L PTS 10 Cancun
28.09.83 Rodolfo Alvarado L RSC 10 Merida
16.12.83 Javier Guerrero W PTS 10 Chetumal
03.02.84 Antonio Lopez W RSC 6 Chetumal
16.05.84 Raul Dominguez W CO 4 Mexico City
27.09.84 Gilberto Sosa W CO 1 Mexico City
27.10.84 Fernando Varguez W PTS 10 Merida
02.02.85 Emilio Santos W PTS 10 Mexico City
21.04.85 Wilibaldo Salazar W RSC 5 Merida
25.05.85 Hilario Duran L PTS 10 Mexico City
18.08.85 Ismael Benitez W PTS 10 Mexico City
28.09.85 Pedro Moreno W PTS 10 Merida
30.11.85 Hilario Duran W PTS 10 Merida
01.03.86 Javier Guerrero L PTS 10 Mexico City
10.05.86 Javier Alonso W PTS 10 Mexico City
26.07.86 Luis Hernandez W RSC 8 Mexico City
18.10.86 Memo Flores W RSC 6 Mexico City
06.12.86 Emilio Santos L PTS 10 Mexico City
07.03.87 German Torres L PTS 10 Mexico City
13.06.87 Humberto Gonzalez L RSC 8 Mexico City
14.08.87 Jorge Rivera L PTS 10 Chetumal
26.09.87 Javier Alonso W PTS 10 Merida
14.11.87 Luis Hernandez W PTS 10 Cancun
30.01.88 Justo Zuniga W PTS 10 Merida
30.04.88 Evaristo Morales W CO 2 Merida
11.06.88 Javier Guerrero W PTS 10 Merida
19.11.88 Evaristo Morales W RTD 3 Chetumal
18.02.89 Javier Varguez L RSC 12 Merida
(Mexican L. Flyweight Title Challenge)
29.04.89 Raul Acosta W PTS 10 Merida
Summary: 47 contests, won 34, drew 1, lost 12.

Luis (Chicanero) Mendoza
San Onofre, Colombia. *Born* 1965
Former Undefeated Colombian Bantamweight & S. Bantamweight Champion

02.02.85 Luis Berrio W PTS 6 Cartagena
29.03.85 Onofre Valiente W CO 4 Cartagena
21.04.85 Valerio Zea W PTS 10 Cartagena
15.11.85 Darryl Pinckney W RSC 1 Miami
03.12.85 Luis Monzote W PTS 6 Miami
13.12.85 Jesse Williams L PTS 6 Miami
15.02.86 Tomas Maza W CO 4 San Andres
14.06.86 Ezequiel Hernandez W PTS 8 San Andres
05.07.86 Manuel Salgado W PTS 6 Cartagena
18.07.86 Alejandro Pastrana W CO 1 San Andres
12.09.86 Albeiro Arboleda W RSC 6 Cartagena
03.10.86 Miguel Ariza W CO 1 Cartagena
(Vacant Colombian Bantamweight Title)
31.10.86 Gustavo Zabala W RSC 9 Monteria
(Colombian Bantamweight Title Defence)
21.12.86 Ezequiel Hernandez W PTS 10 Cartagena
20.02.87 Alirio Macias W CO 2 Cartagena
13.03.87 Rafael Martinez W CO 1 Cartagena
03.04.87 Eduo Bermudez W CO 3 Cartagena
15.05.87 Moises Fuentes W PTS 10 Cartagena
(Colombian S. Bantamweight Title Challenge)
31.07.87 Gilberto Barcenas W CO 4 San Andres
04.09.87 Daniel Blanco W PTS 10 Cartagena
11.12.87 Enrique Sanchez W PTS 10 Cartagena
26.02.88 Miguel Maturana W RTD 4 Cartagena
03.09.88 Jaime Castellon W RTD 3 Cartagena
30.09.88 Salatiel Palacio W CO 2 Cartagena
23.12.88 Enrique Sanchez W PTS 10 Cartagena
18.02.89 Manuel Vilchez W PTS 10 Cartagena
15.04.89 Azael Moran W PTS 10 Barranquilla
Summary: 27 contests, won 26, lost 1.

Sergio Merani
Villa Maria, Argentine. *Born* 30.07.62
L. Heavyweight

20.07.84 Miguel Mosna W PTS 6 Villa Maria
16.11.84 Guarino Carraro W PTS 6 Villa Maria
14.12.84 Guarino Carraro W PTS 8 Tancacha
22.02.85 Anibal Romero W PTS 8 Tio Pujio
08.03.85 Marcos Perez W CO 1 Pozo del Molle
10.08.85 Mario Melo W PTS 10 General Madariaga
05.10.85 Nestor Giovannini DREW 8 Buenos Aires
08.03.86 Miguel Mosna DREW 10 General Madariaga
15.08.86 Jose Helguera W PTS 10 Tucuman
23.12.86 Victor Robledo W PTS 10 Cordoba
15.05.87 Ed Contreras W RTD 6 Rivadavia
28.10.87 Joe Lasisi L CO 2 Las Vegas
26.03.88 Mario Melo L RSC 9 General Madariaga
06.05.88 Walter Bustos W CO 1 Tio Pujio
24.06.88 Victor Robledo W CO 3 Heranado
08.07.88 Rodrigo Benech W PTS 10 Paysandu
05.08.88 Julio Lamela W CO 4 Tio Pujio
09.09.88 Enrique Coronel W RTD 4 Rio Tercero
07.10.88 Emmanuel Brites W CO 2 Villa Maria
19.11.88 Miguel Mosna W PTS 10 Buenos Aires
10.02.89 Marcel Figueroa W PTS 10 Mar del Plata
Summary: 21 contests, won 17, drew 2, lost 2.

Bernardo Mercado
Cartagena, Colombia. *Born* 16.07.53
Former Undefeated Con. Am. Heavyweight Champion

15.11.75 Henry Washington W CO 1 Los Angeles
11.12.75 Ken Charles W CO 1 Los Angeles
08.01.76 Marv Johnson W CO 1 Los Angeles
12.02.76 David Martinez W RSC 3 Los Angeles
26.02.76 Mark White W CO 1 Reno
13.05.76 Manuel Ramos W CO 5 Albuquerque
19.08.76 Johnny Mac W PTS 8 Reno
22.09.76 Bob Smith W RSC 1 Las Vegas
28.09.76 James J. Woody W RSC 3 New York
06.10.76 Earl McLeary W RSC 4 Lake Tahoe
13.10.76 Dan Johnson W RSC 5 Las Vegas
03.11.76 John Poucha W CO 2 Las Vegas
15.02.77 King Solomon W CO 1 Sacramento
10.03.77 Dan Johnson W RSC 7 Los Angeles
29.04.77 Randy Stephens W CO 1 Fort Worth
11.05.77 Horace Robinson W PTS 6 New York
24.07.77 Bud Smith W CO 2 Cartagena
30.09.77 Roger Russell W CO 1 New York
18.11.77 Fili Moala W RSC 8 Las Vegas
25.02.78 Horace Robinson W PTS 10 Las Vegas
23.06.78 John Tate L RSC 2 New York
22.10.78 Mike Weaver L RSC 5 Reno
14.02.79 Tony Pulu W CO 8 Salt Lake City
03.04.79 Trevor Berbick W CO 1 Halifax
25.05.79 Fili Moala W RSC 5 San Diego
03.08.79 Henry Clark W PTS 10 Santa Monica
02.02.80 Tony Pulu W CO 8 Salt Lake City
14.08.80 Tom Prater W RSC 12 Bogota
(Vacant Con. Am. Heavyweight Title)
02.10.80 Leon Spinks L RSC 9 Las Vegas
13.06.81 Gilberto Acuna W RSC 1 Miami
06.11.81 Randy Cobb L PTS 10 Pittsburgh
07.05.83 Fernando Montes W RSC 5 Cartagena
04.09.86 Fernando Montes W RSC 4 Cartagena
06.11.86 Jose Gonzalez W CO 1 Los Angeles
28.05.88 Conroy Nelson W PTS 8 Saskatoon
02.08.88 Wes Smith W CO 4 Oklahoma City
13.08.88 Wesley Watson W RSC 1 Bristol
Summary: 37 contests, won 33, lost 4.

Bernardo Mercado

Peter Goldfield/USA

Miguel Mercedes
La Romana, Dominican Republic. *Born* 14.05.60
Fecarbox Flyweight Champion

.83 Juan Sierra L PTS 6 Santiago
03.03.83 Alex Silva W CO 4 Los Angeles
12.07.84 Jose Diaz W CO 4 Los Angeles
13.09.84 Tony Flores W RSC 5 Los Angeles
17.11.84 Tony Escobar W PTS 10 Los Angeles
27.05.85 Yoshi Kurashita W RSC 5 Tokyo
05.12.85 Rae-Ki Ahn L PTS 10 Seoul
11.10.86 Armando Velasco W RSC 3 Mexico City
15.11.86 Alvaro Mercado W CO 2 Barranquilla
(Vacant Fecarbox Flyweight Title)
30.01.87 Carlos Diaz W CO 5 La Romana
18.06.87 Manuel Trujillo W CO 2 Los Angeles
12.11.87 Javier Diaz W PTS 10 Los Angeles
29.05.88 Yul-Woo Lee W PTS 10 Youchon
03.03.89 Elvis Alvarez L PTS 12 Medellin
(Vacant WBO Flyweight Title)
Summary: 14 contests, won 11, lost 3.

Nate Miller

Peter Goldfield/USA

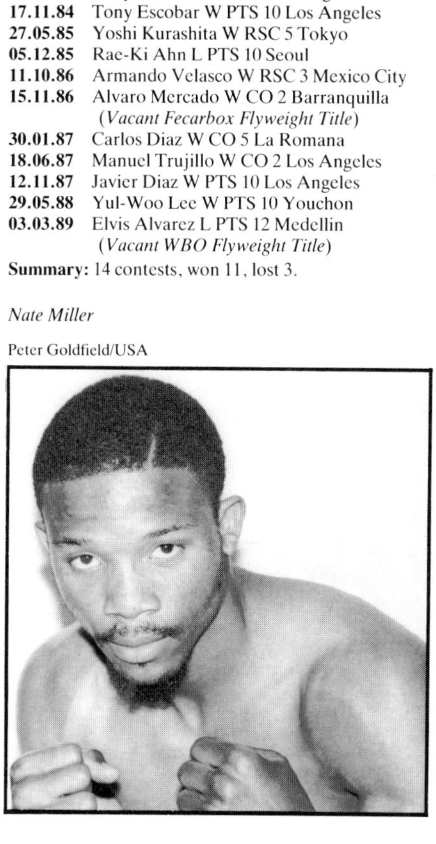

Nate Miller
Philadelphia, USA. *Born* 1963
NABF Cruiserweight Champion

30.09.86 Tony Jackson W RSC 1 Philadelphia
27.01.87 Harry Savage W CO 1 Philadelphia
10.02.87 Johnny Williams W RSC 2 Philadelphia
31.03.87 Ricardo Spain W PTS 6 Philadelphia
11.06.87 George Wilson W RSC 1 Philadelphia
01.08.87 Harry Savage W RSC 1 Philadelphia
15.09.87 Dawud Shaw W RSC 2 Philadelphia
11.11.87 Stanley Ross W RSC 5 Philadelphia
08.12.87 Woody Clark W RSC 6 Philadelphia
15.03.88 Ricardo Spain W RSC 2 Philadelphia
19.05.88 Tim Bullock W TD 5 Philadelphia
14.07.88 Lionel Byarm W RSC 2 Philadelphia
16.08.88 Mike Fisher W RSC 7 Philadelphia
21.10.88 Sriki Sanogo L PTS 8 Bordeaux
15.02.89 Bert Cooper W RTD 6 Philadelphia
(*NABF Cruiserweight Title Challenge*)
Summary: 15 contests, won 14, lost 1.

Yung-Chun Min
Chung-Buk, South Korea. *Born* 10.07.68
OPBF Bantamweight Champion

12.12.86 Kyung-Min Oh W PTS 4 Seoul
14.12.86 Dong-Jae Cho W CO 2 Seoul
28.12.86 Yong-Nam Lee W RSC 3 Seoul
22.02.87 Taira Takayuki W CO 2 Seoul
14.03.87 Chun-Hyun Kim W CO 1 Chunchon
17.05.87 Jae-Sun Lim W PTS 8 Busan
16.08.87 Sang-Sok Bang W CO 3 Mokpo
31.10.87 Tae-Sang Chun W CO 2 Jochiwon
27.03.88 Frank Cedeno W RSC 5 Seoul
10.07.88 Dae-Yong Park W RSC 6 Seoul
21.08.88 Kid Tavera W CO 4 Seoul
04.12.88 Luis Espinosa W PTS 10 Kwangju
01.03.89 Dangnuen Kiat Ro W TD 5 Seoul
(*Vacant OPBF Bantamweight Title*)
Summary: 13 contests, won 13.

Frankie Minton

Peter Goldfield/USA

Frankie Minton
Indianapolis, USA. *Born* 04.06.64
L. Heavyweight

29.01.83 Dennis Johnson W PTS 4 Atlantic City
07.04.83 Speedy Brown W RSC 4 Atlantic City
19.05.83 Melvin Epps W PTS 4 Atlantic City
14.06.83 Arthur Ratliff W CO 1 Indianapolis
18.08.83 Iran Barkley L RSC 5 Atlantic City
26.10.83 Akbar Abdullah W RSC 3 St Paul
29.10.83 Ken Bentley W CO 1 Fort Payne
05.11.83 Robert Thomas W PTS 4 Atlantic City
07.02.84 James Wilder W PTS 4 Highland
10.04.84 Tim Anderson W RSC 4 Highland
14.04.84 Orlando Paulding W RSC 4 Tuscaloosa
23.10.84 John Cox W PTS 6 Highland
13.12.84 Rico Ricardo W CO 3 Merrillville
14.02.85 Willie Featherstone L PTS 8 Toronto
30.07.85 James Kinchen L RSC 9 Atlantic City
17.12.85 Bryan Muller L RTD 3 Los Angeles
09.02.86 Danny Blake W PTS 8 Indianapolis
21.06.86 Greg McPherson W CO 4 Chicago
11.07.86 James Kinchen L CO 7 Las Vegas
03.10.86 Gary Thomas W PTS 6 Louisville
17.10.86 James Shavers W PTS 8 Bismark
02.12.86 Henry Milligan W RSC 4 Atlantic City
16.05.87 Jesse Abrams W PTS 6 Newcastle
14.08.87 Art Baylis W PTS 8 Atlantic City
11.09.87 Ben Judah W RSC 2 Davenport
06.11.87 Guy Waters DREW 10 Hobart
28.07.88 Tony Willis L RSC 2 Las Vegas
(*NABF L. Heavyweight Title Challenge*)
Summary: 27 contests, won 20, drew 1, lost 6.

Ray Minus
Bahamas. *Born* 03.07.64
Commonwealth Bantamweight Champion. Former Con. Am. Bantamweight Champion

18.06.82 Angel Torres W RSC 1 Nassau
19.11.82 Cornbread Williams L PTS 6 Freeport
25.02.83 Cornbread Williams W RSC 3 Nassau
30.04.83 Keith Cameron W RSC 2 Nassau
27.05.83 Sal Garcia DREW 6 Nassau
01.07.83 Terry Pizzaro W RSC 6 Nassau
02.09.83 Robert Mullins W RSC 8 Nassau
16.10.83 Osvaldo Acevedo W RTD 7 Nassau
23.12.83 Ron Garret W CO 2 Nassau
02.03.84 Edgar Acevedo W PTS 10 Nassau
31.03.84 Al Adger W CO 1 Nassau
18.05.84 Ray Garza W RSC 10 Freeport
29.06.84 Osvaldo Acevedo W PTS 10 Miami
28.07.84 Eddie Gonzales W CO 6 Nassau
28.09.84 Peter Harris W PTS 10 Nassau
30.11.84 Steve Guess W CO 1 Nassau
22.12.84 Juan Salazar W CO 8 Nassau
08.03.85 Kelvin Seabrooks W CO 3 Nassau
04.04.85 Keith Wallace W RSC 4 Digbeth
17.05.85 Alberto Cruz W CO 2 Nassau
12.07.85 Juan Castellanos W PTS 10 Nassau
09.08.85 Jose Mosqueda NC 4 Nassau
24.09.85 Sam David L CO 12 Atlantic City
(*Vacant Con. Am. Bantamweight Title*)
27.09.86 Paul Ferreri W RTD 10 Nassau
(*Vacant Commonwealth Bantamweight Title*)
06.03.87 Prudencio Cardona W PTS 10 Nassau
01.07.87 Sean Murphy W RSC 5 London
(*Commonwealth Bantamweight Title Defence*)
27.11.87 Miguel Lora L PTS 12 Miami
(*WBC Bantamweight Title Challenge*)
30.01.88 Enrique Sanchez W PTS 12 Nassau
(*Vacant Con. Am Bantamweight Title*)
30.04.88 Morgan Maphosa W CO 3 Nassau
(*Vacant Commonwealth Bantamweight Title*)
25.11.88 Jose Valdez L CO 8 Nassau
(*Con. Am. Bantamweight Title Defence*)
10.03.89 Mike Parris W PTS 12 Nassau
(*Commonwealth Bantamweight Title Defence*)
Summary: 31 contests, won 25, drew 1, lost 4, no contest 1.

Brian Mitchell
South Africa. *Born* 30.08.61
WBA S. Featherweight Champion. Former Undefeated South African S. Featherweight Champion

15.08.81 Josef Monoane W PTS 4 Johannesburg
19.09.81 Bushy Mosoeu W PTS 4 Johannesburg
03.10.81 Tandi Mayisela W PTS 4 Johannesburg
31.10.81 Simon Zondo W RSC 4 Johannesburg
30.11.81 Moses Mthiyane W RSC 4 Durban
06.02.82 Phanuel Mosdane W RSC 2 Johannesburg
01.05.82 Jacob Morake L PTS 10 Kwa Thema
17.05.82 Joseph Tsotetsi W PTS 6 Johannesburg
26.06.82 Moses Sithebe W RSC 3 Orkney
30.07.82 Frank Khonkhobe DREW 6 Sebokeng
15.10.82 Frank Khonkhobe W PTS 10 Diepkloof
14.05.83 Jerome Gumede W PTS 8 Durban
09.04.83 Chris Whiteboy W RSC 9 Orkney
(*South African S. Featherweight Title Challenge*)
02.05.83 Bashew Sibaca W PTS 10 Durban
27.06.83 Graham Gcola W CO 2 Johannesburg
(*South African S. Featherweight Title Defence*)
06.08.83 Jacob Morake W PTS 12 Johannesburg
(*South African S. Featherweight Title Defence*)
21.11.83 Frank Khonkhobe W PTS 12 Johannesburg
(*South African S. Featherweight Title Defence*)
19.12.83 Blessing Ndlele W RSC 1 Durban
02.03.84 Jacob Morake W PTS 12 Springs
(*South African S. Featherweight Title Defence*)
31.03.84 Carlos Rodriguez W RSC 4 Johannesburg
16.04.84 Iland Matthews W PTS 6 Welkom
02.08.84 Nika Khumalo W CO 2 Cape Town
(*South African S. Featherweight Title Defence*)
01.12.84 Aladin Stevens W PTS 8 Sun City
11.02.85 Nyingi Mtya W RSC 3 Boksburg
30.03.85 Carlos Rodriquez W RSC 7 Sun City
27.04.85 Vicente Jorge W RSC 7 Johannesburg
27.07.85 Job Sisanga W PTS 8 Sun City
02.11.85 Jacob Morake W RSC 12 Sun City
(*South African S. Featherweight Title Defence*)
01.03.86 Julio Ruiz W CO 6 Sun City
14.06.86 Bushy Mosoeu W PTS 12 Sun City
(*South African S. Featherweight Title Defence*)
27.09.86 Alfredo Layne W RSC 10 Sun City
(*WBA S. Featherweight Title Challenge*)
27.03.87 Jose Rivera DREW 15 San Juan
(*WBA S. Featherweight Title Defence*)
16.05.87 Aurelio Benitez W RSC 2 Sun City
31.07.87 Francisco Fernandez W RSC 14 Panama City
(*WBA S. Featherweight Title Defence*)
03.10.87 Daniel Londas W PTS 15 Gravelines
(*WBA S. Featherweight Title Defence*)
19.12.87 Salvatore Curcetti W RTD 8 Capo d'Orlando
(*WBA S. Featherweight Title Defence*)
26.04.88 Jose Rivera W PTS 12 Madrid
(*WBA S. Featherweight Title Defence*)
04.06.88 Danilo Cabrera W PTS 10 Johannesburg
02.11.88 Jim McDonnell W PTS 12 London
(*WBA S. Featherweight Title Defence*)
10.02.89 Salvatore Bottiglieri W RSC 8 Capo d'Orlando
(*WBA S. Featherweight Title Defence*)
Summary: 40 contests, won 37, drew 2, lost 1.

Frank Mitchell
Philadelphia, USA. *Born* 17.04.59
S. Featherweight

23.05.83 Paul Farley W PTS 4 Columbus
24.09.83 Harold Williams W CO 1 Columbus
19.12.83 Ed Alexander W PTS 4 Columbus
06.02.84 Paul Rutledge W PTS 6 Columbus
30.03.84 Tony Rutledge W PTS 6 Columbus
08.04.84 Otto Palfy W CO 2 Columbus
21.05.84 Greg Masters W CO 1 Columbus
09.07.84 Dave Neal W CO 1 Columbus
01.09.84 Nick Parker W PTS 4 Struthers

Frank Mitchell

Peter Goldfield/USA

11.02.85 Albert Jones W CO 2 Columbus
30.03.85 Jerry Strickland W CO 1 Columbus
18.09.86 Mario Lesperance W DIS 7 Providence
10.02.87 Mike Brown W PTS 6 Philadelphia
31.03.87 William Reid W RSC 2 Philadelphia
21.04.87 Mike Brown W PTS 6 Philadelphia
11.06.87 Martin Brokenbough W PTS 6 Philadelphia
18.08.87 Doug Pettiford W RSC 1 Philadelphia
01.10.87 Jim Woodhouse W PTS 8 Philadelphia
16.03.88 Tom Hanks W PTS 8 Atlantic City
01.06.88 Billy Young W PTS 10 Atlantic City
Summary: 20 contests, won 20.

Kenny Mitchell
Pensacola, USA. *Born* 07.02.60
WBO S. Bantamweight Champion. USBA Bantamweight Champion

13.01.81 Mario Savala W PTS 6 Sacramento
12.02.81 Nestor Obregon W PTS 8 Los Angeles
26.03.81 James Manning W PTS 8 Portland
17.04.81 Mario Cortez W RSC 4 Stockton
08.05.81 Mario Savala L PTS 6 Sacramento
05.06.81 Jose Panulaya W CO 6 Oakland
11.06.81 Ian Clyde W PTS 6 Los Angeles
21.07.81 Adan Uribe W PTS 6 San Diego
03.10.81 Carlos Bejarno W PTS 8 Atlantic City
31.10.81 Angel Marrero W PTS 8 Atlantic City
07.01.82 Derrick Holmes L PTS 10 Atlantic City
05.03.82 Robert Mullins W PTS 10 Atlantic City
27.04.82 Gabon Yekiso DREW 8 Johannesburg
17.07.82 Kelvin Seabrooks W PTS 8 Atlantic City
02.10.82 Jeff Roberts W PTS 8 Atlantic City
27.01.83 Leonardo Valdez L PTS 10 Las Vegas
29.04.83 Mike Ayala L PTS 12 San Antonio
(*NABF S. Bantamweight Title Challenge*)
14.01.84 Pedro Alindato DREW 8 Atlantic City
13.09.84 Pedro Alindato W PTS 12 New York
08.12.84 Julian Solis L PTS 10 Hato Rey
13.01.86 Jeff Whaley W RSC 8 Los Angeles
10.02.86 Tony Montoya W RSC 1 Los Angeles
21.04.86 Jesus Salud L PTS 10 Los Angeles
13.08.86 Lucilo Nolasco T DRAW 8 Los Angeles
28.11.87 Luigi Camputaro L PTS 10 New Haven
25.03.88 Gaby Canizales W PTS 12 Houston
(*USBA Bantamweight Title Challenge*)
13.07.88 Gilberto Contreras W RSC 8 Los Angeles
(*USBA Bantamweight Title Defence*)
13.02.89 Roland Gomez W PTS 12 Los Angeles
(*USBA Bantamweight Title Defence*)
29.04.89 Julio Gervacio W PTS 12 San Juan
(*Vacant WBO S. Bantamweight Title*)
Summary: 29 contests, won 19, drew 3, lost 7.

Peter Mitrevski
New South Wales, Australia. *Born* 06.07.60
Australian S. Flyweight & Bantamweight Champion

13.07.85 Andy Whitten W CO 4 Sanctuary Point
21.08.85 John Dabbene W RSC 3 Mount Pritchard
04.11.85 Smokey Wills W CO 4 Brisbane
02.02.86 John Dabbene NC 2 Newcastle
10.03.86 John Dabbene W PTS 10 Moore Park
18.09.86 Bobby Williams W RSC 2 Sydney
07.11.86 Billy Deluth W RSC 6 Marrickville
07.12.86 John Dabbene W RSC 4 Marrickville
17.04.87 Neil Garland W RSC 4 Cronulla
24.07.87 Charlie Brown W PTS 8 Sydney
29.08.87 Alan Whitten DREW 12 Goulburn
(*Vacant Australian S. Flyweight Title*)
07.03.88 Charlie Brown W TD 8 Sydney
(*Vacant Australian S. Flyweight Title*)
18.07.88 Charlie Brown W DIS 6 Sydney
(*Vacant Australian Bantamweight Title*)
30.11.88 Billy Deluth W PTS Melbourne
Summary: 14 contests, won 12, drew 1, no contest 1.

Juan (John John) Molina
Fajardo, Puerto Rico. *Born* 1968
WBO S. Featherweight Champion

25.02.86 Job Walters W PTS 4 Atlantic City
02.03.86 Ricky West W PTS 4 Lancaster
09.03.86 Darryl Jacobs W PTS 4 Hampton
03.04.86 John Wesley W RSC 1 New York
12.04.86 Job Walters W PTS 6 Totowa
24.05.86 Jose Gonzalez W RSC 5 San Juan
21.06.86 Floyd Simmons W RSC 2 Atlantic City
12.07.86 Dan Doster W RSC 1 Atlanta
16.08.86 Na'eem Muhammad W RSC 1 Atlantic City
08.11.86 Noris Gautier W CO 1 San Juan
11.12.86 Kevin Marston W PTS 8 New York
20.12.86 Carlos Albuerne W RSC 3 Norfolk
08.02.87 Chris Silva W RSC 3 Providence
19.03.87 Victor Aponte W RSC 10 San Juan
24.05.87 Lupe Suarez L RSC 9 Corpus Christi
25.07.87 Richard Campbell W RSC 2 Norfolk
28.11.87 Fernando Maldonado W RSC 4 San Juan
06.06.88 Rafael Solis W DIS 4 San Juan
16.07.88 Miguel Medina W RSC 8 Stateline
27.10.88 Tony Lopez L PTS 12 Sacramento
(*IBF S. Featherweight Title Challenge*)
29.04.89 Juan Laporte W PTS 12 San Juan
(*Vacant WBO S. Featherweight Title*)
Summary: 21 contests, won 19, lost 2.

Tomas (Ton Molly) Molinares
Cartagena, Colombia. *Born* 06.04.65
Former Undefeated WBA, Fecarbox & Colombian Welterweight Champion.

26.10.84 Arnobis Castro W PTS 6 Cartagena
01.03.85 Cristobal Torres W RSC 4 Barranquilla
29.03.85 Edison Benitez W RSC 5 Barranquilla
03.05.85 Mateo Valdez W PTS 8 Barranquilla
21.06.85 Simon Ramos W RSC 9 Cartagena
(*Colombian Welterweight Title Challenge*)
30.08.85 Jairo Segovia W CO 5 Barranquilla
27.09.85 Glen Savage W RTD 3 Barranquilla
18.10.85 Emiro Olivera W RSC 8 Cartagena
14.12.85 Ezequiel Sanchez W RTD 5 Barranquilla
31.01.86 Saul Julio W CO 5 Cartagena
14.03.86 Ruben Veliz W CO 2 Bogota
30.04.86 Carlos Trujillo W PTS 10 Barranquilla
17.10.86 Edgar Rodriguez W CO 4 Barranquilla
15.11.86 Sergio Sanchez W CO 3 Barranquilla
(*Vacant Fecarbox Welterweight Title*)
21.12.86 Jorge Manchego W RSC 6 Cartagena
13.02.87 Alberto Lindo W CO 4 Barranquilla
04.04.87 Max Cimarra W CO 3 San Andres
19.06.87 Eduardo Batista W RSC 6 Barranquilla
04.09.87 Simon Ramos W CO 2 Cartagena
24.10.87 Fernando Martinez W RSC 4 Miami
18.12.87 Eduardo Rodriguez W RTD 5 Cartagena
16.04.88 Emiro Olivera W CO 2 San Andres
30.04.88 Erik Pera W RSC 4 Cartagena
29.07.88 Marlon Starling W CO 6 Atlantic City
(*WBA Welterweight Title Challenge*)
15.04.89 Horacio Perez L RSC 3 Barranquilla
Summary: 25 contests, won 24, lost 1.

Andre Mongalema
France. *Born* Zaire, 02.05.56
French Middleweight Champion

30.11.79 Giampaolo Piras W PTS 6 Bonnevole
17.02.80 Maurice Renaud DREW 6 Metz
07.03.80 Johnny Cooper DREW 6 Compiegne
22.03.80 Joseph Kossmann W CO 6 Friedewald
26.04.80 Christian Chesini W RSC 3 Luneville
09.05.80 Guido Corpataux W CO 3 Berne
23.05.80 Maurice Bufi W PTS 8 Le Roeulx
24.10.80 Mike McCoy W CO 3 Esch
19.12.80 Ray Langewouters W PTS 8 Molenbeek
31.01.81 Jaques Chinon DREW 8 Compiegne
09.02.81 Agamil Yilderim DREW 8 Vienna
21.02.81 Michel Pagani W RSC 4 Calais
17.03.81 Tony Sibson L PTS 10 Wembley
15.05.81 Agamil Yilderim L PTS 10 Berlin
18.09.81 Marijan Benes L PTS 10 Vienna
05.10.81 Alex Blanchard L RTD 5 Rotterdam
21.12.81 Jose Lozano L PTS 10 Hayange
21.01.82 Loucif Hamani W RTD 4 Paris
06.03.82 Rufino Angulo L CO 8 Paris
09.04.82 Mick Morris W PTS 8 Luxembourg

Juan Molina

07.06.82 Stephane Ferrara L PTS 8 Paris
11.11.82 John Humphreys W PTS 8 Dunkirk
11.03.83 Cliff Gilpin W PTS 8 Petit Synthe
09.04.83 Tarmo Uusivirta L RSC 5 Blendecques
20.05.83 Jacques Chinon W PTS 10 Antibes
17.06.83 Juan Munoz Holgado W CO 2 Antibes
05.08.83 Jose Lozano W CO 1 Nimes
10.10.83 Dick Katende L PTS 8 Paris
09.12.83 Brian Anderson W PTS 8 St Nazaire
27.01.84 Jose Rosemain DREW 8 Aix
17.02.84 Andoni Amana W PTS 10 Antibes
13.04.84 Matteo Salvemini W CO 10 Antibes
14.07.84 Juan Domingo Roldan L PTS 8 Monte Carlo
22.09.84 Maurice Bufi W RSC 5 Monte Carlo
12.10.84 Gratien Tonna W PTS 10 Antibes
29.03.85 Brian Anderson W PTS 8 Antibes
01.06.85 Tony Harrison W PTS 8 Paris
14.07.85 Victor Cordova L PTS 8 Monte Carlo
13.12.86 Christophe Tiozzo L PTS 8 Paris
21.02.87 Tony Meszaros W RSC 7 Perpignon
13.04.87 John van Elteren W RSC 6 Villeurbanne
16.06.87 Jake Torrance W PTS 8 St Nazaire
11.12.87 Klayina Awouitoh W PTS 8 Combourg
13.02.88 Jose Rosemain W PTS 10 Paris
28.03.88 Jean-Noel Camara W CO 5 Paris
(*Vacant French Middleweight Title*)
03.10.88 Paul Tchoue W PTS 8 Paris
19.11.88 Tony Burke W CO 2 Chateau Thierry
02.12.88 Rex Kortram W PTS 8 Combourg
23.01.89 Slugger O'Toole W PTS 8 Paris
Summary: 49 contests, won 32, drew 5, lost 12.

Edgar Monserrat
Panama. *Born* 19.11.63
Panamanian Bantamweight Champion. Former Undefeated Con. Am & Latin American S. Flyweight Champion

18.06.83 Jorge Spalding W PTS 4 Panama City
16.07.83 Eleuterio Munoz W PTS 4 Panama City
13.08.83 Francisco Barco W PTS 4 Panama City
19.11.83 Francisco Barco W RSC 2 Panama City
26.11.83 Armando Rocero L CO 2 Panama City
14.04.84 Pablo Cordova W PTS 4 Panama City
27.10.84 Ali Camacho W PTS 8 Colon
10.12.84 Juan Islas W CO 1 Colon
(*Vacant Con. Am. S. Flyweight Title*)
02.02.85 Bernardino Moreno W RSC 5 Panama City
30.03.85 Jose de la Cruz W CO 1 Panama City
18.05.85 Pedro Romero W RSC 8 Panama City
30.08.85 Luis Newmann W RSC 1 Panama City
05.10.85 Rafael Orono W PTS 10 Panama City
16.11.85 Elpidio de Paula W CO 1 Panama City
(*Vacant Latin American S. Flyweight Title*)
23.12.85 Kaosai Galaxy L RSC 2 Bangkok
(*WBA S. Flyweight Title Challenge*)
01.03.86 Jose Chacon W PTS 10 Panama City
21.03.86 Oscar Bolivar DREW 10 Caracas
15.05.86 Gilberto Roman L PTS 12 Paris
(*WBC S. Flyweight Title Challenge*)
13.09.86 Ernesto Ford W PTS 10 Panama City
20.12.86 Alberto Castro L RSC 7 Panama City
31.07.87 Elvis Alvarez W PTS 10 Panama City
20.02.88 Cesar Salas W RSC 4 Panama City
21.05.88 Jose Chacon W CO 9 Panama City
(*Panamanian Bantamweight Title Challenge*)
25.06.88 Luis Rodriguez W RSC 2 Panama City
16.07.88 Arcelio Diaz W RSC 10 Colon
14.10.88 Emilio Noesi W CO 1 San Pedro
27.11.88 Sung-Il Moon L CO 7 Seoul
(*WBA Bantamweight Title Challenge*)
28.04.89 Luis Malave W PTS 10 Panama City
Summary: 28 contests, won 22, drew 1, lost 5.

John Montes
Los Angeles, USA. *Born* 19.07.61
L. Welterweight

18.10.79 Tim Martinez W RSC 2 Los Angeles
14.12.79 Willie Hall W PTS 5 San Bernardino
04.04.80 Eric Bonilla W PTS 6 San Bernardino
13.05.80 Eric Bonilla W PTS 6 San Bernardino
01.07.80 Gary Vinet W CO 3 San Bernardino
03.07.80 Juan Jiminez W CO 1 Los Angeles
28.08.80 Fidel Fraijo W RSC 6 Los Angeles
16.10.80 Fili Ramirez W PTS 10 Los Angeles
06.11.80 Jose Osuna W RSC 1 Los Angeles
13.12.80 Jerry Venzor W CO 1 El Paso
29.01.81 Carmelo Cruz W CO 2 Los Angeles

11.06.81 Pat Duran W CO 7 Los Angeles
18.07.81 Gustavo Rodriguez W CO 2 Beaumont
24.09.81 Jesus Salcedo W RTD 7 Los Angeles
15.10.81 Roberto Torres W RSC 2 Los Angeles
10.11.81 Arturo Leon W PTS 10 Los Angeles
19.11.81 Memo Arreola W RSC 4 Los Angeles
30.01.82 Rolando Avila W CO 4 Los Angeles
18.03.82 Leo Cruz W RSC 2 Los Angeles
08.04.82 Nacho Jiminez W RTD 2 Los Angeles
22.04.82 Eric Bonilla W RSC 4 Los Angeles
26.06.82 Manuel Abedoy W CO 2 Los Angeles
14.08.82 Hilmer Kenty L PTS 10 Albuquerque
12.02.83 Hector Camacho L CO 1 Anchorage
21.04.83 Dave Sanchez W RSC 2 Los Angeles
26.07.83 Joe Perez W PTS 10 Los Angeles
25.08.83 Sergio Medina W PTS 10 Los Angeles
12.07.84 Sergio Aguirre W RSC 3 Los Angeles
17.10.84 Julio Geraldo W CO 1 Reno
19.12.84 Chuck Peralta W RSC 2 Las Vegas
25.04.85 Tomas Chavez W RSC 4 Los Angeles
14.07.85 Cornelius Boza-Edwards L PTS 10 Tampa
09.03.86 Pernell Whitaker L PTS 10 Hampton
30.06.86 Ricky Lehman W CO 5 Irvine
24.09.86 Ford Jennings W RSC 1 Las Vegas
30.10.86 Martin Quiroz W CO 4 San Jose
12.01.87 Frankie Davis W PTS 10 Long Beach
29.06.87 Eric Martin W PTS 12 Irvine
16.09.87 Walter Sims W CO 2 Long Beach
07.05.88 Octavio Robles W PTS 10 Los Angeles
23.06.88 Miguel Hernandez W CO 4 Los Angeles
16.08.88 Tim Burgess W PTS 10 Los Angeles
22.11.88 Fred Pendleton W RSC 10 Los Angeles
28.02.89 Sammy Fuentes L RSC 7 Los Angeles

Summary: 44 contests, won 39, lost 5.

Jose Montiel
Los Mochis, Mexico. *Born* 1967
Mexican S. Flyweight Champion

14.07.84 Jaime Fernandez W PTS 4 La Paz
10.08.84 Borreguito Ramirez W RSC 2 Hermosillo
31.08.84 Gaby Reyes W RSC 2 Guaymas
02.11.84 Jaime Fernandez DREW 6 La Paz
07.12.84 Leoncio Martinez W RSC 3 Guasave
01.03.85 Danny Vega W PTS 6 Guasave
30.05.85 Jose Juarez W RSC 1 Los Mochis
15.06.85 Edmundo Bernal W RSC 3 Los Mochis
12.07.85 Gaby Cadena W RSC 3 Los Mochis
24.08.85 Baby Chispas L DIS 6 Navojoa
18.10.85 Jose Robles W PTS 8 La Paz
28.02.86 Gabriel Nunez W RSC 2 Guasave
24.04.86 Ranita Robles W PTS 10 Los Mochis
08.05.86 Jose Luis Meza W PTS 10 Huatabampo
20.06.86 Pedro Gamboa W RSC 3 Los Mochis
18.07.86 Moi Martinez W PTS 10 Los Mochis
15.08.86 Marcelo Meza W RSC 3 Los Mochis
05.09.86 Freddy Cruz W RSC 7 Huatabampo
02.10.86 Juan Valenzuela W PTS 10 Huatabampo
21.12.86 Pedro Rabago W PTS 10 Los Mochis
13.03.87 Ubaldo Gonzalez W RSC 2 Los Mochis
10.04.87 Tony Escobar W PTS 10 Los Mochis
25.05.87 Diego Avila W PTS 10 Los Mochis
08.08.87 Jimmy Fernandez L DIS 4 Mexico City
(*Vacant Mexican S. Flyweight Title*)
13.09.87 Adolfo Anguiano W RSC 10 Guasave
04.12.87 Antonio Flores W PTS 10 Guasave
27.12.87 Rafael Alonso W PTS 10 Los Mochis
13.02.88 Armando Castro L RSC 4 Mexico City
(*Mexican S. Flyweight Title Challenge*)
11.04.88 Felipe Torres W CO 3 Tijuana
10.07.88 Armando Castro W PTS 12 Los Mochis
(*Mexican S. Flyweight Title Challenge*)
14.10.88 Armando Castro W RTD 9 Los Mochis
(*Mexican S. Flyweight Title Defence*)
17.12.88 Jose Quirino W PTS 12 Tijuana
(*Mexican S. Flyweight Title Defence*)
03.03.89 Sergio Cornejo W CO 6 Los Mochis
(*Mexican S. Flyweight Title Defence*)
28.04.89 Pedro Rabago W PTS 12 Los Mochis
(*Mexican S. Flyweight Title Defence*)

Summary: 34 contests, won 30, drew 1, lost 3.

Luis (Kid) Monzote
Florida, USA. *Born* Cuba, 21.02.63
Con. Am. L. Flyweight Champion

14.01.83 Rodolfo Moreno L RSC 3 Aguadilla
11.10.84 Jose Ruiz L PTS 4 Aguadilla
21.06.85 Glen Omier L PTS 6 Miami
03.12.85 Luis Mendoza L PTS 6 Miami
04.04.86 Rafael Fortez W PTS 6 Miami
25.04.86 Rafael Fortez L PTS 6 Hialeah
23.05.86 Ramon Pichardo W PTS 4 Miami
27.06.86 Roger Guevara W RSC 6 Miami
16.10.86 Rafael Caban L PTS 10 Aguadilla
06.03.87 Joe Paul W RSC 1 Fort Lauderdale
12.09.87 Prudencio Cardona W PTS 10 Miami
27.11.87 Amado Ursua W PTS 12 Miami
(*Vacant Con. Am. L. Flyweight Title*)
12.02.88 Homero Guel W CO 8 Hialeah
10.06.88 Jaime Olvera W CO 6 Hialeah
16.12.88 Genaro Coronado W RSC 6 Miami

Summary: 15 contests, won 9, lost 6.

Sung-Il Moon
South Korea
WBA Bantamweight Champion

08.03.87 Ric Bajelot W RSC 4 Seoul
17.05.87 Sakdising Singkungthon W CO 3 Pusan
16.08.87 Constancio Dangla W RSC 3 Mokpo
11.12.87 Tepratum Eakchatching W CO 2 Kwangju
21.02.88 Tony Pruitt W CO 3 Seoul
05.06.88 Okie Petrus W CO 4 Ulsan
14.08.88 Kaokor Galaxy W RTD 6 Pusan
(*WBA Bantamweight Title Challenge*)
27.11.88 Edgar Monserrat W CO 7 Seoul
(*WBA Bantamweight Title Defence*)
19.02.89 Chiaki Kobayashi W RSC 5 Taejon
(*WBA Bantamweight Title Defence*)

Summary: 9 contests, won 9.

Michael Moorer
Detroit, USA. *Born* 12.11.67
WBO & Con. Am. L. Heavyweight Champion

04.03.88 Adrian Riggs W RSC 1 Las Vegas
25.03.88 Bill Lee W RSC 1 Detroit
29.04.88 Bret Zywerwinski W RSC 1 Detroit
10.05.88 Dennis Fikes W RSC 3 Phoenix
06.06.88 Keith McMurray W RSC 2 Las Vegas
25.06.88 Lavell Stanley W RSC 2 Detroit
06.08.88 Terry Walker W RSC 4 Las Vegas
12.08.88 Jordan Keepers W CO 2 Milwaukee
07.10.88 Jorge Suero W RSC 2 Auburn Hills
17.10.88 Carl Williams W RSC 1 Tucson
04.11.88 Glenn Kennedy W CO 1 Las Vegas
03.12.88 Ramzi Hassan W RSC 5 Cleveland
(*Vacant Con. Am. & WBO L. Heavyweight Title*)
14.01.89 Victor Claudio W RSC 2 Detroit
(*WBO L. Heavyweight Title Defence*)
19.02.89 Frankie Swindell W RSC 6 Monessen
(*WBO L. Heavyweight Title Defence*)
22.04.89 Fred Delgado W RSC 1 Detroit
(*WBO L. Heavyweight Title Defence*)

Summary: 15 contests, won 15.

Danny (Irish) Morgan
Highland, USA. *Born* 29.05.61
S. Middleweight

01.05.86 Charles Minty W PTS 6 Winnipeg
01.05.87 James Robinson W PTS 4 Grand Forks
10.09.87 Scott Papasadora W PTS 6 St Paul
18.12.87 Tim Lillard W RSC 3 Las Vegas
13.02.88 Billy Shaver W CO 6 Joplin
22.02.88 Billy Pryor W CO 5 Mobile
26.02.88 Wayne Evans W RSC 4 Louisville
01.04.88 Ron Brown W PTS 6 Omaha
03.04.88 Jim Fields W CO 4 Bismark
09.04.88 Willis Green W RSC 6 Joplin
14.04.88 Dick Allen W CO 2 Lincoln
29.06.88 Lonnie Watkins W CO 3 Sioux Falls
05.07.88 Bill Anderson W RSC 3 Oklahoma City
19.07.88 James Littlejohn W CO 10 Oklahoma City
22.07.88 John Featherstone W RSC 9 Louisville
02.08.88 Brad Billings W CO 4 Oklahoma City
12.09.88 Rodney Foster W RSC 4 Louisville
13.09.88 Casey McGonigle W CO 2 Indianapolis
20.09.88 Anthony Adams W DIS 3 Oklahoma City
27.09.88 Ronnie Yeo W RSC 6 St Louis
04.10.88 Wilson Douglas W RSC 4 Oklahoma City

Michael Moorer

Peter Goldfield/USA

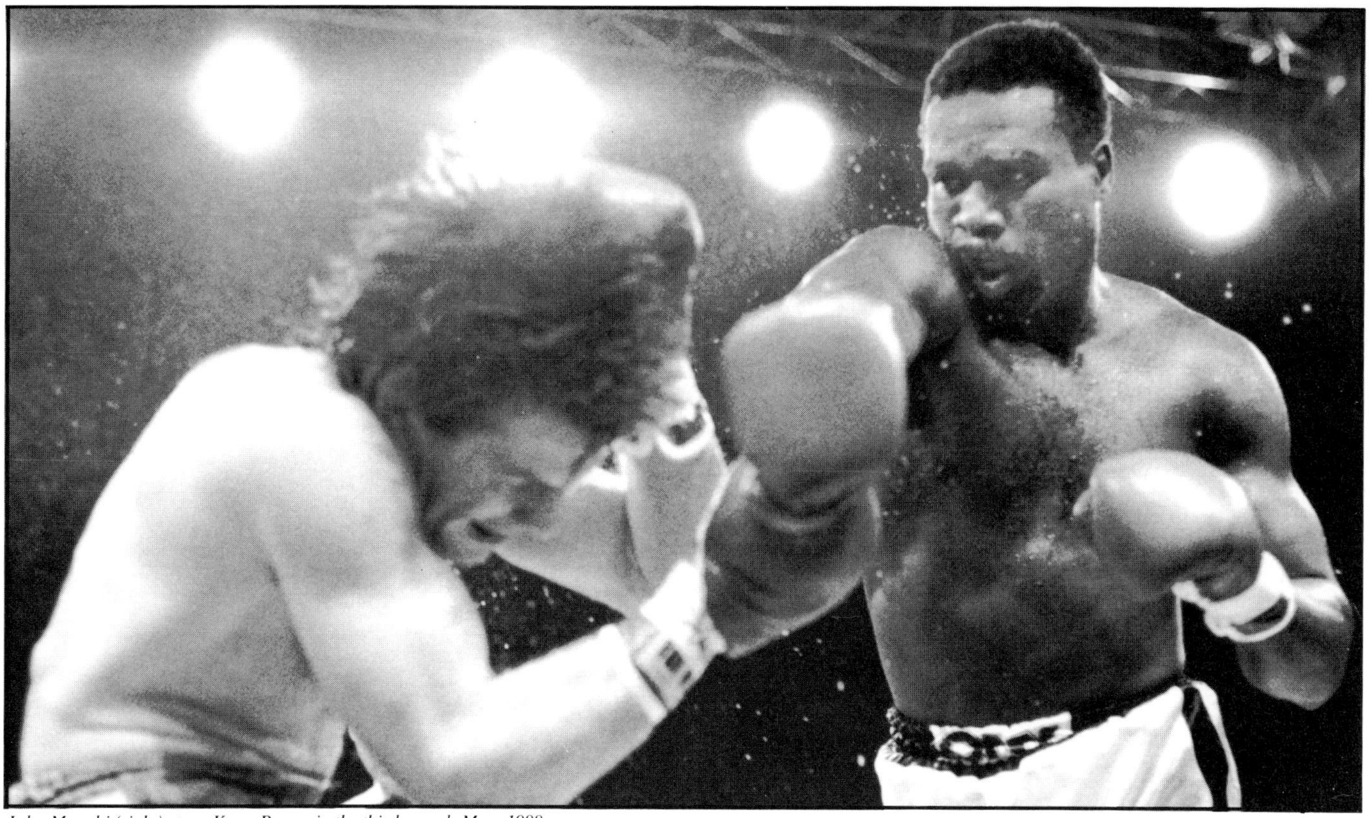

John Mugabi (right) stops Knox Brown in the third round, May, 1988

Tom Casino

18.10.88 Quinton Fox W CO 7 Oklahoma City
01.11.88 Tony Adams W RSC 4 Oklahoma City
15.11.88 Billy Preston W RSC 2 Oklahoma City
06.12.88 Billy Keene W CO 11 Oklahoma City
16.01.89 Bob Richardson W PTS 10 Louisville
Summary: 26 contests, won 26.

John (The Beast) Mugabi
England. *Born* Kampala, Uganda 04.03.60
L. Middleweight

05.12.80 Omar Karadenis W RSC 1 Cologne
13.02.81 Paolo Piras W RSC 2 Kiel
10.04.81 Mauro Hernandez W RTD 4 Kiel
11.05.81 Dennis Pryce W CO 1 London
30.05.81 Pedro Guerrero W RSC 2 Las Vegas
25.09.81 Ron Ford W CO 1 Cologne
31.10.81 John Mwamba W CO 1 Lusaka
16.11.81 Darwin Brewster W RSC 6 London
26.12.81 Sammy Floyd W CO 2 Gelsenkirchen
26.03.82 Curtis Taylor W CO 2 Kiel
02.05.82 Curtis Ramsey W RSC 1 Atlantic City
15.09.82 Steve Williams W RSC 4 New York
23.10.82 Doug Demmings W CO 5 Kiel
15.05.83 Roosevelt Green W RSC 1 Las Vegas
03.07.83 Gary Guiden W RSC 3 Tampa
05.08.83 Jeff Nelson W RSC 2 Tampa
16.09.83 Don Morgan W CO 1 Tampa
08.10.83 Eddie Gazo W RSC 4 Atlantic City
12.11.83 Curtis Parker W RSC 1 Tampa
19.02.84 James Green W RSC 10 Tampa
27.05.84 Wilbert Johnson W RSC 2 Maracaibo
05.08.84 Frank Fletcher W RSC 4 Tampa
25.09.84 Nino Gonzalez W CO 1 London
17.03.85 Earl Hargrove W RSC 1 Tampa
06.08.85 Brian Bradley W RSC 4 Atlantic City
10.03.86 Marvin Hagler L CO 11 Las Vegas
(*World Middleweight Title Challenge*)
05.12.86 Duane Thomas L RSC 3 Las Vegas
(*Vacant WBC L. Middleweight Title*)
22.01.88 Bryan Grant W RSC 2 Atlantic City
05.05.88 Knox Brown W RSC 3 Atlantic City
04.06.88 Gonzalo Montes W RSC 3 Fort Myers
07.07.88 Kenny Snow W RSC 4 Tampa
27.09.88 Mike Sacchetti W CO 3 Sharpsville
05.02.89 Francisco Carballo W CO 2 Las Vegas
23.02.89 Kenny Styles W RSC 1 Detroit
20.03.89 Ralph Smiley W RSC 2 Nogent
Summary: 35 contests, won 33, lost 2.

Takuya Muguruma
Osaka, Japan. *Born* 16.01.61
Former WBA Bantamweight Champion. Former Undefeated Japanese S. Bantamweight Champion

09.04.81 Kenji Miyagi W CO 2 Wakayama
28.05.81 Masamitsu Haruyama W PTS 4 Osaka
21.06.81 Wolf Yoshizaki W RSC 1 Wakayama
12.09.81 Tadashi Kouno W PTS 4 Osaka
07.12.81 Jun Yamaguchi W RSC 4 Kyoto
15.02.82 Mitsuru Sugiya W PTS 6 Osaka
19.06.82 Kenzu Takasugi W PTS 6 Iizuka
23.08.82 Sumihiro Suda W RSC 1 Kochi
01.10.82 Masayoshi Katayama W PTS 8 Tokyo
24.01.83 Kenzu Sugitani W RSC 6 Osaka
24.02.83 Masataka Katayama W RSC 2 Tsu
08.04.83 Fusao Imai W RSC 4 Tokyo
17.05.83 Kazumi Sato W CO 4 Kochi
08.09.83 Shojo Tabata W CO 1 Osaka
29.11.83 Hiroyuki Iwamoto W CO 4 Tokyo
(*Japanese S. Bantamweight Title Challenge*)
15.03.84 Kaoru Yoshioka W CO 3 Osaka
(*Japanese S. Bantamweight Title Defence*)
12.06.84 Kenji Kawamura W PTS 10 Tokyo
(*Japanese S. Bantamweight Title Defence*)
15.09.84 Masahide Ikehara W RSC 4 Osaka
(*Japanese S. Bantamweight Title Defence*)
04.12.84 Eiji Oyama DREW 10 Osaka
(*Japanese S. Bantamweight Title Defence*)
09.03.85 Yun-Kap Choi L PTS 12 Seoul
(*Vacant OPBF S. Bantamweight Title*)
24.06.85 Satoshi Koguchi W RSC 5 Osaka
(*Japanese S. Bantamweight Title Defence*)
29.10.85 Satoshi Okuma W RSC 2 Shiga
(*Japanese S. Bantamweight Title Defence*)
06.02.86 Kazuo Osamu W CO 5 Osaka
(*Japanese S. Bantamweight Title Defence*)
30.03.86 Sam-Yong Kim W CO 3 Itami Shi
21.08.86 Yun-Kap Choi W RSC 2 Osaka
03.12.86 Kyu-Chan Cho W RSC 2 Osaka
29.03.87 Azael Moran W CO 5 Moriguchi
(*Vacant WBA Bantamweight Title*)
24.05.87 Chan-Yung Park L RSC 11 Moriguchi
(*WBA Bantamweight Title Defence*)
09.09.87 Tom Ramos W CO 7 Osaka
17.01.88 Wilfredo Vasquez DREW 12 Osaka
(*WBA Bantamweight Title Challenge*)
15.10.88 Juan J. Estrada L RSC 11 Moriguchi
(*WBA S. Bantamweight Title Challenge*)
Summary: 31 contests, won 26, drew 2, lost 3.

Wali Muhammad
Orange, USA. *Born* 19.04.59
L. Heavyweight

16.08.84 Tony Carbone W RSC 3 Totowa
15.01.85 John Elmore W RSC 1 Atlantic City
12.02.85 Al Shoffner W CO 1 Atlantic City
13.03.85 Alf Tobe W RSC 4 Atlantic City
14.09.85 Demetrius Edwards W PTS 8 Orange
25.11.86 Don Smith W RSC 4 Atlantic City
21.06.87 Ian Mattis W RSC 5 Atlantic City
23.07.87 Frankie Swindell W PTS 8 New York
04.02.88 Mike Belton W PTS 8 Newark
28.09.88 Pat Strachan W RSC 5 Tel Aviv
.89 Richard Mason L CO 5 Tel Aviv
14.02.89 Jeff Lampkin L RSC 10 Atlantic City
(*USBA Cruiserweight Title Challenge*)
Summary: 12 contests, won 10, lost 2.

Wali Muhammad

Peter Goldfield/USA

Shunichi Nakajima
Nagasaki, Japan. *Born* 27.02.61
Japanese S. Flyweight Champion

12.06.84 Michihiro Saga W RSC 3 Tokyo
21.08.84 Kazuichi Murata W RSC 3 Tokyo
25.09.84 Masakatsu Toyooka W PTS 6 Tokyo
29.01.85 Shunji Tsuchiya W CO 2 Tokyo
22.04.85 Kazuki Higa W CO 4 Tokyo
29.06.85 Kwang-Joo Park W CO 3 Seoul
24.09.85 Tadashi Maruo L PTS 10 Tokyo
(*Vacant Japanese S. Flyweight Title*)
03.12.85 Hiroshi Yamamoto W PTS 10 Tokyo
15.03.86 Rae-Ki Ahn L PTS 10 Seoul
23.07.86 Yukhito Tamakuma L PTS 6 Tokyo
21.10.86 Kazuo Katsuma W PTS 10 Tokyo
22.01.87 Hiroshi Yamamoto W PTS 10 Tokyo
26.05.87 Makoto Sawamura W RSC 5 Tokyo
25.06.87 Yasutaka Sakurai W PTS 6 Tokyo
29.08.87 Byong-Kwan Chung L PTS 12 Chungju
(*OPBF S. Flyweight Title Challenge*)
22.10.87 Masayuki Takahashi W CO 5 Tokyo
01.12.87 Shinji Ozawa W RSC 6 Tokyo
01.03.88 Koji Nishikawa W PTS 10 Tokyo
(*Japanese S. Flyweight Title Challenge*)
12.04.88 Jun Hoki W CO 8 Tokyo
(*Japanese S. Flyweight Title Defence*)
02.08.88 Moriaki Arazaki W CO 6 Tokyo
(*Japanese S. Flyweight Title Defence*)
08.11.88 Rolando Protacio W PTS 10 Tokyo
31.01.89 Shigenobu Nakamasa W PTS 10 Tokyo
(*Japanese S. Flyweight Title Defence*)
Summary: 22 contests, won 18, lost 4.

Valerio Nati
Dovadola, Italy. *Born* 11.04.56
Former Undefeated EBU Featherweight Champion. Former EBU Bantamweight Champion. Former Undefeated Italian Bantamweight Champion

07.04.78 Domenico Palumbo W PTS 6 Faenza
19.05.78 Luigi Paravati W RSC 2 Forli
06.07.78 Antonio Franco W RTD 4 Lugo
19.07.78 Domenico Palumbo W RSC 3 Bellaria
21.10.78 Guilio Greco W CO 5 Pesaro
03.11.78 Salvatore Laconi W RSC 3 Forli
26.12.78 Nessim Zebellini W PTS 8 Bologna
13.04.79 Abdelkader Esmain W PTS 8 Forli
08.06.79 Luigi Tessarin W PTS 8 Ravenna
11.10.79 Helenio Ferreira DREW 8 Faenza
30.11.79 Giuseppe Fossati W PTS 12 Forli
(*Italian Bantamweight Title Challenge*)
15.03.80 Claudio Tanda W CO 1 Forli
24.04.80 Franco Buglione W RSC 3 Forli
31.05.80 Eloi da Silva W PTS 8 Sassari
06.08.80 Antonio Franca W RSC 5 Silvi
03.12.80 Juan Francisco Rodriguez W PTS 12 Forli
(*Vacant EBU Bantamweight Title*)
14.02.81 Dominique Cesari W PTS 8 Sassari
01.04.81 Vicente Rodriquez W RSC 5 Rome
(*EBU Bantamweight Title Defence*)
17.06.81 John Feeney W PTS 12 Cervia
(*EBU Bantamweight Title Defence*)
02.09.81 Jean-Jacques Souris W CO 2 Stintino
(*EBU Bantamweight Title Defence*)
20.11.81 Luis de la Sagra W PTS 12 Campobello
(*EBU Bantamweight Title Defence*)
27.01.82 Esteban Eguia W RSC 5 Castrocaro
(*EBU Bantamweight Title Defence*)
28.04.82 Giuseppe Fossati L PTS 12 Lignano
(*EBU Bantamweight Title Defence*)
10.11.82 Richard Saka DREW 8 Sassari
05.01.83 Mariano Garcia W RSC 1 Forio
24.02.83 Giuseppe Fossati DREW 12 Bologna
(*EBU Bantamweight Title Challenge*)
03.06.83 Richard Saka DREW 8 Porto Ferraio
05.08.83 Loris Stecca L PTS 12 Camaiore
(*EBU Featherweight Title Challenge*)
16.11.83 Barry McGuigan L CO 6 Belfast
(*Vacant EBU Featherweight Title*)
13.04.84 Vicente Fernandez W RSC 5 Milan
26.05.84 Orlando Maldonado W RSC 5 Guaynabo
02.07.84 Manuel Santos W PTS 8 Milan
06.10.84 Maurizio Lupino W PTS 8 Carrara
01.03.85 Ley Umba-Sengy W PTS 8 Forli
12.04.85 Julio Garcia W CO 1 Forli
08.06.85 Billy Hardy W RSC 4 Florence
09.07.85 Luis de la Sagra W CO 3 Forli
12.12.85 Ruben Palacios W PTS 10 Milan
26.12.85 Danny Lee W RSC 2 Modena
14.02.86 Steve Cleak W RSC 4 Milan
26.04.86 John Farrell W PTS 8 Lucca
20.06.86 Sonny Long W PTS 8 Paris
10.10.86 Chris Diaz W RSC 7 Cesena
13.03.87 Marc Armand W RSC 2 Forli
(*Vacant EBU Featherweight Title*)
22.05.87 Carlos Segura W CO 1 Jesi
24.07.87 Vincenzo Limatola W DIS 7 Silvi Mariani
(*EBU Featherweight Title Defence*)
21.11.87 Jose Hernandez W RSC 1 Trezzano
27.02.88 Ricky West W CO 2 San Juan
04.06.88 Jose Gallegos W RSC 5 Cagliari
26.11.88 Daniel Zaragoza L CO 5 Forli
(*WBC S. Bantamweight Title Challenge*)
Summary: 50 contests, won 42, drew 4, lost 4.

Rolando (Lando) Navarrete
Santos City, Philippines. *Born* 14.02.57
Former WBC S. Featherweight Champion. Former Undefeated NABF S. Featherweight Champion. Former Philippines Bantamweight Champion. Former Undefeated Philippines Featherweight Champion

17.02.73 Eddie Lementes W PTS 4 Santos City
24.03.73 Quirino Peligro W PTS 6 Santos City
14.04.73 Cris Espinoza W PTS 4 Santos City
23.06.73 Abdel Maratan W PTS 8 Santos City
13.10.73 Cris Espinoza W PTS 8 Santos City
10.11.73 Jimi Verongue DREW 8 Santos City
21.11.73 Fime Sun W RSC 2 Santos City
22.12.73 Mar Belimar W CO 6 Glen
12.06.74 Julius Gonzaga DREW 10 Korondal
10.07.74 Roberto Cinco L PTS 10 Santos City
18.10.74 Willie Abenir W PTS 10 Quezon City
29.11.74 Dobo Quilario W PTS 10 Davao
24.01.75 Rene Cruz Jr W RSC 10 Quezon City
15.02.75 Courado Boy Vasquez W PTS 12 Santos City
(*Philippines Bantamweight Title Challenge*)
01.08.75 Go Mifune W CO 2 Manila
31.08.75 Danny Reyes W CO 8 Santos City
01.10.75 Fernando Cabanela L PTS 12 Manila
(*Philippines Bantamweight Title Defence*)
20.01.76 Bernabe Villacampo W RSC 2 Cebu City
15.05.76 Dommy Mardona W PTS 10 Cebu City
26.06.76 Paul Ferreri L PTS 10 Sydney
31.07.76 San Sacristan W RSC 7 Cebu City
21.08.76 Pol Ladeza W CO 1 Deoro
25.09.76 Rey Paulino W PTS 10 Cebu City
13.11.76 Yung-Shik Kim W RSC 7 Cebu City
29.01.77 Mario Odias W PTS 10 Cebu City
17.06.77 Hyon-Shik Kim L PTS 12 Munwka
(*OPBF Bantamweight Title Challenge*)
12.08.77 Ric Quijano W PTS 10 Davao
12.09.77 Thanomchit Sukhothai L RSC 9 Quezon City
31.12.77 Johnny Sato L RSC 8 Cagayan
28.05.78 Tony Jumoa-as W CO 4 Cebu City
15.07.78 Nene Jun W PTS 12 Santos City
(*Philippines Featherweight Title Challenge*)
19.08.78 Fernando Cabanela W PTS 12 Santos City
(*Philippines Featherweight Title Defence*)
30.09.78 Nene Jun W PTS 12 Davao
(*Philippines Featherweight Title Defence*)
07.01.79 Pete Alferez W CO 2 Cebu City
02.02.79 Ray Tam W RSC 4 Manila
18.03.79 Sukothai Thanonchit DREW 10 Cebu City
19.06.79 Frankie Duarte W PTS 10 Honolulu
24.07.79 Jose Torres W PTS 10 Honolulu
28.08.79 Miguel Meza W RSC 7 Honolulu
09.10.79 Junichi Okubo W RSC 3 Honolulu
18.12.79 Abdul Bey W RSC 7 Honolulu
18.01.80 Frank Ahumada W PTS 10 Manila
01.04.80 Jerome Artis W RSC 7 Honolulu
27.04.80 Alexis Arguello L RSC 4 San Juan
(*WBC S. Featherweight Title Challenge*)
20.01.81 Rosendo Ramirez W RSC 8 Honolulu
10.03.81 Hector Cortez L PTS 10 Honolulu
07.04.81 Refugio Rojas W PTS 10 Honolulu
18.04.81 Arturo Leon W PTS 10 Honolulu
19.05.81 Johnny Sato W PTS 12 Honolulu
(*NABF S. Featherweight Title Challenge*)
21.07.81 Blaine Dickson W PTS 10 Honolulu
29.08.81 Cornelius Boza-Edwards W CO 5 Viareggio
(*WBC S. Featherweight Title Challenge*)
16.01.82 Chung-Il Choi W CO 11 Manila
(*WBC S. Featherweight Title Defence*)
29.05.82 Rafael Limon L CO 12 Las Vegas
(*WBC S. Featherweight Title Defence*)
10.09.82 Young-Sae Oh W RSC 8 Quezon City
29.01.83 Saul Mayren W RSC 6 Manila
29.06.83 Ignacio Jimenez W RSC 6 Honolulu
13.08.83 Dennis Talbot W CO 2 Manila
23.06.84 Mario Martinez L RSC 5 Los Angeles
06.05.88 Elmer Leonardo W CO 2 Manila
22.07.88 Muhammad Juhari W PTS 10 Manila
16.09.88 Bisanti Santos W RSC 2 Manila
05.11.88 Jin-Shik Choi W RSC 6 Quezon City
23.12.88 Rafael Limon W PTS 10 Manila
18.02.89 Dauthong Chuvatana W RSC 1 Manila
22.04.89 Ken Carter W CO 1 Manila
Summary: 65 contests, won 52, drew 3, lost 10.

George (Go Go) Navarro
New Jersey, USA. *Born* 11.05.65
Featherweight

17.05.83 Jim Woodhouse W PTS 4 Atlantic City
15.06.83 Angel Lopez L PTS 4 West Orange
09.08.83 Tony Coleman W RSC 1 Atlantic City
17.01.84 A. D. Wiggins W PTS 4 Atlantic City
01.03.84 Ewart Chance W RSC 1 Atlantic City
08.05.84 Doug Pettiford W PTS 6 Wilmington
04.09.84 Chester Richardson W PTS 6 Atlantic City
23.10.84 Derrick Wilkerson W RSC 3 Atlantic City
05.02.85 Mike Brown W PTS 6 Atlantic City
01.03.85 Mark Perea W RSC 6 Atlantic City
22.08.85 Tom Elston W RSC 5 Chicago
11.10.85 Benny Marquez W PTS 8 Chicago
21.03.86 Rene Resto W PTS 8 Atlantic City
20.06.86 Aristides Acevedo W PTS 10 Atlantic City
15.08.86 Hector Lopez W PTS 12 Atlantic City
16.03.87 Vince Christian W PTS 10 Los Angeles
30.06.87 Jaime Garza W PTS 10 Los Angeles
01.10.87 Hector Lopez L TD 2 Los Angeles
19.08.88 Ed Parker W PTS 10 Atlantic City
30.11.88 Jeff Fenech L RSC 5 Melbourne
(*WBC Featherweight Title Challenge*)
Summary: 20 contests, won 17, lost 3.

George Navarro

Peter Goldfield/USA

Jimmy Navarro
Miami, USA. *Born* 01.12.63
Bantamweight

10.11.84 Mauricio Guadamez W CO 2 Miami
15.12.84 Teo Centeno W RSC 3 Miami
02.02.85 Eddie Leanos W CO 1 Miami
12.02.85 Juan Molina W CO 1 Miami
29.03.85 Jorge Acosta W RSC 4 Miami
10.05.85 Dan Daniels W RSC 1 Miami
24.05.85 Melvin Miller W CO 3 Miami
28.06.85 Terry Pizzaro W RSC 6 Miami
24.08.85 Jorge Acosta W PTS 8 Miami
12.12.85 Teo Centeno W PTS 6 Miami
07.02.86 Ernesto Guerra W CO 3 Hialeah
04.03.86 Tony Pruitt W PTS 6 Atlantic City
18.04.86 Troy Fletcher W RSC 7 Atlantic City
20.06.86 Darryl Thigpen L RSC 4 Atlantic City
12.09.86 Tom Elston W PTS 8 Fort Lauderdale
24.10.86 Joe Paul W CO 1 Fort Lauderdale
14.11.86 Carlos Lopez W CO 6 Fort Lauderdale
30.01.87 Rolando Luna W RSC 4 Fort Lauderdale
20.03.87 Alberto Gonzalez W CO 1 Bridgetown
22.05.87 Temo Villanueva W RSC 2 Miami
18.09.87 David Gauvin W PTS 10 Atlantic City
04.12.87 Mando Trevino W RSC 1 Hialeah
29.11.88 Orlando Canizales L CO 1 San Antonio
(*IBF Bantamweight Title Challenge*)
Summary: 23 contests, won 21, lost 2.

Welcome Ncita
Mdantsane, South Africa. *Born* 21.10.65
South African Flyweight Champion

31.03.84 Vuyani Mngxaso W PTS 4 East London
05.05.84 Bisto Rulashe W PTS 4 Zwelitsha
21.07.84 Mxolisi Majaja W PTS 4 East London
08.09.84 Sizwe Jokiwe W RSC 3 East London
08.12.84 Cosmo Ziqu W PTS 6 East London
05.02.85 Xolile Krabane W RSC 4 East London
18.05.85 Gilbert Makente W PTS 6 Umtata
01.06.85 Tembinkosi Koti W RSC 3 Mdantsane
24.08.85 Basil Ndlazulwana W RSC 2 Mdantsane
30.11.85 Frazier Ndzandze W RSC 7 East London
15.03.86 Johannes Miya W PTS 12 Port Elizabeth
(South African Flyweight Title Challenge)
31.05.86 Kirk Morris W RSC 7 East London
(South African Flyweight Title Defence)
30.10.86 Ricky Diaz W RSC 3 Hartford
22.11.86 Alex Miranda W PTS 8 Johannesburg
07.02.87 Lee Cargle W PTS 10 Sun City
26.04.87 Victor Sonaba W PTS 12 Mdantsane
(South African Flyweight Title Defence)
23.06.87 Johannes Miya W PTS 10 Johannesburg
04.10.87 Johannes Miya W PTS 12 Port Elizabeth
(South African Flyweight Title Defence)
22.02.88 Lincoln Salcedo W RSC 7 Panama City
04.06.88 Juan Rodriguez W PTS 10 Johannesburg
18.12.88 Jaime Olivera W RSC 2 Orlando
Summary: 21 contests, won 21.

Azumah Nelson
Accra Ghana. *Born* 19.07.58
WBC S. Featherweight Champion. Former Undefeated WBC, Ghanaian, ABU & Commonwealth Featherweight Champion

01.12.79 Billy Kwame W PTS 10 Accra
10.02.80 Henry Saddler W CO 9 Accra
(Ghanaian Featherweight Title Challenge)
17.04.80 Henry Optoki W CO 8 Accra
04.07.80 David Capo W PTS 10 Accra
11.09.80 Nii Nuer W CO 3 Accra
13.12.80 Joe Skipper W RSC 10 Accra
(ABU Featherweight Title Challenge)
24.02.81 Bossou Aziza W PTS 10 Lome
02.05.81 Don George W CO 5 Accra
18.08.81 Miguel Ruiz W RSC 3 Bakersfield
26.09.81 Brian Roberts W CO 5 Accra
(Vacant Commonwealth Featherweight Title)
04.12.81 Kabiru Akindele W CO 6 Freetown
(ABU & Commonwealth Featherweight Title Defence)
28.02.82 Charm Chiteule W RSC 10 Lusaka
(ABU & Commonwealth Featherweight Title Defence)
26.06.82 Mukaila Bukare W RSC 6 Accra
21.07.82 Salvador Sanchez L RSC 15 New York
(WBC Featherweight Title Challenge)
31.10.82 Irving Mitchell W RSC 5 McAfee
12.02.83 Ricky Wallace W PTS 10 Cleveland
17.08.83 Alvin Fowler W RSC 2 Las Vegas
23.09.83 Alberto Collazo W RSC 2 Richfield
02.11.83 Kabiru Akindele W CO 9 Lagos
(ABU & Commonwealth Featherweight Title Defence)
09.03.84 Hector Cortez W PTS 10 Las Vegas
08.12.84 Wilfredo Gomez W RSC 11 San Juan
(WBC Featherweight Title Challenge)
06.09.85 Juvenal Ordenes W CO 5 Miami
(WBC Featherweight Title Defence)
12.10.85 Pat Cowdell W CO 1 Birmingham
(WBC Featherweight Title Defence)
25.02.86 Marcos Villasana W PTS 12 Los Angeles
(WBC Featherweight Title Defence)
22.06.86 Danilo Cabrera W RSC 10 San Juan
(WBC Featherweight Title Defence)
07.03.87 Mauro Gutierrez W CO 6 Las Vegas
(WBC Featherweight Title Defence)
29.08.87 Marcos Villasana W PTS 12 Los Angeles
(WBC Featherweight Title Defence)
29.02.88 Mario Martinez W PTS 12 Los Angeles
(Vacant WBC S. Featherweight Title)
25.06.88 Lupe Suarez W RSC 9 Atlantic City
(WBC S. Featherweight Title Defence)
10.12.88 Sidnei dal Rovere W CO 3 Accra
(WBC S. Featherweight Title Defence)
25.02.89 Mario Martinez W RSC 12 Las Vegas
(WBC S. Featherweight Title Defence)
Summary: 31 contests, won 30, lost 1.

Daniel Netto
Coronel Pringles, Argentine. *Born* 16.02.61
Argentinian Cruiserweight Champion

12.11.83 Raul Paez W CO 2 Coronel Pringles
21.09.84 Alberto Ubelar W PTS 6 Parana
20.10.84 Raul Venturelli W PTS 6 Parana
14.12.84 Raul Venturelli W DIS 7 Coronel Pringles
06.09.85 Miguel Cea W CO 3 Trelew
31.01.86 Simon Ramirez W PTS 8 Mar del Plata
08.03.86 Hector Rohr W DIS 2 Coronel Pringles
10.05.86 Victor Robledo DREW 10 Coronel Pringles
07.09.86 Hector Rohr W CO 8 Coronel Pringles
(Argentinian Cruiserweight Title Challenge)
11.12.86 Jose Helguera W PTS 12 Tucuman
(Argentinian Cruiserweight Title Defence)
17.05.87 Anibal Perez W RSC 6 Coronel Pringles
19.07.87 Alberto Barragan W CO 5 Coronel Pringles
18.09.87 Jorge Dascola W PTS 12 Cordoba
(Argentinian Cruiserweight Title Defence)
07.07.88 Emmanuel Brites W PTS 10 Bahia Blanca
16.09.88 Daniel Guibaudo W PTS 10 Concordia
27.02.89 Juan Fernandez W PTS 12 Mar del Plata
(Argentinian Cruiserweight Title Defence)
Summary: 16 contests, won 15, drew 1.

Azumah Nelson (right) successfully defended his WBC super-featherweight title against Lupe Suarez, June, 1988
Tom Casino

Tusikoleta Nkalankete
France. *Born* Zaire 03.03.58
Former EBU L. Welterweight Champion. Former Undefeated French L. Welterweight Champion

26.03.79 Mauricio Fico W PTS 6 Paris
07.06.79 Jean-Marie Kante W PTS 6 Paris
15.06.79 Francis Bailleul W PTS 6 Conde
31.08.79 Isidoro Cabeza DREW 8 Madrid
16.02.80 Roberto Castanon L PTS 8 Leon
07.03.80 Jose Luis Pacheco L PTS 8 Palma
14.03.80 Andre Holyk W PTS 8 Lyons
13.06.80 Perico Fernandez W PTS 8 Palma
14.11.80 Jean Symos W RSC 8 Grivegne
02.02.81 Rene Martin W RSC 2 Paris
28.06.81 Payson Cholwe W PTS 10 Lusaka
21.09.81 Lloyd Hibbert L PTS 8 Wolverhampton
14.12.81 Joey Mack W PTS 8 Paris
14.08.82 Ramon Gomez-Fouz L PTS 8 Gijon
03.12.82 Carlos Foldes W DIS 7 Paris
(Vacant French L. Welterweight Title)
10.09.83 Rene Weller L PTS 8 Cologne
05.11.83 Didier Kowalski W RSC 7 Lille
(French L. Welterweight Title Defence)
02.03.84 Mohamed Lazmany DREW 12 Toulon
(French L. Welterweight Title Defence)
04.09.84 Patrizio Oliva L PTS 12 Acciaroli
(EBU L. Welterweight Title Challenge)
29.03.85 Antoine Vivarelli W RTD 9 Antibes
(French L. Welterweight Title Defence)
07.06.85 Philippe Arrendel W PTS 10 Cleon
(French L. Welterweight Title Defence)
14.03.86 Karim Rabbi W CO 3 Bordeaux
(French L. Welterweight Title Defence)
22.01.86 Terry Marsh L PTS 12 London
(EBU L. Welterweight Title Challenge)
15.05.86 Carlos Prieto DREW 8 Paris
03.08.86 Victor Acosta W RTD 4 Monte Carlo
06.02.87 Tony Laing W RSC 9 Antibes
(Vacant EBU L. Welterweight Title)
22.04.87 Alessandro Scapecchi W RSC 6 Catenia
(EBU L. Welterweight Title Defence)
03.10.87 Mohammed Kawoya W CO 3 Gravelines
(EBU L. Welterweight Title Defence)
26.05.88 Lloyd Christie W CO 6 Paris
(EBU L. Welterweight Title Defence)
25.01.89 Efren Calamati L PTS 12 Arezzo
(EBU L. Welterweight Title Defence)
Summary: 30 contests, won 19, drew 3, lost 8.

Orlin (Boscoe Bear) Norris
Lubbock, USA. *Born* 04.10.65
NABF Heavyweight Champion

16.06.86 Lionel Washington W RSC 3 Bakersfield
25.07.86 Levi Billups W RSC 1 San Diego
02.08.86 Olian Alexander L PTS 4 San Jose
18.09.86 Kenny Mitchell W PTS 4 San Diego
25.09.86 Ricky Reese W RSC 1 Irvine
28.10.86 Mike Bardwell W PTS 6 Reseda
21.11.86 David Smith W PTS 4 Reseda
05.02.87 Roger Troupe W RSC 2 Riverside
12.02.87 Rufus Hadley W PTS 10 Las Vegas
26.02.87 Mike Gans W CO 7 San Diego
20.03.87 Avery Rawls W PTS 10 Las Vegas
03.04.87 Eddie Richardson W CO 2 Las Vegas
27.05.87 Gary Lightbourne W PTS 10 Cleveland
13.08.87 Jean Barbie W CO 1 Los Angeles
04.09.87 Bill Thomas W RSC 3 Las Vegas
25.11.87 Larry Alexander W PTS 12 Las Vegas
(NABF Heavyweight Title Challenge)
23.02.88 Woody Clark W RSC 1 Reseda
19.03.88 Renaldo Snipes W PTS 12 Las Vegas
(NABF Heavyweight Title Defence)
27.05.88 Andy Stokes W PTS 10 Las Vegas
27.07.88 Dwayne Bonds W PTS 12 Los Angeles
(NABF Heavyweight Title Defence)
15.11.88 Jesse Ferguson W PTS 12 San Diego
(NABF Heavyweight Title Defence)
25.04.89 Greg Page W PTS 12 Las Vegas
(NABF Heavyweight Title Defence)
Summary: 22 contests, won 21, lost 1.

Terry Norris
Lubbock, USA. *Born* 17.06.67
NABF L. Middleweight Champion

02.08.86 Jose Cordova W CO 1 San Jose
13.08.86 Carlos Gutierrez W PTS 4 Los Angeles
25.09.86 George Murphy W PTS 4 Los Angeles
07.10.86 Darryl Colquitt W RSC 4 Los Angeles
21.11.86 Carlos Gutierrez W PTS 4 Reseda

03.12.86 Lang McGowan W PTS 4 Los Angeles
05.02.87 Gilbert Baptist W PTS 4 Riverside
26.02.87 Dick Green W RSC 1 San Diego
16.03.87 Tino Leon W RSC 1 Los Angeles
26.03.87 Mauro Veronica W CO 2 Los Angeles
03.04.87 Neto Rayos W CO 1 Las Vegas
27.05.87 Nat Dryer W CO 3 Las Vegas
13.08.87 Derrick Kelly L PTS 10 Los Angeles
04.09.87 Ed Neblett W RSC 6 Las Vegas
25.11.87 Joe Walker L DIS 1 Las Vegas
21.01.88 Roman Nunez W CO 1 San Diego
03.02.88 Richard Aguirre W RSC 3 Riverside
28.03.88 Clayton Hires W RSC 2 Los Angeles
12.08.88 Quincy Taylor W PTS 10 Las Vegas
18.10.88 Gilbert Baptist W PTS 10 San Diego
09.12.88 Steve Little W RSC 6 Las Vegas
(*Vacant NABF L. Middleweight Title*)
27.03.89 Buster Drayton W PTS 12 Las Vegas
(*NABF L. Middleweight Title Defence*)
Summary: 22 contests, won 20, lost 2.

Terry Norris

Michael Nunn
Iowa, USA. *Born* 14.04.63
IBF Middleweight Champion. Former Undefeated NABF Middleweight Champion

20.12.84 John Borman W RSC 1 Las Vegas
08.02.85 Ismael Templos W RSC 4 Stateline
26.03.85 Robert Jackson W CO 1 Reseda
11.04.85 Carlos Campos W RSC 1 Las Vegas
21.05.85 I. W. Johnson W CO 1 Reseda
27.06.85 Larry Davis W RSC 2 Las Vegas
29.07.85 James Waire W RSC 3 Reseda
27.08.85 Marcos Geraldo W RSC 5 Reseda
25.09.85 Charles Campbell W PTS 8 Las Vegas
13.11.85 Jorge Amparo W PTS 8 Las Vegas
10.12.85 Billy Robertson W PTS 10 Los Angeles
28.01.86 Alvaro Granillo W RSC 2 Reseda
10.02.86 Charles Carter W RSC 3 Los Angeles
09.03.86 Carl Jones W PTS 10 Las Vegas
19.05.86 Felipe Vaca W RSC 4 Reseda
25.06.86 Randy Smith W PTS 10 Los Angeles
23.07.86 Charlie Boston W PTS 10 Las Vegas
19.09.86 Mike Tinley W PTS 10 Atlantic City
28.10.86 Orlando Paulding W CO 1 Reseda
21.11.86 Alex Ramos W PTS 12 Reseda
06.02.87 Willie Harris W RSC 6 Reseda
04.04.87 Charles Campbell W RSC 9 Las Vegas
24.04.87 Cecil Pettigrew W RSC 5 Davenport
02.07.87 Jose Duarte W RSC 2 Reseda
11.08.87 Frankie Owens W RSC 9 Las Vegas
11.09.87 Dale Jackson W PTS 10 Davenport
29.10.87 Darnell Knox W RSC 4 Las Vegas
(*Vacant NABF Middleweight Title*)
02.01.88 Kevin Watts W PTS 12 Reseda
(*NABF Middleweight Title Defence*)
19.03.88 Curtis Parker W CO 2 Las Vegas
(*NABF Middleweight Title Defence*)
31.05.88 Ron Daniels W CO 2 Reseda
28.07.88 Frank Tate W RSC 9 Las Vegas
(*IBF Middleweight Title Challenge*)
04.11.88 Juan Domingo Roldan W CO 8 Las Vegas
(*IBF Middleweight Title Defence*)
25.03.89 Sumbu Kalambay W CO 1 Las Vegas
(*IBF Middleweight Title Defence*)
Summary: 33 contests, won 33.

Mohamed Nurhuda
Indonesia. *Born* 22.07.65
WBC International & Indonesian S. Bantamweight Champion. Former Undefeated Indonesian Bantamweight Champion

27.01.85 Arbontek W PTS 4 Surabaya
16.02.85 Margo Sitompul W PTS 6 Banyuwangi
21.07.85 Markus W PTS 8 Surabaya
30.07.85 Atim W PTS 6 Timor
11.08.85 Johannes Matahelemual W PTS 10 Surabaya
05.10.85 Edward Apay W PTS 12 Jakarta
(*Indonesian Bantamweight Title Challenge*)
03.11.85 Chalao Muangsurin W PTS 10 Jakarta
24.01.86 Julius Zapata W PTS 12 Surabaya
(*Indonesian Bantamweight Title Defence*)
22.06.86 Ki-Yul Kang L PTS 12 Surabaya
(*OPBF Bantamweight Title Challenge*)
27.07.86 Ki-Yul Kang L RSC 5 Hongchun
(*OPBF Bantamweight Title Challenge*)
17.10.86 Wim Sapulete W PTS 12 Jakarta
(*Indonesian Bantamweight Title Defence*)
16.11.86 Edward Apay W PTS 12 Surabaya
(*Indonesian Bantamweight Title Defence*)
27.12.86 Monod L PTS 12 Jakarta
(*Indonesian S. Bantamweight Title Challenge*)
08.03.87 Monod W PTS 12 Kudus
(*Indonesian S. Bantamweight Title Challenge*)
05.07.87 Monod DREW 12 Gresik
(*Indonesian S. Bantamweight Title Defence*)
09.08.87 Boy Kelung W PTS 12 Jakarta
(*Indonesian S. Bantamweight Title Defence*)
19.09.87 Bert Granciosa W PTS 10 Jayapura
05.12.87 Sambung W PTS 8 Malang
14.04.88 Joe Hiyas W PTS 12 Jakarta
(*WBC International S. Bantamweight Title Challenge*)
07.07.88 Bert Granciosa W PTS 12 Jakarta
(*WBC International S. Bantamweight Title Defence*)
04.09.88 Tetsuji Shimamoto W PTS 10 Surabaya
19.03.89 Paquito Openo DREW 12 Ujang Pandag
(*WBC International S. Bantamweight Title Defence*)
Summary: 22 contests, won 17, drew 2, lost 3.

Fully Obelmejias
San Jose, Venezuela. *Born* 01.01.53
WBA S. Middleweight Champion. Former Latin American L. Heavyweight Champion.
Former Undefeated Fecarbox Middleweight Champion

30.01.77 Franklyn Suzarra W RSC 1 Caracas
03.04.77 Franklyn Suzarra W RSC 2 Caracas
22.10.77 Jesus Garza W CO 9 Mexico City
18.11.77 Andre Beard W CO 2 San Diego
17.12.77 Rogelio Vera W RTD 2 Mexico City
04.02.78 Vicente Pinon W CO 2 Mexico City
28.02.78 Abel Cordova W PTS 10 Tuxtla
06.04.78 Rudy Robles W RSC 4 Tijuana
30.04.78 Rolando Martinez W RSC 1 Caracas
04.06.78 Jose Anglada W CO 1 Caracas
15.07.78 Sandy Torres W CO 4 Caracas
29.07.78 Willie Warren W RSC 8 Caracas
17.09.78 Johnny Heard W RSC 8 Caracas
12.11.78 Ken Blackwell W RSC 3 Caracas
17.12.78 Carlos Marks W RSC 9 Caracas
(*Fecarbox Middleweight Title Challenge*)
11.02.79 Angel Ortiz W CO 3 Caracas
01.04.79 Jaime Thomas W CO 4 Caracas
07.08.79 Luis Arias W CO 2 Caracas
(*Fecarbox Middleweight Title Defence*)
15.09.79 Sammy Floyd W RSC 10 Caracas
26.10.79 George Lee W RSC 3 Caracas
17.12.79 Ray Phillips W RSC 4 Caracas
03.03.80 Elisha Obed W RSC 3 Caracas
01.04.80 Abel Cordova W CO 2 Caracas
14.04.80 Walter Miranda W CO 1 Caracas
26.05.80 Lamont Lovelady W PTS 10 Caracas
30.06.80 Clifford Wills W RSC 3 Caracas
18.08.80 Felton Marshall W PTS 10 Caracas
10.09.80 Freddie Johnson W RSC 3 San Remo
31.10.80 Leroy Green W RSC 3 Rome
28.11.80 James Waire W RSC 3 Campione
17.01.81 Marvin Hagler L RSC 8 Boston
(*World Middleweight Title Challenge*)
04.05.81 Norberto Cabrera W CO 5 Caracas
30.05.81 Joe Gonsalvez W RSC 2 Caracas
31.08.81 Wayne Barker W RSC 2 Caracas
05.10.81 Eddie Gazo W CO 2 Caracas
07.11.81 Chong-Pal Park W RSC 8 Caracas
15.02.82 Johnny Wise W CO 2 Caracas
14.06.82 Reyes Escalera W CO 2 Barquisimeto
09.08.82 Willie Torres W RSC 8 Porlamar
30.10.82 Marvin Hagler L CO 5 San Remo
(*World Middleweight Title Challenge*)
22.10.83 Raymond Gonzalez W CO 4 St Vincent
14.12.83 Jeff Lampkin W PTS 8 Loano
25.02.84 Jerry Celestine W PTS 8 Paris
24.03.84 Henry Sims W CO 4 Chiavari
28.04.84 Arthel Lawhorne W PTS 8 Naples
14.07.84 Cesar Romero W PTS 8 Monte Carlo
22.09.84 Eric Winbush W PTS 8 Monte Carlo
15.12.84 Leon Taylor W CO 2 Catanzaro
21.07.85 Clarence Osby L PTS 8 Campione
30.05.86 Tomas Polo W PTS 12 Isla Margarita
(*Vacant Latin American L. Heavyweight Title*)
15.11.86 Leslie Stewart L RSC 4 Port of Spain
(*Latin American L. Heavyweight Title Defence*)
18.06.87 Chris Reid W RSC 10 New York
23.05.88 Chong-Pal Park W PTS 12 Suanbao
(*WBA S. Middleweight Title Challenge*)
Summary: 53 contests, won 49, lost 4.

Hideyuki Ohashi
Yokohama, Japan. *Born* 08.03.65
Former Undefeated Japanese L. Flyweight Champion

12.02.85 Masakatsu Aikata W RSC 1 Tokyo
07.05.85 Hideto Osanai W PTS 8 Tokyo
27.08.85 Tadashi Kuramochi W RSC 1 Tokyo
03.12.85 Masato Tanaka W CO 3 Tokyo
20.03.86 Bong-Jun Kim L PTS 10 Tokyo
23.06.86 Yoshiaki Nojima W PTS 10 Tokyo
(*Vacant Japanese L. Flyweight Title*)
14.12.86 Jung-Koo Chang L RSC 5 Inchon
(*WBC L. Flyweight Title Challenge*)
07.04.87 Masato Tanaka W CO 3 Tokyo
08.09.87 Yasutaka Sakurai W PTS 10 Tokyo
11.01.88 Tomohiro Kiyuna W PTS 10 Tokyo
(*Japanese L. Flyweight Title Challenge*)
27.06.88 Jung-Koo Chang L RSC 8 Tokyo
(*WBC L. Flyweight Title Challenge*)
18.10.88 Romy Ceniza W CO 3 Tokyo
07.03.89 Joel Revilla W CO 2 Tokyo
Summary: 13 contests, won 10, lost 3.

Putt Ohyuthanakorn
Chiang Mai, Thailand. *Born* 07.04.66
Thai L. Flyweight Champion. Former Thai M. Flyweight Champion

29.10.83 Smandith Chorsangthorn W CO 1 Bangkok
15.11.83 Chaconpetch Changjirah W PTS 6 Bangkok
03.04.84 Taksing Muangsurin L RSC 4 Bangkok
11.05.84 Sangnoi Sithkempetch W CO 2 Bangkok
27.05.84 Plordphai Sor Burapha W CO 4 Bangkok
16.10.84 Loondednoi Sakcharern W PTS 6 Bangkok
20.11.84 Pongprai Siripong W CO 5 Bangkok
10.12.84 Kongkrun Kiatriangrai L PTS 6 Bangkok
10.01.85 Samuth Sithnaruepol L PTS 6 Bangkok
20.02.85 Rottank Sornrama W RSC 1 Bangkok
17.05.85 Singdum Luadayuthaya W CO 2 Bangkok
28.06.85 Thavat Kiatpongchida W CO 1 Bangkok
(*Thai M. Flyweight Title Challenge*)
24.09.85 Kriangsok Yuthakiat W CO 2 Bangkok
26.12.85 Samuth Sithnaruepol L PTS 10 Bangkok
(*Thai M. Flyweight Title Defence*)
31.01.86 Thangjai Kiattawachai W PTS 6 Bangkok
27.02.86 Praiwan Petchsompong W RSC 4 Bangkok
13.03.86 Thavat Kiatpongchida W PTS 6 Bangkok
03.04.86 Thongtep Patchsriraja W PTS 6 Bangkok
26.06.86 Patchaint Donjaedee W RSC 5 Bangkok
(*Vacant Thai L. Flyweight Title*)
11.08.86 Krairung Lukepayom W PTS 10 Bangkok
(*Thai L. Flyweight Title Defence*)
29.10.86 Krairung Lukepayom W RSC 6 Bangkok
23.12.86 Kenji Matsumura L CO 2 Kakogawa
11.02.87 Kanchai Kiatsontaya W RSC 1 Bangkok
20.03.87 Thanjai Kiatthavatchai W PTS 6 Bangkok

29.04.87 Ded Donjaedee W PTS 6 Bangkok
23.09.87 Maker Sonram W PTS 10 Bangkok
(*Thai L. Flyweight Title Defence*)
11.12.87 Yong-Kang Kim L RSC 10 Kwangju
(*Vacant OPBF L. Flyweight Title*)
19.01.88 Karnchai Kiatsontaya W CO 2 Bangkok
08.03.88 Onkot Sissrimoke W RSC 2 Bangkok
28.04.88 Thanjai Donjaedee W PTS 10 Bangkok
(*Thai L.Flyweight Title Defence*)
02.07.88 Katsumi Komiyama L PTS 10 Osaka
28.08.88 Myung-Woo Yuh L CO 6 Pusan
(*WBA L. Flyweight Title Challenge*)
14.10.88 Jomtamin Suwanmisakawan W RSC 4 Bangkok
Summary: 33 contests, won 25, lost 8.

Michael (The Silk) Olajide
Vancouver, Canada. *Born* Liverpool, England 08.12.63.
Former Undefeated Con. Am. & Canadian Middleweight Champion

17.01.82 Johnny Gaines W CO 1 Victoria
07.02.82 Dale Dorset W RSC 3 Victoria
05.03.82 Don Oversby W CO 1 Victoria
17.06.82 Al Ford W PTS 8 Burnaby
24.03.83 Roosevelt Green W RSC 6 Vancouver
13.08.83 Tom Briscoe W CO 1 Kelowna
13.10.83 Joe Banks W CO 2 New Westminster
25.11.83 Stacy McSwain W PTS 8 Vancouver
12.03.84 Lancelot Innis W CO 4 New Westminster
10.05.84 Leonardo Bermudez W RSC 2 New Westminster
18.08.84 Rosendo Rubalcaba W PTS 10 Burnaby
10.04.85 Wayne Caplette W RSC 9 Vancouver
(*Vacant Canadian Middleweight Title*)
11.07.85 Reyes Escalera W RSC 5 Vancouver
10.08.85 Sakarai Ve W CO 9 Fiji
29.11.85 Elio Diaz W RSC 7 Vancouver
11.01.86 Curtis Parker W PTS 10 Atlantic City
10.04.86 James Green W PTS 10 Atlantic City
05.06.86 Randy Smith W PTS 10 Los Angeles
28.08.86 Knox Brown W RSC 9 New York
30.10.86 Ray Ray Gray W RSC 10 Atlantic City
08.01.87 Richard Burton W RSC 4 New York
(*Vacant Con. Am. Middleweight Title*)
01.02.87 Don Lee W RSC 9 Atlantic City
10.05.87 Troy Darrell W PTS 10 Atlantic City
10.10.87 Frank Tate L PTS 15 Las Vegas
(*Vacant IBF Middleweight Title*)
17.12.87 Frankie Owens W RSC 6 New York
04.02.88 Cecil Pettigrew W PTS 10 New York
06.03.88 Iran Barkley L RSC 5 New York
29.09.88 Troy Watson W RSC 7 New York
Summary: 28 contests, won 26, lost 2.

Fujio Ozaki
Japan. *Born* 07.10.61
OPBF Welterweight Champion. Former Undefeated Japanese Welterweight Champion. Former Japanese Lightweight Champion

19.05.80 Teruo Okuaki W RSC 1 Tokyo
01.07.80 Morio Watanabe W CO 1 Tokyo
30.09.80 Koji Kunisato W PTS 4 Tokyo
28.12.80 Yoshifumi Takeyama W PTS 6 Tokyo
01.03.81 Hidekazu Akai L RSC 3 Tokyo
18.07.81 Masanori Omori W PTS 6 Tokyo
10.10.81 Kazunori Taguchi W CO 1 Tokyo
23.11.81 Yoshihide Sawano W CO 6 Hachinohe
07.05.82 Kojiro Sasaki W RSC 8 Tokyo
06.08.82 Joken Narita W PTS 10 Tokyo
(*Japanese Lightweight Title Challenge*)
09.11.82 Hayao Shiba W CO 8 Tokyo
(*Japanese Lightweight Title Defence*)
22.02.83 Joken Narita W PTS 10 Tokyo
(*Japanese Lightweight Title Defence*)
03.06.83 Cheyenne Yamamoto L PTS 10 Tokyo
(*Japanese Lightweight Title Defence*)
02.09.83 Cheyenne Yamamoto W PTS 10 Tokyo
(*Japanese Lightweight Title Challenge*)
02.12.83 Hikaru Tomonari L CO 7 Tokyo
(*Japanese Lightweight Title Defence*)
19.03.84 Hiroaki Kato W CO 2 Kochi
05.04.84 Noboyuki Tabata W CO 4 Tokyo
02.08.84 Kozo Fukutani W CO 6 Tokyo
10.01.85 Yung-Bae Lee W RSC 8 Tokyo

Fujio Ozaki

06.06.85 Junya Kushikino W PTS 10 Tokyo
(*Japanese Welterweight Title Challenge*)
29.08.85 Junya Kushikino W RSC 8 Tokyo
(*Japanese Welterweight Title Defence*)
04.11.85 Nobutaka Kuwata W CO 8 Naha
(*Japanese Welterweight Title Defence*)
06.02.86 Noboyuki Tabata L PTS 10 Tokyo
(*Japanese Welterweight Title Defence*)
05.06.86 Noboyuki Tabata W CO 5 Tokyo
(*Japanese Welterweight Title Challenge*)
06.11.86 Akinori Yoshida W CO 4 Tokyo
(*Japanese Welterweight Title Defence*)
05.02.87 Hikaru Tomonari W RSC 4 Tokyo
(*Japanese Welterweight Title Defence*)
05.02.88 Marlon Starling L PTS 12 Atlantic City
(*WBA Welterweight Title Challenge*)
07.07.88 Francisco Ferrer W PTS 12 Tokyo
(*Vacant OPBF Welterweight Title*)
18.09.88 Robert Azumah W CO 9 Milo
(*OPBF Welterweight Title Defence*)
11.02.89 Chung-Ok Park W CO 5 Tokyo
(*OPBF Welterweight Title Defence*)
Summary: 30 contests, won 25, lost 5.

Michael Olajide (left) sets up Cecil Pettigrew on his way to a ten-round points win, February, 1988

Tom Casino

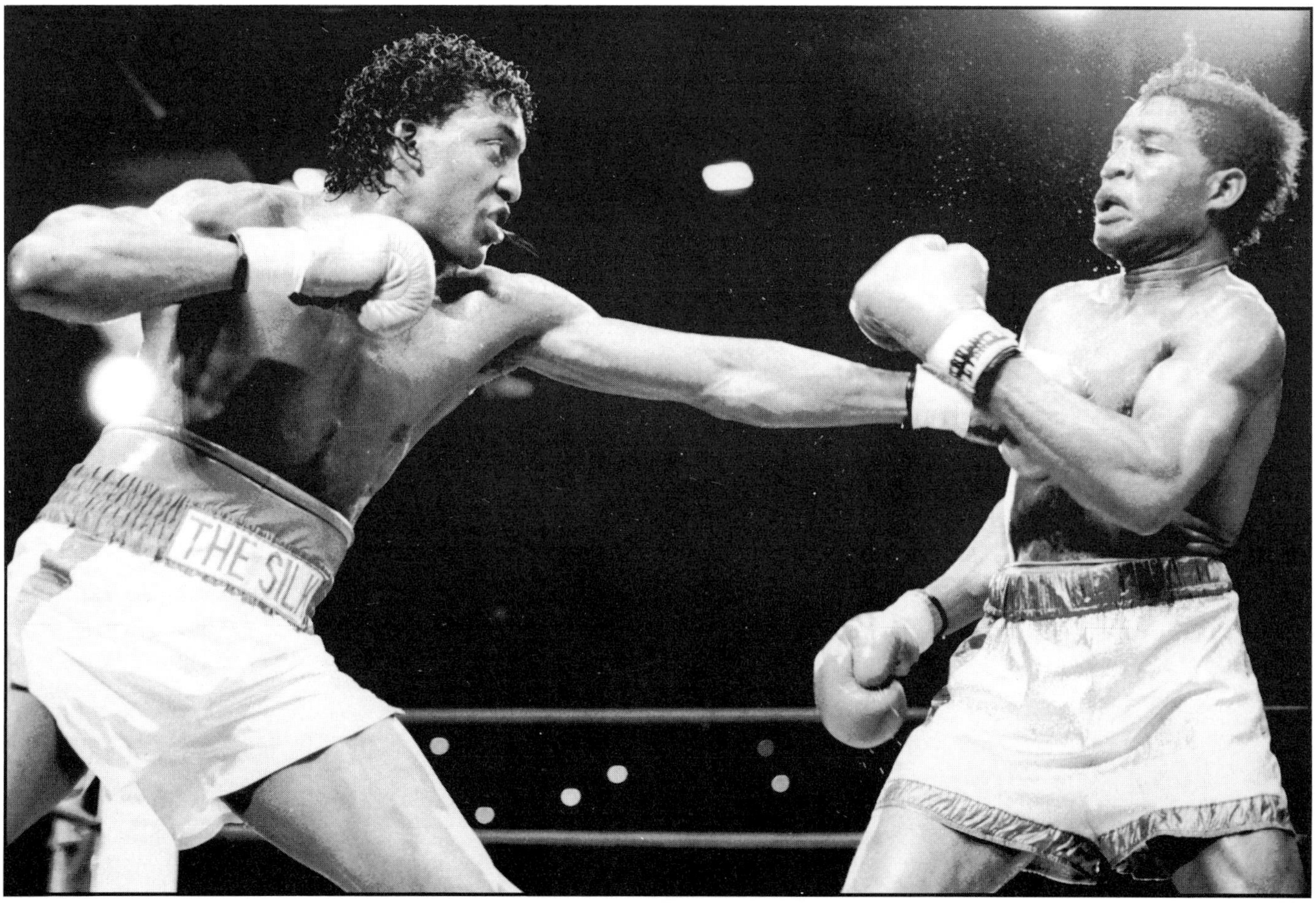

Antonio (Jong-Jong) Pacquing

Cagayan, Philippines
Former OPBF Lightweight Champion. Former Undefeated Philippines Lightweight Champion. Former Philippines S. Bantamweight Champion

16.02.80 Eller Sinoyan W RSC 2 Cagayan
15.03.80 Romy Orobio W RSC 4 Cagayan
05.07.80 Carlos Aradora DREW 10 Butuan
16.08.80 Danny Canada W PTS 10 Cagayan
30.08.80 Erning Querobin W PTS 10 Cagayan
25.10.80 Siony Carupo W PTS 10 Cagayan
30.11.80 Rene Sedayon W PTS 10 Cagayan
27.12.80 Winnie Ampong W PTS 10 Cagayan
28.02.81 Baby Francisco W PTS 10 Cagayan
28.03.81 Divino Inocian W PTS 10 Cagayan
29.05.81 Divino Inocian L PTS 10 Cagayan
04.07.81 Rey Naduma W RSC 10 Cagayan (*Philippines S. Bantamweight Title Challenge*)
24.08.81 Sandy Noora W PTS 10 Cagayan
26.09.81 Ronaldo Sumalis L PTS 10 Cagayan
31.10.81 Ric Diamale L PTS 12 Davao (*Philippines S. Bantamweight Title Defence*)
28.11.81 Nerry Codilla W PTS 10 Cagayan
05.02.82 Melching Maquilan W PTS 10 Cagayan
17.04.82 Ronald Sumalis L PTS 10 Cagayan
28.05.82 Cesar Ligan W PTS 10 Cagayan
10.07.82 Nene Jun W RSC 5 Cebu
02.10.82 Nene Jun W RSC 7 Cagayan
31.10.82 Ric Dolotallas W PTS 10 Misamis
18.12.82 Roger Salas W PTS 10 Cagayan
05.02.83 Del Contado W RSC 8 Cagayan
05.03.83 Ric Dolotallas W PTS 10 Cagayan
16.04.83 Flash Villamer W PTS 12 Cagayan (*Philippines Lightweight Title Challenge*)
30.07.83 Jun Escalera W RSC 5 Cagayan
30.09.83 Amy Pacana L PTS 12 Manila (*Philippines Lightweight Title Defence*)
19.11.83 Bert Lozano W PTS 10 Cagayan
11.02.84 Amy Pacana W PTS 12 Cagayan (*Philippines Lightweight Title Challenge*)
06.04.84 Rolando Aldemir W PTS 10 Cagayan
02.06.84 Johnny Sato L RSC 2 Cagayan
18.08.84 Kyu-Woon Choi L PTS 10 Pohang
23.09.84 Juhari W PTS 12 Jakarta (*Vacant OPBF Lightweight Title*)
13.04.85 Dong-Koo Woo W RSC 4 Chinju (*OPBF Lightweight Title Defence*)
17.02.85 Johannes Msiren W CO 12 Surabaya (*OPBF Lightweight Title Defence*)
15.06.85 Carlos Parcia W RSC 6 Cagayan
07.07.85 Tsuyoshi Hamada L PTS 12 Tokyo (*OPBF Lightweight Title Defence*)
26.08.85 Dale Artango L RSC 5 Brisbane
05.10.85 Fred Panerio W CO 5 Cagayan
01.03.86 Lito Pena W PTS 12 Cagayan (*Philippines Lightweight Title Challenge*)
02.08.86 Amy Pacana W RSC 7 Cagayan (*Philippines Lightweight Title Defence*)
31.01.87 Allan Alegria DREW 10 Cagayan
20.06.87 Jun Ramos W RSC 7 Tagum
23.11.87 Bong-Guk Kendy W RSC 4 Jakarta
08.02.88 Lito Pena W RSC 5 Cagayan
02.07.88 Boy Romero W CO 1 Cagayan
06.08.88 Allan Alegria W PTS 10 Tagum
Summary: 48 contests, won 37, drew 2, lost 9.

Jorge Paez

Mexicali, Mexico. *Born* 27.10.65
IBF Featherweight Champion

16.11.84 Efren Tined W RSC 3 San Luis Rio Colarado
14.12.84 Oscar Duran W San Luis Rio Colorado
30.03.85 Jose Luna W CO 4 Mexicali
16.04.85 Salvador Villavicensio L PTS 4 Tijuana
29.07.85 Mario Rivera DREW 6 Tijuana
01.11.85 Efren Tineo W RSC 1 Mexicali
22.04.86 Salvador Bara W RSC 1 San Luis
27.06.86 Martin Moreno W RSC 6 Mexicali
28.07.86 Miguel Molina L PTS 6 Tijuana
16.09.86 Jesus Rojas W PTS 10 Torreon
03.10.86 Carlos Galan W PTS 10 Mexicali
06.12.86 Noe Gonzalez W RSC 3 Mexicali
01.01.87 Alejandro Mayorga W PTS 10 Mexicali
15.02.87 Jose Millan W CO 2 Mexicali
20.03.87 Marco Santos W RSC 5 Mexicali
25.04.87 Silvestre Castillo W CO 6 Mexico City
22.05.87 Arnel Arrozal W RSC 5 Mexicali
25.07.87 Refugio Alvarado W RSC 7 Mexico City
30.10.87 Robert Lewis W PTS 10 Mexicali
04.12.87 Jesus Lopez W CO 2 Mexicali
18.12.87 Martin Torres W RSC 4 Mexicali
06.02.88 Elpidio Infante W RSC 8 Mexicali
26.02.88 Rocky Alonso W RSC 1 La Paz
04.04.88 Carlos Linares W RSC 3 Tijuana
22.04.88 Rafael Toledo W RSC 2 Mexicali
28.05.88 Martin Garcia W RSC 6 Tijuana
04.08.88 Calvin Grove W PTS 15 Mexicali (*IBF Featherweight Title Challenge*)
30.09.88 Miguel Molina W RSC 6 Juarez
30.03.89 Calvin Grove W CO 11 Mexicali (*IBF Featherweight Title Defence*)
Summary: 29 contests, won 26, drew 1, lost 2.

Chan-Yung Park

South Korea. *Born* 10.06.63
Former WBA Bantamweight Champion

18.11.80 Chang-Sung Choi W CO 3 Seoul
20.11.80 Sang-Ho Choi W PTS 4 Seoul
23.11.80 Sang-Myun Choi W PTS Seoul
29.11.80 Hyung Shik An W PTS 4 Seoul
07.12.80 Kyung-Soo Lee L PTS 6 Seoul
18.01.81 In-Sop Bang W PTS 8 Seoul
02.04.81 Chan-Jung Chun DREW 8 Chunchon
03.06.81 Bong-Ho Lee W PTS 8 Taegu
13.08.81 Hyung-Shik An W PTS 8 Kwangju
03.01.82 Sam-Young Kim DREW 6 Seoul
24.03.82 Shoji Oguma L PTS 10 Tokyo
20.05.82 Yang-Il Shin W RSC 6 Seoul
01.08.82 Chung-Woo Chun W PTS 6 Seoul
03.10.82 Flash Jagdon W PTS 10 Seoul
31.10.82 Suvan Silpaya W PTS 10 Masan
13.01.83 Daonoi Sithsanae W CO 3 Seoul
10.04.83 Adan Uribe Perez W PTS 10 Seoul
17.06.83 Pablo Pepito W PTS 10 Seoul
03.08.83 Kaosai Galaxy L PTS 10 Bangkok
16.10.83 Sung-Moon Choi W PTS 10 Seoul
13.11.83 Neptali Alamag W PTS 10 Inchon
26.02.84 Sak Charsirirta W CO 3 Seoul
03.06.84 Rito Donayre W RSC 3 Seoul
08.07.84 Jorge Ramirez W PTS 10 Seoul
04.12.84 Ernie Cataluna W PTS 10 Seoul
31.03.85 Edgar Apatan W PTS 10 Seoul
25.08.85 Fel Malatag W CO 10 Seoul
02.02.86 Norio Hasegawa W CO 2 Seoul
19.10.86 Little Bangoyan W PTS 10 Seoul
24.05.87 Takuya Muguruma W RSC 11 Moriguchi (*WBA Bantamweight Title Challenge*)
04.10.87 Wilfredo Vasquez L RSC 10 Seoul (*WBA Bantamweight Title Defence*)
12.03.88 Masahatsu Sakuma W RSC 2 Seoul
06.11.88 Robby W CO 4 Seoul
30.04.89 Calim Castro W CO 3 Seoul
Summary: 34 contests, won 28, drew 2, lost 4

Chong-Pal Park

Chunranam-Do, South Korea. *Born* 11.08.60
Former WBA S. Middleweight Champion. Former Undefeated IBF S. Middleweight Champion. Former Undefeated OPBF & South Korean Middleweight Champion

26.11.77 Yong-Soo Chung W CO 1 Pusan
23.12.77 Kyung-Sik Kim W CO 2 Seoul
25.12.77 Seung-Hwan Kang W PTS 6 Seoul
25.03.78 Seung-Hwan Kang DREW 8 Seoul
14.06.78 Hung-Won Kang L RSC 1 Seoul
28.08.78 Kazuo Goshima W CO 1 Tokyo
17.12.78 Chang-Baek Choi W CO 3 Seoul (*South Korean Middleweight Title Challenge*)
03.02.79 Tony Abarca W CO 2 Seoul
17.03.79 Alberto Cruz W CO 2 Taegu
22.04.79 Armando Boniquit W CO 3 Seoul
02.06.79 Michiro Horihata W CO 3 Seoul
22.08.79 Cassius Naito W CO 2 Pusan (*Vacant OPBF Middleweight Title*)
27.01.80 Katsuo Esashi W CO 3 Seoul (*OPBF Middleweight Title Defence*)
18.03.80 Kenji Shibata W CO 5 Seoul (*OPBF Middleweight Title Defence*)
04.05.80 Rocky Joe W CO 8 Jakarta (*OPBF Middleweight Title Defence*)
21.06.80 Fred Pastor W CO 4 Seoul
08.08.80 Peter Piamonte W RTD 4 Seoul (*OPBF Middleweight Title Defence*)
24.09.80 Marcos Torkano W CO 5 Seoul (*OPBF Middleweight Title Defence*)
03.11.80 Phil Davies W RSC 3 Seoul (*OPBF Middleweight Title Defence*)
06.12.80 Joe Willisco W CO 3 Seoul (*OPBF Middleweight Title Defence*)
05.04.81 Caesar Sasaki W CO 6 Seoul (*OPBF Middleweight Title Defence*)
21.06.81 Kenji Shibata W CO 5 Seoul (*OPBF Middleweight Title Defence*)
02.08.81 Sang-Ho Lee W CO 9 Seoul
09.09.81 Mana Pramchai W CO 11 Pusan (*OPBF Middleweight Title Defence*)
07.11.81 Fully Obelmejias L RSC 8 Caracas
03.01.82 Mana Pramchai W CO 4 Seoul (*OPBF Middleweight Title Defence*)
07.03.82 Richie Roberts W CO 8 Seoul (*OPBF Middleweight Title Defence*)
18.04.82 Suwarno W RSC 4 Seoul (*OPBF Middleweight Title Defence*)
18.07.82 Valence Haralan W CO 2 Seoul (*OPBF Middleweight Title Defence*)
26.12.82 Naoto Suzuki W CO 4 Seoul (*OPBF Middleweight Title Defence*)
10.04.83 Antonio Leyva W CO 4 Seoul
29.05.83 Kyung-Min Nah L CO 7 Seoul (*OPBF Middleweight Title Defence*)
04.09.83 Kyung-Min Nah W RSC 4 Chunchon (*OPBF Middleweight Title Challenge*)
06.11.83 Gary Hubble W CO 9 Seoul
04.12.83 Rosendo Ruvalcaba W CO 5 Seoul
05.02.84 Charles Carter W PTS 10 Seoul
17.06.84 Roosevelt Green W RSC 9 Seoul
22.07.84 Murray Sutherland W CO 11 Seoul (*IBF S. Middleweight Title Challenge*)
07.10.84 Wally Carr W PTS 10 Seoul
02.01.85 Roy Gumbs W CO 2 Seoul (*IBF S. Middleweight Title Defence*)
28.04.85 Chang-Hwan Noh W PTS 12 Pusan
30.06.85 Vinnie Curto W PTS 15 Seoul (*IBF S. Middleweight Title Defence*)
02.01.86 Chang-Hwan Noh W CO 9 Seoul
11.04.86 Vinnie Curto W CO 15 Los Angeles (*IBF S. Middleweight Title Defence*)
06.07.86 Lindell Holmes T DRAW 2 Chungju (*IBF S. Middleweight Title Defence*)
14.09.86 Marvin Mack W PTS 15 Pusan (*IBF S. Middleweight Title Defence*)
25.01.87 Doug Sam W RSC 15 Seoul (*IBF S. Middleweight Title Defence*)
03.05.87 Lindell Holmes W PTS 15 Inchon (*IBF S. Middleweight Title Defence*)
26.07.87 Emmanuel Otti W RSC 4 Kwangju (*IBF S. Middleweight Title Defence*)
06.12.87 Jesus Gallardo W RSC 2 Seoul (*Vacant WBA S. Middleweight Title*)
01.03.88 Polly Pasieron W CO 5 Chungju (*WBA S. Middleweight Title Defence*)
23.05.88 Fully Obelmejias L PTS 12 Suanbao (*WBA S. Middleweight Title Defence*)
22.12.88 In-Chul Baek L RSC 9 Seoul
Summary: 53 contests, won 46, drew 2, lost 5.

Cho-Woon Park

South Korea. *Born* 03.01.67
Former Undefeated OPBF & South Korean L. Flyweight Champion

17.04.83 Hi-Suk Kim W RSC 3 Seoul
03.07.83 Eul-Chul Chung DREW 4 Seoul
26.07.83 Dae-Yung Kim W CO 4 Seoul
21.10.83 Jae-Nam Choi W PTS 4 Seoul
12.12.83 Sih-Yuk Chang W PTS 10 Seoul
14.12.83 Chang-Wha Shin W PTS 4 Seoul
16.12.83 Chung-Won Suh W PTS 4 Seoul
07.01.84 Sun-Yong Chung W PTS 4 Seoul
15.01.84 Jae-Chul Kim L PTS 6 Seoul
12.05.84 Chung-Bok Park W PTS 6 Inchon
23.06.84 Sung-Kyu Kim W PTS 6 Seoul
22.09.84 Chang-Yung Chang W PTS 8 Seoul
19.01.85 Dosa Kim W PTS 10 Suwon (*Vacant South Korean L. Flyweight Title*)
06.04.85 Ul-Chul Chung W PTS 10 Taegu (*South Korean L. Flyweight Title Defence*)
17.08.85 Dadoy Anujar W CO 7 Buchon
21.09.85 Chun Huh W PTS 10 Chochiwon (*South Korean L. Flyweight Title Defence*)
11.01.86 Little Baguio DREW 12 Seoul (*Vacant OPBF L. Flyweight Title*)
12.04.86 Little Baguio W PTS 12 Seoul (*Vacant OPBF L. Flyweight Title*)
28.06.86 Junior Thompson W CO 3 Kunsan (*OPBF L. Flyweight Title Defence*)

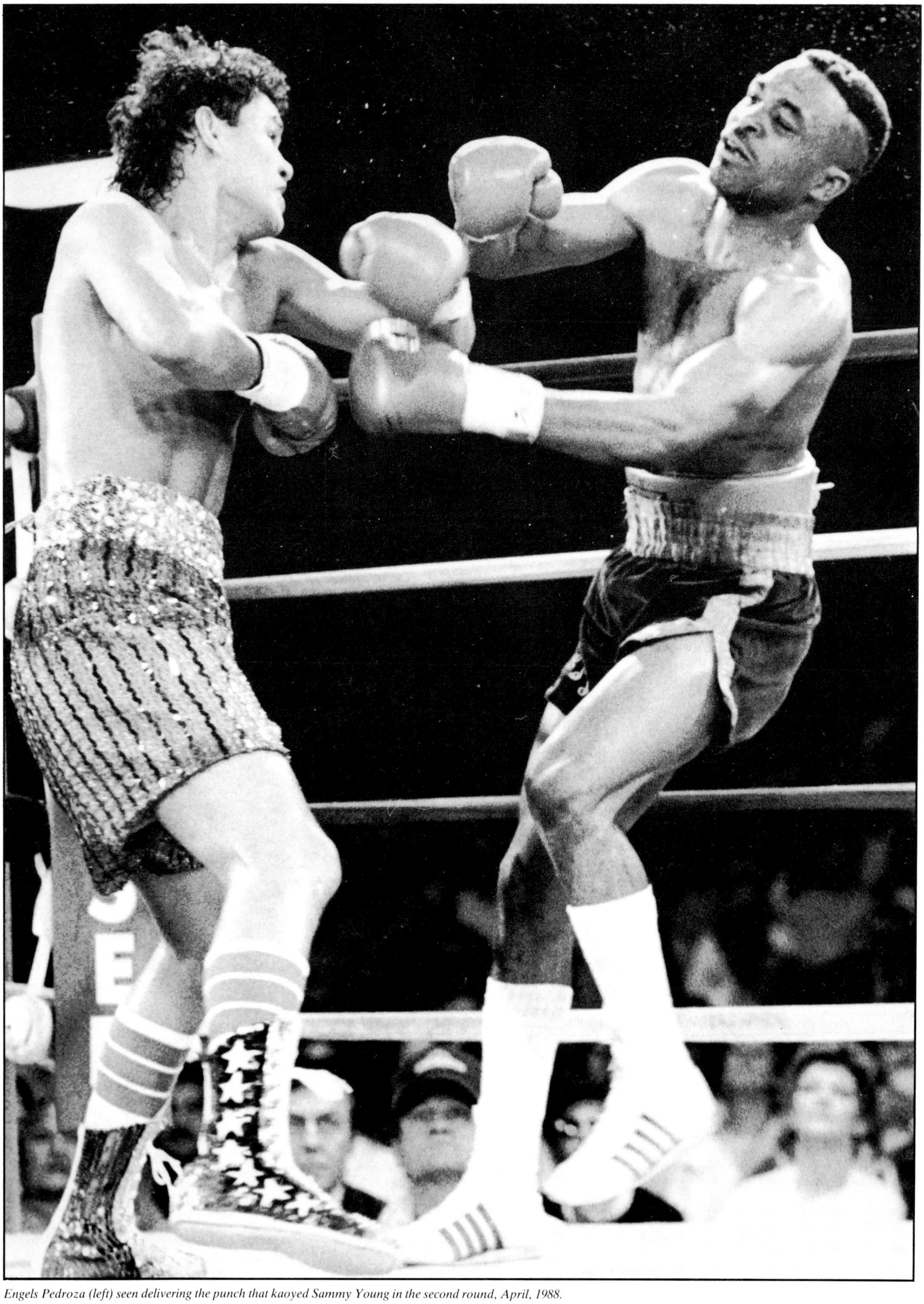

Engels Pedroza (left) seen delivering the punch that kaoyed Sammy Young in the second round, April, 1988.

Christopher M. Farina

07.12.86 Jum-Hwan Choi L PTS 15 Pusan
(*Vacant IBF L. Flyweight Title*)
15.02.87 Rex Rapiso W RSC 12 Seoul
(*Vacant OPBF L. Flyweight Title*)
18.04.87 William Belan DREW 12 Seoul
(*OPBF L. Flyweight Title Defence*)
13.09.87 Ademar Amad W PTS 12 Jinju
(*OPBF L. Flyweight Title Defence*)
21.11.87 Joe Galagran W PTS 10 Eijoungbu
11.02.88 Kenji Matsumura L PTS 12 Himeji
(*OPBF Flyweight Title Challenge*)
06.05.88 Rolando Bohol L PTS 15 Manila
(*IBF Flyweight Title Challenge*)
Summary: 26 contests, won 19, drew 3, lost 4.

Mike Parris
Guyana. *Born* 04.10.57
Guyanan Bantamweight Champion

28.11.82 Rey McBean W PTS 6 Georgetown
19.02.83 Rey McBean W PTS 6 Georgetowm
03.04.83 Oswald Bowen W RSC 4 Georgetown
25.11.83 Anthony Andrews W PTS 12 Georgetown
(*Guyanan Bantamweight Title Challenge*)
24.02.84 Anthony Andrews L RSC 12 Georgetown
(*Guyanan Bantamweight Title Defence*)
02.06.85 Juan Bautista W PTS 10 Georgetown
27.08.85 Darius Ford W RSC 8 Georgetown
(*Vacant Guyanan Bantamweight Title*)
24.02.86 Daryl Pinkney W CO 7 Georgetown
18.05.86 Darius Ford W PTS 12 Georgetown
(*Guyanan Bantamweight Title Defence*)
03.08.86 Juan Polo Perez W PTS 10 Georgetown
31.08.86 Kelvin Smart W PTS 10 Georgetown
13.09.87 Lyndon Profitt W PTS 12 Georgetown
(*Guyanan Bantamweight Title Defence*)
29.11.87 Jesus Bastardo W PTS 10 Georgetown
14.08.88 Wayne Smith W PTS 10 Georgetown
04.12.88 Wayne Smith DREW 12 Georgetown
(*Vacant Guyanan Featherweight Title*)
10.03.89 Ray Minus L PTS 12 Nassau
(*Commonwealth Bantamweight Title Challenge*)
Summary: 16 contests, won 13, drew 1, lost 2.

Tracy Patterson
Peter Goldfield/USA

Tracy Patterson
New York, USA. *Born* 26.12.64
S. Featherweight

19.06.85 Ray Doughty W PTS 4 Totowa
19.07.85 Paul Mays W RSC 1 Poughkeepsie
18.09.85 Paul Moore W CO 1 Atlantic City
30.10.85 Mike Brown W PTS 6 Atlantic City
08.01.86 Darryl Jacobs W RSC 4 Atlantic City
12.02.86 Lamont Buchanan W RSC 5 Detroit
01.03.86 Walter Cowans W PTS 6 Peoria
21.03.86 Darryl Jacobs W PTS 6 Long Beach
26.03.86 Mike Parraz W RSC 1 Detroit
21.05.86 Ricky West W PTS 6 Detroit
21.06.86 James Woodhouse W PTS 6 Atlantic City
28.06.86 Tom Elston W PTS 6 Williamsport
31.10.86 Fred Reed Hall W RSC 1 Atlantic City
02.12.86 Felix Cortez W RSC 1 Atlantic City
13.12.86 Richard Campbell W CO 2 Detroit
16.01.87 Karry Allen W PTS 8 Atlantic City
06.02.87 Eugene Salazar W RSC 3 Reseda
24.04.87 Sonny Long W PTS 8 Davenport
30.06.87 Silford Ashby W RSC 3 Atlantic City
15.08.87 Victor Gonzalez W RSC 4 Reno
09.10.87 Jeff Franklin L PTS 10 Las Vegas
30.01.88 Jeff Hanna W RSC 3 Orlando
01.04.88 Bobby Thomas W CO 2 Omaha
04.06.88 Jay Thomas W RSC 3 Fort Myers
13.08.88 Ronnie Thomas W RSC 4 St Joseph
05.10.88 Tony Hernandez W RSC 1 Orlando
27.10.88 Mario Gonzalez W CO 2 New York
02.12.88 Robinson Sanchez W PTS 10 New York
17.02.89 Allan Makitoki W RSC 4 New York
11.04.89 Kim Jackson W RSC 7 Indianapolis
Summary: 30 contests, won 29, lost 1.

Vinny (The Pazmanian Devil) Pazienza
Cranston, USA. *Born* 16.12.62
Former IBF Lightweight Champion

26.05.83 Chino Rivera W RSC 4 Atlantic City
30.06.83 Keith McCoy W CO 3 Atlantic City
10.07.83 Pat Dangerfield W RSC 2 Atlantic City
16.08.83 Ed Carberry W RSC 2 Atlantic City
31.08.83 Rafael Alicia W RSC 2 Atlantic City
09.09.83 Ricardo Moreno W RSC 3 Las Vegas
24.09.83 Jim Zelinski W RSC 2 Totowa
27.10.83 Bob Stevenson W CO 1 Atlantic City
03.12.83 Emilio Diaz W RTD 3 West Warwick
14.12.83 Jose Ortiz W CO 6 Totowa
26.02.84 David Bell W RSC 4 Beaumont
15.04.84 Mike Golden W PTS 8 Atlantic City
29.08.84 Richie McCain W PTS 8 Atlantic City
09.11.84 Bruno Simili W RSC Riva del Garda
01.12.84 Abdel Marbi L RSC 5 Milan
27.03.85 Antoine Lark W RSC 3 Atlantic City
18.09.85 Jeff Bumphus W PTS 10 Atlantic City
26.11.85 Melvin Paul W CO 2 Atlantic City
05.02.86 Hector Frazier W RSC 7 Providence
18.05.86 Harry Arroyo W PTS 10 Providence
18.09.86 Nelson Bolanos W RSC 6 Providence
08.11.86 Roger Brown W RSC 4 San Juan
08.02.87 Robert Elizondo W RSC 10 Providence
07.06.87 Greg Haugen W PTS 15 Providence
(*IBF Lightweight Title Challenge*)
06.02.88 Greg Haugen L PTS 15 Atlantic City
(*IBF Lightweight Title Defence*)
27.06.88 Felix Dubray W RSC 4 Providence
04.10.88 Ricky Kaiser W RSC 3 Chicago
07.11.88 Roger Mayweather L PTS 12 Las Vegas
(*WBC L. Welterweight Title Challenge*)
14.04.89 Jake Carollo W RSC 2 Atlantic City
Summary: 29 contests, won 26, lost 3.

Engels Pedroza
Venezuela. *Born* 26.09.66
L. Welterweight

17.10.86 Gordon Hanna W RSC 1 Bismark
22.11.86 Dan Hernandez W RSC 2 Las Vegas
24.02.87 Tony Burroughs W RSC 1 Reseda
05.03.87 Floyd Smith W RSC 1 Las Vegas
07.03.87 Jesus Mata W RSC 1 Las Vegas
23.03.87 Roberto Castaneda W RSC 1 Phoenix
03.04.87 Carlos Villareal W CO 1 Las Vegas
15.05.87 Jose L. Mendoza W RSC 1 Las Vegas
30.05.87 Ricardo Rosales W CO 1 Las Vegas
13.06.87 Juan Muniz W RSC 1 Lake Tahoe
21.06.87 Terry Parham W RSC 3 Lexington
05.07.87 John Delpino W RSC 1 Las Vegas
01.08.87 Cecil Taylor W CO 1 Las Vegas
10.09.87 Julian Samaha W RSC 2 Los Angeles
25.11.87 Mario Rodriguez W RSC 2 Las Vegas
12.03.88 Tyrone Cotton W RSC 1 Las Vegas
09.04.88 Javier Juarez W RSC 1 Las Vegas
23.04.88 Sammy Young W CO 2 Las Vegas
19.05.88 Felipe Angulo W CO 5 Las Vegas
17.06.88 Mike Johnson L RSC 9 Las Vegas
13.08.88 Javier Sanchez W RSC 3 Tucson
10.09.88 Manuel de Leon W RSC 2 Las Vegas
05.10.88 Othal Dixon W RSC 1 Los Angeles
22.10.88 Eric Martin W PTS 10 Las Vegas
22.11.88 Jose Rivera L PTS 10 Los Angeles
14.01.89 Jerry Stephens W RSC 2 Las Vegas
24.02.89 C.J. Duffy W RSC 5 Las Vegas
Summary: 27 contests, won 25, lost 2.

Dodie (Boy) Penalosa
Cebu City, Philippines. *Born* 19.11.62
Former IBF Flyweight Champion. Former Undefeated IBF, Philippines & OPBF L. Flyweight Champion

28.02.82 Roger Pilapil W PTS Cebu City
21.03.82 Rolando Navarro W PTS 6 Cebu City
31.03.82 Tony Labrador W PTS 8 Cebu City
08.05.82 Res Cabuenas W PTS 8 San Carlos
19.05.82 Aurel Sagusay W RSC 2 Butuan
05.06.82 Elmer Magallano W PTS 10 Cebu City
30.06.82 Rio Camutan W CO 6 Cebu City
31.07.82 German Ellana W PTS 10 Cebu City
19.09.82 Josue Agcang W PTS 10 Cebu City
26.11.82 Romy Austria W RSC 12 Quezon City
(*Vacant Philippines L. Flyweight Title*)
30.01.83 Fred Guzman T DRAW 4 Cebu City
18.03.83 Sang-Nam Kim W RSC 11 Quezon City
(*Vacant OPBF L. Flyweight Title*)
11.06.83 Katsumi Sato W PTS 12 Manila
(*OPBF L. Flyweight Title Defence*)
10.12.83 Satashi Shingaki W RSC 11 Osaka
(*Vacant IBF L. Flyweight Title*)
13.05.84 Jae-Hong Kim W RSC 9 Seoul
(*IBF L. Flyweight Title Defence*)
16.11.84 Chum-Hwan Choi W PTS 15 Manila
(*IBF L. Flyweight Title Defence*)
19.07.85 Amado Ursua W PTS 10 Manila
12.10.85 Yani Hagler W CO 3 Jakarta
(*IBF L. Flyweight Title Defence*)
21.02.86 Soon-Jung Kang W PTS 10 Manila
05.07.86 Hilario Zapata L PTS 15 Manila
(*WBA Flyweight Title Challenge*)
08.11.86 Young-Il Choi W RSC 5 Manila
22.02.87 Hi-Sup Shin W CO 5 Inchon
(*IBF Flyweight Title Challenge*)
05.09.87 Chang-Ho Choi L CO 11 Manila
(*IBF Flyweight Title Defence*)
15.04.88 Kwanjai Porpenpith W PTS 10 Quezon City
02.09.88 Bi-Won Chung W PTS 10 Manila
04.02.89 Tongpet Sriracha W RSC 8 Pasay
Summary: 26 contests, won 23, drew 1, lost 2.

Fred Pendelton
Philadelphia, USA. *Born* 05.01.63
USBA Lightweight Champion

05.11.81 Ray Evans L PTS 4 Philadelphia
03.12.81 Tony English W CO 2 Philadelphia
11.02.82 Angel Cales L PTS 4 Philadelphia
16.02.82 Rodney Watts L PTS 4 Atlantic City
23.02.82 Felix McKnight W PTS 4 Atlantic City
10.03.82 Jerome Coffee L PTS 8 Nashville
11.05.82 Ray Evans W RSC 4 Atlantic City
20.07.82 Felix McKnight W PTS 6 Atlantic City
15.08.82 Antonio Nieves W PTS 8 Atlantic City
12.10.82 Lloyd Allen W RSC 6 Atlantic City
26.10.82 Gerald Hayes L PTS 8 Atlantic City
27.03.83 Bobby Johnson L PTS 8 Scranton
24.04.83 Jose Rodriguez W PTS 6 Atlantic City
22.05.83 Anthony Fletcher L PTS 8 Atlantic City
05.11.83 Kenny Wills DREW 4 Atlantic City
10.12.83 David Grayton W PTS 8 Andrews
14.01.84 Tim Daniels W PTS 4 Atlantic City
03.03.84 Luis Vega W PTS 4 Atlantic City
19.04.84 Hilmer Kenty L PTS 10 Detroit
28.06.84 Tyrone Trice W RSC 1 Detroit
14.11.84 Adolfo Medel L PTS 10 Atlantic City
04.01.85 Marvin Garris W PTS 8 Philadelphia
19.01.85 Ricky Young L PTS 10 Atlantic City
05.02.85 Joe Manley L PTS 10 Atlantic City
23.03.85 Frankie Randall L RSC 5 Bristol
01.10.85 Darryl Martin W RSC 6 Harrisburg
20.11.85 Jimmy Paul L PTS 10 Atlantic City
24.01.86 Roberto Mendez W RSC 8 Atlantic City
12.03.86 Roger Mayweather W RSC 6 Las Vegas
11.04.86 Shelton Leblanc W PTS 10 Las Vegas
04.07.86 Frankie Randall DREW 12 Atlantic City
(*Vacant USBA Lightweight Title*)
28.08.86 Manuel Hernandez W RSC 3 Los Angeles
07.10.86 Joey Olivera L PTS 10 Los Angeles
02.12.86 Shelton Leblanc L PTS 10 Lafayette
03.04.87 Livingstone Bramble DREW 10 Atlantic City
28.07.87 Ron Haynes W CO 6 Atlantic City
28.09.87 Elvis Perez W RSC 8 Santo Domingo
12.02.88 Sammy Fuentes W RSC 1 Atlantic City

16.03.88 Steve Larrimore W RSC 4 Atlantic City
10.07.88 Livingstone Bramble W RSC 10 Atlantic City
(Vacant USBA Lightweight Title)
13.09.88 Razor Addo W RSC 6 Los Angeles
22.11.88 John Montes L RSC 10 Los Angeles
Summary: 42 contests, won 23, drew 3, lost 16.

Juan Polo Perez
Colombia
Former Undefeated Colombian Flyweight Champion

08.10.82 Arnold Rocha W RSC 1 Santa Marta
05.11.82 Carlos Hernandez W CO 4 Santa Marta
04.02.83 Bombillo Teheran W CO 1 Santa Marta
04.03.83 Sofanor Rodriquez W CO 1 Santa Marta
06.04.83 Victor Tejedor W CO 5 Cartagena
18.06.83 Wilfredo Ruiz W RSC 9 Cartagena
(Colombian Flyweight Title Challenge)
02.07.83 Rafael Julio W RTD 5 Santa Marta
16.09.83 Alberto Castro L PTS 10 Sincelejo
23.12.83 Alberto Castro L PTS 10 Monteria
18.05.84 Alfredo Herrera W RSC 8 Santa Marta
23.06.84 Hilario Zapata L PTS 10 Atlapa
28.07.84 Miguel Maturana L CO 2 Cartagena
02.03.85 Raul Diaz W PTS 10 Cartagena
19.04.85 Alfredo Gomez W RTD 7 Cartagena
03.05.85 Valerio Zea W PTS 8 Cartagena
20.07.85 Jesus Rojas DREW 10 Cartagena
18.10.85 Alex Miranda W RSC 6 Cartagena
31.01.86 Prudencio Cardona W PTS 10 Cartagena
05.07.86 Francisco Alvarez W PTS 10 Cartagena
03.08.86 Mike Parris L PTS 10 Georgetown
19.09.86 Joaquin Caraballo W RSC 4 Cartagena
28.11.86 Heriberto Gelez W PTS 6 Cartagena
12.12.86 Andres Cassiani W PTS 6 Cartagena
23.01.87 Agustin Higirio W PTS 6 Cartagena
14.03.87 Jaime Paternina W CO 2 San Andres
15.05.87 Prudencio Cardona W PTS 10 Cartagena
03.07.87 Alfredo Lugo W PTS 10 Cartagena
31.07.87 Alvaro Mercado W PTS 10 Barranquilla
06.11.87 Efrain Betancourt W RSC 8 Cartagena
26.02.88 Eduo Bermudez DREW 10 Cartagena
28.05.88 Argemiro Colon W RSC 2 Barranquilla
03.09.88 Efrain Betancourt W RSC 3 Cartagena
03.03.89 Alfredo Gomez W CO 2 Medellin
Summary: 33 contests, won 26, drew 2, lost 5.

Raul (Jibaro) Perez
Tijuana, Mexico. *Born* 14.02.67
WBC Bantamweight Champion

29.03.84 Jose Alvarado W RSC 2 Tijuana
12.05.84 Roberto Gatica W PTS 4 Tijuana
10.06.84 Juan J. Lopez W CO 4 Tijuana
23.07.84 Zacarias Hernandez W CO 6 Tijuana
17.08.84 Rufino Lugo W CO 3 Tijuana
29.08.84 Estudiantes Ramirez W CO 3 Tijuana
13.09.84 Jose Borbon W RSC 4 Tijuana
01.10.84 Abraham Garcia W RSC 3 Tijuana
27.10.84 David Bautista W CO 6 Mazatlan
21.11.84 Antonio Flores W RSC 4 Tijuana
10.12.84 Jorge Cons W RSC 3 Tijuana
06.01.85 Canas Lozada W RSC 6 Tijuana
01.02.85 Lupe Acosta W RSC 4 Tijuana
08.03.85 Victor Moreno W RSC 2 Tijuana
25.03.85 Alberto Martinez W PTS 10 Tijuana
06.05.85 Martin Garcia W RSC 9 Tijuana
24.06.85 Carlos de la Paz W RSC 4 Tijuana
27.07.85 Pedro Rodriguez W CO 7 Ensenada
12.08.85 Enrique Aguilar W RSC 9 Tijuana
23.09.85 Eleonico Mercedes W PTS 10 Tijuana
25.11.85 Juan C. Salazar W RSC 7 Tijuana
10.12.85 Lucilo Nolasco W PTS 10 Los Angeles
04.02.86 Lupe Torres W PTS 10 La Paz
24.02.86 Ubaldo Gonzalez W CO 1 San Luis
13.03.86 Lucilo Nolasco W PTS 10 Tijuana
03.05.86 Rodolfo Ortega L PTS 10 Mexico City
16.06.86 Eliseo Olvera W RSC 2 Tijuana
18.07.86 Diego Avila W PTS 10 Tijuana
08.08.86 Miguel Pequeno W CO 3 Tijuana
30.08.86 Prudencio Cardona W PTS 10 Tijuana
10.11.86 Capri Lipkins W PTS 10 Tijuana
08.12.86 James Manning W PTS 10 Tijuana
27.01.87 Tony Escobar W RSC 10 Tijuana
20.03.87 Victor Moreno W CO 1 Mexicali
27.04.87 Calvin Williams W CO 1 Tijuana
06.07.87 Gaby Canizales W RSC 9 Tijuana
10.09.87 Edel Geronimo T DRAW 3 Los Angeles
12.10.87 Jorge Ramirez W PTS 10 Tijuana
07.12.87 Eduardo Torres W CO 1 Tijuana
01.02.88 Rodolfo Ortega W PTS 10 Tijuana
04.04.88 Martin Lopez W RSC 2 Tijuana
01.08.88 Wilfredo Vasquez W PTS 10 Los Angeles
29.10.88 Miguel Lora W PTS 12 Las Vegas
(WBC Bantamweight Title Challenge)
09.03.89 Lucio Lopez W PTS 12 Los Angeles
(WBC Bantamweight Title Defence)
Summary: 44 contests, won 42, drew 1, lost 1.

Tomas Perez
Santa Ana, USA. *Born* 01.05.60
L. Middleweight

20.11.80 Pedro Guerrero W RSC 4 Los Angeles
26.07.81 Paul Gonzales W PTS 4 Las Vegas
06.10.81 Rigo Lopez W RSC 1 Las Vegas
15.10.81 Armando Acosta W PTS 6 Los Angeles
21.11.81 Jahid Kareem W PTS 6 Los Angeles
09.03.82 Paul Gonzales W PTS 6 Las Vegas
17.06.82 Juan Collado W CO 4 Los Angeles
07.10.82 Jerome Kelly W RSC 2 Los Angeles
06.11.82 Mike Ashanti W PTS 6 Los Angeles
03.02.83 Doug James W CO 5 Los Angeles
09.06.83 Jorge Vaca W RSC 8 Los Angeles
10.06.84 Steve Williams W RSC 2 Chicago
27.09.84 Derrick Kelly L PTS 10 Los Angeles
26.08.85 Clinton Reymus W RSC 3 Irvine
29.11.85 Ernie Rabotte W RSC 5 Irvine
31.03.86 Zack Hewitt W RSC 7 Irvine
05.08.86 Luis Santana L PTS 10 Las Vegas
08.04.87 Derrick Kelly L PTS 12 Los Angeles
29.10.87 Gilbert Baptist W TD 7 Irvine
29.02.88 Ray Taylor W RSC 8 Irvine
23.05.88 Joe Walker W RSC 4 Irvine
22.08.88 Kenny Lopez W PTS 12 Irvine
01.12.88 Toby Flores W CO 12 Irvine
23.03.89 Royan Hammond W RSC 11 Irvine
Summary: 24 contests, won 21, lost 3.

Mike Phelps
Beaumont, USA. *Born* 21.03.65
S. Flyweight

14.12.82 Juan Payan W RSC 2 Pasadena
25.01.83 Jaime Herrera W PTS 4 Port Arthur
22.03.83 Federico Rivera W PTS 4 Pasadena
08.07.83 Alberto Mendez W PTS 4 Beaumont
05.08.83 Ruben Chavarria W PTS 4 Beaumont
23.09.83 Rey Nino W PTS 4 Lake Charles
12.11.83 Francisco Arbaiza W PTS 4 Beaumont
24.11.83 Jorge Salas W PTS 4 Pasadena
06.12.83 Francisco Arbaiza W PTS 4 Houston
29.01.84 Felipe Mojica W PTS 4 Beaumont
26.02.84 Carlos Lopez W RSC 3 Beaumont
21.03.84 Felipe Mojica W PTS 6 Pasadena
27.07.84 Willie Covington W RSC 2 Houston
14.08.84 Herman Henderson W RSC 2 Pasadena
11.09.84 Jose Luis Garcia W CO 2 Pasadena
25.09.84 Lee Moore W PTS 4 Metairie
16.10.84 Lee Moore W PTS 6 Pasadena
15.01.85 Eloy Santos W RSC 1 Pasadena
20.02.85 Felipe Mojica T DRAW 3 Beaumont
14.05.85 Jesus Portillo W PTS 8 Beaumont
17.07.85 Lee Cargle W PTS 8 Houston
18.12.85 Juan Muriel W PTS 6 Atlantic City
01.02.86 Ruben Chavarria W CO 1 Beaumont
10.02.86 Jesus Salud L CO 10 Los Angeles
03.04.86 Raymond Medel W PTS 12 Beaumont
02.09.86 Edgar Muniz W PTS 8 Baytown
14.12.86 Eddie Rangel DREW 12 Houston
03.02.88 Eduardo Martin W DIS 6 Houston
02.03.88 Ramon Solis W PTS 8 Houston
29.05.88 Ignacio Duran W RSC 2 Houston
25.02.89 Elly Pical L PTS 12 Singapore
(IBF S. Flyweight Title Challenge)
Summary: 31 contests, won 27, drew 2, lost 2.

Elly Pical
Saparua-Maluku, Indonesia. *Born* 24.03.60
IBF S. Flyweight Champion. Former Undefeated Indonesian & OPBF S. Flyweight Champion

10.12.82 Eddy Rafael W CO 5 Jakarta
19.12.82 Benny Nurianto W CO 6 Malang
06.02.83 Juwarno W CO 1 Malang
15.05.83 Moningko Palungan W CO 2 Malang
24.07.83 Edward Apay L PTS 10 Malang
18.08.83 Munadi W CO 2 Jakarta
11.09.83 Viboon Muangsurin W PTS 10 Jakarta
11.12.83 Wongso Indrajit W PTS 12 Surabaya
(Indonesian S. Flyweight Title Challenge)
30.03.84 Prayurasak Muangsurin W CO 1 Bangkok
19.05.84 Hi-Yun Chung W TD 4 Seoul
(OPBF S. Flyweight Title Challenge)
07.10.84 Matsuo Watanabe W RSC 6 Jakarta
(OPBF S. Flyweight Title Defence)
03.05.85 Joo-Do Chun W RSC 8 Jakarta
(IBF S. Flyweight Title Defence)
25.08.85 Wayne Mulholland W RSC 3 Jakarta
(IBF S. Flyweight Title Defence)
15.02.86 Cesar Polanco L PTS 15 Jakarta
(IBF S. Flyweight Title Defence)
05.07.86 Cesar Polanco W CO 3 Jakarta
(IBF S. Flyweight Title Defence)
03.12.86 Dong-Chun Lee W CO 10 Jakarta
(IBF S. Flyweight Title Defence)
28.02.87 Kaosai Galaxy L CO 14 Jakarta
(WBA S. Flyweight Title Defence)
06.09.87 Sukardi W CO 4 Surabaya
17.10.87 Tae-Il Chang W PTS 15 Jakarta
(IBF S. Flyweight Title Defence)
20.02.88 Raul Diaz W PTS 15 Pontianak
(IBF S. Flyweight Title Defence)
04.09.88 Chang-Ki Kim W PTS 12 Surabaya
(IBF S. Flyweight Title Defence)
25.02.89 Mike Phelps W PTS 12 Singapore
(IBF S. Flyweight Title Defence)
Summary: 22 contests, won 19, lost 3.

Bernardo Pinango
Panama. *Born* Caracas, Venezuela 09.02.60
Former WBA S. Bantamweight Champion. Former Undefeated WBA Bantamweight Champion

01.08.81 Angel Torres DREW 6 Caracas
31.08.81 Angel Torres W RSC 1 Caracas
12.10.81 Nelson Rodriguez W RSC 1 Caracas
12.11.81 Angel Torres W PTS 6 Caracas
26.04.82 William Gonzalez W RSC 3 Caracas
12.07.82 Jimmy Chavez W RSC 7 Polamar
26.07.82 Jose Mosqueda ND 2 Cumana
04.10.82 Antonio Esparragoza DREW 10 Caracas
08.11.82 Tito Roque W RSC 5 Caracas
21.02.83 Arnel Arrozal W PTS 10 Valencia
07.03.83 Orlando Silva W CO 2 Caracas
11.04.83 Rene Aroy W RSC 5 Catia la Mar
02.05.83 Juan Resma W PTS 10 Caracas
08.08.83 Raul Gonzalez L PTS 10 Caracas
17.10.83 Raul Gonzalez W PTS 10 Caracas
06.02.84 Jose Sandoval W RSC 1 Caracas
27.02.84 Hector Vasquez W RSC 2 Caracas
19.03.84 Jesus Flores L PTS 10 Caracas
26.05.84 Milton Torres W PTS 10 Guaynabo
19.07.85 Jose Meneses W CO 5 Panama City
15.12.85 Jose Meneses W CO 5 Panama City
01.03.86 Benito Badilla W CO 8 Panama City
04.06.86 Gaby Canizales W PTS 15 East Rutherford
(WBA Bantamweight Title Challenge)
04.10.86 Ciro de Leva W RSC 10 Turin
(WBA Bantamweight Title Defence)
22.11.86 Simon Skosana W RSC 15 Johannesburg
(WBA Bantamweight Title Defence)
03.02.87 Frankie Duarte W PTS 15 Los Angeles
(WBA Bantamweight Title Defence)
03.10.87 Farid Benredjeb DREW 8 Gravelines
27.02.88 Julio Gervacio W PTS 12 San Juan
(WBA S. Bantamweight Title Challenge)
28.05.88 Juan J. Estrada L PTS 12 Tijuana
(WBA S. Bantamweight Title Defence)
Summary: 29 contests, won 22, drew 3, lost 3, no decision 1.

Rafael Pineda

Peter Goldfield/USA

Rafael (Bombacional) Pineda
Colombia. *Born* 12.01.66
Lightweight

30.04.86 Jose Cassianis W RSC 5 Barranquilla
21.06.86 Jose Morelos W CO 2 San Onofre
25.07.86 Gustave Rodriquez W CO 2 Barranquilla
05.09.86 Santander Vargas W RSC 3 Barranquilla
17.10.86 Alfonso Chamorro W CO 2 Barranquilla
31.10.86 Moises Almanza W RSC 2 Monteria
21.12.86 Julio Llerena W RSC 10 Cartagena
13.02.87 Jesus Espitia W CO 1 Barranquilla
13.03.87 Arnovia Castro W RSC 4 Cartagena
04.04.87 Jose Cassianis W CO 2 San Andres
19.06.87 Fernando Sanchez W CO 1 Barranquilla
31.07.87 Andres Ramos W RSC 3 Barranquilla
04.09.87 Ildemar Paisan W PTS 10 Cartagena
23.10.87 Carlos Mendietta W CO 5 San Andres
18.12.87 Francisco Fernandez W RSC 5 Cartagena
02.04.88 Angel Beltre W CO 2 Atlantic City
15.07.88 Carlos Mantilla W RSC 2 Barranquilla
29.07.88 Juan Manija W CO 5 Atlantic City
03.11.88 Bryan Brown W RSC 2 Las Vegas
05.02.89 Vernon Buchanan W RSC 4 Las Vegas
22.04.89 Mark Breland L RSC 5 Atlantic City
(*WBA Welterweight Title Challenge*)
Summary: 21 contests, won 20, lost 1.

Giampiero Pinna
Castelsardo, Italy. *Born* 27.10.58
WBC International L. Flyweight Champion.
Former Undefeated Italian Flyweight Champion

21.03.80 Roberto d'Aula W RSC 1 Bologna
18.04.80 Armando Guarini W PTS 4 Bologna
22.05.80 Salvatore Laconi NC 1 Bologna
10.10.80 Mario de Prosperis W RTD 4 Sassari
30.04.81 Francisco Garcia W PTS 6 Sassari
02.09.81 Emilio Pireddu W PTS 8 Stintino
07.11.81 Carlo Ravaioli W PTS 8 Sassari
05.02.82 Ciro de Leva L RSC 8 Bologna
21.05.82 Bofunga Eymono W RSC 6 Sassari
10.11.82 Umberto Morri W PTS 8 Sassari
21.12.82 Mariano Garcia W PTS 8 Sassari
22.01.83 Angel Oliver W PTS 8 Sassari
20.05.83 Franco Cherchi L PTS 12 Cagliari
(*Italian Flyweight Title Challenge*)
13.04.84 Franco Cherchi L RSC 4 Milan
(*Italian Flyweight Title Challenge*)
20.10.84 Umberto Morri W PTS 8 Bonorva
14.06.85 Mario Bitetto W PTS 12 Sassari
(*Vacant Italian Flyweight Title*)
17.11.85 Mario Bitetto W PTS 12 Vercelli
(*Italian Flyweight Title Defence*)
29.05.86 Giovanni Camputaro W PTS 12 San Maria
(*Italian Flyweight Title Defence*)
17.12.86 Duke McKenzie L PTS 12 Acqui Terme
(*EBU Flyweight Title Challenge*)
08.07.87 Roberto Cirelli W RSC 11 Lumezzane
(*Vacant Italian Flyweight Title*)
16.12.87 Roberto Cirelli W PTS 12 Villabate
(*Italian Flyweight Title Defence*)
04.06.88 Jaleldine Mastouri W PTS 6 Villabate
13.07.88 Ebo Danquah L RSC 7 Santa Marinelli
(*WBC International L. Flyweight Title Challenge*)
15.10.88 Ebo Danquah W PTS 12 Monte Sarchio
(*WBC International L. Flyweight Title Challenge*)
17.12.88 Charles Enisan W PTS 8 Sassari
Summary: 25 contests, won 19, lost 5, no contest 1.

Cesar (Patico) Polanco
Dominican Republic. *Born* 29.11.67
Former WBC International & IBF S. Flyweight Champion. Former Undefeated Con. Am. Flyweight Champion

25.05.83 Elpidio Jimenez W CO 1 Santiago
25.07.83 Sisia Noesi W PTS 4 Santiago
26.09.83 Rafael Ramos W PTS 6 Santiago
17.10.83 Vicente Arias W PTS 6 Santiago
16.11.83 Juan Maria Ortiz W RSC 1 Santiago
07.12.83 Rafel Ramos W RSC 3 Santiago
12.03.84 Bernardo Diaz W PTS 8 Santiago
13.09.84 Rafael Cabrera DREW 10 Santiago
20.10.84 Victor Espinal W CO 3 Santiago
31.01.85 David Reyes W RSC 4 Santiago
(*Vacant Con. Am. Flyweight Title*)
11.03.85 Isaias Rodriquez W DIS 2 Santiago
16.04.85 Elpidio de Paula W RSC 4 Santiago
16.11.85 Julio Gudino L PTS 10 Panama City
25.11.85 Fernando Mateo W CO 5 Santiago
15.02.86 Elly Pical W PTS 15 Jakarta
(*IBF S. Flyweight Title Challenge*)
05.07.86 Elly Pical L CO 3 Jakarta
(*IBF S. Flyweight Title Defence*)
29.04.87 Alfredo Gomez W CO 3 Curacao
16.08.87 Franco Cherchi W CO 6 Salerno
(*Vacant WBC International S. Flyweight Title*)
25.04.88 Bernardo Diaz W CO 3 Santiago
12.12.88 Luis Malave W PTS 10 Santiago
11.03.89 Nana Yaw Konadu L PTS 12 Accra
(*WBC International S. Flyweight Title Defence*)
Summary: 21 contests, won 17, drew 1, lost 3.

Jesus Poll

Jesus Poll
Caracas, Venezuela. *Born* 01.01.65
NABF S. Bantamweight Champion

31.01.86 Frank Rodriguez W PTS 4 Turmero
22.02.86 Henry Rivas W PTS 4 Caracas
30.04.86 Bernabe Viloria W PTS 6 Barranquilla
30.05.86 Julio Gervacio DREW 6 Curacao
13.09.86 Frank Rodriguez W PTS 8 Caraballera
01.11,86 Richard Wester W RSC 2 Curacao
16.01.87 Galin Georgiev W PTS 4 Phoenix
24.02.87 Daniel Garcia W PTS 8 Reseda
20.03.87 Jeff Franklin DREW 8 Las Vegas
21.05.87 Henry Lugo W PTS 10 Sacramento
05.06.87 Daniel Garcia W PTS 10 Los Angeles
27.06.87 Jorge Rodriquez W RSC 5 Los Angeles
13.08.87 Paul Banke W RSC 7 Los Angeles
10.09.87 Antonio Gonzalez W PTS 10 Los Angeles
23.02.88 Victor Paredes W PTS 10 Reseda
26.04.88 Miguel Juarez W PTS 10 Reseda
27.05.88 Louie Espinosa W PTS 12 Las Vegas
(*NABF S. Bantamweight Title Challenge*)
27.09.88 Allan Makitoki W PTS 10 Reseda
14.10.88 Julian Solis W PTS 12 Las Vegas
(*NABF S. Bantamweight Title Defence*)
04.04.89 Juan J. Estrada L RSC 10 Los Angeles
(*WBA S. Bantamweight Title Challenge*)
Summary: 20 contests, won 17, drew 2, lost 1.

Chris Pyatt
Leicester, England *Born* 03.07.63
Former EBU L. Middleweight Champion. Former Undefeated British L. Middleweight Champion

01.03.83 Paul Murray W RTD 2 London
05.04.83 Billy Waith W RSC 8 London
28.04.83 Lee Hartshorn W RSC 3 Leicester
27.09.83 Darwin Brewster W PTS 8 Wembley
08.10.83 Tyrone Demby W RSC 2 Atlantic City
22.11.83 Tony Britton W RSC 4 Wembley
22.02.84 Judas Clottey W PTS 8 London
15.03.84 Pat Thomas W PTS 10 Leicester
09.05.84 Franki Moro W CO 4 Leicester
23.05.84 Alfonso Redondo W RSC 3 London
16.10.84 John Ridgman W RSC 1 London
16.11.84 Brian Anderson W PTS 12 Leicester
12.02.85 Helier Custos W RSC 5 London
05.06.85 Graeme Ahmed W RSC 3 London
01.07.85 Mosimo Maeleke W RSC 6 London
23.09.85 Sabiyala Diavilia L RSC 4 London
19.02.86 Prince Rodney W CO 9 London
(*British L. Middleweight Title Challenge*)
20.05.86 Thomas Smith W RSC 1 Wembley
17.09.86 John van Elteren W RSC 1 London
(*Vacant EBU L. Middleweight Title*)
25.10.86 Renaldo Hernandez W RSC 3 Paris
28.01.87 Gianfranco Rosi L PTS 12 Perugia
(*EBU L. Middleweight Title Defence*)
18.04.87 Dennis Johnson W CO 2 London
26.05.87 Sammy Floyd W RSC 2 Wembley
28.10.87 Gilbert Josamu W PTS 8 Wembley
28.05.88 Jose Duarte W RSC 4 London
23.11.88 Eddie Hall W RSC 2 London
01.12.88 Knox Brown W RSC 2 London
14.12.88 Tyrone Moore W CO 1 London
15.02.89 Russell Mitchell W RSC 4 London
Summary: 29 contests, won 27, lost 2.

Dwight (Camden Buzzsaw) Muhammad Qawi
Baltimore, USA. *Born* 05.01.53
Con. Am. Cruiserweight Champion. Former WBC L. Heavyweight Champion. Former WBA Cruiserweight Champion

19.04.78 Leonard Langley DREW 6 Washington
03.06.78 Lou Benson W PTS 6 Baltimore
02.11.78 Johnny Davis L PTS 6 New York
25.05.79 Lou Butler W PTS 6 Baltimore
03.07.79 Lou Butler W PTS 8 Atlantic City
26.09.79 Biff Cline W RSC 1 Baltimore
14.11.79 Johnny Wilburn W PTS 8 Baltimore
04.02.80 Theunis Kok W CO 10 Durban
29.03.80 Cornell Chavis W CO 1 Atlantic City
08.05.80 Leonard Langley W RSC 2 Atlantic City
05.06.80 Charlie Smith W RTD 4 Atlantic City
14.08.80 Rick Jester W RSC 3 Chicago
06.11.80 Tony Mesoraca W RTD 6 Atlantic City
08.01.81 Johnny Davis W PTS 10 Atlantic City
05.03.81 Al Bolden W PTS 10 Philadelphia
31.05.81 Mike Rossman W CO 7 Atlantic City
05.09.81 James Scott W PTS 10 Rahway
19.12.81 Matt Saad Muhammad W RSC 10 Atlantic City
(*WBC L. Heavyweight Title Challenge*)
21.03.82 Jerry Martin W RSC 6 Las Vegas
(*WBC L. Heavyweight Title Defence*)
07.08.82 Matt Saad Muhammad W RSC 6 Philadelphia
(*WBC L. Heavyweight Title Defence*)
20.11.82 Eddie Davis W RSC 11 Atlantic City
(*WBC L. Heavyweight Title Defence*)
18.03.83 Michael Spinks L PTS 15 Atlantic City
(*WBC L. Heavyweight Title Defence & WBA L. Heavyweight Title Challenge*)
17.09.83 Johnny Davis W PTS 10 Atlantic City
21.03.84 Vic Valentino W PTS 10 Atlantic City
12.12.84 Stanley Ross W PTS 10 Atlantic City
27.02.85 Michael Greer W PTS 10 Atlantic City
27.07.85 Piet Crous W CO 11 Sun City
(*WBA Cruiserweight Title Challenge*)
08.01.86 Ric Enis W CO 1 Atlantic City
23.03.86 Leon Spinks W RSC 6 Reno
(*WBA Cruiserweight Title Defence*)
12.07.86 Evander Holyfield L PTS 15 Atlanta
(*WBA Cruiserweight Title Defence*)
06.02.87 Sixto Maldonado W CO 4 Atlantic
15.05.87 Ossie Ocasio L PTS 10 Las Vegas
15.08.87 Lee Roy Murphy W RSC 6 St Tropez
05.12.87 Evander Holyfield L CO 4 Atlantic City
(*IBF Cruiserweight Title Challenge*)
19.03.88 George Foreman L RSC 7 Las Vegas
23.11.88 Olian Alexander W RSC 3 Philadelphia
15.02.89 Tyrone Booze W PTS 10 Philadelphia
18.04.89 Andre McCall W PTS 12 Scranton
(*Vacant Con. Am. Cruiserweight Title*)
Summary: 38 contests, won 31, drew 1, lost 6.

Jose (Pepo) Quinones
Puerto Rico. *Born* 13.09.61
Puerto Rican Middleweight Champion. Former Con. Am. Middleweight Champion

16.10.80 Jose Guerrero W CO 1 Los Angeles
20.11.80 Odell Hadley L PTS 4 Los Angeles
26.04.81 Aldo Polesel W RSC 2 Mantova
28.05.81 Jean-Philippe Truchelut W RSC 2 Milan
18.06.81 Paul Muyodi W RSC 1 Milan

28.10.81 Zack Bolden L PTS 4 Las Vegas
04.11.81 Warren Hardy W RSC 1 Las Vegas
14.11.81 Pedro Guerrero W CO 3 Las Vegas
21.11.81 Fred Hutchings L PTS 6 Las Vegas
22.05.82 Luis Palma W PTS 6 Las Vegas
29.05.82 Sumbu Kalambay L CO 2 Milan
21.10.82 Ron Ayers W PTS 6 Cleveland
19.01.83 Al Cook W CO 2 San Juan
16.03.83 Costello King W RSC 2 San Juan
01.05.83 Esteban Pizarro L RSC 4 San Juan
03.02.84 John Burney W PTS 6 Miami
14.03.84 Leroy Moore W RSC 1 Miami
04.04.84 Keith Adams DREW 8 Miami
04.05.84 Ed Flanning W CO 1 Miami
14.08.84 Elvis Parks DREW 8 Miami
30.03.85 Reyes Escalera W RSC 3 Santurce
26.04.85 Horacio Perez W RSC 4 New York
(*Vacant Con. Am. Middleweight Title*)
14.06.85 Arthur Holt W RSC 11 New York
(*Con. Am. Middleweight Title Defence*)
14.12.85 Esteban Pizarro L RSC 6 Catano
(*Con. Am. Middleweight Title Defence*)
01.03.86 Santos Solis W CO 4 Barceloneta
(*Vacant Puerto Rican Middleweight Title*)
29.08.86 Sean Mannion L PTS 10 Lowell
08.11.86 Victor Claudio L PTS 10 San Juan
20.02.87 Doug de Witt W RSC 3 Atlantic City
30.07.87 Gilberto Espinosa W PTS 10 San Juan
28.11.87 Errol Christie W RSC 4 Windsor
10.05.88 Jerome Kelly W RSC 8 Phoenix
09.09.88 Mike Tinley L PTS 10 Atlantic City.
Summary: 32 contests, won 21, drew 2, lost 9.

Jorge (Cocas) Ramirez
Hermosillo, Mexico. *Born* 23.01.65
Mexican S. Featherweight Champion

18.12.82 Ramon Valenzuela W CO 3 Hermosillo
20.01.83 Ivan Lopez W CO 3 Hermosillo
14.02.83 Jorge Zamora W CO 2 Alaman
01.03.83 Sergio Zambrano L RSC 2 Hermosillo
20.03.83 Jorge Zamora W CO 1 Alaman
05.08.83 Grapito Regalado W CO 3 Hermosillo
21.10.83 Vicente Garcia W RSC 1 Caborca
31.10.83 Amado Villegas W RSC 2 Navojoa
11.11.83 Memo Lutz W RSC 4 Obregon
22.11.83 Manuel Chavez W RSC 3 Navojoa
15.12.83 Jorge Aguilar W CO 3 Hermosillo
29.12.83 Salvador Canedo W RSC 6 Penasco
03.02.84 Cosme Suzuki W RSC 2 Penasco
.84 Juan Castro L RSC 1 Navojoa
03.05.84 Joel Valdez W CO 4 Penasco
18.05.84 Mario Fortanel W RSC 9 Penasco
10.06.84 Mariano Bautista W CO 2 Alaman
07.07.84 Roberto Huerta W RSC 1 Navojoa
13.07.84 Torito Morgan W CO 2 Agua Prieto
10.08.84 Tony Lugo W CO 2 Hermosillo
18.08.84 Joel Segura W CO 3 Agua Prieto
24.08.84 Francisco Bojorquez W CO 3 Alaman
10.09.84 Mike Martinez W CO 4 Alaman
29.09.84 Antonio Gonzalez W CO 5 Tijuana
10.10.84 Conrado Lopez W CO 9 Navojoa
27.10.84 Lupe Martinez W CO 2 Nogales
18.12.84 Hector Medina W RSC 6 Hermosillo
21.01.85 Memo Lutz W RSC 2 Tijuana
01.02.85 Jorge Aguilar W CO 3 Nogales
10.02.85 Celso Munoz W CO 6 Navojoa
24.04.85 Rodolfo Martinez DREW 10 Navojoa
31.05.85 Manuel Vazquez W RSC 4 Hermosillo
28.06.85 Lupe Martinez W RSC 3 Hermosillo
11.08.85 Norberto Cabrera DREW 10 Hermosillo
13.09.85 Antonio Paredes W CO 2 Nogales
14.10.85 Oscar Bejines L RSC 9 Tijuana
30.11.85 Norberto Cabrera L PTS 10 Hermosillo
29.12.85 Celso Munoz W RSC 3 Hermosillo
25.01.86 Coreano Lopez W CO 2 Nogales
21.02.86 Boni Flores W CO 2 Hermosillo
21.03.86 Arturo Hernandez W PTS 10 Caborca
17.04.86 Juan Antonio Lopez W PTS 10 Hermosillo
21.05.86 Sergio Bacasegua W PTS 10 Navojoa
15.08.86 Joaquin Acuna W CO 5 Navojoa
26.09.86 Rodolfo Martinez W CO 2 Navojoa
14.10.87 Bruno Rabanales W PTS 10 Navojoa
18.12.87 Salvador Zamora L DIS 6 Obregon
20.02.88 Juan Garcia W CO 2 Obregon
30.04.88 Martin Torres W CO 7 Guaymas
20.06.88 Narciso Valenzuela W CO 7 Hermosillo
24.06.88 Salvador Zamora W PTS 10 Obregon
05.08.88 Besby Dempsey W CO 3 Hermosillo
30.09.88 Roger Arevalo W CO 6 Hermosillo
(*Mexican S. Featherweight Title Challenge*)
03.02.89 Abraham Martinez W CO 3 Hermosillo
(*Mexican S. Featherweight Title Defence*)
08.04.89 Hector Cortez W CO 2 Hermosillo
Summary: 55 contests, won 48, drew 2, lost 5.

Jose Luis Ramirez
Huatabampo, Mexico. *Born* 02.12.58
Former WBC Lightweight Champion. Former Undefeated NABF & Mexican Lightweight Champion

25.03.73 Mario Amparan W RSC 6 Huatabampo
15.04.73 Noe Morales W CO 1 Huatabampo
29.04.73 Roberto Navarrete W CO 1 Huatabampo
15.05.73 Chuy Lopez W RSC 3 Huatabampo
12.07.73 Delfino Mendoza W CO 1 Huatabampo
01.08.73 Delfino Mendoza W PTS 6 Obregon
15.08.73 Lino Munoz W RSC 3 Obregon
30.08.73 Gustavo Guerrero W RSC 5 Huatabampo
20.09.73 Jesse Torres W RSC 1 Huatabampo
10.10.73 Indio Huicosa W PTS 6 Obregon
30.10.73 Chamaco Perez W RSC 5 Obregon
16.03.74 Mario Fontanel W RSC 3 Prieta
29.03.74 Indio Huicosa W RSC 2 Obregon
05.04.74 Gustavo Guerrero W PTS 8 Navojoa
07.05.74 Rudy Sanchez W RSC 2 Huatabampo
12.05.74 Jose Gonzalez W RSC 1 Obregon
17.05.74 Enrique Torres W RSC 3 Navojoa
14.06.74 Salomon Tapia W PTS 8 Navojoa
16.07.74 Pajaro Morales W RSC 5 Huatabampo
21.03.75 Pajaro Morales W RSC 2 Obregon
18.04.75 Jose Lizarraga W RSC 3 Guaymas
30.04.75 Sergio Enriquez L PTS 10 Obregon
21.05.75 Ernesto Castillo W RSC 2 Obregon
18.06.75 Nino Gonzalez W PTS 10 Obregon
15.08.75 Cono Lopez W RSC 3 Obregon
01.10.75 Lorenzo Maldonado W RSC 3 Obregon
13.02.76 Frankie Crawford W RSC 7 Obregon
17.05.76 Roy Esparza W RSC 4 Tijuana
07.06.76 Javier Rios W RSC 1 Culiacan
17.06.76 Nexae Macias W RSC 1 Obregon
06.08.76 Rolando Ramirez W RSC 5 Culiacan
13.09.76 Elio Hernandez W RSC 3 Tijuana
27.09.76 Jesus Delgado W RSC 3 Tijuana
05.11.76 Batoto Salazar W RSC 5 Guaymas
15.11.76 Jesus Lara W CO 4 Tijuana
11.02.77 Ramon Peraza W PTS 10 Los Mochis
12.04.77 Rolando Martinez W CO 1 La Paz
29.06.77 Carlos Ulloa W CO 1 Tijuana
07.07.77 Toluco Munoz W RSC 4 Los Mochis
01.08.77 Aurelio Muniz W PTS 10 Los Mochis
07.12.77 Camilo Ibarra W CO 7 Obregon
07.01.78 Joe Gallardo W CO 7 La Paz
03.02.78 Henry Jacobo W CO 5 Obregon
17.02.78 Indio Perez W CO 4 Obregon
28.04.78 Ruben Olivares L RSC 2 Obregon
23.06.78 Chito Felix W RSC 3 Huatabampo
07.07.78 Bobo Gonzalez W CO 2 Huatabampo
21.07.78 Salvador Torres W RSC 3 Obregon
01.09.78 Leonardo Bermudez W PTS 10 Obregon
20.10.78 David Bernal W CO 3 Tijuana
01.12.78 Cesar Savinon W CO 2 Obregon
02.02.79 Aurelio Muniz W RSC 9 Obregon
07.03.79 Julio Nava W CO 3 Hermosillo
06.04.79 Saul Montana W RSC 7 Guaymas
15.06.79 Beto Gutierrez W RSC 9 Obregon
(*Vacant Mexican Lightweight Title*)
08.07.79 Cachorro Estrella W CO 7 Huatabampo
27.07.79 Antonio Nava W PTS 10 Obregon
20.08.79 Ignacio Campos W RSC 6 Tijuana
28.09.79 Jose Luis Castillo W PTS 12 Obregon
(*Mexican Lightweight Title Defence*)
11.11.79 Joe Gallardo W CO 4 Huatabampo
26.11.79 Ignacio Campos W RSC 12 Tijuana
(*Mexican Lightweight Title Defence*)
19.12.79 Eric Bonilla W CO 4 Obregon
03.02.80 Jose Torres W CO Mexicali
21.03.80 German Cuello W CO 8 Los Angeles
19.06.80 Rafael Nunez W CO 1 Tacoma
09.07.80 Jesus Lara W CO 7 Navojoa
10.08.80 Manuel Sanchez W RSC 6 Huatabampo
23.08.80 Dario de Jesus W CO 1 Los Angeles
11.10.80 Vicente Mijares W RSC 6 Mexico
(*Mexican Lightweight Title Defence*)
14.11.80 Alexis Arguello L PTS 10 Miami
07.02.81 Ernesto Garfias W RSC 7 Los Angeles
27.02.81 Abdul Bey W CO 3 Huatabampo
04.04.81 Celso Limon W CO 1 Hermosillo
10.05.81 Ezequiel Sanchez W PTS 10 Los Angeles
19.07.81 Ray Mancini L PTS 12 Warren
(*NABF Lightweight Title Challenge*)
31.08.81 Jose L. Soberanes W PTS 10 Navojoa
24.10.81 Benny Abarca W CO 6 Tuxtla
(*Mexican Lightweight Title Defence*)
19.03.82 Benny Abarca W CO 3 Culiacan
(*Mexican Lightweight Title Defence*)
08.05.82 Jorge Morales W PTS 10 San Jose
25.06.82 Ricardo Peralta W CO 6 San Jose
(*Mexican Lightweight Title Defence*)
27.08.82 Ernesto Herrera W CO 4 Obregon
10.09.82 Rigoberto Ruiz W CO 5 San Jose
01.10.82 Eleazar Delgado W CO 4 Tijuana
23.10.82 Ramon Avitia W RSC 6 Tijuana
(*Mexican Lightweight Title Defence*)
26.11.82 Frankie Moultrie W RSC 3 Houston
(*Vacant NABF Lightweight Title*)
27.02.83 Jesus Cebreros W CO 3 San Luis
01.05.83 Edwin Rosario L PTS 12 San Juan
(*Vacant WBC Lightweight Title*)
07.10.83 Joe Gallardo W CO 2 Guaymas
04.11.83 Manuel Sanchez W RSC 3 Naucalpan
01.01.84 Victor Kelly W RSC 3 Mazatlan
11.05.84 Hector Medina W CO 4 Mazatlan
02.06.84 Martin Quiroz W PTS 10 Oakland
03.11.84 Edwin Rosario W RSC 4 San Juan
(*WBC Lightweight Title Challenge*)
13.03.85 J. T. Walker W RSC 4 San Jose
06.06.85 Manny Hernandez W PTS 10 Las Vegas
10.08.85 Hector Camacho L PTS 12 Las Vegas
(*WBC Lightweight Title Defence*)
15.09.86 Nick Parker W RSC 6 Paris
25.10.86 Charlie Brown W PTS 10 Paris
10.12.86 John Senegal W RSC 2 Paris
27.03.87 Efrain Nieves W RSC 3 Cannes
16.04.87 Davis Taylor W PTS 10 Marseilles
12.05.87 Roger Brown W RSC 7 Le Mans
26.05.87 Steve Mitchell W CO 5 Villeurbanne
19.07.87 Terrence Alli W PTS 12 St Tropez
(*Vacant WBC Lightweight Title*)
10.10.87 Cornelius Boza-Edwards W CO 5 Paris
(*WBC Lightweight Title Defence*)
19.12.87 John Rafuse W RSC 4 Paris
12.03.88 Pernell Whitaker W PTS 12 Paris
(*WBC Lightweight Title Defence*)
29.10.88 Julio Cesar Chavez L TD 11 Las Vegas
(*WBC Lightweight Title Defence. WBA Lightweight Title Challenge*)
10.03.89 Juan Minaya W DIS 5 Limoges
Summary: 109 contests, won 102, lost 7.

Primo Ramos
Durango, Mexico. *Born* 09.06.60
NABF Lightweight Champion. Former Undefeated Mexican Lightweight Champion

05.06.81 Gary Stallworth W CO 1 Chicago
27.07.81 Wayne Ingram W CO 2 Chicago
21.08.81 Ramon Ochoa W RSC 5 Chicago
02.09.81 Nate Stewart W PTS 6 Chicago
03.11.81 Tony Travis W RSC 6 Chicago
28.11.81 Raul Bencomo W PTS 10 Chihuahua
11.03.82 Gary Brown W RSC 4 Chicago
15.09.82 Bobby Paggie W CO 1 Chicago
16.10.82 Robin Blake L PTS 10 Atlantic City
16.12.82 Terrence Alli L RSC 2 Atlantic City
11.03.83 Mando Cardoso W CO 6 Durango
08.04.83 Canon Hernandez W PTS 10 Durango
30.06.83 Othoniel Lopez W RSC 8 La Paz
15.07.83 Tony Soto W RSC 6 Durango
12.08.83 Tony Perez W RSC 5 Durango
02.09.83 Memin Barcenas W RSC 5 Durango
18.11.83 Ramiro Lozano W CO 8 Durango
08.12.83 Teddy Hatfield W CO 3 Houston
30.12.83 Jose L. Castillo W RSC 5 Durango
07.01.84 Jose Rivera W PTS 10 Houston
02.02.84 Rafael Martinez W CO 2 Durango
25.02.84 Ezequiel Mosqueda L PTS 10 Houston
16.11.84 Melvin Paul L PTS 10 Houston
30.12.84 Gaspar Pool W PTS 10 Durango
05.03.85 Ezzard Charles Adams W RSC 10 Houston
20.04.85 Juan Garcia W PTS 10 Durango
02.06.85 Charles Adams W CO 3 Durango
16.08.85 Martin Galvan W CO 6 Durango
18.10.85 Ricardo Peralta W PTS 10 Durango
20.03.86 Ricardo Peralta W PTS 12 Durango
(*Mexican Lightweight Title Defence*)
06.06.86 Juan Escobar W CO 6 Durango
18.07.86 Jorge Gomez W CO 4 Durango
14.09.86 Herminio Delgado W RSC 10 Villahermosa
(*Mexican Lightweight Title Defence*)
01.01.87 Rocky Balboa W PTS 12 Durango
(*Mexican Lightweight Title Defence*)
19.04.87 Meldrick Taylor L PTS 10 Phoenix
27.07.87 Vernon Buchanan W CO 3 Los Angeles

28.10.87 Frankie Randall W CO 2 Las Vegas
(*Vacant NABF Lightweight Title*)
16.04.88 Kearns Ibarra W RSC 1 Las Vegas
02.09.88 Anthony Jones L PTS 10 Las Vegas
01.11.88 Victorio Belcher W PTS 12 Monterey
(*NABF Lightweight Title Defence*)
17.02.89 Chris Calvin W RSC 6 Albuquerque
(*NABF Lightweight Title Defence*)
Summary: 41 contests, won 35, lost 6.

Frankie (The Surgeon) Randall
Morristown, USA. *Born* 25.09.61
L. Welterweight

04.02.83 Curtis Golston W CO 2 Knoxville
19.02.83 Marcell Wade W RSC 2 Las Vegas
12.03.83 Don Thorps W CO 1 Ashland
02.04.83 Frank Mackey W RSC 2 Lancaster
12.05.83 Charles Sweetenburg W CO 1 Bristol
26.05.83 Charles Sweetenburg W CO 2 Knoxville
25.06.83 Willie Taylor W DIS 4 Pennington Gap
16.09.83 Freddie Guzman W RSC 6 Tampa
21.10.83 Adolfo Marquez W CO 4 Monroe
12.11.83 Richard Lassiter W RSC 5 Tampa
02.12.83 Reese Smith W RSC 4 Tampa
01.02.84 Luis de Jesus W RSC 3 Tampa
15.03.84 Ezequiel Mosquera W PTS 8 Tampa
03.05.84 Jerome Artis W CO 2 Tampa
21.06.84 Jose Rentas W CO 2 Tampa
12.07.84 Steve Mitchell W CO 3 Tampa
30.08.84 Jose Gonzalez W RSC 6 Morristown
11.09.84 Eduardo Lugo W RSC 4 Tampa
17.10.84 Ezzard Charles Adams W PTS 10 Tampa
24.11.84 Shelton Nixon W RSC 2 Bristol
17.01.85 Rashid Aziz W RSC 2 Tampa
23.03.85 Fred Pendleton W RSC 5 Bristol
01.05.85 Davey Brown W PTS 10 Tampa
16.06.85 Edwin Rosario L PTS 10 London
05.10.85 Keith Jackson W CO 4 Morristown
12.12.85 Efrain Nieves W RSC 2 Tampa
30.05.86 Sammy Fuentes W RSC 2 Atlantic City
04.07.86 Fred Pendleton DREW 12 Atlantic City
(*Vacant USBA Lightweight Title*)
03.10.86 Aldemir Mosquera W RSC 3 Atlantic City
16.01.87 Al Martino W RSC 2 Atlantic City
25.03.87 Shelton le Blanc W RTD 5 Atlantic City
09.05.87 Joe Edens W RSC 3 Bristol
09.06.87 Tim Burgess W PTS 10 Atlantic City
28.10.87 Primo Ramos L CO 2 Las Vegas
(*Vacant NABF Lightweight Title*)
19.03.88 Ricardo Cardenas W CO 1 Nashville
10.05.88 Sebastian Wilburn W CO 1 Cleveland
28.07.88 Tony Rorie W RSC 2 Philadelphia
02.12.88 Eduardo Luciano W RSC 1 New York
22.04.89 Derrick McGuire W PTS 8 Detroit
Summary: 39 contests, won 36, drew 1, lost 2.

Sam Reeson
Battersea, England. *Born* 05.01.63
Former Undefeated EBU & British Cruiserweight Champion

19.05.83 Calvin Earlington W PTS 6 London
17.10.83 Glenroy Taylor W PTS 6 London
08.11.83 Alex Romeo W PTS 6 London
28.11.83 Geoff Rymer W PTS 8 London
12.12.83 Eddie Cooper W PTS 6 Bedworth
03.02.84 John Joseph W PTS 8 Maidenhead
27.03.84 Gordon Stacey W PTS 8 London
17.04.84 Steve Lewin W PTS 8 London
18.09.84 Chris Lawson W PTS 8 London
03.10.84 Antonio Harris W PTS 8 Solihull
23.10.84 Michael Armstrong W CO 2 London
20.11.84 Paul Newman W PTS 8 London
24.01.85 Trevor Cattouse W RSC 6 London
26.02.85 Geoff Rymer W RSC 5 London
25.03.85 Theo Josephs W PTS 8 London
09.05.85 Liam Coleman W PTS 8 London
31.10.85 Stewart Lithgo W PTS 12 London
(*Vacant British Cruiserweight Title*)
09.12.85 Rubin Williams W PTS 10 London
10.01.86 Roy Smith W PTS 8 London
15.04.86 Roy Skeldon W PTS 8 London
29.05.86 Louis Pergaud L RSC 4 London
14.03.87 Roy Saffold W PTS 10 London
22.04.87 Manfred Jassman W PTS 12 London
(*Vacant EBU Cruiserweight Title*)
28.11.87 Luigi Ricci W CO 7 Windsor
(*EBU Cruiserweight Title Defence*)
28.05.88 Eric Williams W RSC 8 London
Summary: 25 contests, won 24, lost 1.

Chris (Shamrock Express) Reid
Brooklyn, USA. *Born* 14.03.63
S. Middleweight

30.05.84 Glenn Johnson W RSC 1 Atlantic City
17.06.84 Ron Ayres W RSC 1 Tampa
30.06.84 Chris Coady W RSC 2 Belfast
26.09.84 Pedro Montero W RSC 1 Atlantic City
13.10.84 Paul Newman W RSC 3 Belfast
31.10.84 Ralph Smiles W PTS 6 Atlantic City
13.02.85 Miguel Rosa W RSC 1 Atlantic City
23.02.85 Cordwell Hylton W CO 3 Belfast
13.03.85 Fred Jordan W RSC 4 Atlantic City
24.04.85 Pop Nance T DRAW 2 Atlantic City
18.09.85 David Overton W CO 1 Atlantic City
28.09.85 Hugh Johnson W RSC 7 Belfast
26.11.85 Wesley Reid T DRAW 2 Atlantic City
05.02.86 Maurice Moor W RSC 1 Atlantic City
02.04.86 Darryl Spain W RSC 7 Totowa
14.08.86 Mark Frazie W RSC 7 New York
09.10.86 Marcos Geraldo W RTD 4 New York
08.01.87 Jerome Clouden W RSC 2 New York
09.04.87 Ian Mattis W RSC 6 New York
18.06.87 Fully Obelmejias L RSC 10 New York
12.11.87 Irwin Hines W RSC 4 New York
04.02.88 Doug Kaluza W CO 3 New York
17.03.88 Vince Hopper DREW 10 New York
28.07.88 Carlos Santistevan W RSC 3 New York
07.10.88 Graciano Rocchigiani L RTD 11 Berlin
(*IBF S. Middleweight Title Challenge*)
Summary: 25 contests, won 20, drew 3, lost 2.

Jean-Marc Renard
Huy, Belgium. *Born* 19.04.56
Former Undefeated EBU S. Featherweight Champion.
Former Undefeated EBU & Belgium Featherweight Champion

28.11.80 Marc Armand W PTS 6 Liege
16.01.81 Daniel Champagne W PTS 6 Liege
31.01.81 Claude Kessaci W PTS 6 Liege
28.02.81 Haidar Nourredine W PTS 6 Liege
17.04.81 Daniel Paysserand W RSC 1 Liege
16.05.81 Rafael Blanco W RSC 5 Liege
22.09.81 Barry McGuigan L PTS 8 Belfast
10.12.81 Steve Sammy Sims L PTS 8 Newport
26.02.82 Angelo Licata W PTS 10 Brustem
(*Belgian Featherweight Title Challenge*)
23.03.82 Richie Foster W RSC 5 Belfast
15.05.82 Andre Blanco W PTS 8 Zele
23.06.82 Haidar Nourredine W PTS 8 Bressoux
25.12.82 Dominique Cesari W RTD 4 Izegem
14.01.83 Andre Blanco W PTS 8 Zele
04.02.23 Sammy Meck W PTS 8 Grivegnee
18.03.83 Jose Luis Vicho W PTS 8 Brustem
06.05.83 Mohamed Maalem W RTD 2 Grivegnee
24.09.83 John Sharkey W PTS 8 Oostrobeke
01.11.83 Don George W CO 4 Izegem
25.12.83 Farid Gallouze W RSC 3 Izegem
22.01.84 Steve Pollard W PTS 8 Izegem
12.04.84 Alfredo Raininger W PTS 12 Casavatore
(*EBU S. Featherweight Title Challenge*)
07.07.84 Pat Cowdell L PTS 12 Birmingham
(*EBU S. Featherweight Title Defence*)
01.11.84 Moussa Sangare W PTS 8 Izegem
25.01.85 Sammy Meck W DIS 7 Charleroi
15.02.85 Kamel Djadda W RSC 6 Huy
22.03.85 Mohamed Maalem W RTD 2 Brustem
24.06.85 Jose Maillot W RTD 4 Liege
02.08.85 Vicente Fernandez W RTD 5 Rochefort
19.10.85 Vicente Macias W RSC 4 Middlekerke
29.01.86 Marco Gallo W RSC 8 Catanzaro
(*Vacant EBU S. Featherweight Title*)
18.04.86 Fernando Rodriguez W CO 8 Brustem
(*EBU S. Featherweight Title Defence*)
30.08.86 Pat Doherty W RSC 5 Middlekerke
31.10.86 · Najib Daho W RTD 5 Kortrijk
(*EBU S. Featherweight Title Defence*)

Frankie Randall

Peter Goldfield/USA

Chris Reid (left) in winning action against Mark Frazie, August, 1986

Tom Casino

20.12.86 Daniel Londas DREW 12 St Ouen
(*EBU S. Featherweight Title Defence*)
11.03.87 Antonio Renzo W RSC 8 Cosenza
(*EBU S. Featherweight Title Defence*)
06.06.87 Jeff Roberts W RSC 2 Chaudfontaine
01.11.87 John Farrell W RTD 7 Izegem
05.12.87 Jose Garcia W RSC 6 Natoye
25.12.87 Paul Huggins W RTD 8 Izegem
10.04.88 Kevin Pritchard W RSC 3 Grivegnee
25.06.88 Farid Benredjeb W PTS 12 Compiegne
(*Vacant EBU Featherweight Title*)
16.11.88 Vincenzo Limatola W CO 3 Salerno
(*EBU Featherweight Title Defence*)
25.12.88 Patrick Kamy W RSC 8 Izegem
Summary: 44 contests, won 40, drew 1, lost 3.

Harold Rhodes
Jersey City, USA. *Born* 11.08.63
S. Featherweight

09.07.87 Raul Rivera L RSC 1 New York
25.09.87 Randy Kearse W PTS 4 Atlantic City
14.10.87 David Jones L RSC 1 Atlantic City
04.12.87 Julio Moreno W RSC 2 Atlantic City
29.01.88 Jorge Rivas W PTS 6 Atlantic City
09.04.88 Kenny Lee W CO 1 Stafford
16.04.88 Keely Thompson W PTS 10 Crystal City
27.05.88 Tom Barnes W RSC 1 Atlantic City
09.07.88 Cedric Mingo W PTS 6 Atlantic City
20.07.88 Flip Johnson W PTS 6 Glen Burnie
23.09.88 Billy Young W PTS 10 Atlantic City
29.11.88 Ralph Reyes W RSC 2 San Antonio
Summary: 12 contests, won 10, lost 2.

Harold Rhodes

Peter Goldfield/USA

Jose (Nino) Ribalta
Miami, USA. *Born* 31.03.63
Heavyweight

20.01.82 J. C. Richardson W RSC 2 Fort Lauderdale
05.02.82 Doug Fowler W CO 2 Miami
21.05.82 Ken Davis W PTS 6 Miami
18.06.82 Ken Ring W CO 3 Hialeah
09.07.82 Gabriel Sainz W CO 2 Hialeah
20.07.82 Curtis Gaskins W RSC 2 Fort Lauderdale
03.09.82 Al Leticky W CO 1 Hialeah
21.10.82 John L. Johnson W CO 1 Hialeah
06.11.82 Nate Robinson W RSC 5 Fort Lauderdale
14.01.83 Miles Prince W RSC 2 Hialeah
18.02.83 Ricardo Richardson L RSC 7 Hialeah
29.04.83 Ron Harry W RSC 6 Hialeah
03.06.83 Tom Prater W PTS 8 Hialeah
01.09.83 Robert Evans W PTS 8 Atlantic City
28.10.83 Ishaq Hussein W RSC 6 Atlantic City
15.12.83 Juan Figueroa W DIS 7 Atlantic City
08.03.84 Jim Jones W PTS 8 Miami
26.07.84 Nate Robinson W RSC 2 Miami
18.10.84 Cecil Coffee DREW 10 Atlantic City
29.04.85 James Smith L PTS 10 Buffalo
23.07.85 Ernie Barr W PTS 10 Miami
11.09.85 Marvis Frazier L PTS 10 Atlantic City
04.03.86 Al Houck W RSC 3 Miami
04.04.86 Jeff Feeney W RSC 1 Miami
13.05.86 David Jaco W CO 5 Bloomington
20.06.86 Ricky Keller W CO 1 Miami
17.08.86 Mike Tyson L RSC 10 Atlantic City
26.09.86 Johnny Williams W RSC 2 Miami
17.01.87 Leon Spinks W RSC 1 Miami
16.05.87 Mark Young W PTS 10 Miami
12.09.87 Steve Zouski W PTS 10 Miami
03.06.88 Jose Garcia W CO 1 West Virginia
Summary: 32 contests, won 27, drew 1, lost 4.

Antonio (Tonito) Rivera
Puerto Rico. *Born* 05.12.63
Former IBF Featherweight Champion. Former Puerto Rican S. Bantamweight Champion

26.02.81 Humberto Maldonado W RSC 1 Trujillo
06.03.81 Angel Torres W PTS 4 San Juan
26.03.81 Luis Ramos W RSC 3 Bayamon
22.05.81 Herminio Adorno L PTS 6 San Juan
09.07.81 Herminio Adorno W RSC 1 Trujillo
08.08.81 Elvin Gonzalez L PTS 6 San Juan
24.10.81 Ismael Espinosa W RSC 2 Trujillo
09.01.82 Ramon Canales W CO 3 San Juan
20.05.82 Frankie Granados W RSC 1 San Juan
16.07.82 Antonio Rodriguez W CO 2 Santo Domingo
31.07.82 Elvin Gonzalez W RSC 6 San Juan
09.10.82 Enrique Sanchez L PTS 10 Santo Domingo
12.02.83 Orlando Perez W PTS 12 Canovanas
(*Vacant Puerto Rican S. Bantamweight Title*)
16.04.83 Memo Armengot W CO 2 Trujillo
07.05.83 Feliciano Perez W RSC 5 Guaynabo
14.12.83 Manuel Santos W RSC 8 San Juan
26.07.84 Vince Christian W RSC 5 New York
01.09.84 Juan Veloz L RSC 11 Carolina
(*Puerto Rican S. Bantamweight Title Defence*)
02.02.85 Alberto Mercado W RSC 7 San Juan
12.07.85 Tony Miller DREW 10 Melbourne
05.10.85 Irving Mitchell W RSC 5 Guaynabo
30.08.86 Ki-Yung Chung W RTD 10 Osan
(*IBF Featherweight Title Challenge*)
23.01.88 Calvin Grove L RSC 4 Gamaches
(*IBF Featherweight Title Defence*)
11.07.88 Tomas Rodriguez W RSC 3 San Juan
27.08.88 Margarito Marquez W RSC 6 San Juan
Summary: 25 contests, won 19, drew 1, lost 5.

Jose (Joe) Rivera
Bayamon, Puerto Rico. *Born* 1963
L. Welterweight

14.08.80 Bernabe Montanez DREW 4 San Juan
17.10.80 Monserrat Teron L PTS 4 Trujillo Alto
05.06.82 Enrique Maxwell W CO 1 San Juan
21.03.83 Miguel Santana DREW 6 Bayamon
17.08.83 Nelson Rodriguez W RSC 3 Trujillo Alto
03.09.83 Jose Ortiz W RSC 6 Trujillo Alto
17.03.84 Alberto Batista W CO 2 Hato Rey
23.06.84 Victor Aponte W PTS 6 San Juan
08.12.84 Jose Rosa W RSC 2 San Juan
08.02.85 Chris Anderson W CO 2 San Juan
24.05.85 Rey Estades W PTS 10 San Juan
04.10.85 Luis Rivera W CO 1 San Juan
06.12.85 Edgar Castro W RSC 2 San Juan
27.03.87 Brian Mitchell DREW 15 San Juan
(*WBA S. Featherweight Title Challenge*)
21.11.87 Ramiro Lozano W RSC 2 Las Vegas
26.04.88 Brian Mitchell L PTS 12 Madrid
(*WBA S. Featherweight Title Challenge*)
29.08.88 Martin Quiroz W PTS 10 Los Angeles
22.11.88 Engels Pedroza W PTS 10 Los Angeles
20.03.89 Rodolfo Aguilar L PTS 10 Los Angeles
Summary: 19 contests, won 13, drew 3, lost 3.

Graciano Rocchigiani
Rheinhausen, West Germany. *Born* 29.12.63
IBF S. Middleweight Champion. West German L. Heavyweight Champion. Former Undefeated West German Middleweight Champion

10.09.83 Esperno Postl W RSC 2 Cologne
07.10.83 Marnix Heytens W RSC 1 Frankfurt
05.11.83 Jan Lefeber W PTS 4 Mannheim
14.01.84 Chaed Ringo W RSC 2 Dusseldorf
10.02.84 Mauro da Cruz W PTS 6 Frankfurt

Jose Ribalta

Peter Goldfield/USA

24.02.84 Mick Morris W PTS 4 Hamburg
27.04.84 Franz Dorfer W RTD 2 Berlin
15.09.84 Butangi Nzolameso W PTS 6 Dortmund
05.10.84 Tony Britton W PTS 8 Frankfurt
01.12.84 Philippe Seys W PTS 8 Dusseldorf
09.03.85 T. P. Jenkins W RSC 6 Dusseldorf
26.04.85 Steve Johnson W PTS 10 Frankfurt
31.08.85 Moussa Mukandjo W PTS 10 Berlin
08.11.85 Rudiger Bitterling W RSC 3 Dusseldorf
(*Vacant West German Middleweight Title*)
29.11.85 Antoine Alcantara W CO 2 Frankfurt
01.03.86 James Cook W PTS 8 Cologne
12.05.86 Ian Lazarus W CO 8 Mannheim
03.10.86 Manfred Jassman W PTS 10 Berlin
(*West German L. Heavyweight Title Challenge*)
13.09.87 Ahmed Laghiali W RSC 2 Bad Homburg
03.10.87 Tommy Taylor W PTS 8 Stukenbrock
17.10.87 Laheen Hamdi W RSC 3 Gifhorn
30.10.87 John Held W PTS 8 Bad Homburg
05.12.87 Mustafa Hamsho W CO 1 Dusseldorf
12.03.88 Vince Boulware W RSC 8 Dusseldorf
(*Vacant IBF S. Middleweight Title*)
03.06.88 Nicky Walker W PTS 15 Berlin
(*IBF S. Middleweight Title Defence*)
07.10.88 Chris Reid W RTD 11 Berlin
(*IBF S. Middleweight Title Defence*)
27.01.89 Thulani Malinga L PTS 12 Berlin
(*IBF S. Middleweight Title Defence*)
Summary: 27 contests, won 27.

Ralf Rocchigiani
Rheinhausen, West Germany. *Born* 12.03.63
Former Undefeated West German Cruiserweight Champion

05.11.83 Hans Gimborn W CO 1 Mannheim
02.12.83 Horst Schulze W RSC 1 Stuttgart
14.01.84 Eddy Vandenhouwele W PTS 4 Dusseldorf
06.02.84 Alan Ash W PTS 6 Hamburg
24.02.84 Helmut Ulka W PTS 6 Hamburg
09.03.84 Francesco Campi W RSC 3 Frankfurt
13.04.84 Mike McCoy W PTS 6 Hagen
28.04.84 Liam Coleman DREW 6 Hamburg
08.06.84 Mladen Grubesic W PTS 6 Kassel
22.06.84 Brahim Ferisovic W RSC 3 Munich
15.09.84 Juan A. Barrera W PTS 6 Dortmund
05.10.84 Trevor Cattouse W CO 3 Frankfurt
20.10.84 Paul Muyodi DREW 6 Salzufen
01.12.84 Manfred Jassman L PTS 10 Dusseldorf
(*West German L. Heavyweight Title Challenge*)
10.05.85 Manfred Jassman DREW 10 Berlin
(*West German L. Heavyweight Title Challenge*)
21.08.85 Josef Kossmann W CO 2 Hamburg
(*Vacant West German Cruiserweight Title*)
31.08.85 Jose Seys W PTS 8 Berlin
29.11.85 Tom Collins W PTS 8 Frankfurt
20.12.85 Ibelo Moano W PTS Russelsheim

01.03.86 Mikan Popovic W DIS 7 Cologne
12.05.86 Mladen Grubesic W RSC 2 Mannheim
03.10.86 Alex Blanchard L PTS 12 Berlin
(*EBU L. Heavyweight Title Challenge*)
27.02.87 Alex Zeh DREW 10 Hamburg
(*West German Cruiserweight Title Defence*)
25.09.87 Manfred Jassman W PTS 10 Berlin
(*West German Cruiserweight Title Defence*)
30.10.87 Tommy Taylor W PTS 8 Bad Homburg
05.12.87 Chisanda Mutti W PTS 10 Dusseldorf
23.01.88 Alex Zeh W CO 9 Hamburg
(*West German Cruiserweight Title Defence*)
19.02.88 Agamil Yilderim DREW 8 Berlin
26.04.88 Marvin Camel W PTS 10 Cologne
12.05.88 Vedat Akova W RSC 2 Berlin
29.07.88 Jan Lefeber W PTS 8 Timmendorf
09.04.89 Jan Lefeber DREW 12 Berlin
(*EBU L. Heavyweight Title Challenge*)
Summary: 32 contests, won 24, drew 6, lost 2.

Jose Adilson (Maguila) Rodrigues

Sao Paulo, Brazil. *Born* 12.06.58
Former Undefeated Con. Am. Heavyweight Champion. South American & Brazilian Heavyweight Champion

04.02.83 Jose Tavares W RTD 3 Sao Paulo
19.03.83 Alaerte Vaz W CO 2 Sao Paulo
14.05.83 Francisco Dias W CO 2 Sao Paulo
02.07.83 Waldemar Paulino W CO 1 Sao Paulo
(*Brazilian Heavyweight Title Challenge*)
15.08.83 Eduardo Olivera W CO 2 Sao Paulo
12.09.83 Marcos Tosto W CO 1 Sao Paulo
05.02.84 Domingo d'Elia W RSC 8 Sao Paulo
08.04.84 Antonio Musladino W CO 6 Sao Paulo
13.05.84 Mike White W PTS 10 Sao Paulo
29.07.84 Louis Pergaud W RTD 9 Sao Paulo
09.09.84 Juan Figueroa W CO 1 Sao Paulo
(*South American Heavyweight Title Challenge*)
28.10.84 Georg Butzbach W RSC 1 Sao Paulo
16.12.84 Louis Pergaud W RSC 9 Sao Paulo
10.02.85 Walter Santemore W RTD 5 Sao Paulo
31.03.85 Daniel Falconi L CO 3 Sao Paulo
09.06.85 Nate Robinson W CO 1 Sao Paulo
04.08.85 Peter Mulindwa W CO 2 Sao Paulo
06.10.85 Albert Syben W RTD 6 Sao Paulo
17.11.85 Andre van den Oetelaar L CO 5 Sao Paulo
02.03.86 Vedat Akova W RSC 3 Sao Paulo
18.05.86 Daniel Falconi W CO 7 Sao Paulo
(*South American Heavyweight Title Defence*)
27.07.86 Andre van den Oetelaar W CO 3 Sao Paulo
05.10.86 Melvin Epps W PTS 10 Sao Paulo
21.12.86 Rick Sekorski W PTS 12 Sao Paulo
(*Vacant Con. Am. Heavyweight Title*)
15.03.87 Felipe Rodriguez W CO 7 Sao Paulo
31.05.87 Lorenzo Boyd W CO 2 Curitiba
21.06.87 Mike Jameson W PTS 10 Sao Paulo
09.08.87 James Smith W PTS 10 Sao Paulo
11.10.87 Reggie Gross W PTS 10 Araraquara
20.12.87 Alfredo Evangelista W PTS 10 Rio de Janeiro
14.03.88 Jorge Cambiaso W CO 7 Buenos Aires
(*South American Heavyweight Title Defence*)
12.06.88 Dave Garside W RSC 3 Sao Paulo
14.08.88 Hughroy Currie W RSC 8 Londrina
14.10.88 Mark Lee W RSC 1 Las Vegas
19.12.88 Sam Scaff W CO 2 Sao Paulo
20.03.89 James Tillis W PTS 10 Toledo
Summary: 36 contests, won 34, lost 2.

Mauricio Rodriguez

Miami, USA. *Born* 1958
Fomer Undefeated Con. Am. Welterweight Champion

02.04.81 James Averitt W RSC 3 Tampa
16.04.81 Mitch Thomas W PTS 4 Tampa
10.06.81 Jerome Cox W PTS 4 Tampa
18.07.81 Willie Jenkins W CO 1 Tampa
10.09.81 Roosevelt Moss W RSC 3 Tampa
24.09.81 Rondell Stevenson W RSC 4 Tampa
27.10.81 Manny Vega W CO 1 Tampa
11.11.81 Gene Taylor W PTS 6 Tampa
10.12.81 Ron Smith W PTS 8 Tampa
06.01.82 Paul Gentry W RSC 6 Tampa
11.02.82 Dexter Smith W PTS 8 Tampa
25.02.82 Carlos Santana W PTS 10 Tampa
02.05.82 Carlos Santana L PTS 10 Tampa
18.06.82 Dexter Smith W PTS 10 Hialeah
24.10.82 Anthony Bryant W PTS 6 Tampa
08.12.82 Dario de Jesus W PTS 8 Miami
04.03.83 Randy Mitchum W PTS 8 Tampa
08.07.83 Robert Lee W PTS 8 Tampa
26.08.83 Martin Rojas W PTS 10 Miami
18.11.83 Joe Hawkins W CO 6 Tampa
08.12.83 Adolfo Medel L PTS 8 Miami
01.11.85 William Goodman W PTS 4 Fort Lauderdale
13.12.85 John Stewart W PTS 6 Miami
04.03.86 Clinton Mack W PTS 6 Miami
25.04.86 Lorenzo Guzman W PTS 10 Hialeah
23.05.86 Dario de Jesus W CO 3 Miami
27.06.86 Cornelius Drane W RSC 8 Miami
26.09.86 Martin Rojas W PTS 10 Miami
21.11.86 Aldemar Mosquera W PTS 10 Hialeah
28.02.87 Eduardo Brinoles W PTS 10 Miami
12.09.87 Orlando Orozco W PTS 12 Miami
(*Vacant Con. Am. Welterweight Title*)
15.01.88 Danny Vargas W PTS 10 Miami
11.03.88 Fernando Martinez W RSC 8 Hialeah
10.06.88 Juan Mendoza W CO 1 Hialeah
30.07.88 Felipe Julio W PTS 10 Miami
16.12.88 Mario Coronado W RSC 4 Miami
31.01.89 Roman Nunez W RSC 3 Fort Lauderdale
Summary: 37 contests, won 35, lost 2.

Jesus (Sugar Baby) Rojas

Barranquilla, Colombia. *Born* 01.02.62
Former WBC S. Flyweight Champion. Former Undefeated Con. Am. & Latin American Flyweight Champion

13.02.81 Wilfredo Ruiz W PTS 6 Barranquilla
26.06.81 William Velazquez W PTS 6 Barranquilla
17.07.81 Alfredo Gomez W PTS 6 Barranquilla
18.09.81 Virgilio Palomo W PTS 10 Bogota
30.10.81 Francisco Quiroz W PTS 10 Barranquilla
15.01.82 Rafael Julio W PTS 10 Cartagena
14.05.82 Bernardo Gonzalez W RSC 4 Barranquilla
06.08.82 Rodolfo Flores W PTS 10 Barranquilla
02.10.82 Ramon Perez W RSC 8 Miami
30.10.82 Jose Badilla W CO 4 Miami
19.11.82 Gabriel Sepulveda W RTD 10 Miami
(*Vacant Latin American Flyweight Title*)
18.12.82 Alfonso Lopez W PTS 10 Cartagena
11.03.83 Joe Jackson W RSC 2 Miami
08.04.83 Enrique Guadamez W CO 3 Miami
29.04.83 Juan Ortiz W CO 3 Miami
10.06.83 Steve Whetstone W RSC 8 Miami
29.07.83 Alfonso Lopez W PTS 12 Miami
(*Con. Am. Flyweight Title Challenge*)
26.11.83 Norgi Castro W RSC 8 Miami
27.01.84 Nestor Obregon W RSC 9 Barranquilla
13.03.84 Rudy Crawford W RSC 6 Miami
18.04.84 Felipe Mojica W RSC 8 Miami
28.09.84 Jose Garcia W RSC 4 Miami
12.02.85 Nelson Garcia W CO 3 Miami
24.05.85 Lee Cargle W RSC 7 Miami
20.07.85 Juan Polo Perez DREW 10 Cartagena
26.04.86 Armando Acuna W CO 2 Miami
30.05.86 Juan Pagan W RSC 1 Miami
11.07.86 Rafael Orono W PTS 10 Miami
15.11.86 Jessie Williams W PTS 10 Barranquilla
08.08.87 Santos Laciar W PTS 12 Miami
(*WBC S. Flyweight Title Challenge*)
24.10.87 Gustavo Ballas W RSC 4 Miami
(*WBC S. Flyweight Title Defence*)
08.04.88 Gilberto Roman L PTS 12 Miami
(*WBC S. Flyweight Title Defence*)
07.11.88 Gilberto Roman L PTS 12 Las Vegas
(*WBC S. Flyweight Title Challenge*)
01.03.89 Yun-Un Chin L PTS 10 Seoul
29.04.89 Jose Ruiz L PTS 12 San Juan
(*Vacant WBO S. Flyweight Title*)
Summary: 35 contests, won 30, drew 1, lost 4.

Juan Domingo (Martillo) Roldan

Freyre, Argentine. *Born* 06.03.57
Former Undefeated Argentinian & South American Middleweight Champion

08.12.78 Jorge Servin W RSC 1 San Francisco
26.01.79 Juan Huascarriaga W CO 1 Las Varillas
09.02.79 Luis A. Gutierrez W CO 1 San Francisco
23.03.79 Irineo Cabrera W CO 1 Rafaela
06.04.79 Luis Carcacha W RTD 3 San Francisco
20.04.79 Oscar Lopez W CO 4 Sunchales
11.05.79 Hugo Obregon W PTS 10 Cordoba
24.05.79 Natalio Ibarra W PTS Brinkmann
08.06.79 Hugo Obregon W RSC 11 San Francisco

Juan Domingo Roldan (right) performed creditably against Michael Nunn when challenging for the latter's IBF middleweight title

Tom Casino

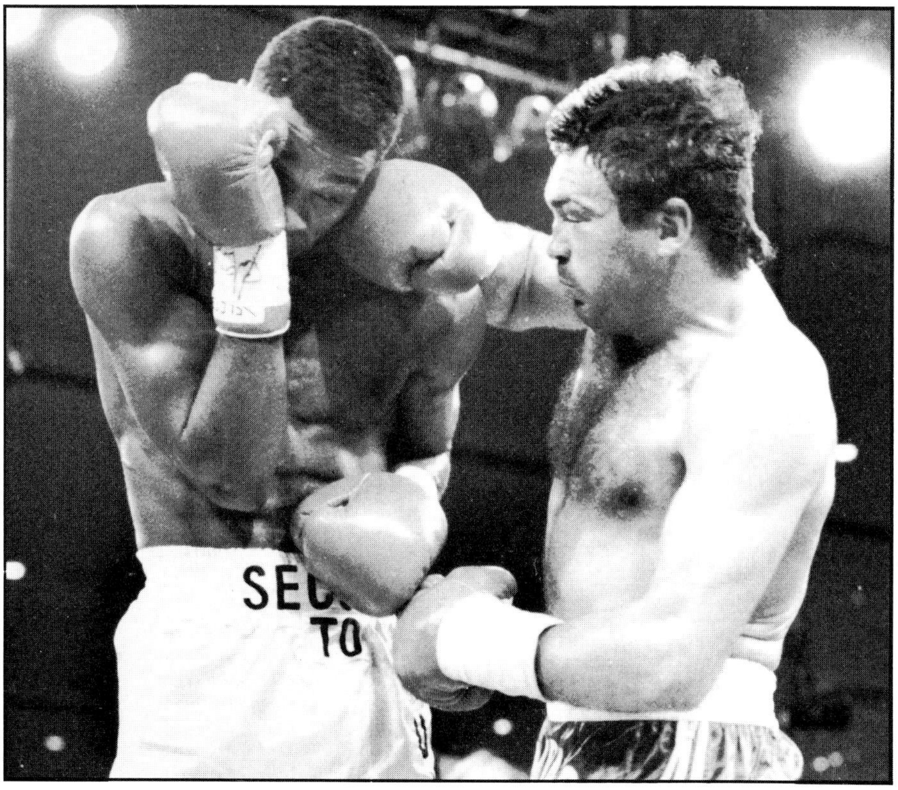

29.06.79 Oscar Perez W CO 2 Rafaela
20.07.79 Alberto Almiron W RTD 5 Cordoba
10.08.79 Ramon Perez W PTS 12 San Francisco
24.08.79 Alberto Cardozo W RSC 3 Morteros
07.09.79 Natalio Ibarra W RTD 4 Freyre
21.09.79 Juan C. Bogado L RTD 8 Cordoba
22.12.79 Alfredo Cruz W RSC 8 Buenos Aires
18.01.80 Roberto Ortiz W CO 2 San Francisco
08.02.80 Juan Bogado W PTS 10 San Francisco
22.02.80 Marcos Perez W CO 6 Morteros
15.03.80 Alfredo Cruz W CO 7 Buenos Aires
11.04.80 Ramon Perez W RSC 8 San Francisco
16.05.80 Ricardo Ortiz W PTS 10 San Francisco
06.06.80 Jorge Salgado W RSC 7 San Francisco
27.06.80 Aldo Carmona W CO 3 Salta
08.07.80 Rogelio Zarza W PTS 10 San Francisco
22.08.80 Roberto Marziali W CO 1 Las Varillas
04.10.80 Ricardo Ortiz W PTS 10 San Francisco
07.11.80 Ramon Perez W PTS 12 Cordoba
21.11.80 Enrique Coronel W RTD 7 Salta
05.12.80 Jose Duran W RTD 6 San Francisco
19.12.80 Carlos Peralta DREW 12 Cordoba
16.01.81 Marcos Perez W PTS 10 Villa Carlos
13.02.81 Manuel Navarro W TD 6 Mar del Plata
13.03.81 Jacinto Fernandez W PTS 12 San Francisco (*Argentinian Middleweight Title Challenge*)
13.06.81 Jose Maria Flores W CO 3 Buenos Aires
26.06.81 Rogelio Zarza W PTS 10 Jujuy
10.07.81 Jose Vega W CO 1 San Francisco
24.07.81 Ric Molina W RTD 5 Tucuman
11.09.81 Julio C. Arancibia W RSC 2 Tucuman
10.10.81 Jacinto Fernandez DREW 10 Buenos Aires
22.01.82 Juan Peralta W PTS 10 Monteros
12.02.82 Carlos Flores W CO 2 Pergamino (*Vacant South American Middleweight Title*)
06.03.82 Ray Phillips W CO 1 Buenos Aires
16.04.82 Marcos Perez W CO 1 Corrientes
11.05.82 Ricardo Arce L DIS 3 Buenos Aires
11.07.82 Ricardo Arce W CO 2 Buenos Aires
13.08.82 Rogelio Zarza W RTD 6 Corrientes
11.09.82 Jacinto Fernandez W CO 2 Buenos Aires
08.10.82 Carlos Peralta W PTS 10 San Francisco
30.10.82 Reggie Ford W CO 1 San Remo
10.12.82 Jose Vega W CO 2 Cordoba
14.01.83 Carlos Peralta ND 3 El Trebol
11.02.83 Wilbur Henderson W RSC 8 Worcester
27.05.83 Teddy Mann W PTS 10 Providence
06.08.83 Roberto Ruiz W CO 8 Buenos Aires
16.09.83 Eduardo Contreras W PTS 10 San Francisco
10.11.83 Frank Fletcher W CO 6 Las Vegas
30.03.84 Marvin Hagler L RSC 10 Las Vegas (*World Middleweight Title Challenge*)
14.07.84 Andre Mongalema W PTS 10 Monte Carlo
14.02.86 Carlos Fernandez W CO 2 Ceres
29.03.86 Angel Caro W CO 6 Villa Angela
10.05.86 Jorge Salgado W PTS 10 Buenos Aires
10.06.86 Eduardo Contreras W PTS 10 Cordoba
01.08.86 Darryl Penn W CO 3 San Francisco
29.08.86 Miguel Maldonado W CO 2 Rosario
13.09.86 Juan C. Gimenez W PTS 10 Buenos Aires
18.10.86 J. B. Williamson W PTS 10 Buenos Aires
13.12.86 Carlos Herrera W RSC 2 Buenos Aires
06.02.87 Tomas Polo W CO 4 Rosario
06.04.87 James Kinchen W RSC 9 Las Vegas
15.05.87 Clarismundo Silva W CO 2 Comodoro
29.10.87 Thomas Hearns L CO 4 Las Vegas (*Vacant WBC Middleweight Title*)
19.08.88 Miguel Maldonado W CO 6 Tucuman
16.09.88 Hugo Corro W CO 1 Mar del Plata
04.11.88 Michael Nunn L CO 8 Las Vegas (*IBF Middleweight Title Challenge*)
Summary: 75 contests, won 67, drew 2, lost 5, no decision 1.

Derrick (Too Sweet) Rolon
Elizabeth, USA. *Born* 17.08.68
Welterweight

18.09.87 Chris Royal W RSC 3 Atlantic City
23.10.87 Charles Jackson W CO 1 Atlantic City
27.11.87 James Holmes W RSC 1 Atlantic City
09.12.87 Khalif Shabazz W PTS 6 Atlantic City
29.01.88 Warren Nelson W PTS 6 Atlantic City
06.03.88 Tony Rorie W PTS 6 New York
15.04.88 Jose Vera W CO 2 Atlantic City
19.05.88 Paul Shorts W RSC 7 Atlantic City
28.07.88 Curtis Baker W RSC 2 Las Vegas
29.11.88 Moses Robinson W RSC 3 San Antonio
10.01.89 Mike Mungin W RSC 9 Atlantic City
11.02.89 Andre Kimbu W PTS 8 Grenoble
14.03.89 Louis Howard W RSC 3 Atlantic City
Summary: 13 contests, won 13.

Adrian Roman
Cordoba, Argentine. *Born* 17.05.60
Former Argentinian Flyweight Champion

21.07.78 Manuel Saucedo W CO 2 Cordoba
01.09.78 Francisco Barrios W PTS 6 Cordoba
29.09.78 Raul Cuevas W DIS Cordoba
27.10.78 Jose Lopez W PTS 8 Cordoba
19.01.79 Raul Cuevas W RSC 2 Salta
02.03.79 Ramon Baez W CO 2 Cordoba
06.04.79 Luis Gomez W CO 9 Cordoba
02.06.79 Jose Ibiris W PTS 10 Cordoba
05.07.79 Jose Ibiris W PTS 10 Cordoba
14.09.79 Jose Ibiris W PTS 10 Tucuman
05.10.79 Luis Gomez W PTS 10 Tucuman
19.10.79 Ruben Condori W TD 7 Cordoba
14.03.80 Jose Izquierdo W PTS 10 Cordoba
19.04.80 Ruben Condori DREW 10 Buenos Aires
06.06.80 Santos Laciar L CO 3 Cordoba
22.08.80 Carlos Sosa W CO 12 Cordoba
15.11.80 Jose Ibiris W RSC 10 Buenos Aires
04.04.81 Miguel Lazarte DREW 10 Buenos Aires
05.06.81 Domingo Aragon W PTS 12 Presedencia
31.07.81 Rodolfo Rodriguez W PTS 10 Cordoba
18.09.81 Federico Condori W CO 2 Salta
09.10.81 Ruben Condori L PTS 12 Salta (*Vacant Argentinian Flyweight Title*)
19.02.82 Ruben Condori W PTS 10 Cordoba
19.03.82 Ramon Rodriguez W RTD 10 Cordoba
10.09.82 Ruben Condori W RSC 7 Salta (*Argentinian Flyweight Title Challenge*)
15.10.82 Rodolfo Rodriguez W RTD 7 Cordoba
12.11.82 Jose Gomez W RTD 8 Cordoba
11.12.82 Gustavo Ballas L PTS 10 Buenos Aires
04.03.83 Mario de Marco W PTS 10 Cordoba
06.04.83 Alberto Pacheco W CO 3 Buenos Aires (*Argentinian Flyweight Title Defence*)
03.06.83 Juan Ivalo W DIS 10 Cordoba
25.11.83 Juan C. Cortes DREW 10 Cordoba
31.12.83 Ruben Condori L PTS 12 Salta (*South American Flyweight Title Challenge*)
16.03.84 Ruben Condori W PTS 12 Cordoba (*Argentinian Flyweight Title Defence*)
14.04.84 Hector Patri W PTS 10 Cordoba
08.06.84 Ramon Albers L PTS 10 Concordia
10.08.84 Juan C. Cortez DREW 10 Cordoba
14.09.84 Ramon Albers L PTS 12 Concordia (*Argentinian Flyweight Title Defence*)
16.11.84 Jaime Miranda W RSC 6 Cordoba
22.01.85 Jose Narvaez DREW 10 La Rioja
08.03.85 Ruben Condori L PTS 10 Salta
10.05.85 Ramon Albers W PTS 10 Sunchales
06.07.85 Alberto Pacheco W CO 9 Dolores (*Argentinian Flyweight Title Challenge*)
04.10.85 Ramon Albers W PTS 12 Concordia (*Argentinian Flyweight Title Defence*)
18.04.86 Jose Cufre W CO 3 Cordoba (*Argentinian Flyweight Title Defence*)
11.07.86 Gustavo Ballas DREW 10 Cordoba
30.08.86 Gilberto Sosa W CO 5 Cordoba
10.10.86 Ramon Albers W PTS 12 Cordoba (*Argentinian Flyweight Title Defence*)
04.04.87 Victor Fuentealba W PTS 10 Trelew
08.08.87 Juan Garcia W RSC 1 Miami
16.10.87 Daniel Lagos W RTD 8 Rawson (*Argentinian Flyweight Title Defence*)
30.01.88 Domingo Aragon W CO 2 Monte Hermoso
08.04.88 Jose Badilla W CO 9 Cordoba
03.06.88 Carlos Laciar DREW 10 Rio Gallegos
18.12.88 Carlos Salazar L PTS 12 Soenz Pena (*Argentinian Flyweight Title Defence*)
11.02.89 Ruben Condori W PTS 12 Villa Carlos Paz
10.04.89 Raul Ojeda W RSC 9 Buenos Aires
Summary: 57 contests, won 42, drew 7, lost 8.

Gilberto Roman
Mexicali, Mexico. *Born* 29.11.61
WBC S. Flyweight Champion

29.08.81 Gilberto Morales W CO 7 Villahermosa
13.09.81 Leonardo Valdez W RSC 8 Mexicali
30.10.81 Leo Castellano W CO 1 Acapulco
09.12.81 Juan Montalvo W CO 1 Mexico City
16.01.82 Juan Zarate W RSC 2 Mexico City
19.02.82 Gil Villacana W RSC 7 Mexicali
19.03.82 Huracan Hernandez W RSC 7 Acapulco
02.04.82 Alejo Garcia W PTS 10 Mexico City
28.05.82 Ciro Cayetano W CO 8 Acapulco
12.06.82 Heriberto Saavedra W PTS 10 Mexico City
03.07.82 Diego Avila L DIS 7 Mexico City
21.08.82 Bobby Ruiz W RSC 6 Mexico City
22.09.82 Fidel Martinez W CO 4 Mexico City
16.10.82 Carlos de la Paz W RSC 5 Mexico City
29.11.82 Ramon Nogueda W CO 4 Tijuana
15.12.82 Lupe Acosta W CO 6 Tijuana
01.02.83 Tony Escobar W RSC 10 Tijuana
14.02.83 Baldo Gonzalez W CO 2 Tijuana
06.03.83 Jimmy Fernandez W RSC 7 Mexicali
15.04.83 Jose Sosa W RSC 3 Mexicali
19.05.83 Jose Torres W PTS 10 Los Angeles
20.06.83 Armando Loredo W PTS 10 Houston
08.07.83 Pedro Rojas W CO 2 Poza Rica
15.09.83 Ron Cisneros W RSC 7 Los Angeles
03.11.83 George Garcia W RSC 9 Los Angeles
02.12.83 Freddie Santos W CO 4 Los Angeles
13.01.84 Rodolfo Martinez W RSC 8 Mexicali
15.03.84 Paul Ferreri W PTS 10 Los Angeles
31.03.84 Manuel Aguilar W CO 6 Mexicali
17.06.84 Berlin Olivetti W RSC 2 Watson Ville
01.10.84 Bernardo Ibarra W PTS 10 Tijuana
30.10.84 Wayne Lyman W CO 2 Culver City
01.12.84 Diego Avila W RSC 8 Mexicali
01.01.85 Antonio Avelar L DIS 5 Mexicali
28.01.85 Jorge Ramirez L PTS 10 Tijuana
30.03.85 Antonio Avelar W RSC 7 Mexicali
04.05.85 Oscar Bolivar W RSC 6 Aruba
07.06.85 Mario Gomez W PTS 10 Nuevo Laredo
06.07.85 Freddy Santos W RSC Mexicali
23.08.85 Armando Marales W CO 5 Carmen
20.09.85 Arnulfo Luna W CO 4 Campeche
20.11.85 Fidel Martinez W CO 2 Acapulco
29.11.85 Arturo Castillo W PTS 10 Aguascalientes
30.03.86 Jiro Watanabe W PTS 12 Osaka (*WBC S. Flyweight Title Challenge*)
15.05.86 Edgar Monserrat W PTS 12 Paris (*WBC S. Flyweight Title Defence*)
18.07.86 Ruben Condori W PTS 12 Salta (*WBC S. Flyweight Title Defence*)
30.08.86 Santos Laciar DREW 12 Cordoba (*WBC S. Flyweight Title Defence*)
15.12.86 Kongtorance Payakarun W PTS 12 Bangkok (*WBC S. Flyweight Title Defence*)
31.01.87 Antoine Montero W RSC 9 Montpelier (*WBC S. Flyweight Title Defence*)
19.03,87 Frank Cedeno W PTS 12 Mexicali (*WBC S. Flyweight Title Defence*)
16.05.87 Santos Laciar L RSC 11 Reims (*WBC S. Flyweight Title Defence*)
30.10.87 Jorge Ramirez W RSC 4 Mexicali
08.04.88 Jesus Rojas W PTS 12 Miami (*WBC S. Flyweight Title Challenge*)
09.07.88 Yoshiyuki Uchida W RSC 5 Kawagoe (*WBC S. Flyweight Title Defence*)
03.09.88 Kiyoshi Hatanaka W PTS 12 Nagoya (*WBC S. Flyweight Title Defence*)
07.11.88 Jesus Rojas W PTS 12 Las Vegas (*WBC S. Flyweight Title Defence*)
Summary: 56 contests, won 51, drew 1, lost 4.

Emil (Matsushima) Romano
Philippines
Flyweight

14.09.85 Arthur Rivera W RSC 2 Pasay
22.03.86 Cris Ramos W PTS 6 Quezon City
04.07.86 Gil Lucban W RSC 4 Manila
25.10.86 Gil Lucban W RSC 1 Quezon City
15.11.86 Sammy Baculong L PTS 10 Baguio
24.01.87 Boy Selda W RSC 5 Manila
02.02.87 Romeo Opriasa W RSC 1 Manila
25.04.87 Bob Arcillas L RSC 6 Quezon City
27.06.87 Rolando Pascua L PTS 10 Manila
22.08.87 Leopard Ari L RSC 3 Los Banos
25.09.87 Wilfredo Mendoza W RSC 9 Manila
07.11.87 Boy Selda W PTS 10 Manila
04.12.87 Dinky Jagdon W PTS 10 Manila
23.01.88 Romeo Opriasa DREW 10 Binmaley
27.02.88 Oh-Kong Son W PTS 10 Kyoto
08.07.88 Seung-Hwa Kang W CO 1 Tokyo
19.09.88 Azadin Anhar W PTS 10 Tokyo
13.11.88 Yong-Kang Kim L PTS 12 Chungju (*WBC Flyweight Title Challenge*)
26.03.89 Takeshi Maeda W RSC 8 Kyoto
Summary: 19 contests, won 13, drew 1, lost 5.

Edwin (Chapo) Rosario

Sancturce, Puerto Rico. *Born* 15.03.63

Former WBA & WBC Lightweight Champion

03.03.79 Jorge Ortega W CO 2 Santo Domingo
03.03.79 Juan Caro W CO 1 Santo Domingo
27.03.79 Enrique Maldonado W CO 3 Santo Domingo
12.05.79 Julio Miranda W CO 4 Santo Domingo
20.07.79 Jose Villegas W CO 5 San Diego
01.08.79 James Sowell W CO 2 Los Angeles
22.09.79 Ramon Cruz W RSC 2 San Juan
18.02.80 Leopoldo Frias W CO 2 Puerto Rico
10.03.80 Pascual Polanco W RSC 4 San Juan
07.07.80 Jose Luis Lara W RSC 2 Bloomington
22.08.80 Javier Flores W RSC 9 Las Vegas
10.04.81 Tony Trys W RSC 4 New York
23.05.81 Jose Resendez W RSC 6 Las Vegas
25.06.81 Refugio Rojas W RSC 2 New York
18.07.81 Rodrigo Aguirre W CO 8 Tampa
16.09.81 James Martinez W PTS 10 Las Vegas
14.11.81 Roberto Garcia W CO 2 Las Vegas
10.12.81 Ernesto Herrera W CO 3 Tampa
30.01.82 Ezzard Charles Adams W CO 3 Las Vegas
21.03.82 Dennis Quimayousie W RSC 1 Las Vegas
22.05.82 Edwin Viruet W RSC 3 Las Vegas
01.05.83 Jose Luis Ramirez W PTS 12 San Juan (*Vacant WBC Lightweight Title*)
17.03.84 Robert Elizondo W RSC 1 San Juan (*WBC Lightweight Title Defence*)
23.06.84 Howard Davis W PTS 12 San Juan (*WBC Lightweight Title Defence*)
03.11.84 Jose Luis Ramirez L RSC 4 San Juan (*WBC Lightweight Title Defence*)
13.03.85 Eduardo Valdez W RSC 3 Atlantic City
15.04.85 Alberto Ramos W RSC 2 New York
16.06.85 Frankie Randall W PTS 10 London
27.12.85 Roque Montoya W RSC 7 Latham
13.06.86 Hector Camacho L PTS 12 New York (*WBC Lightweight Title Challenge*)
26.09.86 Livingstone Bramble W CO 2 Miami (*WBA Lightweight Title Challenge*)
07.03.87 Roger Brown W CO 2 Las Vegas
11.08.87 Juan Nazario W CO 8 Chicago (*WBA Lightweight Title Defence*)
21.11.87 Julio Cesar Chavez L RSC 11 Las Vegas (*WBA Lightweight Title Defence*)
02.06.88 Ramiro Lozano W CO 3 New York
31.07.88 Javier Cerna W CO 1 New York
11.08.88 Rafael Gandarilla W RSC 3 New York
03.09.88 Felipe Angulo W CO 2 New York
27.10.88 Juan Minaya W RSC 4 New York
09.02.89 Jesus Gallardo W RSC 8 New York
16.03.89 Larry Benson W RTD 5 New York

Summary: 41 contests, won 38, lost 3.

Gianfranco Rosi

Assisi, Italy. *Born* 05.08.57

Former WBC L. Middleweight Champion. Former Undefeated EBU L. Middleweight Champion. Former EBU Welterweight Champion. Former Undefeated Italian Welterweight Champion

10.09.79 Francesco Sanna W PTS Perugia
19.10.79 Scipione Colaianni W RSC 2 Perugia
24.11.79 Maurice Renaud W PTS 6 Marsciano
29.12.79 Zdravko Jovicic W RSC 1 Perugia
08.03.80 Patrick Babouran W PTS 6 Spoleto
31.05.80 Nelson Gomez L RSC 7 Spoleto
27.08.80 Jose Ribeiro W DIS 2 Senigallia
14.09.80 Mauro da Cruz W PTS 8 Ellera
29.11.80 Ernesto Ros W PTS 8 Spoleto
17.12.80 Fili Zaccheo W RSC 1 Senigallia
07.03.81 Francesco Galleo W PTS 8 Perugia
10.04.81 Claudio Pereira W PTS 8 Perugia
22.05.81 Piero Spadaccini W PTS 8 Pattoli
12.07.81 Claudio Pereira W PTS 8 Assisi
12.09.81 Antonio Torsello W RSC 2 Perugia
13.11.81 Bechir Jelassi W PTS 8 Rome
04.12.81 Oscar Aparicio W PTS 8 Perugia
16.04.82 Giuseppe di Padova W RTD 7 Perugia (*Italian Welterweight Title Challenge*)
12.06.82 Mosimo Maeleke W PTS 8 Todi
17.07.82 Mosimo Maeleke W PTS 8 Assisi
15.08.82 Antonio Torsello W RSC 2 Alberobello (*Italian Welterweight Title Defence*)
16.09.82 Antonio Antino W PTS 8 Perugia
15.10.82 Everaldo Costa W RSC 7 Perugia (*Italian Welterweight Title Defence*)
11.02.83 Mosimo Maeleke W PTS 8 Perugia
22.04.83 Pierangelo Pira W RTD 5 Perugia (*Italian Welterweight Title Defence*)
01.07.83 Luciano Navarra W PTS 8 Vibo
30.09.83 Francesco Gallo W RSC 8 Modena (*Italian Welterweight Title Defence*)
12.11.83 Mike Essett W DIS 4 Perugia
03.03.84 Manuel de Jesus W PTS 8 Riva del Garda
31.03.84 John Mclean W CO 7 Spoleto
18.05.84 Yvon Segor W PTS 10 Cannes
07.07.84 Perico Fernandez W PTS 12 Perugia (*Vacant EBU Welterweight Title*)
17.11.84 Martin Rojas W PTS 10 Riva del Garda
05.01.85 Lloyd Honeyghan L CO 3 Perugia (*EBU Welterweight Title Defence*)
15.06.85 Inino Bolamba W PTS 8 Spoleto
11.10.85 Domenico Ricci W RTD 3 Perugia
23.11.85 Gaetano Caso W CO 8 Viterbo (*Italian Welterweight Title Challenge*)
28.12.85 Wo Lomani Wo W PTS 10 Terni
15.05.86 Jean-Marie Touatti W PTS 10 Le Cannet
20.06.86 Joaquin Velasquez W PTS 8 Rio Secco
28.01.87 Chris Pyatt W PTS 12 Perugia (*EBU L. Middleweight Title Challenge*)
06.05.87 Emilo Sole W RSC 2 Lucca (*EBU L. Middleweight Title Defence*)
27.05.87 Marc Ruocco W DIS 5 Cannes (*EBU L. Middleweight Title Defence*)
02.10.87 Lupe Aquino W PTS 12 Perugia (*WBC L. Middleweight Title Challenge*)
03.01.88 Duane Thomas W RSC 7 Genoa (*WBC L. Middleweight Title Defence*)
08.07.88 Don Curry L RTD 9 San Remo (*WBC L. Middleweight Title Defence*)
15.02.89 Darryl Anthony W CO 2 Wibo Valentia
22.04.89 Jake Torrance W PTS 8 Perugia

Summary: 48 contests, won 45, lost 3.

Angelo Rottoli

Presezzo, Italy. *Born* 14.12.58

WBC International Cruiserweight Champion. Former Undefeated Italian Heavyweight Champion

04.12.81 Damien Marignan DREW 6 Bergamo

Edwin Rosario (right) thumps in a right-hander to the head of Larry Benson. Benson later retired in the fifth, March, 1989

Tom Casino

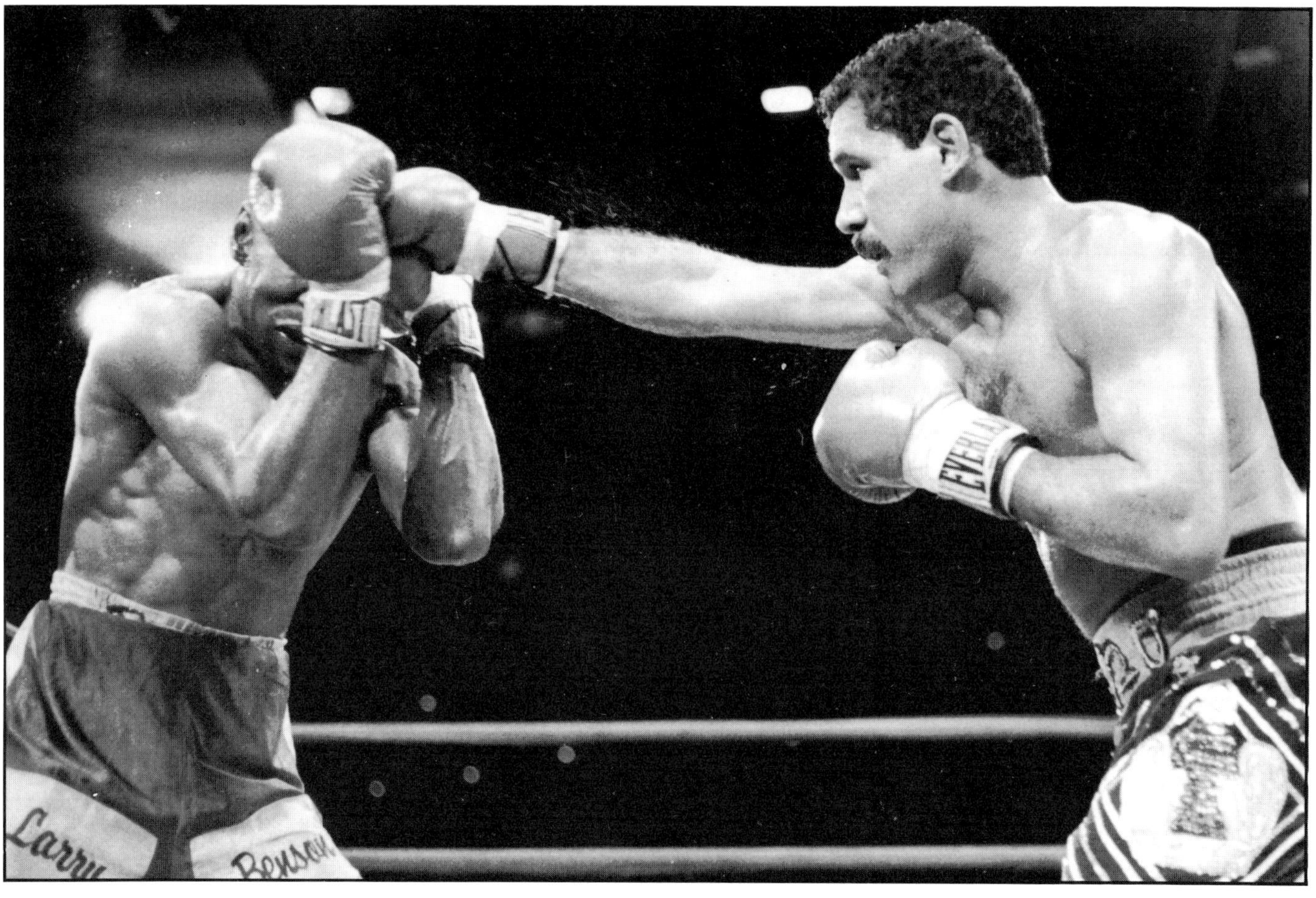

26.12.81 Jose Centa W CO 3 Cremona
06.02.82 Fred Voltine W PTS 6 Boldone
13.03.82 N'Folly Coly W RSC 1 Bergamo
02.04.82 Jose Centa W RSC 3 Bergamo
17.04.82 Damien Marignan W RSC 1 Bergamo
09.07.82 Leo Centorrino W DIS 5 Pineto
30.07.82 Primo Ruberti W RSC 4 Ballabio
14.10.82 Avenamar Peralta W RSC 2 Marano
10.12.82 George Ajio W CO 2 Ferrara
24.03.83 Guido Trane W PTS 8 Bergamo
13.05.83 Peter Mulindwa W PTS 8 Boario
22.09.83 Antxon Iraeta W RSC 4 Roseto
04.11.83 Daniele Laghi W RSC 8 Bergamo
(*Italian Heavyweight Title Challenge*)
30.03.84 Guido Trane W PTS 12 Bergamo
(*Italian Heavyweight Title Defence*)
18.08.84 Rinaldo Pelizzari W CO 11 Gragnano
(*Italian Heavyweight Title Defence*)
21.12.84 Guido Trane DREW 12 Bergamo
(*Italian Heavyweight Title Defence*)
07.04.85 Juan Quintana W PTS 8 Atlantic City
21.06.85 Guido Trane W PTS 12 Verceia
(*Italian Heavyweight Title Defence*)
19.10.85 Henry Sims W PTS 8 Monaco
21.12.85 Richard Lainhart W RSC 1 Pesaro
19.04.86 Narciso Maldonado W PTS 8 San Remo
02.07.86 Pop Nance W DIS 3 Agnone
18.10.86 Steve Mormino W PTS 10 Sella
20.12.86 Bobby Joe Thomas W PTS 10 Lecce
21.02.87 Carlos de Leon L RTD 4 Bergamo
(*WBC Cruiserweight Title Challenge*)
21.06.87 Danny Lawford W PTS 8 Perugia
04.07.87 Mickey Pryor W RSC 1 Ribera
31.10.87 Keith Vining W RSC 6 Bergamo
13.02.88 Mbuyamba Kalongo W RSC 6 Azzano
08.08.88 Bashiru Ali W PTS 12 San Pellegrino
(*WBC International Cruiserweight Title Challenge*)
Summary: 31 contests, won 28, drew 2, lost 1.

Donovan (Razor) Ruddock
Toronto, Canada. *Born* Jamaica 21.12.63
Canadian Heavyweight Champion

20.03.82 Wes Rowe W RSC 4 Toronto
24.04.82 Garland Tipton W CO 2 Toronto
01.06.82 Arthur Hall W PTS 4 Atlantic City
13.08.82 Al Williams W RSC 1 Welland
08.04.83 Bill Hollis W PTS 6 Toronto
26.04.83 Phil Brown DREW 6 Montreal
25.09.83 Conroy Nelson W PTS 10 Toronto
28.02.84 Cedric Parsons W RSC 7 Dartmouth
31.07.84 Ricardo Peterson W PTS 8 Halifax
20.10.84 Oscar Holman W PTS 8 Dartmouth
30.04.85 David Jaco L RSC 7 Dartmouth
25.02.86 Carlton Jones W CO 1 Toronto
28.05.86 John Westgarth W CO 7 London
08.07.86 Al Houck W RSC 1 Halifax
23.08.86 Mike Weaver W PTS 10 Fayetville
16.05.87 Robert Evans W RSC 5 Easton
15.06.87 Carlos Hernandez W DIS 7 Atlantic City
29.08.87 Juan Quintana W RSC 2 Easton
24.11.87 Eddie Richardson W RSC 4 Halifax
26.04.88 Larry Alexander W RSC 2 Camden
28.05.88 Ken Lakusta W CO 1 Saskatoon
(*Vacant Canadian Heavyweight Title*)
27.06.88 Reggie Gross W RSC 2 Atlantic City
06.12.88 James Broad W RSC 1 Halifax
Summary: 23 contests, won 21, drew 1, lost 1.

Jose (Cheito) Ruiz
Puerto Rico
WBO S. Flyweight Champion

13.07.84 Elias Cruz W PTS 4 Trujillo Alto
06.09.84 Marcos Roman W PTS 4 San Juan
11.10.84 Luis Monzote W PTS 4 Aquadillo
23.02.85 Pedro Feliciano L PTS 4 Hato Rey
03.05.86 Jose Vega W PTS 4 Guaynabo
22.06.86 Victor Cruz W PTS 4 San Juan
04.12.86 Marcos Claudio W RSC 1 Trujillo Alto
14.03.87 Pedro Feliciano W PTS 10 San Juan
25.04.87 Jose de Jesus L PTS 10 San Juan
08.08.87 Pedro Feliciano W PTS 10 San Juan
05.12.87 Angel Rosario W PTS 10 Trujillo Alto
11.07.88 Prudencio Cardona W CO 9 San Juan
03.11.88 Bernardo Mendoza W TD 6 San Juan
29.04.89 Jesus Rojas W PTS 12 San Juan
(*Vacant WBO S. Flyweight Title*)
Summary: 14 contests, won 12, lost 2.

Carlos Salazar
Buenos Aires, Argentine. *Born* 05.09.84
Argentinian Flyweight Champion

07.12.85 Roberto Ledesma W RSC 2 Buenos Aires
04.04.86 Ric Escobar W PTS 10 Saenz Pena
12.12.86 Roberto Ledesma W PTS 10 Saenz Pena
10.04.87 Enrique Caro W CO 3 Saenz Pena
08.05.87 Mario Quintana W CO 1 Saenz Pena
18.09.87 Oscar Veraga W PTS 10 Saenz Pena
16.10.87 Oscar Veraga W PTS 10 Saenz Pena
20.11.87 Jose Cufre W RSC 6 Saenz Pena
11.03.88 Jose Cufre W CO 3 Saenz Pena
16.04.88 Julio Olivera W RTD 3 Saenz Pena
14.05.88 Domingo Aragon W PTS 10 Saenz Pena
18.06.88 Domingo Aragon W PTS 10 Saenz Pena
01.07.88 Ruben Condori L PTS 10 Tartagal
02.09.88 Hector Patri W PTS 10 Saenz Pena
14.10.88 Rodolfo Duran W RTD 7 Saenz Pena
18.12.88 Adrian Roman W PTS 12 Saenz Pena
(*Argentinian Flyweight Title Challenge*)
18.03.89 Sergio Carlevaris W PTS 10 Saenz Pena
22.04.89 Carlos Rejala W CO 1 Saenz Pena
Summary: 18 contests, won 17, lost 1.

Donovan Ruddock (right) in action, just prior to second round stoppage win over Juan Quintana, August, 1987
Tom Casino

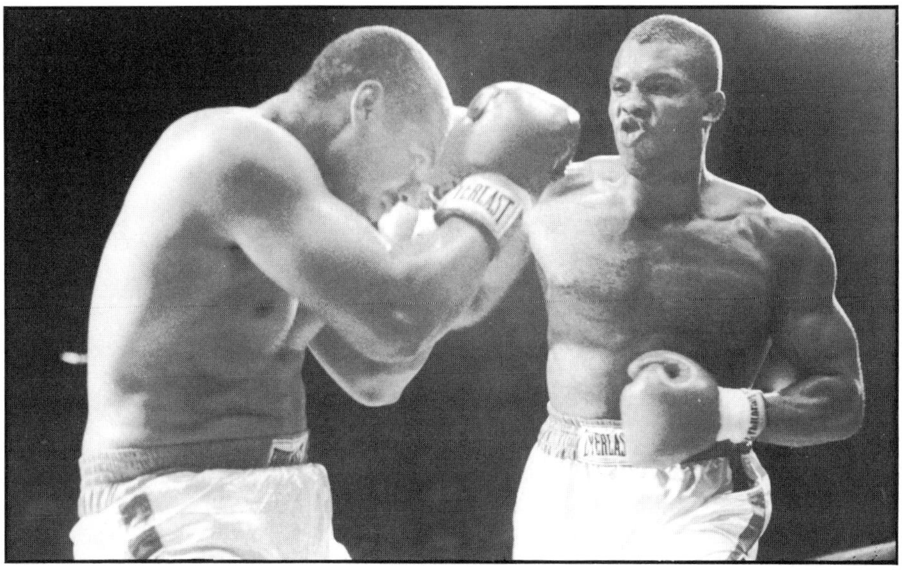

Wilibaldo (Willy) Salazar
Totolan, Mexico. *Born* 1965
NABF L. Flyweight Champion. Mexican Flyweight Champion

14.03.80 Enrique Hernandez W PTS 4 Guadalajara
09.05.80 Manuel Sanchez W CO 2 Guadalajara
18.07.80 Idelfonso Bernal L RSC 4 Guadalajara
22.08.80 Julio Martinez W PTS 8 Guadalajara
12.09.80 Jorge de Alba W RSC 5 Guadalajara
17.10.80 Idelfonso Bernal W PTS 8 Guadalajara
05.12.80 Carlos Carmona W RSC 3 Guadalajara
20.02.81 Ricardo Antonio W RSC 6 Guadalajara
03.04.81 Arturo del Villar W RSC 1 Guadalajara
29.05.81 Augustin Soberanes W RSC 1 Guadalajara
03.07.81 Artemio Ruiz L CO 5 Guadalajara
07.08.81 Enrique Torres L CO 6 Culiacan
12.02.82 Baldomero Santos L PTS 10 Guadalajara
27.05.82 Angel Ortega W RSC 5 Guadalajara
26.06.82 Joel Vazquez W CO 2 Guadalajara
28.08.82 Alberto Martinez L PTS 10 Guadalajara
22.10.82 Miguel Espinoza W RSC 4 Guadalajara
22.02.83 Fidel Martinez L CO 6 Mexico City
01.04.83 Rodolfo Flores L RSC 7 Mexico City
03.06.83 Jesus Portillo DREW 10 Guadalajara
29.10.83 Arturo Tovar W RTD 7 Guadalajara
09.12.83 Rafael Guerra L RSC 2 Guadalajara
07.12.84 Carlos Gomez W PTS 10 Guadalajara
15.02.85 Adolfo Anguiano W PTS 10 Guadalajara
21.04.85 Santiago Mendez L RSC 5 Merida
12.08.85 Javier Guerrero L PTS 10 Mexico City
10.10.85 Anastacios Rosas W RSC 10 Tepic
01.11.85 Rafael Alonso W PTS 10 Guadalajara
16.12.85 Agustin Cardenas W RSC 5 Guadalajara
07.03.86 Antonio Escobar L RSC 9 Guadalajara
05.04.86 Babe Luis W PTS 10 Guadalajara
30.05.86 Abner Arauza W CO 1 Guadalajara
13.06.86 Adolfo Anguiano W PTS 12 Guadalajara
29.08.86 Valente Flores W CO 1 Guadalajara
24.10.86 Gilberto Sosa W CO 2 Guadalajara
27.12.86 Memo Flores W RSC 8 Mexico City
30.01.87 Sergio Garcia W PTS 10 Monterrey
14.03.87 Isidro Perez W RSC 5 Mexico City
24.06.87 Jose Manuel Diaz W PTS 12 Los Angeles
(*Vacant NABF L. Flyweight Title*)
21.08.87 Gilberto Sosa W CO 1 Guadalajara
(*Mexican Flyweight Title Defence*)
09.10.87 Rafael Morales W RSC 9 Guadalajara
(*Mexican Flyweight Title Defence*)
04.12.87 Julio Cardona W RTD 5 Tucson
(*NABF L. Flyweight Title Defence*)
07.02.88 Myung-Woo Yuh L PTS Seoul
(*WBA L. Flyweight Title Challenge*)
22.04.88 Ricardo Mijares W CO 6 Juarez
(*Mexican Flyweight Title Defence*)
09.07.88 Armando Velasco L RSC 2 Mexico City
(*Mexican Flyweight Title Defence*)
30.09.88 Isaias Zamudio W RSC 9 Juarez
(*NABF L. Flyweight Title Defence*)
25.11.88 Gonzalo Villalobos W RSC 8 Guadalajara
(*Vacant Mexican Flyweight Title*)
17.02.89 Valente Flores W CO 1 Guadalajara
(*Mexican Flyweight Title Defence*)
07.04.89 Fernando Varguez W RSC 6 Guadalajara
(*Mexican Flyweight Title Defence*)
Summary: 49 contests, won 35, drew 1, lost 13.

Jesus Salud
Hawaii. *Born* 03.05.63
Bantamweight

28.06.83 Caesar Zulueta W CO 3 Honolulu
23.08.83 Juan Rodriguez W CO 3 Honolulu
04.10.83 Robert Nunez W PTS 5 Honolulu
22.11.83 Randy Dudoit W PTS 6 Honolulu
15.02.84 Anthony Henry W RSC 3 Honolulu
17.04.84 Kali Muhammad W PTS 6 Honolulu
22.05.84 John Norman W RSC 5 Honolulu
14.08.84 Donny Brooks W PTS 8 Honolulu
04.09.84 Gerald Issack W RSC 4 Honolulu
16.10.84 Adolfo Lopez W PTS 6 Honolulu
20.11.84 Troy Townsend W PTS 8 Honolulu
22.01.85 Alfredo Rangel W PTS 10 Honolulu
12.02.85 Jose Salaes W RSC 4 Honolulu
19.03.85 Jeff Hanna W RSC 7 Honolulu
01.05.85 Pedro Rodriguez W RSC 8 Honolulu
11.06.85 Jose Hiyas W PTS 10 Honolulu
23.07.85 Roberto Ramirez W RSC 8 Honolulu
10.12.85 Hugo Partida W RSC 1 Honolulu
10.02.86 Mike Phelps W CO 10 Los Angeles

21.04.86 Kenny Mitchell W PTS 10 Los Angeles
10.07.86 Frankie Duarte L RSC 9 Los Angeles
(*Vacant NABF Bantamweight Title*)
18.11.86 Edel Geronimo W PTS 10 Honolulu
24.02.87 Allan Makitoki W PTS 10 Honolulu
03.09.87 Mario Gomez L RSC 5 Los Angeles
21.04.88 Kirk Harris W CO 8 Los Angeles
13.06.88 Yoo-Woon Park W PTS 10 Los Angeles
27.07.88 Carlos Romero L PTS 10 Los Angeles
19.01.89 Carlos Castro W RSC 3 San Diego
28.02.89 Ramiro Adames W CO 2 Los Angeles
20.04.89 Carlos Salinas W CO 1 San Diego
Summary: 30 contests, won 27, lost 3.

Jose Sanabria
Caracas, Venezuela. *Born* 16.12.63
Former IBF S. Bantamweight Champion

30.03.84 Wilfredo Navas W PTS 4 Chivacoa
13.04.84 Ali Camacho L PTS 4 Barquisimeto
25.05.84 Alfonso Rendon W PTS 4 Chivacoa
16.06.84 Felix Benitez DREW 6 Maracay
13.07.84 Felix Benitez W RSC 2 Carupano
16.08.84 Ali Camacho W PTS 6 Maracay
03.09.84 Jose Villegas W RSC 3 San Felipe
01.03.85 Edgar Alcala W PTS 6 Guigue
08.06.85 Luis Aparicio W RSC 2 Caracas
02.09.85 Felix Guzman W PTS 10 Catia
21.12.85 Rogelio Chacin W PTS 1 Machiquez
31.07.86 James Pipps L PTS 10 Atlantic City
08.11.86 Steve McCrory W RSC 5 Stateline
23.01.87 Hurley Snead W PTS 10 Atlantic City
05.07.87 Robert Shannon W PTS 10 Las Vegas
28.08.87 Aaron Lopez DREW 10 Las Vegas
27.12.87 Seung-Hoon Lee L PTS 15 Pohang
(*IBF S. Bantamweight Title Challenge*)
21.05.88 Moises Fuentes W CO 5 Bucaramanga
(*Vacant IBF S. Bantamweight Title*)
21.08.88 Vincenzo Belcastro W PTS 12 Capo d'Orlando
(*IBF S. Bantamweight Title Defence*)
26.09.88 Fabrice Benichou W RSC 10 Noget sur Marne
(*IBF S. Bantamweight Title Defence*)
11.11.88 Thierry Jacob W RSC 6 Gravelines
(*IBF S. Bantamweight Title Defence*)
10.03.89 Fabrice Benichou L PTS 12 Limoges
(*IBF S. Bantamweight Title Defence*)
Summary: 22 contests, won 16, drew 2, lost 4.

Helio Santana
Brazil. *Born* 05.11.62
Welterweight

12.01.85 Jesie Maciel W RTD 4 Rio de Janeiro
24.01.85 Ismael dos Santos W CO 3 Rio de Janeiro
24.03.85 Roberto Silva W RTD Sao Paulo
27.04.85 Julio Sanchez W PTS 10 Rio de Janeiro
18.08.85 Claudio Pereira W CO 5 Sao Paulo
29.09.85 Eladio Gomez W CO 5 Sao Paulo
29.11.85 Anibal Panteleon W CO 6 Sao Paulo
18.05.86 Ubaldo Figueredo W CO 1 Sao Paulo
27.07.86 Jose Bezerra W PTS 8 Sao Paulo
24.08.86 Alberto Avalos W RTD 4 Campo Grande
05.10.86 Jorge Paredes W CO 2 Sao Paulo
21.12.86 Juan Cruces W PTS 10 Sao Paulo
15.03.87 Ricardo Barrios W RSC 8 Sao Paulo
09.08.87 Ramon Suarez W CO 1 Sao Paulo
15.11.87 Mario Matthysse W PTS 10 Sao Paulo
16.01.88 Enrique Bordon W CO 2 Sao Paulo
06.04.88 Hector Vilte W PTS 10 Sao Paulo
11.04.88 Antonio Juarez W PTS 10 Sao Paulo
01.08.88 Ricardo Espinosa W RTD 3 Sao Paulo
18.12.88 Orlando Orozco W RSC 7 Orlando
Summary: 20 contests, won 20.

Kelvin (The Stinger) Seabrooks
Charlotte, USA. *Born* 10.03.63
Former IBF Bantamweight Champion. Former Undefeated USBA Bantamweight Champion

09.10.81 Peanut Hughes W CO 1 High Point
08.12.81 Rondell Stevenson W RSC 2 Charleston
14.01.82 Vince Christian L PTS 4 Atlantic City
09.03.82 Francis Childs L PTS 4 Chadds Ford
13.05.82 Mike Jeter W CO 1 Anderson
15.06.82 Jerome Coffee L PTS 8 Nashville
17.07.82 Kenny Mitchell L PTS 8 Atlantic City
20.08.82 Terry Pizzaro W PTS 8 Orlando
16.10.82 Donald Alston W RSC 3 Charlotte
16.12.82 Gary Benton W CO 1 Charlotte
15.02.83 Terry Pizzaro W RSC 3 Atlantic City
01.03.83 Rocky Garrett W RSC 2 Charleston
22.03.83 Ewart Chance W RSC 3 Atlantic City
10.05.83 Wilfred Padron W PTS 10 Charleston
21.06.83 Carmelo Negron L RSC 7 Atlantic City
13.12.83 Alfonso Mitchell W RSC 2 Atlantic City
24.01.83 Dave Grayton W PTS 8 Atlantic City
06.03.84 Myron Taylor L PTS 10 Atlantic City
03.04.84 Juan Veloz L PTS 10 Atlantic City
24.05.84 Lane Killian W RSC 5 Nashville
25.08.84 Gaby Canizales L PTS 12 Laredo
(*USBA Bantamweight Title Challenge*)
14.11.84 Chester Richardson W PTS 8 Baltimore
05.12.84 Pat Cowdell L RSC 5 London
04.02.85 Calvin Grove L PTS 10 Atlantic City
08.03.85 Ray Minus W CO 3 Nassau
19.03.85 Lane Killian W RSC 5 Atlantic City
02.05.85 Tommy Cordova L PTS 10 Atlantic City
05.08.85 Fred Reed Hall W RSC 2 Atlantic City
20.08.85 Harold Petty L PTS 12 Atlantic City
(*Vacant Con. Am. Bantamweight Title*)
02.12.85 Rodney Bowman W RSC 3 Sydney
10.12.85 Vernon Buchanan L RSC 6 Atlantic City
10.03.86 Fred Jackson W CO 2 Sydney
15.08.86 Tony Reyes W CO 1 Charlotte
01.03.87 Louis Curtis W PTS 12 Alexandria
(*Vacant USBA Bantamweight Title*)
15.05.87 Miguel Maturana W CO 5 Cartagena
(*Vacant IBF Bantamweight Title*)
04.07.87 Thierry Jacob NC 9 Calais
(*IBF Bantamweight Title Defence*)
18.11.87 Ernie Cataluna W RSC 4 San Cataldo
(*IBF Bantamweight Title Defence*)
06.02.88 Fernando Beltran W RSC 2 Paris
(*IBF Bantamweight Title Defence*)
09.07.88 Orlando Canizales L RSC 15 Atlantic City
(*IBF Bantamweight Title Defence*)
Summary: 39 contests, won 24, lost 14, no contest 1.

Kelvin Seabrooks

Peter Goldfield/USA

John Sichula
Zambia. *Born* 29.07.58
Commonwealth S. Featherweight Champion. Former Undefeated ABU S. Featherweight Champion

28.02.82 Valentine Kangwa W PTS 6 Lusaka
.05.82 Lezza Poko W CO 4 Ndola
04.07.82 Kabiru Akindele W PTS 8 Lagos
02.09.82 David Malo W RSC 3 Ndola
28.11.82 Ray Akway W CO 4 Lusaka
30.01.83 Steve Sting W RSC 4 Lusaka
02.03.83 Valentine Kangwa W RSC 4 Lusaka
.05.83 Prince Harold W CO 2 Lusaka
03.09.83 Safiu Okebadan W RSC 8 Lusaka
(*Vacant ABU S. Featherweight Title*)
04.11.83 Haste Sankisa W RSC 6 Lusaka
.12.83 Bossou Aziza W RSC 6 Lusaka
04.02.84 Langton Tinago W CO 5 Harare
(*Commonwealth S. Featherweight Title Challenge*)
13.04.84 Johnny Rubin DREW 6 Hagen
27.04.84 Hugo Carrizo W PTS 8 Berlin
08.06.84 Haidar Nourredine W RTD 3 Baunatal
22.06.84 Antonio Franca W RSC 3 Munich
25.08.84 Frank Realihno W CO 2 Lusaka
05.10.84 Robert Mullins W RSC 4 Frankfurt
16.11.84 Lester Ellis L PTS 12 Melbourne
(*Commonwealth S. Featherweight Title Defence*)
05.05.85 Modest Napunyi W PTS 6 Lusaka
08.06.85 Haste Sankisa W CO 3 Lusaka
(*Vacant Commonwealth S. Featherweight Title & ABU S. Featherweight Title Defence*)
16.12.85 Lester Ellis W RSC 4 Melbourne
25.10.86 Sam Akromah L PTS 12 Accra
(*Commonwealth & ABU S. Featherweight Title Defence*)
29.08.87 Sam Akromah W PTS 12 Lusaka
(*Commonwealth & ABU S. Featherweight Title Challenge*)
27.11.87 Arturo Hernandez W RSC 4 Russelsheim
26.04.88 Joel Segura W CO 5 Cologne
07.08.88 Johnny Rubin W CO 5 Cologne
21.04.89 Sam Akromah W RSC 9 London
(*Commonwealth S. Featherweight Title Defence*)
Summary: 28 contests, won 25, drew 1, lost 2.

(Rockin') Robbie Sims
Brockton, USA. *Born* 05.11.59
Former Undefeated USBA Middleweight Champion

17.05.80 Troy Vaughn W RSC 4 Las Vegas
18.08.80 Dave Dean W CO 1 Boston
02.10.80 Danny Heath W RSC 1 Boston
25.11.80 Roberto Thomas W RSC 4 Boston
17.01.81 Bill Harrington W RSC 2 Boston
12.02.81 Len Villers W RSC 5 Boston
06.03.81 Jamal Arbubakrr W PTS 8 Worcester
12.04.81 James Green W PTS 8 Atlantic City
13.06.81 Don Dimazio W RSC 2 Boston
06.08.81 Jesus Castro W RSC 3 Atlantic City
16.09.81 Odell Leonard W RTD 6 Boston
23.12.81 Johnny Heard W PTS 10 Providence
17.01.82 Bobby Czyz L PTS 10 Atlantic City
30.04.82 Fred Reed Hall W RSC 5 Yarmouth
10.07.82 Jose Green W CO 4 Warwick
20.08.82 Bruce Thompson W CO 1 Plymouth
16.10.82 Clint Jackson L PTS 10 Atlantic City
04.02.83 Murray Sutherland DREW 10 Worcester
23.03.83 Tony Chiaverini W RSC 5 Worcester
03.08.83 Mike Tinley L PTS 10 Atlantic City
01.09.83 Ted Mann W PTS 10 Atlantic City
25.10.83 Charlie Hecker W CO 2 Portland
06.01.84 Iran Barkley W RSC 6 Atlantic City
29.03.84 Curtis Ramsey W PTS 10 Las Vegas
10.05.84 Danny Long W PTS 12 Brockton
26.07.84 Mike Baker W RSC 5 Miami
01.11.84 Mike Tinley L PTS 10 Atlantic City
30.05.85 Stacey McSwain W CO 4 Portland
30.08.85 Doug de Witt W PTS 10 Atlantic City
06.12.85 Mario Tinco W RSC 4 Las Vegas
09.03.86 John Collins W RSC 1 Las Vegas
(*USBA Middleweight Title Challenge*)
23.06.86 Roberto Duran W PTS 10 Las Vegas
12.02.87 Tim Williams DREW 10 Las Vegas
10.04.87 Lee Sanders W RSC 5 Las Vegas
18.03.88 Ralph Smiley W RSC 9 Boston
12.06.88 Sumbu Kalambay L PTS 12 Ravenna
(*WBA Middleweight Title Challenge*)
18.04.89 Doug de Witt L PTS 12 Atlantic City
(*Vacant WBO Middleweight Title*)
Summary: 37 contests, won 29, drew 2, lost 6.

Tanomsak Singboebae
Thailand. *Born* 15.04.65
Former OPBF Flyweight Champion. Former Undefeated Thai Flyweight Champion

10.06.85 Kamonded Singrungrote W PTS 6 Bangkok
10.09.85 Viboon Kiatsorlos W PTS 6 Bangkok
02.10.85 Utichai Siskempetch W RSC 5 Bangkok
01.11.85 Narong Na Bamrung W PTS 6 Bangkok
05.12.85 Pisit Singrungrote W PTS 6 Bangkok
02.01.86 Wiraded Sor Wateanan W PTS 6 Bangkok
11.02.86 Somded Kiatsonyut W RSC 2 Bangkok
06.03.86 Nongbird Napataya W PTS 10 Bangkok
(*Thai Flyweight Title Challenge*)
12.05.86 Narkalart Kiatsontaya W RSC 5 Bangkok
04.09.86 Prateep Sor Sawadwalee W CO 2 Bangkok

15.10.86 Anburi Sanusi W RSC 4 Bangkok
(*Vacant OPBF Flyweight Title*)
03.12.86 Narkalart Kiatsontaya W CO 4 Bangkok
12.01.87 Sakchai Kiatsontaya W RSC 2 Bangkok
01.03.87 Soon-Jung Kang W PTS 12 Bangkok
(*OPBF Flyweight Title Defence*)
03.05.87 Kenji Matsumura L PTS 12 Kakogawa
(*OPBF Flyweight Title Defence*)
09.07.87 Panchai Kiatsontaya W CO 1 Bangkok
13.08.87 Daonoi Sissaen W CO 3 Bangkok
20.09.87 Louie Gonzalez W CO 2 Bangkok
14.12.87 Frank Cedeno W PTS 10 Bangkok
21.02.88 Nakrob Sorpayathai W CO 3 Bangkok
03.04.88 Al Mariano W RSC 7 Bangkok
19.06.88 Jong-Sup Chun W CO 4 Bangkok
28.08.88 Ippo Gala W PTS 10 Bangkok
23.10.88 Ki-Chang Kim W CO 2 Bangkok
18.12.88 Romeo Opriasa W PTS 10 Bangkok
12.03.89 Tom Ramos W PTS 10 Bangkok
Summary: 26 contests, won 25, lost 1.

Samuth Sithnaruepol
Chonburi, Thailand. *Born* 17.05.59
IBF M. Flyweight Champion. Former Undefeated OPBF & Thai M. Flyweight Champion.

08.05.82 Sirisak Sakcharlat W CO 2 Bangkok
20.06.82 Sentien Sithkempetch W PTS 6 Bangkok
13.08.82 Pomprai Siripong W CO 4 Bangkok
29.08.82 Prayursak Muangsurin L RSC 4 Bangkok
24.10.82 Sarmprang Tienhirang W PTS 6 Bangkok
21.11.82 Pudpard Sithchula W CO 5 Bangkok
10.12.82 Samhunpang Boothavee L RSC 4 Bangkok
09.03.83 Vunjai Sorsanti W CO 2 Bangkok
06.06.83 Narong Pornthavee W PTS 6 Bangkok
25.08.83 Samart Sakadam L RSC 5 Bangkok
14.10.83 Kairung Sithphayak W PTS 6 Bangkok
18.12.83 Dangsak Kiatsonthaya W PTS 6 Bangkok
02.01.84 Nakaraja Kiatsonthaya L PTS 6 Bangkok
11.02.84 Oh-Kong Son L CO 5 Seoul
15.02.84 Sangnarong Sithseemok W CO 2 Bangkok
18.03.84 Nopachai Sakporcharen W CO 2 Bangkok
10.04.84 Thongtep Petchsriraja W CO 2 Bangkok
07.07.84 Narong Nabumrung L RSC 3 Bangkok
16.09.84 Chaiya Singchachvan L PTS 6 Bangkok
25.10.84 Thongthorng Chorsuenanarn W RSC 3 Bangkok
14.11.84 Kongkrung Kiatkliangkai L PTS 8 Bangkok
10.01.85 Putt Ohyuthanakorn W PTS 6 Bangkok
14.02.85 Thavat Kiatpongchinda L PTS 8 Bangkok
02.05.85 Pormongkol Sithkodom W PTS 6 Bangkok
29.06.85 Narong Nabumrung W RSC 4 Bangkok
27.07.85 Kwanjai Sorpengpis L PTS 6 Bangkok
28.08.85 Kongkrung Kiatkliangkai W PTS 6 Bangkok
31.10.85 Kwanjai Sorpengpis W PTS 6 Bangkok
26.12.85 Putt Ohyuthanakorn W PTS 10 Bangkok
(*Thai M. Flyweight Title Challenge*)
19.01.86 Nopachai Sakdipohcharern W CO 2 Bangkok
18.02.86 Thavat Kiatpongchinda W PTS 6 Bangkok
19.03.86 Daonoi Sithprakan W RSC 2 Bangkok
28.04.86 Kenji Ono W PTS 12 Bangkok
(*Vacant OPBF M. Flyweight Title*)
25.12.86 Kwanjai Sorpengpis L PTS 8 Bangkok
19.02.87 Norikazu Kawana W CO 5 Bangkok
(*OPBF M. Flyweight Title Defence*)
29.03.87 Kaopongnoi Thaveerat W CO 2 Bangkok
12.04.87 Thanjai Kiatthavatchai W RSC 3 Bangkok
01.06.87 John Arief DREW 12 Surabaya
(*OPBF M. Flyweight Title Defence*)
29.10.87 Thongthep Petchsriraja W RSC 4 Bangkok
26.11.87 Pornmonkon Chorwaikun W PTS 8 Bangkok
31.12.87 Densor Tranikul W RSC 7 Bangkok
(*OPBF M. Flyweight Title Defence*)
24.03.88 Domingo Lucas W RSC 11 Bangkok
(*Vacant IBF M. Flyweight Title*)
29.08.88 In-Kyu Hwang W PTS 15 Bangkok
(*IBF M. Flyweight Title Defence*)
23.03.89 Nico Thomas DREW 12 Jakorta
(*IBF M. Flyweight Title Defence*)
Summary: 44 contests, won 31, drew 2, lost 11.

Simon Skosana
Springs, South Africa. *Born* 29.12.57
South African Bantamweight Champion

04.05.79 Victor Tladi W PTS 4 Springs
03.08.79 Ben Thusi L RSC 1 Springs
30.03.80 Lucas Nkoana W PTS 4 Springs
01.08.80 James Sibeko W PTS 4 Springs
31.10.80 Richard Modise W PTS 6 Springs
06.02.81 Edison Ramagole L CO 5 Kwa Thema
30.10.81 Joshua Mahlangu W PTS 4 Diepkloof
05.11.82 Edison Ramagole W CO 7 Sebokeng
26.11.82 Paul Tshela W CO 2 Springs
28.01.83 Fransie Badenhorst W PTS 6 Diepkloof
15.04.83 Gift Xalura W CO 4 Springs
05.08.83 Israel Papane W CO 1 Springs
19.08.83 Joseph Ngubane W PTS 8 Sowete
30.09.83 Paulus Tshehla W RSC 6 Natalspruit
28.10.83 Jack Mathys W RSC 2 Springs
03.02.84 Phindile Gaika W PTS 12 Springs
(*South African Bantamweight Title Challenge*)
10.03.84 Roy Somer W RSC 7 Diepkloof
25.05.84 Olvin Mthembu W PTS 8 Springs
10.08.84 Jose de la Cruz Lopez W CO 7 Springs
12.10.84 Richard Smith W RSC 7 Johannesburg
(*South African Bantamweight Title Defence*)
21.09.85 Edgar Roman W PTS 10 Johannesburg
09.11.85 Jeff Hanna W PTS 10 Johannesburg
03.04.86 Fransie Badenhorst W PTS 12 Durban
(*South African Bantamweight Title Defence*)
07.06.86 Phindile Gaika W RSC 7 Springs
(*South African Bantamweight Title Defence*)
06.09.86 Julio Soto Solano W PTS 10 Durban
22.11.86 Bernardo Pinango L RSC 15 Johannesburg
(*WBA Bantamweight Title Challenge*)
24.05.87 Jesus Bastardo W PTS 10 Johannesburg
28.06.87 Fransie Badenhorst W PTS 12 Springs
(*South African Bantamweight Title Defence*)
15.02.88 Tony Pruitt W CO 7 Durban
28.03.88 Fundile Shushwana W RSC 11 Johannesburg
14.06.88 Mark Hammon W CO 4 Durban
15.08.88 Jesse Williams W PTS 10 Durban
20.09.88 Jerome Coffee W PTS 10 Johannesburg
11.02.89 Brian Holmes W PTS 10 Johannesburg
Summary: 34 contests, won 31, lost 3.

Said Skouma
France. *Born* Casablanca 28.08.58
Former Undefeated EBU & French L. Middleweight Champion

06.11.81 Mustapha Yazidi W PTS 6 Tarbes
18.12.81 Mohamed Ghaby W RSC 2 Fumel
15.01.82 Gerard Doizy W RTD 3 Tarbes
12.03.82 Jean-Pierre Moreau W RTD 3 Tarbes
23.04.82 Abdel Ben Ameur W CO 1 Clermont
07.05.82 Wo Lomani Wo W RSC 4 Fumel
28.10.82 Uwe Wissenbach W CO 1 Paris
20.12.82 Dennis Pryce W CO 6 Fumel
04.02.83 Esperno Postl W RSC 5 St Etienne
24.02.83 Lloyd Christie L PTS 8 Paris
19.05.83 Fred Coranson W RTD 8 Paris
01.07.83 Jean-Louis Coquin W PTS 8 Paris
26.11.83 Richard Rodriquez W PTS 12 Nimes
(*Vacant French L. Middleweight Title*)
25.05.84 Jimmy Cable L RSC 11 Toulouse
(*Vacant EBU L. Middleweight Title*)
26.10.84 Philippe Monin W RTD 8 Echirolles
07.12.84 Helier Custos W PTS 8 Bordeaux
25.01.85 Yvon Segor W CO 7 Pointe a Pitre
22.03.85 Germain le Maitre W RTD 5 Tarbes
(*French L. Middleweight Title Challenge*)
18.10.85 Luigi Marini W RSC 4 Antibes
30.11.85 Enrico Scacchia W CO 6 Geneva
(*Vacant EBU L. Middleweight Title*)
10.04.86 Angelo Liquori W RTD 8 Antibes
(*EBU L. Middleweight Title Defence*)
23.05.86 Alfonso Redondo W RSC 4 Bordeaux
(*EBU L. Middleweight Title Defence*)
24.08.86 Kenny Butler W RSC 2 Juan les Pins
25.10.86 Mike McCallum L CO 9 Paris
(*WBA L. Middleweight Title Challenge*)
06.02.87 Judas Clottey L DIS 5 Antibes
28.02.87 Tomas Garcia W RSC 4 Vincennes
27.03.87 Buster Drayton L RTD 10 Cannes
(*IBF L. Middleweight Title Challenge*)
23.06.87 Knox Brown W CO 6 Cannes
06.11.87 Hugo Marinangelli W DIS 7 Antibes
03.03.88 Jake Torrance W RTD 5 Casablanca
03.10.88 Kevin Brazier W CO 3 Paris
19.11.88 Darryl Anthony W RTD 2 Chateau Thierry
23.01.89 Manning Galloway L PTS 10 Paris
13.03.89 Kenny Snow W PTS 10 Paris
Summary: 34 contests, won 28, lost 6.

James (Bonecrusher) Smith
Magnolia, USA. *Born* 03.04.53
Former WBA Heavyweight Champion

05.11.81 James Broad L RSC 4 Atlantic City
30.01.82 Rickey Parkey W PTS 6 Knoxville
22.04.82 Mike Cohen W CO 2 Charleston
31.07.82 Louis Alexander W RSC 2 Atlantic City
11.09.82 Chris McDonald W PTS 8 Atlantic City
16.10.82 Lonnie Chapman W CO 2 Charlotte
14.12.82 Larry Givens W RSC 3 Atlantic City
01.04.83 Nate Robinson W CO 2 Lancaster
23.04.83 Lee Cohen W CO 2 New York
10.05.83 Linwood Jones W RSC 2 Atlantic City
14.06.83 Eugene Cato W CO 4 Charleston
23.08.83 Walter Santemore W RSC 4 Atlantic City
04.11.83 Leroy Boone W RSC 4 Tampa
19.02.84 Ben Griffin W RSC 5 Tampa
13.05.84 Frank Bruno W CO 10 Wembley
09.11.84 Larry Holmes L RSC 12 Las Vegas
(*IBF Heavyweight Title Challenge*)
15.03.85 Tony Tubbs L PTS 10 Las Vegas
29.04.85 Jose Ribalta W PTS 10 Buffalo
15.06.85 Tim Witherspoon L PTS 12 Las Vegas
(*NABF Heavyweight Title Challenge*)
23.02.86 Marvis Frazier L PTS 10 Richmond
05.04.86 Mike Weaver W RSC 1 Latham
07.06.86 Jesse Ferguson W PTS 10 Hamilton
23.08.86 David Bey W PTS 10 Fayetteville
12.12.86 Tim Witherspoon W RSC 1 New York
(*WBA Heavyweight Title Challenge*)
07.03.87 Mike Tyson L PTS 12 Las Vegas
(*WBA Heavyweight Title Defence & WBC Heavyweight Title Challenge*)
09.08.87 Jose Adilson Rodriguez L PTS 10 Sao Paulo
30.07.88 Mike Rouse T DRAW 3 Atlantic City
Summary: 27 contests, won 19, drew 1, lost 7.

Hurley (Dr Prescription) Snead
Detroit, USA. *Born* 29.08.59
Former Undefeated USBA Bantamweight Champion

09.07.81 James Tolliver W CO 6 Detroit
22.08.81 Thomas Elton W RSC 2 Traverse City
17.11.81 Lupe Sanchez W CO 1 Phoenix
17.12.81 Jose Coronado W PTS 6 Phoenix
28.01.82 Jose Coronado W PTS 6 Phoenix
18.02.82 Juan Veloz L PTS 6 Phoenix
16.03.82 Miguel Flores W CO 4 Phoenix
20.04.82 Phil Welther W RSC 1 Phoenix
29.04.82 Brian Johnson W RSC 1 Atlantic City
20.05.82 Danny Young W RSC 2 Phoenix
10.07.82 Jesse Hernandez W CO 1 Phoenix
03.08.82 Rudy Perez T DRAW 1 Phoenix
04.09.82 Victor Arguello W CO 1 Detroit
10.10.82 Sergio Castro W PTS 10 Detroit
19.03.83 Humberto Rodriguez W PTS 8 Reno
12.06.83 Armando Ugalde W PTS 10 Phoenix
23.09.83 James Tolliver W RSC 3 Richfield
14.01.84 Jose Torres W PTS 10 Detroit
11.03.84 Javier Gonzalez W CO 1 Detroit
15.04.84 Manuel Cedeno W PTS 10 Detroit
28.06.84 Norberto Castellano W PTS 10 Detroit
14.11.84 Alfredo Rangel W RSC 2 Detroit
30.01.85 Javier Barajas W RSC 11 Phoenix
18.04.85 Tony Coleman W RSC 4 Detroit
06.06.85 Osvaldo Acevedo W RSC 5 Detroit
(*Vacant USBA Bantamweight Title*)
22.08.85 Ernesto Guevara W CO 1 Detroit
12.09.85 Fred Jackson NC 12 Detroit
(*USBA Bantamweight Title Defence*)
06.12.85 Jose Torres W RSC 4 Las Vegas
10.02.86 Ron Cisneros W PTS 10 Laughlin
26.03.86 Hector Cortez W PTS 10 Las Vegas
15.08.86 Pedro Rodriguez W RSC 5 Detroit
20.11.86 Kenny Butts W RSC 6 Detroit
23.01.87 Jose Sanabria L PTS 10 Atlantic City
27.10.87 Jorge Samona W RSC 4 Detroit
28.01.88 Julio Blanco W PTS 10 Detroit
23.02.88 Mario Lozano W RSC 6 Detroit
30.03.88 Carlos Flores W PTS 10 Detroit
25.05.88 Omar Garcia W CO 1 Detroit
06.09.88 Carlos Flores W RTD 7 Memphis
01.11.88 Edgar Garcia W PTS 10 Memphis

30.11.88 Julian Flores W RSC 8 Detroit
17.01.89 Vincente Castillo W RSC 7 Detroit
Summary: 42 contests, won 38, drew 1, lost 2, no contest 1.

Renaldo (Mr Reindeer) Snipes

Houston, USA. *Born* 15.08.56
Former Undefeated Con. Am Heavyweight Champion.

18.11.78 Carl Halliburton W RSC 1 Chicago
10.12.78 Hal Emerson W PTS 4 White Plains
14.02.79 Sam Miller W CO 3 White Plains
04.03.79 Ron Hope W PTS 4 White Plains
11.04.79 Dave Smith W CO 4 White Plains
23.05.79 Barry Funches W CO 3 White Plains
20.06.79 Charles Cox W PTS 6 White Plains
08.07.79 Eugene Green W PTS 6 New York
10.10.79 Mike Tarasewich W PTS 8 White Plains
05.12.79 Tyrone Harlee W RSC 4 White Plains
16.04.80 Dave Johnson W PTS 8 White Plains
14.05.80 James Reid W CO 3 White Plains
11.06.80 Johnny Warr W PTS 8 White Plains
09.08.80 Robert Coley W CO 1 Atlantic City
17.09.80 Larry Alexander W RSC 2 White Plains
18.10.80 Rodell Dupree W RSC 3 Atlantic City
25.11.80 Malik Dozier W RSC 5 Boston
17.12.80 Dwain Bonds W RSC 8 White Plains
22.01.81 Leroy Boone W PTS 10 White Plains
08.03.81 Floyd Cummings W PTS 10 Atlantic City
17.05.81 Mustafa Muhammad W PTS 10 Atlantic City
09.08.81 Gerrie Coetzee W PTS 10 Tarrytown
06.11.81 Larry Holmes L RSC 11 Pittsburgh (*WBC Heavyweight Title Challenge*)
21.03.82 Scott Frank DREW 10 Atlantic City
05.06.82 Tim Witherspoon L PTS 10 Las Vegas
02.10.82 Trevor Berbick W PTS 10 Atlantic City
20.05.83 Greg Page L PTS 12 Las Vegas (*USBA Heavyweight Title Challenge*)
23.09.83 Alfredo Evangelista L PTS 10 Richfield
30.10.84 Rickey Parkey L PTS 10 Atlantic City
10.07.86 Bobby Crabtree W RSC 5 New York
24.07.86 Dennis Fikes W RSC 2 New York
17.08.86 Donnie Long W PTS 10 Atlantic City
12.12.86 Tyrell Biggs L PTS 10 New York
09.04.87 Melvin Epps W RSC 5 New York
04.06.87 Richard Scott W PTS 10 New York
23.07.87 Terry Anderson W CO 10 New York (*Vacant Con. Am Heavyweight Title*)
19.03.88 Orlin Norris L PTS 12 Las Vegas (*NABF Heavyweight Title Challenge*)
16.06.88 Terry Armstrong W RSC 8 New York
12.08.88 Johnny du Plooy W RSC 7 Milwaukee
15.12.88 Lionel Washington W RSC 4 New York
30.03.89 Andre Crowder W RSC 3 New York
Summary: 41 contests, won 33, drew 1, lost 7.

Tracy Spann

Plainfield, USA. *Born* 07.04.63
Lightweight

23.10.84 Terry Cooney W RSC 1 Atlantic City
20.11.84 Larry Watson W RSC 1 Atlantic City
08.01.85 Chris Bowen W PTS 4 Atlantic City
13.02.85 Mike Brown W PTS 6 Atlantic City
02.04.85 Dick Lasiter W RSC 2 Atlantic City
21.05.85 Frank Mackey W RSC 1 Atlantic City
18.06.85 Leo Lopez W RSC 2 Atlantic City
23.07.85 Jose Gonzalez W PTS 6 Washington
14.09.85 Darryl Richardson W RSC 2 Orange
11.03.86 Kevin Austin W RSC 5 Atlantic City
21.07.86 Bobby Van W CO 3 Atlantic City
21.02.87 Anthony Andrews W PTS 6 Atlantic City
31.03.87 Nick Parker W PTS 8 Erie
27.10.87 Franco Nava W CO 4 New York
30.04.88 Felipe Julio W RSC 2 New York
17.06.88 Raul Salazar W CO 1 Secaucus
16.07.88 Errol West W RSC 3 Kingston
14.10.88 David Taylor W RSC 7 Lausanne
15.12.88 Sebastian Wilburn W CO 6 Rochester
26.01.89 Roger Brown W CO 2 Rochester
11.04.89 Miguel Santana W RSC 2 Philadelphia
Summary: 21 contests, won 21.

Michael (Jinx) Spinks

St Louis, USA. *Born* 13.07.56
Former Undefeated IBF Heavyweight Champion.
Former Undefeated World L. Heavyweight Champion

17.04.77 Eddie Benson W CO 1 Las Vegas
07.05.77 Luis Rodriguez W PTS 6 St Louis
01.06.77 Joe Bordon W CO 2 Montreal
23.08.77 Jasper Brisbane W RSC 1 Philadelphia
13.09.77 Ray Elson W CO 1 Los Angeles
22.10.77 Gary Summerhays W PTS 10 Las Vegas
15.02.78 Tom Bethea W PTS 8 Las Vegas
15.12.78 Eddie Phillips W CO 4 White Plains
24.11.79 Mark Hans W RSC 1 Bloomington
01.02.80 Johnny Wilburn W PTS 8 Louisville
24.02.80 Ramon Ronquillo W RTD 7 Atlantic City
06.05.80 Murray Sutherland W PTS 10 Kaimesha
02.08.80 Dave Conteh W RSC 8 Baton Rouge
18.10.80 Yaqui Lopez W RSC 7 Atlantic City
24.01.81 Willie Taylor W RSC 8 Philadelphia
28.03.81 Marvin Johnson W CO 4 Atlantic City
18.07.81 Mustafa Muhammad W PTS 15 Las Vegas (*WBA L. Heavyweight Title Challenge*)
07.11.81 Vonzell Johnson W RSC 7 Atlantic City (*WBA L. Heavyweight Title Defence*)
13.02.82 Mustapha Wasajja W RSC 6 Atlantic City (*WBA L. Heavyweight Title Defence*)
11.04.82 Murray Sutherland W RSC 8 Atlantic City (*WBA L. Heavyweight Title Defence*)
12.06.82 Jerry Celestine W RSC 8 Atlantic City (*WBA L. Heavyweight Title Defence*)
18.09.82 Johnny Davis W RSC 9 Atlantic City (*WBA L. Heavyweight Title Defence*)
18.03.83 Dwight Muhammad Qawi W PTS 15 Atlantic City (*WBA L. Heavyweight Title Defence & WBC L. Heavyweight Title Challenge*)
25.11.83 Oscar Rivadaneyra W RSC 10 Vancouver (*WBA & WBC L. Heavyweight Title Defence*)
25.02.84 Eddie Davis W PTS 12 Atlantic City (*WBA & WBC L. Heavyweight Title Defence. Vacant IBF L. Heavyweight Title*)
23.02.85 David Sears W RSC 3 Atlantic City (*World L. Heavyweight Title Defence*)
06.06.85 Jim MacDonald W RSC 8 Las Vegas (*World L. Heavyweight Title Defence*)
21.09.85 Larry Holmes W PTS 15 Las Vegas (*IBF Heavyweight Title Challenge*)
19.04.86 Larry Holmes W PTS 15 Las Vegas (*IBF Heavyweight Title Defence*)
06.09.86 Steffen Tangstad W RSC 4 Las Vegas (*IBF Heavyweight Title Defence*)
15.06.87 Gerry Cooney W RSC 5 Atlantic City
27.06.88 Mike Tyson L CO 1 Atlantic City (*World Heavyweight Title Challenge*)
Summary: 32 contests, won 31, lost 1.

Renaldo Snipes walks away after sending Lionel Washington crashing out of the ring and enforcing the referee's intervention

Tom Casino

Marlon (Magic Man) Starling

Hartford, USA. *Born* 29.08.58
WBC Welterweight Champion. Former WBA Welterweight Champion. Former USBA & NABF Welterweight Champion

27.07.79 Tim la Valley W RSC 3 Hartford
07.09.79 Hubert Jackson W PTS 4 Hartford
27.09.79 Jerry North W PTS 4 Hartford
17.10.79 Hector Ortiz W PTS 6 Hartford
05.11.79 John Saxton W RSC 4 Hartford
09.01.80 Charlie Newell W CO 7 Hartford
28.02.80 Frank Minigan W RSC 4 Harford
08.04.80 Feliciano Cintron W RSC 6 Hartford
23.05.80 Eddie Campbell W PTS 8 Hartford
20.06.80 Benji Goldstone W RSC 5 Hartford
03.11.80 Dave Bolden W RSC 3 Hartford
25.11.80 Curtis Taylor W PTS 10 Hartford
16.01.81 Ruby Ortiz W PTS 10 Hartford
09.02.81 Bruce Strauss W CO 2 Hartford
10.04.81 Floyd Mayweather W PTS 10 Hartford
24.04.81 Miguel Hernandez W RSC 8 New York
29.05.81 Johnny Cooper W RSC 1 Hartford
25.06.81 Juan Hidalgo W RSC 5 New York
28.08.81 Jackie Morrell W RSC 2 New York
29.01.82 Danny Paul W PTS 10 Hartford
22.03.82 Jose Santana W CO 1 Hartford
23.04.82 Ricky Camaro W RSC 3 New Haven
05.06.82 Babs McCarthy W CO 9 Hartford
17.07.82 Kevin Morgan W RSC 1 New York (*USBA Welterweight Title Challenge*)
10.09.82 Mao de la Rosa W PTS 10 Hartford
23.10.82 Don Curry L PTS 12 Atlantic City (*USBA Welterweight Title Defence & NABF Welterweight Title Challenge*)
07.01.83 Manuel Madera W RSC 3 Hartford
05.02.83 Jose Baret W CO 4 Atlantic City
23.04.83 Kevin Howard W PTS 12 Hartford (*Vacant NABF and USBA Welterweight Titles*)

24.07.83 Tommy Ayers W PTS 12 Atlantic City
(NABF and USBA Welterweight Title Defence)
10.11.83 Sammy Rookard W RSC 5 Hartford
26.11.83 Bob Graddy W CO 3 Hartford
04.02.84 Don Curry L PTS 15 Atlantic City
(WBA Welterweight Title Challenge & Vacant IBF Welterweight Title)
17.04.84 Lupe Aquino W PTS 12 Atlantic City
(NABF and USBA Welterweight Title Defence)
15.06.84 Pedro Vilella L PTS 12 New York
(NABF Welterweight Title Defence)
26.04.85 Floyd Mayweather W PTS 12 Atlantic City
(USBA Welterweight Title Defence)
07.08.85 Reggie Miller W PTS 10 Atlantic City
22.11.85 Simon Brown W PTS 12 Atlantic City
(USBA Welterweight Title Defence)
24.01.86 Leo Davis W RSC 2 Hartford
07.04.86 Ralph Twinning W RTD 6 Chicago
18.05.86 Johnny Bumphus L TD 6 Providence
(USBA Welterweight Title Defence)
19.09.86 Dexter Smith W RSC 5 Hartford
30.10.86 Roberto Mendez W RSC 4 Hartford
18.02.87 Pedro Vilella W PTS 10 Hartford
05.06.87 Norberto Bueno W CO 3 Hartford
22.08.87 Mark Breland W CO 11 Columbia
(WBA Welterweight Title Challenge)
05.02.88 Fujio Ozaki W PTS 12 Atlantic City
(WBA Welterweight Title Defence)
16.04.88 Mark Breland DREW 12 Las Vegas
(WBA Welterweight Title Defence)
29.07.88 Tomas Molinares L CO 6 Atlantic City
(WBA Welterweight Title Defence)
05.02.89 Lloyd Honeyghan W RSC 9 Las Vegas
(WBC Welterweight Title Challenge)
Summary: 50 contests, won 44, drew 1, lost 5.

Loris Stecca
San Arcangelo, Italy. *Born* 30.03.60
Former WBA S. Bantamweight Champion. Former Undefeated EBU & Italian Featherweight Champion

18.10.80 Angelo Quintavalle W RSC 3 Rimini
14.11.80 Ignazio Fara W RSC 4 Pesaro
03.12.80 Pietro Donati W CO 1 Forli
26.12.80 David Mahmutovic W RSC 1 Bologna
24.01.81 Antonio Franca W CO 4 Padova
07.02.81 Michael Morvan W CO 2 Rimini
20.02.81 Andrea Ricci W DIS 4 Faenza
20.03.81 David Mahmutovic W RSC 3 Ancona
17.04.81 Koichi Oshi W RSC 4 Rimini
29.04.81 Martin Antich W RSC 2 Gatteo
14.05.81 Angel Oliver W PTS 8 Milan
11.06.81 Melquiades da Silva W PTS 8 Milan
24.07.81 Luis de la Sagra W RSC 4 Rimini
09.08.81 Melquiades da Silva W RSC 7 Camaiore
29.08.81 Juan Francisco Rodriguez W RSC 4 Via Reggio
15.10.81 Hector Molina W PTS 8 Milan
13.11.81 Marco Gallo W PTS 12 Rimini
(Italian Featherweight Title Challenge)
26.12.81 Manuel Carrasco W RSC 2 Rimini
09.02.82 Baltazar Arroyo W DIS 2 Las Vegas
18.02.82 Cucu Talamantes W CO 3 Los Angeles
20.03.82 Mariano Rodriguez W RSC 3 Rimini
12.05.82 Pasquale Mazza W RSC 4 L'Aquila
(Italian Featherweight Title Defence)
06.07.82 Alain Lefol W RSC 4 Rimini
04.08.82 Isidoro Cabeza W RSC 5 Rimini
26.08.82 Phil Watford W RSC 5 Los Angeles
02.09.82 Javier Barajas W PTS 10 Los Angeles
09.10.82 Sammy Meck DREW 8 Rimini
02.12.82 Salvatore Melluzzo W RSC 6 Foggia
(Italian Featherweight Title Defence)
28.01.83 Jose Luis Vicho W PTS 8 Morciano
07.04.83 Steve Sammy Sims W RSC 5 Sassari
(Vacant EBU Featherweight Title)
15.06.83 Robert Mullins W PTS 8 Bologna
05.08.83 Valerio Nati W PTS 12 Camaiore
(EBU Featherweight Title Defence)
13.01.84 Jeff Hanna W RSC 5 Riva del Garda
22.02.84 Leonardo Cruz W RSC 12 Milan
(WBA S. Bantamweight Title Challenge)
13.04.84 Victor Bultron W RSC 5 Milan
26.05.84 Victor Callejas L RSC 8 Guaynabo
(WBA S. Bantamweight Title Defence)
16.02.85 Tony Cisneros W RSC 3 Reno
16.03.85 Pat Doherty W RSC 5 Rimini
04.05.85 Mike Huckabee W RSC 3 Feltre
08.06.85 Lane Killian W RSC 5 Castelar
27.07.85 Cleo Garcia W RSC 5 Carrara
08.11.85 Victor Callejas L RTD 6 Rimini
(WBA S. Bantamweight Title Challenge)
04.07.86 Ron Cisneros W PTS 8 Porlezza
03.08.86 Ernesto Guevara W CO 2 Monte Carlo
22.09.86 Ley Umba Sengy W PTS 8 Siracusa
14.11.86 Kirk Stengle W RSC 3 San Giuseppe
19.12.86 Sonny Long W PTS 8 Ancona
13.08.87 Francisco Arreola DREW 8 Forli
11.04.87 Mark Brannon W RSC 6 Bologna
15.05.87 Jose Gonzalez W PTS 8 Geneva
11.07.87 Anthony Williams W CO 6 Corsico
16.08.87 Ricky West W PTS 8 Salerno
28.11.87 Cesar Almonte W DIS 4 Oristano
29.01.88 Jose Gallegos W PTS 8 Rimini
10.04.88 Miguel Pequeno W RSC 4 Iglesias
30.05.88 Jose Segura W RSC 1 Milan
15.09.88 Rocky Lawlor W PTS 8 Milan
29.10.88 Fernando Castaneda W RSC 5 Milan
17.12.88 Jorge Alvarado W RSC 6 Sassari
Summary: 59 contests, won 55, drew 2, lost 2.

Maurizio Stecca
San Arcangelo, Italy. *Born* 19.03.63
WBO Featherweight Champion

01.12.84 Francis Aparicio W RSC 3 Milan
26.12.84 Julio Garcia W PTS 6 Modena
05.01.85 Jean-Paul Guillard W CO 2 Perugia
27.01.85 Haidar Nourredine W PTS 6 Riva del Garda
16.02.85 Kid Castillo W PTS 6 Reno
15.03.85 Vicente Fernandez W PTS 6 Rimini
04.05.85 Dave Murden W PTS 6 Feltre
08.06.85 Don Doster W RSC 2 Castellar
06.07.85 Haidar Nourredine W RSC 6 Ancona
28.09.85 Don Bryant W CO 2 Sassari
12.10.85 Tom Elston W PTS 8 Cesena
13.12.85 John Feeney W PTS 8 Cesena
07.03.86 Jose Luis Vicho W RSC 3 Rimini
02.04.86 Ricky West W PTS 8 Totowa
09.05.86 John Maloney W RTD 1 Sassari
30.05.86 Farid Benredjeb W PTS 8 Abano Terme
03.08.86 Ley Umba Sengi W PTS 8 Roccaraso
19.09.86 Jeff Hanna W PTS 8 Lerici
10.10.86 Felix Cortez W RSC 6 Cesena
28.11.86 Arturo Hernandez W PTS 10 Abano Terme
08.01.87 Cleo Garcia W PTS 8 New York
14.02.87 Juan Muriel W PTS 8 Lucca
27.03.87 Sonny Long W PTS 8 Cagliari
22.04.87 Luis Rodriguez W PTS 8 Catania
12.06.87 Francisco Arreola W PTS 10 Bula
16.08.87 Jose Hernandez W RSC 2 Salerno
09.10.87 Silford Ashby W CO 2 Aosta
28.11.87 Manuel Rodriguez W RSC 7 Oristano
11.12.87 Julian Solis W DIS 6 Livorno
12.03.88 Angel Hernandez W PTS 8 Lerici
22.04.88 Fidel Martinez W RSC 5 Milan
30.07.88 Rafael Gandarilla W PTS 8 Modena
28.09.88 Pedro Nolasco W RSC 6 Milan
(Vacant WBO Featherweight Title)
06.10.88 Rocky Lawlor W RSC 2 Milan
26.11.88 Nigel Haddock W RTD 2 Forli
Summary: 35 contests, won 35.

Alex Stewart

George Kalinsky

Alex Stewart
Jamaica. *Born* London, 28.06.64
Heavyweight

06.09.86 James Walker W RSC 3 Las Vegas
07.05.87 Eric Mitchell W RSC 3 New York
18.06.87 James Little W CO 1 New York
06.08.87 Dennis Cain W CO 2 New York
01.10.87 Tim Morrison W RSC 2 New York
27.10.87 James Harrison W RSC 2 New York
20.11.87 Ernie Poole W RSC 1 Detroit
28.11.87 Juan Quintana W RSC 2 New Haven
17.12.87 John Morton W RSC 4 New York
04.02.88 George Garza W RSC 2 New York
25.03.88 Harry Terrell W CO 1 New York
12.05.88 Mike Jones W RSC 4 New York
20.05.88 James Berry W RSC 1 New York
26.05.88 Aaron Brown W RSC 1 Boston
14.07.88 Calvin Sherman W RSC 1 New York
31.07.88 Conroy Nelson W RSC 2 New York
23.09.88 Tim Adams W RSC 1 New York
27.10.88 Lorenzo Canady W RSC 4 New York
15.12.88 Eddie Richardson W RSC 3 New York
18.02.89 David Jaco W CO 1 Budapest
23.03.89 Arthel Lawhorne W RSC 4 New York
28.04.89 Jack Johnson W RSC 2 Kingston
Summary: 22 contests, won 22.

Leslie Stewart
Trinidad. *Born* 1961
Former WBA L. Heavyweight Champion. Former Undefeated Commonwealth, Latin American & Con. Am. L. Heavyweight Champion

24.01.82 Michael Hospedales W RSC 4 Port of Spain
30.04.82 Ashton Antoine W PTS 8 Marabella
14.05.82 Easy Boy Michael W RSC 2 Port of Spain
30.07.82 Gil Rosario W RSC 9 Port of Spain
30.10.82 Ricardo Richardson W RSC 4 Port of Spain
25.02.83 Zima Baman W RSC 4 Port of Spain
12.05.83 Leon McDonald W RSC 1 Port of Spain
11.09.83 Carlos Flores W RSC 4 Port of Spain
(Latin American L. Heavyweight Title Challenge)
11.11.83 Willie Taylor W PTS 10 Port of Spain
16.12.83 Tom Collins W PTS 10 Port of Spain
16.03.84 Larry Lane W PTS 10 Port of Spain
28.09.84 Elvis Parks W RSC 9 Miami
10.11.84 James Salerno W PTS 10 Miami
01.03.85 Mark Frazie W CO 8 Port of Spain
(Vacant Con. Am. L. Heavyweight Title)
10.05.85 Chris Wells W RSC 6 Fort Lauderdale
29.06.85 Tomas Polo W PTS 10 Port of Spain
12.07.85 Dennis Roberts W RSC 1 Fort Lauderdale
04.08.85 Lottie Mwale W PTS 12 Port of Spain
(Commonwealth L. Heavyweight Title Challenge)
09.02.86 Marvin Johnson L RSC 7 Indianapolis
(Vacant WBA L. Heavyweight Title)
06.05.86 Uriah Grant W PTS 8 Atlantic City
29.07.86 James Salerno W PTS 10 Tampa
18.09.86 Gary Hubble W RSC 5 Sidney
(Commonwealth L. Heavyweight Title Defence)
15.11.86 Fully Obelmejias W RSC 4 Port of Spain
(Latin American L. Heavyweight Title Challenge)
22.03.87 Bobby Thomas W RSC 5 Port of Spain
23.05.87 Marvin Johnson W RTD 8 Port of Spain
(WBA L. Heavyweight Title Challenge)
05.09.87 Virgil Hill L RSC 4 Atlantic City
(WBA L. Heavyweight Title Defence)
27.11.88 Dawud Shaw W RTD 4 Port of Spain
18.03.88 Dean Moore W RSC 9 Miami
29.05.88 Don Lalonde L RSC 5 Port of Spain
(WBC L. Heavyweight Title Challenge)
25.10.88 Bobby Czyz L PTS 10 Atlantic City
22.04.89 Phil Brown W PTS 10 Detroit
Summary: 31 contests, won 27, lost 4.

Lupe Suarez
Corpus Christi, USA. *Born* 29.10.60
S. Featherweight

22.11.81 Hector Valdez W CO 1 Corpus Christi
16.02.82 Antonio Leal W CO 2 Corpus Christi
18.08.82 Ricardo Rodriguez W RSC 1 Alice
29.09.82 Willie Daw W RSC 2 Corpus Christi
25.02.83 Enrique Flores W RSC 2 Corpus Christi
19.03.83 Gilbert Garza W RSC 2 Beaumont

06.04.83 Alejandro Garcia W CO 2 Laredo
11.05.83 James Cleveland W PTS 8 Corpus Christi
08.07.83 Miguel Sanchez W RSC 1 Corpus Christi
12.08.83 Pedro Rodriguez W RSC 2 Corpus Christi
07.12.83 Albert Favella W RSC 6 Corpus Christi
18.01.84 Ricky Avila W RSC 2 Corpus Christi
20.05.84 Leo Martinez W RSC 5 Corpus Christi
27.09.84 Oscar Bejines W PTS 10 Corpus Christi
13.01.85 Robert Mullins W RSC 5 Corpus Christi
20.04.85 Jesus Lopez W RSC 2 Corpus Christi
20.05.85 Myron Taylor W RSC 7 Los Angeles
08.07.85 Rocky Garcia W PTS 10 Los Angeles
21.11.85 Refugio Rojas L RSC 5 Los Angeles
11.05.86 Rafael Gandarilla W PTS 10 Corpus Christi
23.08.86 Carlos Flores W CO 2 Corpus Christi
10.03.87 Ricardo Velasquez W RSC 6 Corpus Christi
24.05.87 Juan Molina W RSC 9 Corpus Christi
05.07.87 Juan Laporte W PTS 10 Las Vegas
04.11.87 Tommy Cordova W RSC 9 Corpus Christi
09.04.88 Rene Constantino W CO 3 Corpus Christi
25.06.88 Azumah Nelson L RSC 9 Atlantic City
(*WBC S. Featherweight Title Challenge*)
06.10.88 Ramon Flores W RSC 3 Corpus Christi
Summary: 28 contests, won 26, lost 2.

Mitsuru Sugiya
Hakodate, Japan. *Born* 15.03.64
Japanese Featherweight Champion

24.01.81 Tadaharu Takahashi W CO 1 Tokyo
14.07.81 Junichi Shibuya W CO 1 Tokyo
17.09.81 Chiyomi Fujita W RSC 1 Tokyo
12.10.81 Kazuo Aomatsu W PTS 4 Tokyo
17.11.81 Masayoshi Kashiwakura W PTS 4 Tokyo
20.12.81 Rasher Kawaguchi W PTS 6 Tokyo
15.02.82 Takuya Mugurama L PTS 6 Osaka
10.04.83 Kazushi Hara W CO 2 Tokyo
10.07.83 Hiromi Oshima W RSC 3 Tokyo
05.09.83 Shigemichi Watasuki W CO 3 Tokyo
30.01.84 Tiger Michigami W RSC 8 Tokyo
25.06.84 Tiger Michigami W RSC 10 Tokyo
10.09.84 Marciano Sekiyama W CO 1 Tokyo
12.11.84 Soon-Hwan Suh W PTS 10 Tokyo
28.01.85 Mitsuteru Higashi W PTS 10 Tokyo
15.07.85 Yun-Sil Kim W CO 1 Tokyo
26.08.85 Keiji Kawamura W PTS 10 Tokyo
14.10.85 Takashi Komori W CO 2 Tokyo
25.02.86 Roberto Arredondo W RSC 8 Tokyo
(*Japanese Featherweight Title Challenge*)
26.05.86 Fusao Imai W RSC 2 Tokyo
(*Japanese Featherweight Title Defence*)
23.08.86 Eijiro Kuruma L CO 7 Himeji
(*Japanese Featherweight Title Defence*)
17.11.86 Masakatsu Sakuma W CO 4 Tokyo
12.01.87 Kenji Iizumi W RSC 3 Tokyo
(*Vacant Japanese Featherweight Title*)
04.04.87 Masayoshi Matsura W RSC 3 Amagasaki
(*Japanese Featherweight Title Defence*)

Mitsuru Sugiya

22.06.87 Lion Ari L PTS 10 Tokyo
17.08.87 Yasuo Jinde W RSC 6 Tokyo
(*Japanese Featherweight Title Defence*)
30.11.87 Yukihiro Kimura W RSC 2 Tokyo
(*Japanese Featherweight Title Defence*)
15.02.88 Kenji Iizumi W PTS 10 Tokyo
(*Japanese Featherweight Title Defence*)
16.05.88 Yasuo Jinde W CO 5 Tokyo
(*Japanese Featherweight Title Defence*)
13.07.88 Minoru Mitsui W CO 4 Sapporo
(*Japanese Featherweight Title Defence*)
24.10.88 Masakatsu Sakuma W CO 10 Tokyo
(*Japanese Featherweight Title Defence*)
25.03.89 Antonio Esparragoza L CO 10 Kawasaki
(*WBA Featherweight Title Challenge*)
Summary: 32 contests, won 28, lost 4.

Apollo Sweet
Australia
OPBF & Australian Cruiserweight Champion

03.04.87 Stan Longinides W PTS 8 Melbourne
20.05.87 Andrew Foster W PTS 6 Mount Pritchard
12.06.87 John Bogolin DREW 10 Dapto
11.09.87 Johnny Taupau W PTS 10 Dapto
20.11.87 Terry Davis W PTS 6 Dapto
16.12.87 Moli Kaufusi W PTS 6 Mount Pritchard
16.03.88 Jeff Harding L PTS 10 Mount Pritchard
15.06.88 Daniel Saylor W PTS 10 Mount Pritchard
03.07.88 Dave Russell W CO 9 Croydon
(*OPBF & Australian Cruiserweight Title Challenge*)
21.10.88 Rudy Darno W RSC 8 Dapto
16.11.88 Kevin Wagstaff W PTS 12 Mount Pritchard
(*OPBF & Australian Cruiserweight Title Defence*)
17.03.89 Daniel Saylor T DRAW 1 Dapto
(*OPBF & Australian Cruiserweight Title Defence*)
Summary: 12 contests, won 9, drew 2, lost 1.

Frankie Swindell
Nashville, USA. *Born* 25.11.63
USBA L. Heavyweight Champion

14.12.85 Charlie Dixon W RSC 2 Chattanooga
31.01.86 Tyrone Venning W RTD 1 Atlantic City
27.03.86 Virgil Nelson W CO 2 Charleston
30.04.86 Jesse Brown W RSC 2 Charleston
31.05.86 Roy Saffold W PTS 6 Bridgeton
05.08.86 Ken Bentley W PTS 12 Memphis
06.09.86 Virgil Nelson W RSC 2 Chattanooga
09.09.86 Charles Dixon W RSC 3 Lexington
07.10.86 Jerome Clouden W CO 6 Los Angeles
03.12.86 Robert Folley L PTS 10 Los Angeles
21.03.87 Alex Stanley W PTS 8 Richmond
09.07.87 Manuel Murillo W CO 1 Houston
23.07.87 Wali Muhammad L PTS 8 New York

Frankie Swindell

Peter Goldfield/USA

23.01.88 Arthel Lawhorne W PTS 8 Detroit
03.02.88 Ed Curry W CO 1 Charleston
26.02.88 Vaughn Hooks NC 12 Philadelphia
(*Vacant USBA L. Heavyweight Title*)
27.05.88 Jeff Thompson W PTS 12 Atlantic City
(*Vacant USBA L. Heavyweight Title*)
21.10.88 Matt Saad Muhammad W RSC 1 Newark
19.02.89 Michael Moorer L RSC 6 Monessen
(*WBO L. Heavyweight Title Challenge*)
Summary: 19 contests, won 15, lost 3, no contest 1.

Naoto Takahashi
Osaka, Japan. *Born* 17.11.67
Japanese S. Bantamweight Champion. Former Undefeated Japanese Bantamweight Champion

07.02.85 Michihiro Saga W RSC 2 Tokyo
02.05.85 Nobuyoshi Ebina W PTS 4 Tokyo
22.08.85 Hiroyuki Gomibuchi W CO 1 Tokyo
07.10.85 Kenichiro Kojo W PTS 4 Tokyo
12.11.85 Shigemitsu Koike W CO 1 Tokyo
21.12.85 Toyokazu Sekito W CO 2 Tokyo
04.03.86 Seiichi Katayama W CO 2 Osaka
22.05.86 Hiroyoshi Yamamoto W PTS 6 Tokyo
23.07.86 Norio Hasegawa W CO 2 Tokyo
25.09.86 Tadashi Shimabukuro W PTS 8 Tokyo
01.02.87 Mitsuo Imazato W CO 5 Tokyo
(*Japanese Bantamweight Title Challenge*)
08.06.87 Mitsuo Imazato W CO 3 Tokyo
(*Japanese Bantamweight Title Defence*)
03.10.87 Chiaki Kobayashi L PTS 10 Tokyo
24.01.88 Tadashi Shimabukuro W PTS 8 Tokyo
(*Japanese Bantamweight Title Defence*)
05.05.88 Somboonyod Singsamang W CO 2 Tokyo
04.08.88 John Matienza W RSC 7 Tokyo
03.11.88 Little Bangoyan W PTS 10 Tokyo
23.01.89 Mark Horikoshi W CO 9 Tokyo
(*Japanese S. Bantamweight Title Challenge*)
Summary: 18 contests, won 17, lost 1.

Yukhito (Leopard) Tamakuma
Aomori, Japan. *Born* 25.01.61
Former Undefeated Japanese Flyweight Champion

24.05.83 Takuto Misawa W PTS 4 Tokyo
08.07.83 Takeshi Go W PTS 4 Tokyo
27.09.83 Koki Oko W PTS 4 Tokyo
10.11.83 Kenji Yokosawa W PTS 4 Tokyo
17.12.83 Seiji Tomari W PTS 6 Tokyo
22.02.84 Kazuhisa Koyama W PTS 6 Osaka
03.05.84 Takahiro Masaki L PTS 8 Tokyo
30.07.84 Hitoshi Taniuchi W RSC 6 Tokyo
12.10.84 Katsu Yoshimoto W PTS 8 Tokyo
10.12.84 Tomohiro Kiyua L RSC 10 Tokyo
28.03.85 Kenji Yokozawa L PTS 10 Tokyo
18.06.85 Yutaka Tsumoda W RSC 7 Tokyo
22.08.85 Kinya Nakamura W PTS 8 Tokyo
24.10.85 Tomoo Matsumoto W RSC 4 Tokyo
27.02.86 Kazuyoshi Funaki W PTS 10 Tokyo
22.05.86 Masayuki Takahashi W CO 3 Tokyo
23.07.86 Shunichi Nakajima W PTS 6 Tokyo
25.09.86 Kentoku Nakama W PTS 8 Tokyo
27.11.86 Masato Tanaka W RSC 7 Tokyo
26.02.87 Koji Nishikawa W PTS 10 Tokyo
(*Japanese Flyweight Title Challenge*)
28.05.87 Koji Nishikawa W PTS 10 Tokyo
(*Japanese Flyweight Title Defence*)
20.07.87 Patchaint Donjaedee W CO 4 Tokyo
21.09.87 Tetsumi Matsushima W CO 7 Tokyo
(*Japanese Flyweight Title Defence*)
30.11.87 Elysser Bautista W RSC 7 Tokyo
25.02.88 Toshio Aikawa W PTS 10 Tokyo
(*Japanese Flyweight Title Defence*)
05.06.88 Hisashi Tokushima W RSC 5 Osaka
(*Japanese Flyweight Title Defence*)
05.03.89 Yong-Kang Kim L PTS 12 Aomari
(*WBC Flyweight Title Challenge*)
Summary: 27 contests, won 23, lost 4.

Frank Tate
Houston, USA. *Born* 27.08.64
Former IBF Middleweight Champion. Former Undefeated USBA Middleweight Champion

07.12.84 Mike Pucciarelli W RSC 1 Houston
08.01.85 Joe McKnight W CO 5 Houston
17.02.85 Phil Jones W CO 4 Houston
04.03.85 Carl Orville W RSC 2 Metairie

Frank Tate (right) staggers Troy Darrell during a points win earlier in his career, July, 1987

Tom Casino

18.03.85 Ronnie Warrior W CO 2 Houston
09.04.85 Calvin Prejan W RSC 4 Houston
05.06.85 David Barrow W PTS 8 Atlantic City
11.08.85 Thomas Smith W PTS 6 Reseda
13.11.85 Bruce Calloway W RSC 3 Houston
17.01.86 Randy Smith W PTS 8 Atlantic City
16.02.86 Jerry Williams W PTS 10 Troy
24.04.86 Ricky Stackhouse W RSC 6 Houston
27.06.86 Brian Muller W RSC 7 Atlantic City
22.08.86 Curtis Parker W PTS 10 Atlantic City
27.12.86 Kevin Watts W PTS 10 Atlantic City
04.03.87 Winston Burnett W RSC 8 Basildon
27.03.87 Marvin Mack W PTS 10 Atlantic City
10.05.87 Mark McPherson W RSC 6 Atlantic City
12.07.87 Troy Darrell W PTS 12 Atlantic City
(*Vacant USBA Middleweight Title*)
10.09.87 James Williams W RSC 6 Houston
10.10.87 Michael Olajide W PTS 15 Las Vegas
(*Vacant IBF Middleweight Title*)
07.02.88 Tony Sibson W CO 10 Stafford
(*IBF Middleweight Title Defence*)
29.05.88 Sanderline Williams W PTS 10 Houston
28.07.88 Michael Nunn L RSC 9 Las Vegas
(*IBF Middleweight Title Defence*)
24.01.89 Jimmy Bills W PTS 10 Great Falls
Summary: 25 contests, won 24, lost 1.

Bernard Taylor
Charlotte, USA. *Born* 26.06.57
NABF Featherweight Champion

04.10.80 Tony Rutledge W PTS 6 Morristown
08.11.80 Danny Cruz W PTS 6 Lake Tahoe
26.12.80 Mike Rodriguez W RSC 3 Las Vegas
16.02.81 Simmie Black W CO 1 Knoxville
22.02.81 Jimmy Washington W RSC 5 Atlantic City
28.03.81 Antonio Nieves W PTS 6 Syracuse
07.05.81 Marcial Santiago W RSC 8 Atlantic City
21.06.81 Jose Pena W RTD 4 Atlantic City
08.08.81 Joe Smith W RSC 2 Knoxville
23.08.81 Tim Lucero W PTS 8 San Antonio
15.10.81 Alberto Collazo W PTS 8 Atlantic City
19.11.81 Gerald Hayes W PTS 10 Atlantic City
27.11.81 Rondell Stephens W RSC 1 Knoxville
30.01.82 Sylvester Price W CO 2 Knoxville
25.02.82 Refugio Rojas W PTS 10 Las Vegas
01.04.82 Jose Vidal W PTS 10 Atlantic City
26.05.82 Ruben Herasme W RSC 6 Charlotte
09.07.82 Paul Rutledge W RSC 5 Knoxville
16.10.82 Eusebio Pedroza DREW 15 Charlotte
(*WBA Featherweight Title Challenge*)
16.12.82 James Martinez W PTS 10 Odessa
13.01.83 Robert Mullins W RSC 1 Bristol
28.04.83 Roosevelt Rico W RSC 3 Atlantic City
25.05.83 Ray Garza W CO 2 Charlotte
12.07.83 Luis Gonzalez W PTS 10 Lafayette
08.10.83 Francisco Fernandez W PTS 10 Los Angeles
06.11.83 Jose Gonzalez W PTS 10 Knoxville
18.02.84 Federico Latino W RSC 3 Los Angeles
22.05.84 Daniel Felizardo W RSC 6 Charlotte
23.08.84 Myron Taylor W PTS 12 Atlantic City
22.11.84 Pedro Montero W PTS 10 St Paul
14.02.85 Gerald Hayes W PTS 10 Atlantic City
25.04.85 Benjamin Marquez W PTS 10 Las Vegas
22.05.85 Jose Mosqueda W PTS 10 Charlotte
11.06.85 Tyrone Downes W PTS 10 Atlantic City
28.09.85 Barry McGuigan L RTD 8 Belfast
(*WBA Featherweight Title Challenge*)
24.02.86 Angel Mayor W RSC 10 Hallandale
21.05.86 Tony Illanil W CO 1 Charlotte
12.09.86 Joe Ruelas W PTS 12 Las Vegas
(*NABF Featherweight Title Challenge*)
22.01.87 Antonio de la Paz W PTS 10 Los Angeles
27.04.87 Hector Lopez L RSC 9 Los Angeles
15.08.87 Javier Marquez W TD 5 Reno
(*NABF Featherweight Title Defence*)
05.02.88 Jeff Franklin DREW 12 Las Vegas
(*NABF Featherweight Title Defence*)
12.01.88 Gary Stallworth W PTS 10 Bristol
02.09.88 Javier Marquez W RSC 10 Mexicali
(*NABF Featherweight Title Defence*)
Summary: 44 contests, won 40, drew 2, lost 2.

Meldrick Taylor
Philadelphia, USA. *Born* 19.10.66
IBF L. Welterweight Champion

15.11.84 Luke Lecce W RSC 1 New York
20.01.85 Dwight Pratchett W PTS 6 Atlantic City
13.03.85 Darryl Curtis W CO 3 Norfolk
06.04.85 Elias Martinez W RSC 5 San Angelo
17.05.85 Neri Reyes W RSC 1 Stateline
29.06.85 Hugo Carrizo W RSC 3 Bellaria
20.07.85 Roberto Medina W PTS 6 Norfolk
16.10.85 Carlos Santana W RSC 4 Atlantic City
21.12.85 Victor Acosta W PTS 8 Virginia Beach
02.02.86 Robin Blake W PTS 10 Lake Charles
03.04.86 Jose Rivera W RSC 6 New York
11.05.86 Harold Brazier W PTS 10 Corpus Christi
16.08.86 Howard Davis DREW 10 Atlantic City
11.12.86 Danny Vargas W RSC 2 New York
06.02.87 Roque Montoya W PTS 10 Atlantic City
19.04.87 Primo Ramos W PTS 10 Phoenix
11.07.87 Irleis Perez W PTS 10 Atlantic City
04.11.87 Richard Fowler W CO 2 Corpus Christi
09.04.88 Ivan Gonzalez W RSC 5 Las Vegas
12.06.88 Martin Quiroz W PTS 10 Villa Park
03.09.88 James McGirt W RSC 12 Atlantic City
(*IBF L. Welterweight Title Challenge*)
21.01.89 John Meekins W RSC 7 Atlantic City
(*IBF L. Welterweight Title Defence*)
Summary: 22 contests, won 21, drew 1.

Myron Taylor
Philadelphia, USA. *Born* 30.11.60
Featherweight

25.08.80 Mike Davis W RSC 2 Philadelphia
09.09.80 Melvin Bethea W RSC 1 Atlantic City
01.10.80 Ben Baker W RSC 1 Atlantic City
06.11.80 Jose Figueroa W RSC 1 Atlantic City
04.12.80 Earl Wilson W RSC 2 Atlantic City
20.01.81 Santos Cruz W PTS 8 Philadelphia
18.05.81 Sylvester Price W CO 2 Philadelphia
30.06.81 Tim Daniels W PTS 8 Atlantic City
31.08.81 Alvin Fowler W RSC 1 Atlantic City
16.10.81 Walter Smith W PTS 8 Philadelphia
10.11.81 Terry Kemp W RSC 2 Atlantic City
27.01.82 Herman Ingram W PTS 8 Philadelphia
28.02.82 Alberto Collazo W PTS 10 Atlantic City
16.05.82 James Martinez DREW 10 Atlantic City
22.09.82 Rafael Gandarilla W PTS 8 Atlantic City
01.12.82 Refugio Rojas L RSC 9 Atlantic City
(*Vacant USBA Featherweight Title*)
27.09.83 Tim Daniels W RSC 4 Atlantic City
18.11.83 Benny Marquez W PTS 8 Tampa
16.12.83 Richard Savage L PTS 10 Tampa
06.03.84 Kelvin Seabrooks W PTS 10 Atlantic City
13.04.84 Tim Daniels W RSC 4 Philadelphia
16.07.84 Antonio Nieves L PTS 10 Atlantic City
23.08.84 Bernard Taylor L PTS 12 Atlantic City
26.10.84 Tom Elston W PTS 8 Philadelphia
27.11.84 Jeff Whaley W RSC 8 Atlantic City
04.03.85 Kenny Baysmore L PTS 12 Atlantic City
(*USBA S. Featherweight Title Challenge*)
20.05.85 Lupe Suarez L RSC 7 Los Angeles
29.06.87 Richard Savage W PTS 10 Secaucus
20.08.87 Richie Otero W PTS 8 New York
12.11.87 Ed Parker DREW 10 New York
24.02.88 Francis Childs W RSC 2 New York
17.05.88 Calvin Grove L PTS 15 Atlantic City
(*IBF Featherweight Title Challenge*)

11.08.88 Dominico Monaco W RSC 7 New York
23.09.88 Alberto Mercado W RSC 5 Atlantic City
03.02.89 Juan Muriel W PTS 10 New York
14.04.89 Curtis Strong W PTS 10 Atlantic City
Summary: 36 contests, won 27, drew 2, lost 7.

Myron Taylor

Peter Goldfield/USA

Francisco Tejedor
Colombia
Fecarbox L. Flyweight Champion

31.01.86 Juan Gomez W RSC 2 Cartagena
28.02.86 Jose Salazar W PTS 6 Santa Marta
06.04.86 Matias Moreno W PTS 6 Barranquilla
30.04.86 Matias Romero W CO 4 Santa Marta
16.05.86 Felipe Medrano W CO 2 Barranquilla
18.07.86 Rafael Lara W RTD 2 Barranquilla
15.08.86 Jesus Geles W CO 2 Riohacha
05.09.86 Carlos Hernandez W RSC 7 Barranquilla
03.10.86 Rafael Julio W PTS 6 Cartagena
15.11.86 Leonardo Paredes W RSC 5 Barranquilla
(*Vacant Fecarbox L. Flyweight Title*)
30.01.87 Manuel Julio W CO 3 Barranquilla
20.02.87 Felix Berrios W PTS 8 Cartagena
06.03.87 Jorge Guevara W CO 6 Cartagena
03.04.87 Arnoldo Vazquez W CO 4 Barranquilla
09.05.87 Hermogenes Murillo W RSC 5 Barranquilla
19.06.87 Uriel Londono W PTS 8 Cartagena
04.09.87 Victor Sierra W RTD 5 Barranquilla
30.10.87 Jose Castillo W PTS 10 Barranquilla
01.12.87 Rafael Julio W RSC 10 Cartagena
30.04.88 Ray Thompson W PTS 10 Cartagena
05.08.88 Orlando Maestre W PTS 10 Barranquilla
28.10.88 Jaime Diaz W CO 7 Barranquilla
25.11.88 Alfredo Cardales W PTS 8 Barranquilla
27.01.89 Eduardo Barrios W CO 3 Barranquilla
15.04.89 Mauricio Bernal W RSC 5 Barranquilla
Summary: 25 contests, won 25.

Nico Thomas
Jakarta, Indonesia
Indonisian M. Flyweight Champion

03.11.86 Kid Manguni W PTS 6 Malang
30.11.86 Little Pono L PTS 8 Gresik
27.12.86 Nana Suharna L PTS 10 Jakarta
10.01.87 Hudi DREW 8 Semalang
05.09.87 Hudi W PTS 8 Malang
31.10.87 John Arief W PTS 8 Surabaya
23.11.87 Romy Austria W CO 8 Jakarta
26.01.88 Napa Kiatwanchai L PTS 12 Jakarta
(*Vacant WBC International M. Flyweight Title*)
16.04.88 John Arief L PTS 12 Malang
(*Indonesian M. Flyweight Title Challenge*)
30.04.88 Kyung-Yung Lee L CO 4 Ulsan
07.07.88 Hudi W PTS 12 Jakarta
(*Vacant Indonesian M. Flyweight Title*)
26.10.88 Nana Suhana W CO 8 Lampung
(*Indonesian M. Flyweight Title Defence*)
26.11.88 Tony Sumawa W PTS 8 Ujung
23.03.89 Samuth Sithnaruepol DREW 12 Jakarta
(*IBF M. Flyweight Title Challenge*)
Summary: 14 contests, won 7, drew 2, lost 5.

Tony Thornton
Glassboro, USA. *Born* 08.11.59
Former USBA Middleweight Champion

15.06.83 Steve Watters W RSC 1 Atlantic City
17.07.83 Jim Barham W CO 1 Atlantic City
27.07.83 Ali Muhammad W RSC 2 Philadelphia
14.06.84 Jesse Goodmond W RSC 1 Atlantic City
18.07.84 Tee-Bop Williams W CO 1 Philadelphia
30.08.84 Pinky Gordon W CO 2 Atlantic City
30.10.84 Pinky Gordon W CO 2 Philadelphia
04.02.85 Jerome Johnson W PTS 8 Atlantic City
01.07.85 Tom Davenport W RSC 2 Atlantic City
05.09.85 Sid Outlaw W RSC 6 Atlantic City
05.11.85 Dave Barrows W RSC 2 Atlantic City
07.02.86 Cecil Pettigrew W RSC 9 Atlantic City
16.05.86 Ernie Jackson W CO 2 Atlantic City
12.08.86 Horacio Perez W RSC 2 Atlantic City
25.11.86 Harry Daniels W CO 2 Atlantic City
05.03.87 Bastante Blanco W RTD 6 Atlantic City
01.06.87 Darryl Spain W RSC 5 Philadelphia
25.08.87 Stacy McSwain DREW 10 Atlantic City
06.11.87 Doug de Witt L PTS 13 Atlantic City
(*Vacant USBA Middleweight Title*)
12.02.88 Tyrone Frazier W PTS 10 Atlantic City
28.07.88 Jerry Holly W RSC 3 Philadelphia
06.10.88 Tim Williams W RSC 5 Philadelphia
10.01.89 Mike Tinley W PTS 12 Atlantic City
(*Vacant USBA Middleweight Title*)
21.03.89 Kevin Watts L PTS 12 Atlantic City
(*USBA Middleweight Title Defence*)
Summary: 24 contests, won 21, drew 1, lost 2.

Mike Tinley
Camden, USA. *Born* 30.05.60
Middleweight

18.06.81 Roy Bostic W CO 2 Totowa
20.08.81 Calvin Taylor W RSC 2 Totowa
02.09.81 Sterling Quick DREW 4 Philadelphia
05.12.81 Brian Matthews W PTS 4 Atlantic City
19.01.82 Claude Steward W RSC 1 Atlantic City
02.02.82 Reg Johnson W CO 2 Atlantic City
24.02.82 Carlton Swift W PTS 6 Atlantic City
07.03.82 Robert Thomas L RSC 3 Atlantic City
11.05.82 Ron Ayers W PTS 6 Atlantic City
23.06.82 Luis Rivera W PTS 8 Atlantic City
26.08.82 Mark McPherson W PTS 8 Atlantic City
05.10.82 Tim Long NC 1 Atlantic City
04.11.82 Herb Willens W RTD 6 Atlantic City
15.03.83 McCarrol Frazier W CO 5 Atlantic City
03.08.83 Robbie Sims W PTS 10 Atlantic City
06.10.83 Bruce Johnson W PTS 12 Atlantic City
30.11.83 Teddy Mann W PTS 12 Atlantic City

Mike Tinley

Peter Goldfield/USA

17.02.84 Doug de Witt L PTS 12 Atlantic City
25.07.84 Jorge Amparo W PTS 10 Atlantic City
13.09.84 Andre Cooper W PTS 12 Atlantic City
01.11.84 Robbie Sims W PTS 10 Atlantic City
09.05.85 Toby Smith W RSC 2 Philadelphia
11.07.85 Ray Ray Gray W PTS 10 Atlantic City
06.12.85 Iran Barkley L PTS 12 New York
(*Vacant Con. Am. Middleweight Title*)
19.09.86 Michael Nunn L PTS 10 Atlantic City
25.06.88 Jo Jo Goodman W RSC 4 Detroit
09.09.88 Jose Quinones W PTS 10 Atlantic City
25.11.88 Ken Releford W RSC 9 Detroit
10.01.89 Tony Thornton L PTS 12 Atlantic City
(*Vacant USBA Middleweight Title*)
Summary: 29 contests, won 22, drew 1, lost 5, no contest 1.

Christophe Tiozzo
St Denis, France. *Born* 01.0.63
Former Undefeated EBU Middleweight Champion

29.10.85 Karl Barwise W PTS 8 Paris
08.12.85 Vint Hammock W RSC 3 Montreal
03.02.86 Danny Vandal W CO 2 Paris
15.03.86 James Shavers W PTS 8 Monte Carlo
15.05.86 Mike Peoples W PTS 8 New York
09.10.86 Wesley Reed W RSC 4 New York
25.10.86 T. P. Jenkins W RTD 4 St Nazaire
07.11.86 Jose Rosemain W RTD 5 Paris
13.12.86 Andre Mongalema W PTS 8 Paris
29.01.87 Troy Watson W PTS 8 New York
27.04.87 Derrick Drane W CO 4 Paris
16.06.87 Jimmy Cable W CO 5 St Nazaire
09.07.87 John Moore W RSC 7 New York
17.09.87 Tim Knight W RSC 4 New York
09.11.87 Jeff Llanas W CO 4 Villeurbanne
21.12.87 Carlos Tite W CO 3 Paris
04.02.88 Charles Campbell W PTS 10 New York
11.03.88 Lester Yarbrough W CO 7 Montbrisson
18.04.88 Pierre Joly W PTS 12 Paris
(*EBU Middleweight Title Challenge*)
13.06.88 Andreas Prox W RSC 9 Lyon
(*EBU Middleweight Title Defence*)
19.09.88 Alfonso Redondo W RSC 7 Corbeil Essone
(*EBU Middleweight Title Defence*)
18.12.88 Sylvester White W CO 8 Orlando
31.03.89 James Kinchen W PTS 10 Paris
Summary: 23 contests, won 23.

German Torres
Celaya, Mexico. *Born* 1958
Former WBC L. Flyweight Champion. Former Undefeated Japanese & Mexican L. Flyweight Champion

27.08.75 Miguel Landin W RSC 5 Mexico City
10.09.75 Fabian Garcia W RSC 2 Mexico City
27.12.75 Amado Ursua L RSC 3 Mexico City
18.02.76 Pedro Hernandez W RSC 3 Mexico City
25.03.76 Chuy Vascasio W RSC 6 Mexico City
23.04.76 Pedro Galaviz L RSC 7 Guadalajara
01.01.77 Antonio Morales W RSC 4 Gomez Palacio
19.02.77 Rocky Mijares L RSC 8 Gomez Palacio
28.07.77 Joel Gatica W CO 2 Tlapehuala
04.10.77 Cecilio Ostos W CO 4 Matamoros
30.11.77 Lupe Madera W PTS 8 Santiago
10.01.78 Jose Guerrero W CO 3 Goahuila
14.03.78 Cecilio Ostos W CO 4 Reynosa
28.04.78 Carlos Cantu W PTS 10 Nuevo Laredo
10.07.78 Esteban Guzman W CO 3 Ciudad Victoria
30.09.78 Cecilio Ostos W RSC 6 Matamoros
23.12.78 Pajarito Frias W RSC 3 Celaya
28.03.79 Leo Santos W CO 4 Mexico City
16.05.79 Pedro Moreno W RSC 5 Mexico City
27.06.79 Alejandro Flores W RSC 7 Mexico City
04.08.79 Candido Tellez W PTS 10 Mexico City
14.09.79 Ganchito Guzman W CO 2 Celaya
05.10.79 Cecilio Cabrera W CO 3 Reynosa
24.11.79 Jose Zavala W RSC 7 Mexico City
(*Vacant Mexican L. Flyweight Title*)
29.12.79 Arturo Tebaqui W CO 3 Hermosillo
26.01.80 Mario Gatica W RSC 2 Mexico City
07.03.80 Jose Zavala W PTS 10 Los Mochis
19.04.80 Tomas Cuellar W CO 3 Mexico City
10.05.80 Armando Perez W RSC 5 Mexico City
22.05.80 Mark Pacheco W RSC 9 Los Angeles
26.07.80 Amado Ursua W RSC 6 Mexico City
(*Mexican L. Flyweight Title Defence*)
09.10.80 Lupe Madera W TD 11 Mexico City
(*Mexican L. Flyweight Title Defence*)

19.12.80 Victor Salcedo W RSC 6 Las Vegas
24.01.81 Jorge Vera DREW 10 Mexico City
28.03.81 Luis Garcia W CO 3 Mexico City
(*Mexican L. Flyweight Title Defence*)
15.08.81 Hilario Zapata L PTS 15 Panama City
(*WBC L. Flyweight Title Challenge*)
31.10.81 Amado Ursua L PTS 12 Campeche
(*Mexican L. Flyweight Title Defence*)
23.01.82 Joey Olivo W PTS 10 Mexico City
27.03.82 Francisco Montiel W RSC 6 Mexico City
(*Vacant Mexican L. Flyweight Title*)
07.06.82 Katsumi Sato W CO 6 Tokyo
06.09.82 Katsumi Taniguchi W CO 3 Tokyo
10.10.82 Yuko Kazaki W CO 6 Tokyo
30.10.82 Chong-Kwan Chung W CO 9 Seoul
13.12.82 Takahashi Nakayama W RSC 6 Tokyo
05.02.83 Chano Muniz W CO 5 Tamaulipas
21.03.83 Soon-Jung Kang W PTS 10 Tokyo
02.06.83 Manabu Irie W CO 4 Okinawa
10.09.83 Jung-Koo Chang L PTS 12 Daejon
(*WBC L. Flyweight Title Challenge*)
12.12.83 Masaharu Inami W RSC 3 Tokyo
(*Japanese L. Flyweight Title Challenge*)
28.01.84 Bernardo Ibarra W PTS 10 Mexico City
15.03.84 Eleoncio Mercedes W RSC 9 Los Angeles
12.04.84 Alfonso Lopez W RSC 6 Los Angeles
14.05.84 Mitsuo Watanabe W CO 4 Tokyo
09.07.84 Bi-Won Chung W PTS 10 Seoul
22.09.84 Dong-Yong Hwan L PTS 10 Seoul
01.01.85 Luis Hernandez W CO 3 Mexico City
22.02.85 Javier Gonzalez W CO 4 Cuernavaca
27.04.85 Jung-Koo Chang L PTS 12 Pusan
(*WBC L. Flyweight Title Challenge*)
06.06.85 Yoshiyuki Uchikoshi W RSC 6 Tokyo
18.08.85 Jorge Cano L PTS 10 Mexico City
01.01.86 Leon Diaz W RSC 4 Torreon
13.04.86 Jung-Koo Chang L PTS 12 Kwangju
(*WBC L. Flyweight Title Challenge*)
07.03.87 Santiago Mendez W PTS 10 Mexico City
01.05.87 Artemio Ruiz W PTS 10 Acapulco
20.06.87 Emilio Santos W CO 2 Mexico City
15.08.87 Rodolfo Alvarado T DRAW 7 Mexico City
14.11.87 Francisco Montiel T DRAW 8 Obregon
25.06.88 Ricardo Mijares W CO 6 Torreon
04.08.88 Ysaias Zamudio W DIS 9 Mexicali
15.10.88 Julio Cardona W PTS 10 Guadalupe
11.12.88 Soon-Jung Kang W PTS 12 Seoul
(*Vacant WBC L. Flyweight Title*)
19.03.89 Yul-Woo Lee L CO 9 Taejon
(*WBC L. Flyweight Title Defence*)
Summary: 72 contests, won 58, drew 3, lost 11.

Tyrone Trice
Milwaukee, USA. *Born* 24.10.63
Welterweight

26.05.83 Rodney Moore W PTS 4 Atlantic City
04.06.83 Fred Tice W RSC 1 Traverse City
12.06.83 Willie Maxwell W CO 1 Phoenix
10.07.83 Manuel Torivio W CO 2 Atlantic City
24.08.83 Dave Odem W PTS 6 Waterford
30.09.83 Leslie Toney W RSC 2 Milwaukee
27.10.83 Victor Gordon W RSC 4 Atlantic City
03.02.84 Nate Stewart W RSC 2 Chicago
11.02.84 Kean McGill W RSC 2 Detroit
15.04.84 Bobby Graddy W RSC 6 Detroit
03.05.84 Teddy Hatfield W RSC 2 Detroit
31.05.84 Pedro Gallardo W RSC 6 Detroit
28.06.84 Fred Pendelton L RSC 1 Detroit
15.08.84 Tyrone Moore W PTS 10 Las Vegas
24.10.84 Anthony Bryant W CO 3 Detroit
06.04.85 Kenny Willis W RSC 3 Atlantic City
22.08.85 Jesus de la Cruz W RSC 1 Detroit
12.09.85 Tyrone Moore W PTS 10 Detroit
21.10.85 Jose Gonzalez W CO 5 Detroit
21.11.85 Dave Odem W RTD 6 Detroit
23.01.86 Mike Bradley W RTD 3 Detroit
28.02.86 Steve Mitchell W RSC 6 Laughlin
22.03.86 Jesse Flores W RSC 4 Reno
24.04.86 Ray Jones W RSC 2 Detroit
10.06.86 Curtis Summitt W RSC 1 Detroit
24.10.86 Dennis Johnson W RSC 7 Detroit
06.08.87 Steve Little W PTS 10 New York
10.10.87 Walter Cowans W RSC 2 Sandusky
20.11.87 Mike English W RSC 1 Detroit
23.04.88 Simon Brown L RSC 14 Berck sur Mer
(*Vacant IBF Welterweight Title*)
13.08.88 Luciano Fernandez W RSC 4 Deauville
24.09.88 Efrain Brown W RSC 6 Berck sur Mer
08.10.88 Francisco Perez W RSC 2 Franconville
09.11.88 Orlando Orozco W RSC 6 Paris
25.03.89 Ron Johnson W RSC 3 Casablanca
Summary: 35 contests, won 33, lost 2.

Tony (TNT) Tubbs
Cincinnati USA. *Born* 15.02.58
Former WBA Heavyweight Champion

14.06.80 Bruce Scott W CO 1 Cincinnati
02.08.80 Jerry Hunter W CO 4 Cincinnati
07.11.80 Ron Draper W PTS 6 San Antonio
14.11.80 John L. Johnson W RSC 1 Miami
22.11.80 Larry Simms W RTD 3 Cincinnati
29.11.80 Mike Creel W RTD 3 Los Angeles
21.08.81 Dennis Wimbley W RSC 2 Elizabeth
21.11.81 Jesse Brown W CO 1 Erlanger
19.12.81 Don Halpin W PTS 8 Pittsburgh
11.04.82 Baker Tinsley W RSC 3 Atlantic City
12.06.82 Claman Parker W RSC 1 Atlantic City
07.08.82 Clarence Hill W PTS 10 Alburquerque
18.09.82 Steve Zouski W RSC 5 Atlantic City
25.02.83 Larry Givens W RSC 7 Cincinnati
10.04.83 Jimmy Young W PTS 10 Pittsburgh
09.09.83 Gordie Racette W PTS 10 Las Vegas
18.03.84 Tom Trimm W RSC 2 Santa Monica
09.11.84 Jerry Williams W RSC 7 Las Vegas
16.01.85 Tim Miller W RSC 2 Las Vegas
15.03.85 James Smith W PTS 10 Las Vegas
29.04.85 Greg Page W PTS 15 Buffalo
(*WBA Heavyweight Title Challenge*)
17.01.86 Tim Witherspoon L PTS 15 Atlanta
(*WBA Heavyweight Title Defence*)
20.04.87 Mike Jameson W PTS 10 Santa Monica
30.05.87 Jerry Halstead W PTS 10 Las Vegas
29.09.87 Eddie Gonzalez W RTD 3 Anaheim
21.03.88 Mike Tyson L RSC 2 Tokyo
(*World Heavyweight Title Challenge*)
20.04.89 Mike Evans W PTS 10 Redondo Beach
Summary: 27 contests, won 25, lost 2.

(Big) Art Tucker
New York, USA. *Born* 29.01.59
Heavyweight

18.02.81 Johnny Warr DREW 6 Rahway
10.08.81 Dwight Triplett W PTS 6 Rahway
04.08.87 Mike Jones W RSC 2 Memphis
23.09.87 Vince delle Chiaie W CO 1 Secaucus
20.10.87 Robbie Robinson W RSC 1 Cleveland
18.12.87 Bruce Johnson W PTS 4 Detroit
21.01.88 Richard Hoard W RSC 1 New York
12.02.88 Donnell Jackson W RSC 5 East Rutherford
20.02.88 Jeff May W CO 1 Detroit
06.03.88 Bruce Johnson W CO 3 New York
30.04.88 John Morton W CO 1 New York
16.06.88 Gary Lightbourne W CO 2 New York
11.08.88 Andre Crowther W CO 1 New York
08.09.88 Eddie Gonzalez W RSC 2 New York
10.11.88 Mark Young W PTS 8 New York
21.04.89 Lucious Kirkley W RSC 3 New York
Summary: 16 contests, won 15, drew 1.

Darryl Tyson
Washington, USA. *Born* 17.10.60
Former Undefeated Con. Am. Lightweight Champion

03.09.82 Wayne Anderson W RSC 5 Washington
15.11.82 John Sawyer W CO 2 Washington
26.11.82 Ed Carberry W RSC 3 Crystal City
18.12.82 David Hamilton W RSC 2 Washington
22.01.83 Richard Gainey W RSC 2 Washington
19.03.83 David Grayton L PTS 8 Baltimore
08.04.83 Mike Monette W RSC 6 Baltimore
05.05.83 Tony Stern W PTS 8 Baltimore
10.08.83 Vinnie Costello W PTS 8 White Plains
18.08.83 Jose Gonzalez W PTS 8 Baltimore
11.10.83 Jimmy Paul W PTS 10 Atlantic City
22.11.83 Jorge Morales W PTS 10 Atlantic City
14.02.84 Carlos Santana W PTS 10 Atlantic City
24.04.84 Anthony English W CO 9 Atlantic City
02.06.84 Dave Odem W RSC 2 Washington
07.08.84 Dwayne Prim W PTS 10 Atlantic City
18.09.84 Dave Brown W PTS 10 Atlantic City
27.11.84 Victor Acosta W CO 6 Atlantic City
09.03.85 Dave Brown W PTS 10 Washington
02.04.85 Gerardo Venzor W RSC 3 Atlantic City
11.05.85 James Martinez W PTS 10 Washington
06.07.85 Melvin Paul W PTS 12 Washington
(*Vacant Con. Am. Lightweight Title*)
03.09.85 Nick Parker W RSC 12 Atlantic City
(*Con. Am. Lightweight Title Defence*)
14.01.86 Sam Johnson W RSC 2 Atlantic City
01.03.86 Freddie Roach W PTS 12 Washington
(*Con. Am. Lightweight Title Defence*)
15.08.86 Jimmy Paul L PTS 15 Detroit
(*IBF Lightweight Title Challenge*)
14.06.87 Chil-Sung Chun L PTS 10 Bukok
25.10.87 Felipe Julio W RSC 4 Tucson
21.03.88 Terrence Alli L PTS 10 Atlantic City
17.09.88 Filiberto Rosas W RSC 10 Dallas
07.02.89 Stanley Longstreet W PTS 10 Atlantic City
Summary: 31 contests won 27, lost 4.

Darryl Tyson

Peter Goldfield/USA

(Iron) Mike Tyson
New York, USA. *Born* 30.06.66
World Heavyweight Champion

06.03.85 Hector Mercedes W CO 1 Albany
10.04.85 Trent Singleton W RSC 1 Albany
23.05.85 Don Halpin W RSC 4 Albany
20.06.85 Rick Spain W CO 1 Atlantic City
11.07.85 John Anderson W RTD 2 Atlantic City
19.07.85 Larry Sims W CO 3 Poughkeepsie
15.08.85 Lorenzo Canady W RSC 1 Atlantic City
05.09.85 Michael Johnson W CO 1 Atlantic City
09.10.85 Donnie Long W RSC 1 Atlantic City
25.10.85 Robert Colay W CO 1 Atlantic City
01.11.85 Sterling Benjamin W RSC 1 Latham
13.11.85 Eddie Richardson W CO 1 Houston
22.11.85 Conroy Nelson W RSC 2 Latham
06.12.85 Sam Scaff W RSC 1 New York
27.12.85 Mark Young W CO 1 Latham
10.01.86 David Jaco W RSC 1 Albany
24.01.86 Mike Jameson W RSC 5 Atlantic City
16.02.86 Jesse Ferguson W RSC 6 Troy
10.03.86 Steve Zouski W CO 3 Nassau
03.05.86 James Tillis W PTS 10 Glens Falls
20.05.86 Mitch Green W PTS 10 New York
13.06.86 Reggie Gross W RSC 1 New York
28.06.86 Bill Hosea W CO 1 Troy
11.07.86 Lorenzo Boyd W CO 2 Swan Lake
26.07.86 Marvis Frazier W CO 1 Glens Falls
17.08.86 Jose Ribalta W RSC 10 Atlantic City
06.09.86 Alfonso Ratliff W RSC 2 Las Vegas
22.11.86 Trevor Berbick W RSC 2 Las Vegas
(*WBC Heavyweight Title Challenge*)
07.03.87 James Smith W PTS 12 Las Vegas
(*WBC Heavyweight Title Defence & WBA Heavyweight Title Challenge*)
30.05.87 Pinklon Thomas W RSC 6 Las Vegas
(*WBA & WBC Heavyweight Title Defence*)
01.08.87 Tony Tucker W PTS 12 Las Vegas
(*WBA & WBC Heavyweight Title Defence. IBF Heavyweight Title Challenge*)
16.10.87 Tyrell Biggs W RSC 7 Atlantic City
(*World Heavyweight Title Defence*)
22.01.88 Larry Holmes W RSC 4 Atlantic City
(*WBA & WBC Heavyweight Title Defence*)
21.03.88 Tony Tubbs W RSC 2 Tokyo
(*World Heavyweight Title Defence*)
27.06.88 Michael Spinks W CO 1 Atlantic City
(*World Heavyweight Title Defence*)
25.02.89 Frank Bruno W RSC 5 Las Vegas
(*World Heavyweight Title Defence*)
Summary: 36 contests, won 36.

Yoshiyuki Uchida
Japan. *Born* 18.05.59
Former Undefeated Japanese S. Flyweight Champion

07.02.81 Hiroyasu Kato L PTS 4 Tokyo
05.04.81 Masanori Kasuya W CO 1 Tokyo
09.06.81 Hiroshi Kiazato W RSC 1 Tokyo
17.09.81 Masayuki Nakamura W CO 3 Tokyo
05.10.81 Muneo Taira W RSC 3 Tokyo
16.11.81 Hiroyasu Kato W CO 1 Tokyo
20.12.81 Norio Ichikawa W RSC 6 Tokyo
15.02.82 Hideo Sakamoto W RSC 6 Osaka
20.06.82 Yasuhiro Kinoshita W RSC 2 Kashima
17.07.82 Masaki Sono W RSC 2 Tokyo
05.10.82 Masaki Sono W CO 2 Shiki
17.01.83 Shinji Takagi W CO 3 Tokyo
16.04.83 Yasuo Azato DREW 10 Nagasaki
12.07.83 Ryuji Ichinomiya W CO 1 Kamifukuoka
18.10.83 Isao Kimura W RSC 3 Osaka
23.02.84 Gonzaburo Nobu W CO 6 Tokyo
27.04.84 Fumito Hasegawa W CO 4 Tokyo
15.06.84 Heishin Tokuchi W PTS 8 Osaka
25.02.85 Tsutomu Kawakami W PTS 10 Tokyo
27.08.85 Koji Kobayashi W CO 7 Tokyo
24.03.86 Jo Shiranui W CO 5 Tokyo
22.05.86 Koji Nishikawa L PTS 10 Tokyo
(*Japanese Flyweight Title Challenge*)
23.02.87 Hiroaki Kanaya W RSC 8 Tokyo
21.09.87 Yon Inazuma W RSC 5 Tokyo
(*Vacant Japanese S. Flyweight Title*)
09.07.88 Gilberto Roman L RSC 5 Kawagoe
(*WBC S. Flyweight Title Challenge*)
Summary: 25 contests, won 21, drew 1, lost 3.

Bahar Udin
Indonesia
Indonesian L. Flyweight Champion

28.04.85 Kid Samora DREW 4 Surabaya
29.07.85 Kid Samora W PTS 4 Surabaya
11.08.85 Hassan W PTS 4 Surabaya
01.09.85 Yulius Leodjan W PTS 6 Surabaya
05.10.85 Bristol Simangunsong L PTS 10 Surabaya
27.04.86 Hudi DREW 8 Malang
10.05.86 Iwan Tubagus Jaya W PTS 10 Surabaya
22.06.86 Little Pono DREW 8 Surabaya
02.08.86 Nana Suhana W PTS 8 Surabaya
07.09.86 Hudi W PTS 8 Surabaya
02.11.86 Sonny Vidal W PTS 10 Surabaya
07.12.86 Iwan Tubagus Jaya W PTS 12 Surabaya
(*Vacant Indonesian L. Flyweight Title*)
28.02.87 Eric Chavez L CO 5 Jakarta
01.06.87 Taufik Bathi W PTS 12 Surabaya
(*Indonesian L. Flyweight Title Defence*)
09.08.87 Demi W RSC 1 Surabaya
(*Indonesian L. Flyweight Title Defence*)
28.11.87 Azadin Anhar W PTS 12 Gor Bandung
(*Indonesian L. Flyweight Title Defence*)
01.03.88 Little Pono W PTS 8 Surabaya
27.05.88 Gim Suyono W PTS 12 Gelora
(*Indonesian L. Flyweight Title Defence*)
10.06.88 Muangchai Kitikasem L PTS 10 Bangkok
04.09.88 Little Baguio DREW 10 Surabaya
23.09.88 Akri Suryaman L PTS 10 Malang
06.11.88 Myung-Woo Yuh L CO 7 Seoul
(*WBA L. Flyweight Title Challenge*)
Summary: 22 contests, won 13, drew 4, lost 5.

Cardenio Ulloa
Puerto Vargas, Chile. *Born* 30.10.56
Latin American Bantamweight Champion. Former Undefeated Con. Am. Bantamweight Champion

23.05.80 Nelson Bustamante W PTS 6 Santiago
09.07.80 Ramon Blanco W CO 5 Santiago
23.07.80 Juan Catanan W CO 1 Santiago
16.08.80 Ramon Blanco W CO 2 Braunau
15.10.80 Jose Carmona W RSC 2 Santiago
29.10.80 Juan Aravena W CO 3 Santiago
26.11.80 Tito Herbert W RSC 1 Santiago
31.01.81 Arturo Neira W PTS 8 El Salvador
06.03.81 Jorge Santis W CO 1 Santiago
03.04.81 Cristobal Ramos W CO 2 Santiago
11.04.81 Guillen Acevedo W RSC 5 El Salvador
22.05.81 Esteban Bustos DREW 8 Santiago
14.10.81 Augustin Ceballos W CO 4 Santiago
18.11.81 Hector Martinez W RSC 2 Santiago
07.12.81 Agustin Ceballos W CO 4 Santiago
26.02.82 Alfredo Herrera W CO 2 Santiago
(*Vacant Con. Am. Bantamweight Title*)
20.03.82 Roberto Condori W PTS 10 Santiago
31.05.82 Juan Rios W PTS 8 Santiago
14.08.82 Humberto Torres W CO 2 Puerto Montt
15.10.82 Jorge Fernandez W RTD 6 Talcahuano
27.11.82 Bernabe Mendez W CO 1 Melipilla
25.03.83 Raul Cuevas W RSC 3 Santiago
21.05.83 Cristobal Ramos W CO 5 Loncoche
17.09.83 Jorge Sepulveda W CO 8 Lebu
11.12.83 Jose Ortiz W CO 1 Miami
20.01.84 Hector Martinez W RSC 7 Miami
24.02.84 Julio Osorio W CO 5 Miami
03.04.84 Jose Lopez W CO 6 Miami
31.07.84 Edgar Muniz W RSC 1 Miami
15.12.84 Richard Sandoval L RSC 8 Miami
(*WBA Bantamweight Title Challenge*)
29.03.85 Diego Avila L PTS 10 Miami
24.05.85 Jorge Franco W RTD 4 Puerto Montt
03.07.85 Armando Romero W PTS 10 Santiago
01.12.85 Benito Badilla L CO 5 Santiago
(*Latin American Bantamweight Title Challenge*)
28.02.86 Juan Garcia W RSC 2 San Felipe
21.03.86 Esteban Bustos W PTS 10 Antofagasta
30.04.86 Benito Badilla W CO 5 Antofagasta
(*Latin American Bantamweight Title Challenge*)
28.05.86 Jose Cabrera W RTD 4 Talca
03.06.86 Javier Brown W CO 3 Santiago
08.08.86 Jose Narvaez W RSC 3 Santiago
13.09.86 Luis Gerez W CO 1 Santiago
29.11.86 Ramon Rodriguez W CO 2 Santiago
08.11.86 Raul Gutierrez W CO 2 Santiago
19.12.86 Roberto Haidar W RSC 3 Santiago
16.01.87 Jorge Monardez W RTD 5 Santiago
(*Latin American Bantamweight Title Defence*)
06.02.87 Eloy Alca W PTS 10 Santiago
27.03.87 Raul Ojeda W PTS 10 Temuco
19.05.87 Ezequiel Hernandez W TD 3 Santiago
24.06.87 Jose Chacon W PTS 10 Santiago
25.07.87 Gliserio Velazco W RSC 4 Santiago
30.10.87 Jose Salazar W CO 2 Santiago
11.12.87 Jose Chacon W PTS 12 Santiago
(*Latin American Bantamweight Title Defence*)
06.02.88 Edwin Ampuero W PTS 10 Copiapo
02.04.88 Carlos Solis W CO 1 Castro
28.06.88 Jose Moreira W PTS 10 Valdivia
15.09.88 Jose Narvaez W CO 5 Oalama
(*Latin American Bantamweight Title Defence*)
23.01.89 Juan Pena W RSC 2 Iquique
15.04.89 Wilson Goncalvez W CO 1 Santiago
Summary: 58 contests, won 54, drew 1, lost 3.

Tarmo Uusivirta
Finland. *Born* 05.02.57
L. Heavyweight

25.06.82 Mick Morris W PTS 6 Hankoo
01.10.82 Deano Wallace W CO 2 Helsinki
09.04.83 Andre Mongalema W RSC 5 Blendecques
18.09.83 Maurice Bufi W RTD 5 Jyvaskyla
05.11.83 Dick Katende L PTS 8 Mannheim
17.12.83 Martin McEwan W CO 2 Mariehamn
18.02.84 Juan M. Holgado W CO 3 Copenhagen
11.05.84 Arthur Holt L PTS 8 New York
21.05.84 Jose Seys L CO 5 Helsinki
27.10.84 Esperno Postl W RSC 4 Mariehamn
09.03.85 Willie Wright W PTS 8 Copenhagen
11.05.85 Paul Tchoue W PTS 8 Vasa
24.11.85 Philippe Seys W CO 2 Vasa
26.03.86 Alex Blanchard DREW 10 Amsterdam
09.11.86 Jimmy Cable W PTS 10 Vasa
21.11.86 Joe Cooper W RSC 2 Copenhagen
26.12.86 Enrico Scacchia DREW 10 Berne
26.10.87 James Cook W PTS 10 Jyvaskyla
15.01.88 Mboyanga Kalombo W PTS 4 Skive
07.02.88 Tony Burke W RTD 8 Laukka
15.05.88 Harry Cowap W RTD 4 Tampere
11.09.88 Gonzalo Mencho W CO 4 Laukka
15.12.88 Alex Blanchard DREW 12 Helsinki
Summary: 23 contests, won 17, drew 3, lost 3.

Jorge Vaca
Guadalajara, Mexico. *Born* 14.12.59
Former WBC Welterweight Champion. Former Undefeated Mexican Welterweight Champion

10.02.78 Luis Piceno W CO 2 Guadalajara
15.03.78 Alfonso Rodriquez W CO 3 Guadalajara
28.04.78 Juan Ramirez W CO 4 Guadalajara
19.05.78 Tony Castillo W CO 2 Guadalajara
16.06.78 Rodolfo Valero L CO 3 Monterrey
01.09.78 Nemesio Ontiveros W RSC 4 Guadalajara
06.10.78 Alejo Agosto W RSC 5 Guadalajara
16.03.79 Alberto Lopez W PTS 10 Guadalajara
15.11.79 Rodolfo Valero L CO 5 Guadalajara
22.08.80 Jesse Blanco W CO 4 Guadalajara
10.10.80 Juan Elizondo L CO 2 Guadalajara
14.11.80 Ranulfo Cardona W RSC 3 Guadalajara
16.01.81 Nicholas Herrera W CO 3 Guadalajara
27.02.81 Juan Elizondo W RSC 7 Guadalajara
28.08.81 Leo Bermudez W CO 4 Guadalajara
09.10.81 Juan Ochoa W RSC 1 Guadalajara
06.11.81 Ramon Beltran W CO 1 Guadalajara
04.12.81 Jose Soberanes W RSC 4 Guadalajara
28.05.82 Jose Alvarez W CO 5 Guadalajara
03.09.82 Jose Soberanes W CO 2 Guadalajara
26.02.83 Sergio Sanchez W RSC 3 Mexico City
09.06.83 Tomas Perez L CO 8 Los Angeles
02.09.83 Lalo Dominguez W RSC 6 Los Angeles
13.01.84 Rocky Granillo DREW 10 Mexicali
28.03.84 Gil Canchola W RSC 2 Tijuana
(*Mexican Welterweight Title Challenge*)
29.05.84 Gerardo Derbez W RSC 2 Tijuana
(*Mexican Welterweight Title Defence*)
12.07.84 Al Long W PTS 10 Los Angeles
11.09.84 Herman Montes L CO 2 Tijuana
26.10.84 Alberto Lopez W RSC 9 Guadalajara
(*Mexican Welterweight Title Defence*)
11.01.85 Ray Morales W CO 1 Juarez
(*Mexican Welterweight Title Defence*)
22.03.85 Gerardo Derbez W RSC 9 Juarez
(*Mexican Welterweight Title Defence*)
02.05.85 Herman Montes W RSC 3 Los Angeles
15.08.85 Tommy Richardson W PTS 10 Los Angeles
29.11.85 Gerardo Derbez W RSC 6 Guadalajara
(*Mexican Welterweight Title Defence*)
10.01.86 Sergio Medina W PTS 12 Guadalajara
(*Mexican Welterweight Title Defence*
25.03.86 Juan Escobar W CO 3 Tijuana
20.06.86 Sergio Medina W RSC 10 Guadalajara
(*Mexican Welterweight Title Defence*)
08.09.86 Ruben Villaman W CO 6 Tijuana
(*Mexican Welterweight Title Defence*)
01.12.86 Roman Nunez W RSC 3 Tijuana
(*Mexican Welterweight Title Defence*)
19.12.86 Pipino Cuevas W CO 2 Guadalajara
21.02.87 Miguel Dominguez W RSC 6 Guadalajara
(*Mexican Welterweight Title Defence*)
27.03.87 David Franklin W CO 2 Guadalajara
25.04.87 Ruben Villaman W RSC 5 Mexico City
(*Mexican Welterweight Title Defence*)
26.06.87 Juan Villa W RSC 2 Guadalajara
(*Mexican Welterweight Title Defence*)
21.08.87 Saoul Mamby W PTS 10 Tijuana
28.10.87 Lloyd Honeyghan W TD 8 Wembley
(*WBC Welterweight Title Challenge*)
29.03.88 Lloyd Honeyghan L CO 3 Wembley
(*WBC Welterweight Title Defence*)
16.07.88 Simon Brown L RSC 3 Kingston
(*IBF Welterweight Title Challenge*)
Summary: 48 contests, won 40, drew 1, lost 7.

Jose (Pepillo) Valdez
Guasave, Mexico.
Con. Am. Bantamweight Champion

14.04.83 Adrian Garcia W CO 2 Guasave
29.04.83 Manny Chavez W CO 8 Guasave
15.05.83 Armando Reyes W CO 3 Guasave
11.06.83 Mari Valenzuela W RSC 4 Guasave
17.06.83 Manuel Mora W PTS 10 Guasave
26.08.83 Oscar Zamora W CO 4 Guasave
18.11.83 Angel Valle W PTS 10 Guasave
06.01.84 Anastasio Rosa W PTS 10 Puerto Vallarta
05.02.84 Rodrigo Villa W CO 2 Los Mochis
30.03.84 Duende Rodriguez W PTS 10 Guasave
08.06.84 Jorge Urbina Diaz L RSC 8 Guadalajara
07.09.84 Sergio Perez W CO 2 Guasave
05.10.84 Moi Martinez W CO 4 Guasave
08.12.84 Ubaldo Gonzalez W RSC 6 Guasave
29.03.85 Ernesto Mata W RSC 7 Guasave
30.05.85 Pedro Castillo W CO 2 Los Mochis
05.07.85 Martin Garcia W RSC 5 Guasave
06.09.85 Candelario Carmona L RSC 9 Los Mochis
15.11.85 Tony Escobar W CO 4 Guasave
03.03.86 Julio Martinez W CO 8 Tijuana
19.04.86 Antonio Gonzalez W PTS 12 Tijuana
16.06.86 Marco Ramirez W PTS 12 Tijuana
19.07.86 Victor Romero W RSC 5 Mexicali
22.08.86 Nanchi Lopez W CO 3 Guasave

26.09.86 Jose Gallegos W CO 5 Guasave
14.11.86 Jorge de Jesus W CO 4 Guasave
20.02.87 Diego Avila W PTS 10 Guasave
03.04.87 Rodolfo Ortega W CO 8 Guasave
29.05.87 Candelario Carmona W PTS 10 Guasave
19.07.87 Edgar Roman W PTS 8 St Tropez
29.01.88 Miguel Cota W CO 2 Guasave
29.04.88 Jose Soto W PTS 10 Guamuchil
17.06.88 Tony Escobar W PTS 10 Mazatlan
14.10.88 Fernie Morales L PTS 12 Juarez
(*Mexican Bantamweight Title Challenge*)
25.11.88 Ray Minus W CO 8 Nassau
(*Con. Am. Bantamweight Title Challenge*)
09.03.89 Jorge Rodriguez W PTS 10 Los Angeles
Summary: 36 contests, won 33, lost 3.

Darrin van Horn
Kentucky, USA. *Born* 07.09.68
IBF L. Middleweight Champion

02.09.84 Leon Kerlinger W CO 2 New Orleans
13.11.84 Reuben Moran W RSC 2 Lafayette
20.11.84 Willie Rimmer W PTS 6 Jefferson
04.12.84 Rodney Jones W RSC 2 St Bernard
18.12.84 Jaime Hobbs W RSC 1 Morgan City
16.01.85 Mike French W CO 1 Lafayette
08.02.85 David Seville W CO 2 Lafayette
21.02.85 James Mitchell W RSC 5 Morgan City
04.03.85 Jesse Hopskins W CO 1 Metairie
07.03.85 Derrick Earvin W PTS 4 Gadsdon
20.03.85 James Sanders W CO 4 Lafayette
18.04.85 Ron Paige W CO 1 Monroe
07.05.85 Wesley Morton W PTS 6 New Orleans
10.06.85 Alonzo Stringfellow W RSC 1 Metairie
26.06.85 Reg Dixon W PTS 6 Lafayette
08.08.85 Robert Manous W RSC 3 Metairie
06.09.85 Earl White W RSC 6 Gretna
17.09.85 Pablo Valdez W CO 4 Metairie
02.10.85 Javier Muniz W RSC 4 Houma
22.10.85 Reg Dixon W PTS 6 Metairie
21.01.86 Ed Montague W PTS 8 Metairie
06.03.86 Norberto Sabater W RSC 2 Metairie
15.04.86 David Ramsey W CO 4 Lafayette
24.06.86 Donald Gwinn W RSC 5 Lexington
01.07.86 Keheven Johnson W RSC 8 New Orleans
09.09.86 Sammy Floyd W PTS 10 Lexington
13.01.87 Danny Thomas W PTS 10 Lexington
24.02.87 James Moore W RSC 6 Lexington
20.04.87 Elio Diaz W PTS 10 Lexington
21.06.87 Luis Santana W PTS 10 Lexington
25.08.87 Greg Taylor W PTS 8 Lexington
17.09.87 Norberto Bueno W CO 3 New York
17.10.87 Juan Alonzo Villa W PTS 10 Atlantic City
05.12.87 Joe Summers W PTS 10 Atlantic City
21.02.88 John Munduga W RSC 7 Frankfurt
05.05.88 Juan Elizondo W RSC 3 Louisville
20.09.88 Jake Torrance W PTS 10 Lexington
03.11.88 Miguel Hernandez W RSC 5 Las Vegas
05.02.89 Robert Hines W PTS 12 Atlantic City
(*IBF L. Middleweight Title Challenge*)
Summary: 39 contests, won 39.

Darrin van Horn
Peter Goldfield/USA

Pedro van Raamsdonk
Amsterdam, Holland. *Born* 02.10.60
Former EBU L. Heavyweight Champion. Former Undefeated Benelux & Dutch L. Heavyweight Champion

17.02.86 Mladen Grubesitz W RSC 2 Arnhem
26.03.86 Serge Bolivard W PTS 6 Amsterdam
13.10.86 Robert Pfischer W CO 1 Scheidam
20.10.86 Joseph Kossmann W RSC 1 Den Bosch
01.12.86 Dave Owens W CO 1 Arnhem
06.04.87 Sergio Bosio W PTS 10 Tilburg
(*Benelux L. Heavyweight Title Challenge*)
18.05.87 Johnny Held W PTS 10 Amsterdam
(*Vacant Dutch L. Heavyweight Title*)
12.10.87 Ray Thomas W PTS 8 Hertogenbosch
16.11.87 Serg Fame W PTS 8 Arnhem
14.03.88 Dennis Banton W CO 1 Arnhem
07.09.88 Tom Collins W RSC 7 Reading
(*EBU L. Heavyweight Title Challenge*)
07.11.88 Jan Lefeber L PTS 12 Rotterdam
(*EBU L. Heavyweight Title Defence*)
20.02.89 Glazz Campbell W PTS 8 Arnhem
Summary: 13 contests, won 12, lost 1.

Jose Varela
Germany. *Born* Spain, 23.04.60
West German L. Middleweight Champion. Former EBU Welterweight Champion. Former Undefeated West German Welterweight Champion

26.02.83 Uwe Wissenbach W CO 1 Mannheim
26.03.83 Giuseppe Agate W PTS 6 Wiesbaden
15.04.83 Eloi de Souza W CO 3 Munich
03.06.83 Esperno Postl W RSC 4 Frankfurt
11.06.83 Rafaelle Salamone W PTS 6 Munich
09.07.83 Ludwig Kammerhofer W RSC 2 Frankfurt
07.10.83 Rudiger Bitterling W RSC 5 Frankfurt
31.10.83 Mohamed Bouziani W PTS 6 Rosenheim
02.12.83 Juergen Broszeit W RSC 1 Rosenheim
14.01.84 Jean Symos W RSC 2 Dusseldorf
10.02.84 Nazario Mariotti W RSC 6 Frankfurt
24.02.84 Billy Waith W RSC 3 Hamburg
09.03.84 Rafaelle Salamone W CO 4 Frankfurt
13.04.84 Rafael Gutierrez W CO 2 Hagen
11.05.84 Jose Ribeiro W CO 2 Stuttgart
08.06.84 Lahcen Hamdi W RSC 3 Baunatal
20.07.84 Mosimo Maeleke W CO 3 Stuttgart
28.09.84 Alaoui Aziz W RSC 2 Munich
05.10.84 Dario de Jesus W PTS 6 Frankfurt
01.12.84 Daniele Zappaterra W RSC 1 Milan
18.01.85 Tony Habermayer W PTS 10 Russelsheim
(*West German Welterweight Title Challenge*)
20.12.85 Martin Rojas W PTS 8 Russelsheim
18.03.86 Mark Mills W CO 4 Russelsheim
03.08.86 Jesus Fernandez W RTD 4 Monte Carlo
10.10.86 Brahim Messaoudi W RSC 5 Russelsheim
(*Vacant EBU Welterweight Title*)
04.04.87 Alfonso Redondo L RTD 9 Dusseldorf
(*EBU Welterweight Title Defence*)
30.10.87 John van Elteren W RSC 3 Mainz
27.11.87 Hardy Jones W CO 1 Russelsheim
16.01.88 Ray Menefee W CO 2 Lubeck
23.01.88 Mike Peoples W CO 1 Hamburg
12.03.88 Mark Stevens W CO 1 Dusseldorf
12.05.88 Sammy Floyd W CO 5 Berlin
16.09.88 Horace Fleary W PTS 8 Berlin
25.02.89 Erwin Heiber W RSC 5 Hamburg
(*West German L. Middleweight Title Challenge*)
Summary: 34 contests, won 33, lost 1.

Javier (Candelita) Varguez
Merida, Mexico.
Mexican L. Flyweight Champion

.81 Maravilla Pinder W CO 1 Huimanguillo
27.02.82 Jorge Rejon DREW 6 Cozumel
21.04.82 Jorge Rejon L RSC 2 Cozumel
.82 Ucan W RSC 3 Cozumel
.82 Jorge Rivera W CO 3 Cozumel
11.09.82 Santiago Mendez W PTS 10 Cancun
.82 Jesus Rivera W PTS 10 Chetumal
29.10.82 Jesus Rivera L PTS 10 Chetumal
21.03.83 Guillermo Flores L PTS 10 Chetumal
17.06.83 Jorge Cano L TD 10 Chetumal
30.09.83 Julio Diaz W PTS 10 Chetumal
16.11.83 Rodolfo Alvarado L PTS 10 Merida
08.10.84 Kid Jorge W RSC 7 Merida
27.02.85 Rosendo Ake L PTS 10 Merida
18.05.85 Jose Figueroa W RSC 7 Cancun
19.12.85 Pastor Brito W RSC 7 Carmen
16.01.87 Polvorita Perez W RSC 5 Campeche
25.02.87 Jacobo Amores W RSC 5 Merida
28.03.87 Mario Perez W RSC 2 Merida
06.05.87 Oscar Sanchez W RSC 1 Merida
23.05.87 Ismael Rodriguez W CO 2 Cancun
13.06.87 Ruben Padilla W PTS 10 Merida
18.07.87 Eduardo Ramirez W PTS 10 Merida
14.11.87 Rosendo Ake W CO 6 Merida
12.12.87 Emilio Santos W RSC 7 Merida
20.02.88 Jorge Rivera W CO 6 Merida
04.06.88 Humberto Gonzalez L RSC 5 Mexico City
(*Mexican L. Flyweight Title Challenge*)
23.07.88 Valerio Olivares W CO 5 Merida
17.09.88 Jose Luis Zepeda W RSC 6 Mexico City
12.11.88 Justo Zuniga W RSC 4 Merida
17.12.88 Jorge Cano W RSC 6 Merida
(*Vacant Mexican L. Flyweight Title*)
18.02.89 Santiago Mendez W RSC 12 Merida
(*Mexican L. Flyweight Title Defence*)
Summary: 32 contests, won 24, drew 1, lost 7.

Julio Vasquez
Santa Fe, Argentina. *Born* 13.06.66
L. Middleweight

07.06.86 Antonio Chancalay W PTS 6 Buenos Aires
04.07.86 Eusebio Escalante W RTD 4 Santa Fe
08.08.86 Jose Diaz W CO 2 Santa Fe
12.09.86 Jose Carabajal W CO 2 Santa Fe
28.11.86 Jose Rivera W CO 2 Salta
13.12.86 Roque Vanos W DIS 4 Buenos Aires
14.03.87 Daniel Altamira W RTD 3 San Genaro
08.05.87 Sergio Combis W PTS 10 Santa Fe
10.07.87 Juan Barbosa W PTS 10 Santa Fe
07.08.87 Ricardo Juarez W PTS 10 Santa Fe
09.10.87 Domingo Sosa W CO 1 Santa Fe
12.11.87 Jorge Tejeda W PTS 10 Santa Fe
04.02.88 Simon Escobar W RSC 5 Santa Fe
07.04.88 Ramon Abeldano W RSC 9 Santa Fe
18.06.88 Ricardo Carballo W CO 8 Buenos Aires
14.10.88 Jorge Pino W PTS 10 Tucuman
10.12.88 Claudio Pereira W CO 1 Buenos Aires
21.01.89 Felipe Guzman W CO 3 Punta del Este
10.03.89 Juan Ortiz W CO 1 Mar del Plata
Summary: 19 contests, won 19.

Wilfredo Vasquez
Bayamon, Puerto Rico. *Born* 02.08.61
Former WBA Bantamweight Champion. Former Undefeated Puerto Rican Bantamweight Champion

29.01.81 William Ramos L PTS 4 Trujillo
26.02.81 Felix Cortez W CO 2 San Juan
26.03.81 Roberto Mercedes W RSC 3 Bayamon
30.04.81 Eusebio Espinal DREW 6 Trujillo
17.06.81 Rey Roque W CO 2 Miami
08.08.81 Herminio Adorno W PTS 6 Trujillo
29.08.81 Pedro Alindato W CO 6 Trujillo
03.03.82 Orlando Perez W RSC 7 San Juan
21.03.82 Rudy Perez W PTS 6 Las Vegas
30.05.82 Ion Traian W RSC 2 Las Vegas
26.06.82 Jose Martinez W CO 2 Las Vegas
06.08.82 Sonny Long W PTS 10 New York
19.10.82 Rudy Perez W RSC 2 Las Vegas
04.02.83 Eugenio Paulino W RSC 5 New York
01.05.83 Andres Torres W CO 8 Puerto Rico
22.07.83 Robert Mullins W CO 3 New York
31.10.83 Ramon Cruz W CO 1 Atlantic City
25.11.83 Pedro Rodriguez W RSC 3 Las Vegas
17.03.84 Juan Torres W RSC 4 San Juan
(*Vacant Puerto Rican Bantamweight Title*)
23.06.84 Julio Guerrero T DRAW 2 San Juan
19.09.84 Javier Barajas W PTS 10 Las Vegas
03.11.84 Norgie Castro W RSC 2 San Juan
13.03.85 Jeff Whaley W RSC 3 Atlantic City
09.08.85 Osvaldo Acevedo W RSC 5 Miami
08.02.86 Miguel Lora L PTS 12 Miami
(*WBC Bantamweight Title Challenge*)
24.05.86 Jose Cervantes W CO 3 San Juan
31.05.86 Antonio Avelar L RSC 8 Miami
04.10.86 Jesus Muniz W CO 8 San Juan
14.03.87 Juan Carazo W CO 1 San Juan
11.04.87 Lee Cargie W RSC 5 San Juan
04.10.87 Chan-Yung Park W RSC 10 Seoul
(*WBA Bantamweight Title Challenge*)

17.01.88 Takuya Muguruma DREW 12 Osaka
(*WBA Bantamweight Title Defence*)
09.05.88 Kaokor Galaxy L PTS 12 Bangkok
(*WBA Bantamweight Title Defence*)
01.08.88 Raul Perez L PTS 10 Los Angeles
Summary: 34 contests, won 26, drew 3, lost 5.

Armando Velasco
Puebla, Mexico. *Born* 09.08.63
Former Undefeated Mexican Flyweight Champion

11.12.82 Miguel Ordonez W RSC 3 Mexico City
25.06.83 Mario Marin L DIS 5 Mexico City
21.09.83 Ricardo Aguilar W RSC 2 Mexico City
05.11.83 Javier Guerrero DREW 8 Mexico City
04.04.84 Miguel Pequeno W CO 2 Mexico City
13.05.84 Neftali Ramirez W RSC 3 Mexico City
04.07.84 Angel Ortega W RSC 8 Mexico City
18.08.84 Valente Flores W RSC 10 Mexico City
19.10.84 Javier Diaz L PTS 10 Nuevo Laredo
20.02.85 Daniel Guillen W RSC 3 Mexico City
29.03.85 Ubaldo Gonzalez W RSC 3 San Luis Potosi
31.05.85 Carlos Gomez W RSC 3 San Luis Potosi
29.06.85 Rafael Alonso W PTS 10 Mexico City
27.08.85 Martin Cardenas W PTS 10 Tijuana
16.11.85 Simon Dominguez W RSC 10 Puebla
29.01.86 Martin A. Ramirez W CO 1 Tijuana
05.04.86 Martin Cardenas L PTS 10 Tijuana
24.06.86 Ray Medel L PTS 10 San Antonio
11.10.86 Miguel Mercedes L RSC 3 Mexico City
14.08.87 Francisco Gonzalez L PTS 10 Tijuana
12.11.87 Orlando Canizales L RSC 4 Houston
(*Vacant NABF Flyweight Title*)
30.01.88 Fernando Varguez W RSC 2 Merida
02.04.88 Mijalio Hernandez W CO 1 Minatitlan
29.04.88 Cesar Soto L DIS 4 Juarez
09.07.88 Wilibaldo Salazar W RSC 2 Mexico City
(*Mexican Flyweight Title Challenge*)
16.12.88 Armando Alvarez W CO 3 Nuevo Laredo
Summary: 26 contests, won 17, drew 1, lost 8.

Kenny Vice
Youngsville, USA. *Born* 15.07.62
Lightweight

24.06.83 Moro Clowney W CO 2 New Iberia
07.07.83 James Sanders W RSC 6 Marrero
12.07.83 Dick Ishmael W PTS 4 Lafayette
13.09.83 Charles Sweetenburg W CO 2 Baker
24.11.83 Albert Favella W PTS 6 Pasadena
28.03.84 Tony Saladin L RSC 2 Atlantic City
10.07.84 Darren Dale W CO 6 Lafayette
20.07.84 Darren Neal W CO 4 Morgan City
11.09.84 Don Robertson W RSC 3 Lafayette
13.11.84 James Sanders W RSC 3 Lafayette
29.11.84 Lee Rockamore W CO 4 Morgan City
21.02.85 Mike Moss W PTS 6 Morgan City
20.03.85 Bryan Rogers W PTS 10 Lafayette
26.06.85 Troy Townsend W RSC 5 Lafayette
11.07.85 Tony Guerro W CO 1 Morgan City
30.07.85 Troy Townsend W PTS 8 Metairie
24.09.85 Jeff Goodwin W RSC 8 Lafayette
28.05.86 Richard Laster W RSC 2 Metairie
12.07.86 Willie Rimmer W CO 2 Franklin
09.03.87 Harold Warren L PTS 8 New Orleans
.87 Jerome Spotsville W RSC 3 Harvey
30.06.87 Victorio Belcher L RSC 6 New Orleans
05.04.88 Vernon Garrett W CO 3 Oklahoma City
14.04.88 James Sanders W CO 1 Lake Charles
05.05.88 Ruben Moran W CO 2 Charenton
14.06.88 Brian Baronet W CO 10 Durban
27.08.88 Jerry Barnes W CO 2 Indianola
03.12.88 Joe Sanchez W CO 2 Indianola
13.04.89 Billy White W RSC 3 Indianola
Summary: 29 contests, won 26, lost 3.

Marcos Villasana
Acapulco, Mexico. *Born* 18.06.60
Former Undefeated Mexican Featherweight Champion

.78 Lucerito Montor W CO 2 Acapulco
.78 Gato Clemente W CO 2 Acapulco
.78 Chato Noqueda W CO 2 Acapulco
.78 Jose Jimenez W CO 3 Acapulco
.78 Victor Banos W CO 1 Acapulco
11.01.78 Roberto Hernandez W CO 3 Acapulco
20.01.78 Flavio Renteria W CO 1 Acapulco
10.02.78 Javier Jimenez W CO 4 Acapulco
21.04.78 David Perez W CO 1 Acapulco
05.78 Victor Banos DREW 10 Acapulco
06.78 Pedro Garcia W CO 6 Acapulco
29.07.78 Arturo Cabrera W CO 3 Acapulco
13.09.78 Ricardo Perez W CO 9 Acapulco
.79 Roberto Martinez W CO 4 Acapulco
.79 Renato Campos W CO 4 Acapulco
23.03.79 Pedro Martinez W RSC 4 Apatzingan
05.79 Juan Jimenez W CO 8 Acapulco
09.06.79 Alfonso Ramirez W PTS 10 Mexico City
14.07.79 Artemio Ramirez L RSC 7 Mexico City
27.10.79 Ambrosio Luna L PTS 10 Mexico City
30.11.79 Ramiro Garcia W PTS 10 Acapulco
25.01.80 Augustin Macias W PTS 10 Acapulco
29.02.80 Jorge Morales W CO 4 Apatzingan
28.03.80 Francisco Parra W CO 8 Acapulco
.05.80 Balam Torres W RSC 4 Acapulco
05.07.80 Pablo Ramirez W RSC 1 Mexico City
24.09.80 Juan Jimenez W CO 2 Mexico City
15.10.80 Carlos Ibarra W RSC 9 Mexico City
03.12.80 Javier Barcenas W RSC 8 Mexico City
31.01.81 Artemio Ramirez W RSC 1 Mexico City
04.04.81 Federico Carreno W RSC 5 Mexico City
27.06.81 Cenobio Nicolas W CO 4 Mexico City
15.08.81 Miguel Alvarez W PTS 10 Mexico City
18.12.81 Justo Garcia W PTS 12 Acapulco
(*Mexican Featherweight Title Challenge*)
19.03.82 Juan Paredes W RSC 8 Acapulco
(*Mexican Featherweight Title Defence*)
19.06.82 Mario Miranda L RSC 8 Cartagena
28.08.82 Norberto Cabrera W CO 2 Mexico City
(*Mexican Featherweight Title Defence*)
13.11.82 Reyes Gonzalez W CO 2 Mexico City
(*Mexican Featherweight Title Defence*)
26.02.83 Gerald Hayes W PTS 10 San Antonio
06.05.83 Santos Moreno W RSC 6 Juarez
(*Mexican Featherweight Title Defence*)
11.07.83 Justo Garcia W RSC 5 Houston
(*Mexican Featherweight Title Defence*)
09.12.83 Maximo Ballesteros W CO 4 Los Angeles
15.03.84 Joaquin Acuna W RSC 6 Los Angeles
(*Mexican Featherweight Title Defence*)
31.03.84 Ruben Herasme W RSC 4 San Juan
17.05.84 Tyrone Downes W RSC 4 Los Angeles
06.07.84 Rosendo Ramirez W RSC 1 Houston
13.09.84 Idabeth Rojas W RSC 9 Los Angeles
17.11.84 Antonio de la Paz W RSC 9 Los Angeles
(*Mexican Featherweight Title Defence*)
02.05.85 Hector Cortes W RSC 7 Los Angeles
06.07.85 Leonardo Valdez L PTS 10 Mexicali
26.09.85 Ricardo Varela W CO 3 Los Angeles
25.02.86 Azumah Nelson L PTS 12 Los Angeles
(*WBC Featherweight Title Challenge*)
03.07.86 Aristides Acevedo T DRAW 1 Los Angeles
12.09.86 Alberto Mercado W PTS 10 Chicago
05.02.87 Angel Hernandez W CO 4 Los Angeles
29.08.87 Azumah Nelson L PTS 12 Los Angeles
(*WBC Featherweight Title Challenge*)
24.03.88 Jaime Garza W CO 5 Los Angeles
23.06.88 Antonio Esparragoza DREW 12 Los Angeles
(*WBA Featherweight Title Challenge*)
08.04.89 Jeff Fenech L PTS 12 Melbourne
(*WBC Featherweight Title Challenge*)
Summary: 59 contests, won 49, drew 3, lost 7.

Nicky Walker
Carson City, USA. *Born* 1962
S. Middleweight

13.05.82 Paddy Wilson W PTS 4 Carson City
27.05.82 Angelo Marchetti W RSC 2 Las Vegas
03.07.82 Kurt Berry W CO 2 Gardnerville
31.07.82 Lester Jackson W CO 1 Lake Tahoe
09.09.82 Tim Felty W RSC 1 Stateline
30.09.82 Billy Brigham W CO 6 Carson City
29.10.82 Danny Coyne W CO 3 Carson City
20.11.82 Hudson Jackson W PTS 6 Everett
22.12.82 Sam Turner W CO 1 Stateline
20.01.83 Ingolf Heitman W CO 2 Santa Rosa
10.02.83 Noe Ramirez L RSC 4 Tonopah
31.03.83 Bob Thomas W CO 3 Carson City
06.04.83 Malachi Malone W CO 2 Stockton
13.04.83 Elden Cress W RSC 4 Reno
30.04.83 Paddy Wilson W RSC 3 Sparks
03.07.83 Jim Cook W RSC 1 Gardnerville
24.08.83 Doug Holliman W PTS 8 Reno
24.09.83 Johnny Nava DREW 10 Stateline
30.10.83 Noe Ramirez W PTS 10 Carson City
09.02.84 Burgess Scruggs W RSC 5 Tonopah
14.04.84 James Shavers W PTS 10 Carson City
20.04.84 Billy Robinson W CO 2 Klamath Falls
12.05.84 Charles Carter L PTS 10 Lake Tahoe
01.09.84 I. W. Johnson W PTS 10 Reno
30.10.84 Ken Johnson W CO 3 Carson City
10.01.85 Doug Holliman W PTS 10 Stateline
23.02.85 Danny Blake DREW 10 Carson City
25.01.86 Tom Covington W PTS 10 Carson City
01.03.86 Tony Golden W PTS 10 Carson City
23.03.86 James Williams W CO 4 Reno
25.04.86 Dwayne Muniz W RSC 5 Stateline
11.07.86 James Williams W PTS 10 Lake Tahoe
17.10.86 Danny Blake W PTS 10 Watsonville
07.02.87 I. W. Johnson W RSC 8 Reno
09.04.87 Rubin Williams W RSC 5 Tonopah
26.04.87 James Waire W PTS 10 Reno
04.09.87 Charles Carter W RSC 5 Reno
30.01.88 Jeff McCall W RSC 5 Carson City
03.06.88 Graciano Rocchigiani L PTS 15 Berlin
(*IBF S. Middleweight Title Challenge*)
23.08.88 Jorge Amparo L RSC 8 Lake Tahoe
13.12.88 Sakkie Horn W PTS 10 Durban
04.03.89 Jimmy Stevens W CO 3 Bismark
16.03.89 Tony Harrison W PTS 10 Reno
Summary: 43 contests, won 37, drew 2, lost 3.

Anaclet Wamba
France. *Born* Congo, 06.01.60
Cruiserweight

27.11.82 Guy Telusson W CO 1 St Brieuc
26.03.83 Fefe Osuna W PTS 6 Joeuf
22.04.83 Achene Reffas W RSC 6 St Brieuc
22.10.83 Luc Goossens W RSC 1 St Brieuc
26.11.83 Marco Vitaglione W PTS 8 St Brieuc
14.01.84 Maurice Gomis W RTD 7 St Brieuc
10.03.84 Rocky Burton W RSC 3 St Brieuc
14.04.84 Winston Allen W PTS 8 Yffiniac
05.05.84 Ali Lukusa W PTS 8 St Brieuc
13.10.84 Louis Pergaud W PTS 8 St Brieuc
26.01.85 Andy Gerrard W PTS 8 St Brieuc
20.04.85 Dave Garside W PTS 8 St Brieuc
27.04.85 Louis Pergaud W PTS 8 Brest
16.10.85 Horace Notice L PTS 8 London
25.01.86 Albert Syben W PTS 8 St Brieuc
20.02.86 John Westgarth W PTS 10 Newcastle
12.04.86 Chris Jacobs W PTS 8 St Brieuc
16.05.86 Joe Kalala W PTS 8 Abidjan
25.10.86 Stuart Lithgo W RSC 2 St Brieuc
10.10.87 K. P. Porter W PTS 8 Paris
23.04.88 Greg Gorrell W RSC 1 Berck sur Mer
25.06.88 Yves Monsieur W PTS 8 Compiegne
21.11.88 Rick Enis W CO 5 Amiens
25.02.89 Siriki Sanogo W PTS 8 St Brieuc
25.03.89 Elvis Parks W CO 2 Casablanca
22.04.89 Dave Muhammed W RSC 4 St Brieuc
Summary: 26 contests, won 25, lost 1.

Frankie (Panchito) Warren
Corpus Christi, USA. *Born* 1959
USBA L. Welterweight Champion

09.10.82 Jack Alvarez W PTS 4 Las Vegas
26.01.83 Ismael Aguilar W RSC 2 Alice
16.06.83 Rodney Sanchez W CO 2 Corpus Christi
08.07.83 Lopez McGee W RSC 3 Corpus Christi
12.08.83 Danny Favella W PTS 6 Corpus Christi
05.10.83 Honorio Valle W RSC 3 Corpus Christi
07.12.83 Frank Govea W RSC 5 Corpus Christi
29.12.83 Enrique Flores W RSC 3 Harlingen
21.03.84 Garland Wright W RSC 6 Atlantic City
20.05.84 Ford Jennings W PTS 8 Corpus Christi
26.09.84 Oscar Caston W RSC 4 Atlantic City
16.11.84 Willie Rodriguez W PTS 10 Corpus Christi
26.12.84 Dave Odem W CO 7 Atlantic City
30.03.85 Dwayne Prim W RSC 8 Dallas
24.04.85 Ricky Kaiser W RSC 3 Atlantic City
10.07.85 Tomas Chavez W RSC 2 Corpus Christi
25.10.85 Michael Bradley W CO 8 Anchorage
19.01.86 Robert Elizondo W RSC 7 Corpus Christi
06.04.86 Sammy Fuentes W PTS 10 Corpus Christi
11.05.86 Ronnie Shields W PTS 12 Corpus Christi
(*Vacant USBA L. Welterweight Title*)
20.07.86 James McGirt W PTS 10 Corpus Christi
19.11.86 Ozzie O'Neal W RSC 5 Atlantic City
(*USBA L. Welterweight Title Defence*)
15.02.87 Gene Hatcher W PTS 10 Sacramento
31.07.87 Efren Nieves W RTD 4 Corpus Christi
07.01.88 Bryan Davenport W CO 1 Houston
14.02.88 James McGirt L RSC 12 Corpus Christi
(*Vacant IBF L. Welterweight Title*)

Frankie Warren (left) storms into Mickey Ward when retaining his USBA light-welterweight title in Atlantic City, January, 1989

Tom Casino

12.06.88 Efrain Nieves W RSC 1 Villa Park
16.07.88 Clarence Coleman W PTS 12 Lake Tahoe
(USBA L. Welterweight Title Defence)
06.10.88 Chuck Glover W CO 2 Corpus Christi
(USBA L. Welterweight Title Defence)
15.01.89 Mickey Ward W PTS 12 Atlantic City
(USBA L. Welterweight Title Defence)
10.04.89 Rogue Montoya W CO 4 Corpus Christi
Summary: 31 contests, won 30, lost 1.

Guy Waters
Australia. *Born* 25.05.64
Commonwealth & Australian L. Heavyweight Champion. Former Undefeated OPBF L. Heavyweight Champion

04.03.85 Geoff Peate L RSC 2 Sydney
19.04.85 John Bogolin W PTS 10 Kanwal
22.11.85 John Bogolin W PTS 10 Gosford
13.06.86 Emmanuel Otti W PTS 10 Gosford
05.02.87 Gary Hubble W PTS 12 Sydney
(Vacant Australian & OPBF L. Heavyweight Title Challenge)
15.08.87 Tommy Taylor W RTD 4 Hobart
06.11.87 Frankie Minton DREW 10 Hobart
06.05.88 Wilbert Johnson W PTS 10 Melbourne
07.10.88 Randy Smith W PTS 10 Adelaide
02.12.88 Gerald Brown W RSC 2 Canberra
25.01.89 Piilva Taito W RSC 1 Ettalong
21.04.89 Willie Featherstone W PTS 12 Sydney
(Commonwealth L. Heavyweight Title Challenge)
Summary: 12 contests, won 10, drew 1, lost 1.

Troy Waters
Sydney, Australia. *Born* London, England 23.04.65
Commonwealth & Australian L. Middleweight Champion

17.10.84 John Piggott W CO 6 Woy Woy
22.02.85 Sean Gray W CO 3 Gosford
26.04.85 Tony Naidu W PTS 6 Sydney
19.07.85 Graeme Locker W PTS 8 Sydney
22.11.85 Tony Campbell W CO 3 Gosford
15.03.86 In-Chull Back L PTS 12 Seoul
(OPBF L. Middleweight Title Challenge)
25.11.86 Paul Toweel W PTS 12 Cardiff
(Vacant Australian L. Middleweight Title)
08.05.87 Dwain Lockman W RSC 7 Sydney
15.08.87 Lloyd Hibbert W RSC 4 Hobart
(Commonwealth L. Middleweight Title Challenge)
06.11.87 Benito Fernandez W RSC 10 Hobart
06.05.88 Jack Callahan W RSC 2 Melbourne
07.10.88 Gilbert Josamu W CO 1 Adelaide
(Commonwealth L. Middleweight Title Defence)
02.12.88 Ricky Stackhouse W PTS 10 Canberra
Summary: 13 contests, won 12, lost 1.

Michael Watson

Michael Watson
Islington, England. *Born* 15.03.65
Middleweight

16.10.84 Winston Wray W RSC 4 London
26.02.85 John Elliott W RSC 8 London
14.04.85 Dennis Sheehan W RSC 3 London
05.06.85 Gary Tomlinson W RSC 4 London
05.11.85 Martin McEwan W RSC 6 Wembley
19.02.86 Karl Barwise W RSC 3 London
07.05.86 Carlton Warren W PTS 6 London
20.05.86 James Cook L PTS 8 Wembley
19.07.86 Simon Collins W CO 1 Wembley
04.11.86 Alan Baptiste W PTS 8 Wembley
19.01.87 Ian Chantler W RTD 4 London
22.02.87 Ralph Smiley W PTS 8 Wembley
19.03.87 Cliff Gilpin W PTS 8 London
05.10.87 Franki Moro W RSC 4 London
28.10.87 Sam Houston W RSC 2 Wembley
03.02.88 Don Lee W RSC 5 Wembley
09.03.88 Kenny Styles W RSC 9 Wembley
13.04.88 Joe McKnight W RSC 4 London
04.05.88 Ricky Stackhouse W RSC 4 Wembley
28.07.88 Israel Cole T DRAW 2 Las Vegas
24.10.88 Reggie Miller W RSC 5 Windsor
18.01.89 James Shavers W RSC 3 London
08.03.89 Frankie Owens W RTD 3 London
Summary: 23 contests, won 21, drew 1, lost 1.

Kevin (Killer) Watts
Pineville, USA. *Born* 09.09.61
USBA Middleweight Champion

08.11.83 David Barrow W RSC 4 Atlantic City
17.01.84 Gene Dixon W CO 1 Atlantic City
08.02.84 Russell Hart W RSC 1 Atlantic City
25.02.84 Keith Todd L RSC 4 Atlantic City
05.06.84 Ali Bilal Bey W RSC 4 Atlantic City
07.08.84 Neil Jackson W PTS 4 Atlantic City
11.09.84 Larry Davis W PTS 6 Atlantic City
23.10.84 Osley Silas W PTS 4 Atlantic City
20.11.84 Jerome Johnson W PTS 8 Atlantic City
15.01.85 Ed Barnes W RSC 4 Atlantic City
15.05.85 William Perry W RSC 5 Atlantic City
19.06.85 Ali Bilal Bey W RSC 5 Atlantic City
22.10.85 Ralph Smiley W RSC 3 Atlantic City
12.11.85 Dwight Walker W PTS 10 Atlantic City
11.02.86 James Green W PTS 10 Atlantic City
15.07.86 Joe McKnight W RSC 6 Atlantic City
02.10.86 Jorge Amparo L PTS 10 Atlantic City
27.12.86 Frank Tate L PTS 10 Atlantic City
26.02.87 Steve Darnell W PTS 10 Atlantic City
10.10.87 Eddie Hall W PTS 8 Las Vegas
20.11.87 Tyrone Frazier DREW 10 Atlantic City
02.01.88 Michael Nunn L PTS 12 Reseda
(NABF Middleweight Title Challenge)
21.03.89 Tony Thornton W PTS 12 Atlantic City
(USBA Middleweight Title Challenge)
Summary: 23 contests, won 18, drew 1, lost 4.

Kevin Watts

Peter Goldfield/USA

Pernell (Sweet Pea) Whitaker
Norfolk, USA. *Born* 02.01.64
IBF Lightweight Champion. Former Undefeated NABF & USBA Lightweight Champion

15.11.84 Farrain Comeaux W RSC 2 New York
20.01.85 Daviel Avery W RSC 4 Atlantic City
13.03.85 Mike Golden W CO 4 Norfolk
20.04.85 Nick Parker W PTS 6 Corpus Christi
20.07.85 John Senegal W RSC 2 Norfolk
30.08.85 Teddy Hatfield W RSC 3 Atlanta
12.11.85 Jesus de la Cruz W CO 1 Houston
09.03.86 John Montes W PTS 10 Hampton
16.08.86 Rafael Williams W PTS 10 Atlantic City
09.10.86 Rafael Gandarilla W PTS 10 New York
19.12.86 Alfredo Layne W PTS 10 Norfolk
28.03.87 Roger Mayweather W PTS 12 Norfolk
(Vacant NABF Lightweight Title)

Pernell Whitaker (right) became the IBF lightweight champion when he defeated Greg Haugen over twelve rounds

Tom Casino

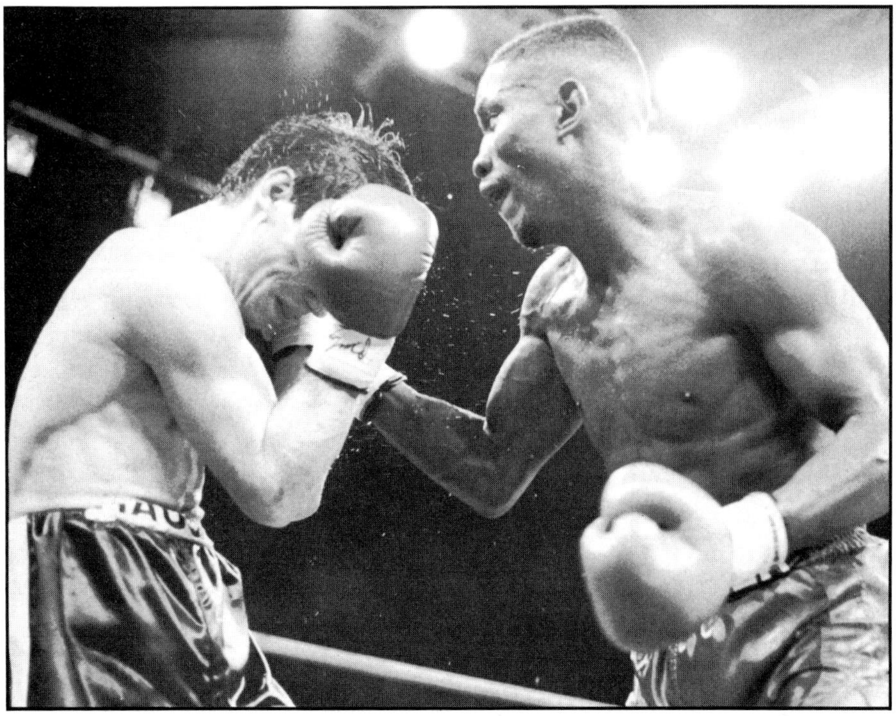

28.06.87 Jim Flores W CO 1 Houston
25.07.87 Miguel Santana W RSC 6 Norfolk
(*Vacant USBA Lightweight Title*)
19.12.87 Davey Montana W RSC 4 Paris
12.03.88 Jose Luis Ramirez L PTS 12 Paris
(*WBC Lightweight Title Challenge*)
02.11.88 Tony Carter W RSC 4 Virginia Beach
18.02.89 Greg Haugen W PTS 12 Hampton
(*IBF Lightweight Title Challenge*)
30.04.89 Louie Lomeli W RSC 3 Norfolk
(*IBF Lightweight Title Defence*)
Summary: 19 contests, won 18, lost 1.

Carl (The Truth) Williams
New York, USA. *Born* 11.11.59
USBA Heavyweight Champion

22.01.82 Greg Stephany W PTS 4 New York
31.03.82 Dwight Triplett W RSC 1 New York
30.04.82 Lou Alexander W RSC 2 New York
28.05.82 Dan Townsend W RSC 1 New York
11.06.82 Barry Funches W RSC 6 New York
20.08.82 Dave Starkey W RSC 3 New York
22.10.82 Michael Greer W RSC 3 New York
08.12.82 Leroy Boone W PTS 8 New York
18.02.83 Richard Cade W RSC 1 New York
24.04.83 Robert Hill W RSC 3 Atlantic City
30.06.83 David Jaco W RTD 1 Atlantic City
16.08.83 Woody Clark W PTS 10 Atlantic City
09.09.83 Percell Davis W RSC 4 Las Vegas
07.03.84 Lou Benson W RSC 2 White Plains
09.08.84 Terry Mims W CO 3 New York
23.10.84 James Tillis W PTS 10 Atlantic City
20.05.85 Larry Holmes L PTS 15 Reno
(*IBF Heavyweight Title Challenge*)
31.08.85 Jesse Ferguson W RSC 10 Atlantic City
16.02.86 Mike Weaver L RSC 2 Troy
21.06.87 Bert Cooper W RTD 7 Atlantic City
(*Vacant USBA Heavyweight Title*)
17.10.87 Mike Gans W RSC 7 Atlantic City
27.01.88 Rodney Frazier W RSC 1 San Diego
(*USBA Heavyweight Title Defence*)
27.06.88 Trevor Berbick W PTS 12 Atlantic City
(*USBA Heavyweight Title Defence*)
10.11.88 Mike Rouse W CO 3 Stateline
Summary: 24 contests, won 22, lost 2.

Charles (Prince) Williams
Cleveland, USA. *Born* 1962
IBF L. Heavyweight Champion. Former Undefeated USBA L. Heavyweight Champion

27.06.78 Henry Bunch L PTS 4 Washington
07.02.79 Mike Hardin DREW 4 Richfield
21.03.79 Willis Crawford W PTS 4 Richfield
27.04.79 Willis Crawford W RSC 3 Dayton
19.05.79 Gus Turner W PTS 4 Findley
20.09.79 Sam Bryant W RSC 1 Richfield
30.04.80 Sylvester Wilder W RSC 1 Struthers
06.05.80 Tim Johnson W CO 1 Canton
17.05.80 Mike Hardin DREW 6 Dayton
13.04.81 Rocky Templeton W RSC 2 Akron
28.05.81 Marc Ball W CO 2 Akron
29.10.81 Jeff Lampkin L RSC 6 Warren
12.12.81 Al Bolden W RSC 4 Monroe
15.12.82 Kemper Morton W PTS 4 Galion
01.03.83 Reggie Gross L RSC 1 Baltimore
24.06.83 Anthony Witherspoon W PTS 8 Warwick
23.09.84 Clarence Osby W RSC 1 Grand Rapids
08.11.84 Marvin Johnson L PTS 10 Indianapolis
02.03.85 Marcus Jackson W PTS 6 Atlantic City
03.06.85 Pop Nance W RSC 1 Atlantic City
05.08.85 Arthur Hall W CO 1 Atlantic City
03.10.85 Mike Fisher W RSC 5 Atlantic City
03.12.85 Jeff Lampkin W PTS 10 Atlantic City
18.04.86 Arthel Lawhorne W RSC 3 Atlantic City
19.08.86 Eric Winbush W PTS 10 Philadelphia
20.09.86 James Salerno W PTS 12 Indianapolis
(*Vacant USBA L. Heavyweight Title*)
14.07.87 Joe Dolphin W RSC 2 Philadelphia
(*USBA L. Heavyweight Title Defence*)
29.10.87 Bobby Czyz W RTD 9 Las Vegas
(*IBF L. Heavyweight Title Challenge*)
18.04.88 James Shavers W RTD 4 Paris
10.06.88 Richard Caramanolis W RTD 11 Annecy
(*IBF L. Heavyweight Title Defence*)
21.10.88 Rufino Angulo W RSC 3 Villeneuve d'Ornon
(*IBF L. Heavyweight Title Defence*)
07.04.89 John Davis W CO 5 Cleveland
Summary: 32 contests, won 26, drew 2, lost 4.

Derek Williams
Battersea, England. *Born* 11.03.65
Commonwealth Heavyweight Champion

24.10.84 Tony Tricker W RSC 6 London
24.01.85 Mike Creasey W RSC 3 London
11.02.85 Barry Ellis W RSC 2 London
25.03.85 Alphonso Forbes W RSC 2 London
20.09.85 Ron Ellis L PTS 8 London
30.01.86 Steve Gee W PTS 6 London
22.02.87 Steve Gee W PTS 6 Wembley
24.03.87 Andrew Gerrard W PTS 6 Wembley
25.06.87 Jess Harding W PTS 6 London
08.10.87 John Westgarth W RSC 7 London

Charles Williams (right) distorts Bobby Czyz's face when winning the IBF light-heavyweight title, October, 1987
Tom Casino

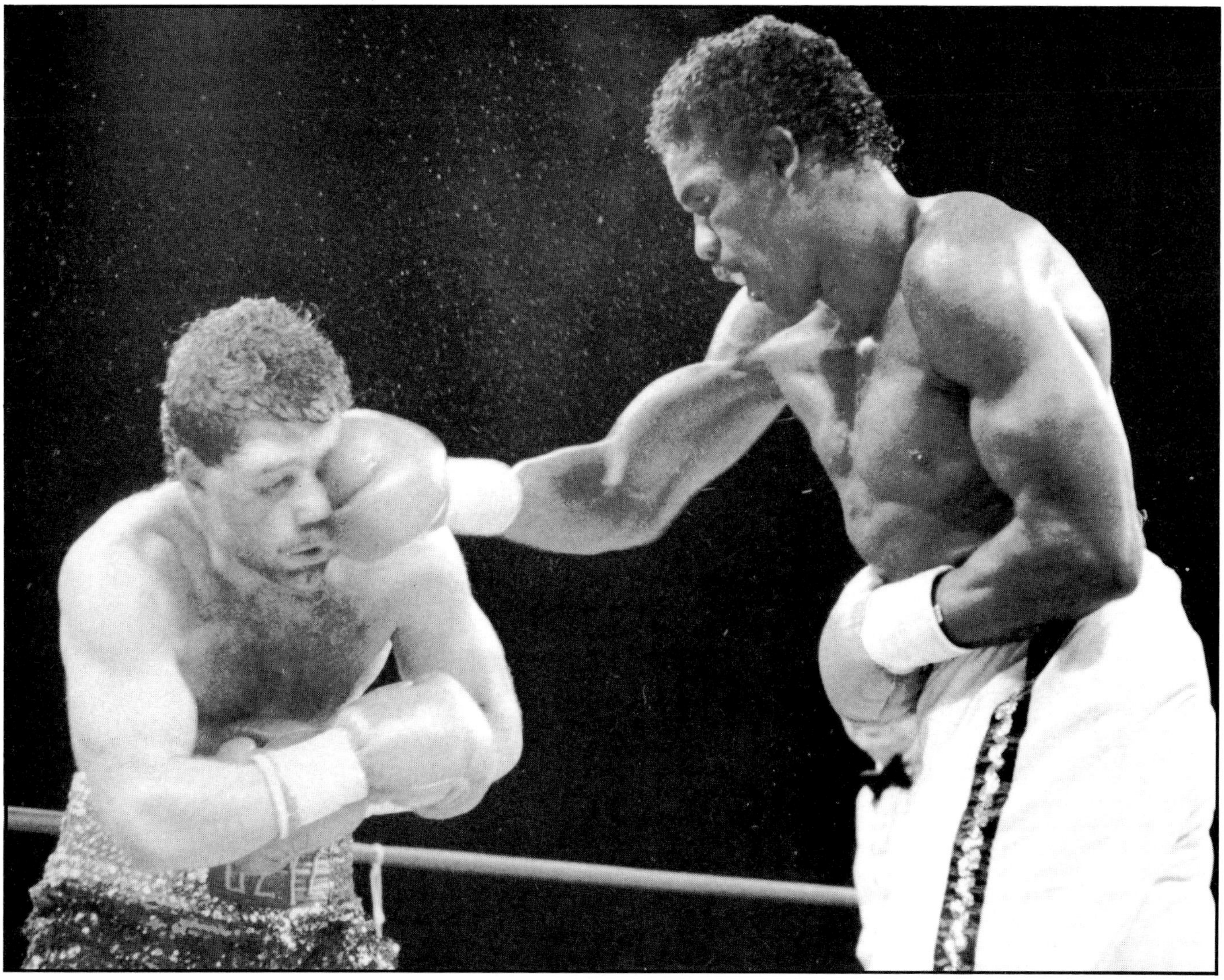

28.01.88 Dave Garside W PTS 10 London
18.05.88 Mark Young W CO 4 Portsmouth
26.10.88 John Westgarth W RSC 2 London
29.11.88 Young Haumona W CO 4 London
(*Vacant Commonwealth Heavyweight Title*)
14.02.89 Noel Quarless W CO 1 London
05.04.89 Al Evans W RSC 2 London
Summary: 16 contests, won 15, lost 1.

Sanderline Williams

Peter Goldfield/USA

Sanderline Williams
Cleveland, USA. *Born* 15.09.58
Middleweight

30.06.82 Tom Houston W RSC 2 Niles
24.07.82 Collins Kellar W PTS 4 Niles
30.08.82 Jack Fain W PTS 6 Niles
13.05.83 Lewis Jones W PTS 6 Youngstown
07.06.83 Andre Cooper L PTS 6 Atlantic City
01.11.83 Vernon Reed W PTS 8 Parma
07.02.84 Ron Ayers W CO 3 Parma
28.03.84 W. C. Honeycutt W CO 3 Parma
08.05.84 Terry Holmes W PTS 10 Atlantic City
23.05.84 Mike Castranova W PTS 8 Parma
07.07.84 Sam Gervins W CO 3 Canton
13.09.84 Al Fracker W RSC 5 Richfield
22.09.84 Nakedo Leftenant W CO 2 Cleveland
27.02.85 Mark Johnson W CO 3 Parma
26.04.85 Stan White W CO 3 Cleveland
06.05.85 Dwight Walker L PTS 10 Atlantic City
29.06.85 Lindell Holmes L RSC 9 Atlantic City
03.12.85 Herol Graham L PTS 10 Belfast
04.02.86 Jessie Carter W RTD 4 Boardman
04.04.86 James Williamson W CO 5 Akron
30.04.86 Terry Holmes W RSC 2 Mentor
27.08.86 Leroy Hester W PTS 10 Mentor
25.02.87 Ray Ray Gray W PTS 10 Akron
24.03.87 Dwight Davison W PTS 10 Cleveland
12.05.87 Jerome Kelly W CO 3 Hillsboro
20.10.87 Anthony Jones W RSC 1 Cleveland
29.01.88 Iran Barkley L PTS 10 Atlantic City
29.05.88 Frank Tate L PTS 10 Houston
29.08.88 Hector Rosario W PTS 10 Cleveland
18.10.88 Ron Essett L PTS 13 Cleveland
(*Vacant NABF Middleweight Title*)
14.04.89 Don Lee L PTS 12 Milwaukee
(*Vacant NABF S. Middleweight Title*)
Summary: 31 contests, won 23, lost 8.

Tony Willis
Maywood, USA. *Born* 04.10.61
NABF L. Heavyweight Champion. Former Undefeated USBA L. Heavyweight Champion

23.10.84 Jerry Harris W CO 3 Highlands
14.12.84 Mike Hildreth W RSC 3 River Grove
31.01.85 Vernon Bridges W PTS 6 Detroit
16.02.85 Tom Lins W RSC 1 Dixon
25.02.85 James McNeal W CO 1 Chicago
12.04.85 Tim Johnson W PTS 6 Chicago
17.07.85 Phil Brown W RSC 1 Akron
08.08.85 James Wilder W RSC 5 Chicago
22.03.86 Larry Burrell W RSC 4 Chicago
25.07.86 Marcos Geraldo W RSC 10 Chicago
09.04.87 Everett Martin W RSC 7 Houston
26.06.87 Willie Edwards W RSC 4 Atlantic City
(*NABF L. Heavyweight Title Challenge*)
13.08.87 Louis Coleman W PTS 10 Houston
24.11.87 Ramzi Hassan W RSC 12 Los Angeles
(*Vacant USBA L. Heavyweight Title*)
29.04.88 Mike Sedillo W PTS 12 Houston
(*NABF L. Heavyweight Title Defence*)
28.07.88 Frankie Minton W RSC 2 Las Vegas
(*NABF L. Heavyweight Title Defence*)
21.02.89 Dennis Andries L RSC 5 Tucson
(*Vacant WBC L. Heavyweight Title*)
Summary: 17 contests, won 16, lost 1.

Mark Wills
Los Angeles, USA. *Born* 10.08.60
Heavyweight

07.11.80 David Carr W PTS 6 Clarksville
26.01.82 Tony Perea L PTS 6 Las Vegas
04.05.82 Tony Fulilangi L RSC 1 Las Vegas
19.11.82 Eddie Wilson W CO 2 Culver City
16.12.82 Tim Lampkin W CO 1 Culver City
31.01.83 Mike Gans L PTS 10 Los Angeles
14.12.83 Mike Mahone W RSC 2 San Bernardino
17.01.85 Rufus Hadley DREW 4 Los Angeles
25.03.85 Tim Witherspoon L RSC 9 Los Angeles
05.11.85 Ken Lakusta W RSC 6 Jakarta
26.02.86 Dee Collier L PTS 12 Reseda
12.06.86 Greg Page W RSC 9 Los Angeles
21.07.86 Rufus Hadley W PTS 10 Los Angeles
25.09.86 Larry Alexander L PTS 12 Los Angeles
09.03.87 Dee Collier L RSC 7 Los Angeles
04.08.87 Tim Witherspoon L RSC 1 Atlantic City
25.04.88 Avery Rawls W CO 8 Irvine
29.09.88 Mike White W RSC 10 Irvine
Summary: 18 contests, won 9, drew 1, lost 8.

Mark Wills

Peter Goldfield/USA

Tony Wilson
Wolverhampton, England. *Born* 25.04.61
Former British L. Heavyweight Champion

12.02.85 Blaine Logsdon W RSC 4 London
28.02.85 Winston Burnett W RSC 5 Wolverhampton
05.06.85 Cordwell Hylton W CO 5 London
14.11.85 Alex Romeo W RSC 2 Dudley
20.01.86 Dave Owens W RSC 2 London
04.03.86 Jonjo Greene W PTS 8 Wembley
20.05.86 Dennis Bailey W RSC 6 Wembley
03.12.86 Simon Harris W RTD 6 London
16.12.86 Pat Strachan W RSC 3 Alfreton
24.03.87 Keith Bristol W CO 1 Nottingham
05.05.87 Jesse Shelby L RSC 2 Leeds
11.11.87 Louis Coleman W RSC 3 Usk
15.12.87 Blaine Logsdon W RSC 6 Cardiff
(*Vacant British L. Heavyweight Title*)
10.05.88 Brian Schumacher W RSC 6 London
(*British L. Heavyweight Title Defence*)
29.11.88 Randy Smith W PTS 10 Manchester
14.12.88 Tony Harrison W PTS 8 London
25.01.89 Brian Schumacher W RSC 3 London
(*British L. Heavyweight Title Defence*)
22.03.89 Tom Collins L RSC 2 Reading
(*British L. Heavyweight Title Defence*)
Summary: 18 contests, won 16, lost 2.

Willie Wilson
Campo, USA. *Born* 18.12.63
S. Middleweight

19.06.86 Joe Moliere W RSC 3 San Diego
25.06.86 Henry Johnson W RSC 1 Los Angeles
29.07.86 Milford Kemp W PTS 4 Reseda
18.09.86 Jeff Medley W RSC 1 San Diego
03.12.86 Justin Leon W PTS 4 Los Angeles
05.02.87 Ron Daniels L RSC 4 Riverside
20.04.87 Tony Chicoine W RSC 2 Santa Monica
27.04.87 Milford Kemp W PTS 6 Los Angeles
18.05.87 Anthony Byrd T DRAW 4 Los Angeles
30.06.87 Israel Cole W PTS 6 Los Angeles
13.08.87 Tino Leon W CO 2 Los Angeles
28.08.87 Mauricio Aldana W CO 1 Mexicali
16.09.87 Ricky Locke W RSC 7 Los Angeles
02.10.87 James Cook L CO 6 Perugia
24.11.87 Doug Laws W RSC 1 Los Angeles
14.01.88 Ricky Locke W RSC 7 Los Angeles
17.03.88 Anthony Byrd L RSC 7 San Diego
07.09.88 Jerry Okorodudu DREW 10 San Bernardino
24.09.88 Abel Cordova W RSC 2 Lancaster
08.12.88 Dwight Davison DREW 10 Detroit
Summary: 20 contests, won 14, drew 3, lost 3.

Frank Winterstein
France. *Born* 10.07.59
Former Undefeated French Middleweight Champion

09.01.80 Joachim Oliveira W RSC 2 Argenteuil
25.01.80 Christian d'Helft W PTS 6 Corbeil
08.03.80 Maurice Renaud W PTS 6 Epinay
05.04.80 Santo Jaconelli W RSC 5 Massy
18.04.80 Cyrille Barbe W RSC 2 St Genevieve
26.04.80 Jean-Philippe Truchelut W RTD 3 Noisy
03.05.80 Eugene Dovin W RSC 1 Paris
06.06.80 Santo Jaconelli W RTD 2 Massy
13.06.80 Jean-Luc Lamy W RSC 6 Coubertin
06.10.80 Bader Ouakhai W RSC 3 Paris
27.10.80 Dragan Tadic W RSC 2 Paris
14.11.80 Felix N'Coumba W CO 2 Paris
27.11.80 Walengua N'Kongo W RTD 1 Paris
08.12.80 Lieti Mandoze W RTD 2 Paris
16.01.81 Mick Morris W CO 2 Paris
29.01.81 Fefe Mobana W RTD 3 Paris
16.02.81 Earl Edwards W PTS 6 Paris
13.03.81 Maurice Renaud W PTS 6 Villeurbanne
04.04.81 Eugene Dovin W RSC 3 St Etienne
10.04.81 Serge Sinelnikov W PTS 6 Villaneuve
15.05.81 Mike Burton W CO 5 Paris
22.05.81 Justin M'Foudi W RSC 2 Nimes
26.09.81 Branko Barakovic W CO 3 Paris
20.11.81 Jose Luis Duran W RSC 5 Nice
26.11.81 Bob Patterson W CO 3 Paris
19.02.82 Fred Coranson W RTD 5 Nice
07.10.82 Sonny Kamunga W CO 3 Paris
04.11.82 Horace McKenzie W CO 3 Bezons
25.11.82 Joel Bonnetaz DREW 8 Marseilles
25.03.83 Louis Acaries L CO 4 Paris
(*EBU Middleweight Title Challenge*)
01.07.83 Joel Bonnetaz W RSC 3 Paris
(*French Middleweight Title Challenge*)
27.11.83 Jacques Chinon W PTS 12 Nimes
(*French Middleweight Title Defence*)
12.11.84 Cliff Gilpin W PTS 10 Paris
04.03.85 Sammy Brennan W RSC 7 St Ouen
29.03.85 Lahcen M'Hamdi W RSC 2 Bordeaux
06.05.85 Doug James W CO 3 Grenoble
14.01.86 Luigi Marini W CO 2 Paris
08.02.86 Tony Britton W RSC 7 Lille
21.02.86 Willie Wright W PTS 8 St Ouen
17.03.86 Bruce Jackson W PTS 8 Paris
28.04.86 Brian Anderson W RSC 8 Paris
13.10.86 Ron Malek W CO 3 Paris
17.11.86 Eddie Smith W RSC 2 Paris
20.12.86 Tony Davenport W RSC 2 St Ouen
18.04.87 Tony Burke W CO 3 Nimes
16.11.87 Sean Mannion W PTS 8 St Ouen
16.05.88 Michael Harris W PTS 8 Levallois
18.11.88 Dwight Hunter W PTS 8 Levallois
Summary: 48 contests, won 46, drew 1, lost 1.

Anthony Witherspoon
Philadelphia, USA. *Born* 1956
Former WBA Americas Cruiserweight Champion

17.06.81 Brian Morrison W CO 1 Philadelphia
30.07.81 Larry Jefferson W RSC 1 Philadelphia

02.09.81 Jim Brown W CO 2 Philadelphia
26.09.81 James van Keuren W RSC 1 Atlantic City
19.12.81 Bernard McLean W RSC 1 Atlantic City
12.06.82 Ed Smith W RSC 2 Atlantic City
24.03.83 Randy Coleman W RTD 2 Newark
24.06.83 Charles Williams L PTS 8 Warwick
10.09.83 Jerry Martin L PTS 10 Atlantic City
11.01.84 Jeff Lampkin W PTS 10 Atlantic City
11.04.84 Reggie Gross W RSC 7 Baltimore
20.09.84 Tim Broady L CO 2 Atlantic City
12.12.84 Charles Price W CO 1 Pikesville
23.02.85 Mike Lee W PTS 8 Atlantic City
06.05.85 Tony Nelson W PTS 10 Atlantic City
05.08.85 James Salerno W PTS 10 Atlantic City
03.10.85 Willie Edwards L PTS 12 Atlantic City
(*NABF L. Heavyweight Title Challenge*)
20.02.87 Al Shoffner W RSC 7 Philadelphia
27.03.87 Robert Obey W RSC 3 Cannes
15.05.87 Ricardo Spain W PTS 8 Las Vegas
24.10.87 Alek Penarski W RSC 1 London
27.06.88 Alex Stanley W RSC 5 Atlantic City
20.10.88 Tyrone Booze L PTS 10 Philadelphia
15.02.89 Bashiru Ali W PTS 12 Philadelphia
(*Vacant WBA Americas Cruiserweight Title*)
18.04.89 Craig Bodzianowski L PTS 12 Scranton
(*WBA Americas Cruiserweight Title Defence*)
Summary: 25 contests, won 19, lost 6.

(Terrible) Tim Witherspoon
Philadelphia, USA. *Born* 27.12.57
Former WBC & WBA Heavyweight Champion. Former Undefeated NABF Heavyweight Champion

30.10.79 Joey Adams W RSC 1 Upper Darby
26.04.80 Robert Ritchie W CO 1 Lynchburg
09.05.80 Robert Evans W PTS 6 Commack
20.07.80 Charles Cox W RSC 5 McAfee
24.10.80 Oliver Wright W RSC 2 Philadelphia
11.12.80 James Reid W RTD 6 Philadelphia
24.01.81 Ed Bednarik W CO 1 Philadelphia
07.02.81 Marvin Stinson W PTS 10 Atlantic City
11.04.81 Dave Johnson W PTS 8 Kiamesha Lake
17.06.81 Bobby Jordan W RSC 4 Philadelphia
30.07.81 Jerry Williams W RTD 7 Philadelphia
07.11.81 Curtis Gaskins W RSC 2 Atlantic City
05.12.81 Alfonso Ratliff W RSC 7 Atlantic City
20.03.82 Luis Acosta W CO 2 Atlantic City
05.06.82 Renaldo Snipes W PTS 10 Las Vegas
20.05.83 Larry Holmes L PTS 12 Las Vegas
(*WBC Heavyweight Title Challenge*)
16.07.83 Floyd Cummings W PTS 10 Las Vegas
23.09.83 James Tillis W RSC 1 Richfield
(*Vacant NABF Heavyweight Title*)
09.03.84 Greg Page W PTS 12 Las Vegas
(*Vacant WBC Heavyweight Title*)
31.08.84 Pinklon Thomas L PTS 12 Las Vegas
(*WBC Heavyweight Title Defence*)
25.03.85 Mark Wills W RSC 9 Los Angeles
29.04.85 James Broad W CO 2 Buffalo
(*NABF Heavyweight Title Challenge*)
15.06.85 James Smith W PTS 12 Las Vegas
(*NABF Heavyweight Title Defence*)
06.09.85 Larry Beilfus W RSC 1 Miami
12.10.85 Sam Scaff W RSC 4 Birmingham
17.01.86 Tony Tubbs W PTS 15 Atlanta
(*WBA Heavyweight Title Challenge*)
19.07.86 Frank Bruno W RSC 11 Wembley
(*WBA Heavyweight Title Defence*)
12.12.86 James Smith L RSC 1 New York
(*WBA Heavyweight Title Defence*)
04.08.87 Mark Wills W RSC 1 Atlantic City
14.10.87 Mike Williams W PTS 10 Atlantic City
17.02.88 Mauricio Villegas W RSC 9 London
26.01.89 Larry Alexander W PTS 10 Las Vegas
Summary: 32 contests, won 29, lost 3.

Bobby Joe Young
Stuebenville, USA. *Born* 04.03.59
Welterweight

29.08.80 Pedro Vilella L PTS 4 New York
09.09.80 Bob Buscombe W RTD 1 Warren
10.10.80 Alf Doubouchet W RSC 2 New York
28.10.80 Efren Sifuentes W RSC 1 Warren
09.12.80 Tony Taylor W RSC 2 Warren
17.12.80 Eddie Campbell W CO 3 Steubenville
07.01.81 Danny Chapman W RSC 4 New York
28.02.81 Papo Figueroa W CO 3 Atlantic City
12.03.81 Willie Thomas W RSC 2 New York
08.05.81 Greg Harper W CO 4 Fairmont
31.05.81 Curtis Taylor W RSC 1 Atlantic City
30.06.81 Mike Herron W PTS 8 Philadelphia
25.07.81 Leotis Burgess W RSC 5 Atlantic City
06.11.81 Mike Blunt W RSC 2 Pittsburgh
10.12.81 Babs McCarthy W RSC 5 Atlantic City
28.02.82 Don Morgan W RSC 7 Atlantic City
27.03.82 Kevin Howard L PTS 10 Philadelphia
09.07.82 Pedro Acosta W RSC 2 Bridgeport
19.07.82 Pete Seward W RSC 1 Atlantic City
22.09.82 Raul Hernandez W RSC 3 Atlantic City
23.10.82 Mark Harris W PTS 10 Lancaster
03.03.83 Jose Vallejo W PTS 10 Ambridge
10.04.83 Nino la Rocca L RSC 8 San Remo
10.07.83 Darrell Chambers W RSC 9 Atlantic City
23.09.83 Jeff Malcolm L PTS 10 Cleveland
03.03.84 Sam Lantion W RSC 6 Hamilton
06.04.84 Eduardo Romero W CO 2 New York
08.11.84 Dennis Fain W RSC 8 Steubenville
12.01.85 Darryl Anthony L RSC 9 Atlantic City
17.04.85 Larry McCall W RSC 8 Steubenville
31.05.85 Donald Gwynne W CO 2 Wheeling
23.07.85 Gary Roemhild W PTS 10 Atlantic City
08.10.85 Ken Shannon W PTS 10 Atlantic City
22.05.86 Felipe Montellano W PTS 10 Atlantic City
16.09.86 Matt Farrago DREW 10 Syracuse
03.05.87 David Noel W TD 8 Atlantic City
30.06.87 Charles Nwokolo L PTS 10 Los Angeles
08.08.87 Aaron Pryor W CO 7 Sunrise
14.07.88 Ali Salaam W PTS 10 New York
Summary: 39 contests, won 32, drew 1, lost 6.

Bobby Joe Young

Peter Goldfield/USA

Myung-Woo Yuh
South Korea. *Born* 10.01.64
WBA L. Flyweight Champion. Former Undefeated OPBF L. Flyweight Champion

28.03.82 Byung-Boum Choi W PTS 4 Chinju
28.04.82 Joo-Young Lee W PTS 4 Seoul
16.05.82 Chang-Yung Chang W PTS 4 Seoul
21.05.82 Joo-Ho Kwon W PTS 4 Seoul
23.05.82 Youn-Ri Moon W PTS 4 Seoul
25.05.82 Ki-Soo Kim W PTS 4 Seoul
05.06.82 Nam-Sok Yun W PTS 4 Seoul
31.07.82 Hyo-Young Park W PTS 6 Seoul
30.10.82 Ki-Chang Kim W PTS 8 Taegu
05.12.82 Ki-Yung Kim W PTS 8 Chinju
23.01.83 Kyung-Shik Park W PTS 10 Daejon
05.03.83 Rae-Ki Ahn W PTS 8 Seoul
04.12.83 Ha-Shik Lim W PTS 8 Seoul
15.04.84 Little Baguio W CO 2 Seoul
27.05.84 Bi-Won Chung W PTS 10 Seoul
02.12.84 Edwin Inocencio W CO 3 Seoul
(*Vacant OPBF L. Flyweight Title*)
24.02.85 Tagabus Jaya W CO 3 Seoul
(*OPBF L. Flyweight Title Defence*)
08.09.85 Oh-Kong Son W RSC 7 Seoul
08.12.85 Joey Olivo W PTS 15 Seoul
(*WBA L. Flyweight Title Challenge*)
09.03.86 Jose de Jesus W PTS 15 Suwon
(*WBA L. Flyweight Title Defence*)
14.06.86 Tomohiro Kiyuna W RSC 12 Inchon
(*WBA L. Flyweight Title Defence*)
30.11.86 Mario de Marco W PTS 15 Seoul
(*WBA L. Flyweight Title Defence*)
01.03.87 Eduardo Tunon W RSC 1 Seoul
(*WBA L. Flyweight Title Defence*)
07.06.87 Benedicto Murillo W RSC 15 Pusan
(*WBA L. Flyweight Title Defence*)
20.09.87 Rodolfo Blanco W CO 8 Inchon
(*WBA L. Flyweight Title Defence*)
07.02.88 Wilibaldo Salazar W PTS 12 Seoul
(*WBA L. Flyweight Title Defence*)
12.06.88 Jose de Jesus W PTS 12 Seoul
(*WBA L. Flyweight Title Defence*)
28.08.88 Putt Ohyuthanakorn W CO 6 Pusan
(*WBA L. Flyweight Title Defence*)
06.11.88 Bahar Udin W CO 7 Seoul
(*WBA L. Flyweight Title Defence*)
12.02.89 Katsumi Komiyama W RSC 10 Chungju
(*WBA L. Flyweight Title Defence*)
Summary: 30 contests, won 30.

Hilario Zapata
Panama City, Panama. *Born* 19.08.58
Former WBC L. Flyweight Champion. Former WBA Flyweight Champion

28.10.77 Victor Lopez W RSC 3 Colon
26.11.77 Cesar Becerra W RSC 3 Panama City
04.03.78 Humberto Mayorga W PTS 4 Panama City
15.04.78 Alfredo Thomas W RSC 3 Panama City
02.06.78 Juan Guzman W RSC 10 Panama City
19.08.78 Yong-Hwang Kim W PTS 10 Seoul
28.10.78 Alfonso Lopez L PTS 12 Panama City
(*Vacant Latin American L. Flyweight Title*)
14.01.79 Ramon Perez W RSC 9 San Juan
07.04.79 Nestor Obregon W PTS 10 Panama City
23.06.79 Freddie Castillo W PTS 12 Panama City
06.10.79 Jose Ricardo W RSC 7 Colon
24.03.80 Shigeo Nakajima W PTS 15 Tokyo
(*WBC L. Flyweight Title Challenge*)
07.06.80 Chi-Bok Kim W PTS 15 Seoul
(*WBC L. Flyweight Title Defence*)
04.08.80 Hector Melendez W PTS 15 Caracas
(*WBC L. Flyweight Title Defence*)
17.09.80 Shigeo Nakajima W RSC 11 Gifu
(*WBC L. Flyweight Title Defence*)
01.12.80 Reynaldo Becerra W PTS 15 Caracas
(*WBC L. Flyweight Title Defence*)
08.02.81 Joey Olivo W RSC 13 Panama City
(*WBC L. Flyweight Title Defence*)
24.04.81 Rudy Crawford W PTS 15 San Francisco
(*WBC L. Flyweight Title Defence*)
15.08.81 German Torres W PTS 15 Panama City
(*WBC L. Flyweight Title Defence*)
06.11.81 Sor Vorasingh W RSC 10 Korat
(*WBC L. Flyweight Title Defence*)
06.02.82 Amado Ursua L CO 2 Panama City
(*WBC L. Flyweight Title Defence*)
20.07.82 Tadashi Tomori W PTS 15 Kanazawa
(*WBC L. Flyweight Title Challenge*)
18.09.82 Jung-Koo Chang W PTS 15 Chonju
(*WBC L. Flyweight Title Defence*)
30.11.82 Tadashi Tomori W RSC 8 Tokyo
(*WBC L. Flyweight Title Defence*)
26.03.83 Jung-Koo Chang L RSC 3 Daejon
(*WBC L. Flyweight Title Defence*)
09.11.83 Harold Petty L RSC 10 Las Vegas
(*NABF Bantamweight Title Challenge*)
23.06.84 Juan Polo Perez W PTS 10 Atlapa
14.07.84 Ramon Nery W PTS 10 Panama City
01.09.84 Alex Miranda W RSC 9 Panama City
10.10.84 Alberto Castro W PTS 10 Isla Margarita
08.12.84 Santos Laciar L PTS 15 Buenos Aires
(*WBC Flyweight Title Challenge*)
28.12.84 Rafael Cabrera W PTS 10 Panama City
02.02.85 Ramon Espinal W RSC 1 Panama City
30.03.85 Alonzo Gonzales W PTS 10 Panama City
05.10.85 Alonzo Gonzales W PTS 15 Panama City
(*Vacant WBA Flyweight Title*)
31.01.86 Javier Lucas W PTS 15 Panama City
(*WBA Flyweight Title Defence*)
07.04.86 Shuichi Hozumi W PTS 15 Nirasaki
(*WBA Flyweight Title Defence*)
05.07.86 Dodie Penalosa W PTS 15 Manila
(*WBA Flyweight Title Defence*)
13.09.86 Alberto Castro W PTS 15 Panama City
(*WBA Flyweight Title Defence*)

06.12.86 Claudemir Dias W PTS 15 Salvador
(*WBA Flyweight Title Defence*)
13.02.87 Fidel Bassa L PTS 15 Barranquilla
(*WBA Flyweight Title Defence*)
15.08.87 Fidel Bassa DREW 15 Panama City
(*WBA Flyweight Title Challenge*)
02.12.88 Julio Gudino L PTS 10 Panama City
22.04.89 Pedro Romero L PTS 10 Panama City
Summary: 44 contests, won 35, drew 1, lost 8.

Daniel Zaragoza
Mexico City, Mexico. *Born* 11.12.57
WBC S. Bantamweight Champion. Former Undefeated NABF S. Bantamweight Champion. Former WBC Bantamweight Champion. Former Undefeated Mexican Bantamweight Champion

17.10.80 Ernesto Gutierrez W CO 4 Poza Rica
18.12.80 Porifiro Urrutia W RSC 3 Tampico
21.02.81 Joel Segura W CO 3 Meridan
29.03.81 Jesus Maravilla W CO 2 Villahermosa
15.05.81 Jose Zapata W PTS 10 Villahermosa
27.06.81 Roque Guillen W RSC 3 Tuxtla
22.07.81 Alonzo Gonzales W PTS 10 Los Angeles
28.08.81 Rayito Gonzalez W CO 4 Campeche
13.09.81 Javier Marquez W RSC 8 Mexicali
30.10.81 Julio Avendano W CO 5 Acapulco
20.11.81 Mario Chavez W PTS 10 Mexicali
12.02.82 Miguel Juarez W PTS 10 Acapulco
05.03.82 Franciso Mago W RSC 5 Acapulco
23.04.82 Ramon Concha W RSC 2 Acapulco
29.07.82 Harold Petty L PTS 10 Las Vegas
04.09.82 Jorge Ramirez W PTS 12 Mexico City
(*Mexican Bantamweight Title Challenge*)
29.11.82 Jesus Lopez W PTS 12 Tijuana
(*Mexican Bantamweight Title Defence*)
29.01.83 Lorenzo Ramirez W PTS 10 Los Angeles
18.03.83 Rigoberto Estrada W PTS 12 Juarez
(*Mexican Bantamweight Title Defence*)
27.05.83 Jesus Lopez W PTS 12 Juarez
(*Mexican Bantamweight Title Defence*)
08.08.83 Harold Petty L PTS 12 Houston
(*NABF Bantamweight Title Challenge*)
26.09.83 Martin Torres W RSC 5 Tijuana
(*Mexican Bantamweight Title Defence*)
30.10.83 Rodolfo Martinez W RSC 11 Guadalajara
(*Mexican Bantamweight Title Defence*)
16.12.83 Rigoberto Estrada W PTS 12 Juarez
(*Mexican Bantamweight Title Defence*)
18.02.84 Javier Marquez W RSC 5 Mexicali
(*Mexican Bantamweight Title Defence*)
17.03.84 Patrick Young W CO 4 Mexicali
21.05.84 Mario Gomez W RSC 3 Tijuana
(*Mexican Bantamweight Title Defence*)
21.09.84 Jorge Ramirez W DIS 11 Juarez
(*Mexican Bantamweight Title Defence*)
30.11.84 Jorge Ramirez W PTS 12 La Paz
(*Mexican Bantamweight Title Defence*)
04.05.85 Fred Jackson W DIS 7 Aruba
(*Vacant WBC Bantamweight Title*)
09.08.85 Miguel Lora L PTS 12 Miami
(*WBC Bantamweight Title Defence*)
11.04.86 Jeff Fenech L PTS 10 Sydney
04.07.86 Antonio Gonzalez W PTS 10 Tijuana
29.08.86 Raul Negrete W TD 7 Tijuana
06.12.86 Mike Ayala W CO 7 San Antonio
(*NABF S. Bantamweight Title Challenge*)
03.04.87 Aaron Lopez W PTS 12 San Antonio
(*NABF S. Bantamweight Title Defence*)
28.06.87 Ramiro Adames W RSC 5 Houston
31.07.87 Darryl Thigpen W PTS 12 San Antonio
(*NABF S. Bantamweight Title Defence*)
17.12.87 Noe Gonzalez W RSC 7 Naucalpan
29.02.88 Carlos Zarate W RSC 10 Los Angeles
(*Vacant WBC S. Bantamweight Title*)
29.05.88 Seung-Hoon Lee DREW 12 Youchan
(*WBC S. Bantamweight Title Defence*)
26.11.88 Valerio Nati W CO 5 Forli
(*WBC S. Bantamweight Title Defence*)
Summary: 42 contests, won 37, drew 1, lost 4.

Rafael Zuniga
Cartagena, Colombia
Featherweight

26.10.84 Bernabe Viloria W RSC 3 Cartagena
02.03.85 Alfredo Herrera W RSC 3 Cartagena
29.03.85 Juan Ordonez W CO 7 Cartagena
21.04.85 Robinson Herrera W PTS 6 Cartagena
15.11.85 Jose Gonzalez W PTS 6 Miami
13.12.85 Jesus Garcia W RSC 1 Miami
03.10.86 Pedro Perez DREW 6 Cartagena
30.01.87 Pedro Mendoza W PTS 6 Barranquilla
20.02.87 Alvaro Narvaez W CO 4 Cartagena
15.05.87 Ruben Palacios W CO 2 Cartagena
31.07.87 Daniel Delgado W PTS 8 San Andres
04.09.87 Moises Almanza W RSC 5 Cartagena
18.12.87 Pedro Perez W PTS 8 Cartagena
04.03.88 Alfonso de Leon W CO 3 Barranquilla
16.04.88 Arnovis Castro W PTS 10 San Andres
30.04.88 Hugo Ramirez W PTS 10 Cartagena
15.07.88 Lizardo Ortiz W CO 2 Barranquilla
03.09.88 Alfonso de Leon W PTS 6 Cartagena
18.11.88 Angel Guerra W PTS 6 Barranquilla
31.03.89 Tomas Arguello W PTS 10 Cartagena
Summary: 20 contests, won 19, drew 1.

Hilario Zapata

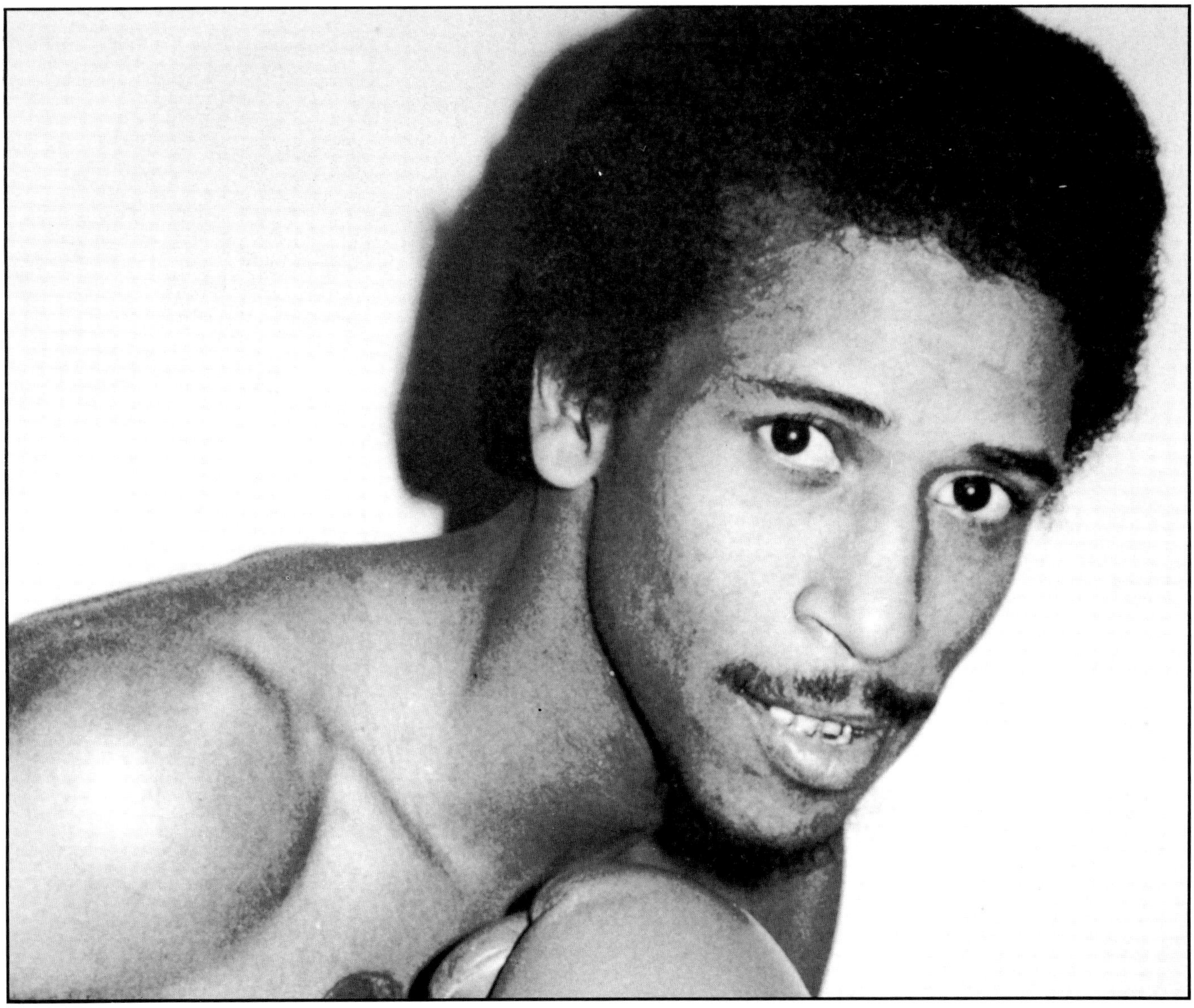

Hall of Fame

Twelve of the all-time greats as seen through the eyes of Ron Olver a leading boxing historian.

LOU AMBERS

Lou Ambers must have felt a little apprehensive on 10 May, 1935, when he faced the great Tony Canzoneri for the vacant world lightweight title. After all, he had been one of Tony's sparring-partners only a couple of years before. Whether this affected his performance, only he knew, but he was floored three times, eventually losing on points.

However, Lou learned a lot from that fight. The following year they fought again, and this time he won on points to take the title. They met yet again in 1937, and he won even more convincingly. At last he had got Tony out of his system, and proved himself a worthy world champion.

Luigi Guiseppe d'Ambrosio was born in Herkimer, New York, on 8 November, 1913. His parents had emigrated from Italy, and he was one of ten children. His father had a saloon, but Luigi wasn't keen on any sort of work. He preferred to spend his time picking fights on street corners, was often missing from home, and spent the odd night in prison, principally to keep warm.

When he was around 16 years of age he started to box in clubs, which were known as "bootleg" shows. They were not licensed professional promotions, but the fighters were paid anything from five to fifteen dollars.

Luigi boxed every two or three weeks, and dutifully took his purse monies home to mother. His father's business had failed, and his contribution to the family budget was invaluable.

His progress as a fighter was rapid. Without tuition he just went forward throwing punches. But as time went on he improved his defences, and his biggest asset was a tough chin. Nobody — but nobody — stopped him until the end of his career.

A friend named Skid Enright got him started, and immediately changed Luigi's name to Otis Paradise, and later to Lou Ambers, which stuck to him for the rest of his career, and indeed for the rest of his life. Nicknamed the "Herkimer Hurricane", his managers were Nicanor Rafael (1932–33), Dave Steinberg (1933–34), and Al Weill (1934–41).

Lou dropped just one six-round decision in his first three years, and after beating Harry Dublinsky, Sammy Fuller, and Harold Hughes in successive fights at the beginning of 1935 he was matched with Canzoneri, as previously mentioned.

Manager Al Weill threw him in at the deep end, when just a couple of months after the Canzoneri defeat he matched him with Fritzie Zivic, who would go on to win the world welter title. When Lou's jaw was broken in round seven, his manager wanted him to quit, but instead he took the fight to Zivic and won on points! Just one example of his determination.

He had an operation, his jaw was wired for six weeks, and he was out of action for five months. Then he came back as if nothing had happened, to resume his successful career and clinch a return with Canzoneri.

This time it was a different Ambers. He was more experienced, and Al Weill had obtained the services of ace trainer Charley Goldman, who planned the fight to the last detail. He won handily on points, and after four years of tough campaigning, was lightweight champion of the world.

In September, 1937, promoter Mike Jacobs staged the Carnival of Champions, which included four world title fights, with Lou defending against Pedro Montanez. Although the show was not a financial success, he came away with $82,500, which was the biggest purse of his career.

The partnership between Lou and Al was more like a father-son relationship, and his victory over the previously undefeated Montanez was one of the high-spots.

Unfortunately for Lou, there was a gentleman named Henry Armstrong around at that time. He had already annexed the featherweight and welterweight titles, and wanted Lou's crown to set up a record of holding three world championships simultaneously.

They were due to meet at the New York Polo Grounds, but it rained incessantly, and the fight was shifted to the indoor venue of Madison Square Garden. The delay was one week, and it eventually took place in July, 1938. Following one of the greatest fights ever seen, Armstrong got the verdict on a split decision, although Lou thought *he* deserved the decision.

A return was inevitable, and it took place at the Yankee Stadium in August, 1939. It was another crowd-pleaser, with Armstrong being penalised for low punches five times in the first eleven rounds, which could well have cost him the fight. In any case, Lou got the verdict, and regained his title.

There was to have been a third fight between these two all-time greats, but it never materialised. Lou had five straight wins before defending his crown against Lew Jenkins in May, 1940, but it was obvious that the two clashes with Armstrong had taken a lot out of him, and he went down four times before it was stopped.

Still he thought he could get that title back and in February, 1941, he tackled Jenkins again. Alas, the result was the same. Al Weill threw in the towel in round seven after Lou had been floored and, although Lou protested that he could have continued, the writing was on the wall. He could see the punches coming, but he could no longer avoid them.

The time had now come to retire, and he joined the American Coast Guard during World War II. After it was all over he settled down with his wife, and their three children to a normal life in Phoenix, Arizona.

Lou not only won a world title, but he defeated, in championship fights, two of the greatest of all time, namely Tony Canzoneri and Henry Armstrong.

He was elected to Boxing's Hall Of Fame in 1964.

Both Lou Ambers (right) and the defending champion, Tony Canzoneri, exchange left leads during their world lightweight title bout, 3 September, 1936. Lou, a former sparring partner to Canzoneri, became the new title-holder at the end of fifteen hard fought rounds

CARMEN BASILIO

Carmen Basilio certainly did it the hard way. He had no less than eleven "world" title fights, and met the best. "Sugar" Ray Robinson, Gene Fullmer, Johnny Saxton, Tony de Marco, Kid Gavilan and Billy Graham were just a few of the top stars with whom he clashed in a career of 79 bouts, and only one man stopped him — Fullmer, who did so twice.

Carmen was born on 2 April, 1927, at Canastota, near Syracuse in New York State. His parents were both Italian, who met and settled in America to grow onions. There were four sons and six daughters.

He was interested in boxing at an early age, when his father used to talk about another Italian, Primo Carnera, who had won the world heavyweight crown. The boys, and sometimes the girls, used to spar around with ordinary gloves on, but eventually father purchased some proper boxing gloves, and from then on it was boxing, boxing, all the way.

Carmen had no great successes as an amateur, serving with the American Marines in the Pacific, and having only three contests, which he won.

In 1948 he was discharged, taking a job in a factory, but the pay was small, so he decided to earn a bit more by turning pro, making his debut in 1948.

Also that year he met Kay Simpkins, who was a waitress in his favourite restaurant, and they were married in 1950. This happened when he was training for a fight with Gaby Ferland, with whom he had already drawn. So Carmen and Kay slipped away for a quiet wedding, and he celebrated by stopping Ferland in one round.

Most of his early fights were at Syracuse. He was managed by Johnny de John and Joe Netro, and had dropped only two verdicts in 22 bouts when he outpointed the former world lightweight champion Lew Jenkins. This was a fine win after only just over a year as a pro.

Then just as things seemed to be taking off, there were setbacks, Kay lost her job through running away to get married, and then had a long illness. Carmen contracted bursitis of his left elbow and shoulder, but had to continue fighting in order to pay Kay's doctor's bills.

But the time came when his injuries forced him to give up boxing, and from September, 1951 to February, 1952 he had to lay off. Then in May, 1952 he was matched with up-and-coming college boy Chuck Davey, who was being talked about as a title prospect. Carmen won on points, only to have the decision reversed the following day when an error was found on the score-card, the result being amended to a draw.

There was even more disappointment when they met again two months later, Chuck getting the verdict. Carmen also lost the next one, to Billy Graham. However, in January, 1953 he beat the former lightweight champion Ike Williams, and in June, 1953 he outpointed Graham to win the New York State welterweight title, and retained it the following month, also against Graham.

In September, 1953 came the big one — a fight with champion Kid Gavilan for the world title. And he actually put Gavilan on the deck for just the second time in his career, only for the latter to get up, fight back, and win on points by a split decision.

So it was back to square one, but he progressed quickly, being unbeaten in 1954, and in June, 1955, stopped Tony de Marco to win the world title. Through all the setbacks Kay had been his inspiration, looking after his diet, driving their car to accompany him on his roadwork, and being at

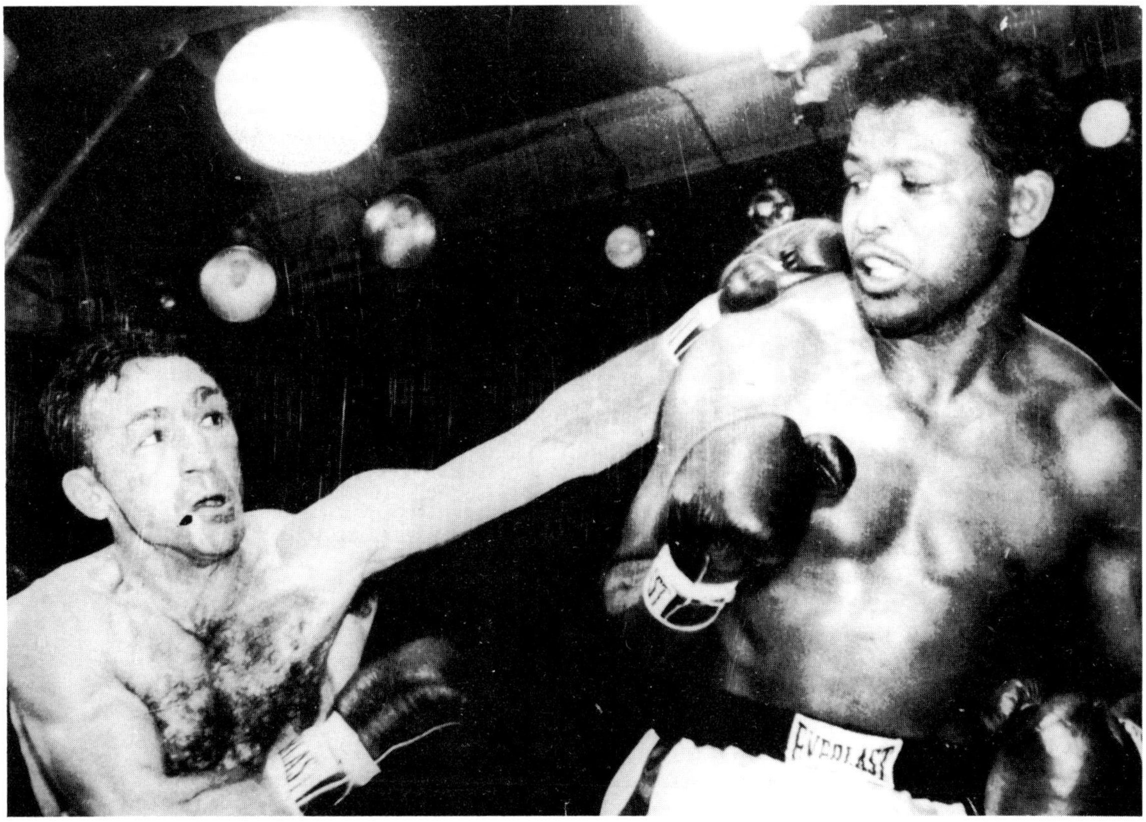

Carmen (left) in action against the legendary "Sugar" Ray Robinson. The Pair had two memorable battles for the middleweight title between 1957 and 1958, winning one apiece

ringside for all his fights. They moved to a six-roomed house at Chittenango, near Syracuse, and he became a pillar of the community, giving talks and tuition to youngsters and also becoming a scout-master.

From then on it was title fight after title fight. In November, 1955 he stopped de Marco to keep his crown, only to lose it to Johnny Saxton in March, 1956, and then regain it from Saxton the following September.

But Carmen was after bigger fish. He had his eye on "Sugar" Ray Robinson's middleweight title, and they clashed in September, 1957. It was alleged in some quarters that Carmen hated Robinson because back in 1948 at Stillman's Gym young Carmen had spoken to the champ, but had been ignored.

True or false, Carmen certainly gave everything that night, and won a narrow decision on points, only to lose it back to Robinson in March, 1958, also a close one. They were so evenly matched, these two, but "Sugar" Ray had the physical advantage, standing 5ft 11½in, while Carmen only scaled 5ft 7in.

According to the rules, Carmen had to give up the welter crown when he won the middleweight title, so he kept going in the heavier division. In August, 1959 he was stopped in round fourteen by Gene Fullmer for the vacant NBA middleweight title. They met again in June 1960 and this time Basilio was stopped in twelve.

Carmen always said these were the hardest two fights of his career. Each was a "survival of the fittest". He was proud of the fact that he had only been down twice in his career, and had never been counted out.

In 1961 he had three fights, outpointing both Gaspar Ortega and a former world welter champ, Don Jordan, then losing on points to the Boston fireman, Paul Pender, in yet another tilt at the world middleweight title.

He had made up his mind before the bout that he would retire, but afterwards said he wished he had changed his mind. However, Kay had been urging him to call it a day, so he kept his word.

The Basilios had all sorts of plans. Carmen was keen on raising hunting dogs; Kay wanted to set up a clothing store. Carmen was proving a fine after-dinner speaker, and the story goes that on one occasion he was presented with a gun. Pointing it at the Syracuse boxing promoter Norm Rothchild, he said: "If you'll step outside we'll discuss the percentage for my next fight."

Later, Carmen was employed as a Physical Education coach at LeMoyne College, Syracuse, also having interests in a motel, and a project that was extremely popular, the Carmen Basilio Italian Sausages.

His hero was always Jimmy Braddock, a fighter who came up the hard way, and won the world heavyweight title. Carmen, too, never had it easy and consequently was one of the toughest champions of all time, as his record proves, with 27 of his 56 victories being inside the distance.

In 1969 Carmen was elected to Boxing's Hall Of Fame.

JACK "KID" BERG

There must have been many proud moments in the life of former world junior-welterweight champion Jack "Kid" Berg, but I am willing to bet that Jack would consider one of the proudest, was that day, early in 1989, when he was made president of the London Ex-Boxers' Association. On that occasion he told me what an honour it was, and how nice it was to be remembered in this manner, nearly 60 years after winning the title.

At 79, Jack has the body of a man half his age, and is extremely alert, mentally as well as physically. In the '30s, he went to America to show them just how good British fighters were, and his exploits there are legendary. He became known as the "Whitechapel Whirlwind".

He was born on 28 June, 1909, in the East End of London, the son of Judah and Mildred Bergman, who had come from Russia as Jewish immigrants. He was later christened Judah, after his father.

As a youngster he was involved in the usual street fights, and when he left school had a variety of jobs, none of which he particularly fancied. All he wanted to do was fight.

His chance came at Premierland in 1924, a venue where he eventually had over 50 contests. He adopted the ring name of Jack "Kid" Berg, and that's the way it stayed throughout his long and illustrious career. His idol was that other great Jewish fighter, Ted "Kid" Lewis, another who went to America and showed the Yanks just how good British fighters were.

Promoter Victor Berliner soon realised how popular Jack was, and right through to 1927 he averaged 20 fights a year at Premierland. His first defeat came in March, 1925, when he was outpointed by the more experienced Johnny Cuthbert, and three months later they met again, the result being the same.

Undaunted, Jack asked for a third fight with Cuthbert, and in October, 1925, beat Johnny in eleven rounds, before outpointing Johnny Curley. He was still only 16.

The highlights of 1926 were his three fights with Harry Corbett, losing the first, drawing the second, and winning the third. There were also two fine victories over talented Frenchman André Routis, who went on to win the world featherweight title. Against Routis, Jack earned his biggest purse to date — £200.

His "go forward" style endeared him to the fans, but he seemed to be getting nowhere in Britain. Then with much alacrity he accepted an offer to campaign in the United States, and off he went. Accompanied by brother Willie, he teamed up with managers Sol Gold and Frankie Jacobs.

His trainer was the great Ray Arcel, and they struck up a wonderful partnership. A couple of years ago Ray made a surprise appearance in London when "This is Your Life" featured Jack on TV. The tears flowed freely as they embraced, and in 1988 Jack made a special trip to America to help celebrate Ray's birthday.

Jack first arrived in America in early 1928, and he was to make another seven trips. He took to the United States like a duck takes to water, and the

"Kid" Berg was always a welcome visitor to American shores. Here he is pictured (right) backing up Herman Perlick against the ropes in Madison Square Garden, 1931, while on his way to a ten-round points victory

Yanks took to him.

In his opening campaign he had seven fights, winning six and losing one, to Billy Petrolle, with whom he had already drawn. When I interviewed Jack on a video at a meeting of the London Ex-Boxers' Association, I told him that I assumed his toughest opponent was Tony Canzoneri.

"Not likely," he replied. "Billy Petrolle put me down ten times in five rounds. He was the toughest."

His first meeting with Canzoneri was in 1930, Jack winning on points. A year earlier, Jack had outpointed Mushy Callahan, and immediately after the Canzoneri fight he came back to London to meet Mushy for the latter's world junior-welterweight title.

This was a weight division not recognised in Britain. It had originated in America, and Callahan had become the holder in 1926, by beating Pinkey Mitchell, although some sources state he won it the previous year by beating Red Herring.

When the MC announced the Callahan-Berg fight as being for the world junior-welterweight title, no less a personage than Lord Lonsdale got up and said: "Don't be absurd. There is no such thing as a junior championship!" But this surprise outburst didn't cut any ice with the fans, who were eagerly looking forward to this all-Jewish encounter.

After an exciting, bruising battle, Callahan retired at the end of round ten. "Yiddle", as Jack was affectionately known, was now champion of the world, and he immediately returned to America, defeating among others Kid Chocolate, Joe Glick and Billy Petrolle.

In April, 1931 he met Canzoneri for the world lightweight title, walked into a right hand in round three, and was knocked out. Jack had no excuses. USA sources described this fight as also being for Jack's world junior-welter crown, but Jack protested.

Again, in the return fight in September, 1931, it was regarded as being for two titles. In round eight a punch landed palpably low, and down went Jack. Under the "No Foul" rule in America, all he could do was get up and fight on, otherwise he would have been counted out. He did his best, and although badly hurt, was still there at the end of fifteen rounds, only to be adjudged a points loser.

In April, 1931, the National Boxing Association presented Jack with a magnificent belt for winning the world junior title, which he still possesses. From then on he spent most of his time at home, although occasionally going back to America for further visits.

In 1934 he won the British lightweight title by beating Harry Mizler, only to lose it to Jimmy Walsh in 1936. He also had a crack at the Empire Crown, but was outpointed by Laurie Stevens.

During World War II, Jack served in the Royal Air Force and boxed as often as he could. He had threatened to retire on several occasions, but finally did so in 1945, winning his last three fights, two of them inside the distance.

He led a colourful life, enjoying every moment of his boxing and the adulation that went along with it. He was married to Bunty in 1933, but their union was dissolved in 1943, and he immediately married his present wife Morya (pronounced "Moira").

Louis Golding wrote a novel entitled *Magnolia Street,* said to be based on Jack's life, and a film entitled *Money Talks,* based on the book, featured Jack playing the role himself. I also remember him appearing in the theatre, in a comedy, with a boxing theme entitled *Is Zat So?* He also did a lot of stunting for films.

These days his interest in the fight game is as keen as ever, and he once said to me: "Ron, I think they appreciate me more in America than they do here." And do you know, he could be right. Most of his major successes were gained in the United States, and it was said that he fought more like an American than a British boxer.

Also, out of nearly 200 fights, almost half took place in America. But the fact remains that Jack is as British as the Union Jack, is proud of being so, and has been, and indeed still is, one of our best ambassadors for the great sport of boxing.

JIMMY BRADDOCK

It was the legendary writer Damon Runyon who dubbed James J. Braddock the Cinderella Man. And not without reason. One day he was just another fighter, trying to make a living, getting the odd job at the docks, with his family on the equivalent of our Social Security, the next day he was a contender for the world heavyweight title. And it couldn't have happened to a nicer man.

I was fortunate to meet Jimmy in London in the late '60s, when he came over to make a few personal appearances, and although by now he was a rich man, he seemed so humble, so down-to-earth, so grateful for everything that happened to him. And he was only too happy to talk about his boxing career, and to pay tribute to all who helped him along the way.

James Walker Braddock was born in New York, in the area known as Hell's Kitchen, on 7 June, 1906. There were five boys and two girls, and it was elder brother Joe who taught him the basics of the sport.

He had many amateur fights, turning professional in 1926 with Joe Gould, who spotted him working out at the gym run by the former heavyweight star Joe Jeanette. It proved to be a long, sometimes hopeless, but eventually fruitful partnership.

Jimmy started like a house afire. In that first year he won eight fights in the first round, and quickly established himself as a force to be reckoned with. In 1928 he beat tough opponents like Paul Swiderski, Tuffy Griffiths, and Pete Latzo, and in March, 1929, stopped Jimmy Slattery to earn himself a crack at Tommy Loughran's world light-heavyweight crown, but was outpointed.

After that he found it difficult to get fights, and

even when he did, several verdicts went against him. In 1929 he lost four of his eight bouts, in 1930 he lost three out of six, in 1931 he lost three out of seven and in 1932 he lost six out of eight.

He was going nowhere — fast, yet it should be remembered that among those with whom he went the distance were John Henry Lewis, Ernie Schaaf, Maxie Rosenbloom, Al Gainer, Tony Shucco and Charlie Retzlaff, all top men.

At the time he had a wife and three children to support, and was finding it difficult. But 1933 promised to be a busier year, with four defeats in nine contests. But after September the fights dried up, and nine months went by without as much as a smell of liniment.

Then in June, 1934, Primo Carnera was due to defend his world heavyweight title against Max Baer. It was planned to feature the up-and-coming Corn Griffin in the chief support. But who could they match him against? It had to be someone who would give Corn a good fight, but who wouldn't be likely to beat him.

It was manager Joe Gould who went to Jimmy Johnston and pleaded with him to give Braddock a chance. Johnston was reluctant, for last time out Braddock had been involved in a "No Contest" with Abe Feldman, after injuring his right hand on Abe's head, and the referee ruled them both out for "not trying".

Finally Johnston agreed, but the New York State Athletic Commission were far from happy, until eventually Johnston persuaded them that Braddock could last six rounds. His purse was $250.

Johnston covered his head with his hands as Jimmy went down from a right hand, but he got up and immediately floored Griffin. Although already tired from his own efforts to finish off his man, Jimmy twice put Griffin down in round three and the bout was stopped in his favour.

Another five months passed without a fight, until they wanted an opponent for a young John Henry Lewis on the Maxie Rosenbloom-Bob Olin world light-heavyweight title show. In came Jimmy, to deck his man twice, and win on points. His purse — $750, of which he was able to pay back the $300 he had received from social security, or "welfare", as it was known in the United States.

James J. Braddock's last contest resulted in a debatable points victory over Britain's Tommy Farr. In a scene from the 1938 action, Jimmy (left) parries the jab and prepares to counter with a left hook

So to March, 1935. Max Baer was world champion and they wanted a challenger. Art Lasky was favoured, so to show him off at Madison Square Garden they chose as his opponent — yes, the 29-year-old "evergreen" Jimmy Braddock, who proceeded to give Lasky the father and mother of a beating, winning eleven of the fifteen rounds!

So Jimmy was selected to meet Baer in June, 1935, at Long Island City. None of the critics gave him a chance. The betting was 10-1, added to which, Jimmy had problems: arthritis in his left side, which affected his punching, forcing him to wear a padded steel corset in sparring. However, with treatment, all seemed well by the time fightday came round.

The story of the fight is well-known. Whether Max had underestimated his opponent will never be known, but the champ did his usual share of clowning and lost several rounds for illegal tactics. As for Jimmy, he just stuck to his boxing, made a mess of Maxie's face with his persistent left jabbing, and at the end of it all a new world heavyweight champion was crowned.

It was two years before Jimmy boxed again. The first defence of his title was against Joe Louis. And yet again Jimmy provided the initial shock, as he dumped Joe on the canvas in the opening round. Although there was no fairy-tale ending this time, Jimmy refused to give in, told his manager not to stop it, and took a lot of punishment before being kayoed in round eight. And he got a bigger ovation than Joe, going out like a champion.

There was just one fight left. When Tommy Farr came to America and put up such a good scrap against the champion Louis, he stayed for more fights, and in January, 1938, met Braddock at the Madison Square Garden. And Jimmy got the verdict, which many alleged was a sentimental one. Be that as it may, he went out on a winning note, realising that all good things must come to an end.

His share of the fight with Louis amounted to $293,660, which was very nice. But there was something even nicer. One of the terms of the agreement made when Jimmy met Louis, was that for the next ten years, Jimmy was to receive ten per cent of all Mike Jacobs' promotions in which Louis was involved.

Joe Gould was the man who negotiated this agreement and their partnership was a great team effort. Joe too had to make a lot of sacrifices in order to keep faith with Jimmy, in his struggle to get to the top, and in the end it all worked out.

Jimmy and Mae had three children, Jay, Howard and Rose Marie, and on winning the title he bought a house in North Bergen, New Jersey. Upon retiring, he continued to work on the docks, did a bit of refereeing, was involved in marine equipment Army surplus, and was also with the Operating Engineering's Union.

In a career of 86 fights he lost only twice inside the distance, to Joe Louis and Lou Scozza.

He was elected to Boxing's Hall Of Fame in 1964, and died at North Bergen in 1974.

BILLY CONN

Just a few seconds of folly, and sheer stupidity, cost Billy Conn the world heavyweight title. In June, 1941, he met champion Joe Louis, and according to two of the three judges, at the end of round twelve, he was boxing Joe's ears off. One judge scored it 7-4-1 and another 7-5, both for Conn. The third official surprisingly cast it 6-6, but it appeared that all Billy had to do was to keep boxing for the last three rounds and the title would be his.

It was then that "The Pittsburgh Kid", as Billy was known, had a rush of blood to the head. So convinced was he of his superiority that in round thirteen he tried to knock Joe out, a tactic which Joe quickly turned to his advantage. And after two minutes and 58 seconds of the round it was Billy who was knocked out.

There was a second meeting for the title in 1946, but we'll come to that one later.

William David Conn Junior was born in East Liberty, Pittsburgh, on 8 October, 1917. His parents, who were Irish, had emigrated to America soon after their marriage.

His father was a steam-fitter, and as they lived in a tough area, was anxious that Billy should be able to look after himself. So he took him to the gym of Johnny Ray, an old fighter, who taught him the basics.

Billy needed no prompting. Already he was used to hanging around the gyms, and he just wanted to fight. He was never an amateur, going straight into the pro ranks in June, 1934, under Johnny's management. He lost his four-rounds début to Dick Woodward on points, earning just two and a half dollars.

From December, 1936, to December, 1937, he had ten bouts, winning seven. But consider his opponents — Fritzie Zivic, Babe Risko, Vince Dundee, Oscar Rankins, Teddy Yarosz (twice), Young Corbett III (twice) and Solly Krieger. *All but Rankins won world titles at some time or another and Billy was still only 19 years old!*

Billy quickly developed into an accomplished boxer, with speed of punch and of foot. He was never a lethal puncher, with only fourteen quick wins in 76 fights, but he was beating the best. He avenged the Krieger loss by outscoring him twice, and he also twice defeated another world champ, Fred Apostoli.

These successes brought him a fight with Melio Bettina for the vacant world light-heavyweight title in July, 1939, which he won on points. They met again two months later, with Billy confirming his previous win and in his third title fight, later that year, he outpointed Gus Lesnevich.

The United States were still not involved in World War II, and in 1940 Billy again successfully defended his crown against Lesnevich. But he quickly realised that the big money was in the heavyweight division.

Billy knew he didn't have the weight. The most he had scaled in his four title fights was 12st 5½lb, but he didn't lack confidence, and knew that his skills and speed would help to keep him out of trouble against the big boys.

Surprisingly, he not only beat heavyweights like Gus Dorazio, Bob Pastor and Buddy Knox — he stopped them. He also outpointed Lee Savold, and when they were beginning to run out of opponents for champion Joe Louis, Conn was an obvious choice. He was good-looking, a fine boxer, had plenty of charisma, and above all, had a fantastic Irish following.

The fight took place at the New York Polo Grounds. Louis weighed 14st 3½lb, Conn 12st 6lb, and as already described, Billy was skating it when he got too cocky, and paid the penalty.

However, with a gate of 54,487, there were compensations. Louis got $153,905, and Conn $70,000. Soon after, both men were drafted into the US Army, thus foiling promoter Mike Jacobs' plans of an immediate rematch.

Billy managed just three fights in 1942, outpointing Henry Cooper, J.D. Turner, and scoring an impressive win over world middleweight champion Tony Zale. Then he served four years in the Army, before resuming in June, 1946, and right into the deep end — that return with Louis.

It took place at New York's Yankee Stadium. The gate was 45,266, receipts grossed over a million dollars, with Louis receiving $625,916 and Conn $325,958. Both got extra payments for film rights.

Unfortunately the fight was a flop. Neither had taken part in a serious contest for several years,

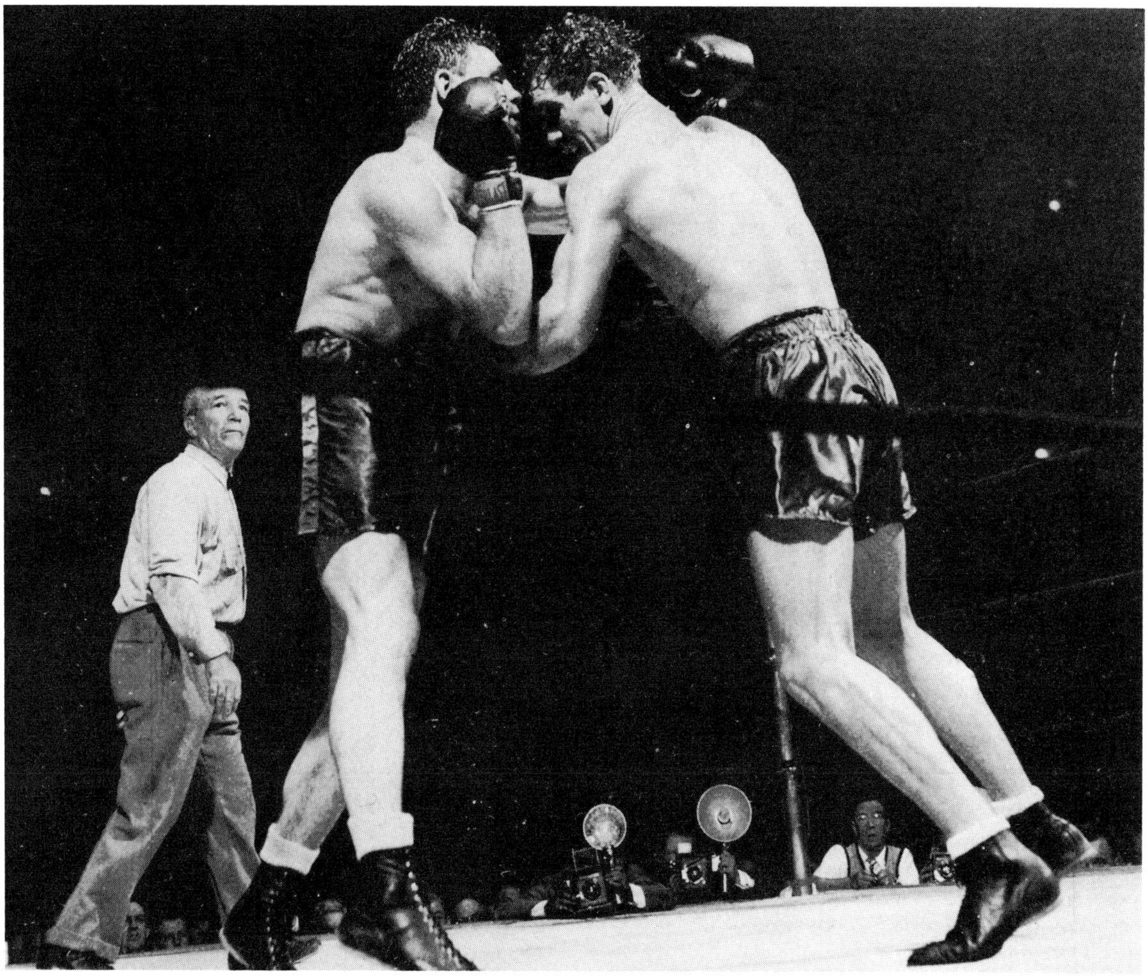

Following a successful defence of his world light-heavyweight title against Gus Lesnevich in 1940, Billy Conn (right) startled the heavier men with a resounding thirteenth round stoppage win over Bob Pastor. Note Pastor wincing as a left to the body gets home

but at least Louis had engaged in many exhibitions. Billy was stopped in round eight of a dull contest.

To all intents and purposes this was the end of his career, although he did return in 1948 to stop Mike O'Dowd and Jackie Lyons. And in December of that year, he boxed an exhibition with Joe Louis. They became good friends, and there were frequent get-togethers and correspondence.

Billy never did anything else but box. He often said he disliked work, but he did make an oil strike in Texas, and even tried to persuade Joe to invest. Joe refused, and lost himself a lot of money.

There were other business involvements, and the family eventually settled in Pittsburgh. Several years ago he came to Britain to make a few personal appearances, and I had the pleasure of meeting him. I found him charming to talk to, and inevitably we chatted about the first Louis fight. "I blew it," he said, "but I was beaten by a great champion."

Apart from Tommy Loughran, I regard Billy as the most skilful boxer to win the world light-heavyweight title, which I am sure he could have held indefinitely if he had not decided to go for the heavyweight crown.

Although he was no Harry Greb, Billy was never averse to "returning the compliment" if he was hit low or punched illegally. He would return as good (or as bad) as he got. But there was no more dedicated boxer than Billy, who assimilated everything he could read about the Noble Art, and would spend hours just practising and improving one particular punch.

He hated the Army, but he did his stint. And of course, one reason for hating the Army was that the time he spent there could well have been better spent continuing a fight career that was taking off in fine style. After all, who knows what might have happened if the return with Louis had taken place soon after their first encounter, instead of five years later?

He was elected to Boxing's Hall of Fame in 1965 and the following year refereed the world lightweight title fight between Carlos Ortiz and Sugar Ramos in Mexico, where Ramos had settled after being exiled from Cuba.

The fight ended in a riot after Billy had stopped it in round five when Ramos sustained a bad cut over the left eye. Ortiz' manager Billy Daly had two broken ribs and was hit on the head with a bottle.

Ramos' cut required 28 stitches, which seemed to vindicate Billy. He had asked the doctor to come and examine the injury as early as round four, but conscious of the weight of the Ramos support, the medic stayed in his seat, and told Billy to make his own decision.

Said Billy: "I had to save Ramos' eye. That is what the referee is for. Yeah, I was afraid I would get hit by the mob, but somebody had to do it. I knew they would try and beat me up, but so what? I had to do it."

Billy's action was a brave one. But then, he was never one to shirk responsibility.

INGEMAR JOHANSSON

Most of the Swedish media labelled Ingemar Johansson a coward after the 1952 Helsinki Olympic Games. They alleged that he had let Sweden down, let himself down, and let the sport down. And what was Ingo's "crime"? He had been disqualified in the final of the heavyweight division, and came away without a medal of any kind.

The facts were these. He was up against the American Sanders, who, like Ingo, was a good counter-puncher. So Ingo decided not to play into his opponent's hands by attacking. Sanders appeared to make up his mind to do the same. At the end of round one, both were warned to put more action into it.

Nothing much happened in round two, but it was Ingo who got the warning, and at the end of the session he was disqualified for "not giving of his best". Just 18 years old at the time, how could he be expected to take the criticism that had been piled upon him? And it was by no means clear that he deserved it.

It was alleged afterwards that Sanders had been ordered to go in with guard up and wait for Ingo to be disqualified. Also, many onlookers felt that the referee could have handled the situation better.

Be that as it may, the stigma remained. What the general public didn't know was that Ingo had made up his mind long before the Olympics to turn pro, and wasn't really keen on competing in the Olympics. He didn't think he was that good, and it came as a big surprise to find himself in the final.

In recent years, after controversy upon controversy, he received his silver medal, which probably meant as much to him as winning the world heavyweight title as a professional. But more of that later.

Ingo was born on 16 October, 1932, at Gothenburg, Sweden, to proud parents Ebba and Jens, and by the age of eleven, to help the family budget, he took a job as a grocer's errand-boy. When he was twelve he saw his first professional promotion, having saved enough money from his job to afford a ticket for the cheapest seats, and then and there he knew he wanted to be a boxer.

So he went to as many promotions as he could afford, and soon got himself a hero — Swedish fighter Olle Bengtsson. When he was thirteen he joined the Redbergslid's Boxing Club, telling them he was fourteen. At that time he weighed ten stones, but within two years he had developed into a heavyweight.

When he was fifteen he went to Hindas to spar with some of Edwin Ahlquist's fighters, and it was there that he met his hero Olle Bengtsson. And not only met him, but sparred with him.

In 1948 the famous Finnish heavyweight Gunnar Barlund was in the process of making a comeback, and trained at Ingo's gym. Ingo was landing so many left hands that Barlund took umbrage, started to make it a proper fight. The two were pulled apart, but Johansson said he enjoyed the experience.

From then on Ingo had many jobs, sweeping snow, humping around bunches of bananas, working on the harbour, but all the time dreaming of the day when he would hopefully become a professional boxer.

But first came his career as an amateur, during which he had 71 bouts, winning 61 (32 inside schedule), losing nine on points and being disqualified once. He became Swedish champion, boxed in several internationals, and was an automatic choice for the Olympics. But strangely enough this wasn't an event to which he was looking forward. His mind was on the professional code.

Following the Olympics, Ingo had a few exhibition bouts in a tour of Norrland, the northernmost province of Sweden, eventually making his pro dębut in December, 1952, in Gothenburg, stopping Robert Masson in four rounds. Things went very much according to plan, and after beating tough men like Joe Bygraves, Hein Ten Hoff and Uber Bacilieri, he stopped Franco Cavvichi to win the European title in September, 1956. It was only Ingo's fifteenth fight.

There were successful defences against Henry Cooper and Joe Erskine, both inside the distance, then in September, 1958, came the crunch, a meeting with world contender Eddie Machen. They came from far and wide to watch this fight at Gothenburg and the hall was packed.

Ingo didn't let them down. He put Machen down three times, and was battering him freely on the ropes when he fell to the canvas to be counted out by referee Andrew Smyth, in the opening round.

Ahlquist then set out to arrange a fight against

world champion Floyd Patterson, and after months of negotiation it was set for June, 1959. The American press were unkind to the Swede, alleging that he was not a worthy contender, and had no business in the same ring as Floyd.

This only made Ingo the more determined to succeed. To him, Patterson was just another opponent. After two rounds of weighing each other up, Ingo put his opponent down several times in round three, before the bout was stopped.

The Swedish boxer was world champion, and the right hand with which he had tagged Patterson so many times was dubbed "Ingo's Bingo".

It was his only bout in 1959, and he wouldn't have another until his return with Patterson twelve months later, in June, 1960. This time everything happened in round five. Ingo was floored, was down for nine, then got up to be caught by a right hand that put him down for the full count.

In March, 1961, they met for the third time, and there was a dramatic first round, in which Patterson was down twice, but got up to floor the former champion. Both had eye injuries and in round six Ingo went down from a right hand, and just failed to beat the count.

He didn't box again for twelve months, returning in 1962 to stop Joe Bygraves and Wim Snoek, then kayoed Dick Richardson in eight to take the latter's European title.

There was just one fight left. In April, 1963, he met Brian London in a twelve-round non-title fight. Nothing much happened for eleven rounds. Then, in the final minute of the final session, a right to the head put Ingo on the canvas.

The bell rang with Ingo still on the canvas. Opinions vary as to how far the count had proceeded. Referee Andrew Smyth said "four", timekeeper Bror Carlsson said "eight", and London thought it was "nine". But all this was academic, because Ingo got the verdict on points. He never boxed again.

It had been a short career. Just 28 bouts, and the only two he lost were against Patterson. However, in that time Ingo had amassed himself a lot of money.

His share of the first world title fight was $281,426. For the second contest he received $283,045 for his 35%; $177,482 from his share of the gate, and $132,580 from his share of radio and movie rights. Also, he owned the complete radio and movie rights for Scandinavia estimated at $50,000.

For the third Patterson fight he earned $112,500 as his share of the gate, plus $540,000 from the TV, movie, and radio rights, which all added up to a nice little sum on which to retire.

Ingo went into the haulage business, was married to Birgit, and as far as I know, is still rich and healthy. There is an Ex-Boxers' Association in Sweden, of which he is a prominent member. This I know because two other prominent members, Kurt and Benny, are also members of the London Ex-Boxers' Association, and attend meetings from time to time.

He will be remembered as one of only four European-born boxers to win the world heavyweight title, and indeed no European boxer has won it since.

He was awarded the Edward J. Neil Trophy in 1959.

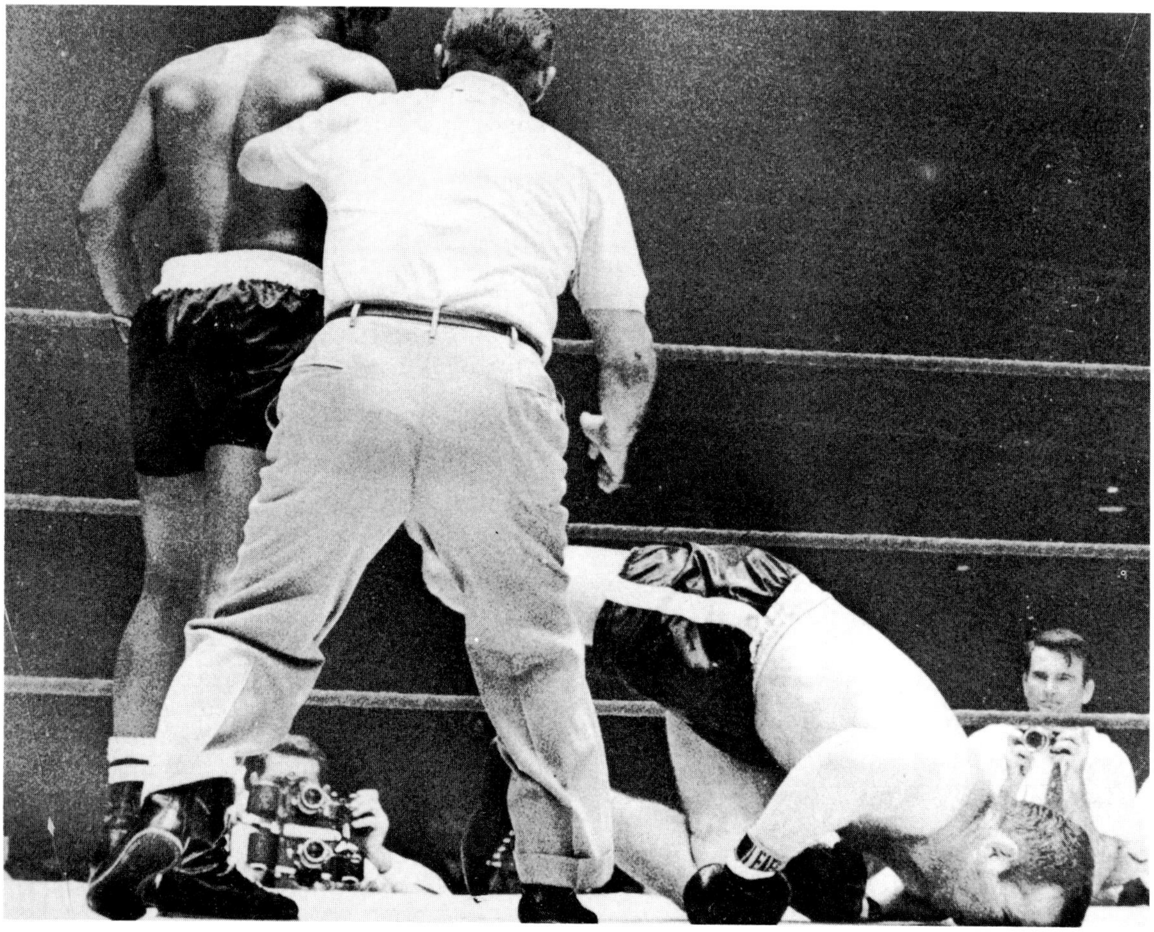

"Ingo" bites the dust in a bid to recapture his old heavyweight title. Floyd Patterson is escorted to a neutral corner by the referee, before Johansson can be counted out, during the sixth round of their 1961 Miami Beach battle

TED "KID" LEWIS

Not for nothing did they call him "The Bashing, Crashing, Dashing Kid". For the legendary Ted Kid Lewis was all of those things. Arguably, he was the greatest fighting machine Britain has ever produced, and his popularity remained right up to the time of his death in 1970.

Why was Ted so popular? Firstly, because of his aggressive, crowd-pleasing style, secondly, because he won the world welterweight title and last, but not least, because he did Britain proud with an American record of nearly 100 fights. He won his world title in the United States, lost it, and recaptured it, all in the USA.

He was born Gershon Mendeloff, at 56 Umberton Street, St George's, in the East End, on 24 October, 1894, where his parents had emigrated from Russia. His father was a cabinet-maker, and Ted used to help him after coming home from the Jews' Free School.

There were eight children, and at an early age Ted was involved in the streets fights for which the East End was noted at that time. In fact, at fourteen he became a gang leader, and one day while having a difference of opinion with another lad, a policeman suggested that they would be better occupied at the local Judean Club, settling their differences with the regulation gloves.

Ted duly turned up, but his opponent didn't. However, Ted got his fight, lost on points, and received the princely sum of sixpence. His opponent was Johnny Sharpe, who later became a top manager and agent, and from whom I took over as British correspondent of the American monthly fight magazine *The Ring*.

Now Ted didn't want his father to know he had been fighting, so when asked for his name he spotted a copy of the *Sporting Life*, mentioning the famous American fighter Harry Lewis. So he said he was "Kid Lewis", and later added "Ted" to that *nom-de-ring*.

He weighed seven stones, joined the Judean Club to learn the basics, and was launched on a professional career. He duly won a cup in a competition, plus five shillings, but when his father found out he was pleased at first, then realised the implications, and told Ted he must decide — settle down to a "proper" job or leave home.

The decision was virtually taken out of his hands when one night he came home with a cauliflower ear. His mother fainted, and he didn't hang around to let his father have a look — he left. For a time he helped fighter Alf Mansfield to sell papers on Commercial Street, and then came his big moment. He was due to have his first fight at Wonderland, with his name on the bill.

The fight was scheduled for August, 1911, but on that night Wonderland burned down. So it was off to Premierland, where Harry Jacobs gave him a contract for twelve contests, varying from ten to twelve rounds each, for a total sum of £88. Not bad for a lad of 17, and from then on he averaged 30 fights a year for the first three years, culminating in him winning the British featherweight title in 1913, by stopping Alec Lambert.

The following year he won the European crown, beating Paul Til, and then he left to campaign in Australia, where he had five fights, winning four and losing on points to Herb McCoy, whom he also beat. He was still there when war broke out, but decided to return home via America, a decision that was to change his whole life.

His affairs were taken over by an American manager, Charles Harvey, and he could no longer make the featherweight limit. He would have loved a shot at Freddie Welsh's world lightweight title, but Freddie wasn't available.

At that time, the world welterweight title situation was a little unclear, but some sources recognised Jack Britton's win over Mike Glover in June, 1915, for the title. Three months earlier Ted had got the better of Jack in a "no-decision" bout.

Two months later, Britton and Lewis met in a return, and some record-books still state that this was for the world welterweight title. However, nothing could be further from the truth. Ted, himself, confirmed that this match was made at the lightweight limit of 9st 9lb, so could not possibly have involved a title at a larger weight.

However, there was to be a decision at the end of this one, and it went to Ted, who afterwards recalled that Britton tried every trick in the book in order to make things difficult. First he refused to weigh in, then he objected to the gloves, then to the bandages, and finally to the fact that Ted was wearing a gumshield.

There was a lot of arguing between the principals and their mentors, and eventually Ted

The incomparable Ted "Kid" Lewis (right) tears into action against Australia's Frankie Burns during their bout for the British Empire middleweight title at the Holland Park Rink in 1922. Burns was counted out in the eleventh round, following a heavy bombardment

agreed to box without a gumshield. The following month they met for the third time, and after Britton had weighed in, Ted had his own back by refusing to do so, and again won on points.

In all Lewis and Britton met on 20 occasions. Lewis won three, Britton four, one was drawn and twelve were "no decision".

After losing his title to Britton in 1916, Ted and Elsie were married, and the following year a son, Morton, was born. In 1918 he joined the US Army as an instructor, but contracted yellow jaundice, and by the time he had recovered, the Armistice had been signed and the war was over.

Ted won back his world title from Jack, only to lose it to him in 1919. Their last meeting was a title fight in 1921, which Britton won on points.

On the home front Ted continued to collect titles. In addition to British and European featherweight honours, he won the Empire, European and British welterweight, and the European, Empire and British middleweight crowns.

He beat champions like Matt Wells, Tom Gummer, Jack Bloomfield, Johnny Basham, Gus Platts, Frank Moody, and Johnny Brown. And in America, he got the better of world champions Willie Ritchie and Benny Leonard, in "no-decision" bouts.

However, one of the fights for which he will be most remembered was a losing one. In May, 1922, he met legendary Frenchman Georges Carpentier at a packed Olympia. As always, Ted forced the issue from the first bell, but Carpentier held at every opportunity until the referee stepped between them and said the clinching must stop. It was still round one.

Ted dropped his arms to his sides and protested that it was not his fault. As he did so, Carpentier caught him with a right hand, and knocked him out. Now, there is an old boxing axiom which states that a boxer must defend himself at all times, but as Ted said afterwards, surely this does not apply when both boxers are being spoken to by the referee, and no order to "Box On" had been given.

It was Ted's greatest regret that he had let down his many fans, but it did not detract from his popularity. Indeed, there was much sympathy for what was considered an unsportsmanlike action. Ted tried hard to get a return with Carpentier, but in vain. He retired in 1929, after nearly 300 fights.

Sadly Elsie died in the early '60s after 45 happy married years, and their son became a top man in the film industry. Ted eventually went to reside at the Home For Aged Jews in South London.

He has yet another claim to fame, being the first British fighter to wear a gumshield. His biggest regret was not winning a Lonsdale Belt outright. He made enough British title defences, but some of them were not at the National Sporting Club, so they didn't qualify for the belt. So incensed were some of his supporters that they had a special belt made and presented it to him. The cost of this belt was around £1,000, which compared favourably with the NSC Belts, worth around £200 each.

He must have earned a fortune, but was a generous man, and gave much of it away to friends in need, and, indeed, to anyone who happened to mention that they were down on their luck. He also donated frequently to charities.

In 1965 he received a Special Award from the British Boxing Writers' Club, and in 1970 at the World Sporting Club, he and Ken Buchanan were presented with silver salvers by *Boxing News*, as the only two British boxers in the last 50 years to win world titles abroad.

Ted died on 20 October, 1970, after a short illness, and was laid to rest at East Ham Cemetery.

He was elected to Boxing's Hall Of Fame in 1964.

TOMMY LOUGHRAN

I have always appreciated the special skills, which world light-heavyweight champion Tommy had in plenty, and I marvelled when he conceded over six stones to Primo Carnera, and was only beaten by sheer weight in this "pygmy versus giant" encounter.

So imagine how excited I was to learn that Tommy was coming to Britain for the 1975 International Convention of Ex-Boxers, organised by the late Jerry Dunn. We duly met, and he was one of the most charming men I have ever interviewed: pleasant, modest and unassuming.

Also present on that occasion, was the former British heavyweight Frank Bell, who once kayoed Tommy Farr, and the three of us had a lot to talk about. Tommy said he had been sent over to represent the Veteran Boxers' Association of the United States, and they couldn't have chosen a better ambassador.

He was born in Philadelphia on 29 November, 1902, and at the age of twelve had his first taste of fisticuffs when set upon by the local bully. Having won this one convincingly, he decided that when he was old enough he would like to make boxing his career. But a lot was to happen before then.

During World War I, when he was fourteen, and full of the stuff that heroes are made of, he ran away from home to join the United States Army. However, as soon as his parents discovered what had happened, they informed the powers-that-be and he was returned to them safe and sound.

It took a long time for Tommy to get over that disappointment, and he spent hours around the local gyms until he felt he was ready to turn pro. Joe Smith became his manager, and in December, 1919, at the age of 17, he won his first paid fight, stopping Eddie Carter.

In those days many fights were "no decision" affairs, according to the rules then applying, and under these conditions, in 1922, Tommy met four boxers, who at one time or another held world titles, namely Mike McTigue, Harry Greb, Gene Tunney, and Bryan Downey. All went the full distance.

Tommy was of Irish extraction and had a large following. In 1923 he met rough, tough Harry Greb four times, winning one, losing two, with one "no decision". And he beat a couple of British good 'uns in Ted Moore and Roland Todd. He boxed Greb again the following year, the result being a draw.

In 1925 he drew with Jack Delaney, yet another world champion, but the following year came the highspot so far, a victory over legendary Frenchman Georges Carpentier, just two fights after Georges had been stopped in the fifteenth round by Gene Tunney. Reports at that time stated that it was one of the most scientific bouts ever witnessed. The Frenchman afterwards said he had boxed at his best, but his best had not been good enough. Two fights later Carpentier retired from the ring.

After that no-one could deny Tommy a shot at the world light-heavyweight title, and in October, 1927, he took the vacant crown by outpointing Mike McTigue, retaining it three times in 1928, against Leo Lomski, and Pete Latzo (twice).

In 1929, two more successful defences followed, against Mickey Walker and Jimmy Braddock, making it six world title fights in just over 21 months. Then, due to weight problems, he gave up his crown, and moved into the heavyweight division with immediate disastrous results.

In September, 1929, he was matched with Jack Sharkey, who stopped him in three rounds. Tommy said he never saw the punch coming. The following year Sharkey was beaten by Max Schmeling in the only world heavyweight title fight to end by a disqualification.

He gradually crept up the heavyweight ratings ladder, but it wasn't easy, invariably having to concede weight. However, he beat top contenders like Max Baer, and in 1933 gained his revenge over Sharkey, who had won and lost the world title. He beat Ernie Schaaf twice, but Ernie beat him twice. He beat Steve Hamas twice, but Steve beat him twice. He beat King Levinsky, but lost the return.

Meanwhile, Primo Carnera had won the world title by stopping Jack Sharkey, had successfully defended it against Paolino Uzcudun, and was looking for another lamb to be led to the slaughter. Loughran was the choice, and the difference in weight was ludicrous.

It didn't bother Tommy. He was convinced he could outbox the slow-moving Italian, and there were many who agreed with him. And he might still have won had it not been for the frequent occasions when Primo kept stepping on his feet. At the end of fifteen rounds, he was limping badly, and Carnera duly received the verdict.

It was the start of a difficult period. After Carnera, he was successively outpointed by Walter Neusel, Johnny Risko, and José Caratolli. He made a tour of South America in 1935, then came to Europe, where he decisioned Maurice Strickland, André Lenglet, and Jack London, but was outpointed by Tommy Farr and Ben Foord.

In December, 1936, when he was beaten by Sonny Boy Walker (Sonny Boy Who?), he postponed his retirement so that he could have a return match. This came in January, 1937, Tommy winning on points, and retiring gracefully. Only two defeats inside the distance in 173 fights is proof indeed of his skills, and he was undoubtedly one of the greatest light-heavyweights of all time. Not for nothing was he known as "The Philly Ghost".

Tommy was a devout Catholic, and spent a lot of time teaching the youngsters to box in Catholic Boys' Clubs. In 1942 he joined the Marine Corps, becoming a Sergeant Instructor in Physical Training. Here he met referee Joe McGuigan, who in 1944 got Tommy a job as a sugar salesman. This proved an immediate success, and he eventually became a sugar broker with the William Hogan Company, staying for 25 years until his retirement.

After that he excelled at public speaking, talking to organisations all over the country about his boxing experiences, or indeed any other subject. To the best of my knowledge Tommy never married, and never drank or smoked. He set his own high standards, and did his best to live up to them.

He was elected to Boxing's Hall Of Fame in 1956, and died in 1982.

Tommy Loughran, a brilliant light-heavyweight champion, was really too small to fight heavyweights, but always gave a good account. Unfortunately, in a contest for the vacant American title, in 1929, he was kaoyed by Jack Sharkey inside three rounds, despite being shown (left) on the attack only moments from the finish

MAXIE ROSENBLOOM

When the then Cassius Clay came to Britain for the first time, Promoter Jack Solomons organised a breakfast-reception at the top of the Post Office Tower in London, and I was among the members of the press who were invited.

On arrival, I entered the lift, and just before it closed, a gentleman slipped in quickly. We were the only two occupants, and when I turned around to face him it was the unmistakeable figure of actor George Raft. We struck up a conversation, which continued practically throughout the reception, during the course of which, I asked him about his association with Maxie Rosenbloom, who held the world light-heavyweight title for such a long time.

I couldn't have chosen a better subject. We talked for ages about Maxie, and I suppose the latter must have been George's closest friend. A friendship formed after meeting in a peculiar fashion.

Maxie, born on 6 September, 1904, a Jewish-American, as a youth, frequently got involved in street fights. On one occasion it appeared he was outnumbered, only for unexpected help to arrive from another youngster — George Raft.

George was a vaudeville dancer, and was impressed by Maxie's performance in flooring the leader of the gang, and told him he could earn money with his fists.

Maxie was interested, and as a result took part in several "amateur" fights which earned him money. Sometimes George acted as his second, and they became firm pals.

Then he linked up with manager Frank Bachman, the start of a fine partnership which took Maxie right to the top. He averaged around 20 fights a year for the whole of his career, was alleged to have spent more time in night clubs than in the gym, didn't smoke or drink, but freely confessed he loved the women.

Known as "Slapsie Maxie", because of his habit of hitting with the open glove, he found he could

extend his reach by doing so. But I often wonder how he would fare these days, when referees are strict on this offence.

He turned pro in 1923, and four years later had his first title bout, being outpointed by Jimmy Slattery for the vacant National Boxing Association crown.

The following year he came to Britain for a couple of fights, and although kayoed by Tommy Milligan, a fortnight later he outpointed Roland Todd. The following month he was back in America, beating the great Ted "Kid" Lewis on a disqualification. That win was the start of a fantastic run of 40 fights, of which he lost only two, one to Jimmy Slattery and the other to Fred Lenhart, before making his second title challenge.

"Slapsy" Maxie (left) seen crouching under a Jimmy Slattery attack, in an effort to claim the inside position. The world light-heavyweight champion made a successful defence over fifteen rounds in August, 1931, against the man he had previously defeated for the title

Almost every year he boxed Slattery at least once, and in June, 1930, they met again for the world title, which Slattery had won just four months earlier by beating Lou Scozza. The fact that Maxie had only once beaten Jimmy in five clashes meant nothing on this occasion, and he won handily on points.

His clowning methods in the ring, and his lifestyle out of it, didn't meet with the approval of the NBA, who frowned upon the choice of Abie Bain as his first title challenger. Maxie disposed of Abie in eleven, and in 1931 successfully defended against Slattery, who was a handful of fights away from retirement.

Meanwhile the NBA had declared Lou Scozza as their champion, but in July, 1932, Maxie outpointed Lou to become undisputed world champ. There were successful defences against Adolf Heuser, Bob Godwin, Mickey Walker, Joe Knight (draw), before losing the title to Bob Olin in November, 1934. Even so, the verdict was hotly disputed.

Maxie was then 30 years old, but retire? "You must be joking," he said, and proceeded to carve out a whole new career as a heavyweight, still keeping up the average of 20 fights a year.

He beat top men like Tony Shucco, Charley Massera, Abe Feldman, John Henry Lewis, Lee Ramage, Bob Nestell, Roscoe Toles and King Levinsky. By the end of 1937 it appeared that he had retired, but after five months out of the ring he returned, to provide a grandstand finale to his career, with wins over Odell Polee and Al Ettore, both inside the distance, plus a draw with contender Bob Pastor, and a points win over Lou Nova, another top man.

Maxie had a remarkable record of 299 fights, losing only two inside the distance, one to Milligan, the other to Jimmy Adamick, near the end of his career.

Settling in California, his last three fights were in Hollywood, it was there that he opened a night club. He called it — yes, "Slapsie Maxie's". He also embarked on an acting career, normally playing the "dumb" role, and making many films.

Maxie was a natural comedian, and was soon being sought for dates in various clubs. He also teamed up with Max Baer for a time, but there was always an argument as to whose name should appear first on the bills. But Maxie was much in demand for TV and club dates, and became an integral part of Show Biz.

It was the great Damon Runyon who tagged him "Slapsie Maxie", but don't get the impression that he wasn't a worthy world champion. On the contrary, he was an excellent boxer, with clever footwork, who had a solid defence, and who could block, parry, duck and weave as well as anyone.

He became a world champion in spite of his lack of punch, only 19 of his victories coming inside the distance, but he more than compensated by his skill.

Maxie was elected to Boxing's Hall Of Fame in 1972, and died in South Pasadena in 1976.

SANDY SADDLER

Sandy Saddler had four world featherweight title fights with Willie Pep, who was regarded as one of the most skilful boxers of all time. The records show that Saddler won three, all inside the distance, Pep winning the other on points, which will give you some idea of just how good Sandy was.

Sandy was born on 23 June, 1926, at Boston, and when still at school, used to train at the Police Athletic League gym. He represented them in amateur bouts, and lost only a handful of his 50 contests.

Soon he ran out of opposition, and decided to turn pro. Willie Pep tells the story of how his manager Lou Viscusi was friendly with the Johnston brothers, Jimmy, Ned, Charley, and Bill, all of whom were managers.

One day Bill came to Lou, and said he had a youngster ready to make his début, and could Lou help. So Lou did, and the youngster won on points. Bill asked Lou to get him another bout. Lou did, and the youngster was stopped in three rounds. That youngster was Sandy Saddler.

Sandy's first victim was New England State champion Earl Roys, and the man who stopped Sandy was Jock Leslie. Sandy's version is that he was supposed to get a return with Roys, but the latter was in the Navy, and was unavailable. Leslie was far more experienced.

Apart from one disqualification, this was the only time in Sandy's career of 162 bouts that he lost inside the distance, an outstanding record. And he lost only fourteen on points.

During that first year of 1944, Sandy had 22 fights with 24 the following year. In that period the only other man to beat him was Lou Alter. They drew the return, but he never got the chance of a rematch with Leslie. From March, 1945, to August, 1945, Sandy achieved fourteen successive wins inside the distance. He was now managed by Charley Johnston, who was showing him all over the United States.

There were a couple of hiccups in 1946. He was decisioned by Bobby McQuillar, and also by former featherweight champion Phil Terranova, who the previous year had been outpointed in a world title fight by Willie Pep. But all the time Sandy was gaining experience, and in 1947, within the space of one month had three bouts. He stopped Joe Brown and drew with Jimmy Carter, both of whom would go on to annex the world lightweight title, and he also outpointed Melvin Bartholomew.

Still averaging around 20 bouts per year, his form improved by leaps and bounds until, in October, 1948, he was matched with Willie Pep for the world title, stopping the champion in four. It was a surprise to many people, but not to Sandy, who had been taking advice from Archie Moore, and was convinced that the right way to beat Willie was to keep on top of him, and not give him a chance to use his long-range skills.

However, Willie had learned something extra from their first meeting, and when the return came in February, 1949, he kept away from Sandy, and although the latter tried his best to crowd him out, it was Willie who got the verdict.

It was soon after that when Sandy made his one and only appearance in Britain, stopping Jim Keery in four rounds in London. Later that year he beat former bantam champ Harold Dade, and stopped future lightweight champ Paddy de Marco. And Sandy wasn't finished yet. In December he won the vacant world junior-lightweight title, outpointing Orlando Zulueta.

The Saddler-Pep series continued in September, 1950, but before that Sandy retained his junior crown by retiring Lauro Salas. Then he beat Willie for the second time, stopping him in eight. By now there was a lot of needle between the two, and the exchanges had become rough, to say the least. Willie said he hurt his shoulder and couldn't lift his arm.

So Sandy was champion again, and after being outpointed by Del Flanagan, at the end of the year, he chalked up ten straight wins, eight inside the distance, including a junior title defence, stopping Diego Sosa.

Sandy was only human, being outpointed by Paddy de Marco in August, 1951, prior to meeting Pep, the following month, for the fourth time. I watched the film of this fight and it was without doubt the dirtiest bout I have ever witnessed. It ended in round nine when Willie's left eye was closed.

Saddler and Pep were suspended by the New

A new champion is crowned. Sandy (right) took the world featherweight title from the brilliant Willie Pep in October, 1948, when, following a driving attack, he scored a tremendous fourth round knockout win

York State Athletic Commission for an indefinite period, but, of course, that didn't stop either boxer from competing outside New York.

Just three fights for Sandy in 1952, before he started his stint in the US Army, which kept him out of action for the whole of 1953. His world featherweight title was frozen, and he came back in 1954 with just one defeat during the year (to Frenchman Hoacine Khalfi) and eight wins (including a stoppage victory over legendary Frenchman Ray Famechon), seven of them inside the distance.

He started 1955 by stopping Lulu Perez, then in February outpointed Teddy "Red Top" Davis in defence of his world crown. He then lost to Joey Lopes and Flash Elorde, but stopped Kenny Davis, Shigeji Kaneko and Davey Gallardo.

Unaware that 1956 would be his last year, Sandy successfully defended his title against Flash Elorde in January, beat Curley Monroe in February, then was surprisingly outpointed by the in-experienced Larry Boardman.

Next came the incident that was to change his whole life. He was riding in a taxi that was involved in an accident, and sustained a serious eye injury, which forced his retirement from the ring, still holding the world title.

He took a job as Physical Director of the National Maritime Union gymnasium in New York, and went to live in Manhattan, training and giving advice to amateurs and pros, including former world heavyweight champion, George Foreman. I understand that the eye problem has worsened considerably in recent years.

Sandy was beautifully-built for a featherweight, standing 5ft 8½in, had a long reach, and punched hard with both hands, as witness his 103 quick wins from a total of 144 victories.

His series with Willie will go down in history, not only for the skill and power shown by both men, but for the "needle" element which resulted, especially in their last contest.

Pep and Saddler have always made it plain that there was, and is, no animosity between them. Willie states he had nothing but respect for Sandy, who said he and Willie were good friends, but when they were in the ring it was every man for himself.

Sandy never drank or smoked and often said how much he owed to Archie Moore for teaching him the tricks of the trade. He was one of the select band who retired still holding a world title, and one of the busiest boxers ever to hold one.

Only two boxers who won world titles have scored more quick wins, namely Archie Moore and "Sugar" Ray Robinson.

In 1971 Sandy was elected to Boxing's Hall Of Fame.

MICKEY WALKER

Mickey Walker was one of the select few who won the world welter and middleweight titles, boxed unsuccessfully for the world light-heavyweight crown, and even boxed a draw with a former heavyweight champion, Jack Sharkey. He started life as an architect, went on to become an architect and an artist in the ring, and finished as an artist whose paintings made him a lot of money.

He was born Edward Patrick Walker in Elizabeth, New Jersey, on 13 July, 1901. His mother had wanted a girl and would arrange his hair in curls. This didn't go down too well with the local lads in the Keighry Head district, which was predominantly Irish, so he learned to fight in the local freight yards, where it was a case of every man (or boy) for himself.

He left school at fourteen, got a job as a messenger boy in an architect's office, and graduated to become a member of a draughtsman's firm. But this ended when another member of the firm took the "mickey" out of him. So Mickey chinned him.

It is not clear why he took the ring name of "Mickey", but apparently that was what he had always been called, maybe because of the Irish connection. And why the nickname of the "Toy Bulldog"? He was given it by Francis Albertini, sports editor of the New York *Mail*, and could well have been because he had a nose that resembled that of a bulldog.

As a youngster his hero was Jack Dempsey, and it was after watching a film of the world title fight between Jack and Jess Willard, that he got the urge to become a professional fighter.

His first recorded bout was in February, 1919, a "no-decision" affair with Dominic Orsini, in his hometown of Elizabeth, the venue of all his early fights. But having given up a $90 a week job, he came a cropper in his eighth outing, being kayoed in one round by Phil Delmont, a setback he never got the chance to reverse.

According to the records, Mickey had five managers during his career, Johnny Anthea (1919–20), Jack Bulger (1920–23), Joe Diegnan (1923–25), Jack "Doc" Kearns (1925–34) and Bill Duffy (1934–35). But Mickey often said that Jack Dempsey had also managed him at one period.

Most of his contests were "no-decision" affairs, governed by the laws at that time, and in one of these he boxed twelve rounds with welter champion Jack Britton. He also stopped title contender Dave Shade, and in 1922 was matched with Britton, for the latter's world title.

Mickey could consider himself a trifle lucky to get this chance, for in his previous seven bouts he had won only two, lost two by disqualifications, lost to Lou Bogash and Jock Malone on points, and boxed a "no-decision" with Georgie Ward, in which the critics voted against him.

However, what had gone before didn't matter on 1 November, 1922, when he outpointed Britton to take the welter crown. He won by a street, and even had the champion down in round ten.

His biggest disadvantage was his height, or lack of it, scaling only 5ft 7in, and after defending the title several times he experienced weight problems. During this period he had the temerity to challenge Harry Greb for the latter's world middleweight crown, and was outpointed. This took place in July, 1925, and there are stories of a subsequent clash between the two later that night (or early the following morning) at a restaurant.

Despite allegations that there was no such fracas, and that it was just a newspaper hype, Walker said it was perfectly true, and that it was he who started it, by telling Greb that he would never have won had he not stuck his thumb in Mickey's eye. Harry took offence, as Harry would, and as they were taking their coats off Mickey said he hit Greb and knocked him down. What might have happened is anyone's guess, but a policeman broke it up.

In 1926 Mickey lost his welter title to Pete Latzo on points. He had already defeated Latzo, but was well beaten on this occasion, and immediately moved up into the middleweight division. Only

five fights and seven months later he won the middleweight crown, outpointing Tiger Flowers.

In June, 1927, he went to London to defend his title against Britisher Tommy Milligan, for the promoter, impressario C.B. Cochran. Mickey and Doc Kearns bet the whole of their purse on victory, and Milligan was stopped in round ten. But the story goes that they spent so much on the subsequent celebrations that they arrived home broke.

In March, 1929, while still holding the middleweight title, he had a shot at Tommy Loughran's light-heavyweight crown, but was outpointed. And after making two successful defences of his middleweight title, both against Ace Hudkins, Doc Kearns announced he was launching him into the heavyweight division.

It didn't seem a very good idea, taking into account Mickey's lack of height and weight, but he beat a few "names", like Johnny Risko, KO Christner, and Bearcat Wright, who weighed 20 stones (280 pounds). This brought him a match with former champion Jack Sharkey, and for this he relinquished his world middleweight title.

Against all the odds, Mickey held Jack to a draw, and most ringsiders thought he deserved the verdict. He then beat top heavies like Paolino Uzcudun and King Levinsky, but was stopped by Max Schmeling. In November, 1933 he was outpointed by "Slapsie" Maxie Rosenbloom for the world light-heavyweight title, and that was his last championship contest, even though in May, 1934, he beat Rosenbloom in a non-title affair.

His career came to an end in December, 1935, when he was stopped by the German Erich Seelig, although in June, 1939, he stopped Red Bush in what was termed an "exhibition".

On retirement, Mickey managed bars in his hometown of Elizabeth and also in New York, and was even sports editor of the *Police Gazette*, one of the very old and traditional fight magazines.

It was the George Sanders film, *The Moon and Sixpence*, based on the life of painter Paul Gauguin, that inspired him to take up painting, and although it took time, he eventually became very good, and his work was accepted by the Associated American Artists' Gallery.

There was a drink problem, but he beat it. Although married six times, he finished up on his own, but was very proud of his son Mike, who became an architectural engineer. He often said that he had enjoyed life to the full and would not have changed anything.

Mickey died on 28 April, 1981, at Freehold, New Jersey. He was elected to Boxing's Hall Of Fame in 1955.

Coming to London in 1927, Mickey Walker put his world iiddleweight crown on ie line against Tommy Milligan. The champion just had a bit too much for the game Scot, winning by a kayo in the tenth

FRITZIE ZIVIC

Fritzie Zivic and Harry Greb had two things in common. Both became world champions, and both perfected the use of the butt, the elbow, and the thumb to a fine art. To them it was "the survival of the fittest".

Fritzie was the youngest of five sons, the other four were Jack, Pete, Joe, and Eddie, born to Tomas Zivic and his wife, who came from Croatia. Starting life at Lawrenceville in the town of Pittsburgh, on 8 May, 1913, Fritzie didn't survive his first day at school without trouble. He was set on by half a dozen much older boys, who also insulted his family.

The family honour had to be avenged. So the following day his mum took the precaution of including a few bricks in his satchel. When the gang again tried to bully him he used the bricks to good effect, and had no further trouble.

His father too had to put up with bullying in the steel mill at which he worked. They told him to go back from whence he had come. However, his sons all knew how to use their fists, and Tomas was in no danger when they showed up.

Fritzie's brothers all boxed, the most famous being Pete and Jack. Both represented America in the 1920 Olympic Games, Pete reaching the quarter-finals in the flyweight division, and Jack the semi-finals of the featherweights. And both boxed for pay with success.

It was only natural that Fritzie wanted to emulate his brothers, and he turned pro in 1931, under manager Luke Carney, who also guided his brothers. In fact one of Luke's protégés was heavyweight Frank Moran, who met Jack Johnson for the world title.

Most of Fritzie's early fights were in Pittsburgh, and all went well until 1935-36, when he dropped eight decisions in a row. But he soon got back on the winning trail again, and in December, 1936, met Billy Conn, who went on to win the world light-heavyweight title, and indeed came within a few rounds of taking away Joe Louis' heavyweight crown.

It was quite a fight, the split decision going to Conn, although Fritzie thought he had won. The conditions were unusual. There was a $1,000 forfeit if Fritzie weighed less than 10st 10lb (150 pounds), and if Conn weighed more than 11st 6lb (160 pounds).

Fritzie fought hard, and often, averaging more than 20 bouts per year. In 1938 he defeated top men like Charley Burley, Tommy Bland, and Frankie Blair, and the following year he gained wins over Eddie Booker, and Charlie Bell.

There's quite a story about that fight. Fritzie's brother Eddie was due to meet Bell, but had to pull out due to an ear injury. So Fritzie offered to substitute. Bell's manager agreed, but stipulated that his boxer should not be knocked out in the first two rounds. So Fritzie had to hold him up for the first two sessions, and then kayoed him in the third!

Also in 1939, Fritzie outpointed Mexican Kid Azteca, who holds the world record of long service in a professional career that extended from 1929 to the early '60s.

By 1940 Fritzie had fought his way into title contention, and in October he outpointed the great Henry Armstrong to win the world welter crown. It was a rough, tough, no-holds-barred fight. It was also Fritzie's first fifteen-rounder, and he had paced it well.

A return was a "natural", and it took place the following January. This time Fritzie won even more convincingly, stopping Henry in twelve. The champ loved his new life-style, loved spending money, and of course there were always those who were only too willing to help him spend it.

In July, 1941, he lost his title to Freddie "Red" Cochrane. It was a close one, held in Cochrane's own State of New Jersey, where the referee rendered the decision and Fritzie thought he had won. Many ringsiders also thought it was a "hometown" verdict. But there were also stories that Fritzie had underestimated his opponent, and had been going to parties.

Fortunately, he had a good trainer in Freddy Fierro, who licked him into shape in spite of his occasional lapses, and in 1942 there was a return, with Cochrane, which Fritzie won on points. Unfortunately, it was a non-title affair. From then until 1949, he was managed by Louis Stokan.

Fritzie was still averaging 20 fights per year, and although he never again challenged for a world title, he met some of the best in the business. Only three months after losing his title, he lost a close points decision to "Sugar" Ray Robinson, and in a second meeting, in January, 1942, Fritzie was stopped in ten.

They don't come any tougher than Jake la Motta and they met three times in 1943. Jake won the first, Fritzie the second and Jake the third. All went the distance, and all were close.

By 1945 the spirit was still willing, but the body was getting weaker. There was a period from July of that year until the end of 1947, when Fritzie had 29 fights, and lost all but nine.

He ended his career in 1949, winning both his fights, against Al Reid and Eddie Steele. There were reports that his investments failed, and that he had several jobs, at one time working on the highway with a pick and shovel, later becoming a boilermaker in Pittsburgh, where he had settled with his wife Helen and family.

If you look at his record, and see that he lost 65, this may seem a lot of defeats, but after all he did have 232 fights against some of the best around, including several world champions. And he had one of the best fighting hearts of all time.

He was elected to Boxing's Hall Of Fame in 1972, and died at Pittsburgh on 16 May, 1984.

The referee rushes in to save a badly battered Henry Armstrong from further punishment at the hands of Fritzie, during the thirteenth round of their return battle for the world welterweight title in January, 1940

World championship Boxing, 1890–1989

The following records attempt to set out by weight division every champion and championship bout contested under Queensberry Rules since the beginning of gloves (2 oz minimum).

Boxing grew up in Great Britain, and quickly spread to the USA, but it was not until the champions of these two countries came together in the latter part of the last century that it developed on an international scale. Organisations then came into existence solely for the purpose of controlling professional boxing. The National Sporting Club of Britain was formed in 1891, later to be amalgamated into the British Boxing Board of Control during 1929. By the early part of the century the sport had also begun to boom among the French, who in 1911 were instrumental in setting up the International Boxing Union to look after the interests of boxing in Europe. Following World War II the body became known as the European Boxing Union. In America many states had allowed boxing to take place, but in 1920 the New York State Athletic Commission was legally constituted under the Walker Law to govern the sport. Also at the same time several of the independent states of America became affiliated to form the National Boxing Association, which by 1962 was re-named the World Boxing Association. In an effort to create a balance of power, Britain supported the setting up of the World Boxing Council, formed in 1963, which brought together New York and its satellite states, with the BBBC, the Commonwealth and the EBU. Recently the International Boxing Federation, an offshoot of the WBA, has sprung into prominence on the world boxing stage.

Over the years many new weight divisions have been formed and original classes have been restructured. For example the bantamweight division limit, which in 1890 stood at 112 lbs, was gradually increased until it reached an internationally accepted 118 lbs in 1909. Similarly other weight limits rose, e.g. featherweight: 1890 (118 lbs) – 1909 (126 lbs); welterweight: 1892 (142 lbs) – 1909 (147 lbs); middleweight: 1891 (154 lbs) – 1909 (160 lbs).

The following data does not include "No Decision" bouts, champions awarded titles without a contest, or claimants with no realistic backing. Note that the champions in bold are accorded universal recognition.

Championship Status Code:
AUST = Australia; CALIF = California; EBU = European Boxing Union; FR = France; GB = Great Britain; IBF = International Boxing Federation; IBU = International Boxing Union; LOUIS = Louisiana; MARY = Maryland; MASS = Massachusetts; NBA = National Boxing Association; NY = New York; PEN = Pennsylvania; USA = United States; WBA = World Boxing Association; WBC = World Boxing Council.

Current World Bodies: weight classifications

Lbs	WBA	WBC	IBF
105	Mini-Flyweight	Straw-Weight	Straw-Weight
108	Junior-Flyweight	Light-Flyweight	Junior-Flyweight
112	Flyweight	Flyweight	Flyweight
115	Junior-Bantamweight	Super-Flyweight	Junior-Bantamweight
118	Bantamweight	Bantamweight	Bantamweight
122	Junior-Featherweight	Super-Bantamweight	Junior-Featherweight
126	Featherweight	Featherweight	Featherweight
130	Junior-Lightweight	Super-Featherweight	Junior-Lightweight
135	Lightweight	Lightweight	Lightweight
140	Junior-Welterweight	Super-Lightweight	Junior-Welterweight
147	Welterweight	Welterweight	Welterweight
154	Junior-Middleweight	Super-Welterweight	Junior-Middleweight
160	Middleweight	Middleweight	Middleweight
168	Super-Middleweight	Super-Middleweight	Super-Middleweight
175	Light-Heavyweight	Light-Heavyweight	Light-Heavyweight
190	Junior-Heavyweight	—	Cruiserweight
195	—	Cruiserweight	—
†	Heavyweight	Heavyweight	Heavyweight

* Undefeated champions (does not include title holders who were stripped or lost recognition)

Mini-Flyweight (105 lbs)

Title Holders

	Birthplace	Tenure	Status
Kyung-Yung Lee*	S Korea	1987–1988	IBF
Hiroki Ioka	Japan	1987–1988	WBC
Luis Gamez*	Venezuela	1988–1989	WBA
Samuth Sithnaruepol	Thailand	1988–	IBF
Napa Kiatwanchai	Thailand	1988–	WBC
Bong-Jun Kim	S Korea	1989–	WBA

Title Bouts

14.06.87 Kyung-Yung Lee W CO 2 Masaharu Kawakami, Bujok, S Korea (IBF)
Kyung-Yung Lee relinquished IBF version of title (contested vacant WBC title)
18.10.87 Kiroki Ioka W PTS 12 Mai Thornburifarm, Osaka, Japan (WBC)
10.01.88 Luis Gamez W PTS 12 Bong-Jun Kim, Pusan, S Korea (WBA)
31.01.88 Hiroki Ioka W RSC 12 Kyung-Yung Lee, Osaka, Japan (WBC)
24.03.88 Samuth Sithnaruepol W RSC 11 Domingo Lucas, Bangkok (IBF)
24.04.88 Luis Gamez W RSC 3 Kenji Yokozawa, Tokyo, Japan (WBA)
Luis Gamez relinquished WBA version of the title (due to increased weight problems)
05.06.88 Hiroki Ioka DREW 12 Napa Kiatwanchai, Osaka, Japan (WBC)
29.08.88 Samuth Sithnaruepol W PTS 15 In-Kyu Hwang, Bangkok, Thailand (IBF)
13.11.88 Napa Kiatwanchai W PTS 12 Hiroki Ioka, Osaka, Japan (WBC)
11.02.89 Napa Kiatwanchai W PTS 12 John Arief, Bangkok, Thailand (WBC)
23.03.89 Samuth Sithnaruepol DREW 12 Nico Thomas, Jakarta, Indonesia (IBF)
16.04.89 Bong-Jun Kim W RSC 7 Agustin Garcia, Seoul, S Korea (WBA)

Light-Flyweight (108 lbs)

Title Holders

	Birthplace	Tenure	Status
Franco Udella	Italy	1975	WBC
Jaime Rios	Panama	1975–1976	WBA
Luis Estaba	Venezuela	1975–1978	WBC
Juan Guzman	Dom Republic	1976	WBA
Yoko Gushiken	Japan	1976–1981	WBA
Freddie Castillo	Mexico	1978	WBC
Sor Vorasingh	Thailand	1978	WBC
Sung-Jun Kim	S Korea	1978–1980	WBC
Shigeo Nakajima	Japan	1980	WBC
Hilario Zapata	Panama	1980–1982	WBC
Pedro Flores	Mexico	1981	WBA
Hwan-Jin Kim	S Korea	1981	WBA
Katsuo Tokashiki	Japan	1981–1983	WBA
Amado Ursua	Mexico	1982	WBC
Tadashi Tomori	Japan	1982	WBC
Hilario Zapata	Panama	1982–1983	WBC
Jung-Koo Chang*	S Korea	1983–1988	WBC
Lupe Madera	Mexico	1983–1984	WBA
Dodie Penalosa	Philippines	1983–1986	IBF
Francisco Quiroz	Dom Republic	1984–1985	WBA
Joey Olivo	USA	1985	WBA
Myung-Woo Yuh	S Korea	1985–	WBA
Jum-Hwan Choi	S Korea	1987–1988	IBF
Tacy Macalos	Philippines	1988–	IBF
German Torres	Mexico	1988–1989	WBC
Yul-Woo Lee	S Korea	1989–	WBC

Title Bouts

04.04.75 Franco Udella W DIS 12 Valentin Martinez, Milan, Italy (WBC)
Franco Udella forfeited WBC recognition (failure to defend against Rafael Lovera)
23.08.75 Jaime Rios W PTS 15 Rigoberto Marcano, Panama C, Panama (WBA)
13.09.75 Luis Estaba W CO 4 Rafael Lovera, Caracas, Venezuela (WBC)
17.12.75 Luis Estaba W RSC 10 Takenobu Shimabakuro, Okinawa, Japan (WBC)
03.01.76 Jaime Rios W PTS 15 Kazunori Tenryu, Kagoshima, Japan (WBA)
14.02.76 Luis Estaba W PTS 15 Leo Palacios, Caracas, Venezuela (WBC)
02.05.76 Luis Estaba W PTS 15 Juan Alvarez, Caracas, Venezuela (WBC)
01.07.76 Juan Guzman W PTS 15 Jaime Rios, St Domingo, Dom Republic (WBA)
17.07.76 Luis Estaba W CO 3 Franco Udella, Maracay, Venezuela (WBC)
26.09.76 Luis Estaba W RTD 10 Rodolfo Rodriguez, Caracas, Venezuela (WBC)
10.10.76 Yoko Gushiken W CO 7 Juan Guzman, Kofu, Japan (WBA)
21.11.76 Luis Estaba W RSC 10 Valentin Martinez, Caracas, Venezuela (WBC)
30.01.77 Yoko Gushiken W PTS 15 Jaime Rios, Tokyo, Japan (WBA)
15.05.77 Luis Estaba W PTS 15 Rafael Pedroza, Caracas, Venezuela (WBC)
22.05.77 Yoko Gushiken W PTS 15 Rigoberto Marcano, Sapporo, Japan (WBA)
17.07.77 Luis Estaba W PTS 15 Ricardo Estupinan, Cruz, Venezuela (WBC)

21.08.77 Luis Estaba W RSC 11 Juan Alvarez, Cruz, Venezeula (WBC)
18.09.77 Luis Estaba W CO 15 Orlando Hernandez, Caracas, Venezuela (WBC)
09.10.77 Yoko Gushiken W RSC 4 Montsayarm Mahachai, Oita, Japan (WBA)
30.10.77 Luis Estaba W PTS 15 Sor Vorasingh, Caracas, Venezuela (WBC)
29.01.78 Yoko Gushiken W RSC 14 Aniceto Vargas, Nagoya, Japan (WBA)
19.02.78 Freddie Castillo W RSC 14 Luis Estaba, Caracas, Venezuela (WBC)
06.05.78 Sor Vorasingh W PTS 15 Freddie Castillo, Bangkok, Thailand (WBC)
07.05.78 Yoko Gushiken W RSC 13 Jaime Rios, Hiroshima, Japan (WBA)
29.07.78 Sor Vorasingh W RTD 5 Luis Estaba, Caracas, Venezuela (WBC)
30.09.78 Sung-Jun Kim W CO 3 Sor Vorasingh, Seoul, S Korea (WBC)
15.10.78 Yoko Gushiken W CO 4 Sang-Il Chung, Tokyo, Japan (WBA)
07.01.79 Yoko Gushiken W CO 7 Rigoberto Marcano, Kawasaki, Japan (WBA)
31.03.79 Sung-Jun Kim DREW 15 Hector Melendez, Seoul, S Korea (WBC)
08.04.79 Yoko Gushiken W RSC 7 Alfonso Lopez, Tokyo, Japan (WBA)
28.07.79 Sung-Jun Kim W PTS 15 Stony Carupo, Seoul, S Korea (WBC)
29.07.79 Yoko Gushiken W PTS 15 Rafael Pedroza, Kitakyushi, Japan (WBA)
21.10.79 Sung-Jun Kim W PTS 15 Hector Melendez, Seoul, S Korea (WBC)
28.10.79 Yoko Gushiken W RSC 7 Tito Abella, Tokyo, Japan (WBA)
03.01.80 Shigeo Nakajima W PTS 15 Sung-Jun Kim, Tokyo, Japan (WBC)
27.01.80 Yoko Gushiken W PTS 15 Yong-Hyun Kim, Osaka, Japan (WBA)
24.03.80 Hilario Zapata W PTS 15 Shigeo Nakajima, Tokyo, Japan (WBC)
01.06.80 Yoko Gushiken W RSC 8 Martin Vargas, Kochi C, Japan (WBA)
07.06.80 Hilario Zapata W PTS 15 Chi-Bok Kim, Seoul, S Korea (WBC)
04.08.80 Hilario Zapata W PTS 15 Hector Melendez, Caracas, Venezuela (WBC)
17.09.80 Hilario Zapata W RSC 11 Shigeo Nakajima, Gifu, Japan (WBC)
12.10.80 Yoko Gushiken W PTS 15 Pedro Flores, Kanazawa, Japan (WBA)
01.12.80 Hilario Zapata W PTS 15 Reynaldo Becerra, Caracas, Venezuela (WBC)
08.02.81 Hilario Zapata W RSC 13 Joey Olivo, Panama C, Panama (WBC)
08.03.81 Pedro Flores W RTD 12 Yoko Gushiken, Gushikawa, Japan (WBA)
24.04.81 Hilario Zapata W PTS 15 Rudy Crawford, San Francisco, USA (WBC)
19.07.81 Hwan-Jin Kim W RSC 13 Pedro Flores, Taegu, S Korea (WBA)
15.08.81 Hilario Zapata W PTS 15 German Torres, Panama C, Panama (WBC)
11.10.81 Hwan-Jin Kim W PTS 15 Alfonso Lopez, Daejon,S Korea (WBA)
06.11.81 Hilario Zapata W RSC 10 Sor Vorasingh, Korat, Thailand (WBC)
16.12.81 Katsuo Tokashiki W PTS 15 Hwan-Jin Kim, Sendai, Japan (WBA)
06.02.82 Amado Ursua W CO 2 Hilario Zapata, Panama C, Panama (WBC)
04.04.82 Katsuo Tokashiki W PTS 15 Lupe Madera, Sendai, Japan (WBA)
13.04.82 Tadashi Tomori W PTS 15 Amado Ursua, Tokyo, Japan (WBC)
07.07.82 Katsuo Tokashiki W CO 8 Masahara Inami, Tokyo, Japan (WBA)
20.07.82 Hilario Zapata W PTS 15 Tadashi Tomori, Kanazawa, Japan (WBC)
18.09.82 Hilario Zapata W PTS 15 Jung-Koo Chang, Chonju, S Korea (WBC)
10.10.82 Katsuo Tokashiki W PTS 15 Sung-Nam Kim, Tokyo, Japan (WBA)
30.11.82 Hilario Zapata W RSC 8 Tadashi Tomori, Tokyo, Japan (WBC)
09.01.83 Katsuo Tokashiki W PTS 15 Hwan-Jin Kim, Kyoto, Japan (WBA)
26.03.83 Jung-Koo Chang W RSC 3 Hilario Zapata, Daejon, S Korea (WBC)
10.04.83 Katsuo Tokashiki DREW 15 Lupe Madera, Tokyo, Japan (WBA)
11.06.83 Jung-Koo Chang W RSC 2 Masaharu Iha, Taegu, S Korea (WBC)
10.07.83 Lupe Madera W RSC 4 Katsuo Tokashiki, Tokyo, Japan (WBA)
10.09.83 Jung-Koo Chang W PTS 12 German Torres, Daejon, S Korea (WBC)
23.10.83 Lupe Madera W PTS 12 Katsuo Tokashiki, Sapporo, Japan (WBA)
10.12.83 Dodie Penalosa W RSC 11 Satoshi Shingaki, Osaka, Japan (IBF)
31.03.84 Jung-Koo Chang W PTS 12 Sot Chitalada, Pusan, S Korea (WBC)
13.05.84 Dodie Penalosa W RSC 9 Jae-Hong Kim, Seoul, S Korea (IBF)
19.05.84 Francisco Quiroz W CO 9 Lupe Madera, Maracaibo, Venezuela (WBA)
18.08.84 Jung-Koo Chang W RSC 9 Katsuo Tokashiki, Pohang, S Korea (WBC)
18.08.84 Francisco Quiroz W CO 2 Victor Sierra, Panama C, Panama (WBA)
16.11.84 Dodie Penalosa W PTS 15 Jum-Hwan Choi, Manila, Philippines (IBF)
15.12.84 Jung-Koo Chang W PTS 12 Tadashi Kuramochi, Pusan, S Korea (WBC)
29.03.85 Joey Olivo W PTS 15 Francisco Quiroz, Miami, USA (WBA)
27.04.85 Jung-Koo Chang W PTS 12 German Torres, Ulsan, S Korea (WBC)
28.07.85 Joey Olivo W PTS 15 Moon-Jin Choi, Seoul, S Korea (WBA)
03.08.85 Jung-Koo Chang W PTS 15 Francisco Montiel, Seoul, S Korea (WBC)
12.10.85 Dodie Penalosa W CO 3 Yani Hagler, Jakarta, Indonesia (IBF)
Dodie Penalosa forfeited title (challenged Hilario Zapata for the WBA flyweight title)
10.11.85 Jung-Koo Chang W PTS 12 Jorge Cano, Daejon, S Korea (WBC)
08.12.85 Myung-Woo Yuh W PTS 15 Joey Olivo, Seoul, S Korea (WBA)
09.03.86 Myung-Woo Yuh W PTS 15 Jose de Jesus, Suwon, S Korea (WBA)
13.04.86 Jung-Koo Chang W PTS 12 German Torres, Kwangju, S Korea (WBC)
14.06.86 Myung-Woo Yuh W RSC 12 Tomohiro Kiyuna, Inchon, S Korea (WBA)
13.09.86 Jung-Koo Chang W PTS 12 Francisco Montiel, Seoul, S Korea (WBC)
30.11.86 Myung-Woo Yuh W PTS 15 Mario de Marco, Seoul, S Korea (WBA)
07.12.86 Jum-Hwan Choi W PTS 15 Cho-Woon Park, Pusan, S Korea (IBF)
14.12.86 Jung-Koo Chang W RSC 5 Hideyuki Ohashi, Inchon, S Korea (WBC)
01.03.87 Myung-Woo Yuh W RSC 1 Eduardo Tunon, Seoul, S Korea (WBA)
29.03.87 Jum-Hwan Choi W PTS 15 Tacy Macalos, Seoul, S Korea (IBF)
19.04.87 Jung-Koo Chang W RSC 6 Efren Pinto, Seoul, S Korea (WBC)
07.06.87 Myung-Woo Yuh W RSC 15 Benedicto Murillo, Pusan, S Korea (WBA)
28.06.87 Jung-Koo Chang W RSC 10 Agustin Garcia, Seoul, S Korea (WBC)
05.07.87 Jum-Hwan Choi W RSC 4 Toshihiko Matsuta, Seoul, S Korea (IBF)
09.08.87 Jum-Hwan Choi W RSC 3 Azadin Anhar, Jakarta, Indonesia (IBF)
20.09.87 Myung-Woo Yuh W CO 8 Rodolfo Blanco, Inchon, S Korea (WBA)
13.12.87 Jung-Koo Chang W PTS 12 Isidro Perez, Seoul, S Korea (WBC)
07.02.88 Myung-Woo Yuh W PTS 12 Wilibaldo Salazar, Seoul, S Korea (WBA)
12.06.88 Myung-Woo Yuh W PTS 12 Jose de Jesus, Seoul, Thailand (WBA)
27.06.88 Jung-Koo Chang W RSC 8 Hideyuki Ohashi, Tokyo, Japan (WBC)
(Jung-Koo Chang relinquished title (retired through ill health)
28.08.88 Myung-Woo Yuh W CO 6 Putt Ohyuthanakorn, Pusan, S Korea (WBA)
05.11.88 Tacy Macalos W PTS 12 Jum-Hwan Choi, Manila, Philippines (IBF)
06.11.88 Myung-Woo Yuh W CO 7 Bahar Udin, Seoul, S Korea (WBA)
11.12.88 German Torres W PTS 12 Soon-Jung Kang, Seoul, S Korea (WBC)
12.02.89 Myung-Woo Yuh W RSC 10 Katsumi Komiyama, Chungju, S Korea (WBA)
19.03.89 Yul-Woo Lee W CO 9 German Torres, Taejon, S Korea (WBC)

Flyweight (112 lbs)

Title Holders

	Birthplace	Tenure	Status
Sid Smith	England	1913	GB/IBU
Bill Ladbury	England	1913–1914	GB/IBU
Percy Jones	Wales	1914	GB/IBU
Tancy Lee	Scotland	1915	GB/IBU
Joe Symonds	England	1915–1916	GB/IBU
Jimmy Wilde	Wales	1916	GB/IBU
Jimmy Wilde	Wales	1916–1923	
Pancho Villa*	Philippines	1923–1925	
Fidel la Barba	USA	1925–1927	USA
Fidel la Barba*	USA	1927	
Johnny McCoy	USA	1927–1928	CALIF
Frenchy Belanger	Canada	1927–1928	NBA
Izzy Schwartz	USA	1927–1929	NY
Newsboy Brown	Russia	1928	CALIF
Frankie Genaro	USA	1928–1929	NBA
Johnny Hill	Scotland	1928–1929	GB/CALIF
Emile Pladner	France	1929	NBA/IBU
Frankie Genaro	USA	1929–1931	NBA/IBU
Willie la Morte	USA	1929–1930	NY
Midget Wolgast	USA	1930–1935	NY
Young Perez	Tunisia	1931–1932	NBA/IBU
Jackie Brown	England	1932–1935	NBA/IBU
Benny Lynch	Scotland	1935–1937	NBA
Small Montana	Philippines	1935–1937	NY/CALIF
Valentin Angelmann	France	1936–1937	IBU
Benny Lynch	Scotland	1937	
Peter Kane	England	1938–1943	
Jackie Paterson	Scotland	1943–1947	
Jackie Paterson	Scotland	1947–1948	GB/NY
Rinty Monaghan	Ireland	1947–1948	NBA
Rinty Monaghan*	Ireland	1948–1950	
Terry Allen	England	1950	
Dado Marino	Hawaii	1950–1952	
Yoshio Shirai	Japan	1952–1954	
Pascual Perez	Argentine	1954–1960	
Pone Kingpetch	Thailand	1960–1962	
Fighting Harada	Japan	1962–1963	
Pone Kingpetch	Thailand	1963	
Hiroyuki Ebihara	Japan	1963–1964	
Pone Kingpetch	Thailand	1964–1965	
Salvatore Burruni	Italy	1965	
Salvatore Burruni	Italy	1965–1966	WBC
Horacio Accavallo*	Argentine	1966–1968	WBA
Walter McGowan	Scotland	1966	WBC
Chartchai Chionoi	Thailand	1966–1969	WBC
Efren Torres	Mexico	1969–1970	WBC
Hiroyuki Ebihara	Japan	1969	WBA
Bernabe Villacampo	Philippines	1969–1970	WBA
Chartchai Chionoi	Thailand	1970	WBC
Berkrerk Chartvanchai	Thailand	1970	WBA
Masao Ohba*	Japan	1970–1973	WBA
Erbito Salavarria	Philippines	1970–1971	WBC
Betulio Gonzalez	Venezuela	1972	WBC
Venice Borkorsor*	Thailand	1972–1973	WBC
Chartchai Chionoi	Thailand	1973–1974	WBA
Betulio Gonzalez	Venezuela	1973–1974	WBC
Shoji Oguma	Japan	1974–1975	WBC
Susumu Hanagata	Japan	1974–1975	WBA
Miguel Canto	Mexico	1975–1979	WBC
Erbito Salavarria	Philippines	1975–1976	WBA
Alfonso Lopez	Panama	1976	WBA
Guty Espadas	Mexico	1976–1978	WBA
Betulio Gonzalez	Venezuela	1978–1979	WBA
Chan-Hee Park	S Korea	1979–1980	WBC
Luis Ibarra	Panama	1979–1980	WBA
Tae-Shik Kim	S Korea	1980	WBA
Shoji Oguma	Japan	1980–1981	WBC
Peter Mathebula	S Africa	1980–1981	WBA
Santos Laciar	Argentine	1981	WBA
Antonio Avelar	Mexico	1981–1982	WBC
Luis Ibarra	Panama	1981	WBA
Juan Herrera	Mexico	1981–1982	WBA
Prudencio Cardona	Colombia	1982	WBC
Santos Laciar*	Argentine	1982–1985	WBA
Freddie Castillo	Mexico	1982	WBC
Eleoncio Mercedes	Dom Republic	1982–1983	WBC
Charlie Magri	Tunisia	1983	WBC
Frank Cedeno	Philippines	1983–1984	WBC
Soon-Chun Kwon	S Korea	1983–1985	IBF
Koji Kobayashi	Japan	1984	WBC
Gabriel Bernal	Mexico	1984	WBC
Sot Chitalada	Thailand	1984–1988	WBC
Hilario Zapata	Panama	1985–1987	WBA
Chong-Kwan Chung	S Korea	1985–1986	IBF
Bi-Won Chung	S Korea	1986	IBF
Hi-Sup Shin	S Korea	1986–1987	IBF
Fidel Bassa	Colombia	1987–	WBA
Dodie Penalosa	Philippines	1987	IBF

Chang-Ho Choi	S Korea	1987–1988	IBF
Rolando Bohol	Philippines	1988	IBF
Yong-Kang Kim	S Korea	1988–	WBC
Duke McKenzie	England	1988–	IBF

Title Bouts

11.04.13 Sid Smith W PTS 20 Eugene Criqui, Paris, France (GB/IBU)
02.06.13 Bill Ladbury W RSC 11 Sid Smith, London, England (GB/IBU)
26.01.14 Percy Jones W PTS 20 Bill Ladbury, London, England (GB/IBU)
26.03.14 Percy Jones W PTS 20 Eugene Criqui, Liverpool, England (GB/IBU)
Percy Jones forfeited GB/IBU recognition (overweight for defence against Joe Symonds)
25.01.15 Tancy Lee W RSC 17 Jimmy Wilde, London, England (GB/IBU)
18.10.15 Joe Symonds W RSC 16 Tancy Lee, London, England (GB/IBU)
14.02.16 Jimmy Wilde W RSC 12 Joe Symonds, London, England (GB/IBU)
24.04.16 Jimmy Wilde W RTD 11 Johnny Rosner, Liverpool, England (GB/IBU)
26.06.16 Jimmy Wilde W RSC 11 Tancy Lee, London, England (GN/IBU)
31.07.16 Jimmy Wilde W CO 10 Johnny Hughes, London, England (GB/IBU)
18.12.16 Jimmy Wilde W CO 11 Young Zulu Kid, London, England
12.03.17 Jimmy Wilde W RTD 4 George Clark, London, England
18.06.23 Pancho Villa W CO 7 Jimmy Wilde, New York C, USA
13.10.23 Pancho Villa W PTS 15 Benny Schwartz, Baltimore, USA
08.02.24 Pancho Villa W PTS 15 Georgie Marks, New York C, USA
30.05.24 Pancho Villa W PTS 15 Frankie Ash, New York C, USA
01.05.25 Pancho Villa W PTS 15 Clever Sencio, Manila, Philippines
Pancho Villa left title vacant (died from blood poisoning)
22.08.25 Fidel la Barba W PTS 10 Frankie Genaro, Los Angeles, USA (USA)
08.07.26 Fidel la Barba W PTS 10 Georgie Rivers, Los Angeles, USA (USA)
21.01.27 Fidel la Barba W PTS 12 Elky Clark, New York C, USA
Fidel la Barba relinquished title (entered university)
28.10.27 Johnny McCoy W PTS 10 Tommy Hughes, Los Angeles, USA (CALIF)
28.11.27 Frenchy Belanger W PTS 10 Frankie Genaro, Toronto, Canada (NBA)
16.12.27 Izzy Schwartz W PTS 15 Newsboy Brown, New York C, USA (NY)
19.12.27 Frenchy Belanger W PTS 12 Ernie Jarvis, Toronto, Canada (NBA)
03.01.28 Newsboy Brown W PTS 10 Johnny McCoy, Los Angeles, USA (CALIF)
06.02.28 Frankie Genaro W PTS 10 Frenchy Belanger, Toronto, Canada (NBA)
09.04.28 Izzy Schwartz W PTS 15 Routier Parra, New York C, USA (NY)
20.07.28 Izzy Schwartz W DIS 4 Frisco Grande, New York C, USA (NY)
03.08.28 Izzy Schwartz W CO 4 Little Jeff Smith, New York C, USA (NY)
29.08.28 Johnny Hill W PTS 15 Newsboy Brown, London, England (GB/CALIF)
Johnny Hill ceased to be recognised by the GB/Californian authorities (this followed a defeat by Emile Pladner in a non-title bout, February, 1929)
02.03.29 Emile Pladner W CO 1 Frankie Genaro, Paris, France (NBA/IBU)
12.03.29 Izzy Schwartz W PTS 12 Frenchy Belanger, Toronto, Canada (NY)
18.04.29 Frankie Genaro W DIS 5 Emile Pladner, Paris, France (NBA/IBU)
22.08.29 Willie la Morte W PTS 15 Izzy Schwartz, Newark, USA (NY)
17.10.29 Frankie Genaro W PTS 15 Ernie Jarvis, London, England (NBA/IBU)
21.11.29 Willie la Morte W CO 7 Frisco Grande, Paterson, USA (NY)
Willie la Morte forfeited NY recognition (failure to meet Midget Wolgast)
18.01.30 Frankie Genaro W RTD 12 Yvon Trevidic, Paris, France (NBA/IBU)
21.03.30 Midget Wolgast W PTS 15 Black Bill, New York C, USA (NY)
16.05.30 Midget Wolgast W CO 6 Willie la Morte, New York C, USA (NY)
10.06.30 Frankie Genaro W PTS 10 Frenchy Belanger, Toronto, Canada (NBA/IBU)
06.08.30 Frankie Genaro W PTS 10 Willie la Morte, Newark, USA (NBA/IBU)
26.12.30 Frankie Genaro DREW 15 Midget Wolgast, New York C, USA
25.03.31 Frankie Genaro DREW 15 Victor Ferrand, Madrid, Spain (NBA/IBU)
13.07.31 Midget Wolgast W PTS 15 Ruby Bradley, New York C, USA (NY)
30.07.31 Frankie Genaro W CO 6 Jackie Harmon, Waterbury, USA (NBA/IBU)
03.10.31 Frankie Genaro W PTS 15 Valentin Angelmann, Paris, France (NBA/IBU)
27.10.31 Young Perez W CO 2 Frankie Genaro, Paris, France (NBA/IBU)
31.10.32 Jackie Brown W RSC 13 Young Perez, Manchester, England (NBA/IBU)
12.06.33 Jackie Brown W PTS 15 Valentin Angelmann, London, England (NBA/IBU)
11.12.33 Jackie Brown W PTS 15 Ginger Foran, Manchester, England (NBA/IBU)
18.06.34 Jackie Brown DREW 15 Valentin Angelmann, Manchester, England (NBA/IBU)
Jackie Brown forfeited IBU recognition (failure to defend against Valentin Angelmann)
09.09.35 Benny Lynch W RTD 2 Jackie Brown, Manchester, England (NBA)
16.09.35 Small Montana W PTS 10 Midget Wolgast, Oakland, USA (NY/CALIF)
06.01.36 Valentin Angelmann W RTD 5 Kid David, Paris, France (IBU)
16.09.36 Benny Lynch W CO 8 Pat Palmer, Glasgow, Scotland (NBA)
12.12.36 Valentin Angelmann W PTS 15 Ernst Weiss, Paris, France (IBU)
Valentin Angelmann ceased to be recognised by the IBU (increasing weight)
19.01.37 Benny Lynch W PTS 15 Small Montana, Wembley, England
13.10.37 Benny Lynch W CO 13 Peter Kane, Glasgow, Scotland
Benny Lynch forfeited title (overweight for scheduled defence against Jackie Jurich)
22.09.38 Peter Kane W PTS 15 Jackie Jurich, Liverpool, England
19.06.43 Jackie Paterson W CO 1 Peter Kane, Glasgow, Scotland
10.07.46 Jackie Paterson W PTS 15 Joe Curran, Glasgow, Scotland
Jackie Paterson forfeited NBA recognition (overweight for scheduled defence against Dado Marino)
20.10.47 Rinty Monaghan W PTS 15 Dado Marino, London, England (NBA)
23.03.48 Rinty Monaghan W CO 7 Jackie Paterson, Belfast, Ireland
05.04.49 Rinty Monaghan W PTS 15 Maurice Sandeyron, Belfast, Ireland
30.09.49 Rinty Monaghan DREW 15 Terry Allen, Belfast, Ireland
Rinty Monaghan relinquished title (retired)
25.04.50 Terry Allen W PTS 15 Honore Pratesi, London, England
01.08.50 Dado Marino W PTS 15 Terry Allen, Honolulu, Hawaii
01.11.51 Dado Marino W PTS 15 Terry Allen, Honolulu, Hawaii
19.05.52 Yoshio Shirai W PTS 15 Dado Marino, Tokyo, Japan
15.11.52 Yoshio Shirai W PTS 15 Dado Marino, Tokyo, Japan
18.05.53 Yoshio Shirai W PTS 15 Tanny Campo, Tokyo, Japan
27.10.53 Yoshio Shirai W PTS 15 Terry Allen, Tokyo, Japan
23.05.54 Yoshio Shirai W PTS 15 Leo Espinosa, Tokyo, Japan
26.11.54 Pascual Perez W PTS 15 Yoshio Shirai, Tokyo, Japan
30.05.55 Pascual Perez W CO 5 Yoshio Shirai, Tokyo, Japan
11.01.56 Pascual Perez W PTS 15 Leo Espinosa, Bs Aires, Argentine
30.06.56 Pascual Perez W RTD 11 Oscar Suarez, Montevideo, Uruguay
03.08.56 Pascual Perez W RSC 5 Ricardo Valdez, Tandil, Argentine
30.03.57 Pascual Perez W CO 1 Dai Dower, Bs Aires, Argentine
07.12.57 Pascual Perez W CO 3 Young Martin, Bs Aires, Argentine
19.04.58 Pascual Perez W PTS 15 Ramon Arias, Caracas, Venezuela
15.12.58 Pascual Perez W PTS 15 Dommy Ursua, Manila, Philippines
10.08.59 Pascual Perez W PTS 15 Kenji Yonekura, Tokyo, Japan
05.11.59 Pascual Perez W CO 13 Sadao Yaoita, Osaka, Japan
16.04.60 Pone Kingpetch W PTS 15 Pascual Perez, Bangkok, Thailand
22.09.60 Pone Kingpetch W RSC 8 Pascual Perez, Los Angeles, USA
27.06.61 Pone Kingpetch W PTS 15 Mitsunori Seki, Tokyo, Japan
30.05.62 Pone Kingpetch W PTS 15 Kyo Noguchi, Tokyo, Japan
10.10.62 Fighting Harada W CO 11 Pone Kingpetch, Tokyo, Japan
12.01.63 Pone Kingpetch W PTS 15 Fighting Harada, Tokyo, Japan
18.09.63 Hiroyuki Ebihara W CO 1 Pone Kingpetch, Tokyo, Japan
23.01.64 Pone Kingpetch W PTS 15 Hiroyuki Ebihara, Bangkok, Thailand
23.04.65 Salvatore Burruni W PTS 15 Pone Kingpetch, Rome, Italy
Salvator Burruni forfeited WBA recognition (failure to defend against Horacio Accavallo)
02.12.65 Salvatore Burruni W CO 13 Rocky Gattellari, Sydney, Australia (WBC)
01.03.66 Horacio Accavallo W PTS 15 Katsuyoshi Takayama, Tokyo, Japan (WBA)
14.06.66 Walter McGowan W PTS 15 Salvatore Burruni, Wembley, England (WBC)
15.07.66 Horacio Accavallo W PTS 15 Hiroyuki Ebihara, Bs Aires, Argentine (WBA)
10.12.66 Horacio Accavallo W PTS 15 Efren Torres, Bs Aires, Argentine (WBA)
30.12.66 Chartchai Chionoi W RSC 9 Walter McGowan, Bangkok, Thailand (WBC)
26.07.67 Chartchai Chionoi W CO 3 Puntip Keosuriya, Bangkok, Thailand (WBC)
13.08.67 Horacio Accavallo W PTS 15 Hiroyuki Ebihara, Bs Aires, Argentine (WBA)
Horacio Accavallo relinquished WBA version of title (retired)
19.09.67 Chartchai Chionoi W RSC 7 Walter McGowan, Wembley, England (WBC)
28.01.68 Chartchai Chionoi W RSC 13 Efren Torres, Mexico C, Mexico (WBC)
10.11.68 Chartchai Chionoi W PTS 15 Bernabe Villacampo, Bangkok, Thailand (WBC)
23.02.69 Efren Torres W RSC 8 Chartchai Chionoi, Mexico C, Mexico (WBC)
30.03.69 Hiroyuki Ebihara W PTS 15 Jose Severino, Sapporo, Japan (WBA)
19.10.69 Bernabe Villacampo W PTS 15 Hiroyuki Ebihara, Tokyo, Japan (WBA)
28.11.69 Efren Torres W PTS 15 Susumu Hanagata, Guadalajara, Mexico (WBC)
20.03.70 Chartchai Chionoi W PTS 15 Efren Torres, Bangkok, Thailand (WBC)
06.04.70 Berkrerk Chartvanchai W PTS 15 Bernabe Villacampo, Bangkok (WBA)
21.10.70 Masao Ohba W RSC 13 Berkrerk Chartvanchai, Tokyo, Japan (WBA)
07.12.70 Erbito Salavarria W RSC 2 Chartchai Chionoi, Bangkok, Thailand (WBC)
01.04.71 Masao Ohba W PTS 15 Betulio Gonzalez, Tokyo, Japan (WBA)
30.04.71 Erbito Salavarria W PTS 15 Susumu Hanagata, Manila, Philippines (WBC)
23.10.71 Masao Ohba W PTS 15 Fernando Cabanela, Tokyo, Japan (WBA)
20.11.71 Erbito Salavarria DREW 15 Betulio Gonzalez, Caracas, Venezuela (WBC)
Erbito Salavarria forfeited WBC recognition (allegedly used an illegal stimulant)
04.03.72 Masao Ohba W PTS 15 Susumu Hanagata, Tokyo, Japan (WBA)
03.06.72 Betulio Gonzalez W CO 4 Socrates Batoto, Caracas, Venezuela (WBC)
20.06.72 Masao Ohba W CO 5 Orlando Amores, Tokyo, Japan (WBA)
29.09.72 Venice Borkorsor W RTD 10 Betulio Gonzalez, Bangkok, Thailand (WBC)
02.01.73 Masao Ohba W RSC 12 Chartchai Chionoi, Tokyo, Japan (WBA)
Masao Ohba left WBA version of title vacant (died in a road accident)
09.02.73 Venice Borkorsor W PTS 15 Erbito Salavarria, Bangkok, Thailand (WBC)
Venice Borkorsor relinquished WBC version of title (moved up to bantamweight)
17.05.73 Chartchai Chionoi W RSC 4 Fritz Chervet, Bangkok, Thailand (WBA)
04.08.73 Betulio Gonzalez W PTS 15 Miguel Canto, Caracas, Venezuela (WBC)
27.10.73 Chartchai Chionoi W PTS 15 Susumu Hanagata, Bangkok, Thailand (WBA)
17.11.73 Betulio Gonzalez W RSC 11 Alberto Morales, Caracas, Venezuela (WBC)
27.04.74 Chartchai Chionoi W PTS 15 Fritz Chervet, Zurich, Switzerland (WBA)
20.07.74 Betulio Gonzalez W RSC 10 Franco Udella, Sabbiadoro, Italy (WBC)
01.10.74 Shoji Oguma W PTS 15 Betulio Gonzalez, Tokyo, Japan (WBC)
18.10.74 Susumu Hanagata W RSC 6 Chartchai Chionoi, Yokohama, Japan (WBA)
08.01.75 Miguel Canto W PTS 15 Shoji Oguma, Sendai, Japan (WBC)
01.04.75 Erbito Salavarria W PTS 15 Susumu Hanagata, Toyama, Japan (WBA)
24.05.75 Miguel Canto W PTS 15 Betulio Gonzalez, Monterrey, Mexico (WBC)
23.08.75 Miguel Canto W RSC 11 Jiro Takada, Merida, Mexico (WBC)
07.10.75 Erbito Salavarria W PTS 15 Susumu Hanagata, Yokohama, Japan (WBA)
13.12.75 Miguel Canto W PTS 15 Ignacio Espinal, Merida, Mexico (WBC)
27.02.76 Alfonso Lopez W RSC 15 Erbito Salavarria, Manila, Philippines (WBA)
21.04.76 Alfonso Lopez W PTS 15 Shoji Oguma, Tokyo, Japan (WBA)
15.05.76 Miguel Canto W PTS 15 Susumu Hanagata, Merida, Mexico (WBC)
02.10.76 Guty Espadas W RSC 13 Alfonso Lopez, Los Angeles, USA (WBA)
03.10.76 Miguel Canto W PTS 15 Betulio Gonzalez, Caracas, Venezuela (WBC)
19.11.76 Miguel Canto W PTS 15 Orlando Javierta, Los Angeles, USA (WBC)
01.01.77 Guty Espadas W RTD 7 Jiro Takada, Tokyo, Japan (WBA)
24.04.77 Miguel Canto W PTS 15 Reyes Arnal, Caracas, Venezuela (WBC)
30.04.77 Guty Espadas W RSC 13 Alfonso Lopez, Merida, Mexico (WBA)
15.06.77 Miguel Canto W PTS 15 Kimio Furesawa, Tokyo, Japan (WBC)
17.09.77 Miguel Canto W PTS 15 Martin Vargas, Merida, Mexico (WBC)
19.11.77 Guty Espadas W CO 8 Alex Santana, Los Angeles, USA (WBA)
30.11.77 Miguel Canto W PTS 15 Martin Vargas, Santiago, Chile (WBC)
02.01.78 Guty Espadas W RSC 7 Kimio Furesawa, Tokyo, Japan (WBA)
04.01.78 Miguel Canto W PTS 15 Shoji Oguma, Tokyo, Japan (WBC)
18.04.78 Miguel Canto W PTS 15 Shoji Oguma, Tokyo, Japan (WBC)
13.08.78 Betulio Gonzalez W PTS 15 Guty Espadas, Maracay, Venezuela (WBA)
04.11.78 Betulio Gonzalez W RSC 12 Martin Vargas, Maracay, Venezuela (WBA)
20.11.78 Miguel Canto W PTS 15 Tacomron Vibonchai, Houston, USA (WBC)
29.01.79 Betulio Gonzalez DREW 15 Shoji Oguma, Hamamatsu, Japan (WBA)
10.02.79 Miguel Canto W PTS 15 Antonio Avelar, Merida, Mexico (WBC)

13.03.79 Chan-He Park W PTS 15 Miguel Canto, Pusan, S Korea (WBC)
19.05.79 Chan-He Park W PTS 15 Tsutomo Igarashi, Seoul, S Korea (WBC)
06.07.79 Betulio Gonzalez W CO 12 Shoji Oguma, Utsunomiya, Japan (WBA)
09.09.79 Chan-He Park DREW 15 Miguel Canto, Seoul, S Korea (WBC)
16.11.79 Luis Ibarra W PTS 15 Betulio Gonzalez, Maracay, Venezuela (WBA)
16.12.79 Chan-He Park W CO 2 Guty Espadas, Pusan, S Korea (WBC)
09.02.80 Chan-He Park W PTS 15 Arnel Arrozal, Seoul, S Korea (WBC)
16.02.80 Tae-Shik Kim W CO 2 Luis Ibarra, Seoul, S Korea (WBA)
13.04.80 Chan-He Park W PTS 15 Alberto Morales, Taegu, S Korea (WBC)
18.05.80 Shoji Oguma W CO 9 Chan-He Park, Seoul, S Korea (WBC)
29.06.80 Tae-Shik Kim W PTS 15 Arnel Arrozal, Seoul, S Korea (WBA)
28.07.80 Shoji Oguma W PTS 15 Sung-Jun Kim, Tokyo, Japan (WBC)
18.10.80 Shoji Oguma W PTS 15 Chan-He Park, Sendai, Japan (WBC)
13.12.80 Peter Mathebula W PTS 15 Tae-Shik Kim, Los Angeles, USA (WBA)
03.02.81 Shoji Oguma W PTS 15 Chan-He Park, Tokyo, Japan (WBC)
28.03.81 Santos Laciar W RSC 7 Peter Mathebula, Orlando, Soweto (WBA)
12.05.81 Antonio Avelar W CO 7 Shoji Oguma, Mito C, Japan (WBC)
06.06.81 Luis Ibarra W PTS 15 Santos Laciar, Bs Aires, Argentine (WBA)
30.08.81 Antonio Avelar W CO 2 Tae-Shik Kim, Seoul, S Korea (WBC)
26.09.81 Juan Herrera W CO 11 Luis Ibarra, Merida, Mexico (WBA)
26.12.81 Juan Herrera W RSC 7 Betulio Gonzalez, Merida, Mexico (WBA)
20.03.82 Prudencio Cardona W CO 1 Antonio Avelar, Tampico, Mexico (WBC)
01.05.82 Santos Laciar W RSC 13 Juan Herrera, Merida, Mexico (WBA)
24.07.82 Freddie Castillo W PTS 15 Prudencio Cardona, Merida, Mexico (WBC)
14.08.82 Santos Laciar W PTS 15 Betulio Gonzalez, Maracaibo, Venezuela (WBA)
05.11.82 Santos Laciar W RSC 13 Steve Muchoki, Copenhagen, Denmark (WBA)
06.11.82 Eleoncio Mercedes W PTS 15 Freddie Castillo, Los Angeles, USA (WBC)
04.03.83 Santos Laciar W CO 9 Ramon Neri, Cordoba, Argentine (WBA)
15.03.83 Charlie Magri W RSC 7 Eleoncio Mercedes, Wembley, England (WBC)
05.05.83 Santos Laciar W RSC 2 Shuichi Hozumi, Shizuoka, Japan (WBA)
17.07.83 Santos Laciar W CO 1 Hi-Sup Shin, Cheju, S Korea (WBA)
27.09.83 Frank Cedeno W RSC 6 Charlie Magri, Wembley, England (WBC)
24.12.83 Soon-Chun Kwon W CO 5 Rene Busayong, Seoul, S Korea (IBF)
18.01.84 Koji Kobayashi W RSC 2 Frank Cedeno, Tokyo, Japan (WBC)
28.01.84 Santos Laciar W PTS 15 Juan Herrera, Marsala, Italy (WBA)
25.02.84 Soon-Chun Kwon W CO 12 Roger Castillo, Seoul, S Korea (IBF)
09.04.84 Gabriel Bernal W CO 2 Koji Kobayashi, Tokyo, Japan (WBC)
19.05.84 Soon-Chun Kwon W PTS 15 Ian Clyde, Daejon, S Korea (IBF)
01.06.84 Gabriel Bernal W RSC 11 Antoine Montero, Nimes, France (WBC)
07.09.84 Soon-Chun Kwon NC 12 Joaquin Caraballo, Chungju, S Korea (IBF)
15.09.84 Santos Laciar W CO 10 Prudencio Cardona, Cordoba, Argentine (WBA)
08.10.84 Sot Chitalada W PTS 12 Gabriel Bernal, Bangkok, Thailand (WBC)
08.12.84 Santos Laciar W PTS 15 Hilario Zapata, Bs Aires, Argentine (WBA)
25.01.85 Soon-Chun Kwon DREW 15 Chong-Kwang Chung, Daejon, S Korea (IBF)
20.02.85 Sot Chitalada W RTD 4 Charlie Magri, London, England (WBC)
14.04.85 Soon-Chun Kwon W CO 3 Shinobu Kawashima, Pohang, S Korea (IBF)
06.05.85 Santos Laciar W PTS 15 Antoine Montero, Grenoble, France (WBA)
Santos Laciar relinquished WBA version of title (moved up to super-flyweight)
22.06.85 Sot Chitalada DREW 12 Gabriel Bernal, Bangkok, Thailand (WBC)
17.07.85 Soon-Chun Kwon DREW 15 Chong-Kwan Chung, Masan, S Korea (IBF)
05.10.85 Hilario Zapata W PTS 15 Alonzo Gonzales, Panama C, Panama (WBA)
20.12.85 Chong-Kwan Chung W RSC 4 Soon-Chun Kwon, Taegu, S Korea (IBF)
31.01.86 Hilario Zapata W PTS 15 Javier Lucas, Panama C, Panama (WBA)
22.02.86 Sot Chitalada W PTS 12 Freddie Castillo, Kuwait (WBC)
07.04.86 Hilario Zapata W PTS 15 Suichi Hozumi, Nirasaki, Japan (WBA)
27.04.86 Bi-Won Chung W PTS 15 Chong-Kwan Chung, Pusan, S Korea (IBF)
05.07.86 Hilario Zapata W PTS 15 Dodie Penalosa, Manila, Philippines (WBA)
02.08.86 Hi-Sup Shin W RSC 15 Bi-Won Chung, Inchon, S Korea (IBF)
13.09.86 Hilario Zapata W PTS 15 Alberto Castro, Panama C, Panama (WBA)
22.11.86 Hi-Sup Shin W RSC 13 Henry Brent, Chunchon, S Korea (IBF)
06.12.86 Hilario Zapata W PTS 15 Claudemir Dias, Salvador, Brazil (WBA)
10.12.86 Sot Chitalada W PTS 12 Gabriel Bernal, Bangkok, Thailand (WBC)
13.02.87 Fidel Bassa W PTS 15 Hilario Zapata, Barranquilla, Colombia (WBA)
22.02.87 Dodie Penalosa W CO 5 Hi-Sup Shin, Inchon, S Korea (IBF)
25.04.87 Fidel Bassa W CO 13 Dave McAuley, Belfast, Ireland (WBA)
15.08.87 Fidel Bassa DREW 15 Hilario Zapata, Panama C, Panama (WBA)
05.09.87 Chang-Ho Choi W CO 11 Dodie Penalosa, Manila, Philippines (IBF)
05.09.87 Sot Chitalada W CO 4 Rae-Ki Ahn, Bangkok, Thailand (WBC)
18.12.87 Fidel Bassa W PTS 12 Felix Marty, Cartagena, Colombia (WBA)
16.01.88 Rolando Bohol W PTS 15 Chang-Ho Choi, Manila, Philippines (IBF)
31.01.88 Sot Chitalada W RSC 7 Hideaki Kamishiro, Osaka, Japan (WBC)
26.03.88 Fidel Bassa W PTS 12 Dave McAuley, Belfast, Ireland (WBA)
06.05.88 Rolando Bohol W PTS 15 Cho-Woon Park, Manila, Philippines (IBF)
23.07.88 Yong-Kang Kim W PTS 12 Sot Chitalada, Pohang, S Korea (WBC)
02.10.88 Fidel Bassa W PTS 12 Raymond Medel, San Antonio, USA (WBA)
05.10.88 Duke McKenzie W CO 11 Rolando Bohol, Wembley, England (IBF)
13.11.88 Yong-Kang Kim W PTS 12 Emil Romano, Chungju, S Korea (WBC)
05.03.89 Yong-Kang Kim W PTS 12 Yukhito Tamakuma, Aomori, Japan (WBC)
08.03.89 Duke McKenzie W RSC 4 Tony de Luca, London, England (IBF)
15.04.89 Fidel Bassa W RSC 6 Julio Gudino, Barranquilla, Colombia (WBA)

Super-Flyweight (115 lbs)

Title Holders

	Birthplace	Tenure	Status
Rafael Orono	Venezuela	1980–1981	WBC
Chul-Ho Kim	S Korea	1981–1982	WBC
Gustavo Ballas	Argentine	1981	WBA
Rafael Pedroza	Panama	1981–1982	WBA
Jiro Watanabe	Japan	1982–1984	WBA
Rafael Orono	Venezuela	1982–1983	WBC
Payao Poontarat	Thailand	1983–1984	WBC
Joo-Do Chun	S Korea	1983–1985	IBF
Jiro Watanabe	Japan	1984–1986	WBC
Elly Pical	Indonesia	1985–1986	IBF
Kaosai Galaxy	Thailand	1984–	WBA
Cesar Polanco	Dom Republic	1986	IBF
Gilberto Roman	Mexico	1986–1987	WBC
Elly Pical	Indonesia	1986–1987	IBF
Santos Laciar	Argentine	1987	WBC
Tae-Il Chang	S Korea	1987	IBF
Jesus Rojas	Colombia	1987–1988	WBC
Elly Pical	Indonesia	1987–	IBF
Gilberto Roman	Mexico	1988–	WBC

Title Bouts

02.02.80 Rafael Orono W PTS 15 Seung-Hoon Lee, Caracas, Venezuela (WBC)
14.04.80 Rafael Orono W PTS 15 Ramon Soria, Caracas, Venezuela (WBC)
28.07.80 Rafael Orono DREW 15 Willie Jensen, Caracas, Venezuela (WBC)
15.09.80 Rafael Orono W RSC 3 Jovito Rengifo, Barquisimeto, Venezuela (WBC)
24.01.81 Chul-Ho Kim W CO 9 Rafael Orono, San Christobal, Venezuela (WBC)
22.04.81 Chul-Ho Kim W PTS 15 Jiro Watanabe, Seoul, S Korea (WBC)
29.07.81 Chul-Ho Kim W CO 13 Willie Jensen, Pusan, S Korea (WBC)
12.09.81 Gustavo Ballas W RSC 8 Sok-Chul Baek, Bs Aires, Argentine (WBA)
18.11.81 Chul-Ho Kim W RSC 9 Jackal Maruyama, Pusan, S Korea (WBC)
05.12.81 Rafael Pedroza W PTS 15 Gustavo Ballas, Panama C, Panama (WBA)
10.02.82 Chul-Ho Kim W CO 8 Koki Ishii, Taegu, S Korea (WBC)
08.04.82 Jiro Watanabe W PTS 15 Rafael Pedroza, Osaka, Japan (WBA)
04.07.82 Chul-Ho Kim DREW 15 Raul Valdez, Daejon, S Korea (WBC)
29.07.82 Jiro Watanabe W RSC 9 Gustavo Ballas, Osaka, Japan (WBA)
11.11.82 Jiro Watanabe W RTD 12 Shoji Oguma, Hamamatsu, Japan (WBA)
28.11.82 Rafael Orono W CO 6 Chul-Ho Kim, Seoul, S Korea (WBC)
31.01.83 Rafael Orono W CO 4 Pedro Romero, Caracas, Venezuela (WBC)
24.02.83 Jiro Watanabe W CO 8 Luis Ibanez, Tsu C, Japan (WBA)
09.05.83 Rafael Orono W PTS 12 Raul Valdez, Caracas, Venezuela (WBC)
23.06.83 Jiro Watanabe W PTS 15 Roberto Ramirez, Sendai, Japan (WBA)
06.10.83 Jiro Watanabe W RTD 11 Soon-Chun Kwon, Osaka, Japan (WBA)
29.10.83 Rafael Orono W RSC 5 Orlando Maldonado, Caracas, Venezuela (WBC)
27.11.83 Payao Poontarat W PTS 12 Rafael Orono, Pattaya, Thailand (WBC)
10.12.83 Joo-Do Chun W CO 5 Ken Kasugai, Osaka, Japan (IBF)
28.01.84 Joo-Do Chun W CO 12 Prayoonsak Muangsurin, Seoul, S Korea (IBF)
15.03.84 Jiro Watanabe W RSC 15 Celso Chavez, Osaka, Japan (WBA)
Jiro Watanabe forfeited WBA recognition (failure to defend against Kaosai Galaxy)
17.03.84 Joo-Do Chun W CO 1 Diego de Villa, Kwangju, S Korea (IBF)
28.03.84 Payao Poontarat W RSC 10 Guty Espadas, Bangkok, Thailand (WBC)
26.05.84 Joo-Do Chun W RSC 6 Felix Marques, Wonju, S Korea (IBF)
05.07.84 Jiro Watanabe W PTS 12 Payao Poontarat, Osaka, Japan (WBC)
20.07.84 Joo-Do Chun W CO 7 William Develos, Pusan, S Korea (IBF)
21.11.84 Kaosai Galaxy W CO 6 Eusebio Espinal, Bangkok, Thailand (WBA)
29.11.84 Jiro Watanabe W RSC 11 Payao Poontarat, Kumamoto, Japan (WBC)
06.01.85 Joo-Do Chun W CO 15 Kwang-Gu Park, Ulsan, S Korea (IBF)
06.03.85 Kaosai Galaxy W CO 7 Dong-Chun Lee, Bangkok, Thailand (WBA)
03.05.85 Elly Pical W RSC 8 Joo-Do Chun, Jakarta, Indonesia (IBF)
09.05.85 Jiro Watanabe W PTS 12 Julio Solano, Tokyo, Japan (WBC)
17.07.85 Kaosai Galaxy W RSC 5 Rafael Orono, Bangkok, Thailand (WBA)
25.08.85 Elly Pical W RSC 3 Wayne Mulholland, Jakarta, Indonesia (IBF)
17.09.85 Jiro Watanabe W RSC 7 Katsuo Katsuma, Osaka, Japan (WBC)
13.12.85 Jiro Watanabe W CO 5 Yun-Sok Hwang, Taegu, S Korea (WBC)
23.12.85 Kaosai Galaxy W RSC 2 Edgar Monserrat, Bangkok, Thailand (WBA)
15.02.86 Cesar Polanco W PTS 15 Elly Pical, Jakarta, Indonesia (IBF)
30.03.86 Gilberto Roman W PTS 12 Jiro Watanabe, Osaka, Japan (WBC)
15.05.86 Gilberto Roman W PTS 12 Edgar Monserrat, Paris, France (WBC)
05.07.86 Elly Pical W CO 3 Cesar Polanco, Jakarta, Indonesia (IBF)
18.07.86 Gilberto Roman W PTS 12 Ruben Condori, Salta, Argentine (WBC)
30.08.86 Gilberto Roman DREW 12 Santos Laciar, Cordoba, Argentine (WBC)
01.11.86 Kaosai Galaxy W CO 5 Israel Contreras, Curacao, DWI (WBA)
03.12.86 Elly Pical W CO 10 Dong-Chun Lee, Jakarta, Indonesia (IBF)
Elly Pical forfeited title (challenged for the WBA S. flyweight title)
15.12.86 Gilberto Roman W PTS 12 Kongtoranee Payakarun, Bangkok, Thailand (WBC)
31.01.87 Gilberto Roman W RSC 9 Antoine Montero, Montpelier, France (WBC)
28.02.87 Kaosai Galaxy W CO 14 Elly Pical, Jakarta, Indonesia (WBA)
19.03.87 Gilberto Roman W PTS 12 Frank Cedeno, Mexicali, Mexico (WBC)
16.05.87 Santos Laciar W RSC 11 Gilberto Roman, Reims, France (WBC)
17.05.87 Tae-Il Chang W PTS 15 Soon-Chun Kwon, Pusan, S Korea (IBF)
08.08.87 Jesus Rojas W PTS 12 Santos Laciar, Miami, USA (WBC)
12.10.87 Kaosai Galaxy W RSC 3 Byong-Kwan Chung, Bangkok, Thailand (WBA)
17.10.87 Elly Pical W PTS 15 Tae-Il Chang, Jakarta, Indonesia (IBF)
24.10.87 Jesus Rojas W RSC 4 Gustavo Ballas, Miami, USA (WBC)
26.01.88 Kaosai Galaxy W PTS 12 Kongtoranee Payakarun, Bangkok, Thailand (WBA)
20.02.88 Elly Pical W PTS 15 Raul Diaz, Pontianak, Indonesia (IBF)
08.04.88 Gilberto Roman W PTS 12 Jesus Rojas, Miami, USA (WBC)
09.07.88 Gilberto Roman W RSC 5 Yoshiyuki Uchida, Kawagoe, Japan (WBC)
03.09.88 Elly Pical W PTS 12 Chang-Ki Kim, Surabaya, Indonesia (IBF)
03.09.88 Gilberto Roman W PTS 12 Kiyoshi Hatanaka, Nagoya, Japan (WBC)
09.10.88 Kaosai Galaxy W CO 8 Chang-Ho Choi, Seoul, S Korea (WBA)
07.11.88 Gilberto Roman W PTS 12 Jesus Rojas, Las Vegas, USA (WBC)
15.01.89 Kaosai Galaxy W CO 2 Tae-Il Chang, Bangkok, Thailand (WBA)
25.02.89 Elly Pical W PTS 12 Mike Phelps, Singapore (IBF)
08.04.89 Kaosai Galaxy W PTS 12 Kenji Matsumura, Yokahama, Japan (WBA)

Bantamweight (118 lbs)

Title Holders

	Birthplace	Tenure	Status
Billy Plimmer	England	1892–1895	
Pedlar Palmer	England	1895–1899	
Terry McGovern*	USA	1899–1900	
Dan Dougherty	USA	1900–1901	
Harry Forbes	USA	1901–1903	
Frankie Neil	USA	1903–1904	
Joe Bowker*	England	1904–1905	
Jimmy Walsh*	USA	1905–1907	
Owen Moran	England	1907	GB
Monte Attell	USA	1909–1910	CALIF
Johnny Coulon	Canada	1910–1911	LOUIS
Frankie Conley	Italy	1910–1911	CALIF
Johnny Coulon	Canada	1911–1914	USA
Digger Stanley	England	1910–1912	GB/IBU
Charles Ledoux	France	1912–1913	GB/IBU
Eddie Campi	USA	1913–1914	GB/IBU
Kid Williams	Denmark	1914	GB/IBU
Kid Williams	Denmark	1914–1917	
Pete Herman	USA	1917–1920	
Joe Lynch	USA	1920–1921	
Pete Herman	USA	1921	
Johnny Buff	USA	1921–1922	
Joe Lynch	USA	1922–1923	
Joe Lynch	USA	1923–1924	NBA
Abe Goldstein	USA	1923–1924	NY
Abe Goldstein	USA	1924	
Eddie Martin	USA	1924–1925	
Charlie Rosenberg	USA	1925–1927	
Teddy Baldock	England	1927	GB
Bud Taylor*	USA	1927–1928	NBA
Willie Smith	S Africa	1927–1929	GB
Bushy Graham*	Italy	1928–1929	NY
Al Brown	Panama	1929–1931	NY/IBU
Pete Sanstol	Norway	1931	NBA
Al Brown	Panama	1931–1934	
Sixto Escobar	Puerto Rico	1934–1935	NBA
Al Brown	Panama	1934–1935	NY/IBU
Baltazar Sangchilli	Spain	1935–1936	NY/IBU
Lou Salica	USA	1935	NBA
Sixto Escobar	Puerto Rico	1935–1936	NBA
Tony Marino	USA	1936	NY/IBU
Sixto Escobar	Puerto Rico	1936–1937	
Harry Jeffra	USA	1937–1938	
Sixto Escobar*	Puerto Rico	1938–1939	
Lou Salica	USA	1940–1942	
Manuel Ortiz	USA	1942–1947	
Harold Dade	USA	1947	
Manuel Ortiz	USA	1947–1950	
Vic Toweel	S Africa	1950–1952	
Jimmy Carruthers*	Australia	1952–1954	
Robert Cohen	Algeria	1954–1956	
Raton Macias	Mexico	1955–1957	NY/EBU
Mario D'Agata	Italy	1956–1957	NBA
Alphonse Halimi	Algeria	1957	NY/EBU
Alphonse Halimi	Algeria	1957–1959	NY/EBU
Joe Becerra*	Mexico	1959–1960	
Alphonse Halimi	Algeria	1960–1961	
Eder Jofre	Brazil	1960–1962	EBU
Johnny Caldwell	Ireland	1961–1962	NBA
Eder Jofre	Brazil	1962–1965	EBU
Fighting Harada	Japan	1965–1968	
Lionel Rose	Australia	1968–1969	
Ruben Olivares	Mexico	1969–1970	
Chuchu Castillo	Mexico	1970–1971	
Ruben Olivares	Mexico	1971–1972	
Rafael Herrera	Mexico	1972	
Enrique Pinder	Panama	1972	
Enrique Pinder	Panama	1972–1973	
Romeo Anaya	Mexico	1973	WBC
Rafael Herrera	Mexico	1973–1974	WBA
Arnold Taylor	S Africa	1973–1974	WBC
Soo-Hwan Hong	S Korea	1974–1975	WBA
Rodolfo Martinez	Mexico	1974–1976	WBA
Alfonso Zamora	Mexico	1975–1977	WBC
Carlos Zarate	Mexico	1976–1979	WBA
Jorge Lujan	Panama	1977–1980	WBC
Lupe Pintor	Mexico	1979–1983	WBA
Julian Solis	Puerto Rico	1980	WBC
Jeff Chandller	USA	1980–1984	WBA
Albert Davila*	USA	1983–1985	WBA
Richard Sandoval	USA	1984–1986	WBC
Satoshi Shingaki	Japan	1984–1985	WBA
Jeff Fenech*	Australia	1985–1987	IBF
Daniel Zaragoza	Mexico	1985	IBF
Miguel Lora	Colombia	1985–1988	WBC
Gaby Canizales	USA	1986	WBC
Bernardo Pinango*	Venezuela	1986–1987	WBA
Takuya Muguruma	Japan	1987	WBA
Kelvin Seabrooks	USA	1987–1988	WBA
Chan-Yung Park	S Korea	1987	IBF
Wilfredo Vasquez	Puerto Rico	1987–1988	WBA
Kaokor Galaxy	Thailand	1988	WBA
Orlando Canizales	USA	1988–	WBA
Sung-Il Moon	S Korea	1988–	IBF
Raul Perez	Mexico	1988–	WBA
			WBC

Title Bouts

09.05.92 Billy Plimmer W PTS 10 Tommy Kelly, New York C, USA
28.12.92 Billy Plimmer W 8 Joe McGrath, New York C, USA
24.09.94 Billy Plimmer DREW 25 Johnny Murphy, New Orleans, USA
26.11.94 Billy Plimmer W CO 3 Charley Kelly, New York C, USA
28.05.95 Billy Plimmer W CO 7 George Corfield, London, England
25.11.95 Pedlar Palmer W DIS 14 Billy Plimmer, London, England
18.10.97 Pedlar Palmer W PTS 20 Dave Sullivan, London, England
12.12.98 Pedlar Palmer W RSC 17 Billy Plimmer, London, England
17.04.99 Pedlar Palmer W RSC 3 Billy Rotchford, London, England
22.09.99 Terry McGovern W CO 1 Pedlar Palmer, Tuckahoe, USA
22.12.99 Terry McGovern W CO 2 Harry Forbes, New York C, USA
Terry McGovern relinquished title (moved up to featherweight)
26.05.00 Dan Dougherty W PTS 20 Tommy Feltz, New York C, USA
04.08.00 Dan Dougherty W PTS 25 Tommy Feltz, New York C, USA
11.11.01 Harry Forbes W CO 2 Dan Dougherty, St Louis, USA
23.01.02 Harry Forbes W CO 4 Dan Dougherty, St Louis, USA
27.02.02 Harry Forbes W PTS 15 Tommy Feltz, St Louis, USA
01.05.02 Harry Forbes DREW 20 Johnny Reagan, St Louis, USA
23.12.02 Harry Forbes W RSC 7 Frankie Neil, Oakland, USA
27.02.03 Harry Forbes W PTS 10 Andrew Tokell, Detroit, USA
13.08.03 Frankie Neil W CO 2 Harry Forbes, San Francisco, USA
04.09.03 Frankie Neil W CO 15 Billy de Coursey, Los Angeles, USA
16.10.03 Frankie Neil DREW 20 Johnny Reagan, Los Angeles, USA
17.06.04 Frankie Neil W CO 3 Harry Forbes, Chicago, USA
17.10.04 Joe Bowker W PTS 20 Frankie Neil, London, England
29.05.05 Joe Bowker W PTS 20 Pinky Evans, London, England
Jow Bowker relinquished title (moved up to featherweight)
20.10.05 Jimmy Walsh W PTS 15 Digger Stanley, Chelsea, Mass, USA
Jimmy Walsh relinquished title (moved up to featherweight)
22.04.07 Owen Moran W PTS 20 Al Delmont, London, England (GB)
Owen Moran ceased to be recognised by GB (unable to make the weight he campaigned as a featherweight)
19.06.09 Monte Attell W CO 18 Frankie Neil, San Francisco, USA (CALIF)
17.12.09 Monte Attell DREW 20 Danny Webster, San Francisco, USA (CALIF)
19.02.10 Johnny Coulon W PTS 10 Jim Kendrick, New Orleans, USA (LOUIS)
22.02.10 Frankie Conley W CO 42 Monte Attell, Los Angeles, USA (CALIF)
06.03.10 Johnny Coulon W CO 19 Jim Kendrick, New Orleans, USA (LOUIS)
17.10.10 Digger Stanley W CO 8 Joe Bowker, London, England (GB)
05.12.10 Digger Stanley W PTS 20 Johnny Condon, London, England (GB)
19.12.10 Johnny Coulon NC 3 Earl Denning, Memphis, USA (LOUIS)
26.02.11 Johnny Coulon W PTS 20 Frankie Conley, New Orleans, USA (USA)
14.09.11 Digger Stanley W PTS 20 Ike Bradley, Liverpool, England (GB)
03.02.12 Johnny Coulon W PTS 20 Frankie Conley, Los Angeles, USA (USA)
18.02.12 Johnny Coulon W PTS 20 Frankie Burns, New Orleans, USA (USA)
22.04.12 Digger Stanley W PTS 20 Charles Ledoux, London, England (GB/IBU)
23.06.12 Charles Ledoux W CO 7 Digger Stanley, Dieppe, France (GB/IBU)
24.06.13 Eddie Campi W PTS 20 Charles Ledoux, Los Angeles, USA (GB/IBU)
31.01.14 Kid Williams W CO 12 Eddie Campi, Los Angeles, USA (GB/IBU)
09.06.14 Kid Williams W CO 3 Johnny Coulon, Los Angeles, USA
28.09.14 Kid Williams W CO 4 Kid Herman, Philadelphia, USA
06.12.15 Kid Williams DREW 20 Frankie Burns, New Orleans, USA
07.02.16 Kid Williams DREW 20 Pete Herman, New Orleans, USA
09.01.17 Pete Herman W PTS 20 Kid Williams, New Orleans, USA
05.11.17 Pete Herman W PTS 20 Frankie Burns, New Orleans, USA
22.12.20 Joe Lynch W PTS 15 Pete Herman, New York C, USA
25.07.21 Pete Herman W PTS 15 Joe Lynch, New York C, USA
23.09.21 Johnny Buff W PTS 15 Pete Herman, New York C, USA
10.11.21 Johnny Buff W PTS 15 Jackie Sharkey, New York C, USA
10.07.22 Joe Lynch W RTD 14 Johnny Buff, New York C, USA
22.12.22 Joe Lynch W PTS 15 Midget Smith, New York C, USA
Joe Lynch forfeited NY recognition (withdrew from a scheduled defence against Joe Burman)
10.10.23 Abe Goldstein W PTS 12 Joe Burman, New York C, USA (NY)
21.03.24 Abe Goldstein W PTS 15 Joe Lynch, New York C, USA
16.07.24 Abe Goldstein W PTS 15 Charles Ledoux, New York C, USA
08.09.24 Abe Goldstein W PTS 15 Tommy Ryan, New York C, USA
19.12.24 Eddie Martin W PTS 15 Abe Goldstein, New York C, USA
20.03.25 Charlie Rosenberg W PTS 15 Eddie Martin, New York C, USA
23.07.25 Charlie Rosenberg W CO 4 Eddie Shea, New York C, USA
02.03.26 Charlie Rosenberg W PTS 10 George Butch, St Louis, USA
Charlie Rosenberg forfeited title (overweight for defence against Bushy Graham)
26.03.27 Bud Taylor DREW 10 Tony Canzoneri, Chicago, USA (NBA)
05.05.27 Teddy Baldock W PTS 15 Archie Bell, London, England (GB)
24.06.27 Bud Taylor W PTS 10 Tony Canzoneri, Chicago, USA (NBA)
Bud Taylor relinquished NBA version of title (weight making difficulties)
06.10.27 Willie Smith W PTS 15 Teddy Baldock, London, England (GB)
Willie Smith ceased to be recognised in GB (made no effort to defend)
23.05.28 Bushy Graham W PTS 15 Izzy Schwartz, New York C, USA (NY)
Bushy Graham relinquished NY version of title (weight making difficulties)
18.06.29 Al Brown W PTS 15 Vidal Gregorio, New York C, USA (NY)
28.08.29 Al Brown W PTS 10 Knud Larsen, Copenhagen, Denmark (NY/IBU)

08.02.30 Al Brown W DIS 4 Johnny Erickson, New York C, USA (NY/IBU)
04.10.30 Al Brown W PTS 15 Eugene Huat, Paris, France (NY/IBU)
11.02.31 Al Brown W PTS 10 Nick Bensa, Paris, France (NY/IBU)
20.05.31 Pete Sanstol W PTS 10 Archie Bell, Montreal, Canada (NBA)
25.08.31 Al Brown W PTS 15 Pete Sanstol, Montreal, Canada
27.10.31 Al Brown W PTS 15 Eugene Huat, Montreal, Canada
10.07.32 Al Brown W PTS 15 Kid Francis, Marseilles, France
19.09.32 Al Brown W CO 1 Emile Pladner, Toronto, Canada
18.03.33 Al Brown W PTS 12 Dom Bernasconi, Milan, Italy
03.07.33 Al Brown W PTS 15 Johnny King, Manchester, England
19.02.34 Al Brown W PTS 15 Young Perez, Paris, France
Al Brown forfeited NBA recognition (failure to defend against Baby Casanova)
26.06.34 Sixto Escobar W CO 9 Baby Casanova, Montreal, Canada (NBA)
08.08.34 Sixto Escobar W PTS 15 Eugene Huat, Montreal, Canada (NBA)
01.11.34 Al Brown W CO 10 Young Perez, Tunis, Tunisia (NY/IBU)
01.06.35 Baltazar Sangchilli W PTS 15 Al Brown, Valencia, Spain (NY/IBU)
26.08.35 Lou Salica W PTS 15 Sixto Escobar, New York C, USA (NBA)
15.11.35 Sixto Escobar W PTS 15 Lou Salica, New York C, USA (NBA)
29.06.36 Tony Marino W CO 14 Baltazar Sangchilli, New York C, USA (NY/IBU)
31.08.36 Sixto Escobar W RSC 13 Tony Marino, New York C, USA
13.10.36 Sixto Escobar W CO 1 Carlos Quintana, New York C, USA
21.02.37 Sixto Escobar W PTS 15 Lou Salica, San Juan, Puerto Rico
23.09.37 Harry Jeffra W PTS 15 Sixto Escobar, New York C, USA
20.02.38 Sixto Escobar W PTS 15 Harry Jeffra, San Juan, Puerto Rico
02.04.39 Sixto Escobar W PTS 15 Kayo Morgan, San Juan, Puerto Rico
Sixto Escobar relinquished title (weight making difficulties)
04.03.40 Lou Salica DREW 15 George Pace, Toronto, Canada (NBA)
24.09.40 Lou Salica W PTS 15 George Pace, New York C, USA
13.01.41 Lou Salica W PTS 15 Tommy Forte, Philadelphia, USA
25.04.41 Lou Salica W PTS 15 Lou Transparenti, Baltimore, USA
16.06.41 Lou Salica W PTS 15 Tommy Forte, Philadelphia, USA
07.08.42 Manuel Ortiz W PTS 12 Lou Salica, Los Angeles, USA
01.01.43 Manuel Ortiz W PTS 10 Kenny Lindsay, Portland, USA
27.01.43 Manuel Ortiz W RSC 10 George Freitas, Oakland, USA
10.03.43 Manuel Ortiz W RSC 11 Lou Salica, Oakland, USA
28.04.43 Manuel Ortiz W CO 6 Lupe Cordoza, Fort Worth, USA
26.05.43 Manuel Ortiz W PTS 15 Joe Robleto, Los Angeles, USA
12.07.43 Manuel Ortiz W CO 7 Joe Robleto, Seattle, USA
01.10.43 Manuel Ortiz W CO 4 Leonardo Lopez, Los Angeles, USA
23.11.43 Manuel Ortiz W PTS 15 Benny Goldberg, Los Angeles, USA
14.03.44 Manuel Ortiz W PTS 15 Ernesto Aguilar, Los Angeles, USA
04.04.44 Manuel Ortiz W PTS 15 Tony Olivera, Los Angeles, USA
12.09.44 Manuel Ortiz W CO 4 Luis Castillo, Los Angeles, USA
14.11.44 Manuel Ortiz W RSC 9 Luis Castillo, Los Angeles, USA
25.02.46 Manuel Ortiz W CO 13 Luis Castillo, San Francisco, USA
18.05.46 Manuel Ortiz W CO 5 Kenny Lindsay, Los Angeles, USA
10.06.46 Manuel Ortiz W CO 11 Jackie Jurich, San Francisco, USA
06.01.47 Harold Dade W PTS 15 Manuel Ortiz, San Francisco, USA
11.03.47 Manuel Ortiz W PTS 15 Harold Dade, Los Angeles, USA
30.05.47 Manuel Ortiz W PTS 15 Kui Kong Young, Honolulu, Hawaii
20.12.47 Manuel Ortiz W PTS 15 Tirso del Rosario, Manila, Philippines
04.07.48 Manuel Ortiz W RSC 8 Memo Valero, Mexicali, Mexico
01.03.49 Manuel Ortiz W PTS 15 Dado Marino, Honolulu, Hawaii
31.05.50 Vic Toweel W PTS 15 Manuel Ortiz, Johannesburg, S Africa
02.12.50 Vic Toweel W RTD 10 Danny O'Sullivan, Johannesburg, S Africa
17.11.51 Vic Toweel W PTS 15 Luis Romero, Johannesburg, S Africa
26.01.52 Vic Toweel W PTS 15 Peter Keenan, Johannesburg, S Africa
15.11.52 Jimmy Carruthers W CO 1 Vic Toweel, Johannesburg, S Africa
21.03.53 Jimmy Carruthers W CO 10 Vic Toweel, Johannesburg, S Africa
13.11.53 Jimmy Carruthers W PTS 15 Pappy Gault, Sydney, Australia
02.05.54 Jimmy Carruthers W PTS 12 Chamrern Songkitrat, Bangkok, Thailand
Jimmy Carruthers relinquished title (retired)
19.09.54 Robert Cohen W PTS 15 Chamrern Songkitrat, Bangkok, Thailand (NY/EBU)
09.03.55 Raton Macias W RSC 11 Chamrern Songkitrat, San Francisco, USA (NBA)
03.09.55 Robert Cohen DREW 15 Willie Toweel, Johannesburg, S Africa (NY/EBU)
25.03.56 Raton Macias W CO 10 Leo Espinosa, Mexico C, Mexico (NBA)
29.06.56 Mario D'Agata W RTD 6 Robert Cohen, Rome, Italy (NY/EBU)
01.04.57 Alphonse Halimi W PTS 15 Mario D'Agata, Paris, France (NY/EBU)
15.06.57 Raton Macias W RSC 11 Dommy Ursua, San Francisco, USA (NBA)
06.11.57 Alphonse Halimi W PTS 15 Raton Macias, Los Angeles, USA
08.07.59 Joe Becerra W CO 8 Alphonse Halimi, Los Angeles, USA
04.02.60 Joe Becerra W CO 9 Alphonse Halimi, Los Angeles, USA
23.05.60 Joe Becerra W PTS 15 Kenji Yonekura, Tokyo, Japan
Joe Becerra relinquished title (retired)
25.10.60 Alphonse Halimi W PTS 15 Freddie Gilroy, Wembley, England (EBU)
18.11.60 Eder Jofre W CO 6 Eloy Sanchez, Los Angeles, USA (NBA)
25.03.61 Eder Jofre W RTD 9 Piero Rollo, Rio de Janeiro, Brazil (NBA)
30.05.61 Johnny Caldwell W PTS 15 Alphonse Halimi, Wembley, England (EBU)
19.08.61 Eder Jofre W RSC 7 Ramon Arias, Caracas, Venezuela (NBA)
31.10.61 Johnny Caldwell W PTS 15 Alphonse Halimi, Wembley, England (EBU)
18.01.62 Eder Jofre W RTD 10 Johnny Caldwell, Sao Paulo, Brazil
04.05.62 Eder Jofre W RSC 10 Herman Marquez, San Francisco, USA
11.09.62 Eder Jofre W CO 6 Joe Medel, Sao Paulo, Brazil
04.04.63 Eder Jofre W CO 3 Katsutoshi Aoki, Tokyo, Japan
18.05.63 Eder Jofre W RTD 11 Johnny Jamito, Quezon C, Philippines
27.11.64 Eder Jofre W CO 7 Bernardo Caraballo, Bogota, Colombia
17.05.65 Fighting Harada W PTS 15 Eder Jofre, Nagoya, Japan
30.11.65 Fighting Harada W PTS 15 Alan Rudkin, Tokyo, Japan
01.06.66 Fighting Harada W PTS 15 Eder Jofre, Tokyo, Japan
03.01.67 Fighting Harada W PTS 15 Joe Medel, Nagoya, Japan
04.07.67 Fighting Harada W PTS 15 Bernardo Caraballo, Tokyo, Japan
26.02.68 Lionel Rose W PTS 15 Fighting Harada, Tokyo, Japan
02.07.68 Lionel Rose W PTS 15 Takao Sakurai, Tokyo, Japan
06.12.68 Lionel Rose W PTS 15 Chuchu Castillo, Los Angeles, USA
08.03.69 Lionel Rose W PTS 15 Alan Rudkin, Melbourne, Australia
22.08.69 Ruben Olivares W CO 5 Lionel Rose, Los Angeles, USA
12.12.69 Ruben Olivares W RSC 2 Alan Rudkin, Los Angeles, USA
18.04.70 Ruben Olivares W PTS 15 Chuchu Castillo, Los Angeles, USA
16.10.70 Chuchu Castillo W RSC 14 Ruben Olivares, Los Angeles, USA
03.04.71 Ruben Olivares W PTS 15 Chucho Castillo, Los Angeles, USA
25.10.71 Ruben Olivares W RSC 14 Katsutoshi Kanazawa, Nagoya, Japan
14.12.71 Ruben Olivares W RSC 11 Jesus Pimental, Los Angeles, USA
19.03.72 Rafael Herrera W CO 8 Ruben Olivares, Mexico C, Mexico
30.07.72 Enrique Pinder W PTS 15 Rafael Herrera, Panama C, Panama
Enrique Pinder forfeited WBC recognition (failure to defend against the stipulated challenger)
20.01.73 Romeo Anaya W CO 3 Enrique Pinder, Panama C, Panama (WBA)
15.04.73 Rafael Herrera W RSC 12 Rodolfo Martinez, Monterrey, Mexico (WBC)
28.04.73 Romeo Anaya W PTS 15 Rogelio Lara, Los Angeles, USA (WBA)
18.08.73 Romeo Anaya W CO 3 Enrique Pinder, Los Angeles, USA (WBA)
13.10.73 Rafael Herrera W PTS 15 Venice Borkorsor, Los Angeles, USA (WBC)
03.11.73 Arnold Taylor W CO 14 Romeo Anaya, Johannesburg, S Africa (WBA)
25.05.74 Rafael Herrera W CO 6 Romeo Anaya, Mexico C, Mexico (WBC)
03.07.74 Soo-Hwan Hong W PTS 15 Arnold Taylor, Durban, S Africa (WBA)
07.12.74 Rodolfo Martinez W RSC 4 Rafael Herrera, Merida, Mexico (WBC)
28.12.74 Soo-Hwan Hong W PTS 15 Fernando Canabela, Seoul, S Korea (WBA)
14.03.75 Alfonso Zamora W CO 4 Soo-Hwan Hong, Los Angeles, USA (WBA)
31.05.75 Rodolfo Martinez W RSC 7 Nestor Jiminez, Bogota, Colombia (WBC)
30.08.75 Alfonso Zamora W CO 4 Thanomjit Sukhothhai, Los Angeles, USA (WBA)
08.10.75 Rodolfo Martinez W PTS 15 Hisami Numata, Sendai, Japan (WBC)
06.12.75 Alfonso Zamora W CO 1 Socrates Batoto, Mexico C, Mexico (WBA)
30.01.76 Rodolfo Martinez W PTS 15 Venice Borkorsor, Bangkok, Thailand (WBC)
03.04.76 Alfonso Zamora W CO 2 Eusebio Pedroza, Mexicali, Mexico (WBA)
08.05.76 Carlos Zarate W CO 9 Rodolfo Martinez, Los Angeles, USA (WBC)
10.07.76 Alfonso Zamora W CO 3 Gilberto Illueca, Juarez, Mexico (WBA)
28.08.76 Carlos Zarate W RSC 12 Paul Ferreri, Los Angeles, USA (WBC)
16.10.76 Alfonso Zamora W RSC 12 Soo-Hwan Hong, Inchon, S Korea (WBA)
13.11.76 Carloz Zarate W CO 4 Waruinge Nakayama, Culiacan, Mexico (WBC)
05.02.77 Carlos Zarate W RSC 3 Fernando Cabanela, Mexico C, Mexico (WBC)
29.10.77 Carlos Zarate W RSC 6 Danilio Batista, Los Angeles, USA (WBC)
19.11.77 Jorge Lujan W CO 10 Alfonso Zamora, Los Angeles, USA (WBA)
02.12.77 Carlos Zarate W RSC 5 Juan Francisco Rodriguez, Madrid, Spain (WBC)
25.02.78 Carlos Zarate W RSC 8 Albert Davila, Los Angeles, USA (WBC)
18.03.78 Jorge Lujan W RTD 11 Roberto Rubaldino, San Antonio, USA (WBA)
22.04.78 Carlos Zarate W RSC 13 Andres Hernandez, San Juan, Puerto Rico (WBC)
09.06.78 Carlos Zarate W CO 4 Emilio Hernandez, Las Vegas, USA (WBC)
15.09.78 Jorge Lujan W PTS 15 Albert Davila, New Orleans, USA (WBA)
10.03.79 Carlos Zarate W CO 3 Mensah Kpalongo, Los Angeles, USA (WBC)
08.04.79 Jorge Lujan W RSC 15 Cleo Garcia, Las Vegas, USA (WBA)
02.06.79 Lupe Pintor W PTS 15 Carlos Zarate, Las Vegas, USA (WBC)
06.10.79 Jorge Lujan W CO 15 Roberto Rubaldino, McAllen, USA (WBA)
09.02.80 Lupe Pintor W RSC 12 Alberto Sandoval, Los Angeles, USA (WBC)
02.04.80 Jorge Lujan W RSC 9 Shuichi Isogami, Tokyo, Japan (WBA)
11.06.80 Lupe Pintor DREW 15 Eijiro Murata, Tokyo, Japan (WBC)
29.08.80 Julian Solis W PTS 15 Jorge Lujan, Miami, USA (WBA)
19.09.80 Lupe Pintor W CO 12 Johnny Owen, Los Angeles, USA (WBC)
14.11.80 Jeff Chandler W RSC 14 Julian Solis, Miami, USA (WBA)
19.12.80 Lupe Pintor W PTS 15 Albert Davila, Las Vegas, USA (WBC)
31.01.81 Jeff Chandler W PTS 15 Jorge Lujan, Philadelphia, USA (WBA)
22.02.81 Lupe Pintor W PTS 15 Jose Uziga, Houston, USA (WBC)
05.04.81 Jeff Chandler DREW 15 Eijiro Murata, Tokyo, Japan (WBA)
25.07.81 Jeff Chandler W CO 7 Julian Solis, Atlantic C, USA (WBA)
26.07.81 Lupe Pintor W RSC 8 Jovito Rengifo, Las Vegas, USA (WBC)
22.09.81 Lupe Pintor W CO 15 Hurricane Teru, Nagoya, Japan (WBC)
10.12.81 Jeff Chandler W RSC 13 Eijiro Murata, Atlantic C, USA (WBA)
27.03.82 Jeff Chandler W RSC 6 Johnny Carter, Philadelphia, USA (WBA)
03.06.82 Lupe Pintor W RSC 11 Seung-Hoon Lee, Los Angeles, USA (WBC)
Lupe Pintor forfeited WBC recognition (unable to defend due to a motorcycle accident)
27.10.82 Jeff Chandler W RSC 9 Miguel Iriarle, Atlantic C, USA (WBA)
13.03.83 Jeff Chandler W PTS 15 Gaby Canizales, Atlantic C, USA (WBA)
01.09.83 Albert Davila W CO 12 Kiko Bejines, Los Angeles, USA (WBC)
11.09.83 Jeff Chandler W RSC 10 Eijiro Murata, Tokyo, Japan (WBA)
17.12.83 Jeff Chandler W RSC 7 Oscar Muniz, Atlantic C, USA (WBA)
07.04.84 Richard Sandoval W RSC 15 Jeff Chandler, Atlantic C, USA (WBA)
16.04.84 Satoshi Shingaki W RSC 8 Elmer Magallano, Kashiwara, Japan (IBF)
26.05.84 Albert Davila W RSC 11 Enrique Sanchez, Miami, USA (WBC)
Albert Davila relinquished WBC version of title (back injury)
04.08.84 Satoshi Shingaki W PTS 15 Joves de la Puz, Naha C, Japan (IBF)
22.09.84 Richard Sandoval W PTS 15 Edgar Roman, Monte Carlo (WBA)
15.12.84 Richard Sandoval W RSC 8 Cardenio Ulloa, Miami, USA (WBA)
26.04.85 Jeff Fenech W RSC 9 Satoshi Shingaki, Sydney, Australia (IBF)
04.05.85 Daniel Zaragoza W DIS 7 Fred Jackson, Aruba, DWI (WBC)
09.08.85 Miguel Lora W PTS 12 Daniel Zaragoza, Miami, USA (WBC)
23.08.85 Jeff Fenech W CO 3 Satoshi Shingaki, Sydney, Australia (IBF)
02.12.85 Jeff Fenech W PTS 15 Jerome Coffee, Sydney, Australia (IBF)
08.02.86 Miguel Lora W PTS 12 Wilfredo Vasquez, Miami, USA (WBC)
10.03.86 Gaby Canizales W RSC 7 Richard Sandoval, Las Vegas, USA (WBA)
04.06.86 Bernardo Pinango W PTS 15 Gaby Canizales, E Rutherford, USA (WBA)
18.07.86 Jeff Fenech W RSC 14 Steve McCrory, Sydney, Australia (IBF)
Jeff Fenech relinquished title (challenged for the WBC super-bantamweight title)
23.08.86 Miguel Lora W RSC 6 Enrique Sanchez, Miami, USA (WBC)
04.10.86 Bernardo Pinango W RSC 10 Ciro de Leva, Turin, Italy (WBA)
15.11.86 Miguel Lora W PTS 12 Albert Davila, Barranquilla, Colombia (WBC)

22.11.86 Bernardo Pinango W RSC 15 Simon Skosana, Johannesburg, S Africa (WBA)
03.02.87 Bernardo Pinango W PTS 15 Frankie Duarte, Los Angeles, USA (WBA)
Bernardo Pinango relinquished title (retired)
29.03.87 Takuya Muguruma W CO 5 Azael Moran, Moriguchi, Japan (WBA)
15.05.87 Kelvin Seabrooks W CO 5 Miguel Maturana, Cartagena, Colombia (IBF)
24.05.87 Chan-Yung Park W RSC 11 Takuya Muguruma, Moriguchi, Japan (WBA)
04.07.87 Kelvin Seabrooks NC 9 Thierry Jacob, Calais, France (IBF)
25.07.87 Miguel Lora W RSC 4 Antonio Avelar, Miami, USA (WBC)
04.10.87 Wilfredo Vasquez W RSC 10 Chan-Yung Park, Seoul, S Korea (WBA)
18.11.87 Kelvin Seabrooks W RSC 4 Ernie Cataluna, San Cataldo, Italy (IBF)
27.11.87 Miguel Lora W PTS 12 Ray Minus, Miami, USA (WBC)
17.01.88 Wilfredo Vasquez DREW 12 Takuya Maguruma, Osaka, Japan (WBA)
06.02.88 Kelvin Seabrooks W RSC 2 Fernando Beltran, Paris, France (IBF)
30.04.88 Miguel Lora W PTS 12 Lucio Lopez, Cartagena, Colombia (WBC)
09.05.88 Kaokor Galaxy W PTS 12 Wilfredo Vasquez, Bangkok, Thailand (WBA)
07.07.88 Orlando Canizales W RSC 15 Kelvin Seabrooks, Atlantic C, USA (IBF)
01.08.88 Miguel Lora W PTS 12 Albert Davila, Los Angeles, USA (WBC)
14.08.88 Sung-Il Moon W TD 6 Kaokor Galaxy, Pusan, S Korea (WBA)
29.10.88 Raul Perez W PTS 12 Miguel Lora, Las Vegas, USA (WBC)
27.10.88 Sung-Il Moon W CO 7 Edgar Monserrat, Seoul, S Korea (WBA)
29.11.88 Orlando Canizales W CO 1 Jimmy Navarro, San Antonio, USA (IBF)
19.02.89 Sung-Il Moon W RSC 5 Chaiki Kobayashi, Taejon, S Korea (WBA)
09.03.89 Raul Perez W PTS 12 Lucio Lopez, Los Angeles, USA (WBC)

Super-Bantamweight (122 lbs)

Title Holders

	Birthplace	Tenure	Status
Jack Kid Wolfe	USA	1922–1923	NY
Rigoberto Riasco	Panama	1976	WBC
Royal Kobayashi	Japan	1976	WBC
Dong-Kyun Yum	S Korea	1976–1977	WBC
Wilfredo Gomez*	Puerto Rico	1977–1983	WBC
Soo-Hwan Hong	S Korea	1977–1978	WBA
Ricardo Cardona	Colombia	1978–1980	WBA
Leo Randolph	USA	1980	WBA
Sergio Palma	Argentine	1980–1982	WBA
Leonardo Cruz	Dom Republic	1982–1984	WBA
Jaime Garza	USA	1983–1984	WBC
Bobby Berna	Philippines	1983–1984	IBF
Loris Stecca	Italy	1984	WBA
Seung-In Suh	S Korea	1984–1985	IBF
Victor Callejas	Puerto Rico	1984–1986	WBA
Juan Meza	Mexico	1984–1985	WBC
Ji-Won Kim*	S Korea	1985–1986	IBF
Lupe Pintor	Mexico	1985–1986	WBC
Samart Payakarun	Thailand	1986–1987	WBC
Louie Espinosa	USA	1987	WBA
Seung-Hoon Lee*	S Korea	1987–1988	IBF
Jeff Fenech*	Australia	1987–1988	WBC
Julio Gervacio	Dom Republic	1987–1988	WBA
Bernardo Pinango	Venezuela	1988	WBA
Daniel Zaragoza	Mexico	1988–	WBC
Jose Sanabria	Venezuela	1988–1989	IBF
Juan J. Estrada	Mexico	1988–	WBA
Fabrice Benichou	France	1989–	IBF

Title Bouts

21.09.22 Jack Kid Wolfe W PTS 15 Joe Lynch, New York C, USA (NY)
Jack Kid Wolfe ceased to be recognised by NY (overweight for defence against Carl Duane – title fell into disuse)
03.04.76 Rigoberto Riasco W RTD 8 Waruinge Nakayama, Panama C, Panama (WBC)
12.06.76 Rigoberto Riasco W CO 10 Livio Nolasco, Panama C, Panama (WBC)
01.08.76 Rigoberto Riasco W PTS 15 Dong-Kyun Yum, Pusan, S Korea (WBC)
10.10.76 Royal Kobayashi W RSC 8 Rigoberto Riasco, Tokyo, Japan (WBC)
24.11.76 Dong-Kyun Yum W PTS 15 Royal Kobayashi, Seoul, S Korea (WBC)
13.02.77 Dong-Kyun Yum W PTS 15 Jose Cervantes, Seoul, S Korea (WBC)
21.05.77 Wilfredo Gomez W CO 12 Dong-Kyun Yum, San Juan, Puerto Rico (WBC)
11.07.77 Wilfredo Gomez W CO 5 Raol Tirado, San Juan, Puerto Rico (WBC)
26.11.77 Soo-Hwan Hong W CO 3 Hector Carrasquilla, Panama C, Panama (WBA)
19.01.78 Wilfredo Gomez W CO 3 Royal Kobayashi, Kitakyushu, Japan (WBC)
01.02.78 Soo-Hwan Hong W PTS 15 Yu Kasahara, Tokyo, Japan (WBA)
08.04.78 Wilfredo Gomez W RSC 7 Juan Antonio Lopez, Bayamon, Puerto Rico (WBC)
06.05.78 Ricardo Cardona W RSC 12 Soo-Hwan Hong, Seoul, S Korea (WBA)
02.06.78 Wilfredo Gomez W RSC 3 Sakad Petchyindee, Korat, Thailand (WBC)
02.09.78 Ricardo Cardona W PTS 15 Ruben Valdez, Cartagena, Colombia (WBA)
09.09.78 Wilfredo Gomez W RSC 13 Leonardo Cruz, San Juan, Puerto Rico (WBC)
28.10.78 Wilfredo Gomez W RSC 5 Carlos Zarate, San Juan, Puerto Rico (WBC)
12.11.78 Ricardo Cardona W PTS 15 Soon-Hyun Chung, Seoul, S Korea (WBA)
09.03.79 Wilfredo Gomez W RSC 5 Nestor Jimenez, New York C, USA (WBC)
16.06.79 Wilfredo Gomez W RSC 5 Jesus Hernandez, San Juan, Puerto Rico (WBC)
23.06.79 Ricardo Cardona W PTS 15 Soon-Hyun Chung, Seoul, S Korea (WBA)
06.09.79 Ricardo Cardona W PTS 15 Yukio Segawa, Hachinohe, Japan (WBA)
28.09.79 Wilfredo Gomez W RSC 10 Carlos Mendoza, Las Vegas, USA (WBC)
26.10.79 Wilfredo Gomez W RSC 5 Nicky Perez, New York C, USA (WBC)
15.12.79 Ricardo Cardona W PTS 15 Sergio Palma, Barranquilla, Colombia (WBA)
03.02.80 Wilfredo Gomez W RTD 6 Ruben Valdez, Las Vegas, USA (WBC)
04.05.80 Leo Randolph W RSC 15 Ricardo Cardona, Seattle, USA (WBA)
09.08.80 Sergio Palma W CO 6 Leo Randolph, Washington, USA (WBA)
22.08.80 Wilfredo Gomez W RSC 5 Derrick Holmes, Las Vegas, USA (WBC)
08.11.80 Sergio Palma W RSC 9 Ulisses Morales, Bs Aires, Argentine (WBA)
13.12.80 Wilfredo Gomez W CO 3 Jose Cervantes, Miami, USA (WBC)
04.04.81 Sergio Palma W PTS 15 Leonardo Cruz, Bs Aires, Argentine (WBA)
15.08.81 Sergio Palma W RSC 12 Ricardo Cardona, Bs Aires, Argentine (WBA)
03.10.81 Sergio Palma W PTS 15 Vichit Muangroi-et, Bs Aires, Argentine (WBA)
15.01.82 Sergio Palma W PTS 15 Jorge Lujan, Cordoba, Argentine (WBA)
27.03.82 Wilfredo Gomez W RSC 6 Juan Meza, Atlantic C, USA (WBC)
11.06.82 Wilfredo Gomez W CO 10 Juan Antonio Lopez, Las Vegas, USA (WBC)
12.06.82 Leonardo Cruz W PTS 15 Sergio Palma, Miami, USA (WBA)
18.08.82 Wilfredo Gomez W RTD 7 Roberto Rubaldino, San Juan, Puerto Rico (WBC)
13.11.82 Leonardo Cruz W CO 8 Benito Badilla, San Juan, Puerto Rico (WBA)
03.12.82 Wilfredo Gomez W RSC 14 Lupe Pintor, New Orleans, USA (WBC)
Wilfredo Gomez reliquished WBC version of title (moved up to featherweight)
16.03.83 Leonardo Cruz W PTS 15 Soon-Hyun Chung, San Juan, Puerto Rico (WBA)
15.06.83 Jaime Garza W RSC 2 Bobby Berna, Los Angeles, USA (WBC)
26.08.83 Leonardo Cruz W PTS 15 Cleo Garcia, St Domingo, Dom Republic (WBA)
04.12.83 Bobby Berna W RTD 11 Seung-In Suh, Seoul, S Korea (IBF)
22.02.84 Loris Stecca W RSC 12 Leonardo Cruz, Milan, Italy (WBA)
15.04.84 Seung-In Suh W CO 10 Bobby Berna, Seoul, S Korea (IBF)
26.05.84 Jaime Garza W CO 3 Felipe Orozco, Miami, USA (WBC)
26.05.84 Victor Callejas W RSC 8 Loris Stecca, Guaynabo, Peurto Rico (WBA)
08.07.84 Seung-In Suh W CO 4 Cleo Garcia, Seoul, S Korea (IBF)
03.11.84 Juan Meza W CO 1 Jaime Garza, Kingston NY, USA (WBC)
03.01.85 Ji-Won Kim W CO 10 Seung-In Suh, Seoul, S Korea (IBF)
02.02.85 Victor Callejas W PTS 15 Seung-Hoon Lee, San Juan, Puerto Rico (WBA)
30.03.85 Ji-Won Kim W PTS 15 Ruben Palacios, Suwon, S Korea (IBF)
19.04.85 Juan Meza W RSC 6 Mike Ayala, Los Angeles, USA (WBC)
28.06.85 Ji-Won Kim W CO 4 Bobby Berna, Pusan, S Korea (IBF)
18.08.85 Lupe Pintor W PTS 12 Juan Meza, Mexico C, Mexico (WBC)
09.10.85 Ji-Won Kim W CO 1 Seung-In Suh, Seoul, S Korea (IBF)
08.11.85 Victor Callejas W RTD 6 Loris Stecca, Rimini, Italy (WBA)
Victor Callejas forfeited WBA recognition (failure to defend against Louie Espinosa)
18.01.86 Samart Pakayarun W CO 5 Lupe Pintor, Bangkok, Thailand (WBC)
01.06.86 Ji-Won Kim W CO 2 Rudy Casicas, Inchon, S Korea (IBF)
Ji-Won Kim relinquished title (retired)
10.12.86 Samart Payakarun W CO 12 Juan Meza, Bangkok, Thailand (WBC)
16.01.87 Louie Espinosa W RSC 4 Tommy Valoy, Phoenix, USA (WBA)
18.01.87 Seung-Hoon Lee W CO 9 Prayoonsak Muangsurin, Pohang, S Korea (IBF)
05.04.87 Seung-Hoon Lee W CO 10 Jorge Urbina Diaz, Seoul, S Korea (IBF)
08.05.87 Jeff Fenech W RSC 4 Samart Payakarun, Sydney, Australia (WBC)
10.07.87 Jeff Fenech W RTD 5 Greg Richardson, Sydney, Australia (WBC)
15.07.87 Louie Espinosa W RSC 15 Manuel Vilchez, Phoenix, USA (WBA)
19.07.87 Seung-Hoon Lee W CO 5 Lion Collins, Seoul, S Korea (IBF)
15.08.87 Louie Espinosa W CO 9 Mike Ayala, San Antonio, USA (WBA)
16.10.87 Jeff Fenech W TD 4 Carlos Zarate, Sydney, Australia (WBC)
Jeff Fenech relinquished WBC version of title (weightmaking difficulties)
28.11.87 Julio Gervacio W PTS 12 Louie Espinosa, San Juan, Puerto Rico (WBA)
27.12.87 Seung-Hoon Lee W PTS 15 Jose Sanabria, Pohang, S Korea (IBF)
Seung-Hoon Lee relinquished IBF version of title (challenged for the WBC super-bantamweight title)
27.02.88 Bernardo Pinango W PTS 12 Julio Gervacio, San Juan, Puerto Rico (WBA)
29.02.88 Daniel Zaragoza W RSC 10 Carlos Zarate, Los Angeles, USA (WBC)
21.05.88 Jose Sanabria W CO 5 Moises Fuentes, Bucaramanga, Colombia (IBF)
28.05.88 Juan J. Estrada W PTS 12 Bernardo Pinango, Tijuana, Mexico (WBA)
29.05.88 Daniel Zaragoza DREW 12 Seung-Hoon Lee, Youchan, S Korea (WBC)
21.08.88 Jose Sanabria W PTS 12 Vincenzo Belcastro, Capo d'Orlando, Italy (IBF)
26.09.88 Jose Sanabria W RSC 10 Fabrice Benichou, Noget sur Marne, France (IBF)
15.10.88 Juan J. Estrada W RSC 11 Takuya Muguruma, Moriguchi, Japan (WBA)
11.11.88 Jose Sanabria W RSC 6 Thierry Jacob, Gravelines, France (IBF)
26.11.88 Daniel Zaragoza W CO 5 Valerio Nati, Forli, Italy (WBC)
10.03.89 Fabrice Benichou W PTS 12 Jose Sanabria, Limoges, France (IBF)
04.04.89 Juan J. Estrada W RSC 10 Jesus Poll, Los Angeles, USA (WBA)

Featherweight (126 lbs)

Title Holders

	Birthplace	Tenure	Status
George Dixon	Canada	1890–1897	
Solly Smith	USA	1897–1898	USA
Ben Jordan	England	1898–1899	GB
Dave Sullivan	Ireland	1898	USA
George Dixon	Canada	1898–1899	USA
George Dixon	Canada	1899–1900	
Terry McGovern	USA	1900–1901	
Young Corbett II	USA	1901–1903	
Abe Attell	USA	1903–1904	
Tommy Sullivan	USA	1904–1905	
Abe Attell	USA	1906–1912	
Abe Attell	USA	1912	USA
Jim Driscoll	Wales	1912–1913	GB/IBU
Johnny Kilbane	USA	1912–1913	USA
Johnny Kilbane	USA	1913–1922	
Johnny Kilbane	USA	1922–1923	NBA
Johnny Dundee	Italy	1922–1923	NY
Eugene Criqui	France	1923	
Johnny Dundee*	Italy	1923–1924	
Kid Kaplan*	Russia	1925–1926	MASS
Honeyboy Finnegan	USA	1926–1927	NBA
Benny Bass	Russia	1927–1928	NY

Tony Canzoneri	USA	1927–1928	
Tony Canzoneri	USA	1928	
Andre Routis	France	1928–1929	
Bat Battalino	USA	1929–1932	NBA
Tommy Paul	USA	1932–1933	NY
Kid Chocolate	Cuba	1932–1933	NBA
Freddie Miller	USA	1933–1936	NY
Baby Arizmendi	Mexico	1934–1935	CALIF
Baby Arizmendi	Mexico	1935–1936	NY
Mike Belloise	USA	1936	NBA
Petey Sarron	USA	1936–1937	CALIF
Henry Armstrong	USA	1936–1937	NBA/NY
Henry Armstrong*	USA	1937–1938	IBU
Maurice Holtzer	France	1937–1938	NBA
Leo Rodak	USA	1938–1939	NY
Joey Archibald	USA	1938–1939	
Joey Archibald	USA	1939–1940	NY
Joey Archibald	USA	1940	LOUIS
Jimmy Perrin	USA	1940	NBA
Petey Scalzo	USA	1940–1941	NY
Harry Jeffra	USA	1940–1941	NY
Joey Archibald	USA	1941	NBA
Richie Lemos	USA	1941	NY
Chalky Wright	Mexico	1941–1942	MARY
Harry Jeffra	USA	1941–1942	NBA
Jackie Wilson	USA	1941–1943	NY
Willie Pep	USA	1942–1946	NBA
Jackie Callura	Canada	1943	NBA
Phil Terranova	USA	1943–1944	NBA
Sal Bartolo	USA	1944–1946	
Willie Pep	USA	1946–1948	
Sandy Saddler	USA	1948–1949	
Willie Pep	USA	1949–1950	
Sandy Saddler*	USA	1950–1957	
Hogan Kid Bassey	Nigeria	1957–1959	
Davey Moore	USA	1959–1963	
Sugar Ramos	Cuba	1963–1964	
Vincente Saldivar*	Mexico	1964–1967	WBA
Raul Rojas	USA	1967–1968	WBC
Howard Winstone	Wales	1968	WBC
Jose Legra	Cuba	1968–1969	WBA
Shozo Saijyo	Japan	1968–1971	WBC
Johnny Famechon	France	1969–1970	
Vicente Saldivar	Mexico	1970	WBC
Kuniaki Shibata	Japan	1970–1972	WBC
Antonio Gomez	Venezuela	1971–1972	WBA
Clemente Sanchez	Mexico	1972	WBC
Ernesto Marcel*	Panama	1972–1974	WBA
Jose Legra	Cuba	1972–1973	WBC
Eder Jofre	Brazil	1973–1974	WBC
Ruben Olivares	Mexico	1974	WBA
Bobby Chacon	USA	1974–1975	WBC
Alexis Arguello*	Nicaragua	1974–1977	WBA
Ruben Olivares	Mexico	1975	WBC
David Kotey	Ghana	1975–1976	WBC
Danny Lopez	USA	1976–1980	WBC
Rafael Ortega	Panama	1977	WBA
Cecilio Lastra	Spain	1977–1978	WBA
Eusebio Pedroza	Panama	1978–1985	WBA
Salvador Sanchez*	Mexico	1980–1982	WBC
Juan Laporte	Puerto Rico	1982–1984	WBC
Min-Keun Chung	S Korea	1984–1985	IBF
Wilfredo Gomez	Puerto Rico	1984	WBC
Azumah Nelson*	Ghana	1984–1987	WBC
Barry McGuigan	Ireland	1985–1986	WBA
Ki-Yung Chung	S Korea	1985–1986	IBF
Steve Cruz	USA	1986–1987	WBA
Antonio Rivera	Puerto Rico	1986–1987	IBF
Antonio Esparragoza	Venezuela	1987–	WBA
Calvin Grove	USA	1988	IBF
Jeff Fenech*	Australia	1988–	WBC
Jorge Paez	Mexico	1988–	IBF

Title Bouts

27.06.90 George Dixon W RTD 18 Nunc Wallace, London, England
23.10.90 George Dixon W RSC 40 Johnny Murphy, Providence, USA
31.03.91 George Dixon W RSC 22 Cal McCarthy, Troy, USA
28.07.91 George Dixon W CO 5 Abe Willis, San Francisco, USA
27.06.92 George Dixon W CO 14 Fred Johnson, New York C, USA
06.09.92 George Dixon W CO 8 Jack Skelly, New Orleans, USA
07.08.93 George Dixon W CO 3 Eddie Pierce, New York C, USA
25.09.93 George Dixon W CO 7 Solly Smith, New York C, USA
27.08.95 George Dixon W PTS 25 Johnny Griffin, Boston, USA
05.12.95 George Dixon DREW 10 Frank Erne, New York C, USA
17.03.96 George Dixon W 8 Jerry Marshall, Boston, USA
16.06.96 George Dixon DREW 20 Martin Flaherty, Boston, USA
25.09.96 George Dixon DREW 20 Tommy White, New York C, USA
22.01.97 George Dixon W CO 6 Billy Murphy, New York C, USA
15.02.97 George Dixon DREW 20 Jack Downey, New York C, USA
26.04.97 George Dixon W PTS 20 Johnny Griffin, New York C, USA
23.07.97 George Dixon DREW 20 Dal Hawkins, San Francisco, USA
04.10.97 Solly Smith W PTS 20 George Dixon, San Francisco, USA (USA)
01.07.98 Ben Jordan W PTS 25 George Dixon, New York C, USA (GB)
07.07.98 Solly Smith W DIS 7 Billy O'Donnell, Buffalo, USA (USA)
01.08.98 Solly Smith DREW 25 Tommy White, New York C, USA (USA)
26.09.98 Dave Sullivan W RTD 5 Solly Smith, New York C, USA (USA)
11.11.98 George Dixon W DIS 10 Dave Sullivan, New York C, USA (USA)
29.11.98 George Dixon W PTS 25 Oscar Gardner, New York C, USA (USA)
17.01.99 George Dixon W CO 10 Young Pluto, New York C, USA (USA)
15.05.99 George Dixon W PTS 20 Kid Broad, Buffalo, USA (USA)
29.05.99 Ben Jordan W CO 9 Harry Greenfield, London, England (GB)
Ben Jordan ceased to be recognised by GB (this followed a defeat by Eddie Santry in October, 1899)
02.06.99 George Dixon W PTS 25 Joe Bernstein, New York C, USA (USA)
11.07.99 George Dixon W PTS 20 Tommy White, Denver, USA (USA)
11.08.99 George Dixon DREW 20 Eddie Santry, New York C, USA (USA)
02.11.99 George Dixon W PTS 25 Will Curley, New York C, USA
21.11.99 George Dixon W PTS 25 Eddie Lenny, New York C, USA
09.01.00 Terry McGovern W RSC 9 George Dixon, New York C, USA
01.02.00 Terry McGovern W CO 5 Eddie Santry, Chicago, USA
09.03.00 Terry McGovern W CO 3 Oscar Gardner, New York C, USA
12.06.00 Terry McGovern W CO 3 Tommy White, New York C, USA
02.11.00 Terry McGovern W CO 7 Joe Bernstein, Louisville, USA
30.04.01 Terry McGovern W CO 4 Oscar Gardner, San Francisco, USA
29.05.01 Terry McGovern W CO 5 Aurelio Herrera, San Francisco, USA
28.11.01 Young Corbett W CO 2 Terry McGovern, Hartford, USA
16.10.02 Young Corbett II W RTD 8 Joe Bernstein, Baltimore, USA
14.01.03 Young Corbett II W 18 Austin Rice, Hot Springs, USA
26.02.03 Young Corbett II DREW 20 Eddie Hanlon, San Francisco, USA
31.03.03 Young Corbett II W CO 11 Terry McGovern, San Francisco, USA
Young Corbett II lost general recognition (weight making difficulties)
03.09.03 Abe Attell W PTS 20 Johhny Reagan, St Louis, USA
01.02.04 Abe Attell W RSC 5 Harry Forbes, St Louis, USA
23.06.04 Abe Attell W PTS 20 Johnny Reagan, St Louis, USA
13.10.04 Tommy Sullivan W CO 5 Abe Attell, St Louis, USA
Tommy Sullivan forfeited title (inactivity)
22.02.06 Abe Attell W PTS 15 Jimmy Walsh, Chelsea, Mass, USA
15.03.06 Abe Attell W DIS 3 Tony Moran, Baltimore, USA
11.05.06 Abe Attell DREW 20 Kid Herman, Los Angeles, USA
04.07.06 Abe Attell W PTS 20 Frankie Neil, Los Angeles, USA
30.10.06 Abe Attell W PTS 20 Harry Baker, Los Angeles, USA
16.11.06 Abe Attell W PTS 15 Billy de Coursey, San Diego, USA
07.12.06 Abe Attell W CO 8 Jimmy Walsh, Los Angeles, USA
18.01.07 Abe Attell W CO 8 Harry Baker, Los Angeles, USA
24.05.07 Abe Attell W PTS 20 Kid Solomon, Los Angeles, USA
29.10.07 Abe Attell W CO 4 Freddie Weeks, Los Angeles, USA
01.01.08 Abe Attell DREW 25 Owen Moran, San Francisco, USA
31.01.88 Abe Attell W RTD 13 Frankie Neil, San Francisco, USA
28.02.08 Abe Attell W CO 7 Eddie Kelly, San Francisco, USA
30.04.08 Abe Attell W CO 4 Tommy Sullivan, San Francisco, USA
07.09.08 Abe Attell DREW 23 Owen Moran, San Francisco, USA
14.01.09 Abe Attell W CO 10 Freddie Weeks, Goldfield, USA
04.02.09 Abe Attell W CO 7 Eddie Kelly, New Orleans, USA
26.03.09 Abe Attell W CO 8 Frankie White, Dayton, USA
28.02.10 Abe Attell W CO 6 Harry Forbes, New York C, USA
22.08.10 Abe Attell W CO 3 Eddie Marino, Calgary, Canada
05.09.10 Abe Attell W CO 17 Billy Lauder, Calgary, Canada
24.10.10 Abe Attell W PTS 10 Johnny Kilbane, Kansas City, USA
13.11.10 Abe Attell DREW 15 Frankie Conley, New Orleans, USA
Abe Attell forfeited GB/IBU recognition (failure to defend against Driscoll)
22.02.12 Johnny Kilbane W PTS 10 Abe Attell, Los Angeles, USA (USA)
21.05.12 Johnny Kilbane DREW 12 Jimmy Walsh, Boston, USA (USA)
03.06.12 Jim Driscoll W CO 12 Jean Poesy, London, England (GB/IBU)
14.10.12 Johnny Kilbane W PTS 12 Eddie O'Keefe, Cleveland, USA (USA)
03.12.12 Johnny Kilbane W RSC 8 Monte Attell, Cleveland, USA (USA)
27.01.13 Jim Driscoll DREW 20 Owen Moran, London, England (GB/IBU)
Jim Driscoll ceased to be recognised by the IBU/GB (he relinquished the European featherweight title in July 1913)
29.04.13 Johnny Kilbane DREW 20 Johnny Dundee, Los Angeles, USA (USA)
16.09.13 Johnny Kilbane W PTS 12 Jimmy Walsh, Boston, USA
04.09.16 Johnny Kilbane W CO 3 K. O. Chaney, Cedar Point, USA
26.03.17 Johnny Kilbane DREW 12 Eddie Wallace, Bridgeport, USA
21.04.20 Johnny Kilbane W CO 7 Alvie Miller, Lorain, USA
17.09.21 Johnny Kilbane W CO 7 Danny Frush, Cleveland, USA
15.08.22 Johnny Dundee W CO 9 Danny Frush, New York C, USA (NY)
02.06.23 Eugene Criqui W CO 6 Johnny Kilbane, New York C, USA
26.07.23 Johnny Dundee W PTS 15 Eugene Criqui, New York C, USA
Johnny Dundee relinquished title (moved up to super-featherweight)
02.01.25 Kid Kaplan W RTD 9 Danny Kramer, New York C, USA
27.08.25 Kid Kaplan DREW 15 Babe Herman, Waterbury, USA
18.12.25 Kid Kaplan W PTS 15 Babe Herman, New York C, USA
28.06.26 Kid Kaplan W CO 10 Bobby Garcia, Hartford, USA
Kid Kaplan relinquished title (weight making difficulties)
15.11.26 Honeyboy Finnegan W PTS 10 Chick Suggs, Boston, USA (MASS)
Honeyboy Finnegan ceased to be recognised by Massachusetts (unable to make the weight any longer)
12.09.27 Benny Bass W PTS 10 Red Chapman, Philadelphia, USA (NBA)
24.10.27 Tony Canzoneri W PTS 15 Johnny Dundee, New York C, USA (NY)
10.02.28 Tony Canzoneri W PTS 15 Benny Bass, New York C, USA
28.09.28 Andre Routis W PTS 15 Tony Canzoneri, New York C, USA
27.05.29 Andre Routis W RSC 3 Buster Brown, Baltimore, USA
23.09.29 Bat Battalino W PTS 15 Andre Routis, Hartford, USA
15.07.30 Bat Battalino W CO 5 Ignacio Fernandez, Hartford, USA
12.12.30 Bat Battalino W PTS 15 Kid Chocolate, New York C, USA

22.05.31 Bat Battalino W PTS 15 Fidel la Barba, New York C, USA
01.07.31 Bat Battalino W PTS 10 Bobby Brady, Jersey C, USA
23.07.31 Bat Battalino W PTS 10 Freddie Miller, Cincinnati, USA
04.11.31 Bat Battalino W PTS 10 Earl Maestro, Chicago, USA
Bat Battalino forefeited title (overweight for a defence against Freddie Miller)
26.05.32 Tommy Paul W PTS 10 Johnny Pena, Detroit, USA (NBA)
13.10.32 Kid Chocolate W CO 12 Lew Feldman, New York C, USA (NY)
09.12.32 Kid Chocolate W PTS 15 Fidel la Barba, New York C, USA (NY)
13.01.33 Freddie Miller W PTS 10 Tommy Paul, Chicago, USA (NBA)
28.02.33 Freddie Miller W PTS 10 Baby Arizmendi, Los Angeles, USA (NBA)
21.03.33 Freddie Miller W PTS 10 Speedy Dado, Los Angeles, USA (NBA)
19.05.33 Kid Chocolate W PTS 15 Seaman Tommy Watson, New York C, USA (NY)
Kid Chocolate forfeited NY recognition (failure to defend against Frankie Klick)
01.01.34 Freddie Miller W PTS 10 Jackie Sharkey, Cincinnati, USA (NBA)
30.08.34 Baby Arizmendi W PTS 15 Mike Belloise, New York C, USA (NY)
Baby Arizmendi forfeited NY recognition (He contested the Californian version without NY authority)
21.09.34 Freddie Miller W PTS 15 Nel Tarleton, Liverpool, England (NBA)
01.01.35 Baby Arizmendi W PTS 12 Henry Armstrong, Mexico C, Mexico (CALIF)
17.02.35 Freddie Miller W CO 1 Jose Girones, Barcelona, Spain (NBA)
12.06.35 Freddie Miller W PTS 15 Nel Tarleton, Liverpool, England (NBA)
22.10.35 Freddie Miller W PTS 15 Vernon Cormier, Boston, USA (NBA)
18.02.36 Freddie Miller W PTS 12 Johnny Pena, Seattle, USA (NBA)
02.03.36 Freddie Miller W PTS 15 Petey Sarron, Miami, USA (NBA)
11.05.36 Petey Sarron W PTS 15 Freddie Miller, Washington, USA (NBA)
22.07.36 Petey Sarron W PTS 15 Baby Manuel, Dallas, USA (NBA)
04.08.36 Henry Armstrong W PTS 10 Baby Arizmendi, Los Angeles, USA (CALIF)
03.09.36 Mike Belloise W CO 9 Dave Crowley, New York C, USA (NY)
Mike Belloise ceased to be recognised by NY (this followed the defeat by Henry Armstrong in October, 1936)
27.10.36 Henry Armstrong W PTS 10 Mike Belloise, Los Angeles, USA (CALIF)
04.09.37 Petey Sarron W PTS 12 Freddie Miller, Johannesburg, S Africa (NBA)
05.10.37 Maurice Holtzer W PTS 15 Phil Dolhem, Algiers, Algeria (IBU)
29.10.37 Henry Armstrong W CO 6 Petey Sarron, New York C, USA (NY/NBA)
Henry Armstrong relinquished NY/NBA version of title (he began to campaign in a higher weight division)
19.02.38 Maurice Holtzer DREW 15 Maurice Dubois, Geneva, Switzerland (IBU)
Maurice Holtzer ceased to be recognised by the IBU (he relinquished the EBU featherweight title in July, 1938)
17.06.38 Leo Rodak W PTS 15 Jackie Wilson, Baltimore, USA (NBA)
17.10.38 Joey Archibald W PTS 15 Mike Belloise, New York C, USA (NY)
24.10.38 Leo Rodak W PTS 15 Freddie Miller, Washington, USA (NBA)
18.04.39 Joey Archibald W PTS 15 Leo Rodak, Providence, USA
Joey Archibald forfeited NBA recognition (refused to defend against Petey Scalzo)
28.09.39 Joey Archibald W PTS 15 Harry Jeffra, Washington, USA (NY)
08.05.40 Jimmy Perrin W PTS 15 Bobby Ruffin, New Orleans, USA (LOUIS)
Jimmy Perrin ceased to be recognised by Louisiana (this followed a defeat by Petey Scalzo in a non-title bout, August, 1940)
15.05.40 Petey Scalzo W CO 6 Frankie Covelli, Washington, USA (NBA)
20.05.40 Harry Jeffra W PTS 15 Joey Archibald, Baltimore, USA (NY)
10.07.40 Petey Scalzo W RSC 15 Bobby Poison Ivy, Hartford, USA (NBA)
29.07.40 Harry Jeffra W PTS 15 Spider Armstrong, Baltimore, USA (NY)
12.05.41 Joey Archibald W PTS 15 Harry Jeffra, Washington, USA (NY)
19.05.41 Petey Scalzo W PTS 15 Phil Zwick, Milwaukee, USA (NBA)
01.07.41 Richie Lemos W CO 5 Petey Scalzo, Los Angeles, USA (NBA)
11.09.41 Chalky Wright W CO 11 Joey Archibald, Washington, USA (NY)
15.09.41 Harry Jeffra W PTS 12 Lou Transparenti, Baltimore, USA (MARY)
18.11.41 Jackie Wilson W PTS 12 Richie Lemos, Los Angeles, USA (NBA)
16.12.41 Jackie Wilson W PTS 12 Richie Lemos, Los Angeles, USA (NBA)
19.06.42 Chalky Wright W RSC 10 Harry Jeffra, Baltimore, USA (NY)
25.09.42 Chalky Wright W PTS 15 Lulu Constantino, New York C, USA (NY)
20.11.42 Willie Pep W PTS 15 Chalky Wright, New York C, USA (NY)
18.01.43 Jackie Callura W PTS 15 Jackie Wilson, Providence, USA (NBA)
18.03.43 Jackie Callura W PTS 15 Jackie Wilson, Boston, USA (NBA)
08.06.43 Willie Pep W PTS 15 Sal Bartolo, Boston, USA (NY)
16.08.43 Phil Terranova W CO 8 Jackie Callura, New Orleans, USA (NBA)
27.12.43 Phil Terranova W RSC 6 Jackie Callura, New Orleans, USA (NBA)
10.03.44 Sal Bartolo W PTS 15 Phil Terranova, Boston, USA (NBA)
05.05.44 Sal Bartolo W PTS 15 Phil Terranova, Boston, USA (NBA)
29.09.44 Willie Pep W PTS 15 Chalky Wright, New York C, USA (NY)
15.12.44 Sal Bartolo W PTS 15 Willie Roache, Boston, USA (NBA)
19.02.45 Willie Pep W PTS 15 Phil Terranova, New York C, USA (NY)
03.05.46 Sal Bartolo W CO 6 Spider Armstrong, Boston, USA (NBA)
07.06.46 Willie Pep W CO 12 Sal Bartolo, New York C, USA
22.08.47 Willie Pep W CO 12 Jock Leslie, Flint, USA
24.02.48 Willie Pep W RSC 10 Humberto Sierra, Miami, USA
29.10.48 Sandy Saddler W CO 4 Willie Pep, New York C, USA
11.02.49 Willie Pep W PTS 15 Sandy Saddler, New York C, USA
20.09.49 Willie Pep W RSC 7 Eddie Compo, Waterbury, USA
16.01.50 Willie Pep W CO 5 Charley Riley, St Louis, USA
17.03.50 Willie Pep W PTS 15 Ray Famechon, New York C, USA
08.09.50 Sandy Saddler W RTD 8 Willie Pep, New York C, USA
26.09.51 Sandy Saddler W RTD 9 Willie Pep, New York C, USA
25.02.55 Sandy Saddler W PTS 15 Teddy Davis, New York C, USA
18.01.56 Sandy Saddler W RSC 13 Flash Elorde, San Francisco, USA
Sandy Saddler relinquished title (retired)
24.06.57 Hogan Kid Bassey W RSC 10 Cherif Hamia, Paris, France
01.04.58 Hogan Kid Bassey W CO 3 Ricardo Moreno, Los Angeles, USA
18.03.59 Davey Moore W RTD 13 Hogan Kid Bassey, Los Angeles, USA
19.08.59 Davey Moore W RTD 10 Hogan Kid Bassey, Los Angeles, USA
29.08.60 Davey Moore W PTS 15 Kazuo Takayama, Tokyo, Japan
08.04.61 Davey Moore W CO 1 Danny Valdez, Los Angeles, USA
13.11.61 Davey Moore W PTS 15 Kuzuo Takayama, Tokyo, Japan
17.08.62 Davey Moore W RSC 2 Olli Maki, Helsinki, Finland
21.03.63 Sugar Ramos W RTD 10 Davey Moore, Los Angeles, USA
13.07.63 Sugar Ramos W PTS 15 Rafiu King, Mexico C, Mexico
28.02.64 Sugar Ramos W RTD 6 Mitsunori Seki, Tokyo, Japan
09.05.64 Sugar Ramos W PTS 15 Floyd Robertson, Accra, Ghana
26.09.64 Vincente Saldivar W RTD 11 Sugar Ramos, Mexico C, Mexico
06.12.64 Vincente Saldivar W RSC 11 Delfino Rosales, Guanajuato, Mexico
07.05.65 Vincente Saldivar W RSC 15 Raul Rojas, Los Angeles, USA
07.09.65 Vincente Saldivar W PTS 15 Howard Winstone, London, England
12.02.66 Vincente Saldivar W CO 2 Floyd Robertson, Mexico C, Mexico
07.08.66 Vincente Saldivar W PTS 15 Mitsunori Seki, Mexico C, Mexico
29.01.67 Vincente Saldivar W RSC 7 Mitsunori Seki, Mexico C, Mexico
15.06.67 Vincente Saldivar W PTS 15 Howard Winstone, Cardiff, Wales
14.10.67 Vincente Saldivar W RTD 12 Howard Winstone, Mexico C, Mexico
Vincente Saldivar relinquished title (retired)
14.12.67 Raul Rojas W PTS 15 Antonio Herrera, Los Angeles, USA (WBA)
23.01.68 Howard Winstone W RSC 9 Mitsunori Seki, London, England (WBC)
28.03.68 Raul Rojas W PTS 15 Enrique Higgins, Los Angeles, USA (WBA)
24.07.68 Jose Legra W RSC 5 Howard Winstone, Porthcawl, Wales (WBC)
28.09.68 Shozo Saijyo W PTS 15 Raul Rojas, Los Angeles, USA (WBA)
21.01.69 Johnny Famechon W PTS 15 Jose Legra, London, England (WBC)
09.02.69 Shozo Saijyo W PTS 15 Pedro Gomez, Tokyo, Japan (WBA)
28.07.69 Johnny Famechon W PTS 15 Fighting Harada, Sydney, Australia (WBC)
07.09.69 Shozo Saijyo W CO 2 Jose Pimental, Sapporo, Japan (WBA)
06.01.70 Johnny Famechon W CO 14 Fighting Harada, Tokyo, Japan (WBC)
08.02.70 Shozo Saijyo W PTS 15 Godfrey Stevens, Tokyo, Japan (WBA)
09.05.70 Vincente Saldivar W PTS 15 Johnny Famechon, Rome, Italy (WBC)
05.07.70 Shozo Saijyo W PTS 15 Frankie Crawford, Sendai, Japan (WBA)
11.12.70 Kuniaki Shibata W RSC 12 Vincente Saldivar, Tijuana, Mexico (WBC)
28.02.71 Shozo Saijyo W PTS 15 Frankie Crawford, Utsonomuja, Japan (WBA)
03.06.71 Kuniaki Shibata W CO 1 Raul Cruz, Tokyo, Japan (WBC)
02.09.71 Antonio Gomez W RSC 5 Shozo Saijyo, Tokyo, Japan (WBA)
11.11.71 Kuniaki Shibata DREW 15 Ernesto Marcel, Matsuyama, Japan (WBC)
06.02.72 Antonio Gomez W CO 7 Raul Martinez, Maracay, Venezuela (WBA)
19.05.72 Clemente Sanchez W CO 3 Kuniaki Shibata, Tokyo, Japan (WBC)
19.08.72 Ernesto Marcel W PTS 15 Antonio Gomez, Maracay, Venezuela (WBA)
03.12.72 Ernesto Marcel W RSC 6 Enrique Garcia, Panama C, Panama (WBA)
16.12.72 Jose Legra W RSC 10 Clemente Sanchez, Monterrey, Mexico (WBC)
05.05.73 Eder Jofre W PTS 15 Jose Legra, Brasilia, Brazil (WBC)
14.07.73 Ernesto Marcel W RTD 11 Antonio Gomez, Panama C, Panama (WBA)
08.09.73 Ernesto Marcel W CO 9 Spider Nemoto, Panama C, Panama (WBA)
21.10.73 Eder Jofre W CO 4 Vincente Saldivar, Salvador, Brazil (WBC)
Eder Jofre forfeited WBC recognition (failure to defend against Alfredo Marcano)
16.02.74 Ernesto Marcel W PTS 15 Alexis Arguello, Panama C, Panama (WBA)
Ernesto Marcel relinquished WBA version of title (retired)
09.07.74 Ruben Olivares W RSC 7 Zensuke Utagawa, Los Angeles, USA (WBA)
07.09.74 Bobby Chacon W RSC 9 Alfredo Marcano, Los Angeles, USA (WBC)
23.11.74 Alexis Arguello W CO 13 Ruben Olivares, Los Angeles, USA (WBA)
01.03.75 Bobby Chacon W CO 2 Jesus Estrada, Los Angeles, USA (WBC)
15.03.75 Alexis Arguello W RSC 8 Leonel Hernandez, Caracas, Venezuela (WBA)
31.05.75 Alexis Arguello W RSC 2 Rigoberto Riasco, Managua, Nicaragua (WBA)
20.06.75 Ruben Olivares W RSC 2 Bobby Chacon, Los Angeles, USA (WBC)
20.09.75 David Kotey W PTS 15 Ruben Olivares, Los Angeles, USA (WBC)
12.10.75 Alexis Arguello W CO 5 Royal Kobayashi, Tokyo, Japan (WBA)
06.03.76 David Kotey W RSC 12 Flipper Uehara, Accra, Ghana (WBC)
19.06.76 Alexis Arguello W CO 3 Salvatore Torres, Los Angeles, USA (WBA)
Alexis Arguello relinquished WBA version of title (moved up to super-featherweight)
16.07.76 David Kotey W RSC 3 Shig Fukuyama, Tokyo, Japan (WBC)
05.11.76 Danny Lopez W PTS 15 David Kotey, Accra, Ghana (WBC)
15.01.77 Rafael Ortega W PTS 15 Francisco Coronado, Panama C, Panama (WBA)
29.05.77 Rafael Ortega W PTS 15 Flipper Uehara, Okinawa, Japan (WBA)
13.09.77 Danny Lopez W RSC 7 Jose Torres, Los Angeles, USA (WBC)
17.12.77 Cecilio Lastra W PTS 15 Rafael Ortega, Torrelavega, Spain (WBA)
15.02.78 Danny Lopez W RSC 6 David Kotey, Las Vegas, USA (WBC)
15.04.78 Eusebio Pedroza W CO 13 Cecilio Lastra, Panama C, Panama (WBA)
23.04.78 Danny Lopez W RSC 6 Jose de Paula, Los Angeles, USA (WBC)
02.07.78 Eusebio Pedroza W RSC 12 Ernesto Herrera, Panama C, Panama (WBA)
15.09.78 Danny Lopez W CO 2 Juan Malvarez, New Orleans, USA (WBC)
21.10.78 Danny Lopez W DIS 4 Fel Clemente, Pesaro, Italy (WBC)
27.11.78 Eusebio Pedroza W PTS 15 Enrique Solis, San Juan, Puerto Rico (WBA)
09.01.79 Eusebio Pedroza W RTD 13 Royal Kobayashi, Tokyo, Japan (WBA)
10.03.79 Danny Lopez W CO 2 Danny Castanon, Salt Lake C, USA (WBC)
08.04.79 Eusebio Pedroza W RSC 11 Hector Carrasquilla, Panama C, Panama (WBA)
17.06.79 Danny Lopez W CO 15 Mike Ayala, San Antonio, USA (WBC)
21.07.79 Eusebio Pedroza W RSC 12 Ruben Olivares, Houston, USA (WBA)
25.09.79 Danny Lopez W RSC 3 Jose Caba, Los Angeles, USA (WBC)
17.11.79 Eusebio Pedroza W RSC 11 Johnny Aba, Port Moresby, P N Guinea (WBA)
22.01.80 Eusebio Pedroza W PTS 15 Spider Nemoto, Tokyo, Japan (WBA)
02.02.80 Salvador Sanchez W RSC 13 Danny Lopez, Phoenix, USA (WBC)
29.03.80 Eusebio Pedroza W CO 9 Juan Malvarez, Panama C, Panama (WBA)
12.04.80 Salvador Sanchez W PTS 15 Ruben Castillo, Tucson, USA (WBC)
21.06.80 Salvador Sanchez W RSC 14 Danny Lopez, Las Vegas, USA (WBC)
20.07.80 Eusebio Pedroza W CO 9 Sa-Wang Kim, Seoul, S Korea (WBA)
13.09.80 Salvador Sanchez W PTS 15 Pat Ford, San Antonio, USA (WBC)
04.10.80 Eusebio Pedroza W PTS 15 Rocky Lockridge, McAfee, USA (WBA)
13.12.80 Salvador Sanchez W PTS 15 Juan Laporte, El Paso, USA (WBC)
14.02.81 Eusebio Pedroza W CO 13 Pat Ford, Panama C, Panama (WBA)
22.03.81 Salvador Sanchez W RSC 10 Roberto Castanon, Las Vegas, USA (WBC)
01.08.81 Eusebio Pedroza W CO 7 Carlos Pinango, Caracas, Venezuela (WBA)
21.08.81 Salvador Sanchez W RSC 8 Wilfredo Gomez, Las Vegas, USA (WBC)
05.12.81 Eusebio Pedroza W CO 5 Bashew Sibaca, Panama C, Panama (WBA)

12.12.81 Salvador Sanchez W PTS 15 Pat Cowdell, Houston, USA (WBC)
24.01.82 Eusebio Pedroza W PTS 15 Juan Laporte, Atlantic C, USA (WBA)
08.05.82 Salvador Sanchez W PTS 15 Rocky Garcia, Dallas, USA (WBC)
21.07.82 Salvador Sanchez W RSC 15 Azumah Nelson, New York C, USA (WBC)
Salvador Sanchez left WBC version of title vacant (killed in a road crash)

15.09.82 Juan Laporte W RTD 10 Mario Miranda, New York C, USA (WBC)
16.10.82 Eusebio Pedroza DREW 15 Bernard Taylor, Charlotte, USA (WBA)
20.02.83 Juan Laporte W PTS 12 Ruben Castillo, San Juan, Puerto Rico (WBC)
24.04.83 Eusebio Pedroza W PTS 15 Rocky Lockridge, Liguma, Italy (WBA)
25.06.83 Juan Laporte W PTS 12 Johnny de la Rosa, San Juan, Puerto Rico (WBC)
22.10.83 Eusebio Pedroza W PTS 15 Jose Caba, San Remo, Italy (WBA)
04.03.84 Min-Keun Oh W CO 2 Joko Arter, Seoul, S Korea (IBF)
31.03.84 Wilfredo Gomez W PTS 12 Juan Laporte, San Juan, Puerto Rico (WBC)
27.05.84 Eusebio Pedroza W PTS 15 Angel Mayor, Maracaibo, Venezuela (WBA)
10.06.84 Min-Keun Oh W PTS 15 Kelvin Lampkin, Seoul, S Korea (IBF)
08.12.84 Azumah Nelson W RSC 11 Wilfredo Gomez, San Juan, Puerto Rico (WBC)
02.02.85 Eusebio Pedroza W PTS 15 Jorge Lujan, Panama C, Panama (WBA)
07.04.85 Min-Keun Oh W PTS 15 Irving Mitchell, Pusan, S Korea (IBF)
08.06.85 Barry McGuigan W PTS 15 Eusebio Pedroza, London, England (WBA)
06.09.85 Azumah Nelson W CO 5 Juvenal Ordenes, Miami, USA (WBC)
28.09.85 Barry McGuigan W RTD 8 Bernard Taylor, Belfast, Ireland (WBA)
12.10.85 Azumah Nelson W CO 1 Pat Cowdell, Birmingham, England (WBC)
29.11.85 Ki-Yung Chung W RSC 15 Min-Keun Oh, Chonju, S Korea (IBF)
15.02.86 Barry McGuigan W RSC 14 Danilo Cabrera, Dublin, Ireland (WBA)
16.02.86 Ki-Yung Chung W RTD 6 Tyrone Jackson, Ulsan, S Korea (IBF)
25.02.86 Azumah Nelson W PTS 12 Marcos Villasana, Los Angeles, USA (WBC)
18.05.86 Ki-Yung Chung W PTS 15 Richard Savage, Taegu, S Korea (IBF)
22.06.86 Azumah Nelson W RSC 10 Danilo Cabrera, San Juan, Puerto Rico (WBC)
23.06.86 Steve Cruz W PTS 15 Barry McGuigan, Las Vegas, USA (WBA)
30.08.86 Antonio Rivera W RTD 10 Ki-Yung Chung, Osan, S Korea (IBF)
06.03.87 Antonio Esparragoza W RSC 12 Steve Cruz, Fort Worth, USA (WBA)
07.03.87 Azumah Nelson W CO 6 Mauro Gutierrez, Las Vegas, USA (WBC)
26.07.87 Antonio Esparragoza W CO 10 Pascual Aranda, Houston, USA (WBA)
29.08.87 Azumah Nelson W PTS 12 Marcos Villasana, Los Angeles, USA (WBC)
Azumah Nelson relinquished WBC version of title (weight making difficulties)
23.01.88 Calvin Grove W RSC 4 Antonio Rivera, Gamaches, France (IBF)
07.03.88 Jeff Fenech W RSC 10 Victor Callejas, Sydney, Australia (WBC)
17.05.88 Calvin Grove W PTS 15 Myron Taylor, Atlantic C, USA (IBF)
23.06.88 Antonio Esparragoza DREW 12 Marcos Villasana, Los Angeles, USA (WBA)
04.08.88 Jorge Paez W PTS 15 Calvin Grove, Mexicali, Mexico (IBF)
12.08.88 Jeff Fenech W RSC 5 Tyrone Downes, Melbourne, Australia (WBC)
05.11.88 Antonio Esparragoza W CO 8 Jose Marmolejo, Marsala, Italy (WBA)
30.11.88 Jeff Fenech W RSC 5 George Navarro, Melbourne, Australia (WBC)
25.03.89 Antonio Esparragoza W CO 10 Mitsuru Sugiya, Kawasaki, Japan (WBA)
30.03.89 Jorge Paez W CO 11 Calvin Grove, Mexicali, Mexico (IBF)
08.04.89 Jeff Fenech W PTS 12 Marcos Villasana, Melbourne, Australia (WBC)
Jeff Fenech relinquished WBC version of title (retired)

Super-Featherweight (130 lbs)

Title Holders

	Birthplace	Tenure	Status
Johnny Dundee	Italy	1921–1923	NY
Jack Bernstein	USA	1923	NBA/NY
Johnny Dundee	Italy	1923–1924	NBA/NY
Kid Sullivan	USA	1924–1925	NBA/NY
Mike Ballerino	USA	1925	NBA/NY
Tod Morgan	USA	1925–1929	NBA/NY
Benny Bass	USA	1929	NBA/NY
Benny Bass	Russia	1929–1931	NBA
Kid Chocolate	Cuba	1931–1933	NBA
Frankie Klick	USA	1933–1934	NBA
Sandy Saddler	USA	1949–1950	OHIO
Harold Gomes	USA	1959–1960	NBA
Flash Elorde	Philippines	1960–1965	NBA
Flash Elorde	Philippines	1965–1967	
Yoshiaki Numata	Japan	1967	
Hiroshi Kobayashi	Japan	1967–1969	
Hiroshi Kobayashi	Japan	1969–1971	WBA
Rene Barrientos	Philippines	1969–1970	WBC
Yoshiaki Numata	Japan	1970–1971	WBC
Alfredo Marcano	Venezuela	1971–1972	WBA
Ricardo Arredondo	Mexico	1971–1974	WBC
Ben Villaflor	Philippines	1972–1973	WBA
Kuniaki Shibata	Japan	1973	WBA
Ben Villaflor	Philippines	1973–1976	WBA
Kuniaki Shibata	Japan	1974–1975	WBC
Alfredo Escalera	Puerto Rico	1975–1978	WBC
Sam Serrano	Puerto Rico	1976–1980	WBA
Alexis Arguello*	Nicaragua	1978–1980	WBC
Yasutsune Uehara	Japan	1980–1981	WBA
Rafael Limon	Mexico	1980–1981	WBC
Cornelius Boza-Edwards	Uganda	1981	WBC
Sam Serrano	Puerto Rico	1981–1983	WBA
Rolando Navarrete	Philippines	1981–1982	WBC
Rafael Limon	Mexico	1982	WBC
Bobby Chacon	USA	1982–1983	WBC
Roger Mayweather	USA	1983–1984	WBA
Hector Camacho*	Puerto Rico	1983–1984	WBC
Rocky Lockridge	USA	1984–1985	WBA
Hwan-Kil Yuh	S Korea	1984–1985	IBF
Julio Cesar Chavez*	Mexico	1984–1987	WBC
Lester Ellis	England	1985	IBF
Wilfredo Gomez	Puerto Rico	1985–1986	WBA
Barry Michael	England	1985–1987	IBF
Alfredo Layne	Panama	1986	WBA
Brian Mitchell	S Africa	1986–	WBA
Rocky Lockridge	USA	1987–1988	IBF
Azumah Nelson	Ghana	1988–	WBC
Tony Lopez	USA	1988–	IBF

Title Bouts

18.11.21 Johnny Dundee W DIS 5 K. O. Chaney, New York C, USA (NY)
06.07.22 Johnny Dundee W PTS 15 Jackie Sharkey, New York C, USA (NY)
28.08.22 Johnny Dundee W PTS 15 Pepper Martin, New York C, USA (NY)
02.02.23 Johnny Dundee W PTS 15 Elino Flores, New York C, USA (NY)
30.05.23 Jack Bernstein W PTS 15 Johnny Dundee, New York C, USA (NY/NBA)
25.06.23 Jack Bernstein W CO 5 Freddie Jacks, Philadelphia, USA (NY/NBA)
17.12.23 Johnny Dundee W PTS 15 Jack Bernstein, New York C, USA (NY/NBA)
20.06.24 Kid Sullivan W RTD 9 Johnny Dundee, New York C, USA (NY/NBA)
18.08.24 Kid Sullivan W PTS 15 Pepper Martin, New York C, USA (NY/NBA)
15.10.24 Kid Sullivan W CO 5 Mike Ballerino, New York C, USA (NY/NBA)
01.04.25 Mike Ballerino W PTS 10 Kid Sullivan, Philadelphia, USA (NY/NBA)
06.07.25 Mike Ballerino W PTS 15 Pepper Martin, New York C, USA (NY/NBA)
02.12.25 Tod Morgan W RTD 10 Mike Ballerino, Los Angeles, USA (NY/NBA)
03.06.26 Tod Morgan W RTD 6 Kid Sullivan, New York C, USA (NY/NBA)
30.09.26 Tod Morgan W PTS 15 Joe Glick, New York C, USA (NY/NBA)
19.10.26 Tod Morgan W PTS 10 Johnny Dundee, San Francisco, USA (NY/NBA)
19.11.26 Tod Morgan W PTS 15 Carl Duane, New York C, USA (NY/NBA)
28.05.27 Tod Morgan W PTS 12 Vic Foley, Vancouver, Canada (NY/NBA)
16.12.27 Tod Morgan W DIS 14 Joe Glick, New York C, USA (NY/NBA)
24.05.28 Tod Morgan W PTS 15 Eddie Martin, New York C, USA (NY/NBA)
18.07.28 Tod Morgan W PTS 15 Eddie Martin, New York C, USA (NY/NBA)
03.12.28 Tod Morgan DREW 10 Santiago Zorilla, San Francisco, USA (NY/NBA)
05.04.29 Tod Morgan W PTS 10 Santiago Zorilla, Los Angeles, USA (NY/NBA)
20.05.29 Tod Morgan W PTS 10 Baby Sal Sorio, Los Angeles, USA (NY/NBA)
20.12.29 Benny Bass W CO 2 Tod Morgan, New York C, USA (NY/NBA)
Benny Bass ceased to be recognised by NY (NY abolished weight division)
03.02.30 Benny Bass W RSC 4 Davey Abad, St Louis, USA (NBA)
05.01.31 Benny Bass W PTS 10 Lew Massey, Philadelphia, USA (NBA)
15.07.31 Kid Chocolate W RSC 7 Benny Bass, Philadelphia, USA (NBA)
10.04.32 Kid Chocolate W PTS 15 Davey Abad, Havana, Cuba (NBA)
04.08.32 Kid Chocolate W PTS 10 Eddie Shea, Chicago, USA (NBA)
01.05.33 Kid Chocolate W PTS 10 Johnny Farr, Philadelphia, USA (NBA)
04.12.33 Kid Chocolate W PTS 10 Frankie Wallace, Cleveland, USA (NBA)
25.12.33 Frankie Klick W RSC 7 Kid Chocolate, Philadelphia, USA (NBA)
Frankie Klick ceased to be recognised by the NBA (title fell into disuse)
06.12.49 Sandy Saddler W PTS 10 Orlando Zulueta, Cleveland, USA (OHIO)
18.04.50 Sandy Saddler W RSC 9 Lauro Salas, Cleveland, USA (OHIO)
28.02.51 Sandy Saddler W CO 2 Diego Sosa, Havana, Cuba (OHIO)
Sandy Saddler ceased to be recognised by Ohio (failure to defend in Cleveland after regaining the featherweight title)
20.07.59 Harold Gomes W PTS 15 Paul Jorgensen, Providence, USA (NBA)
16.03.60 Flash Elorde W CO 7 Harold Gomes, Quezon C, Philippines (NBA)
17.08.60 Flash Elorde W CO 1 Harold Gomes, San Francisco, USA (NBA)
19.03.61 Flash Elorde W PTS 15 Joey Lopes, Manila, Philippines (NBA)
16.12.61 Flash Elorde W RSC 1 Sergio Caprari, Manila, Philippines (NBA)
23.06.62 Flash Elorde W PTS 15 Auburn Copeland, Manila, Philippines (NBA)
16.02.63 Flash Elorde W PTS 15 Johnny Bizzarro, Manila, Philippines (WBA)
16.11.63 Flash Elorde W DIS 11 Love Allotey, Quezon C, Philippines (WBA)
27.07.64 Flash Elorde W RSC 12 Teruo Kosaka, Tokyo, Japan (WBA)
05.06.65 Flash Elorde W CO 15 Teruo Kosaka, Quezon C, Philippines
04.12.65 Flash Elorde W PTS 15 Kang-Il Suh, Quezon C, Philippines
22.10.66 Flash Elorde W PTS 15 Vincente Derado, Quezon C, Philippines
15.06.67 Yoshiaki Numata W PTS 15 Flash Elorde, Tokyo, Japan
14.12.67 Hiroshi Kobayashi W CO 12 Yoshiaki Numata, Tokyo, Japan
30.03.68 Hiroshi Kobayashi DREW 15 Rene Barrientos, Tokyo, Japan
06.10.68 Hiroshi Kobayashi W PTS 15 Jaime Valladeres, Tokyo, Japan
Hiroshi Kobayashi forfeited WBC recognition (failure to defend against Rene Barrientos)
15.02.69 Rene Barrientos W PTS 15 Ruben Navarro, Quezon C, Philippines (WBC)
06.04.69 Hiroshi Kobayashi W PTS 15 Antonio Amaya, Tokyo, Japan (WBA)
09.11.69 Hiroshi Kobayashi W PTS 15 Carlos Canete, Tokyo, Japan (WBA)
05.04.70 Yoshiaki Numata W PTS 15 Rene Barrientos, Tokyo, Japan (WBC)
23.08.70 Hiroshi Kobayashi W PTS 15 Antonio Amaya, Tokyo, Japan (WBA)
27.09.70 Yoshiaki Numata W CO 5 Raul Rojas, Tokyo, Japan (WBC)
03.01.71 Yoshiaki Numata W PTS 15 Rene Barrientos, Shizuaka, Japan (WBC)
03.03.71 Hiroshi Kobayashi W PTS 15 Ricardo Arredondo, Tokyo, Japan (WBA)
30.05.71 Yoshiaki Numata W PTS 15 Lionel Rose, Hiroshima, Japan (WBC)
29.07.71 Alfredo Marcano W RTD 10 Hiroshi Kobayashi, Aomori, Japan (WBA)
10.10.71 Ricardo Arredondo W CO 10 Yoshiaki Numata, Sendai, Japan (WBC)
07.11.71 Alfredo Marcano W RSC 4 Kenji Iwata, Caracas, Venezuela (WBA)
29.01.72 Ricardo Arredondo W PTS 15 Jose Marin, San Jose, Costa Rica (WBC)
22.04.72 Ricardo Arredondo W CO 5 William Martinez, Mexico C, Mexico (WBC)
25.04.72 Ben Villaflor W PTS 15 Alfredo Marcano, Honolulu, Hawaii (WBA)
05.09.72 Ben Villaflor DREW 15 Victor Echegaray, Honolulu, Hawaii (WBA)
15.09.72 Ricardo Arredondo W CO 12 Susumu Okabe, Tokyo, Japan (WBC)
06.03.73 Ricardo Arredondo W PTS 15 Apollo Yoshio, Fukuoka C, Japan (WBC)
12.03.73 Kuniaki Shibata W PTS 15 Ben Villaflor, Honolulu, Hawaii (WBA)
19.06.73 Kuniaki Shibata W PTS 15 Victor Echegaray, Tokyo, Japan (WBA)
01.09.73 Ricardo Arredondo W RSC 6 Morito Kashiwaba, Tokyo, Japan (WBC)

18.10.73 Ben Villaflor W CO 1 Kuniaki Shibata, Honolulu, Hawaii (WBA)
28.02.74 Kuniaki Shibata W PTS 15 Ricardo Arredondo, Tokyo, Japan (WBC)
14.03.74 Ben Villaflor DREW 15 Apollo Yoshio, Toyama, Japan (WBA)
27.06.74 Kuniaki Shibata W PTS 15 Antonio Amaya, Tokyo, Japan (WBC)
03.08.74 Kuniaki Shibata W RSC 15 Ramiro Bolanos, Tokyo, Japan (WBC)
24.08.74 Ben Villaflor W RSC 2 Yasutsune Uehara, Honololu, Hawaii (WBA)
13.03.75 Ben Villaflor W PTS 15 Hyun-Chi Kim, Quezon C, Philippines (WBA)
27.03.75 Kuniaki Shibata W PTS 15 Ould Makloufi, Fukuoka C, Japan (WBC)
05.07.75 Alfredo Escalera W CO 2 Kuniaki Shibata, Kasamatsu, Japan (WBC)
20.09.75 Alfredo Escalera DREW 15 Leonel Hernandez, Caracas, Venezuela (WBC)
12.12.75 Alfredo Escalera W RSC 9 Sven-Erik Paulsen, Oslo, Norway (WBC)
12.01.76 Ben Villaflor W RSC 13 Morito Kashiwaba, Tokyo, Japan (WBA)
20.02.76 Alfredo Escalera W RSC 13 Jose Fernandez, San Juan, Puerto Rico (WBC)
01.04.76 Alfredo Escalera W RSC 6 Buzzsaw Yamabe, Nara, Japan (WBC)
13.04.76 Ben Villaflor DREW 15 Sam Serrano, Honolulu, Hawaii (WBA)
01.07.76 Alfredo Escalera W PTS 15 Buzzsaw Yamabe, Nara, Japan (WBC)
18.09.76 Alfredo Escalera W RTD 12 Ray Lunny, San Juan, Puerto Rico (WBC)
16.10.76 Sam Serrano W PTS 15 Ben Villaflor, San Juan, Puerto Rico (WBA)
30.11.76 Alfredo Escalera W PTS 15 Tyrone Everett, Philadelphia, USA (WBC)
15.01.77 Sam Serrano W RSC 11 Alberto Herrera, Guayaquil, Ecuador (WBA)
17.03.77 Alfredo Escalera W RSC 6 Ronnie McGarvey, San Juan, Puerto Rico (WBC)
16.05.77 Alfredo Escalera W CO 8 Carlos Becerril, Landover, USA (WBC)
26.06.77 Sam Serrano W PTS 15 Leonel Hernandez, Cruz, Venezuela (WBA)
27.08.77 Sam Serrano W PTS 15 Apollo Yoshio, San Juan, Puerto Rico (WBA)
10.09.77 Alfredo Escalera W PTS 15 Sigfredo Rodriguez, San Juan, Puerto Rico (WBC)
19.11.77 Sam Serrano W RSC 10 Tae-Ho Kim, San Juan, Puerto Rico (WBA)
28.01.78 Alexis Arguello W RSC 13 Alfredo Escalera, Bayamon, Puerto Rico (WBC)
18.02.78 Sam Serrano W PTS 15 Mario Martinez, San Juan, Puerto Rico (WBA)
29.04.78 Alexis Arguello W RSC 5 Rey Tam, Los Angeles, USA (WBC)
03.06.78 Alexis Arguello W CO 1 Diego Alcala, San Juan, Puerto Rico (WBC)
08.07.78 Sam Serrano W RSC 9 Yong-Ho Oh, San Juan, Puerto Rico (WBA)
10.11.78 Alexis Arguello W PTS 15 Arturo Leon, Las Vegas, USA (WBC)
29.11.78 Sam Serrano W PTS 15 Takas Maruki, Nagoya, Japan (WBA)
04.02.79 Alexis Arguello W CO 13 Alfredo Escalera, Rimini, Italy (WBC)
18.02.79 Sam Serrano W PTS 15 Julio Valdez, San Juan, Puerto Rico (WBA)
14.04.79 Sam Serrano W RSC 8 Nkosana Mgxaji, Capetown, S Africa (WBA)
08.07.79 Alexis Arguello W RSC 11 Rafael Limon, New York C, USA (WBC)
16.11.79 Alexis Arguello W RTD 7 Bobby Chacon, Los Angeles, USA (WBC)
20.01.80 Alexis Arguello W RSC 11 Ruben Castillo, Tucson, USA (WBC)
03.04.80 Sam Serrano W RSC 13 Battle Hawk Kazama, Nara, Japan (WBA)
27.04.80 Alexis Arguello W RSC 4 Rolando Navarrete, San Juan, Puerto Rico (WBC)
Alexis Arguello relinquished WBC version of title (moved up to lightweight)
02.08.80 Yasutsune Uehara W CO 6 Sam Serrano, Detroit, USA (WBA)
20.11.80 Yasutsune Uehara W PTS 15 Leonel Hernandez, Tokyo, Japan (WBA)
11.12.80 Rafael Limon W RSC 15 Ildefonso Bethelmy, Los Angeles, USA (WBC)
08.03.81 Cornelius Boza-Edwards W PTS 15 Rafael Limon, Stockton, USA (WBC)
09.04.81 Sam Serrano W PTS 15 Yasutsune Uehara, Wakayama, Japan (WBA)
30.05.81 Cornelius Boza-Edwards W RTD 13 Bobby Chacon, Las Vegas, USA (WBC)
29.06.81 Sam Serrano W PTS 15 Leonel Hernandez, Caracas, Venezuela (WBA)
29.08.81 Rolando Navarrete W CO 5 Cornelius Boza-Edwards, Reggio, Italy (WBC)
10.12.81 Sam Serrano W RSC 12 Hikaru Tomonari, San Juan, Puerto Rico (WBA)
16.01.82 Rolando Navarrete W CO 11 Chung-Il Choi, Manila, Philippines (WBC)
29.05.82 Rafael Limon W CO 12 Rolando Navarrete, Las Vegas, USA (WBC)
05.06.82 Sam Serrano NC 11 Benedicto Villablanca, Santiago, Chile (WBA)
18.09.82 Rafael Limon W RSC 7 Chung-Il Choi, Los Angeles, USA (WBC)
11.12.82 Bobby Chacon W PTS 15 Rafael Limon, Sacramento, USA (WBC)
19.01.83 Roger Mayweather W CO 8 Sam Serrano, San Juan, Puerto Rico (WBA)
20.04.83 Roger Mayweather W RSC 8 Jorge Alvarado, San Jose, USA (WBA)
15.05.83 Bobby Chacon W PTS 12 Cornelius Boza-Edwards, Las Vegas, USA (WBC)
Bobby Chacon forfeited recognition (contractual dispute)
07.08.83 Hector Camacho W RSC 5 Rafael Limon, San Juan, Puerto Rico (WBC)
17.08.83 Roger Mayweather W CO 1 Benedicto Villablanca, Las Vegas, USA (WBA)
18.11.83 Hector Camacho W CO 5 Rafael Solis, San Juan, Puerto Rico (WBC)
Hector Camacho relinquished WBC version of title (moved up to lightweight)
26.02.84 Rocky Lockridge W CO 1 Roger Mayweather, Beaumont, USA (WBA)
22.04.84 Hwan-Kil Yuh W PTS 15 Rod Sequenan, Seoul, S Korea (IBF)
12.06.84 Rocky Lockridge W RSC 11 Taej-In Moon, Anchorage, Alaska (WBA)
13.09.84 Julio Cesar Chavez W RSC 8 Mario Martinez, Los Angeles, USA (WBC)
16.09.84 Hwan-Kil Yuh W CO 6 Sak Galexi, Pohang, S Korea (IBF)
27.01.85 Rocky Lockridge W RSC 6 Kamel Bou Ali, Riva del Garda, Italy (WBA)
15.02.85 Lester Ellis W PTS 15 Hwan-Kil Yuh, Melbourne, Australia (IBF)
19.04.85 Julio Cesar Chavez W RSC 6 Ruben Castillo, Los Angeles, USA (WBC)
26.04.85 Lester Ellis W CO 13 Rod Sequenan, Melbourne, Australia (IBF)
19.05.85 Wilfredo Gomez W PTS 15 Rocky Lockridge, San Juan, Puerto Rico (WBA)
07.07.85 Julio Cesar Chavez W RSC 2 Roger Mayweather, Las Vegas, USA (WBC)
12.07.85 Barry Michael W PTS 15 Lester Ellis, Melbourne, Australia (IBF)
22.09.85 Julio Cesar Chavez W PTS 12 Dwight Pratchett, Las Vegas, USA (WBC)
18.10.85 Barry Michael W RSC 4 Jin-Shik Choi, Darwin, Australia (IBF)
15.05.86 Julio Cesar Chavez W RSC 5 Faustino Barrios, Paris, France (WBC)
23.05.86 Barry Michael W RSC 4 Mark Fernandez, Melbourne, Australia (IBF)
24.05.86 Alfredo Layne W RSC 9 Wilfredo Gomez, San Juan, Puerto Rico (WBA)
13.06.86 Julio Cesar Chavez W RSC 7 Refugio Rojas, New York C, USA (WBC)
03.08.86 Julio Cesar Chavez W PTS 12 Rocky Lockridge, Monte Carlo (WBC)
23.08.86 Barry Michael W PTS 12 Najib Daho, Manchester, England (IBF)
27.09.86 Brian Mitchell W RSC 10 Alfredo Layne, Sun C, S Africa (WBA)
12.12.86 Julio Cesar Chavez W PTS 12 Juan Laporte, New York C, USA (WBC)
27.03.87 Brian Mitchell DREW 15 Jose Rivera, San Juan, Puerto Rico (WBA)
18.04.87 Julio Cesar Chavez W RSC 3 Francisco Tomas Cruz, Nimes, France (WBC)
31.07.87 Brian Mitchell W RSC 14 Francisco Fernandez, Panama C (WBA)
09.08.87 Rocky Lockridge W RTD 8 Barry Michael, Windsor, England (IBF)
21.08.87 Julio Cesar Chavez W PTS 12 Danilo Cabrera, Tijuana, Mexico (WBC)
Julio Cesar Chavez relinquished WBC version of title (won WBA lightweight title)
03.10.87 Brian Mitchell W PTS 15 Daniel Londas, Gravelines, France (WBA)
25.10.87 Rocky Lockridge W RSC 10 Johnny de la Rosa, Tucson, USA (IBF)
19.12.87 Brian Mitchell W RTD 8 Salvatore Curcetti, Capo d'Orlando, Italy (WBA)
29.02.88 Azumah Nelson W PTS 12 Mario Martinez, Los Angeles, USA (WBC)
02.04.88 Rocky Lockridge W PTS 15 Harold Knight, Atlantic C, USA (IBF)
26.04.88 Brian Mitchell W PTS 12 Jose Rivera, Madrid, Spain (WBA)
25.06.88 Azumah Nelson W RSC 9 Lupe Suarez, Atlantic C, USA (WBC)
27.07.88 Tony Lopez W PTS 12 Rocky Lockridge, Sacramento, USA (IBF)
27.10.88 Tony Lopez W PTS 12 Juan Molina, Sacramento, USA (IBF)
02.11.88 Brian Mitchell W PTS 12 Jim McDonnell, London, England (WBA)
10.12.88 Azumah Nelson W CO 3 Sydnei dal Rovere, Accra, Ghana (WBC)
10.02.89 Brian Mitchell W RSC 8 Salvatore Bottiglieri, Capo d'Orlando, Italy (WBA)
25.02.89 Azumah Nelson W RSC 12 Mario Martinez, Las Vegas, USA (WBC)
05.03.89 Tony Lopez W PTS 12 Rocky Lockridge, Sacramento, USA (IBF)

Lightweight (135 lbs)

Title Holders

	Birthplace	Tenure	Status
George Lavigne	USA	1896–1899	
Frank Erne	Switzerland	1899–1902	
Joe Gans	USA	1902–1904	
Jimmy Britt	USA	1904–1905	
Battling Nelson	Denmark	1905–1906	
Joe Gans	USA	1906–1908	
Battling Nelson	Denmark	1908–1910	
Ad Wolgast	USA	1910–1912	
Willie Ritchie	USA	1912–1914	
Freddie Welsh	Wales	1914–1917	
Benny Leonard*	USA	1917–1925	
Jimmy Goodrich	USA	1925	NY
Rocky Kansas	USA	1925–1926	
Sammy Mandell	USA	1926–1930	
Al Singer	USA	1930	
Tony Canzoneri	USA	1930–1933	
Barney Ross*	USA	1933–1935	
Tony Canzeroni	USA	1935–1936	
Lou Ambers	USA	1936–1938	
Henry Armstrong	USA	1938–1939	
Lou Ambers	USA	1939–1940	
Sammy Angott	USA	1940–1941	NBA
Lew Jenkins	USA	1940–1941	NY
Sammy Angott*	USA	1941–1942	
Beau Jack	USA	1942–1943	NY
Slugger White	USA	1943	MARY
Bob Montgomery	USA	1943	NY
Sammy Angott	USA	1943–1944	NBA
Beau Jack	USA	1943–1944	NY
Bob Montgomery	USA	1944–1947	NY
Juan Zurita	Mexico	1944–1945	NBA
Ike Williams	USA	1945–1947	NBA
Ike Williams	USA	1947–1951	
Jimmy Carter	USA	1951–1952	
Lauro Salas	Mexico	1952	
Jimmy Carter	USA	1952–1954	
Paddy de Marco	USA	1954	
Jimmy Carter	USA	1954–1955	
Wallace Bud Smith	USA	1955–1956	
Joe Brown	USA	1956–1962	
Carlos Ortiz	Puerto Rico	1962–1965	
Ismael Laguna	Panama	1965	
Carlos Ortiz	Puerto Rico	1965–1968	
Carlos Teo Cruz	Dom Republic	1968–1969	
Mando Ramos	USA	1969–1970	
Ismael Laguna	Panama	1970	
Ken Buchanan	Scotland	1970–1971	
Ken Buchanan	Scotland	1971–1972	WBA
Pedro Carrasco	Spain	1971–1972	WBC
Mando Ramos	USA	1972	WBC
Roberto Duran	Panama	1972–1978	WBA
Chango Carmona	Mexico	1972	WBC
Rodolfo Gonzalez	Mexico	1972–1974	WBC
Guts Ishimatsu	Japan	1974–1976	WBC
Esteban de Jesus	Puerto Rico	1976–1978	WBC
Roberto Duran*	Panama	1978–1979	
Jim Watt	Scotland	1979–1981	WBC
Ernesto Espana	Venezuela	1979–1980	WBA
Hilmer Kenty	USA	1980–1981	WBA
Sean O'Grady	USA	1981	WBA
Alexis Arguello*	Nicaragua	1981–1983	WBC
Claude Noel	Trinidad	1981	WBA
Arturo Frias	USA	1981–1982	WBA
Ray Mancini	USA	1982–1984	WBA
Edwin Rosario	Puerto Rico	1983–1984	WBC
Charlie Brown	USA	1984	IBF
Harry Arroyo	USA	1984–1985	IBF
Livingstone Bramble	USA	1984–1986	WBA
Jose Luis Ramirez	Mexico	1984–1985	WBC
Jimmy Paul	USA	1985–1986	IBF
Hector Camacho*	Puerto Rico	1985–1987	WBC
Edwin Rosario	Puerto Rico	1986–1987	WBA

Greg Haugen	USA	1986–1987	IBF
Vinny Pazienza	USA	1987–1988	IBF
Jose Luis Ramirez	Mexico	1987–1988	WBC
Julio Cesar Chavez	Mexico	1987–1988	WBA
Greg Haugen	USA	1988–1989	IBF
Julio Cesar Chavez	Mexico	1988–	WBA/WBC
Pernell Whitaker	USA	1989–	IBF

Title Bouts

01.09.96 George Lavigne W CO 17 Dick Burge, London, England
27.10.96 George Lavigne W CO 24 Jack Everhardt, New York C, USA
08.02.97 George Lavigne W PTS 25 Kid McPartland, New York C, USA
28.04.97 George Lavigne W 11 Eddie Connolly, New York C, USA
29.10.97 George Lavigne W RTD 12 Joe Walcott, San Francisco, USA
17.03.98 George Lavigne DREW 20 Jack Daly, Cleveland, USA
28.09.98 George Lavigne DREW 20 Frank Erne, New York C, USA
25.11.98 George Lavigne W PTS 20 Tom Tracy, San Francisco, USA
03.07.99 Frank Erne W PTS 20 George Lavigne, Buffalo, USA
04.12.99 Frank Erne DREW 25 Jack O'Brien, New York C, USA
23.03.00 Frank Erne W RTD 12 Joe Gans, New York C, USA
12.05.02 Joe Gans W CO 1 Frank Erne, Fort Erie, Canada
27.06.02 Joe Gans W CO 3 George McFadden, San Francisco, USA
24.07.02 Joe Gans W CO 15 Rufe Turner, Oakland, USA
17.09.02 Joe Gans W CO 5 Gus Gardner, Baltimore, USA
13.10.02 Joe Gans W CO 5 Kid McPartland, Fort Erie, Canada
01.01.03 Joe Gans W DIS 11 Gus Gardner, New Britain, USA
11.03.03 Joe Gans W RTD 11 Steve Crosby, Hot Springs, USA
29.05.03 Joe Gans W CO 10 Willie Fitzgerald, San Francisco, USA
04.07.03 Joe Gans W CO 5 Buddy King, Butte, USA
12.01.04 Joe Gans W PTS 10 Willie Fitzgerald, Detroit, USA
31.10.04 Joe Gans W DIS 5 Jimmy Britt, San Francisco, USA
Joe Gans lost general recognition (refused to make the weight)
20.12.04 Jimmy Britt W PTS 20 Battling Nelson, San Francisco, USA
05.05.05 Jimmy Britt W PTS 20 Jabez White, San Francisco, USA
21.07.05 Jimmy Britt W PTS 20 Kid Sullivan, San Francisco, USA
09.09.05 Battling Nelson W CO 18 Jimmy Britt, San Francisco, USA
03.09.06 Joe Gans W DIS 42 Battling Nelson, Goldfield, USA
01.01.07 Joe Gans W CO 8 Kid Herman, Tonopah, USA
09.09.07 Joe Gans W RTD 6 Jimmy Britt, San Francisco, USA
27.09.07 Joe Gans W PTS 20 George Memsic, Los Angeles, USA
01.04.08 Joe Gans W CO 3 Spike Robson, Philadelphia, USA
14.05.08 Joe Gans W RSC 11 Rudy Unholz, San Francisco, USA
04.07.08 Battling Nelson W CO 17 Joe Gans, San Francisco, USA
09.09.08 Battling Nelson W CO 21 Joe Gans, San Francisco, USA
29.05.09 Battling Nelson W CO 23 Dick Hyland, San Francisco, USA
22.06.09 Battling Nelson W CO 5 Jack Clifford, Oklahoma C, USA
22.02.10 Ad Wolgast W RSC 40 Battling Nelson, Richmond, USA
17.03.11 Ad Wolgast W RSC 9 George Memsic, Los Angeles, USA
31.03.11 Ad Wolgast W RTD 5 Antonio la Grave, San Francisco, USA
26.04.11 Ad Wolgast W RSC 2 One-Round Hogan, New York C, USA
27.05.11 Ad Wolgast W RTD 17 Frankie Burns, San Francisco, USA
04.07.11 Ad Wolgast W CO 13 Owen Moran, San Francisco, USA
04.07.12 Ad Wolgast W CO 13 Joe Rivers, Los Angeles, USA
28.11.12 Willie Ritchie W DIS 16 Ad Wolgast, San Francisco, USA
04.07.13 Willie Ritchie W CO 11 Joe Rivers, San Francisco, USA
17.04.14 Willie Ritchie W PTS 20 Tommy Murphy, San Francisco, USA
07.07.14 Freddie Welsh W PTS 20 Willie Ritchie, London, England
04.07.16 Freddie Welsh W DIS 11 Ad Wolgast, Denver, USA
04.09.16 Freddie Welsh W PTS 20 Charley White, Colorado Springs, USA
28.05.17 Benny Leonard W RSC 9 Freddie Welsh, New York C, USA
25.07.17 Benny Leonard W CO 3 Johnny Kilbane, Philadelphia, USA
05.07.20 Benny Leonard W CO 9 Charley White, Benton Harbor, USA
26.11.20 Benny Leonard W RSC 14 Joe Welling, New York C, USA
14.01.21 Benny Leonard W RSC 6 Richie Mitchell, New York C, USA
10.02.22 Benny Leonard W PTS 15 Rocky Kansas, New York C, USA
04.07.22 Benny Leonard W RSC 8 Rocky Kansas, Michigan C, USA
23.07.23 Benny Leonard W PTS 15 Lew Tendler, New York C, USA
Benny Leonard relinquished title (retired)
13.07.25 Jimmy Goodrich W RSC 2 Stanislaus Loayza, New York C, USA (NY)
07.12.25 Rocky Kansas W PTS 15 Jimmy Goodrich, Buffalo, USA
03.07.26 Sammy Mandell W PTS 10 Rocky Kansas, Chicago, USA
21.05.28 Sammy Mandell W PTS 15 Jimmy McLarnin, New York C, USA
02.08.29 Sammy Mandell W PTS 10 Tony Canzoneri, Chicago, USA
17.07.30 Al Singer W CO 1 Sammy Mandell, New York C, USA
14.11.30 Tony Canzoneri W CO 1 Al Singer, New York C, USA
24.04.31 Tony Canzoneri W CO 3 Jackie Kid Berg, Chicago, USA
10.09.31 Tony Canzoneri W PTS 15 Jackie Kid Berg, New York C, USA
20.11.31 Tony Canzoneri W PTS 15 Kid Chocolate, New York C, USA
04.11.32 Tony Canzoneri W PTS 15 Billy Petrolle, New York C, USA
23.06.33 Barney Ross W PTS 10 Tony Canzoneri, Chicago, USA
12.09.33 Barney Ross W PTS 15 Tony Canzoneri, New York C, USA
Barney Ross relinquished title (moved up to welterweight)
10.05.35 Tony Canzoneri W PTS 15 Lou Ambers, New York C, USA
04.10.35 Tony Canzoneri W PTS 15 Al Roth, New York C, USA
03.09.36 Lou Ambers W PTS 15 Tony Canzoneri, New York C, USA
07.05.37 Lou Ambers W PTS 15 Tony Canzoneri, New York C, USA
23.09.37 Lou Ambers W PTS 15 Pedro Montanez, New York C, USA
17.08.38 Henry Armstrong W PTS 15 Lou Ambers, New York C, USA
22.08.39 Lou Ambers W PTS 15 Henry Armstrong, New York C, USA
Lou Ambers forfeited NBA recognition (failure to defend against Davey Day)
03.05.40 Sammy Angott W PTS 15 Davey Day, Louisville, USA (NBA)
10.05.40 Lew Jenkins W RSC 3 Lou Ambers, New York C, USA (NY)
22.11.40 Lew Jenkins W RSC 2 Pete Lello, New York C, USA (NY)
02.05.41 Sammy Angott W PTS 12 Dave Castilloux, Louisville, USA (NBA)
19.12.41 Sammy Angott W PTS 15 Lew Jenkins, New York C, USA
15.05.42 Sammy Angott W PTS 15 Allie Stolz, New York C, USA
Sammy Angott relinquished title (retired)
18.12.42 Beau Jack W CO 3 Tippy Larkin, New York C, USA (NY)
04.01.43 Slugger White W PTS 15 Willie Joyce, Baltimore, USA (MARY)
21.05.43 Bob Montgomery W PTS 15 Beau Jack, New York C, USA (NY)
27.10.43 Sammy Angott W PTS 15 Slugger White, Los Angeles, USA (NBA)
19.11.43 Beau Jack W PTS 15 Bob Montgomery, New York C, USA (NY)
03.03.44 Bob Montgomery W PTS 15 Beau Jack, New York C, USA (NY)
08.03.44 Juan Zurita W PTS 15 Sammy Angott, Los Angeles, USA (NBA)
18.04.45 Ike Williams W CO 2 Juan Zurita, Mexico C, Mexico (NBA)
30.04.46 Ike Williams W RSC 8 Enrique Bolanos, Los Angeles, USA (NBA)
28.06.46 Bob Montgomery W CO 13 Allie Stolz, New York C, USA (NY)
04.09.46 Ike Williams W CO 9 Ronnie James, Cardiff, Wales (NBA)
26.11.46 Bob Montgomery W CO 8 Wesley Mouzon, Philadelphia, USA (NY)
04.08.47 Ike Williams W CO 6 Bob Montgomery, Philadelphia, USA
25.05.48 Ike Williams W PTS 15 Enrique Bolanos, Los Angeles, USA
12.07.48 Ike Williams W RSC 6 Beau Jack, Philadelphia, USA
23.09.48 Ike Williams W CO 10 Jesse Flores, New York C, USA
21.07.49 Ike Williams W RSC 4 Enrique Bolanos, Los Angeles, USA
05.12.49 Ike Williams W PTS 15 Freddie Dawson, Philadelphia, USA
25.05.51 Jimmy Carter W RSC 14 Ike Williams, New York C, USA
14.11.51 Jimmy Carter W PTS 15 Art Aragon, Los Angeles, USA
01.04.52 Jimmy Carter W PTS 15 Lauro Salas, Los Angeles, USA
14.05.52 Lauro Salas W PTS 15 Jimmy Carter, Los Angeles, USA
15.10.52 Jimmy Carter W PTS 15 Lauro Salas, Chicago, USA
24.04.53 Jimmy Carter W RSC 4 Tommy Collins, Boston, USA
12.06.53 Jimmy Carter W RSC 13 George Araujo, New York C, USA
11.11.53 Jimmy Carter W CO 5 Armand Savoie, Montreal, Canada
05.03.54 Paddy de Marco W PTS 15 Jimmy Carter, New York C, USA
17.11.54 Jimmy Carter W RSC 15 Paddy de Marco, San Francisco, USA
29.06.55 Wallace Bud Smith W PTS 15 Jimmy Carter, Boston, USA
19.10.55 Wallace Bud Smith W PTS 15 Jimmy Carter, Cincinnati, USA
24.08.56 Joe Brown W PTS 15 Wallace Bud Smith, New Orleans, USA
13.02.57 Joe Brown W RSC 10 Wallace Bud Smith, Miami, USA
19.06.57 Joe Brown W RSC 15 Orlando Zulueta, Denver, USA
04.12.57 Joe Brown W RSC 11 Joey Lopes, Chicago, USA
07.05.58 Joe Brown W RSC 8 Ralph Dupas, Houston, USA
23.07.58 Joe Brown W PTS 15 Kenny Lane, Houston, USA
11.02.59 Joe Brown W PTS 15 Johnny Busso, Houston, USA
03.06.59 Joe Brown W RTD 8 Paolo Rossi, Washington, USA
02.12.59 Joe Brown W RTD 5 Dave Charnley, Houston, USA
28.10.60 Joe Brown W PTS 15 Cisco Andrade, Los Angeles, USA
18.04.61 Joe Brown W PTS 15 Dave Charnley, London, England
28.10.61 Joe Brown W PTS 15 Bert Somodio, Quezon C, Philippines
21.04.62 Carlos Ortiz W PTS 15 Joe Brown, Las Vegas, USA
03.12.62 Carlos Ortiz W CO 5 Teruo Kosaka, Tokyo, Japan
07.04.63 Carlos Ortiz W RSC 13 Doug Vaillant, San Juan, Puerto Rico
15.02.64 Carlos Ortiz W RSC 14 Flash Elorde, Manila, Philippines
11.04.64 Carlos Ortiz W PTS 15 Kenny Lane, San Juan, Puerto Rico
10.04.65 Ismael Laguna W PTS 15 Carlos Ortiz, Panama C, Panama
13.11.65 Carlos Ortiz W PTS 15 Ismael Laguna, San Juan, Puerto Rico
20.06.66 Carlos Ortiz W RSC 12 Johnny Bizzarro, Pittsburgh, USA
22.10.66 Carlos Ortiz W RSC 5 Sugar Ramos, Mexico C, Mexico
28.11.66 Carlos Ortiz W CO 14 Flash Elorde, New York C, USA
01.07.67 Carlos Ortiz W RSC 4 Sugar Ramos, San Juan, Puerto Rico
16.08.67 Carlos Ortiz W PTS 15 Ismael Laguna, New York C, USA
29.06.68 Carlos Teo Cruz W PTS 15 Carlos Ortiz, St Domingo, Puerto Rico
28.09.68 Carlos Teo Cruz W PTS 15 Mando Ramos, Los Angeles, USA
18.02.69 Mando Ramos W RSC 11 Carlos Teo Cruz, Los Angeles, USA
04.10.69 Mando Ramos W RSC 6 Yoshiaki Numata, Los Angeles, USA
03.03.70 Ismael Laguna W RTD 9 Mando Ramos, Los Angeles, USA
07.06.70 Ismael Laguna W RSC 13 Guts Ishimatsu, Panama C, Panama
26.09.70 Ken Buchanan W PTS 15 Ismael Laguna, San Juan, Puerto Rico
12.02.71 Ken Buchanan W PTS 15 Ruben Navarro, Los Angeles, USA
Ken Buchanan forfeited WBC recognition (failure to defend against Pedro Carrasco)
13.09.71 Ken Buchanan W PTS 15 Ismael Laguna, New York C, USA (WBA)
05.11.71 Pedro Carrasco W DIS 11 Mando Ramos, Madrid, Spain (WBC)
18.02.72 Mando Ramos W PTS 15 Pedro Carrasco, Los Angeles, USA (WBC)
26.06.72 Roberto Duran W RSC 13 Ken Buchanan, New York C, USA (WBA)
28.06.72 Mando Ramos W PTS 15 Pedro Carrasco, Madrid, Spain (WBC)
15.09.72 Chango Carmona W RSC 8 Mando Ramos, Los Angeles, USA (WBC)
10.11.72 Rodolfo Gonzalez W RTD 12 Chango Carmona, Los Angeles, USA (WBC)
20.01.73 Roberto Duran W CO 5 Jimmy Robertson, Panama C, Panama (WBA)
17.03.73 Rodolfo Gonzalez W RSC 9 Ruben Navarro, Los Angeles, USA (WBC)
02.06.73 Roberto Duran W RSC 8 Hector Thompson, Panama C, Panama (WBA)
08.09.73 Roberto Duran W RSC 10 Guts Ishimatsu, Panama C, Panama (WBA)
27.10.73 Rodolfo Gonzalez W RTD 10 Antonio Puddu, Los Angeles, USA (WBC)
16.03.74 Roberto Duran W RSC 11 Estban de Jesus, Panama C, Panama (WBA)
11.04.74 Guts Ishimatsu W CO 8 Rodolfo Gonzalez, Tokyo, Japan (WBC)
13.09.74 Guts Ishimatsu DREW 15 Tury Pineda, Nagoya, Japan (WBC)
28.11.74 Guts Ishimatsu W CO 12 Rodolfo Gonzalez, Osaka, Japan (WBC)
21.12.74 Roberto Duran W RSC 1 Masataka Takayama, San Jose, Costa Rica (WBA)
27.02.75 Guts Ishimatsu W PTS 15 Ken Buchanan, Tokyo, Japan (WBC)
02.03.75 Roberto Duran W CO 14 Ray Lampkin, Panama C, Panama (WBA)
05.06.75 Guts Ishimatsu W PTS 15 Tury Pineda, Osaka, Japan (WBC)
04.12.75 Guts Ishimatsu W CO 14 Alvaro Rojas, Tokyo, Japan (WBC)
14.12.75 Roberto Duran W CO 15 Leoncio Ortiz, San Juan, Puerto Rico (WBA)
08.05.76 Esteban de Jesus W PTS 15 Guts Ishimatsu, Bayamon, Puerto Rico (WBC)

22.05.76 Roberto Duran W CO 14 Lou Bizzarro, Erie, USA (WBA)
10.09.76 Esteban de Jesus W CO 7 Hector Medina, Bayamon, Puerto Rico (WBC)
15.10.76 Roberto Duran W CO 1 Alvaro Rojas, Los Angeles, USA (WBA)
29.01.77 Roberto Duran W CO 13 Vilomar Fernandez, Miami, USA (WBA)
12.02.77 Esteban de Jesus W RSC 6 Buzzsaw Yamabe, Bayamon, Puerto Rico (WBC)
25.06.77 Esteban de Jesus W CO 11 Vincente Mijares, Bayamon, Puerto Rico (WBC)
17.09.77 Roberto Duran W PTS 15 Edwin Viruet, Philadelphia, USA (WBA)
21.01.78 Roberto Duran W CO 12 Esteban de Jesus, Las Vegas, USA
Roberto Duran relinquished title (moved up to welterweight)
17.04.79 Jim Watt W RSC 12 Alfredo Pitalua, Glasgow, Scotland (WBC)
16.06.79 Ernesto Espana W CO 13 Claude Noel, San Juan, Puerto Rico (WBA)
04.08.79 Ernesto Espana W RSC 9 Johnny Lira, Chicago, USA (WBA)
03.11.79 Jim Watt W RSC 9 Roberto Vasquez, Glasgow, Scotland (WBC)
02.03.80 Hilmer Kenty W RSC 9 Ernesto Espana, Detroit, USA (WBA)
14.03.80 Jim Watt W RSC 4 Charlie Nash, Glasgow, Scotland (WBC)
07.06.80 Jim Watt W PTS 15 Howard Davis, Glasgow, Scotland (WBC)
02.08.80 Hilmer Kenty W RSC 9 Yong-Ho Oh, Detroit, USA (WBA)
20.09.80 Hilmer Kenty W RSC 4 Ernesto Espana, San Juan, Puerto Rico (WBA)
01.11.80 Jim Watt W RSC 12 Sean O'Grady, Glasgow, Scotland (WBC)
08.11.80 Hilmer Kenty W PTS 15 Vilomar Fernandez, Detroit, USA (WBA)
12.04.81 Sean O'Grady W PTS 15 Hilmer Kenty, Atlantic C, USA (WBA)
Sean O'Grady forfeited WBA recognition (contractual dispute)
20.06.81 Alexis Arguello W PTS 15 Jim Watt, Wembley, England (WBC)
12.09.81 Claude Noel W PTS 15 Gato Gonzalez, Atlantic C, USA (WBA)
03.10.81 Alexis Arguello W RSC 14 Ray Mancini, Atlantic C, USA (WBC)
21.11.81 Alexis Arguello W CO 7 Robert Elizondo, Las Vegas, USA (WBC)
05.12.81 Arturo Frias W CO 8 Claude Noel, Las Vegas, USA (WBA)
30.01.82 Arturo Frias W TD 9 Ernesto Espana, Atlantic C, USA (WBA)
13.02.82 Alexis Arguello W RSC 6 Bubba Busceme, Beaumont, USA (WBC)
08.05.82 Ray Mancini W RSC 1 Arturo Frias, Las Vegas, USA (WBA)
22.05.82 Alexis Arguello W CO 5 Andy Ganigan, Las Vegas, USA (WBC)
Alexis Arguello relinquished WBC version of title (moved up to light-welterweight)
24.07.82 Ray Mancini W RSC 6 Ernesto Espana, Warren, USA (WBA)
13.11.82 Ray Mancini W RSC 14 Deuk-Koo Kim, Las Vegas, USA (WBA)
01.05.83 Edwin Rosario W PTS 12 Jose Luis Ramirez, San Juan, Puerto Rico (WBC)
15.09.83 Ray Mancini W CO 9 Orlando Romero, New York C, USA (WBA)
14.01.84 Ray Mancini W RSC 3 Bobby Chacon, Reno, USA (WBA)
30.01.84 Charlie Choo Choo Brown W PTS 15 Melvin Paul, Atlantic C, USA (IBF)
17.03.84 Edwin Rosario W RSC 1 Robert Elizondo, San Juan, Puerto Rico (WBC)
15.04.84 Harry Arroyo W RSC 14 Charlie Choo Choo Brown, Atlantic C, USA (IBF)
01.06.84 Livingstone Bramble W RSC 14 Ray Mancini, Buffalo, USA (WBA)
23.06.84 Edwin Rosario W PTS 12 Howard Davis, San Juan, Puerto Rico (WBC)
01.09.84 Harry Arroyo W RSC 8 Charlie W. L. Brown, Youngstown, USA (IBF)
03.11.84 Jose Luis Ramirez W RSC 4 Edwin Rosario, San Juan, Puerto Rico (WBC)
12.01.85 Harry Arroyo W RSC 11 Terrence Ali, Atlantic C, USA (IBF)
16.02.85 Livingstone Bramble W PTS 15 Ray Mancini, Reno, USA (WBA)
06.04.85 Jimmy Paul W PTS 15 Harry Arroyo, Atlantic C, USA (IBF)
30.06.85 Jimmy Paul W RSC 14 Robin Blake, Las Vegas, USA (IBF)
10.08.85 Hector Camacho W PTS 12 Jose Luis Ramirez, Las Vegas, USA (WBC)
16.02.86 Livingstone Bramble W RSC 13 Tyrone Crawley, Reno, USA (WBA)
04.06.86 Jimmy Paul W PTS 15 Irleis Perez, E Rutherford, USA (IBF)
13.06.86 Hector Camacho W PTS 12 Edwin Rosario, New York C, USA (WBC)
15.08.86 Jimmy Paul W PTS 15 Darryl Tyson, Detroit, USA (IBF)
26.09.86 Hector Camacho W PTS 12 Cornelius Boza-Edwards, Miami, USA (WBC)
Hector Camacho relinquished WBC version of title (moved up to light-welterweight)
26.09.86 Edwin Rosario W CO 2 Livingstone Bramble, Miami, USA (WBA)
05.12.86 Greg Haugen W PTS 15 Jimmy Paul, Las Vegas, USA (IBF)
07.06.87 Vinny Pazienza W PTS 15 Greg Haugen, Providence, USA (IBF)
19.07.87 Jose Luis Ramirez W PTS 12 Terrence Alli, St Tropez, France (WBC)
11.08.87 Edwin Rosario W CO 8 Juan Nazario, Chicago, USA (WBA)
10.10.87 Jose Luis Ramirez W CO 5 Cornelius Boza-Edwards, Paris, France (WBC)
21.11.87 Julio Cesar Chavez W RSC 11 Edwin Rosario, Las Vegas, USA (WBA)
06.02.88 Greg Haugen W PTS 15 Vinny Pazienza, Atlantic C, USA (IBF)
12.03.88 Jose Luis Ramirez W PTS 12 Pernell Whitaker, Paris, France (WBC)
11.04.88 Greg Haugen W TD 11 Miguel Santana, Tacoma, USA (IBF)
16.04.88 Julio Cesar Chavez W RSC 6 Rodolfo Aguilar, Las Vegas, USA (WBA)
28.10.88 Greg Haugen W RTD 10 Gert Bo Jacobsen, Copenhagen, Denmark (IBF)
29.10.88 Julio Cesar Chavez W TD 11 Jose Luis Ramirez, Las Vegas, USA (WBA/WBC)
18.02.89 Pernell Whitaker W PTS 12 Greg Haugen, Hampton, USA (IBF)
30.04.89 Pernell Whitaker W RSC 3 Louie Lomeli, Norfolk, USA (IBF)

Light-Welterweight (140 lbs)

Title Holders

	Birthplace	Tenure	Status
Mushy Callahan	USA	1926–1929	NBA/NYA
Mushy Callahan	USA	1929–1930	NBA
Jackie Kid Berg	England	1930–1931	NBA
Tony Canzoneri	USA	1931–1932	NBA
Johnny Jadick	USA	1932–1933	NBA
Battling Shaw	Mexico	1933	NBA
Tony Canzoneri	USA	1933	NBA
Barney Ross*	USA	1933–1935	NBA
Tippy Larkin	USA	1946–1947	MASS/NY
Carlos Ortiz	Puerto Rico	1959–1960	NBA
Duilio Loi	Italy	1960–1962	NBA
Eddie Perkins	USA	1962	NBA
Duilio Loi*	Italy	1962–1963	NBA
Roberto Cruz	Philippines	1963	WBA
Eddie Perkins	USA	1963–1965	WBA
Eddie Perkins	USA	1965	
Carlos Hernandez	Venezuela	1965–1966	
Sandro Lopopolo	Italy	1966–1967	
Paul Fujii	Hawaii	1967–1968	
Paul Fujii	Hawaii	1968	WBA
Nicolino Loche	Argentine	1968–1972	WBA
Pedro Adigue	Philippines	1968–1970	WBC
Bruno Arcari*	Italy	1970–1974	WBC
Alfonoso Frazer	Panama	1972	WBA
Antonio Cervantes	Colombia	1972–1976	WBA
Perico Fernandez	Spain	1974–1975	WBC
Saensak Muangsurin	Thailand	1975–1976	WBC
Wilfred Benitez	USA	1976–1977	WBA
Miguel Velasquez	Spain	1976	WBC
Saensak Muangsurin	Thailand	1976–1978	WBC
Antonio Cervantes	Colombia	1977–1980	WBA
Wilfred Benitez	USA	1977	NY
Sang-Hyun Kim	S Korea	1978–1980	WBC
Saoul Mamby	USA	1980–1982	WBC
Aaron Pryor*	USA	1980–1983	WBA
Leroy Haley	USA	1982–1983	WBC
Bruce Curry	USA	1983–1984	WBC
Johnny Bumphus	USA	1984	WBA
Bill Costello	USA	1984–1985	WBC
Gene Hatcher	USA	1984–1985	WBA
Aaron Pryor	USA	1984–1986	IBF
Ubaldo Sacco	Argentine	1985–1986	WBA
Lonnie Smith	USA	1985–1986	WBC
Patrizio Oliva	Italy	1986–1987	WBA
Gary Hinton	USA	1986	IBF
Rene Arredondo	Mexico	1986	WBC
Tsuyoshi Hamada	Japan	1986–1987	WBC
Joe Manley	USA	1986–1987	IBF
Terry Marsh*	England	1987	IBF
Juan M. Coggi	Argentine	1987–	WBA
Rene Arredondo	Mexico	1987	WBC
Roger Mayweather	USA	1987–	WBC
James McGirt	USA	1988	IBF
Meldrick Taylor	USA	1988–	IBF

Title Bouts

21.09.26 Mushy Callahan W PTS 10 Pinkey Mitchell, Los Angeles, USA (NY/NB)
14.03.27 Mushy Callahan W CO 2 Andy Divodi, New York C, USA (NY/NBA)
31.05.27 Mushy Callahan W PTS 10 Spug Myers, Chicago, USA (NY/NBA)
28.05.29 Mushy Callahan W CO 3 Fred Mahan, Los Angeles, USA (NY/NBA)
Mushy Callahan ceased to be recognised by NY (NY abolished weight division)
18.02.30 Jackie Kid Berg W RTD 10 Mushy Callahan, London, England (NBA)
29.05.30 Jackie Kid Berg W RSC 4 Al Delmont, Newark, USA (NBA)
03.09.30 Jackie Kid Berg W PTS 10 Buster Brown, Newark, USA (NBA)
23.01.31 Jackie Kid Berg W PTS 10 Goldie Hess, Chicago, USA (NBA)
10.04.31 Jackie Kid Berg W PTS 10 Billy Wallace, Detroit, USA (NBA)
24.04.31 Tony Canzoneri W CO 3 Jackie Kid Berg, Chicago, USA (NBA)
13.07.31 Tony Canzoneri W PTS 10 Cecil Payne, Los Angeles, USA (NBA)
29.10.31 Tony Canzoneri W PTS 10 Phillie Griffin, Newark, USA (NBA)
18.01.32 Johnny Jadick W PTS 10 Tony Canzoneri, Philadelphia, USA (NBA)
18.07.32 Johnny Jadick W PTS 10 Tony Canzoneri, Philadelphia, USA (NBA)
20.02.33 Battling Shaw W PTS 10 Johnny Jadick, New Orleans, USA (NBA)
21.05.33 Tony Canzoneri W PTS 10 Battling Shaw, New Orleans, USA (NBA)
23.06.33 Barney Ross W PTS 10 Tony Canzoneri, Chicago, USA (NBA)
26.07.33 Barney Ross W RSC 6 Johnny Farr, Kansas C, USA (NBA)
17.11.33 Barney Ross W PTS 10 Sammy Fuller, Chicago, USA (NBA)
07.02.34 Barney Ross W PTS 12 Pete Nebo, New Orleans, USA (NBA)
05.03.34 Barney Ross DREW 10 Frankie Klick, San Francisco, USA (NBA)
27.03.34 Barney Ross W PTS 10 Bobby Pacho, Los Angeles, USA (NBA)
10.12.34 Barney Ross W PTS 12 Bobby Pacho, Cleveland, USA (NBA)
28.01.35 Barney Ross W PTS 10 Frankie Klick, Miami, USA (NBA)
09.04.35 Barney Ross W PTS 12 Harry Woods, Seattle, USA (NBA)
Barney Ross relinquished NBA version of title (he decided to concentrate on the welterweight decision – title fell into disuse)
29.04.46 Tippy Larkin W PTS 12 Willie Joyce, Boston, USA (MASS)
13.09.46 Tippy Larkin W PTS 12 Willie Joyce, New York C, USA (MASS/NY)
Tippy Larkin ceased to be recognised by NY and Massachusetts (this followed a defeat by Ike Williams in a non-title bout, June, 1947)
12.06.59 Carlos Ortiz W RTD 2 Kenny Lane, New York C, USA (NBA)
04.02.60 Carlos Ortiz W CO 10 Battling Torres, Los Angeles, USA (NBA)
15.06.60 Carlos Ortiz W PTS 15 Duilio Loi, San Francisco, USA (NBA)
01.09.60 Duilio Loi W PTS 15 Carlos Ortiz, Milan, Italy (NBA)
10.05.61 Duilio Loi W PTS 15 Carlos Ortiz, Milan, Italy (NBA)
21.10.61 Duilio Loi DREW 15 Eddie Perkins, Milan, Italy (NBA)
14.09.62 Eddie Perkins W PTS 15 Duilio Loi, Milan, Italy (NBA)
15.12.62 Duilio Loi W PTS 15 Eddie Perkins, Milan, Italy (NBA)
Duilio Loi relinquished NBA version of title (retired)
21.03.63 Roberto Cruz W CO 1 Battling Torres, Los Angeles, USA (WBA)
15.06.63 Eddie Perkins W PTS 15 Roberto Cruz, Manila, Philippines (WBA)
04.01.64 Eddie Perkins W RSC 13 Yoshinori Takahashi, Tokyo, Japan (WBA)
18.04.64 Eddie Perkins W PTS 15 Bunny Grant, Kingston, Jamaica (WBA)
18.01.65 Carlos Hernandez W PTS 15 Eddie Perkins, Caracas, Venezuela
15.05.65 Carlos Hernandez W RSC 4 Mario Rossito, Maracaibo, Venezuela
10.07.65 Carlos Hernandez W CO 3 Percy Hayles, Kingston, Jamaica
30.04.66 Sandro Lopopolo W PTS 15 Carlos Hernandez, Rome, Italy
21.10.66 Sandro Lopopolo W RSC 7 Vicente Rivas, Rome, Italy
30.04.67 Paul Fujii W RTD 2 Sandro Lopopolo, Tokyo, Japan

16.11.67 Paul Fujii W CO 4 Willi Quatuor, Tokyo, Japan
Paul Fujii forfeited WBC recognition (failure to defend against Pedro Adigue)
12.12.68 Nicolino Loche W RTD 9 Paul Fujii, Tokyo, Japan (WBA)
14.12.68 Pedro Adigue W PTS 15 Adolph Pruitt, Quezon C, Philippines (WBC)
03.05.69 Nicolino Loche W PTS 15 Carlos Hernandez, Bs Aires, Argentine (WBA)
11.10.69 Nicolino Loche W PTS 15 Joao Henrique, Bs Aires, Argentine (WBA)
01.02.70 Bruno Arcari W PTS 15 Pedro Adigue, Rome, Italy (WBC)
16.05.70 Nicolino Loche W PTS 15 Adolph Pruitt, Bs Aires, Argentine (WBA)
10.07.70 Bruno Arcari W DIS 6 Rene Roque, Lignano, Italy (WBC)
30.10.70 Bruno Arcari W CO 3 Raymundo Dias, Genoa, Italy (WBC)
06.03.71 Bruno Arcari W PTS 15 Joao Henrique, Rome, Italy (WBC)
03.04.71 Nicolino Loche W PTS 15 Domingo Barrera, Bs Aires, Argentine (WBA)
26.06.71 Bruno Arcari W RSC 9 Enrique Jana, Palermo, Italy (WBC)
10.10.71 Bruno Arcari W CO 10 Domingo Corpas, Genoa, Italy (WBC)
11.12.71 Nicolino Loche W PTS 15 Antonio Cervantes, Bs Aires, Argentine (WBA)
10.03.72 Alfonso Frazer W PTS 15 Nicolino Loche, Panama C, Panama (WBA)
10.06.72 Bruno Arcari W CO 12 Joao Henrique, Genoa, Italy (WBC)
17.06.72 Alfonso Frazer W RTD 4 Al Ford, Panama C, Panama (WBA)
28.10.72 Antonio Cervantes W CO 10 Alfonso Frazer, Panama C, Panama (WBA)
02.12.72 Bruno Arcari W PTS 15 Costa Azevedo, Turin, Italy (WBC)
16.02.73 Antonio Cervantes W PTS 15 Josua Marquez, San Juan, Puerto Rico (WBA)
17.03.73 Antonio Cervantes W RTD 9 Nicolino Loche, Maracay, Venezuela (WBA)
19.05.73 Antonio Cervantes W RSC 5 Alfonso Frazer, Panama C, Panama (WBA)
08.09.73 Antonio Cervantes W RSC 5 Carlos Giminez, Bogota, Colombia (WBA)
04.12.73 Antonio Cervantes W PTS 15 Lion Furuyama, Panama C, Panama (WBA)
16.02.74 Bruno Arcari W DIS 8 Tony Ortiz, Turin, Italy (WBC)
Bruno Arcari relinquished WBC version of title (weight making difficulties)
02.03.74 Antonio Cervantes W CO 6 Chang-Kil Lee, Cartagena, Colombia (WBA)
27.07.74 Antonio Cervantes W CO 2 Victor Ortiz, Cartagena, Colombia (WBA)
21.09.74 Perico Fernandez W PTS 15 Lion Furuyama, Rome, Italy (WBC)
26.10.74 Antonio Cervantes W CO 8 Shinchi Kadoto, Tokyo, Japan (WBA)
19.04.75 Perico Fernandez W CO 9 Joao Henrique, Barcelona, Spain (WBC)
17.05.75 Antonio Cervantes W PTS 15 Esteban de Jesus, Panama C, Panama (WBA)
15.07.75 Saensak Muangsurin W RTD 8 Perico Fernandez, Bangkok, Thailand (WBC)
15.11.75 Antonio Cervantes W RTD 7 Hector Thompson, Panama C, Panama (WBA)
25.01.76 Saensak Muangsurin W PTS 15 Lion Furuyama, Tokyo, Japan (WBC)
06.03.76 Wilfred Benitez W PTS 15 Antonio Cervantes, San Juan, Puerto Rico (WBA)
31.05.76 Wilfred Benitez W PTS 15 Emiliano Villa, San Juan, Puerto Rico (WBA)
30.06.76 Miguel Velasquez W DIS 4 Saensak Muangsurin, Madrid, Spain (WBC)
16.10.76 Wilfred Benitez W RSC 3 Tony Petronelli, San Juan, Puerto Rico (WBA)
Wilfred Benitez forfeited WBA recognition (failure to defend against Antonio Cervantes)
29.10.76 Saensak Muangsurin W RSC 2 Miguel Velasquez, Segovia, Spain (WBC)
15.01.77 Saensak Muangsurin W RSC 15 Monroe Brooks, Chiang, Thailand (WBC)
02.04.77 Saensak Muangsurin W CO 6 Guts Ishimatsu, Tokyo, Japan (WBC)
17.06.77 Saensak Muangsurin W PTS 15 Perico Fernandez, Madrid, Spain (WBC)
25.06.77 Antonio Cervantes W RSC 5 Carlos Giminez, Maracaibo, Venezuela (WBA)
03.08.77 Wilfred Benitez W RSC 15 Guerrero Chavez, New York C, USA (NY)
Wilfred Benitez ceased to be recognised by NY (moved up to welterweight)
20.08.77 Saensak Muangsurin W RSC 6 Mike Everett, Roi-Et, Thailand (WBC)
22.10.77 Saensak Muangsurin W PTS 15 Saoul Mamby, Korat, Thailand (WBC)
05.11.77 Antonio Cervantes W PTS 15 Adriano Marrero, Maracay, Venezuela (WBA)
29.12.77 Saensak Muangsurin W RTD 13 Jo Kimpuani, Chanthabun, Thailand (WBC)
08.04.78 Saensak Muangsurin W CO 13 Francisco Moreno, Hat Yai, Thailand (WBC)
28.04.78 Antonio Cervantes W CO 6 Tonga Kiatvayupakdi, Udon, Thailand (WBA)
26.08.78 Antonio Cervantes W RSC 9 Norman Sekgapane, Botswana (WBA)
30.12.78 Sang-Hyun Kim W CO 13 Saensak Muangsurin, Seoul, S Korea (WBC)
18.01.79 Antonio Cervantes W PTS 15 Miguel Montilla, New York C, USA (WBA)
03.06.79 Sang-Hyun Kim W PTS 15 Fitzroy Guisseppi, Seoul, S Korea (WBC)
25.08.79 Antonio Cervantes W PTS 15 Kwang-Min Kim, Seoul, S Korea (WBA)
04.10.79 Sang-Hyun Kim W CO 11 Masahiro Yokai, Tokyo, Japan (WBC)
23.02.80 Saoul Mamby W CO 14 Sang-Hyun Kim, Seoul, S Korea (WBC)
29.03.80 Antonio Cervantes W RSC 7 Miguel Montilla, Cartagena, Colombia (WBA)
07.07.80 Saoul Mamby W RSC 13 Esteban de Jesus, Bloomington, USA (WBC)
02.08.80 Aaron Pryor W CO 4 Antonio Cervantes, Cincinnati, USA (WBA)
02.10.80 Saoul Mamby W PTS 15 Maurice Watkins, Las Vegas, USA (WBC)
22.11.80 Aaron Pryor W RSC 6 Gaetan Hart, Cincinnati, USA (WBA)
12.06.81 Saoul Mamby W PTS 15 Jo Kimpuani, Detroit, USA (WBC)
27.06.81 Aaron Pryor W RSC 2 Lennox Blackmore, Las Vegas, USA (WBA)
29.08.81 Saoul Mamby W PTS 15 Thomas Americo, Jakarta, Indonesia (WBC)
14.11.81 Aaron Pryor W RSC 7 Dujuan Johnson, Cleveland, USA (WBA)
20.12.81 Saoul Mamby W PTS 15 Obisia Nwankpa, Lagos, Nigeria (WBC)
21.03.82 Aaron Pryor W RSC 12 Miguel Montilla, Atlantic C, USA (WBA)
26.06.82 Leroy Haley W PTS 15 Saoul Mamby, Cleveland, USA (WBC)
04.07.82 Aaron Pryor W RSC 6 Akio Kameda, Cincinnati, USA (WBA)
20.10.82 Leroy Haley W PTS 15 Juan Giminez, Cleveland, USA (WBC)
12.11.82 Aaron Pryor W RSC 14 Alexis Arguello, Miami, USA (WBA)
13.02.83 Leroy Haley W PTS 12 Saoul Mamby, Cleveland, USA (WBC)
02.04.83 Aaron Pryor W RSC 3 Sang-Hyun Kim, Atlantic C, USA (WBA)
18.05.83 Bruce Curry W PTS 12 Leroy Haley, Las Vegas, USA (WBC)
07.07.83 Bruce Curry W RSC 7 Hidekazu Akai, Osaka, Japan (WBC)
09.09.83 Aaron Pryor W CO 10 Alexis Arguello, Las Vegas, USA (WBA)
Aaron Pryor relinquished WBA version of title (retired)
19.10.83 Bruce Curry W PTS 12 Leroy Haley, Las Vegas, USA (WBC)
22.01.84 Johnny Bumphus W PTS 15 Lorenzo Garcia, Atlantic C, USA (WBA)
29.01.84 Bill Costello W RSC 10 Bruce Curry, Beaumont, USA (WBC)
01.06.84 Gene Hatcher W RSC 11 Johnny Bumphus, Buffalo, USA (WBA)
22.06.84 Aaron Pryor W PTS 15 Nicky Furlano, Toronto, Canada (IBF)
15.07.84 Bill Costello W PTS 12 Ronnie Shields, Kingston, NY, USA (WBC)
03.11.84 Bill Costello W PTS 12 Saoul Mamby, Kingston NY, USA (WBC)
15.12.84 Gene Hatcher W PTS 15 Ubaldo Sacco, Fort Worth, USA (WBA)
16.02.85 Bill Costello W PTS 12 Leroy Haley, Kingston NY, USA (WBC)
02.03.85 Aaron Pryor W PTS 15 Gary Hinton, Atlantic C, USA (IBF)
Aaron Pryor forfeited title (inactive)
21.07.85 Ubaldo Sacco W RSC 9 Gene Hatcher, Campione, Italy (WBA)
21.08.85 Lonnie Smith W RSC 8 Bill Costello, New York C, USA (WBC)
15.03.86 Patrizio Oliva W PTS 15 Ubaldo Sacco, Monte Carlo (WBA)
26.04.86 Gary Hinton W PTS 15 Antonio Reyes Cruz, Lucca, Italy (IBF)
05.05.86 Rene Arredondo W RSC 5 Lonnie Smith, Los Angeles, USA (WBC)
24.07.86 Tsuyoshi Hamada W CO 1 Rene Arredondo, Tokyo, Japan (WBC)
06.09.86 Patrizio Oliva W RSC 3 Brian Brunette, Naples, Italy (WBA)
30.10.86 Joe Manley W CO 10 Gary Hinton, Hartford, USA (IBF)
02.12.86 Tsuyoshi Hamada W PTS 12 Ronnie Shields, Tokyo, Japan (WBC)
10.01.87 Patrizio Oliva W PTS 15 Rodolfo Gonzalez, Agrigento, Italy (WBA)
04.03.87 Terry Marsh W RSC 10 Joe Manley, Basildon, England (IBF)
01.07.87 Terry Marsh W RTD 6 Akio Kameda, London, England (IBF)
Terry Marsh relinquished IBF version of title (retired)
04.07.87 Juan M. Coggi W CO 3 Patrizio Oliva, Ribera, Italy (WBA)
22.07.87 Rene Arredondo W RSC 6 Tsuyoshi Hamada, Tokyo, Japan (WBC)
12.11.87 Roger Mayweather W RSC 6 Rene Arredondo, Los Angeles, USA (WBC)
14.02.88 James McGirt W RSC 12 Frankie Warren, Corpus Christi, USA (IBF)
24.03.88 Roger Mayweather W CO 3 Mauricio Aceves, Los Angeles, USA (WBC)
07.05.88 Juan M. Coggi W CO 2 Sang-Ho Lee, Roseto, Italy (WBA)
06.06.88 Roger Mayweather W PTS 12 Harold Brazier, Las Vegas, USA (WBC)
31.07.88 James McGirt W CO 1 Howard Davis, New York C, USA (IBF)
03.09.88 Meldrick Taylor W RSC 12 James McGirt, Atlantic C, USA (IBF)
22.09.88 Roger Mayweather W RSC 12 Rodolfo Gonzalez, Los Angeles, USA (WBC)
07.11.88 Roger Mayweather W PTS 12 Vinny Pazienza, Las Vegas, USA (WBC)
21.01.89 Juan M. Coggi W PTS 12 Harold Brazier, Vasto, Italy (WBA)
21.01.89 Meldrick Taylor W RSC 7 John Meekins, Atlantic C, USA (IBF)
29.04.89 Juan M. Coggi W PTS 12 Akinobu Hiranaka, Vasto, Italy (WBA)

Welterweight (147 lbs)

Title Holders

	Birthplace	Tenure	Status
Mysterious Billy Smith	USA	1892–1894	
Tommy Ryan*	USA	1894–1898	
Mysterious Billy Smith	USSA	1898–1900	
Rube Ferns	USA	1900	
Matty Matthews	USA	1900–1901	
Rube Ferns	USA	1901	
Joe Walcott	Barbados	1901–1904	
Dixie Kid	USA	1904–1905	
Honey Mellody	USA	1906–1907	
Mike Twin Sullivan*	USA	1907–1908	
Jimmy Gardner	USA	1908–1910	USA
Harry Lewis	USA	1910–1912	GB/FR
Jimmy Clabby	USA	1910–1912	USA/AUSTR
Waldemar Holberg	Denmark	1914	AUSTR
Tom McCormick	Ireland	1914	AUSTR
Matt Wells	England	1914–1915	AUSTR
Mike Glover	USA	1915	USA
Jack Britton	USA	1915	USA
Ted Kid Lewis	England	1915–1916	
Jack Britton	USA	1916–1917	
Ted Kid Lewis	England	1917–1919	
Jack Britton	USA	1919–1922	
Mickey Walker	USA	1922–1926	
Pete Latzo	USA	1926–1927	
Joe Dundee	Italy	1927–1929	
Joe Dundee	Italy	1929	NY
Jackie Fields	USA	1929	NBA
Jackie Fields	USA	1929–1930	
Young Jack Thompson	USA	1930	
Tommy Freeman	USA	1930–1931	
Young Jack Thompson	USA	1931	
Lou Brouillard	Canada	1931–1932	
Jackie Fields	USA	1932–1933	
Young Corbett III	Italy	1933	
Jimmy McLarnin	Ireland	1933–1934	
Barney Ross	USA	1934	
Jimmy McLarnin	Ireland	1934–1935	
Barney Ross	USA	1935–1938	
Henry Armstrong	USA	1938–1940	
Fritzie Zivic	USA	1940–1941	
Red Cochrane	USA	1941–1946	
Marty Servo*	USA	1946	
Sugar Ray Robinson*	USA	1946–1951	
Johnny Bratton	USA	1951	NBA
Kid Gavilan	Cuba	1951–1952	NBA/NY
Kid Gavilan	Cuba	1952–1954	
Johnny Saxton	USA	1954–1955	
Tony de Marco	USA	1955	
Carmen Basilio	USA	1955–1956	
Johnny Saxton	USA	1956	
Carmen Basilio*	USA	1956–1957	
Virgil Akins	USA	1958	
Don Jordan	USA	1958–1960	
Benny Kid Paret	Dom Republic	1960–1961	
Emile Griffith	Cuba	1961	
Benny Kid Paret	Virgin Islands	1961–1962	
Emile Griffith	Cuba	1962–1963	

Luis Rodriguez	Virgin Islands	1963	
Emile Griffith*	Cuba	1963–1966	
Curtis Cokes	Virgin Islands	1966–1967	WBA
Charley Shipes	USA	1966–1967	CALIF
Curtis Cokes	USA	1967–1969	
Jose Napoles	USA	1969–1970	
Billy Backus	Cuba	1970–1971	
Jose Napoles*	USA	1971–1975	
Hedgemon Lewis	Cuba	1972–1974	NY
Jose Napoles	USA	1975	WBC
Angel Espada	Cuba	1975–1976	WBA
John H. Stracey	Puerto Rico	1975–1976	WBC
Carlos Palomino	England	1976–1979	WBC
Pipino Cuevas	Mexico	1976–1980	WBA
Wilfred Benitez	Mexico	1979	WBC
Sugar Ray Leonard	USA	1979–1980	WBC
Roberto Duran	USA	1980	WBC
Thomas Hearns	Panama	1980–1981	WBA
Sugar Ray Leonard	USA	1980–1981	WBC
Sugar Ray Leonard*	USA	1981–1982	
Don Curry	USA	1983–1984	WBA
Don Curry	USA	1984–1985	WBA/IBF
Milton McCrory	USA	1983–1985	WBC
Don Curry	USA	1985–1986	
Lloyd Honeyghan	USA	1986	
Lloyd Honeyghan	Jamaica	1986–1987	WBC/IBF
Mark Breland	Jamaica	1987	WBA
Marlon Starling	USA	1987–1988	WBA
Jorge Vaca	Mexico	1987–1988	WBC
Lloyd Honeyghan	Jamaica	1988–1989	WBC
Simon Brown	Jamaica	1988–	IBF
Tomas Molinares*	Colombia	1988	WBA
Mark Breland	USA	1989–	WBA
Marlon Starling	USA	1989–	WBC

Title Bouts

14.12.92 Mysterious Billy Smith W CO 14 Danny Needham, San Francisco, USA
17.04.93 Mysterious Billy Smith W CO 2 Tom Williams, New York C, USA
26.07.94 Tommy Ryan W PTS 20 Mysterious Billy Smith, Minneapolis, USA
18.01.95 Tommy Ryan W 3 Nonpareil Jack Dempsey, New York C, USA
27.05.95 Tommy Ryan NC 18 Mysterious Billy Smith, New York C, USA
25.11.96 Tommy Ryan W DIS 9 Mysterious Billy Smith, New York C, USA
23.12.96 Tommy Ryan W CO 4 Bill Payne, Syracuse, USA
24.02.97 Tommy Ryan W CO 9 Tom Tracy, Syracuse, USA
Tommy Ryan reliquished title (moved up to middleweight)
04.04.98 Mysterious Billy Smith DREW 25 Joe Walcott, Bridgeport, USA
29.07.98 Mysterious Billy Smith W PTS 25 George Green, New York C, USA
25.08.98 Mysterious Billy Smith W PTS 25 Matty Matthews, New York C, USA
05.09.98 Mysterious Billy Smith DREW 25 Andy Walsh, New York C, USA
03.10.98 Mysterious Billy Smith W CO 20 Jim Judge, Scranton, USA
07.10.98 Mysterious Billy Smith W PTS 25 Charley McKeever, New York C, USA
06.12.98 Mysterious Billy Smith W PTS 20 Joe Walcott, New York C, USA
24.01.99 Mysterious Billy Smith W CO 14 Billy Edwards, New York C, USA
10.03.99 Mysterious Billy Smith W RSC 14 George Lavigne, San Francisco, USA
29.06.99 Mysterious Billy Smith DREW 20 Charley McKeever, New York C, USA
04.08.99 Mysterious Billy Smith DREW 25 Andy Walsh, New York C, USA
08.11.99 Mysterious Billy Smith W PTS 20 Charley McKeever, New York C, USA
15.01.00 Rube Ferns W DIS 21 Mysterious Billy Smith, Buffalo, USA
13.08.00 Rube Ferns W RTD 15 Eddie Connolly, Buffalo, USA
01.09.00 Rube Ferns W PTS 15 Matty Matthews, Detroit, USA
16.10.00 Matty Matthews W PTS 15 Rube Ferns, Detroit, USA
29.04.01 Matty Matthews W PTS 20 Tom Couhig, Louisville, USA
24.05.01 Rube Ferns W CO 10 Matty Matthews, Toronto, Canada
23.09.01 Rube Ferns W CO 9 Frank Erne, Fort Erie, Canada
18.12.01 Joe Walcott W RSC 5 Rube Ferns, Fort Erie, Canada
23.06.02 Joe Walcott W PTS 15 Tommy West, London, England
02.04.03 Joe Walcott DREW 20 Billy Woods, Los Angeles, USA
29.04.04 Dixie Kid W DIS 20 Joe Walcott, San Francisco, USA
12.05.04 Dixie Kid DREW 20 Joe Walcott, San Francisco, USA
Dixie Kid lost general recognition (failure to defend the title within a reasonable period)
30.09.04 Joe Walcott DREW 20 Joe Gans, San Francisco, USA
16.10.06 Honey Mellody W PTS 15 Joe Walcott, Chelsea, Mass, USA
29.11.06 Honey Mellody W RSC 12 Joe Walcott, Chelsea, Mass, USA
23.04.07 Mike Twin Sullivan W PTS 20 Honey Mellody, Los Angeles, USA
01.11.07 Mike Twin Sullivan W PTS 20 Frank Field, Goldfield, USA
27.11.07 Mike Twin Sullivan W CO 13 Kid Farmer, Los Angeles, USA
23.04.08 Mike Twin Sullivan W PTS 25 Jimmy Gardner, Los Angeles, USA
Mike Twin Sullivan relinquished title (eye injury)
07.11.08 Jimmy Gardner W PTS 15 Jimmy Clabby, New Orleans, USA (USA)
26.11.08 Jimmy Gardner DREW 20 Jimmy Clabby, New Orleans, USA (USA)
Jimmy Gardner ceased to be recognised in the USA (unable to make the weight)
19.02.10 Harry Lewis DREW 25 Willie Lewis, Paris, France (FR)
23.04.10 Harry Lewis DREW 25 Willie Lewis, Paris, France (FR)
04.05.10 Harry Lewis W CO 3 Peter Brown, Paris, France (FR)
27.06.10 Harry Lewis W RTD 7 Young Joseph, London, England (GB/FR)
05.09.10 Jimmy Clabby W CO 13 Guy Buckles, Sheridan, USA (USA)
02.11.10 Jimmy Clabby W RSC 7 Bob Bryant, Sydney, Australia (USA/AUSTR)
26.12.10 Jimmy Clabby W CO 1 Gus Devitt, Brisbane, Australia (USA/AUSTR)
Jimmy Clabby ceased to be recognised by Australia/USA (he grew into a fully fledged middleweight before being able to consolidate his claim)
25.01.11 Harry Lewis W CO 4 Johnny Summers, London, England (GB/FR)
(Harry Lewis ceased to be recognised in GB and France (this followed two losing contests against Johnny Mathieson in 1912)
01.01.14 Waldemar Holberg W PTS 20 Ray Bronson, Melbourne, Australia (AUSTR)
24.01.14 Tom McCormick W DIS 6 Waldemar Holberg, Melbourne, Australia (AUSTR)
14.02.14 Tom McCormick W CO 1 Johnny Summers, Sydney, Australia (AUSTR)
21.03.14 Matt Wells W PTS 20 Tom McCormick, Sydney, Australia (AUSTR)
01.06.15 Mike Glover W PTS 12 Matt Wells, Boston, USA (USA)
22.06.15 Jack Britton W PTS 12 Mike Glover, Boston, USA (USA)
31.08.15 Ted Kid Lewis W PTS 12 Jack Britton, Boston, USA
27.09.15 Ted Kid Lewis W PTS 12 Jack Britton, Boston, USA
26.10.15 Ted Kid Lewis W PTS 12 Joe Mandot, Boston, USA
02.11.15 Ted Kid Lewis W PTS 12 Milburn Saylor, Boston, USA
23.11.15 Ted Kid Lewis W CO 1 Jimmy Duffy, Boston, USA
01.03.16 Ted Kid Lewis W PTS 20 Harry Stone, New Orleans, USA
24.04.16 Jack Britton W PTS 20 Ted Kid Lewis, New Orleans, USA
06.06.16 Jack Britton W PTS 12 Mike O'Dowd, Boston, USA
17.10.16 Jack Britton W PTS 12 Ted Kid Lewis, Boston, USA
14.11.16 Jack Britton DREW 12 Ted Kid Lewis, Boston, USA
21.11.16 Jack Britton W PTS 12 Charley White, Boston, USA
25.06.17 Ted Kid Lewis W PTS 20 Jack Britton, Dayton, USA
13.11.17 Ted Kid Lewis W RSC 4 Johnny McCarthy, San Francisco, USA
17.05.18 Ted Kid Lewis W PTS 20 Johnny Tillman, Denver, USA
17.03.19 Jack Britton W CO 9 Ted Kid Lewis, Canton, USA
01.12.19 Jack Britton W CO 11 Billy Ryan, Canton, USA
31.05.20 Jack Britton W PTS 15 Johnny Griffiths, Akron, USA
23.08.20 Jack Britton DREW 12 Lou Bogash, Bridgeport, USA
06.09.20 Jack Britton W PTS 10 Ray Bronson, Cedar Point, USA
07.02.21 Jack Britton W PTS 15 Ted Kid Lewis, New York C, USA
03.06.21 Jack Britton DREW 10 Dave Shade, Portland, USA
10.06.21 Jack Britton DREW 10 Frank Barrieau, Portland, USA
17.02.22 Jack Britton DREW 15 Dave Shade, New York C, USA
26.06.22 Jack Britton W DIS 13 Benny Leonard, New York C, USA
01.11.22 Mickey Walker W PTS 15 Jack Britton, New York C, USA
08.10.23 Mickey Walker NC 9 Jimmy Jones, Newark, USA
02.06.24 Mickey Walker W PTS 10 Lew Tendler, Philadelphia, USA
01.10.24 Mickey Walker W CO 6 Bobby Barrett, Philadelphia, USA
21.09.25 Mickey Walker W PTS 15 Dave Shade, New York C, USA
20.05.26 Pete Latzo W PTS 10 Mickey Walker, Scranton, USA
29.06.26 Pete Latzo W CO 5 Willie Harmon, Newark, USA
09.07.26 Pete Latzo W DIS 4 George Levine, New York C, USA
03.06.27 Joe Dundee W PTS 15 Pete Latzo, New York C, USA
07.07.28 Joe Dundee W CO 8 Hilario Martinez, Philadelphia, USA
25.03.29 Jackie Fields W PTS 10 Young Jack Thompson, Chicago, USA (NBA)
25.07.29 Jackie Fields W DIS 2 Joe Dundee, Detroit, USA
09.05.30 Young Jack Thompson W PTS 15 Jackie Fields, Detroit, USA
05.09.30 Tommy Freeman W PTS 15 Young Jack Thompson, Cleveland, USA
09.01.31 Tommy Freeman W PTS 10 Pete August, Hot Springs, USA
26.01.31 Tommy Freeman W PTS 10 Eddie Murdoch, Oklahoma C, USA
05.02.31 Tommy Freeman W CO 5 Duke Trammel, Memphis, USA
09.02.31 Tommy Freeman W CO 5 Al Kid Kober, New Orleans, USA
01.03.31 Tommy Freeman W PTS 10 Alfredo Gaona, Mexico C, Mexico
14.04.31 Young Jack Thompson W RTD 12 Tommy Freeman, Cleveland, USA
23.10.31 Lou Brouillard W PTS 15 Young Jack Thompson, Boston, USA
28.01.32 Jackie Fields W PTS 10 Lou Brouillard, Chicago, USA
22.02.33 Young Corbett III W PTS 10 Jackie Fields, San Francisco, USA
29.05.33 Jimmy McLarnin W CO 1 Young Corbett III, Los Angeles, USA
28.05.34 Barney Ross W PTS 15 Jimmy McLarnin, New York C, USA
17.09.34 Jimmy McLarnin W PTS 15 Barney Ross, New York C, USA
28.05.35 Barney Ross W PTS 15 Jimmy McLarnin, New York C, USA
27.11.36 Barney Ross W PTS 15 Izzy Jannazzo, New York C, USA
23.09.37 Barney Ross W PTS 15 Ceferino Garcia, New York C, USA
31.05.38 Henry Armstrong W PTS 15 Barney Ross, New York C, USA
25.11.38 Henry Armstrong W PTS 15 Ceferino Garcia, New York C, USA
05.12.38 Henry Armstrong W RSC 3 Al Manfredo, Cleveland, USA
10.01.39 Henry Armstrong W PTS 10 Baby Arizmendi, Los Angeles, USA
04.03.39 Henry Armstrong W RSC 4 Bobby Pacho, Havana, Cuba
16.03.39 Henry Armstrong W CO 1 Lew Feldman, St Louis, USA
31.03.39 Henry Armstrong W CO 12 Davey Day, New York C, USA
25.05.39 Henry Armstrong W PTS 15 Ernie Roderick, London, England
09.10.39 Henry Armstrong W RSC 4 Al Manfredo, Des Moines, USA
13.10.39 Henry Armstrong W CO 2 Howard Scott, Minneapolis, USA
20.10.39 Henry Armstrong W CO 3 Richie Fontaine, Seattle, USA
24.10.39 Henry Armstrong W PTS 10 Jimmy Garrison, Los Angeles, USA
30.10.39 Henry Armstrong W RSC 4 Bobby Pacho, Denver, USA
11.12.39 Henry Armstrong W CO 7 Jimmy Garrison, Cleveland, USA
04.01.40 Henry Armstrong W CO 5 Joe Ghnouly, St Louis, USA
24.01.40 Henry Armstrong W RSC 9 Pedro Montanez, New York C, USA
26.04.40 Henry Armstrong W RSC 7 Paul Junior, Boston, USA
24.05.40 Henry Armstrong W RSC 5 Ralph Zanelli, Boston, USA
21.06.40 Henry Armstrong W RSC 3 Paul Junior, Portland, USA
23.09.40 Henry Armstrong W CO 4 Phil Furr, Washington, USA
04.10.40 Fritzie Zivic W PTS 15 Henry Armstrong, New York C, USA
17.01.41 Fritzie Zivic W RSC 12 Henry Armstrong, New York C, USA
29.07.41 Red Cochrane W PTS 15 Fritzie Zivic, Newark, USA
01.02.46 Marty Servo W CO 4 Red Cochrane, New York C, USA
Marty Servo relinquished title (retired)
20.12.46 Sugar Ray Robinson W PTS 15 Tommy Bell, New York C, USA
24.06.47 Sugar Ray Robinson W RSC 8 Jimmy Doyle, Cleveland, USA
19.12.47 Sugar Ray Robinson W RSC 6 Chuck Taylor, Detroit, USA
28.06.48 Sugar Ray Robinson W PTS 15 Bernard Docusen, Chicago, USA
11.07.49 Sugar Ray Robinson W PTS 15 Kid Gavilan, Philadelphia, USA
09.08.50 Sugar Ray Robinson W PTS 15 Charlie Fusari, Jersey C, USA
Sugar Ray Robinson relinquished title (moved up to middleweight)

14.03.51 Johnny Bratton W PTS 15 Charlie Fusari, Chicago, USA (NBA)
18.05.51 Kid Gavilan W PTS 15 Johnny Bratton, New York C, USA (NBA/NY)
29.08.51 Kid Gavilan W PTS 15 Billy Graham, New York C, USA (NBA/NY)
04.02.52 Kid Gavilan W PTS 15 Bobby Dykes, Miami, USA (NBA/NY)
07.07.52 Kid Gavilan W RSC 11 Gil Turner, Philadelphia, USA
05.10.52 Kid Gavilan W PTS 15 Billy Graham, Havana, Cuba
11.02.53 Kid Gavilan W RTD 9 Chuck Davey, Chicago, USA
18.09.53 Kid Gavilan W PTS 15 Carmen Basilio, Syracuse, USA
13.11.53 Kid Gavilan W PTS 15 Johnny Bratton, Chicago, USA
20.10.54 Johnny Saxton W PTS 15 Kid Gavilan, Philadelphia, USA
01.04.55 Tony de Marco W RSC 14 Johnny Saxton, Boston, USA
10.06.55 Carmen Basilio W RSC 12 Tony de Marco, Syracuse, USA
30.11.55 Carmen Basilio W RSC 12 Tony de Marco, Boston, USA
14.03.56 Johnny Saxton W PTS 15 Carmen Basilio, Chicago, USA
12.09.56 Carmen Basilio W RSC 9 Johnny Saxton, Syracuse, USA
22.02.57 Carmen Basilio W CO 2 Johnny Saxton, Cleveland, USA
Carmen Basilio relinquished title (moved up to middleweight)
05.06.58 Virgil Akins W RSC 4 Vince Martinez, St Louis, USA
05.12.58 Don Jordan W PTS 15 Virgil Akins, Los Angeles, USA
24.04.59 Don Jordan W PTS 15 Virgil Akins, St Louis, USA
10.07.59 Don Jordan W PTS 15 Denny Moyer, Portland, USA
27.05.60 Benny Kid Paret W PTS 15 Don Jordan, Las Vegas, USA
10.12.60 Benny Kid Paret W PTS 15 Federico Thompson, New York C, USA
01.04.61 Emile Griffith W CO 13 Benny Kid Paret, Miami, USA
03.06.61 Emile Griffith W RSC 12 Gaspar Ortega, Los Angeles, USA
30.09.61 Benny Kid Paret W PTS 15 Emile Griffith, New York C, USA
24.03.62 Emile Griffith W RSC 12 Benny Kid Paret, New York C, USA
13.07.62 Emile Griffith W PTS 15 Ralph Dupas, Las Vegas, USA
08.12.62 Emile Griffith W RTD 9 Jorge Fernandez, Las Vegas, USA
21.03.63 Luis Rodriguez W PTS 15 Emile Griffith, Los Angeles, USA
08.06.63 Emile Griffith W PTS 15 Luis Rodriguez, New York C, USA
12.06.64 Emile Griffith W PTS 15 Luis Rodriguez, Las Vegas, USA
22.09.64 Emile Griffith W PTS 15 Brian Curvis, Wembley, England
30.03.65 Emile Griffith W PTS 15 Jose Stable, New York C, USA
10.12.65 Emile Griffith W PTS 15 Manuel Gonzalez, New York C, USA
Emile Griffith relinquished title (moved up to middleweight)
24.08.66 Curtis Cokes W PTS 15 Manuel Gonzalez, New Orleans, USA (WBA)
28.11.66 Curtis Cokes W PTS 15 Jean Josselin, Dallas, USA (WBA)
07.12.66 Charlie Shipes W RSC 10 Percy Manning, Hayward, USA (CALIF)
19.05.67 Curtis Cokes W RSC 10 Francois Pavilla, Dallas, USA (WBA)
02.10.67 Curtis Cokes W RSC 8 Charlie Shipes, Oakland, USA
16.04.68 Curtis Cokes W RSC 5 Willie Ludick, Dallas, USA
21.10.68 Curtis Cokes W PTS 15 Ramon la Cruz, New Orleans, USA
18.04.69 Jose Napoles W RSC 13 Curtis Cokes, Los Angeles, USA
29.06.69 Jose Napoles W RTD 10 Curtis Cokes, Mexico C, Mexico
17.10.69 Jose Napoles W PTS 15 Emile Griffith, Los Angeles, USA
15.02.70 Jose Napoles W RSC 15 Ernie Lopez, Los Angeles, USA
03.12.70 Billy Backus W RSC 4 Jose Napoles, Syracuse, USA
04.06.71 Jose Napoles W RSC 8 Billy Backus, Los Angeles, USA
14.12.71 Jose Napoles W PTS 15 Hedgemon Lewis, Los Angeles, USA
28.03.72 Jose Napoles W CO 7 Ralph Charles, Wembley, England
10.06.72 Jose Napoles W RSC 2 Adolph Pruitt, Monterrey, Mexico
16.06.72 Hedgemon Lewis W PTS 15 Billy Backus, Syracuse, USA (NY)
08.12.72 Hedgemon Lewis W PTS 15 Billy Backus, Syracuse, USA (NY)
28.02.73 Jose Napoles W CO 7 Ernie Lopez, Los Angeles, USA
23.06.73 Jose Napoles W PTS 15 Roger Menetrey, Grenoble, France
22.09.73 Jose Napoles W PTS 15 Clyde Gray, Toronto, Canada
03.08.74 Jose Napoles W RSC 9 Hedgemon Lewis, Mexico C, Mexico
14.12.74 Jose Napoles W CO 3 Horacio Saldano, Mexico C, Mexico
30.03.75 Jose Napoles W TD 12 Armando Muniz, Acapulco, Mexico
Jose Napoles relinquished WBA version of title (the WBC defence requirement clashed with that of the WBA)
28.06.75 Angel Espada W PTS 15 Clyde Gray, San Juan, Puerto Rico (WBA)
12.07.75 Jose Napoles W PTS 15 Armando Muniz, Mexico C, Mexico (WBC)
11.10.75 Angel Espada W PTS 15 Johnny Gant, San Juan, Puerto Rico (WBA)
06.12.75 John H. Stracey W RSC 6 Jose Napoles, Mexico C, Mexico (WBC)
20.03.76 John H. Stracey W RSC 10 Hedgemon Lewis, Wembley, England (WBC)
27.04.76 Angel Espada W RSC 8 Alfonso Hayman, San Juan, Puerto Rico (WBA)
22.06.76 Carlos Palomino W RSC 12 John H. Stracey, Wembley, England (WBC)
17.07.76 Pipino Cuevas W RSC 2 Angel Espada, Mexicali, Mexico (WBA)
22.10.76 Pipino Cuevas W CO 2 Shoji Tsujimoto, Kanazawa, Japan (WBA)
22.01.77 Carlos Palomino W RSC 15 Armando Muniz, Los Angeles, USA (WBC)
12.03.77 Pipino Cuevas W CO 2 Miguel Campanino, Mexico C, Mexico (WBA)
14.06.77 Carlos Palomino W CO 11 Dave Boy Green, Wembley, England (WBC)
06.08.77 Pipino Cuevas W CO 2 Clyde Gray, Los Angeles, USA (WBA)
13.09.77 Carlos Palomino W PTS 15 Everaldo Azevedo, Los Angeles, USA (WBC)
19.11.77 Pipino Cuevas W RSC 11 Angel Espada, San Juan, Puerto Rico (WBA)
10.12.77 Carlos Palomino W CO 13 Jose Palacios, Los Angeles, USA (WBC)
11.02.78 Carlos Palomino W CO 7 Ryu Sorimachi, Las Vegas, USA (WBC)
04.03.78 Pipino Cuevas W RSC 9 Harold Weston, Los Angeles, USA (WBA)
18.03.78 Carlos Palomino W RSC 9 Mimoun Mohatar, Las Vegas, USA (WBC)
20.05.78 Pipino Cuevas W RSC 1 Billy Backus, Los Angeles, USA (WBA)
27.05.78 Carlos Palomino W PTS 15 Armando Muniz, Los Angeles, USA (WBC)
09.09.78 Pipino Cuevas W RSC 2 Pete Ranzany, Sacramento, USA (WBA)
14.01.79 Wilfred Benitez W PTS 15 Carlos Palomino, San Juan, Puerto Rico (WBC)
29.01.79 Pipino Cuevas W RSC 2 Scott Clark, Los Angeles, USA (WBA)
25.03.79 Wilfred Benitez W PTS 15 Harold Weston, San Juan, Puerto Rico (WBC)
30.07.79 Pipino Cuevas W PTS 15 Randy Shields, Chicago, USA (WBA)
30.11.79 Sugar Ray Leonard W RSC 15 Wilfred Benitez, Las Vegas, USA (WBC)
08.12.79 Pipino Cuevas W RSC 10 Angel Espada, Los Angeles, USA (WBA)
31.03.80 Sugar Ray Leonard W CO 4 Dave Boy Green, Landover, USA (WBC)
06.04.80 Pipino Cuevas W CO 5 Harold Volbrecht, Houston, USA (WBA)
20.06.80 Roberto Duran W PTS 15 Sugar Ray Leonard, Montreal, Canada (WBC)
02.08.80 Thomas Hearns W RSC 2 Pipino Cuevas, Detroit, USA (WBA)
25.11.80 Sugar Ray Leonard W RTD 8 Roberto Duran, New Orleans, USA (WBC)
06.12.80 Thomas Hearns W CO 6 Luis Primera, Detroit, USA (WBA)
28.03.81 Sugar Ray Leonard W RSC 10 Larry Bonds, Syracuse, USA (WBC)
25.04.81 Thomas Hearns W RSC 12 Randy Shields, Phoenix, USA (WBA)
25.06.81 Thomas Hearns W RSC 4 Pablo Baez, Houston, USA (WBA)
16.09.81 Sugar Ray Leonard W RSC 14 Thomas Hearns, Las Vegas, USA
15.02.82 Sugar Ray Leonard W RSC 3 Bruce Finch, Reno, USA
Sugar Ray Leonard relinquished title (retired)
13.02.83 Don Curry W PTS 15 Jun-Sok Hwang, Fort Worth, USA (WBA)
19.03.83 Milton McCrory DREW 12 Colin Jones, Reno, USA (WBC)
13.08.83 Milton McCrory W PTS 12 Colin Jones, Las Vegas, USA (WBC)
03.09.83 Don Curry W RSC 1 Roger Stafford, Marsala, Italy (WBA)
14.01.84 Milton McCrory W RSC 6 Milton Guest, Detroit, USA (WBC)
04.02.84 Don Curry W PTS 15 Marlon Starling, Atlantic C, USA (WBA/IBF)
15.04.84 Milton McCrory W RSC 6 Gilles Ebilia, Detroit, USA (WBC)
21.04.84 Don Curry W RTD 7 Elio Diaz, Fort Worth, USA (WBA/IBF)
22.09.84 Don Curry W RSC 6 Nino la Rocca, Monte Carlo (WBA/IBF)
19.01.85 Don Curry W RSC 4 Colin Jones, Birmingham, England (WBA/IBF)
09.03.85 Milton McCrory W PTS 12 Pedro Vilella, Paris, France (WBC)
14.07.85 Milton McCrory W RSC 3 Carlos Trujillo, Monte Carlo (WBC)
06.12.85 Don Curry W CO 2 Milton McCrory, Las Vegas, USA (WBA/WBC)
09.03.86 Don Curry W CO 2 Eduardo Rodriguez, Forth Worth, USA (WBA)
27.09.86 Lloyd Honeyghan W RTD 6 Don Curry, Atlantic C, USA
Lloyd Honeyghan relinquished WBA version of title (wanted to avoid a meeting with the WBA's leading contender Harold Volbrecht on the grounds of apartheid)
06.02.87 Mark Breland W CO 7 Harold Volbrecht, Atlantic C, USA (WBA)
22.02.87 Lloyd Honeyghan W RSC 2 Johhny Bumphus, Wembley, England (IBF)
18.04.87 Lloyd Honeyghan W PTS 12 Maurice Blocker, London, England (WBC)
22.08.87 Marlon Starling W CO 11 Mark Breland, Columbia, USA (WBA)
30.08.87 Lloyd Honeyghan W RSC 1 Gene Hatcher, Marbella, Spain (WBC)
28.10.87 Jorge Vaca W TD 8 Lloyd Honeyghan, Wembley, England (WBC)
Lloyd Honeyghan forfeited IBF recognition (title vacated following Vaca defeat)
05.02.88 Marlon Starling W PTS 12 Fujio Ozaki, Atlantic C, USA (WBA)
29.03.88 Lloyd Honeyghan W CO 3 Jorge Vaca, Wembley, England (WBC)
16.04.88 Marlon Starling DREW 12 Mark Breland, Las Vegas, USA (WBA)
23.04.88 Simon Brown W RSC 14 Tyrone Trice, Berck sur Mer, France (IBF)
16.07.88 Simon Brown W RSC 3 Jorge Vaca, Kingston, Jamaica (IBF)
29.07.88 Tomas Molinares W CO 6 Marlon Starling, Atlantic C, USA (WBA)
(Tomas Molinares relinquished title (inability to make the weight)
29.07.88 Lloyd Honeyghan W RSC 5 Yung-Kil Chung, Atlantic C, USA (WBC)
14.10.88 Simon Brown W PTS 12 Mauro Martelli, Lausanne, Switzerland (IBF)
05.02.89 Mark Breland W RSC 1 Seung-Soon Lee, Las Vegas, USA (WBA)
05.02.89 Marlon Starling W RSC 9 Lloyd Honeyghan, Las Vegas, USA (WBC)
18.02.89 Simon Brown W RSC 3 Jorge Maysonet, Budapest, Hungary (IBF)
22.04.89 Mark Breland W RSC 5 Rafael Pineda, Atlantic C, USA (WBA)
27.04.89 Simon Brown W CO 7 Al Long, Washington, USA (IBF)

Light-Middleweight (154 lbs)

Title Holders

	Birthplace	Tenure	Status
Denny Moyer	USA	1962–1963	
Ralph Dupas	USA	1963	WBA
Sandro Mazzinghi	Italy	1963–1965	WBA
Nino Benvenuti	Italy	1965–1966	WBA
Ki-Soo Kim	S Korea	1966–1968	WBA
Sandro Mazzinghi	Italy	1968–1969	WBA
Freddie Little	USA	1969–1970	WBA
Carmelo Bossi	Italy	1970–1971	
Koichi Wajima	Japan	1971–1974	
Oscar Albarado	USA	1974–1975	
Koichi Wajima	Japan	1975	
Koichi Wajima	Japan	1975	
Miguel de Oliveira	Brazil	1975	WBA
Jae-Do Yuh	S Korea	1975–1976	WBC
Elisha Obed	Bahamas	1975–1976	WBA
Koichi Wajima	Japan	1976	WBC
Jose Duran	Spain	1976	WBA
Eckhard Dagge	W Germany	1976–1977	WBA
Miguel Castellini	Argentine	1976–1977	WBC
Eddie Gazo	Nicaragua		WBA
Rocky Mattioli	Italy	1977–1978	WBA
Masashi Kudo	Japan	1977–1979	WBC
Maurice Hope	Antigua	1978–1979	WBA
Ayub Kalule	Uganda	1979–1981	WBC
Wilfred Benitez	USA	1979–1981	WBA
Sugar Ray Leonard*	USA	1981–1982	WBC
Tadashi Mihara	Japan	1981	WBA
Davey Moore	USA	1981–1982	WBA
Thomas Hearns*	USA	1982–1983	WBA
Roberto Duran*	Panama	1982–1986	WBC
Mark Medal	USA	1983–1984	WBA
Mike McCallum*	Jamaica	1984	IBF
Carlos Santos	Puerto Rico	1984–1987	WBA
Buster Drayton	USA	1984–1986	IBF
Duane Thomas	USA	1986–1987	IBF
Matthew Hilton	Canada	1986–1987	WBC
Lupe Aquino	Mexico	1987–1988	IBF
Gianfranco Rosi	Italy	1987	WBC

Julian Jackson	Virgin Islands	1987–1988	WBC
Don Curry	USA	1987–	WBA
Robert Hines	USA	1988–1989	WBC
Darrin van Horn	USA	1988–1989	IBF
Rene Jacqot	France	1989–	IBF
		1989–	WBC

Title Bouts

20.10.62 Denny Moyer W PTS 15 Joey Giambra, Portland, USA (WBA)
19.02.63 Denny Moyer W PTS 15 Stan Harrington, Honolulu, Hawaii (WBA)
29.04.63 Ralph Dupas W PTS 15 Denny Moyer, New Orleans, USA (WBA)
17.06.63 Ralph Dupas W PTS 15 Denny Moyer, Baltimore, USA (WBA)
07.09.63 Sandro Mazzinghi W CO 9 Ralph Dupas, Milan, Italy (WBA)
02.12.63 Sandro Mazzinghi W RSC 13 Ralph Dupas, Sydney, Australia (WBA)
03.10.64 Sandro Mazzinghi W RSC 12 Tony Montano, Genoa, Italy (WBA)
11.12.64 Sandro Mazzinghi W PTS 15 Fortunato Manca, Rome, Italy (WBA)
08.06.65 Nino Benvenuti W CO 6 Sandro Mazzinghi, Milan, Italy (WBA)
17.12.65 Nino Benvenuti W PTS 15 Sandro Mazzinghi, Rome, Italy (WBA)
25.06.66 Ki-Soo Kim W PTS 15 Nino Benvenuti, Seoul, S Korea (WBA)
17.12.66 Ki-Soo Kim W PTS 15 Stan Harrington, Seoul, S Korea (WBA)
03.10.67 Ki-Soo Kim W PTS 15 Freddie Little, Seoul, S Korea (WBA)
25.05.68 Sandro Mazzinghi W PTS 15 Ki-Soo Kim, Milan, Italy (WBA)
25.10.68 Sandro Mazzinghi NC 9 Freddie Little, Rome, Italy (WBA)
Sandro Mazzinghi forfeited WBA recognition (failure to defend against Freddie Little)
17.03.69 Freddie Little W PTS 15 Stan Hayward, Las Vegas, USA
09.09.69 Freddie Little W CO 2 Hisao Minami, Osaka, Japan
20.03.70 Freddie Little W PTS 15 Gerhard Piaskowy, Berlin, W Germany
09.07.70 Carmelo Bossi W PTS 15 Freddie Little, Monza, Italy
29.04.71 Carmelo Bossi DREW 15 Jose Hernandez, Madrid, Spain
31.10.71 Koichi Wajima W PTS 15 Carmelo Bossi, Tokyo, Japan
07.05.72 Koichi Wajima W CO 1 Domenico Tiberia, Tokyo, Japan
03.10.72 Koichi Wajima W CO 3 Matt Donovan, Tokyo, Japan
09.01.73 Koichi Wajima DREW 15 Miguel de Oliviera, Tokyo, Japan
19.04.73 Koichi Wajima W PTS 15 Ryu Sorimachi, Osaka, Japan
14.08.73 Koichi Wajima W RTD 12 Silvani Bertini, Sapporo, Japan
05.02.74 Koichi Wajima W PTS 15 Miguel de Oliviera, Tokyo, Japan
03.06.74 Oscar Albarado W CO 15 Koichi Wajima, Tokyo, Japan
08.10.74 Oscar Albarado W RSC 7 Ryu Sorimachi, Tokyo, Japan
21.01.75 Koichi Wajima W PTS 15 Oscar Albarado, Tokyo, Japan
Koichi Wajima forfeited WBC recognition (failure to defend against Miguel de Oliviera)
07.05.75 Miguel de Oliviera W PTS 15 Jose Duran, Monte Carlo (WBC)
07.06.75 Jae-Do Yuh W RSC 7 Koichi Wajima, Kitakyushi, Japan (WBA)
11.11.75 Jae-Do Yuh W RSC 6 Masahiro Misako, Shizuoka, Japan (WBA)
13.11.75 Elisha Obed W RTD 10 Miguel de Oliviera, Paris, France (WBC)
17.02.76 Koichi Wajima W CO 15 Jae-Do Yuh, Tokyo, Japan (WBA)
28.02.76 Elisha Obed W CO 2 Tony Gardner, Nassau, Bahamas (WBC)
25.04.76 Elisha Obed W PTS 15 Sea Robinson, Abidjan, Ivory Coast (WBC)
18.05.76 Jose Duran W CO 14 Koichi Wajima, Tokyo, Japan (WBA)
18.06.76 Eckhard Dagge W RTD 10 Elisha Obed, Berlin, W Germany (WBC)
18.09.76 Eckhard Dagge W PTS 15 Emile Griffith, Berlin, W Germany (WBC)
08.10.76 Miguel Castellini W PTS 15 Jose Duran, Madrid, Spain (WBA)
05.03.77 Eddie Gazo W PTS 15 Miguel Castellini, Managua, Nicaragua (WBA)
15.03.77 Eckhard Dagge DREW 15 Maurice Hope, Berlin, W Germany (WBC)
07.06.77 Eddie Gazo W RSC 11 Koichi Wajima, Tokyo, Japan (WBA)
06.08.77 Rocky Mattioli W CO 5 Eckhard Dagge, Berlin, W Germany (WBC)
13.09.77 Eddie Gazo W PTS 15 Kenji Shibata, Tokyo, Japan (WBA)
18.12.77 Eddie Gazo W PTS 15 Chae-Keun Lim, Inchon, S Korea (WBA)
11.03.78 Rocky Mattioli W CO 7 Elisha Obed, Melbourne, Australia (WBC)
14.05.78 Rocky Mattioli W RSC 5 Jose Duran, Pescara, Italy (WBC)
09.08.78 Masashi Kudo W PTS 15 Eddie Gazo, Akita, Japan (WBA)
13.12.78 Masashi Kudo W PTS 15 Ho-In Joo, Osaka, Japan (WBA)
04.03.79 Maurice Hope W RTD 8 Rocky Mattioli, San Remo, Italy (WBC)
13.03.79 Masashi Kudo W PTS 15 Manuel Gonzalez, Tokyo, Japan (WBA)
20.06.79 Masashi Kudo W RSC 12 Manuel Gonzalez, Yokkaichi, Japan (WBA)
25.09.79 Maurice Hope W RSC 7 Mike Baker, Wembley, England (WBC)
24.10.79 Ayub Kalule W PTS 15 Masashi Kudo, Akita, Japan (WBA)
06.12.79 Ayub Kalule W PTS 15 Steve Gregory, Copenhagen, Denmark (WBA)
17.04.80 Ayub Kalule W RTD 11 Emiliano Villa, Copenhagen, Denmark (WBA)
12.06.80 Ayub Kalule W PTS 15 Marijan Benes, Randers, Denmark (WBA)
12.07.80 Maurice Hope W RSC 11 Rocky Mattioli, Wembley, England (WBC)
06.09.80 Ayub Kalule W PTS 15 Bushy Bester, Aarhus, Denmark (WBA)
26.11.80 Maurice Hope W PTS 15 Carlos Herrera, Wembley, England (WBC)
24.05.81 Wilfred Benitez W CO 12 Maurice Hope, Las Vegas, USA (WBC)
25.06.81 Sugar Ray Leonard W RSC 9 Ayub Kalule, Houston, USA (WBA)
Sugar Ray Leonard relinquished WBA version of title (he decided to concentrate on the welterweight division)
07.11.81 Tadashi Mihara W PTS 15 Rocky Fratto, Rochester, USA (WBA)
14.11.81 Wilfred Benitez W PTS 15 Carlos Santos, Las Vegas, USA (WBC)
30.01.82 Wilfred Benitez W PTS 15 Roberto Duran, Las Vegas, USA (WBC)
02.02.82 Davey Moore W RSC 6 Tadashi Mihara, Tokyo, Japan (WBA)
26.04.82 Davey Moore W CO 5 Charlie Weir, Johannesburg, S Africa (WBA)
17.07.82 Davey Moore W RSC 10 Ayub Kalule, Atlantic C, USA (WBA)
03.12.82 Thomas Hearns W PTS 15 Wilfred Benitez, New Orleans, USA (WBC)
29.01.83 Davey Moore W CO 4 Gary Guiden, Atlantic C, USA (WBA)
16.06.83 Roberto Duran W RSC 8 Davey Moore, New York C, USA (WBA)
Roberto Duran relinquished WBA version of title (retired)
11.02.84 Thomas Hearns W PTS 12 Luigi Minchillo, Detroit, USA (WBC)
11.03.84 Mark Medal W RSC 5 Earl Hargrove, Atlantic C, USA (IBF)
15.06.84 Thomas Hearns W CO 2 Roberto Duran, Las Vegas, USA (WBC)
15.09.84 Thomas Hearns W RSC 3 Fred Hutchings, Saginaw, USA (WBC)
19.10.84 Mike McCallum W PTS 15 Sean Mannion, New York C, USA (WBA)
02.11.84 Carlos Santos W PTS 15 Mark Medal, New York C, USA (IBF)
01.12.84 Mike McCallum W RSC 14 Luigi Minchillo, Milan, Italy (WBA)
01.06.85 Carlos Santos W PTS 15 Louis Acaries, Paris, France (IBF)
Carlos Santos forfeited title (failure to defend against Davey Moore)
28.07.85 Mike McCallum W RSC 8 David Braxton, Miami, USA (WBA)
04.06.86 Buster Drayton W PTS 15 Carlos Santos, E Rutherford, USA (IBF)
23.06.86 Thomas Hearns W RSC 8 Mark Medal, Las Vegas, USA (WBC)
Thomas Hearns relinquished WBC version of title (moved up to middleweight)
23.08.86 Mike McCallum W RSC 2 Julian Jackson, Miami, USA (WBA)
24.08.86 Buster Drayton W RSC 10 Davey Moore, Juan les Pins, France (IBF)
25.10.86 Mike McCallum W CO 9 Said Skouma, Paris, France (WBA)
05.12.86 Duane Thomas W RSC 3 John Mugabi, Las Vegas, USA (WBC)
27.03.87 Buster Drayton W RTD 10 Said Skouma, Cannes, France (IBF)
19.04.87 Mike McCallum W RSC 10 Milton McCrory, Phoenix, USA (WBA)
27.06.87 Matthew Hilton W PTS 15 Buster Drayton, Montreal, Canada (IBF)
12.07.87 Lupe Aquino W PTS 12 Duane Thomas, Bordeaux, France (WBC)
18.07.87 Mike McCallum W CO 5 Don Curry, Las Vegas, USA (WBA)
Mike McCallum relinquished WBA version of title (moved up to challenge for WBA middlweight title)
02.10.87 Gianfranco Rosi W PTS 12 Lupe Aquino, Perugia, Italy (WBC)
16.10.87 Matthew Hilton W RTD 2 Jack Callahan, Atlantic C, USA (IBF)
21.11.87 Julian Jackson W RSC 3 In-Chul Baek, Las Vegas, USA (WBA)
03.01.88 Gianfranco Rosi W RSC 7 Duane Thomas, Genoa, Italy (WBC)
08.07.88 Don Curry W RTD 9 Gianfranco Rosi, San Remo, Italy (WBC)
30.07.88 Julian Jackson W RSC 3 Buster Drayton, Atlantic C, USA (WBA)
04.11.88 Robert Hines W PTS 12 Matthew Hilton, Las Vegas, USA (IBF)
05.02.89 Darrin van Horn W PTS 12 Robert Hines, Atlantic C, USA (IBF)
11.02.89 Rene Jacquot W PTS 12 Don Curry, Grenoble, France (WBC)
25.02.89 Julian Jackson W CO 8 Francisco de Jesus, Las Vegas, USA (WBA)

Middleweight (160 lbs)

Title Holders

	Birthplace	Tenure	Status
Bob Fitzsimmons*	England	1891–1897	
Kid McCoy	USA	1897–1898	
Tommy Ryan*	USA	1898–1907	
Stanley Ketchel	USA	1907–1908	
Billy Papke	USA	1908	
Stanley Ketchel*	USA	1908–1910	
Billy Papke	USA	1911–1912	GB
Frank Mantell	USA	1912–1913	USA
Billy Papke	USA	1912–1913	IBU
Frank Klaus	USA	1913	IBU
George Chip	USA	1913–1914	USA
Eddie McGoorty	USA	1914	AUSTR
Jeff Smith	USA	1914	AUSTR
Al McCoy	USA	1914–1917	USA
Mick King	Australia	1914	AUSTR
Jeff Smith	USA	1914–1915	AUSTR
Les Darcy*	Australia	1915–1917	AUSTR
Mike O'Dowd	USA	1917–1920	
Johnny Wilson	USA	1920–1923	
Bryan Downey	USA	1922	OHIO
Dave Rosenberg	USA	1922	NY
Jock Malone	USA	1922–1923	OHIO
Mike O'Dowd*	USA	1922–1923	NY
Harry Greb	USA	1923–1926	
Tiger Flowers	USA	1926	
Mickey Walker*	USA	1926–1931	
Gorilla Jones	USA	1931–1932	NBA
Marcel Thil	France	1932	NBA/IBU
Marcel Thil	France	1932–1937	IBU
Ben Jeby	USA	1933	NY
Gorilla Jones	USA	1933	NBA
Lou Brouillard	Canada	1933	NY/NBA
Vince Dundee	USA	1933–1934	NY/NBA
Teddy Yarosz	USA	1934–1935	NY/NBA
Babe Risko	USA	1935–1936	NY/NBA
Freddie Steele	USA	1936–1937	NY/NBA
Freddie Steele	USA	1937–1938	NBA
Fred Apostoli	USA	1937–1938	IBU
Fred Apostoli	USA	1937–1939	NY
Edouard Tenet	France	1938	IBU
Al Hostak	USA	1938	NBA
Solly Krieger	USA	1938–1939	NBA
Al Hostak	USA	1939–1940	NBA
Ceferino Garcia	Philippines	1939–1940	NY
Ken Overlin	USA	1940–1941	NY
Tony Zale	USA	1940–1941	NBA
Billy Soose	USA	1941	NY
Tony Zale	USA	1941–1947	
Rocky Graziano	USA	1947–1948	
Tony Zale	USA	1948	
Marcel Cerdan	Algeria	1948–1949	
Jake la Motta	USA	1949–1950	
Jake la Motta	USA	1950–1951	NY/NBA
Sugar Ray Robinson	USA	1950–1951	PEN
Sugar Ray Robinson	USA	1951	
Randy Turpin	England	1951	
Sugar Ray Robinson*	USA	1951–1952	

Randy Turpin	England	1953	EBU
Carl Bobo Olson	Hawaii	1953–1955	
Sugar Ray Robinson	USA	1955–1957	
Gene Fullmer	USA	1957	
Sugar Ray Robinson	USA	1957	
Carmen Basilio	USA	1957–1958	
Sugar Ray Robinson	USA	1958–1959	
Sugar Ray Robinson	USA	1959–1960	NY/EBU
Gene Fullmer	USA	1959–1962	NBA
Paul Pender	USA	1960–1961	NY/EBU
Terry Downes	England	1961–1962	NY/EBU
Paul Pender	USA	1962–1963	NY/EBU
Dick Tiger	Nigeria	1962–1963	NBA
Dick Tiger	Nigeria	1963	
Joey Giardello	USA	1963–1965	
Dick Tiger	Nigeria	1965–1966	
Emile Griffith	Virgin Islands	1966–1967	
Nino Benvenuti	Italy	1967	
Emile Griffith	Virgin Islands	1967–1968	
Nino Benvenuti	Italy	1968–1970	
Carlos Monzon	Argentine	1970–1974	
Carlos Monzon	Argentine	1974–1976	WBA
Rodrigo Valdez	Colombia	1974–1976	WBC
Carlos Monzon*	Argentine	1976–1977	
Rodrigo Valdez	Colombia	1977–1978	
Hugo Corro	Argentine	1978–1979	
Vito Antuofermo	Italy	1979–1980	
Alan Minter	England	1980	
Marvin Hagler	USA	1980–1987	
Marvin Hagler	USA	1987	WBC/IBF
Sugar Ray Leonard*	USA	1987	WBC
Frank Tate	USA	1987–1988	IBF
Sumbu Kalambay	Zaire	1987–1989	WBA
Thomas Hearns	USA	1987–1988	WBC
Iran Barkley	USA	1988–1989	WBC
Michael Nunn	USA	1988–	IBF
Roberto Duran	Panama	1989–	WBC

Title Bouts

14.01.91 Bob Fitzsimmons W CO 13 Nonpareil Jack Dempsey, New Orleans, USA
26.09.94 Bob Fitzsimmons W CO 2 Dan Creedon, New Orleans, USA
Bob Fitzsimmons relinquished title (moved up to heavyweight)
17.12.97 Kid McCoy W PTS 15 Dan Creedon, New York C, USA
Kid McCoy lost general recognition (this came about when the Kid elected to campaign in the heavyweight division)
25.02.98 Tommy Ryan W CO 18 George Green, San Francisco, USA
13.06.98 Tommy Ryan W RSC 14 Tommy West, New York C, USA
24.10.98 Tommy Ryan W PTS 20 Jack Bonner, New York C, USA
18.09.99 Tommy Ryan W 10 Frank Craig, New York C, USA
04.03.01 Tommy Ryan W RTD 17 Tommy West, Louisville, USA
24.06.02 Tommy Ryan W CO 3 Johnny Gorman, London, England
15.09.02 Tommy Ryan W CO 6 Kid Carter, Fort Erie, Canada
Tommy Ryan relinquished title (retired)
04.07.07 Stanley Ketchel DREW 20 Joe Thomas, Marysville, USA
02.09.07 Stanley Ketchel W CO 32 Joe Thomas, San Francisco, USA
12.12.07 Stanley Ketchel W PTS 20 Joe Thomas, San Francisco, USA
22.02.08 Stanley Ketchel W CO 1 Mike Twin Sullivan, San Francisco, USA
09.05.08 Stanley Ketchel W CO 20 Jack Twin Sullivan, San Francisco, USA
04.06.08 Stanley Ketchel W PTS 10 Billy Papke, Milwaukee, USA
31.07.08 Stanley Ketchel W CO 3 Hugo Kelly, San Francisco, USA
18.08.08 Stanley Ketchel W CO 2 Joe Thomas, San Francisco, USA
07.09.08 Billy Papke W RSC 12 Stanley Ketchel, Los Angeles, USA
26.11.08 Stanley Ketchel W CO 11 Billy Papke, San Francisco, USA
02.06.09 Stanley Ketchel W CO 4 Tony Caponi, Schnectady, USA
09.06.09 Stanley Ketchel W RSC 3 Jack O'Brien, Philadelphia, USA
05.07.09 Stanley Ketchel W PTS 20 Billy Papke, San Francisco, USA
27.05.10 Stanley Ketchel W CO 2 Willie Lewis, New York C, USA
10.06.10 Stanley Ketchel W CO 5 Jim Smith, New York C, USA
Stanley Ketchel left title vacant (murdered in shooting incident)
08.06.11 Billy Papke W RTD 9 Jim Sullivan, London, England (GB)
22.02.12 Frank Mantell W PTS 20 Billy Papke, Sacramento, USA (USA)
30.03.12 Frank Mantell W PTS 20 Jack Henrick, Los Angeles, USA (USA)
Frank Mantell ceased to be recognised in the USA (this followed several bad defeats)
29.06.12 Billy Papke W RSC 16 Marcel Moreau, Paris, France (IBU)
23.10.12 Billy Papke W DIS 17 Georges Carpentier, Paris, France (IBU)
04.12.12 Billy Papke W CO 7 George Bernard, Paris, France (IBU)
05.03.13 Frank Klaus W DIS 15 Billy Papke, Paris, France (IBU)
11.10.13 George Chip W CO 6 Frank Klaus, Pittsburgh, USA (USA)
23.12.13 George Chip W CO 5 Frank Klaus, Pittsburgh, USA (USA)
01.01.14 Eddie McGoorty W CO 1 Dave Smith, Sydney, Australia (AUSTR)
07.02.14 Eddie McGoorty W PTS 20 Pat Bradley, Sydney, Australia (AUSTR)
14.03.14 Jeff Smith W PTS 20 Eddie McGoorty, Sydney, Australia (AUSTR)
06.04.14 Al McCoy W CO 1 George Chip, New York C, USA (USA)
13.04.14 Jeff Smith W CO 16 Pat Bradley, Sydney, Australia (AUSTR)
06.06.14 Jeff Smith W PTS 20 Jimmy Clabby, Sydney, Australia (AUSTR)
28.11.14 Mick King W PTS 20 Jeff Smith, Sydney, Australia (AUSTR)
26.12.14 Jeff Smith W PTS 20 Mick King, Sydney, Australia (AUSTR)
23.01.15 Jeff Smith W DIS 5 Les Darcy, Sydney, Australia (AUSTR)
20.02.15 Jeff Smith W PTS 20 Mick King, Melbourne, Australia (AUSTR)
23.05.15 Les Darcy W DIS 2 Jeff Smith, Sydney, Australia (AUSTR)
12.06.15 Les Darcy W RTD 10 Mick King, Sydney, Australia (AUSTR)
31.07.14 Les Darcy W RSC 15 Eddie McGoorty, Sydney, Australia (AUSTR)
04.09.15 Les Darcy W PTS 20 Billy Murray, Sydney, Australia (AUSTR)
09.10.15 Les Darcy W RTD 6 Fred Dyer, Sydney, Australia (AUSTR)
23.10.15 Les Darcy W PTS 20 Jimmy Clabby, Sydney, Australia (AUSTR)
27.12.15 Les Darcy W RTD 8 Eddie McGoorty, Sydney, Australia (AUSTR)
15.01.16 Les Darcy W PTS 20 George Brown, Sydney, Australia (AUSTR)
25.03.16 Les Darcy W CO 7 Les O'Donnell, Sydney, Australia (AUSTR)
08.04.16 Les Darcy W PTS 20 George Brown, Sydney, Australia (AUSTR)
13.05.16 Les Darcy W RTD 4 Alex Costica, Sydney, Australia (AUSTR)
03.06.16 Les Darcy W CO 2 Buck Crouse, Sydney, Australia (AUSTR)
24.06.16 Les Darcy W CO 12 Dave Smith, Sydney, Australia (AUSTR)
26.06.16 Al McCoy W PTS 15 Hugh Ross, Bridgeport, USA (USA)
09.09.16 Les Darcy W PTS 20 Jimmy Clabby, Sydney, Australia (AUSTR)
30.09.16 Les Darcy W CO 9 George Chip, Sydney, Australia (AUSTR)
Les Darcy left Australian version of the title vacant (died from pneumonia)
14.11.17 Mike O'Dowd W CO 6 Al McCoy, New York C, USA
17.07.19 Mike O'Dowd W CO 3 Al McCoy, St Paul, USA
06.11.19 Mike O'Dowd W CO 2 Billy Kramer, Paterson, USA
01.03.20 Mike O'Dowd W CO 2 Jack McCarron, Philadelphia, USA
30.03.20 Mike O'Dowd W CO 5 Joe Eagan, Boston, USA
06.05.20 Johnny Wilson W PTS 12 Mike O'Dowd, Boston, USA
17.03.21 Johnny Wilson W PTS 15 Mike O'Dowd, New York C, USA
27.02.21 Johnny Wilson W DIS 7 Bryan Downey, Cleveland, USA
22.02.22 Bryan Downey W PTS 12 Frank Carbone, Canton, USA (OHIO)
15.05.22 Bryan Downey W PTS 12 Mike O'Dowd, Columbus, USA (OHIO)
14.08.22 Dave Rosenberg W PTS 15 Phil Krug, New York C, USA (NY)
18.09.22 Jock Malone W PTS 12 Bryan Downey, Columbus, USA (OHIO)
30.11.22 Mike O'Dowd W DIS 8 Dave Rosenberg, New York C, USA (NY)
Mike O'Dowd relinquished NY version of title (retired)
24.07.23 Jock Malone W PTS 12 Bryan Downey, Columbus, USA (OHIO)
Jock Malone ceased to be recognised by Ohio (this followed a defeat by Lou Bogash in a non-title bout, October, 1923)
31.08.23 Harry Greb W PTS 15 Johnny Wilson, New York C, USA
03.12.23 Harry Greb W PTS 10 Bryan Downey, Pittsburgh, USA
18.01.24 Harry Greb W PTS 15 Johnny Wilson, New York C, USA
24.03.24 Harry Greb W RSC 12 Fay Keiser, Baltimore, USA
26.06.24 Harry Greb W PTS 15 Ted Moore, New York C, USA
02.07.25 Harry Greb W PTS 15 Mickey Walker, New York C, USA
13.11.25 Harry Greb W PTS 15 Tony Marullo, New Orleans, USA
26.02.26 Tiger Flowers W PTS 15 Harry Greb, New York C, USA
19.08.26 Tiger Flowers W PTS 15 Harry Greb, New York C, USA
03.12.26 Mickey Walker W PTS 10 Tiger Flowers, Chicago, USA
30.06.27 Mickey Walker W CO 10 Tommy Milligan, London, England
21.06.28 Mickey Walker W PTS 10 Ace Hudkins, Chicago, USA
29.10.29 Mickey Walker W PTS 10 Ace Hudkins, Los Angeles, USA
30.07.30 Mickey Walker W CO 3 Willie Oster, Newark, USA
Mickey Walker relinquished title (moved up to heavyweight)
25.08.31 Gorilla Jones W PTS 10 Tiger Thomas, Milwaukee, USA (NBA)
25.01.32 Gorilla Jones W RSC 6 Oddone Piazza, Milwaukee, USA (NBA)
26.04.32 Gorilla Jones W PTS 12 Young Terry, Trenton, USA (NBA)
11.06.32 Marcel Thil W DIS 11 Gorilla Jones, Paris, France (NBA/IBU)
04.07.32 Marcel Thil W PTS 15 Len Harvey, London, England (NBA/IBU)
Marcel Thil ceased to be recognised by the NBA (the authority once again supported the claims of Gorilla Jones)
11.11.32 Ben Jeby W PTS 15 Chuck Devlin, New York C, USA (NY)
13.01.33 Ben Jeby W RSC 12 Frank Battaglia, New York C, USA (NY)
30.01.33 Gorilla Jones W CO 7 Sammy Slaughter, Cleveland, USA (NBA)
Gorilla Jones ceased to be recognised by the NBA (failure to defend)
17.03.33 Ben Jeby DREW 15 Vince Dundee, New York C, USA (NY)
10.07.33 Ben Jeby W PTS 15 Young Terry, Newark, USA (NY)
09.08.33 Lou Brouillard W CO 7 Ben Jeby, New York C, USA (NY/NBA)
02.10.33 Marcel Thil W PTS 15 Kid Tunero, Paris, France (IBU)
30.10.33 Vince Dundee W PTS 15 Lou Brouillard, Boston, USA (NY/NBA)
08.12.33 Vince Dundee W PTS 15 Andy Callahan, Boston, USA (NY/NBA)
26.02.34 Marcel Thil W PTS 15 Ignacio Ara, Paris, France (IBU)
01.05.34 Vince Dundee W PTS 15 Al Diamond, Paterson, USA (NY/NBA)
03.05.34 Marcel Thil W PTS 15 Gustav Roth, Paris, USA (IBU)
11.09.34 Teddy Yarosz W PTS 15 Vince Dundee, Pittsburgh, USA (NY/NBA)
15.10.34 Marcel Thil DREW 15 Carmelo Candel, Paris, France (IBU)
04.05.35 Marcel Thil W RTD 14 Vilda Jaks, Paris, France (IBU)
03.06.35 Marcel Thil W PTS 15 Ignacio Ara, Madrid, Spain (IBU)
28.06.35 Marcel Thil W PTS 10 Carmelo Candel, Paris, France (IBU)
19.09.35 Babe Risko W PTS 15 Teddy Yarosz, Pittsburgh, USA (NY/NBA)
20.01.36 Marcel Thil W DIS 4 Lou Brouillard, Paris, France (IBU)
10.02.36 Babe Risko W PTS 15 Tony Fisher, Newark, USA (NY/NBA)
11.07.36 Freddie Steele W PTS 15 Babe Risko, Seattle, USA (NY/NBA)
01.01.37 Freddie Steele W PTS 10 Gorilla Jones, Milwaukee, USA (NY/NBA)
15.02.37 Marcel Thil W DIS 6 Lou Brouillard, Paris, France (IBU)
19.02.37 Freddie Steele W PTS 15 Babe Risko, New York C, USA (NY/NBA)
11.05.37 Freddie Steele W CO 3 Frank Battaglia, Seattle, USA (NY/NBA)
11.09.37 Freddie Steele W CO 4 Ken Overlin, Seattle, USA (NY/NBA)
Freddie Steele ceased to be recognised by NY (failure to defend against Fred Apostoli)
23.09.37 Fred Apostoli W RSC 10 Marcel Thil, New York C, USA (IBU)
Fred Apostoli forfeited IBU recognition (Thil was stripped of the European title and the IBU recognised the winner of the Tenet/Besselmann contest)
19.02.38 Freddie Steele W RTD 7 Carmen Barth, Cleveland, USA (NBA)
01.04.38 Fred Apostoli W PTS 15 Glen Lee, New York C, USA (NY)
07.04.38 Edouard Tenet W RTD 12 Josef Besselmann, Berlin, Germany (IBU)
Edouard Tenet ceased to be recognised by the IBU (this followed a defeat by Bep van Klaveren in a European title defence, July, 1938)
26.07.38 Al Hostak W CO 1 Freddie Steele, Seattle, USA (NBA)
01.11.38 Solly Krieger W PTS 15 Al Hostak, Seattle, USA (NBA)
18.11.38 Fred Apostoli W RSC 8 Young Corbett III, New York C, USA (NY)

Sugar Ray Leonard acknowledges the cheers of the crowd following his wonderful middleweight title win over Marvin Hagler, April, 1987.

Tom Casino

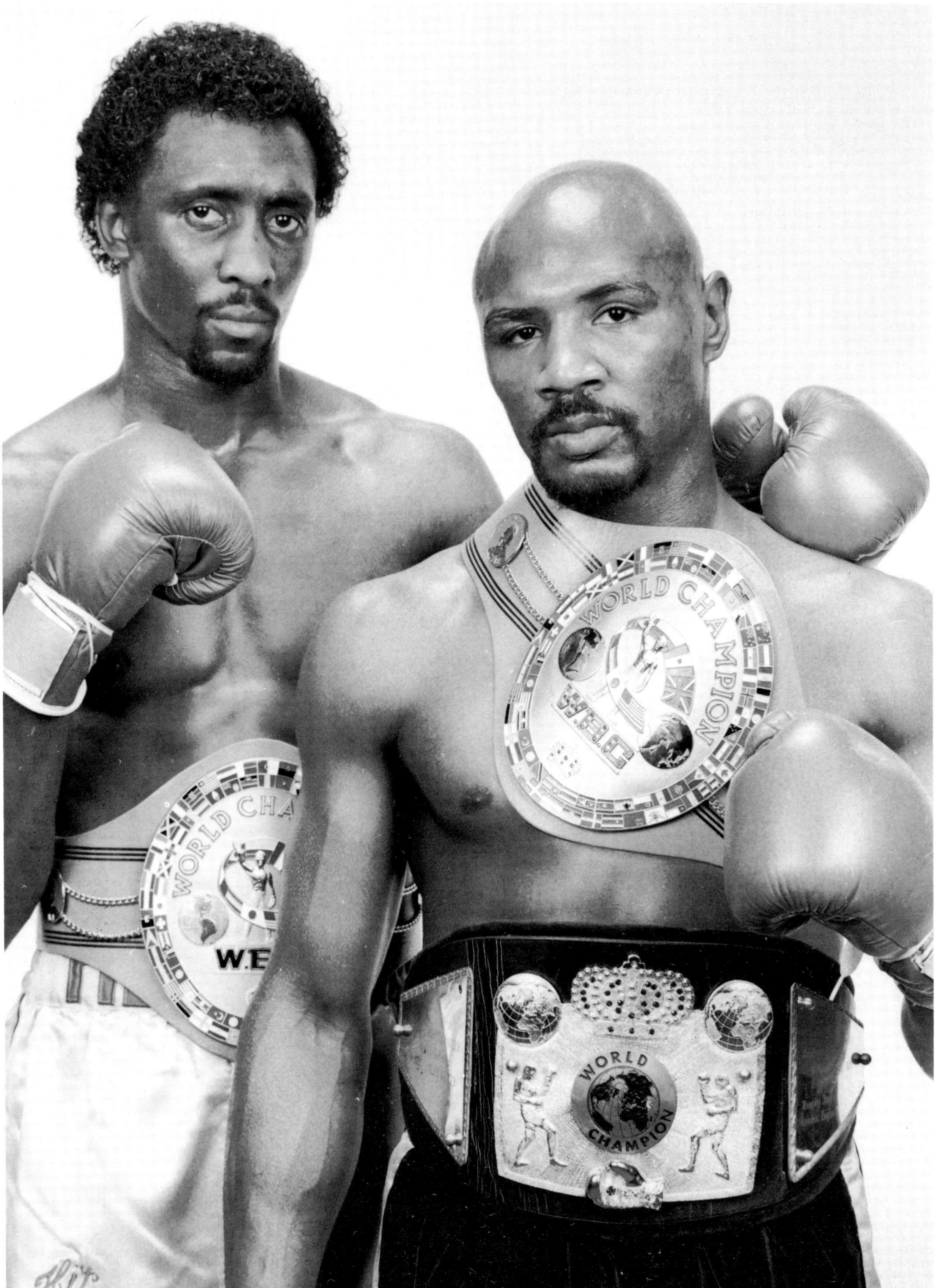

Two middleweight greats — Thomas Hearns (left) and Marvin Hagler.

Peter Goldfield/USA

27.06.39 Al Hostak W RSC 4 Solly Krieger, Seattle, USA (NBA)
02.10.39 Ceferino Garcia W RSC 7 Fred Apostoli, New York C, USA (NY)
11.12.39 Al Hostak W CO 1 Eric Seelig, Cleveland, USA (NBA)
23.12.39 Ceferino Garcia W CO 13 Glen Lee, Manila, Philippines (NY)
01.03.40 Ceferino Garcia DREW 10 Henry Armstrong, Los Angeles, USA (NY)
23.05.40 Ken Overlin W PTS 15 Ceferino Garcia, New York C, USA (NY)
19.07.40 Tony Zale W RTD 13 Al Hostak, Seattle, USA (NBA)
01.11.40 Ken Overlin W PTS 15 Steve Belloise, New York C, USA (NY)
13.12.40 Ken Overlin W PTS 15 Steve Belloise, New York C, USA (NY)
21.02.41 Tony Zale W CO 14 Steve Mamakos, Chicago, USA (NBA)
09.05.41 Billy Soose W PTS 15 Ken Overlin, New York C, USA (NY)
Billy Soose ceased to be recognised by NY (this followed a defeat by George Abrams in a non-title bout, July, 1941 and increasing weight problems)
28.05.41 Tony Zale W CO 2 Al Hostak, Chicago, USA (NBA)
28.11.41 Tony Zale W PTS 15 Georgie Abrams, New York C, USA
27.09.46 Tony Zale W CO 6 Rocky Graziano, New York C, USA
16.07.47 Rocky Graziano W RSC 6 Tony Zale, Chicago, USA
10.06.48 Tony Zale W CO 3 Rocky Graziano, Newark, USA
21.09.48 Marcel Cerdan W RSC 12 Tony Zale, Jersey C, USA
16.06.49 Jake la Motta W RTD 10 Marcel Cerdan, Detroit, USA
05.06.50 Sugar Ray Robinson W PTS 15 Robert Villemain, Philadelphia, USA (PEN)
12.07.50 Jake la Motta W PTS 15 Tiberio Mitri, New York C, USA (NY/NBA)
25.08.50 Sugar Ray Robinson W CO 1 Jose Basora, Scranton, USA (PEN)
13.09.50 Jake la Motta W CO 15 Laurent Dauthuille, Detroit, USA (NY/NBA)
26.10.50 Sugar Ray Robinson W CO 12 Carl Bobo Olson, Philadelphia, USA (PEN)
14.02.51 Sugar Ray Robinson W RSC 13 Jake la Motta, Chicago, USA
10.07.51 Randy Turpin W PTS 15 Sugar Ray Robinson, London, England
12.09.51 Sugar Ray Robinson W RSC 10 Randy Turpin, New York C, USA
13.03.52 Sugar Ray Robinson W PTS 15 Carl Bobo Olson, San Francisco, USA
16.04.52 Sugar Ray Robinson W CO 3 Rocky Graziano, Chicago, USA
Sugar Ray Robinson relinquished title (retired)
09.06.53 Randy Turpin W PTS 15 Charles Humez, London, England (EBU)
21.10.53 Carl Bobo Olson W PTS 15 Randy Turpin, New York C, USA
02.04.54 Carl Bobo Olson W PTS 15 Kid Gavilan, Chicago, USA
20.08.54 Carl Bobo Olson W PTS 15 Rocky Castellani, San Francisco, USA
15.12.54 Carl Bobo Olson W RSC 11 Pierre Langlois, San Francisco, USA
09.12.55 Sugar Ray Robinson W CO 2 Carl Bobo Olson, Chicago, USA
18.05.56 Sugar Ray Robinson W CO 4 Carl Bob Olson, Los Angeles, USA
02.01.57 Gene Fullmer W PTS 15 Sugar Ray Robinson, New York C, USA
01.05.57 Sugar Ray Robinson W CO 5 Gene Fullmer, Chicago, USA
23.09.57 Carmen Basilio W PTS 15 Sugar Ray Robinson, New York C, USA
25.03.58 Sugar Ray Robinson W PTS 15 Carmen Basilio, Chicago, USA
Sugar Ray Robinson forfeited NBA recognition (inactivity)
28.08.59 Gene Fullmer W RSC 14 Carmen Basilio, San Francisco, USA (NBA)
04.12.59 Gene Fullmer W PTS 15 Spider Webb, Logan, USA (NBA)
22.01.60 Paul Pender W PTS 15 Sugar Ray Robinson, Boston, USA (NY/EBU)
20.04.60 Gene Fullmer DREW 15 Joey Giardello, Bozeman, USA (NBA)
10.06.60 Paul Pender W PTS 15 Sugar Ray Robinson, Boston, USA (NY/EBU)
29.06.60 Gene Fullmer W RSC 12 Carmen Basilio, Salt Lake C, USA (NBA)
03.12.60 Gene Fullmer DREW 15 Sugar Ray Robinson, Los Angeles, USA (NBA)
14.01.61 Paul Pender W RSC 7 Terry Downes, Boston, USA (NY/EBU)
04.03.61 Gene Fullmer W PTS 15 Sugar Ray Robinson, Las Vegas, USA (NBA)
22.04.61 Paul Pender W PTS 15 Carmen Basilio, Boston, USA (NY/EBU)
11.07.61 Terry Downes W RTD 9 Paul Pender, Wembley, England (NY/EBU)
05.08.61 Gene Fullmer W PTS 15 Florentino Fernandez, Ogden, USA (NBA)
09.12.61 Gene Fullmer W CO 10 Benny Kid Paret, Las Vegas, USA (NBA)
07.04.62 Paul Pender W PTS 15 Terry Downes, Boston, USA (NY/EBU)
Paul Pender forfeited NY/EBU recognition (failure to defend within stipulated period)
23.10.62 Dick Tiger W PTS 15 Gene Fullmer, San Francisco, USA (NBA)
23.02.63 Dick Tiger DREW 15 Gene Fullmer, Las Vegas, USA (NBA)
10.08.63 Dick Tiger W RTD 7 Gene Fullmer, Ibadan, Nigeria
07.12.63 Joey Giardello W PTS 15 Dick Tiger, Atlantic C, USA
14.12.64 Joey Giardello W PTS 15 Ruben Carter, Philadelphia, USA
21.10.65 Dick Tiger W PTS 15 Joey Giardello, New York C, USA
25.04.66 Emile Griffith W PTS 15 Dick Tiger, New York C, USA
13.07.66 Emile Griffith W PTS 15 Joey Archer, New York C, USA
23.01.67 Emile Griffith W PTS 15 Joey Archer, New York C, USA
17.04.67 Nino Benvenuti W PTS 15 Emile Griffith, New York C, USA
29.09.67 Emile Griffith W PTS 15 Nino Benvenuti, New York C, USA
04.03.68 Nino Benvenuti W PTS 15 Emile Griffith, New York C, USA
14.12.68 Nino Benvenuti W PTS 15 Don Fullmer, San Remo, Italy
04.10.69 Nino Benvenuti W DIS 7 Fraser Scott, Naples, Italy
22.11.69 Nino Benvenuti W CO 1 Luis Rodriguez, Rome, Italy
23.05.70 Nino Benvenuti W CO 8 Tom Bethea, Umag, Yugoslavia
07.11.70 Carlos Monzon W CO 12 Nino Benvenuti, Rome, Italy
08.05.71 Carlos Monzon W RSC 3 Nino Benvenuti, Monte Carlo
25.09.71 Carlos Monzon W RSC 14 Emile Griffith, Bs Aires, Argentine
04.03.72 Carlos Monzon W RSC 5 Denny Moyer, Rome, Italy
17.06.72 Carlos Monzon W RTD 12 Jean-Claude Bouttier, Colombes, France
19.08.72 Carlos Monzon W RSC 5 Tom Bogs, Copenhagen, Denmark
11.11.72 Carlos Monzon W PTS 15 Bennie Briscoe, Bs Aires, Argentine
02.06.73 Carlos Monzon W PTS 15 Emile Griffith, Monte Carlo
29.09.73 Carlos Monzon W PTS 15 Jean-Claude Bouttier, Paris, France
09.02.74 Carlos Monzon W RTD 6 Jose Napoles, Paris, France
Carlos Monzon forfeited WBC recognition (failure to defend against Rodrigo Valdez)
25.05.74 Rodrigo Valdez W CO 7 Bennie Briscoe, Monte Carlo (WBC)
05.10.74 Carlos Monzon W CO 7 Tony Mundine, Bs Aires, Argentine (WBA)
30.11.74 Rodrigo Valdez W CO 11 Gratien Tonna, Paris, France (WBC)
31.05.75 Rodrigo Valdez W RSC 8 Ramon Mendez, Cali, Colombia (WBC)
30.06.75 Carlos Monzon W RSC 10 Tony Licata, New York C, USA (WBA)
16.08.75 Rodrigo Valdez W PTS 15 Rudy Robles, Cartagena, Colombia (WBC)
13.12.75 Carlos Monzon W CO 5 Gratien Tonna, Paris, France (WBA)
28.03.75 Rodrigo Valdez W RTD 4 Nessim Cohen, Paris, France (WBC)
26.06.76 Carlos Monzon W PTS 15 Rodrigo Valdez, Monte Carlo
30.07.77 Carlos Monzon W PTS 15 Rodrigo Valdez, Monte Carlo
Carlos Monzon relinquished title (retired)
05.11.77 Rodrigo Valdez W PTS 15 Bennie Briscoe, Campione, Italy
22.04.78 Hugo Corro W PTS 15 Rodrigo Valdez, San Remo, Italy
05.08.78 Hugo Corro W PTS 15 Ronnie Harris, Bs Aires, Argentine
11.11.78 Hugo Corro W PTS 15 Rodrigo Valdez, Bs Aires, Argentine
30.06.79 Vito Antuofermo W PTS 15 Hugo Corro, Monte Carlo
30.11.79 Vito Antuofermo DREW 15 Marvin Hagler, Las Vegas, USA
16.03.80 Alan Minter W PTS 15 Vito Antuofermo, Las Vegas, USA
28.06.80 Alan Minter W RTD 8 Vito Antuofermo, Wembley, England
27.09.80 Marvin Hagler W RSC 3 Alan Minter, Wembley, England
17.01.81 Marvin Hagler W RSC 8 Fully Obelmejias, Boston, USA
13.06.81 Marvin Hagler W RTD 4 Vito Antuofermo, Boston, USA
03.10.81 Marvin Hagler W RSC 11 Mustafa Hamsho, Rosemont, USA
07.03.82 Marvin Hagler W RSC 1 Caveman Lee, Atlantic C, USA
30.10.82 Marvin Hagler W RSC 5 Fully Obelmejias, San Remo, Italy
11.02.83 Marvin Hagler W RSC 6 Tony Sibson, Worcester, USA
27.05.83 Marvin Hagler W CO 4 Wilford Scypion, Providence, USA
10.11.83 Marvin Hagler W PTS 15 Roberto Duran, Las Vegas, USA
30.03.84 Marvin Hagler W RSC 10 Juan Domingo Roldan, Las Vegas, USA
19.10.84 Marvin Hagler W RSC 3 Mustafa Hamsho, New York C, USA
16.04.85 Marvin Hagler W RSC 3 Thomas Hearns, Las Vegas, USA
10.03.86 Marvin Hagler W CO 11 John Mugabi, Las Vegas, USA
Marvin Hagler forfeited WBA/IBF recognition (failure to meet Herol Graham inside the stipulated period and subsequently boxing Leonard)
06.04.87 Sugar Ray Leonard W PTS 12 Marvin Hagler, Las Vegas, USA (WBC)
Sugar Ray Leonard relinquished WBC version of title (retired)
10.10.87 Frank Tate W PTS 15 Michael Olajide, Las Vegas, USA (IBF)
23.10.87 Sumbu Kalambay W PTS 15 Iran Barkley, Livorno, Italy (WBA)
29.10.87 Thomas Hearns W CO 4 Juan Domingo Roldan, Las Vegas, USA (WBC)
07.02.88 Frank Tate W CO 10 Tony Sibson, Stafford, England (IBF)
01.03.88 Sumbu Kalambay W PTS 12 Mike McCallum, Pesaro, Italy (WBA)
06.06.88 Iran Barkley W RSC 3 Thomas Hearns, Las Vegas, USA (WBC)
12.06.88 Sumbu Kalambay W PTS 12 Robbie Sims, Ravenna, Italy (WBA)
28.07.88 Michael Nunn W RSC 9 Frank Tate, Las Vegas, USA (IBF)
04.11.88 Michael Nunn W CO 8 Juan Domingo Roldan, Las Vegas, USA (IBF)
08.11.88 Sumbu Kalambay W RSC 7 Doug de Witt, Monte Carlo (WBA)
Sumbu Kalambay forfeited WBA recognition (failure to sign for defence against Herol Graham)
24.02.89 Roberto Duran W PTS 12 Iran Barkley, Atlantic C, USA (WBC)
25.03.89 Michael Nunn W CO 1 Sumbu Kalambay, Las Vegas, USA (IBF)

Super-Middleweight (168 lbs)

Title Holders

	Birthplace	Tenure	Status
Murray Sutherland	Scotland	1984	IBF
Chong-Pal Park*	S Korea	1984–1987	IBF
Chong-Pal Park	S Korea	1987–1988	WBA
Graciano Rocchigiani	W Germany	1988–	IBF
Fully Obelmejias	Venezuela	1988–	WBA
Sugar Ray Leonard	USA	1988–	WBC

Title Bouts

28.03.84 Murray Sutherland W PTS 15 Ernie Singletary, Atlantic C, USA (IBF)
22.07.84 Chong-Pal Park W CO 11 Murray Sutherland, Seoul, S Korea (IBF)
02.01.85 Chong-Pal Park W CO 2 Roy Gumbs, Seoul, S Korea (IBF)
30.06.85 Chong-Pal Park W PTS 15 Vinnie Curto, Seoul, S Korea (IBF)
11.04.86 Chong-Pal Park W CO 15 Vinnie Curto, Los Angeles, USA (IBF)
06.07.86 Chong-Pal Park T DRAW 2 Lindell Holmes, Chungju, S Korea (IBF)
14.09.86 Chong-Pal Park W PTS 15 Marvin Mack, Pusan, S Korea (IBF)
25.01.87 Chong-Pal Park W RSC 15 Doug Sam, Seoul, S Korea (IBF)
03.05.87 Chong-Pal Park W PTS 15 Lindell Holmes, Inchon, S Korea (IBF)
26.07.87 Chong-Pal Park W RSC 4 Emmanuel Otti, Kwangju, S Korea (IBF)
Chong-Pal Park relinquished title (contested the WBA version of the title)
06.12.87 Chong-Pal Park W RSC 2 Jesus Gallardo, Seoul, S Korea (WBA)
01.03.88 Chong-Pal Park W CO 5 Polly Pasieron, Chungju, S Korea (WBA)
12.03.88 Graciano Rocchigiani W RSC 8 Vince Boulware, Dusseldorf, W Germany (IBF)
23.05.88 Fully Obelmejias W PTS 12 Chong-Pal Park, Suanbao, S Korea (WBA)
03.06.88 Graciano Rocchigiani W PTS 15 Nicky Walker, Berlin, W Germany (IBF)
07.10.88 Graciano Rocchigiani W RTD 11 Chris Reid, Berlin, W Germany (IBF)
07.11.88 Sugar Ray Leonard W RSC 9 Don Lalonde, Las Vegas, USA (WBC)
27.01.89 Graciano Rocchigiani W PTS 12 Thulani Malinga, Berlin, W Germany (IBF)

Light-Heavyweight (175 lbs)

Title Holders

	Birthplace	Tenure	Status
Jack Root	Austria	1903	USA
George Gardner	Ireland	1903	USA
Bob Fitzsimmons	England	1903–1905	
Jack O'Brien*	USA	1905–1912	
Jack Dillon	USA	1912–1916	
Battling Levinsky	USA	1916–1920	
Georges Carpentier	France	1920–1922	
Battling Siki	Senegal	1922–1923	

Mike McTigue	Ireland	1923–1925	
Paul Berlenbach	USA	1925–1926	
Jack Delaney*	Canada	1926–1927	
Jimmy Slattery	USA	1927	NBA
Tommy Loughran	USA	1927	NY
Tommy Loughran*	USA	1927–1929	
Jimmy Slattery	USA	1930	NY
Maxie Rosenbloom	USA	1930–1933	NY
George Nichols	USA	1932	NBA
Bob Godwin	USA	1933	NBA
Maxie Rosenbloom	USA	1933–1934	
Bob Olin	USA	1934–1935	
John Henry Lewis*	USA	1935–1938	
Tiger Jack Fox	USA	1938–1939	NY
Melio Bettina	USA	1939	NY
Len Harvey	England	1939	GB
Billy Conn*	USA	1939–1940	
Anton Christoforidis	Greece	1941	NBA
Gus Lesnevich	USA	1941–1942	
Gus Lesnevich	USA	1942–1946	NY/NBA
Freddie Mills	England	1942–1946	GB
Freddie Mills	England	1948–1950	
Joey Maxim	USA	1950–1952	
Archie Moore	USA	1952–1961	
Archie Moore	USA	1961–1962	NY/EBU
Harold Johnson	USA	1961–1962	NBA
Harold Johnson	Puerto Rico	1962–1963	
Willie Pastrano	Nigeria	1963–1965	
Jose Torres	USA	1965–1966	
Dick Tiger	USA	1966–1968	
Bob Foster	Venezuela	1968–1971	
Bob Foster	USA	1971–1972	WBC
Vicente Rondon	England	1971–1972	WBA
Bob Foster*	Argentine	1972–1974	
John Conteh	Argentine	1974–1977	WBC
Victor Galindez	Yugoslavia	1974–1978	WBA
Miguel Cuello	USA	1977–1978	WBC
Mate Parlov	USA	1978	WBC
Mike Rossman	Argentine	1978–1979	WBA
Marvin Johnson	USA	1978–1979	WBC
Victor Galindez	USA	1979	WBA
Matt Saad Muhammad	USA	1979–1981	WBC
Marvin Johnson	USA	1979–1980	WBA
Mustafa Muhammad	USA	1980–1981	WBA
Michael Spinks	USA	1981–1983	WBA
Dwight Muhammad Qawi	USA	1981–1983	WBC
Michael Spinks*	Yugoslavia	1983–1985	
J. B. Williamson	USA	1985–1986	WBC
Slobodan Kacar	Guyana	1985–1986	IBF
Marvin Johnson	USA	1986–1987	WBA
Dennis Andries	USA	1986–1987	WBC
Bobby Czyz	Guyana	1986–1987	IBF
Thomas Hearns*	USA	1987	WBC
Leslie Stewart	Trinidad	1987	WBA
Virgil Hill	USA	1987–	WBA
Charles Williams	USA	1987–	IBF
Don Lalonde	Canada	1987–1988	WBC
Sugar Ray Leonard*	USA	1988	WBC
Dennis Andries	Guyana	1989–	WBC

Title Bouts

22.04.03 Jack Root W PTS 10 Kid McCoy, Detroit, USA (USA)
04.07.03 George Gardner W CO 12 Jack Root, Fort Erie, Canada (USA)
25.11.03 Bob Fitzsimmons W PTS 20 George Gardner, San Francisco, USA
20.12.05 Jack O'Brien W RTD 13 Bob Fitzsimmons, San Francisco, USA
28.11.06 Jack O'Brien DREW 20 Tommy Burns, Los Angeles, USA
Jack O'Brien relinquished title (retired)
28.05.12 Jack Dillon W CO 3 Hugo Kelly, Indianapolis, USA
28.04.14 Jack Dillon W PTS 10 Al Norton, Kansas C, USA
25.04.16 Jack Dillon W PTS 15 Battling Levinsky, Kansas C, USA
24.10.16 Battling Levinsky W PTS 12 Jack Dillon, Boston, USA
03.05.20 Battling Levinsky W PTS 12 Clay Turner, Portland, USA
12.10.20 Georges Carpentier W CO 4 Battling Levinsky, Jersey C, USA
11.05.22 Georges Carpentier W CO 1 Ted Kid Lewis, London, England
24.09.22 Battling Siki W CO 6 Georges Carpentier, Paris, France
17.03.23 Mike McTigue W PTS 20 Battling Siki, Dublin, Ireland
04.10.23 Mike McTigue DREW 10 Young Stribling, Columbus, USA
30.05.25 Paul Berlenbach W PTS 15 Mike McTigue, New York C, USA
11.09.25 Paul Berlenbach W RSC 11 Jimmy Slattery, New York C, USA
11.12.25 Paul Berlenbach W PTS 15 Jack Delaney, New York C, USA
10.06.26 Paul Berlenbach W PTS 15 Young Stribling, New York C, USA
16.07.26 Jack Delaney W PTS 15 Paul Berlenbach, New York C, USA
Jack Delaney relinquished title (moved up to heavyweight)
30.08.27 Jimmy Slattery W PTS 10 Maxie Rosenbloom, Hartford, USA (NBA)
07.10.27 Tommy Loughran W PTS 15 Mike McTigue, New York C, USA (NY)
12.12.27 Tommy Loughran W PTS 15 Jimmy Slattery, New York C, USA
06.01.28 Tommy Loughran W PTS 15 Leo Lomski, New York C, USA
01.06.28 Tommy Loughran W PTS 15 Pete Latzo, New York C, USA
16.07.28 Tommy Loughran W PTS 10 Pete Latzo, Wilkes Barre, USA
08.03.29 Tommy Loughran W PTS 10 Mickey Walker, Chicago, USA
18.07.29 Tommy Loughran W PTS 15 James J. Braddock, New York C, USA
Tommy Loughran relinquished title (moved up to heavyweight)
10.02.30 Jimmy Slattery W PTS 15 Lou Scozza, Buffalo, USA (NY)
25.06.30 Maxie Rosenbloom W PTS 15 Jimmy Slattery, Buffalo, USA (NY)
22.10.30 Maxie Rosenbloom W RSC 11 Abe Bain, New York C, USA (NY)
05.08.31 Maxie Rosenbloom W PTS 15 Jimmy Slattery, New York C, USA (NY)
18.03.32 George Nichols W PTS 10 Dave Maier, Chicago, USA (NBA)
George Nichols ceased to be recognised by the NBA (this followed a defeat by Lou Scozza in a non-title bout, May, 1932)
14.07.32 Maxie Rosenbloom W PTS 15 Lou Scozza, Buffalo, USA (NY)
22.02.33 Maxie Rosenbloom W PTS 10 Al Stillman, St Louis, USA (NY)
01.03.33 Bob Godwin W PTS 10 Joe Knight, Palm Beach, USA (NBA)
10.03.33 Maxie Rosenbloom W PTS 15 Adolf Heuser, New York C, USA (NY)
24.03.33 Maxie Rosenbloom W RSC 4 Bob Godwin, New York C, USA
03.11.33 Maxie Rosenbloom W PTS 15 Mickey Walker, New York C, USA
05.02.34 Maxie Rosenbloom DREW 15 Joe Knight, Miami, USA
16.11.34 Bob Olin W PTS 15 Maxie Rosenbloom, New York C, USA
31.10.35 John Henry Lewis W PTS 15 Bob Olin, St Louis, USA
13.03.36 John Henry Lewis W PTS 15 Jock McAvoy, New York C, USA
09.11.36 John Henry Lewis W PTS 15 Len Harvey, Wembley, England
03.06.37 John Henry Lewis W RSC 8 Bob Olin, St Louis, USA
25.04.38 John Henry Lewis W CO 4 Emilio Martinez, Minneapolis, USA
28.10.38 John Henry Lewis W PTS 15 Al Gainer, New Haven, USA
John Henry Lewis relinquished title (retired)
29.11.38 Tiger Jack Fox W PTS 15 Al Gainer, New York C, USA (NY)
03.02.39 Melio Bettina W RSC 9 Tiger Jack Fox, New York C, USA (NY)
10.07.39 Len Harvey W PTS 15 Jock McAvoy, London, England (GB)
Len Harvey failed to capitalise on GB recognition (wartime inactivity)
13.07.39 Billy Conn W PTS 15 Melio Bettina, New York C, USA
25.09.39 Billy Conn W PTS 15 Melio Bettina, Pittsburgh, USA
17.11.39 Billy Conn W PTS 15 Gus Lesnevich, New York C, USA
05.06.40 Billy Conn W PTS 15 Gus Lesnevich, Detroit, USA
Billy Conn relinquished title (moved up to heavyweight)
13.01.41 Anton Christoforidis W PTS 15 Melio Bettina, Cleveland, USA (NBA)
22.05.41 Gus Lesnevich W PTS 15 Anton Christoforidis, New York C, USA
26.08.41 Gus Lesnevich W PTS 15 Tami Mauriello, New York C, USA
14.11.41 Gus Lesnevich W PTS 15 Tami Mauriello, New York C, USA
20.06.42 Freddie Mills W CO 2 Len Harvey, London, England (GB)
14.05.46 Gus Lesnevich W RSC 10 Freddie Mills, London, England
28.02.47 Gus Lesnevich W RSC 10 Billy Fox, New York C, USA
05.03.48 Gus Lesnevich W CO 1 Billy Fox, New York C, USA
26.07.48 Freddie Mills W PTS 15 Gus Lesnevich, London, England
24.01.50 Joey Maxim W CO 10 Freddie Mills, London, England
22.08.51 Joey Maxim W PTS 15 Bob Murphy, New York C, USA
25.06.52 Joey Maxim W RTD 13 Sugar Ray Robinson, New York C, USA
17.12.52 Archie Moore W PTS 15 Joey Maxim, St Louis, USA
24.06.53 Archie Moore W PTS 15 Joey Maxim, Ogden, USA
27.01.54 Archie Moore W PTS 15 Joey Maxim, Miami, USA
11.08.54 Archie Moore W RSC 14 Harold Johnson, New York C, USA
22.06.55 Archie Moore W CO 3 Carl Bobo Olson, New York C, USA
05.06.56 Archie Moore W RSC 10 Yolande Pompey, London, England
20.09.57 Archie Moore W RSC 7 Tony Anthony, Los Angeles, USA
10.12.58 Archie Moore W CO 11 Yvon Durelle, Montreal, Canada
12.08.59 Archie Moore W CO 3 Yvon Durelle, Montreal, Canada
Archie Moore forfeited NBA recognition (inactivity)
07.02.61 Harold Johnson W RSC 9 Jesse Bowdry, Miami, USA (NBA)
24.04.61 Harold Johnson W RSC 2 Von Clay, Philadelphia, USA (NBA)
10.06.61 Archie Moore W PTS 15 Giulio Rinaldi, New York C, USA (NY/EBU)
Archie Moore forfeited NY/EBU recognition (failure to defend against either Harold Johnson or Doug Jones)
29.08.61 Harold Johnson W PTS 15 Eddie Cotton, Seattle, USA (NBA)
12.05.62 Harold Johnson W PTS 15 Doug Jones, Philadelphia, USA
23.06.62 Harold Johnson W PTS 15 Gustav Scholz, Berlin, W Germany
01.06.63 Willie Pastrano W PTS 15 Harold Johnson, Las Vegas, USA
10.04.64 Willie Pastrano W RSC 5 Greg Peralta, New Orleans, USA
30.11.64 Willie Pastrano W RSC 11 Terry Downes, Manchester, England
30.03.65 Jose Torres W RSC 9 Willie Pastrano, New York C, USA
21.05.66 Jose Torres W PTS 15 Wayne Thornton, New York C, USA
15.08.66 Jose Torres W PTS 15 Eddie Cotton, Las Vegas, USA
15.10.66 Jose Torres W CO 2 Chic Calderwood, San Juan, Puerto Rico
16.12.66 Dick Tiger W PTS 15 Jose Torres, New York C, USA
16.05.67 Dick Tiger W PTS 15 Jose Torres, New York C, USA
17.11.67 Dick Tiger W RSC 12 Roger Rouse, Las Vegas, USA
24.05.68 Bob Foster W CO 4 Dick Tiger, New York C, USA
23.01.69 Bob Foster W RSC 1 Frankie de Paula, New York C, USA
24.05.69 Bob Foster W RSC 4 Andy Kendall, Springfield, USA
04.04.70 Bob Foster W RSC 3 Roger Rouse, Missoula, USA
27.06.70 Bob Foster W CO 10 Mark Tessman, Baltimore, USA
Bob Foster forfeited WBA recognition (failure to defend against Jimmy Dupree)
27.02.71 Vicente Rondon W RSC 6 Jimmy Dupree, Caracas, Venezuela (WBA)
02.03.71 Bob Foster W CO 4 Hal Carroll, Scranton, USA (WBC)
24.04.71 Bob Foster W PTS 15 Ray Anderson, Tampa, USA (WBC)
05.06.71 Vicente Rondon W CO 1 Piero del Papa, Caracas, Venezuela (WBA)
21.08.71 Vicente Rondon W PTS 15 Eddie Jones, Caracas, Venezuela (WBA)
26.10.71 Vicente Rondon W RSC 12 Gomeo Brennan, Miami, USA (WBA)
29.10.71 Bob Foster W RSC 8 Tommy Hicks, Scranton, USA (WBC)
15.12.71 Vicente Rondon W CO 8 Doyle Baird, Cleveland, USA (WBA)
16.12.71 Bob Foster W RSC 3 Brian Kelly, Oklahoma C, USA (WBC)
07.04.72 Bob Foster W CO 2 Vicente Rondon, Miami, USA
27.06.72 Bob Foster W CO 4 Mike Quarry, Las Vegas, USA
26.09.72 Bob Foster W CO 14 Chris Finnegan, Wembley, England
21.08.73 Bob Foster W PTS 15 Pierre Fourie, Alburquerque, USA
01.12.73 Bob Foster W PTS 15 Pierre Fourie, Johannesburg, S Africa

17.06.74 Bob Foster DREW 15 Jorge Ahumada, Alburquerque, USA
Bob Foster relinquished title (retired)
01.10.74 John Conteh W PTS 15 Jorge Ahumada, Wembley, England (WBC)
07.12.74 Victor Galindez W RTD 12 Len Hutchins, Bs Aires, Argentine (WBA)
11.03.75 John Conteh W RSC 5 Lonnie Bennett, Wembley, England (WBC)
07.04.75 Victor Galindez W PTS 15 Pierre Fourie, Johannesburg, S Africa (WBA)
30.06.75 Victor Galindez W PTS 15 Jorge Ahumada, New York C, USA (WBA)
13.09.75 Victor Galindez W PTS 15 Pierre Fourie, Johannesburg, S Africa (WBA)
28.03.76 Victor Galindez W RTD 3 Harald Skog, Oslo, Norway (WBA)
22.05.76 Victor Galindez W CO 15 Richie Kates, Johannesburg, S Africa (WBA)
05.10.76 Victor Galindez W PTS 15 Kosie Smith, Johannesburg, S Africa (WBA)
09.10.76 John Conteh W PTS 15 Yaqui Lopez, Copenhagen, Denmark (WBC)
05.03.77 John Conteh W RSC 3 Len Hutchins, Liverpool, England (WBC)
John Conteh forfeited WBC version of title (withdrew from a scheduled defence against Miguel Cuello)
21.05.77 Miguel Cuello W CO 9 Jesse Burnett, Monte Carlo (WBC)
18.06.77 Victor Galindez W PTS 15 Richie Kates, Rome, Italy (WBA)
17.09.77 Victor Galindez W PTS 15 Yaqui Lopez, Rome, Italy (WBA)
20.11.77 Victor Galindez W PTS 15 Mustapha Muhammad, Turin, Italy (WBA)
07.01.78 Mate Parlov W CO 9 Miguel Cuello, Milan, Italy (WBC)
06.05.78 Victor Galindez W PTS 15 Yaqui Lopez, Reggio, Italy (WBA)
17.06.78 Mate Parlov W PTS 15 John Conteh, Belgrade, Yugoslavia (WBC)
15.09.78 Mike Rossman W RSC 13 Victor Galindez, New Orleans, USA (WBA)
02.12.78 Marvin Johnson W RSC 10 Mate Parlov, Marsala, Italy (WBC)
05.12.78 Mike Rossman W RSC 6 Aldo Traversaro, Philadelphia, USA (WBA)
14.04.79 Victor Galindez W RTD 9 Mike Rossman, New Orleans, USA (WBA)
22.04.79 Matt Saad Muhammad W RSC 8 Marvin Johnson, Indianapolis, USA (WBC)
18.08.79 Matt Saad Muhammad W PTS 15 John Conteh, Atlantic C, USA (WBC)
30.11.79 Marvin Johnson W RSC 11 Victor Galindez, New Orleans, USA (WBA)
29.03.80 Matt Saad Muhammad W RSC 4 John Conteh, Atlantic C, USA (WBC)
31.03.80 Mustapha Muhammad W RSC 11 Marvin Johnson, Knoxville, USA (WBA)
11.05.80 Matt Saad Muhammad W RSC 5 Louis Pergaud, Halifax, Canada (WBC)
13.07.80 Matt Saad Muhammad W RSC 14 Yaqui Lopez, McAfee, USA (WBC)
20.07.80 Mustapha Muhammad W RSC 10 Jerry Martin, McAfee, USA (WBA)
28.11.80 Matt Saad Muhammad W CO 4 Lotte Mwale, San Diego, USA (WBC)
29.11.80 Mustapha Muhammad W RSC 3 Rudi Koopmans, Los Angeles, USA (WBA)
28.02.81 Matt Saad Muhammad W RSC 11 Vonzell Johnson, Atlantic C, USA (WBC)
25.04.81 Matt Saad Muhammad W CO 9 Murray Sutherland, Atlantic C, USA (WBC)
18.07.81 Michael Spinks W PTS 15 Mustapha Muhammad, Las Vegas, USA (WBA)
26.09.81 Matt Saad Muhammad W RSC 11 Jerry Martin, Atlantic C, USA (WBC)
07.11.81 Michael Spinks W RSC 7 Vonzell Johnson, Atlantic C, USA (WBA)
19.12.81 Dwight Muhammad Qawi W RSC 10 Matt Saad Muhammad, Atlantic C, USA (WBC)
13.02.82 Michael Spinks W RSC 6 Mustapha Wasajja, Atlantic C, USA (WBA)
21.03.82 Dwight Muhammad Qawi W RSC 6 Jerry Martin, Las Vegas, USA (WBC)
11.04.82 Michael Spinks W RSC 8 Murray Sutherland, Atlantic C, USA (WBA)
12.06.82 Michael Spinks W RSC 8 Jerry Celestine, Atlantic C, USA (WBA)
07.08.82 Dwight Muhammad Qawi W RSC 6 Matt Saad Muhammad, Philadelphia, USA (WBC)
18.09.82 Michael Spinks W RSC 9 Johnny Davis, Atlantic C, USA (WBA)
20.11.82 Dwight Muhammad Qawi W RSC 11 Eddie Davis, Atlantic C, USA (WBC)
18.03.83 Michael Spinks W PTS 15 Dwight Muhammad Qawi, Atlantic C, USA
25.11.83 Michael Spinks W RSC 10 Oscar Rivadeneyra, Vancouver, Canada
25.02.84 Michael Spinks W PTS 12 Eddie Davis, Atlantic C, USA
23.02.85 Michael Spinks W RSC 3 David Sears, Atlantic C, USA
06.06.85 Michael Spinks W RSC 8 Jim MacDonald, Las Vegas, USA
Michael Spinks relinquished title (moved up to heavyweight)
10.12.85 J. B. Williamson W PTS 12 Prince Muhammed, Los Angeles, USA (WBC)
21.12.85 Slobodan Kacar W PTS 15 Mustafa Muhammad, Pesaro, Italy (IBF)
09.02.86 Marvin Johnson W RSC 7 Leslie Stewart, Indianapolis, USA (WBA)
30.04.86 Dennis Andries W PTS 12 J. B. Williamson, London, England (WBC)
06.09.86 Bobby Czyz W RSC 5 Slobodan Kacar, Las Vegas, USA (IBF)
10.09.86 Dennis Andries W RSC 9 Tony Sibson, London, England (WBC)
20.09.86 Marvin Johnson W RSC 13 Jean-Marie Emebe, Indianapolis, USA (WBA)
26.12.86 Bobby Czyz W RSC 1 David Sears, West Orange, USA (IBF)
21.02.87 Bobby Czyz W CO 2 Willie Edwards, Atlantic C, USA (IBF)
07.03.87 Thomas Hearns W RSC 10 Dennis Andries, Detroit, USA (WBC)
Thomas Hearns relinquished WBC version of title (moved down to the middleweight division)
03.05.87 Bobby Czyz W RSC 6 Jim MacDonald, Atlantic C, USA (IBF)
23.05.87 Leslie Stewart W RTD 8 Marvin Johnson, Port of Spain, Trinidad (WBA)
05.09.87 Virgil Hill W RSC 4 Leslie Stewart, Atlantic C, USA (WBA)
29.10.87 Charles Williams W RTD 9 Bobby Czyz, Las Vegas, USA (IBF)
21.11.87 Virgil Hill W PTS 12 Rufino Angulo, Paris, France (WBA)
27.11.87 Don Lalonde W RSC 2 Eddie Davis, Port of Spain, Trinidad (WBC)
03.04.88 Virgil Hill W RSC 11 Jean-Marie Emebe, Bismark, USA (WBA)
29.05.88 Don Lalonde W RSC 5 Leslie Stewart, Port of Spain, Trinidad (WBC)
06.06.88 Virgil Hill W PTS 12 Ramzi Hassan, Las Vegas, USA (WBA)
10.06.88 Charles Williams W RTD 11 Richard Caramanolis, Annecy, France (IBF)
21.10.88 Charles Williams W RSC 3 Rufino Angulo, Villeneuve d'Ornon, France (IBF)
07.11.88 Sugar Ray Leonard W RSC 9 Don Lalonde, Las Vegas, USA (WBC)
Sugar Ray Leonard relinquished title (decided to concentrate on defending the super-middleweight title)
11.11.88 Virgil Hill W RSC 10 Willie Featherstone, Bismark, USA (WBA)
21.02.89 Dennis Andries W RSC 5 Tony Willis, Tucson, USA (WBC)
04.03.89 Virgil Hill W PTS 12 Bobby Czyz, Bismark, USA (WBA)

Cruiserweight (190/195 lbs)

Title Holders

	Birthplace	Tenure	Status
Marvin Camel	USA	1979–1980	WBC
Carlos de Leon	Puerto Rico	1980–1982	WBC
Ossie Ocasio	Puerto Rico	1982–1984	WBA
S. T. Gordon	USA	1982–1983	WBC
Marvin Camel	USA	1983–1984	IBF
Carlos de Leon	Puerto Rico	1983–1985	WBC
Lee Roy Murphy	USA	1984–1986	IBF
Piet Crous	S Africa	1984–1985	WBA
Alfonso Ratliff	USA	1985	WBC
Dwight Muhammad Qawi	USA	1985–1986	WBA
Bernard Benton	USA	1985–1986	WBC
Carlos de Leon	Puerto Rico	1986–1988	WBC
Rickey Parkey	USA	1986–1987	IBF
Evander Holyfield	USA	1986–1987	WBA
Evander Holyfield	USA	1987–1988	WBA/IBF
Evander Holyfield*	USA	1988	
Taoufik Belbouli	France	1989–	WBA

Title Bouts

08.12.79 Marvin Camel DREW 15 Mate Parlov, Split, Yogoslavia (WBC)
31.03.80 Marvin Camel W PTS 15 Mate Parlov, Las Vegas, USA (WBC)
25.11.80 Carlos de Leon W PTS 15 Marvin Camel, New Orleans, USA (WBC)
13.02.82 Ossie Ocasio W PTS 15 Robbie Williams, Johannesburg, S Africa (WBA)
24.02.82 Carlos de Leon W RSC 8 Marvin Camel, Atlantic C, USA (WBC)
27.06.82 S. T. Gordon W RSC 2 Carlos de Leon, Cleveland, USA (WBC)
15.12.82 Ossie Ocasio W PTS 15 Young Joe Louis, Chicago, USA (WBA)
16.02.83 S. T. Gordon W RSC 8 Jesse Burnett, E Rutherford, USA (WBC)
20.05.83 Ossie Ocasio W PTS 15 Randy Stephens, Las Vegas, USA (WBA)
21.05.83 Marvin Camel W RSC 9 Rick Sekorski, Billings, USA (IBF)
17.07.83 Carlos de Leon W PTS 12 S. T. Gordon, Las Vegas, USA (WBC)
21.09.83 Carlos de Leon W RSC 4 Yaqui Lopez, San Jose, USA (WBC)
13.12.83 Marvin Camel W RSC 5 Rod MacDonald, Halifax, Canada (IBF)
09.03.84 Carlos de Leon W PTS 12 Anthony Davis, Las Vegas, USA (WBC)
05.05.84 Ossie Ocasio W RSC 15 John Odhiambo, San Juan, Puerto Rico (WBA)
02.06.84 Carlos de Leon W PTS 12 Bashiru Ali, Oakland, USA (WBC)
06.10.84 Lee Roy Murphy W RSC 14 Marvin Camel, Billings, USA (IBF)
01.12.84 Piet Crous W PTS 15 Ossie Ocasio, Sun C, S Africa (WBA)
20.12.84 Lee Roy Murphy W RSC 12 Young Joe Louis, Chicago, USA (IBF)
30.03.85 Piet Crous W RSC 3 Randy Stephens, Sun C, S Africa (WBA)
06.06.85 Alfonso Ratliff W PTS 12 Carlos de Leon, Las Vegas, USA (WBC)
27.07.85 Dwight Muhammad Qawi W RSC 11 Piet Crous, Sun C, S Africa (WBA)
21.09.85 Bernard Benton W PTS 12 Alfonso Ratliff, Las Vegas, USA (WBC)
19.10.85 Lee Roy Murphy W CO 12 Chisanda Mutti, Monte Carlo (IBF)
22.03.86 Carlos de Leon W PTS 12 Bernard Benton, Las Vegas, USA (WBC)
23.03.86 Dwight Muhammad Qawi W RSC 6 Leon Spinks, Reno, USA (WBA)
19.04.86 Lee Roy Murphy W CO 9 Dorcey Gaymon, San Remo, Italy (IBF)
12.07.86 Evander Holyfield W PTS 15 Dwight Muhammad Qawi, Atlanta, USA (WBA)
10.08.86 Carlos de Leon W RSC 8 Michael Greer, Giardini Naxos, Italy (WBC)
25.10.86 Ricky Parkey W RSC 10 Lee Roy Murphy, Marsala, Italy (IBF)
14.02.87 Evander Holyfield W RSC 7 Henry Tillman, Reno, USA (WBA)
21.02.87 Carlos de Leon W RTD 4 Angelo Rottoli, Bergamo, Italy (WBC)
28.03.87 Rickey Parkey W RSC 12 Chisanda Mutti, Camaiore, Italy (IBF)
15.05.87 Evander Holyfield W RSC 3 Rickey Parkey, Las Vegas, USA (IBF)
15.08.87 Evander Holyfield W RSC 11 Ossie Ocasio, St Tropez, France (IBF/WBA)
05.12.87 Evander Holyfield W CO 4 Dwight Muhammad Qawi, Atlantic C, USA (IBF)
22.01.88 Carlos de Leon W PTS 12 Jose Mario Flores, Atlantic C, USA (WBC)
09.04.88 Evander Holyfield W RSC 8 Carlos de Leon, Las Vegas, USA
Evander Holyfield relinquished title (moved up to heavyweight)
25.03.89 Taoufik Belbouli W RSC 8 Michael Greer, Casablanca, Morocco (WBA)

Heavyweight (190/195 lbs +)

Title Holders

	Birthplace	Tenure	Status
James J. Corbett	USA	1892–1897	
Bob Fitzsimmons	England	1897–1899	
James J. Jeffries*	USA	1899–1905	
Marvin Hart	USA	1905–1906	
Tommy Burns	Canada	1906–1908	
Jack Johnson	USA	1908–1915	
Jess Willard	USA	1915–1919	
Jack Dempsey	USA	1919–1926	
Gene Tunney*	USA	1926–1928	
Max Schmeling	Germany	1930–1932	
Jack Sharkey	USA	1932–1933	
Primo Carnera	Italy	1933–1934	
Max Baer	USA	1934–1935	
James J. Braddock	USA	1935–1937	
Joe Louis*	USA	1937–1949	
Ezzard Charles	USA	1949–1950	NBA
Lee Savold	USA	1950	GB/EBU
Ezzard Charles	USA	1950–1951	
Jersey Joe Walcott	USA	1951–1952	
Rocky Marciano*	USA	1952–1956	
Floyd Patterson	USA	1956–1959	
Ingemar Johansson	Sweden	1959–1960	
Floyd Patterson	USA	1960–1962	
Sonny Liston	USA	1962–1964	
Muhammad Ali	USA	1964–1965	
Muhammad Ali	USA	1965–1967	WBC
Ernie Terrell	USA	1965–1967	WBA
Muhammad Ali	USA	1967	
Joe Frazier	USA	1968–1970	WBC

Jimmy Ellis	USA	1968–1970	WBA
Joe Frazier	USA	1970–1973	
George Foreman	USA	1973–1974	
Muhammad Ali	USA	1974–1978	
Leon Spinks	USA	1978	
Leon Spinks	USA	1978	WBA
Larry Holmes*	USA	1978–1983	WBC
Muhammad Ali*	USA	1978–1979	WBA
John Tate	USA	1979–1980	WBA
Mike Weaver	USA	1980–1982	WBA
Michael Dokes	USA	1982–1983	WBA
Gerrie Coetzee	S Africa	1983–1984	WBA
Tim Witherspoon	USA	1984	WBC
Pinklon Thomas	USA	1984–1986	WBC
Larry Holmes	USA	1984–1985	IBF
Greg Page	USA	1984–1985	WBA
Tony Tubbs	USA	1985–1986	WBA
Michael Spinks	USA	1985–1987	IBF
Tim Witherspoon	USA	1986	WBA
Trevor Berbick	Jamaica	1986	WBC
Mike Tyson	USA	1986–1987	WBC
James Smith	USA	1986–1987	WBA
Mike Tyson	USA	1987	WBA/WBC
Tony Tucker	USA	1987	IBF
Mike Tyson	USA	1987–	

Title Bouts

07.09.92 James J. Corbett W CO 21 John L. Sullivan, New Orleans, USA
25.01.94 James J. Corbett W CO 3 Charley Mitchell, Jacksonville, USA
17.03.97 Bob Fitzsimmons W CO 14 James J. Corbett, Carson C, USA
09.06.99 James J. Jeffries W CO 11 Bob Fitzsimmons, New York C, USA
03.11.99 James J. Jeffries W PTS 25 Tom Sharkey, New York C, USA
06.04.00 James J. Jeffries W CO 1 Jack Finnegan, Detroit, USA
11.05.00 James J. Jeffries W CO 23 James J. Corbett, New York C, USA
15.11.01 James J. Jeffries W RTD 5 Gus Ruhlin, San Francisco, USA
25.07.02 James J. Jeffries W CO 8 Bob Fitzsimmons, San Francisco, USA
14.08.03 James J. Jeffries W CO 10 James J. Corbett, San Francisco, USA
26.08.04 James J. Jeffries W CO 2 Jack Munroe, San Francisco, USA
James J. Jeffries relinquished title (retired)
03.07.05 Marvin Hart W RSC 12 Jack Root, Reno, USA
23.02.06 Tommy Burns W PTS 20 Marvin Hart, Los Angeles, USA
02.10.06 Tommy Burns W CO 15 Jim Flynn, Los Angeles, USA
28.11.06 Tommy Burns DREW 20 Jack O'Brien, Los Angeles, USA
08.05.07 Tommy Burns W PTS 20 Jack O'Brien, Los Angeles, USA
04.07.07 Tommy Burns W CO 1 Bill Squires, Los Angeles, USA
02.12.07 Tommy Burns W CO 10 Gunner Moir, London, England
10.02.08 Tommy Burns W CO 4 Jack Palmer, London, England
17.03.08 Tommy Burns W CO 1 Jem Roche, Dublin, Ireland
18.04.08 Tommy Burns W CO 5 Jewey Smith, Paris, France
13.06.08 Tommy Burns W CO 8 Bill Squires, Paris, France
24.08.08 Tommy Burns W CO 13 Bill Squires, Sydney, Australia
02.09.08 Tommy Burns W CO 6 Bill Lang, Melbourne, Australia
26.12.08 Jack Johnson W RSC 14 Tommy Burns, Sydney, Australia
16.10.09 Jack Johnson W CO 12 Stanley Ketchell, Los Angeles, USA
04.07.10 Jack Johnson W RSC 15 James J. Jeffries, Reno, USA
04.07.12 Jack Johnson W RSC 9 Jim Flynn, Las Vegas, USA
19.12.13 Jack Johnson DREW 10 Jim Johnson, Paris, France
27.06.14 Jack Johnson W PTS 20 Frank Moran, Paris, France
05.04.15 Jess Willard W CO 26 Jack Johnson, Havana, Cuba
04.07.19 Jack Dempsey W RTD 3 Jess Willard, Toledo, USA
06.09.20 Jack Dempsey W CO 3 Billy Miske, Benton Harbor, USA
14.12.20 Jack Dempsey W CO 12 Bill Brennan, New York C, USA
02.07.21 Jack Dempsey W CO 4 Georges Carpentier, Jersey C, USA
04.07.23 Jack Dempsey W PTS 15 Tommy Gibbons, Shelby, USA
14.09.23 Jack Dempsey W CO 2 Angel Firpo, New York C, USA
23.09.26 Gene Tunney W PTS 10 Jack Dempsey, Philadelphia, USA
22.09.27 Gene Tunney W PTS 10 Jack Dempsey, Chicago, USA
26.07.28 Gene Tunney W RSC 11 Tom Heeney, New York C, USA
Gene Tunney relinquished title (retired)
12.06.30 Max Schmeling W DIS 4 Jack Sharkey, New York C, USA
03.07.31 Max Schmeling W RSC 15 Young Stribling, Cleveland, USA
21.06.32 Jack Sharkey W PTS 15 Max Schmeling, New York C, USA
29.06.33 Primo Carnera W CO 6 Jack Sharkey, New York C, USA
22.10.33 Primo Carnera W PTS 15 Paolino Uzcudun, Rome, Italy
01.03.34 Primo Carnera W PTS 15 Tommy Loughran, Miami, USA
14.06.34 Max Baer W RSC 11 Primo Carnera, New York C, USA
13.06.35 James J. Braddock W PTS 15 Max Baer, New York C, USA
22.06.37 Joe Louis W CO 8 James J. Braddock, Chicago, USA
30.08.37 Joe Louis W PTS 15 Tommy Farr, New York C, USA
23.02.38 Joe Louis W CO 3 Nathan Mann, New York C, USA
01.04.38 Joe Louis W CO 5 Harry Thomas, Chicago, USA
22.06.38 Joe Louis W CO 1 Max Schmeling, New York C, USA
25.01.39 Joe Louis W RSC 1 John Henry Lewis, New York C, USA
17.04.39 Joe Louis W CO 1 Jack Roper, Los Angeles, USA
28.06.39 Joe Louis W RSC 4 Tony Galento, New York C, USA
20.09.39 Joe Louis W CO 11 Bob Pastor, Detroit, USA
09.02.40 Joe Louis W PTS 15 Arturo Godoy, New York C, USA
29.03.40 Joe Louis W CO 2 Johnny Paychek, New York C, USA
20.06.40 Joe Louis W RSC 8 Arturo Godoy, New York C, USA
16.12.40 Joe Louis W RTD 6 Al McCoy, Boston, USA
31.01.41 Joe Louis W CO 5 Red Burman, New York C, USA
17.02.41 Joe Louis W CO 2 Gus Dorazio, Philadelphia, USA
21.03.41 Joe Louis W RSC 13 Abe Simon, Detroit, USA
08.04.41 Joe Louis W RSC 9 Tony Musto, St Louis, USA
23.05.41 Joe Louis W DIS 7 Buddy Baer, Washington, USA
18.06.41 Joe Louis W CO 13 Billy Conn, New York C, USA
29.09.41 Joe Louis W RSC 6 Lou Nova, New York C, USA
09.01.42 Joe Louis W CO 1 Buddy Baer, New York C, USA
27.03.42 Joe Louis W CO 6 Abe Simon, New York C, USA
19.06.46 Joe Louis W CO 8 Billy Conn, New York C, USA
18.09.46 Joe Louis W CO 1 Tami Mauriello, New York C, USA
05.12.47 Joe Louis W PTS 15 Jersey Joe Walcott, New York C, USA
25.06.48 Joe Louis W CO 11 Jersey Joe Walcott, New York C, USA
Joe Louis relinquished title (retired)
22.06.49 Ezzard Charles W PTS 15 Jersey Joe Walcott, Chicago, USA (NBA)
10.08.49 Ezzard Charles W RSC 7 Gus Lesnevich, New York C, USA (NBA)
14.10.49 Ezzard Charles W CO 8 Pat Valentino, San Francisco, USA (NBA)
06.06.50 Lee Savold W RTD 4 Bruce Woodcock, London, England (GB/EBU)
Lee Savold ceased to be recognised by GB/EBU (this followed the announcement that Joe Louis was making a comeback)
15.08.50 Ezzard Charles W RSC 14 Freddie Beshore, Buffalo, USA (NBA)
27.09.50 Ezzard Charles W PTS 15 Joe Louis, New York C, USA
05.12.50 Ezzard Charles W CO 11 Nick Barone, Cincinnati, USA
12.01.51 Ezzard Charles W RSC 10 Lee Oma, New York C, USA
07.03.51 Ezzard Charles W PTS 15 Jersey Joe Walcott, Detroit, USA
30.05.51 Ezzard Charles W PTS 15 Joey Maxim, Chicago, USA
18.07.51 Jersey Joe Walcott W CO 7 Ezzard Charles, Pittsburgh, USA
05.06.52 Jersey Joe Walcott W PTS 15 Ezzard Charles, Philadelphia, USA
23.09.52 Rocky Marciano W CO 13 Jersey Joe Walcott, Philadelphia, USA
15.05.53 Rocky Marciano W CO 1 Jersey Joe Walcott, Chicago, USA
24.09.53 Rocky Marciano W RSC 11 Roland la Starza, New York C, USA
17.06.54 Rocky Marciano W PTS 15 Ezzard Charles, New York C, USA
17.09.54 Rocky Marciano W CO 8 Ezzard Charles, New York C, USA
16.05.55 Rocky Marciano W RSC 9 Don Cockell, San Francisco, USA
21.09.55 Rocky Marciano W CO 9 Archie Moore, New York C, USA
Rocky Marciano relinquished title (retired)
30.11.56 Floyd Patterson W CO 5 Archie Moore, Chicago, USA
29.07.57 Floyd Patterson W RSC 10 Tommy Jackson, New York C, USA
22.08.57 Floyd Patterson W CO 6 Pete Rademacher, Seattle, USA
18.08.58 Floyd Patterson W RTD 12 Roy Harris, Los Angeles, USA
01.05.59 Floyd Patterson W CO 11 Brian London, Indianapolis, USA
26.06.59 Ingemar Johansson W RSC 3 Floyd Patterson, New York C, USA
20.06.60 Floyd Patterson W CO 5 Ingemar Johansson, New York C. USA
13.03.61 Floyd Patterson W CO 6 Ingemar Johansson, Miami, USA
04.12.61 Floyd Patterson W CO 4 Tom McNeeley, Toronto, Canada
25.09.62 Sonny Liston W CO 1 Floyd Patterson, Chicago, USA
22.07.63 Sonny Liston W CO 1 Floyd Patterson, Las Vegas, USA
25.02.64 Muhammad Ali W RTD 6 Sonny Liston, Miami, USA
Muhammad Ali forfeited recognition (contractual dispute)
05.03.65 Ernie Terrell W PTS 15 Eddie Machen, Chicago, USA (WBA)
25.05.65 Muhammad Ali W CO 1 Sonny Liston, Lewiston, USA (WBC)
01.11.65 Ernie Terrell W PTS 15 George Chuvalo, Toronto, Canada (WBA)
22.11.65 Muhammad Ali W RSC 12 Floyd Patterson, Las Vegas, USA (WBC)
29.03.66 Muhammad Ali W PTS 15 George Chuvalo, Toronto, Canada (WBC)
21.05.66 Muhammad Ali W RSC 6 Henry Cooper, London, England (WBC)
28.06.66 Ernie Terrell W PTS 15 Doug Jones, Houston, USA (WBA)
06.08.66 Muhammad Ali W CO 3 Brian London, London, England (WBC)
10.09.66 Muhammad Ali W RSC 12 Karl Mildenberger, Frankfurt, W Germany (WBC)
14.11.66 Muhammad Ali W RSC 3 Cleveland Williams, Houston, USA (WBC)
06.02.67 Muhammad Ali W PTS 15 Ernie Terrell, Houston, USA
22.03.67 Muhammad Ali W CO 7 Zora Folley, New York C, USA
Muhammad Ali forfeited title (inactivity)
04.03.68 Joe Frazier W RSC 11 Buster Mathis, New York C, USA (WBC)
27.04.68 Jimmy Ellis W PTS 15 Jerry Quarry, Oakland, USA (WBA)
24.06.68 Joe Frazier W RTD 2 Manuel Ramos, New York C, USA (WBC)
14.09.68 Jimmy Ellis W PTS 15 Floyd Patterson, Stockholm, Sweden (WBA)
10.12.68 Joe Frazier W PTS 15 Oscar Bonavena, Philadelphia, USA (WBC)
22.04.69 Joe Frazier W CO 1 Dave Zyglewicz, Houston, USA (WBC)
23.06.69 Joe Frazier W RSC 7 Jerry Quarry, New York C, USA (WBC)
16.02.70 Joe Frazier W RTD 4 Jimmy Ellis, New York C, USA
18.11.70 Joe Frazier W CO 2 Bob Foster, Detroit, USA
08.03.71 Joe Frazier W PTS 15 Muhammad Ali, New York C, USA
15.01.72 Joe Frazier W RSC 4 Terry Daniels, New Orleans, USA
26.05.72 Joe Frazier W RSC 4 Don Stander, Omaha, USA
22.01.73 George Foreman W RSC 2 Joe Frazier, Kingston, Jamaica
01.09.73 George Foreman W CO 1 Jose Roman, Tokyo, Japan
26.03.74 George Foreman W RSC 2 Ken Norton, Caracas, Venezuela
30.10.74 Muhammad Ali W CO 8 George Foreman, Kinshasha, Zaire
24.03.75 Muhammad Ali W RSC 15 Chuck Wepner, Cleveland, USA
16.05.75 Muhammad Ali W RSC 11 Ron Lyle, Las Vegas, USA
01.07.75 Muhammad Ali W PTS 15 Joe Bugner, Kuala Lumpur, Malaysia
01.10.75 Muhammad Ali W RTD 14 Joe Frazier, Manila, Philippines
20.02.76 Muhammad Ali W CO 5 Jean-Pierre Coopman, San Juan, Puerto Rico
30.04.76 Muhammad Ali W PTS 15 Jimmy Young, Landover, USA
25.05.76 Muhammad Ali W RSC 5 Richard Dunn, Munich, W Germany
28.09.76 Muhammad Ali W PTS 15 Ken Norton, New York C, USA
16.05.77 Muhammad Ali W PTS 15 Alfredo Evangelista, Landover, USA
29.09.77 Muhammad Ali W PTS 15 Ernie Shavers, New York C, USA
15.02.78 Leon Spinks W PTS 15 Muhammad Ali, Las Vegas, USA
Leon Spinks forfeited WBC recognition (failure to defend against Ken Norton)
09.06.78 Larry Holmes W PTS 15 Ken Norton, Las Vegas, USA (WBC)
15.09.78 Muhammad Ali W PTS 15 Leon Spinks, New Orleans, USA (WBA)
Muhammad Ali relinquished WBA version of title (retired)
10.11.78 Larry Holmes W CO 7 Alfredo Evangelista, Las Vegas (WBC)

23.03.79 Larry Holmes W RSC 7 Ossie Ocasio, Las Vegas, USA (WBC)
22.06.79 Larry Holmes W RSC 12 Mike Weaver, New York C, USA (WBC)
28.09.79 Larry Holmes W RSC 11 Ernie Shavers, Las Vegas, USA (WBC)
20.10.79 John Tate W PTS 15 Gerrie Coetzee, Pretoria, S Africa (WBA)
03.02.80 Larry Holmes W CO 6 Lorenzo Zanon, Las Vegas, USA (WBC)
31.03.80 Mike Weaver W CO 15 John Tate, Knoxville, USA (WBA)
31.03.80 Larry Holmes W RSC 8 Leroy Jones, Las Vegas, USA (WBC)
07.07.80 Larry Holmes W RSC 7 Scott Ledoux, Minneapolis, USA (WBC)
02.10.80 Larry Holmes W RTD 10 Muhammad Ali, Las Vegas, USA (WBC)
25.10.80 Mike Weaver W CO 13 Gerrie Coetzee, Sun C, S Africa (WBA)
11.04.81 Larry Holmes W PTS 15 Trevor Berbick, Las Vegas, USA (WBC)
12.06.81 Larry Holmes W RSC 3 Leon Spinks, Detroit, USA (WBC)
03.10.81 Mike Weaver W PTS 15 James Tillis, Rosemont, USA (WBA)
06.11.81 Larry Holmes W RSC 11 Renaldo Snipes, Pittsburgh, USA (WBC)
11.06.82 Larry Holmes W RSC 13 Gerrry Cooney, Las Vegas, USA (WBC)
26.11.82 Larry Holmes W PTS 15 Tex Cobb,Houston, USA (WBC)
10.12.82 Michael Dokes W RSC 1 Mike Weaver, Las Vegas, USA (WBA)
27.03.83 Larry Holmes W PTS 12 Lucien Rodriguez, Scranton, USA (WBC)
20.05.83 Michael Dokes DREW 15 Mike Weaver, Las Vegas, USA (WBA)
20.05.83 Larry Holmes W PTS 12 Tim Witherspoon, Las Vegas, USA (WBC)
10.09.83 Larry Holmes W RSC 5 Scott Frank, Atlantic C, USA (WBC)
23.09.83 Gerrie Coetzee W CO 10 Michael Dokes, Richfield, USA (WBA)
25.11.83 Larry Holmes W RSC 1 Marvis Frazier, Las Vegas, USA (WBC)
Larry Holmes relinquished WBC version of title (decided to box exclusively for the IBF)
09.03.84 Tim Witherspoon W PTS 12 Greg Page, Las Vegas, USA (WBC)
31.08.84 Pinklon Thomas W PTS 12 Tim Witherspoon, Las Vegas, USA (WBC)
09.11.84 Larry Holmes W RSC 12 James Smith, Las Vegas, USA (IBF)
01.12.84 Greg Page W CO 8 Gerrie Coetzee, Sun C, S Africa (WBA)
15.03.85 Larry Holmes W RSC 10 David Bey, Las Vegas, USA (IBF)
29.04.85 Tony Tubbs W PTS 15 Greg Page, Buffalo, USA (WBA)
20.05.85 Larry Holmes W PTS 15 Carl Williams, Reno, USA (IBF)
15.06.85 Pinklon Thomas W CO 8 Mike Weaver, Las Vegas, USA (WBC)
21.09.85 Michael Spinks W PTS 15 Larry Holmes, Las Vegas, USA (IBF)
17.01.86 Tim Witherspoon W PTS 15 Tony Tubbs, Atlanta, USA (WBA)
22.03.86 Trevor Berbick W PTS 12 Pinklon Thomas, Las Vegas, USA (WBC)
19.04.86 Michael Spinks W PTS 15 Larry Holmes, Las Vegas, USA (IBF)
19.07.86 Tim Witherspoon W RSC 11 Frank Bruno, Wembley, England (WBA)
06.09.86 Michael Spinks W RSC 4 Steffen Tangstad, Las Vegas, USA (IBF)
Michael Spinks forfeited title (refusal to defend against Tony Tucker)
22.11.86 Mike Tyson W RSC 2 Trevor Berbick, Las Vegas, USA (WBC)
12.12.86 James Smith W RSC 1 Tim Witherspoon, New York C, USA (WBA)
07.03.87 Mike Tyson W PTS 12 James Smith, Las Vegas, USA (WBA/WBC)
30.05.87 Mike Tyson W RSC 6 Pinklon Thomas, Las Vegas, USA (WBA/WBC)
30.05.87 Tony Tucker W RSC 10 James Douglas, Las Vegas, USA (IBF)
01.08.87 Mike Tyson W PTS 12 Tony Tucker, Las Vegas, USA
16.10.87 Mike Tyson W RSC 7 Tyrell Biggs, Atlantic C, USA
22.01.88 Mike Tyson W RSC 4 Larry Holmes, Atlantic C, USA (WBC/WBA)
21.03.88 Mike Tyson W RSC 2 Tony Tubbs, Tokyo, Japan (WBC/WBA)
27.06.88 Mike Tyson W CO 1 Michael Spinks, Atlantic C, USA
25.02.89 Mike Tyson W RSC 5 Frank Bruno, Las Vegas, USA (WBC)

Making the seventh defence of his heavyweight crown, Mike Tyson utterly destroyed the title aspirations of Michael Spinks inside 91 seconds, June, 1988.

Tom Casino

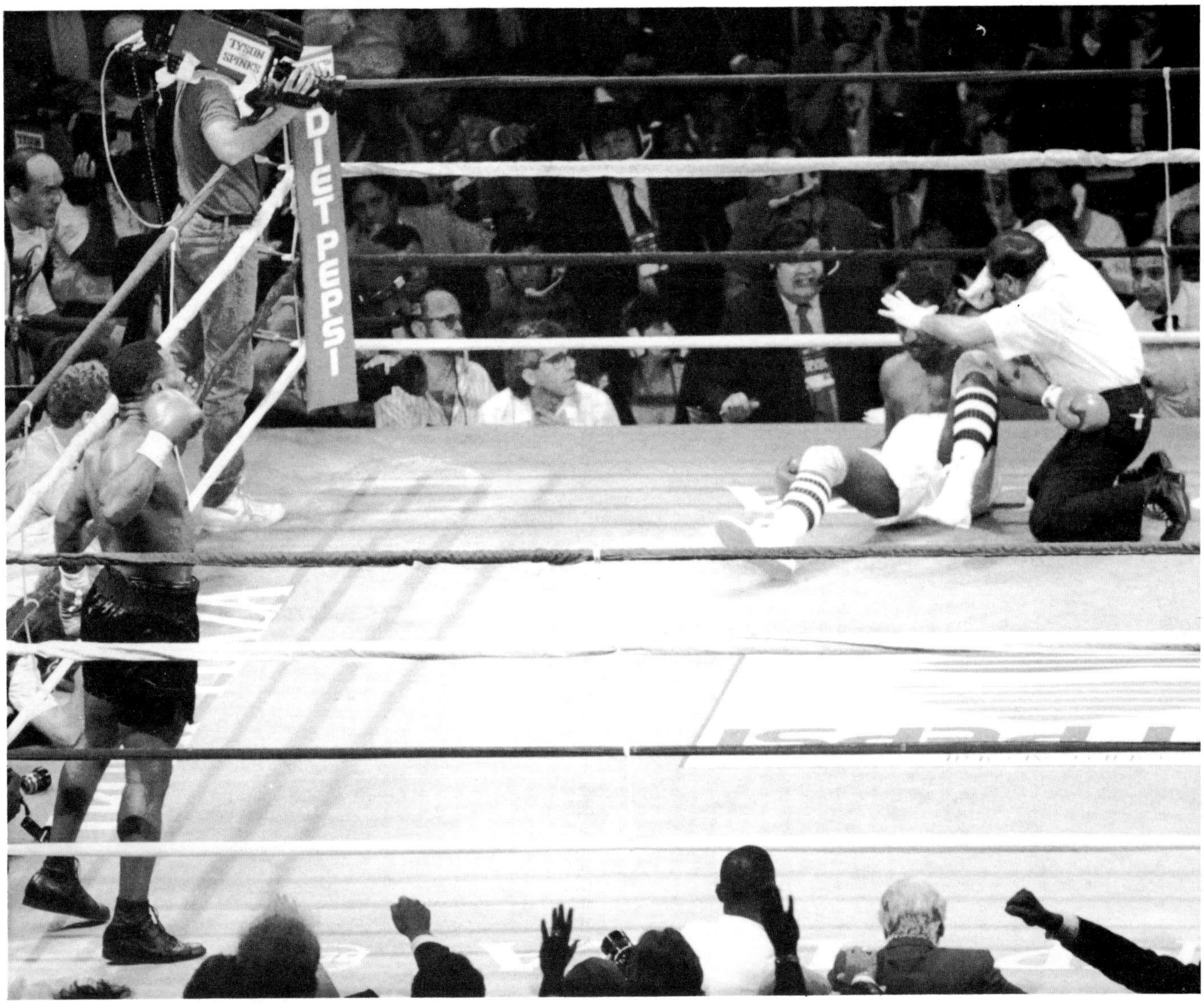

The legendary Muhammad Ali

Harry Goodwin

Boxers' Record Index

Page numbers are show *in italic* and where illustrations, **in bold**

General Index

Page numbers are show *in italic* and where illustrations, **in bold**